ST☾TE
OF THE NATION
South Africa 2004–2005

Edited by John Daniel,
Roger Southall & Jessica Lutchman

Compiled by the Democracy and Governance Research Programme,
Human Sciences Research Council

First published in South Africa by HSRC Press
Private Bag X9182, Cape Town, 8000, South Africa
www.hsrcpress.ac.za

Published in the rest of the world by Michigan State University Press
East Lansing, Michigan, 48823-5202, United States of America

Copy editing by Vaun Cornell
Typeset by Christabel Hardacre
Cover design by Flame Design
Cover photograph by Yassir Booley
Production by comPress
Printed in the Republic of South Africa by Paarl Print

Distributed in South Africa by Blue Weaver Marketing and Distribution
PO Box 30370, Tokai, Cape Town, 7966, South Africa.
Tel: +27 +21 701-4477
Fax: +27 +21 701-7302
email: orders@blueweaver.co.za

In South Africa
ISBN 0-7969-2086-9

In the rest of the world
ISBN 0-87013-716-6

Contents

List of tables

List of figures

Foreword

State of the Nation: South Africa 2004–2005 is the second issue of what, last year, the Human Sciences Research Council (HSRC) announced would become an annual set of original essays dedicated to reviewing developments in South Africa. Recalling the format of the *South African Review* that was edited by Glenn Moss and others in the 1980s, and drawing inspiration from the presidential 'State of the Nation' speeches which have become a feature of our new democracy, these annual collections seek to provide empirically-based analysis and assessment of contemporary events and trends from a developmental perspective, reflecting the values that are embedded in the Constitution.

The founding *State of the Nation* collection attracted widespread interest. It was commended for the quality and coverage of the contributions and the vigorous argument that they occasioned. The current volume constitutes a worthy successor, and is sure to have a similar effect. It is a project of the Democracy and Governance Research Programme of the HSRC. But it draws upon original and stimulating work also undertaken elsewhere within the organisation and, in addition, features contributions by a spread of analysts from universities and civil society. As such, it powerfully illustrates both the breadth of the expanded HSRC's own capabilities and its commitment to undertaking such work in active collaboration with publicly and privately funded research partners.

The importance of the annual *State of the Nation* volumes in promoting public debate in South Africa has been recognised by five donor organisations. Atlantic Philanthropy, the Ford Foundation and the Mott Foundation have generously provided funding for the project over three years. Without their assistance, the production of the book would not have been possible. The Konrad Adenauer Foundation and the Durban-based Democracy Development Programme helped to ensure that the first volume entered the mainstream of national policy discourse by providing funding for a series of three launch workshops. They have generously agreed to repeat the exercise for the present collection. Without the extensive supplementation of its parliamentary grant by partners such as these, the HSRC would be far less able to discharge its statutory mandate of undertaking social-scientific research of relevance to public policy, public knowledge and public debate.

The HSRC's mandate is a distinctively challenging one. Any scientific research that is interesting and profound will engender controversy, in itself and its applications. But this is notably true of social research, which deals with politics, the economy, and society, both locally and internationally. It thus covers matters which participants engaged in their respective institutions – such as politicians, managers and employees, activists, and diplomats – as well as thoughtful citizens engaged in their everyday lives, may wish to apply in their decision-making. These participants and citizens are thus as intensely concerned to assess the research as the analysts who produce it. The special contribution, and obligation, of the latter is to provide considered analyses that are based on empirical evidence and the scholarly insights of their disciplines.

In this regard the editors of this second volume of *State of the Nation* – John Daniel, Roger Southall and Jessica Lutchman – and all its contributors, beyond and within the HSRC, continue to serve us well. They are to be thanked for providing a wide-ranging work of intellectual substance that will help to advance democracy and development in our country and on our continent by provoking relevant reflection and lively discussion.

Dr FM Orkin

President and Chief Executive Officer
HSRC

Acronyms

ABET	Adult Basic Education and Training
ACDP	African Christian Democratic Party
Actag	Arts and Culture Task Group
AG	Auditor General
AGOA	African Growth and Opportunity Act
AIDS	Acquired immune deficiency syndrome
AMA	Africa Muslim Agency
Amps	All-Media and Products Survey (produced by the South African Advertising Research Foundation [SAARF])
ANC	African National Congress
Apla	Azanian Peoples' Liberation Army
ART	Anti-retroviral treatment
AU	African Union
BASA	Business and the Arts
BEE	Black economic empowerment
BEEC	Black Economic Empowerment Commission
BIG	Basic income grant
BMATT	British Military Advisory and Training Team
BNC	Bi-national Commission (South Africa-Nigeria)
Cals	Centre for Applied Legal Studies
CAP	Community Arts Project
CEDAW	United Nations Convention on the Elimination of All Forms of Discrimination Against Women
CEO	Chief Executive Officer
CESM	Classification educational subject matter
CII	Channel Islam International
CLRB	Communal Land Rights Bill
Codesa	Convention for a Democratic South Africa
Contralesa	Congress of Traditional Leaders of South Africa
COP	Community-oriented policing
Cosatu	Congress of South African Trade Unions
CPF	Community police forum
CPI	Consumer price index
CSANDF	Chief of the South African National Defence Force

CTA	Ciskei Territorial Authority
DA	Democratic Alliance
DAC	Department of Arts and Culture, South Africa
DACST	Department of Arts, Culture, Science and Technology, South Africa
DEAT	Department of Environmental Affairs and Tourism, South Africa
DFA	Department of Foreign Affairs, South Africa
DG	Director General
DISA	Digital Imaging Project of South Africa
DLA	Department of Land Affairs, South Africa
DoD	Department of Defence, South Africa
DoE	Department of Education
DoH	Department of Health, South Africa
DoHA	Department of Home Affairs, South Africa
DoL	Department of Labour, South Africa
DoSD	Department of Social Development, South Africa
DoSS	Department of Safety and Security, South Africa
DP	Democratic Party
DPLG	Department of Provincial and Local Government, South Africa
DPRU	Development Policy Research Unit
DPSA	Department of Public Service and Administration, South Africa
DRC	Democratic Republic of the Congo
DSAC	Department of Sport, Arts and Culture, Eastern Cape
DTI	Department of Trade and Industry, South Africa
DWAF	Department of Water Affairs and Forestry, South Africa
ECD	Early Childhood Development
ELSEN	Education for Learners with Special Needs
EMIS	Education Management Information System
EMS	Economic and management sciences
EU	European Union
FDI	Foreign direct investment
FET	Further education and training
FF+	Freedom Front Plus
GCIS	Government Communications and Information System
GDP	Gross domestic product
GEAR	Growth, Employment, and Redistribution strategy
GET	General Education and Training
GNU	Government of National Unity
HDI	Human Development Index
HE	Higher Education
HIV	Human immunodeficiency virus
HSRC	Human Sciences Research Council

HBU	Historically black universities
HWU	Historically white universities
IBA	Independent Broadcasting Authority
ICT	Information and communications technology
ICVS	International crime victim survey
ID	Independent Democrats
Idasa	Institute for Democracy in South Africa
IDC	Industrial Development Corporation
IEC	Independent Electoral Commission
IES	Income and expenditure survey
IFP	Inkatha Freedom Party
IJS	Integrated Justice System
INCD	International Network for Cultural Diversity
INCP	The International Network for Cultural Policy
IPCI	Islamic Propagation Centre International
ISS	Institute for Security Studies
IT	Information technology
IUC	Islamic Unity Conference
JMC	Joint Monitoring Committee on the Improvement of the Quality of Life and Status of Women
JSE	Johannesburg Stock Exchange
KZN	KwaZulu-Natal
LFPR	labour force participation rate
LFS	Labour force survey
LPM	Landless People's Movement
LPPPD	Litres of water per person per day
LSM	Living standard measure
MDC	Movement for Democratic Change
MDG	Millennium Development Goals
MK	Umkhonto we Sizwe
MoD	Minister of Defence
MTEF	Medium-term expenditure framework
MJC	Muslim Judicial Council
MP	Member of Parliament
MPL	Muslim Personal Law
MVA	Manufacturing value added
MYM	Muslim Youth Movement
NAC	National Arts Council
NACCA	National Action Committee for Children Infected and Affected by HIV/AIDS
Nacosa	National AIDS Committee of South Africa
Nacsa	Network for Arts and Culture in South Africa

Naptosa	National Association of Professional Teachers' Associations of South Africa
NASA	National Archives of South Africa
NCCS	National Crime Combating Strategy
NCOP	National Council of Provinces
NCPS	National Crime Prevention Strategy
NDPP	National Director of Public Prosecutions
NDR	National democratic revolution
Nedlac	National Economic Development and Labour Council
NEP	New Economic Policy
Nepad	New Partnership for Africa's Development
NGO	non-governmental organisation
NLC	National Land Committee
NNP	New National Party
NP	National Party
NQF	National Qualifictions Framework
NSB	National Sorghum Breweries
NVQ	National Vocational Qualification
NYSE	New York Stock Exchange
OAMU	Organisation of African Muslim Unity
OAU	Organisation of African Unity
OHS	October household survey
OSW	Office of the Status of Women
PAC	Pan Africanist Congress
Pagad	People against Gangsterism and Drugs
Pansa	Performing Arts Network of South Africa
PAT	After-tax profit
PCAS	Presidential Policy Co-ordination and Advisory Services
PCPD	Portfolio Committee of Parliament on Defence
PEP	Post-exposure prophylaxis
PFMA	Public Finance Management Act
PIR	Poverty and Inequality Report
PL	Poverty line
PLAAS	Programme for Land and Agrarian Studies
PMTCT	Prevention of mother-to-child transmission
PR	Proportional representation
PSC	Public Service Commission
RDP	Reconstruction and Development Programme
RWM	Rural Women's Movement
SAA	South African Airways
SACP	South African Communist Party
SACU	Southern African Customs Union

SADC	Southern African Development Community
SADET	South African Democracy Education Trust
SADF	South African Defence Force
Sadtu	South African Democratic Teachers' Union
SAHRC	South African Human Rights Commission
SALC	South African Law Commission
Saldru	South African Labour Development Research Unit
SAMP	South African Migration Project
Sanac	South African National AIDS Council
SANDF	South African National Defence Force
SAOU	Suid Afrikaanse Onderwysers' Unie
SAP	South African Police
SAPS	South African Police Service
SAQA	South African Qualifications Authority
SARB	South African Reserve Bank
SAR&H	South African Railways and Harbours
SARS	South African Revenue Service
SASAS	South African social attitude survey
Scopa	Standing Committee on Public Accounts
SDI	Spatial Development Initiative
SDP	Strategic Defence Package
SEE	Survey of earnings and employment
SGB	Standards generating bodies
SIU	Special Investigation Unit
SOE	State-owned enterprises
SRNS	School register of needs survey
Stats SA	Statistics South Africa
STD	Sexually transmitted disease
Swapo	South West African Peoples' Organisation
TAC	Treatment Action Campaign
TI 2003	Transparency International corruption perception index
TIPS	Trade and Industry Policy Strategies
Trac	Transvaal Rural Action Committee
TRC	Truth and Reconciliation Commission
UCDP	United Christian Democratic Party
UCT	University of Cape Town
UDM	United Democratic Movement
UDW	University of Durban-Westville
UMNO	United Malays' National Organisation
UN	United Nations
UNDP	United Nations Development Programme

UNODC	United Nations Office on Drugs and Crime
Unicef	United Nations Children's Fund
Unita	National Union for the Total Independence of Angola
VIPs	Ventilated improved privies
WC	Western Cape
WTO	World Trade Organization
Zanu-PF	Zimbabwe African National Union-Patriotic Front

Introduction: President Mbeki's second term: opening the golden door?

John Daniel, Roger Southall and Jessica Lutchman

> The era's beginning: are these ruined shacks,
> these poor schools, these people still in rags and tatters,
> this cloddish insecurity of my poor families,
> is all this the day?
> The Century's beginning, the golden door?
> *Citation by President Thabo Mbeki of Chilean poet,*
> *Pablo Neruda, in Parliament, 5 February 2004*

The celebrations of ten years of democracy in South Africa are continuing, and rightly so. The elections of 1994 marked the most significant juncture ever in South African history, away from a society which employed race as its fundamental organising principle and which condemned the majority of people to poverty and oppression on grounds of colour, to one which aspires to the abolition of race as a criterion of status, class and wealth, to political equality and to 'a better life for all'.

In 2004, South Africa remains confronted by a wholly formidable raft of problems: the majority of people are still appallingly poor, economic growth is insufficient to guarantee mass improvement, social inequality remains rife, and democracy itself faces major challenges. And yet South Africa is a different country, a country which compared to ten years ago is more united, more peaceful, more optimistic, more self-confident and more ambitious. Lest we forget, it is a fundamentally better and morally far superior place than it was in 1994. Yet it is also one where progress towards a better future cannot be guaranteed, and depends significantly upon the choices that are made by government. It is therefore of considerable relevance that 2004 was a year in which the African National Congress (ANC) government of President Thabo Mbeki appeared to confirm a significant change in direction. But how big a change was it? And where is it likely to lead?

2004: a year of two speeches

The end of South Africa's first decade of democracy was concurrent with the holding of a third general election, which took place on April 14. The expected return of the ANC to power would also see the beginning of Thabo Mbeki's second, and under the Constitution, his concluding term as president. These were all key factors which rendered 2004 a year of not just the customary one but of two presidential speeches on 'The State of the Nation'. The first was delivered on 6 February at the beginning of the last session of the outgoing Parliament; the second on 21 May at the opening of the first session of the new (Mbeki 2004a, 2004b). They were significantly different in style and content. The first celebrated achievement, reflecting Mbeki the seer, the visionary and the poet; the second recorded ambition, emphasising Mbeki the leader and the technocrat determined to make his mark on history.

During the latter half of 2003, the government had undertaken a ten-year review of its record since taking power (PCAS 2003). This was to inform Mbeki's first presentation, but only after he had recalled the triumph over apartheid and the way that it had 'radically and irrevocably' changed people's lives. For the black, especially African majority, he declared, liberation in 1994 had augured 'a new dawn (that) proclaimed the coming of a bright day', where previously they had only known despair. Despite having been victims of racism and violence, the masses had stood side by side with their former oppressors at the voting booths and embraced dialogue, reconciliation and peace. In so doing, they began the process of overcoming the fears of those – like Afrikaans journalist Rian Malan – who had predicted majority rule as ushering in an apocalypse. As demanded by Nelson Mandela when he had delivered his own first 'State of the Nation' speech in 1994, South African democracy had achieved 'the frontiers of human fulfillment, and the continuous extension of the frontiers of freedom'.

Borrowing from the ten-year review, Mbeki trumpeted the official statistics of achievement. Between 1994 and 2004, over 1.9 million housing subsidies had been provided and 1.6 million houses built for the poor; more than 70 per cent of households had become electrified and an additional nine million people had been provided access to clean water. By 2004, 63 per cent of households had access to sanitation, the previously racially divided education system had been integrated (even though there was urgent need for more resource allocation and capacity building in rural areas), secondary school enrolment had reached 85 per cent, and nutrition and early childhood interventions had been established to improve the lives of children from poor backgrounds. He could also have added, had he drawn more heavily from the ten-year review, that 1.8 million hectares of land had been redistributed, and 1.6 million jobs had been created (even though unemployment had increased because of job losses in established industries and the high rate of inflow of new entrants to the labour market), and poverty rates had declined significantly. But he did also stress that these delivery gains had been matched by the reduction of a two-decade rate of double-digit inflation to less than 4 per cent, a move from negative to the longest period of consistently positive growth since the 1940s, and the transition from South Africa being a country constantly in debt to one which was now in surplus. Much remained to be done to meet outstanding challenges, and to eradicate poverty and underdevelopment, but the policies needed to meet them were in place, and there was no foreseeable reason to change them. What was now needed was their vigorous implementation to create a 'winning people-centred society'. The first decade of democracy, proclaimed Mbeki (before concluding his speech with the quotation from Chilean poet Pablo Neruda which is cited earlier), had laid the sure foundation for even greater advances in the second.

Mbeki's elegant first speech was more presidential than partisan, yet nonetheless presented the ANC's platform for the forthcoming election. Not surprisingly, with the polls in view, it put a strongly positive spin on the government's performance, glossed over its failures, and was strangely silent – no, monstrously silent – on the challenges presented by HIV/AIDS. Yet it also stressed continuity over change, obscuring changes which had already begun to take place in economic policy.

The story of the incoming ANC-led government's shift from the social democratically-inclined Reconstruction and Development Programme (RDP) to the conservative Growth, Employment and Redistribution strategy (GEAR) is a familiar one. According to the government's more radical critics, many of whom reside within its partners in the Tripartite Alliance, the Congress of South African Trade Unions (Cosatu) and the South African Communist Party (SACP), it either 'sold-out' its liberatory ideals or buckled under pressure from international, 'neo-liberal' forces (notably the International Monetary Fund and World Bank). The outcome was its adoption of a home-grown structural adjustment programme which, at the cost of jobs and the needs of the poor, stressed debt reduction and inflation control, privatisation, deregulation of financial controls, trade liberalisation, export promotion, and labour-market flexibility in order to achieve a more internationally competitive economy. For its part, the government maintained that global economic realities dictated the need for it to arrest the alarming decline of an economy battered by years of international isolation and domestic turmoil, and to win international confidence. Only by addressing the country's macroeconomic fundamentals could the objectives of the RDP be realised. These issues and those discussed in the two paragraphs that follow are examined in more detail in the chapters by Stephen Gelb, Reg Rumney and Miriam Altman in the economy section of this volume.

The government's (relative) success in transforming a previously highly-protected, inward-looking and inefficient economy to one that is financially well-managed, market-driven and more competitive has become the stuff of international fiscal legend. Furthermore, whatever their misgivings about the conservative nature of policy, the majority of South Africans were apprecia-tive of a government that was, in macroeconomic terms, self-evidently com-petent, and much more so than the National Party (NP) government which had preceded it. Not for nothing was Finance Minister Trevor Manuel able to compound his high standing in international financial circles with immense popularity within the ANC. However, the problem that increasingly confronted the government was that its conservative strategies failed to deliver the returns that global economic orthodoxy promised for it.

However much the government could redefine employment (to argue, in essence, that job losses in declining industries were more than compensated for by new ones in service industries and the informal sector), unemploy-ment went on increasing (to a level of over 40 per cent in 2003). However much it sought to tackle poverty (and the statistics are impressive that it did), the government's own instrument to examine the need and potential for a comprehensive system of social security (the Taylor Commission for the Department of Social Development) was to admit in 2002 that between 45 and 55 per cent of the population were poor, that 10 per cent of the African population were malnourished and that 25 per cent of African chil-dren are born stunted. And however much the government preached greater equality, it was faced by the news that whilst income differentials between white and black were narrowing, those within the African population and the country as a whole were widening (SAIRR 2001:374 citing Stats SA 2000). The United Nations Development Progamme (UNDP) reported that the percentage of the population living below US$1 per day had increased from 9.4 per cent in 1995 (3.7 million) to 10.5 per cent in 2002 (4.7 million), and that the extent of poverty in South Africa had increased absolutely between those years (UNDP 2003:42). Alarmingly, too, life-expectancy had declined from 57 to 55 years. For all the government's macroeconomic 'responsibility', economic growth was insufficient to keep pace with South Africa's minimum demands, domestic saving remained low (16 per cent in 2002) (SARB 2003:19), and international investors continued to look askance. Indeed, between 1994 and 2002, the average flows of incoming foreign direct investment (FDI) amounted to only 1.4 per cent of gross domestic product (GDP).

Faced by strong indications of policy failure and mounting domestic political pressures (notably around poverty and jobs), the government began to quietly question its own orthodoxy in favour of a more interventionist economic strategy. In the words of the *Mail & Guardian* (20–26.02.04), budgets from 2001 onward registered a thawing of the government's self-imposed 'ideological ice age' and 'acceptance that an active state role in the economy is inevitable in a country like South Africa'. This shift culminated in a pre-election budget in February 2004 which featured a 9 per cent growth in government expenditure featuring, *inter alia*, a large-scale public works programme, at a cost to the state of over R15 billion over four years, and an increase in welfare and social spending of 14 per cent over the next three years, following a 22 per cent rise between 2002 and 2004. If market forces alone cannot resolve the problems of poverty and unemployment, Mbeki had mused in mid-2003, then the government would have to intervene in the economy more directly. The public works programme would be implemented through the private sector, which would be invited to tender for labour-intensive infrastructural projects, yet the government's thinking now also stressed an increased role for the public sector, with privatisation now taking second place to reform of the parastatals (such as Eskom and Transnet) and public-private partnerships. 'With the renewed focus on poverty eradication,' noted the prominent analyst Robyn Chalmers (*Business Day* 31.05.04), 'government has decided a new approach is required, with the focus on parastatal investment rather than big asset sales' – all at the same time as giving assurances to foreign investors that it has not abandoned its privatisation policy! From 2000 onwards, meanwhile, the government had also begun to adopt a more vigorous set of policies towards black economic empowerment (BEE), taking the view that if white capital was not able or willing to create a new class of black, 'patriotic' entrepreneurs, they should be propelled and assisted into doing so. For more discussion of BEE, see Roger Southall's chapter in the economy section of this volume.

The *Mail & Guardian* (20–26.02.04) had opined that the language of the Finance Minister's pre-election budget speech had harked back to the 'halcyon days of the Reconstruction and Development Programme'. Mbeki's post-election address at the inauguration of the new Parliament confirmed that the state was about to play a considerably more activist economic role. The government's response to poverty and underdevelopment, he declared, rested on three pillars, namely, encouraging the growth and development of the 'first economy', increasing its potential to create jobs; addressing the challenges of the 'second economy';[1] and building a social security net to meet the objective of poverty alleviation.

What was so thoroughly remarkable about Mbeki's plans for the first economy was that although they promised greater efforts at attracting greater domestic and foreign investment, the overwhelming emphasis was placed upon government and public-sector action. In recognition of the low rate of domestic saving, institutional investors would be 'engaged' to locate five per cent of their funds in the 'real economy' (that is, labour-intensive investments); the state-owned enterprises (SOEs) would announce new plans for investment in September; the cost of doing business would be aggressively tackled through the restructuring of the public infrastructure, notably the ports, railways and electricity provision; there would be more official attention to the development of small and medium business, and the Agricultural Credit Scheme re-established to provide capital for agriculture; and more would be done to speed skills development, assist exports and increase research and development. A Black Economic Advisory Council would be established as a matter of urgency, and the National Empowerment Fund would announce new measures within the next three months, mindful of the government's provision of R10 billion for BEE over the next five years.

Plans for the second economy included the launch of the Expanded Public Works Programme in September, concentrating on the 21 urban and rural nodes identified by the government's Urban Renewal and Integrated and Sustainable Rural Development Programmes. The state's extension of micro-credit would soon come on track, and the Department of Agriculture would intensify its support to agricultural activities in communal land areas and for co-operative enterprises.

However, it was very much the target setting for poverty alleviation which invited media comment that Mbeki meant serious business over the course of his second term. Government, he declared, *will* work to ensure that social grants reach all 7.7 million beneficiaries; it *will* add about 3.2 million children to the child support grants register as the upper-age limit is raised to children turning 14; it *will* allocate R166 billion over three years for social security; it *will* ensure that all households have easy access to clean running water within the next five years; it *will* provide 300 000 households with basic sanitation during the current year; it *will* ensure that each household has access to electricity within the next eight years. Other targets, notably within the health sphere (including a promise that 113 health facilities would be fully operational by March 2005 to cope with the Comprehensive Plan on HIV and AIDS) and with regard to safety and security, were also proclaimed.

This time round, a concluding poetical flourish was eschewed in favour of a blunt instruction to the South African people to 'get down to work'.

Mbeki, opined one columnist, was 'a man in a hurry'. Unlike his predecessor, Nelson Mandela, he had not had sainthood thrust upon him, and he had a single remaining term to make his mark on history. But why set up such tight deadlines? Because in three years the battle for the succession within the ANC would be raging, and he would be a lame-duck president. Unless he secured rapid achievements, he would, according to Justice Malala, become 'a blip in South Africa's history' (*ThisDay* 25.04.04).

Mbeki's embarkation upon his final term was clearly a major factor in defining the pace and direction of the government's priorities. However, the bigger question is whether the second 'State of the Nation' speech represents merely a pragmatic shift in government strategy or points to the consolidation of a grander vision for South Africa's transformation.

Towards a developmental state?

There is a growing sense that South Africa stands on the cusp of a significant change, perhaps even a paradigm shift, in the direction of public policy. There has been a careful review by government of the experiences of the first ten years of democracy; there is a clear indication of a reconsideration of GEAR; there has been an election campaign in which the issues of equality and poverty ranked high upon the agenda; the ANC was returned with an increased majority, and unarguably, has a mandate to pursue transformative policies; and, at the beginning of his second term, Mbeki is generally regarded, with perhaps three exceptions, as having favoured merit and ability to deliver over party standing in his appointment of a new Cabinet and new premiers. The ground seems to have been cleared for something big.

There is one line of thought that, after encountering the inadequacies of GEAR, the government is swinging back to the RDP. The ANC leadership's rapprochement with Cosatu and the SACP within the Tripartite Alliance which took place in 2003, after the tensions of the previous year when the latter organisations were accused of being 'ultra-left', is also sometimes taken as indication that the government is reverting to a more redistributive or even 'socialist' platform. Indeed, this has even prompted the suggestion that the Mbeki government is opting for third-way-style social democracy.

This latter view was encouraged by Thabo Mbeki joining leading politicians of the centre-left, including Prime Minister Tony Blair, at a second 'progressive governance' conference summit organised under the banner of the 'Third Way' in July 2003. The first such meeting had taken place six years previously, and had brought together centre-left governments and parties with similarly-minded governments from southern countries such as Brazil, Argentina, Chile, Taiwan and South Korea. South Africa's invitation to the second of these gatherings was viewed as public testimony to the ANC's social-democratic inclinations.

The third way is a descendant of the 'revisionist socialism' of the early twentieth century. Its guiding principles have been the realisation of the classic goals of social democracy (such as social equality, pluralism, human rights and workers' participation) through democratic means, and politically, it has favoured pragmatism over dogmatism. In its more recent manifestations, associated with the philosophies of Blair and former US president Bill

Clinton, the third way argues the need to cope with globalisation by combining the benefits of the free market (economic efficiency, growth and competition) with a renovation of the welfare state to materialise sustainable conditions of economic growth in ways that do not imperil the improvement, of social justice, social cohesion and individual liberty. The rights of both individual and corporate citizens (that is, business) are said to be balanced against responsibilities (Blair 1998; Giddens 1998).

From this perspective, the ANC can be said to be following the third way because, under its rule:

- South Africa has embraced progressive governance policies with sound macroeconomic policies which seek to reap the benefits of globalisation and market efficiency.
- The relationship between state, market and civil society has been redefined, so that market-oriented policies are articulated with the promotion of democracy, engagement with civil society, and the protection of the most vulnerable in society. The government pursues a social compact with all major 'stakeholders' through such devices as the National Economic Development and Labour Council (Nedlac), Growth and Development Summits and so on.
- South Africa pursues progressive policies in the international arena, most notably with regard to its central role in the promotion of the New Partnership for Africa's Development (Nepad), which seeks to pursue third-way strategies revolving around market efficiency and good governance continentally. Mbeki has emerged as an African statesman determined to reshape the architecture of global political and economic governance in order to cater for the needs of Africa, the South and the global poor.

A third-way interpretation of the ANC's strategy is not without merit, not least because it points to broad outlooks on the world which it shares with the European centre-left, most notably the vision of 'New Labour' as presented by Tony Blair. Importantly, it also offers a counterpoint to views which characterise the government's policy as neo-liberal, ignoring its very real commitment to poverty alleviation and redistribution to achieve greater racial equality. More obliquely, it also raises important questions about the ideological reorientation not only of the ANC but also of its ally the SACP, which remains shy about defining its relationship to social democracy following the collapse of Soviet-style communism. However, given the numerous objections to what is widely perceived to be the incoherence and vagueness of the third way, and in recent times the alignment of its most eminent practitioner, Tony Blair, with American imperialism in Iraq, it does not seem to take us very far. This is apart from the fact that Mbeki can be arguably more strongly identified with other projects such as the 'African Renaissance' and Pan-Africanism, whose relationship to third-wayism needs to be more elaborately defined.

At a more directly policy level, too, the social-democratic credentials of the government have been queried by Nicoli Nattrass in an important article in the *Mail & Guardian* (21–27.11.03). It may have empowered rather than weakened trade unions, but – in contrast to social democracies, which are characterised by high levels of taxation to pay for correspondingly high levels of equalising social spending – the ANC continues to pursue an economic strategy which hopes that low taxation and small budget deficits will boost growth and thereby alleviate poverty. Trevor Manuel's latest budget may have announced the new public works programme and promised to provide funding for the comprehensive roll-out of anti-retroviral drugs in the war against AIDS, but his allowing the budget deficit to increase over the short term for manifestly electoral reasons should not be confused with a major shift in economic direction. The option of raising taxation was not placed on the agenda, and the government remains committed to 'trickle-down' economics rather than social democracy. It also remains firmly committed to lowering the cost of business and offering incentives for business development.

Even if the depiction of the government as pursuing a third way or social democratic agenda is not convincing, a credible argument can be made that its recent economic policy shifts have been more than pragmatic, and that they articulate with a comprehensive agenda of transformation that Mbeki, now a second and final-term president, is particularly concerned to pursue. This would seem to draw inspiration far less from socialism than from the idea of an Asian-style (capitalist) 'developmental state'. Most particularly, it would appear to borrow from the experience of Malaysia, which has been particularly influential in shaping the ANC's ideas about how to combine growth with racial redistribution.

A debate in the literature on the reasons for the success of high-performing East and South-East Asian economies matches a neo-classical viewpoint against revisionism. The former argues that the high-performing countries got 'the basics right', by which is meant that they provided a stable macro-economic environment, a reliable legal framework and incentives for export orientation, whilst refraining from interfering with price formation, foreign trade and the economic functioning of private enterprises. In addition, their governments also invested heavily in health and education. In contrast, revisionists like Amsden (1989) and Wade (1990) propose that these states have governed the markets in critical ways, notably by consciously manipulating prices to promote selective sector development. 'The revisionists contend that the East Asian governments have consistently and deliberately remedied market failures and altered the incentive structure to boost industries that would not otherwise have thrived' (Martinussen 1999:269). Overall, there is a high level of government intervention, yet the interventionism is different from that which has normally obtained in post-colonial Africa. Whereas the latter has emphasised restrictions and control, the developmental states have provided a policy framework for competition, growth and export.

Without being unduly mechanistic, it is arguable that the Mbeki government is in the throes of a shift away from the neo-classical to the revisionist stance. Having provided a stable and investor-friendly macroeconomic environment under GEAR and deregulated the economy in order to equip it to compete in an unforgiving global arena, the government has been pleased by the visible extent of its progress and the favourable reception it has received from business. However, it has been disappointed by the returns in terms of both growth and the redistribution of ownership and wealth between whites and blacks, and it is uncomfortably aware that these relative failures present a serious threat to long-term stability (and hence threaten to endanger its earlier achievements and return the country to square one). Given additional difficulties such as the problems presented by privatisation (which, contradictorily, requires extensive state financing if the desirable end of black ownership is to be achieved), the government is therefore shifting towards a more interventionist posture which will see a reinvigorated, stimulating role for public-sector enterprises and a more concerted effort to promote employment, growth and exports by its manipulating the market. If overall the government will remain fiscally cautious and conservative, it will nonetheless combine this with a greater sense of adventure.

This interpretation blends in with the ANC's own particular perspective that its task – as well as transforming the economy – has been to fashion a modern, democratic state out of the backward-looking inheritance of apartheid. This has entailed the fashioning of an efficient machinery of governance out of the amalgam of a racially-divided central authority and 'self-governing' and juridically 'independent' African homelands which existed prior to 1994. This has entailed, *inter alia*, the pursuit of a fairly centralised model of rule. During the negotiations process, the ANC had had to compromise upon its preference for a central state by agreement to the creation of the nine new provinces. However, since being in power, the ANC has been determined to ensure that the provinces, most of which have incorporated former homelands, shall not become obstacles to a common vision of identity, growth and development for the 'new South Africa'. Through central appointment rather than local election of premiers, and through assertion of presidential and party disciplines, the ANC has not so much threatened democracy (as federalist-inclined parties like the Democratic Alliance [DA] and Inkatha Freedom Party [IFP] imply) as ensured that development and delivery shall not be inhibited by the growth of provincial baronies. From this perspective, the ANC's political dominance is an expression of democratic will and modernisation, rather than the instrument of potential dictatorship and developmental stagnation that some of its critics imply.

The relationship between the three levels of power (national, provincial and local) prescribed by the 1996 Constitution is that of co-operative governance, yet the ANC's vision, in practice, is that of highly centralised co-operation. This accords closely to the model of centralised federalism which obtains in Malaysia, where since the adoption of its New Economic Policy (NEP) in 1970, the ruling United Malays' National Organisation (UMNO) has used its status as a dominant party to combine its oversight and stimulation of the rapid growth of the economy with a significant transfer of ownership and wealth away from the minority Chinese (37 per cent of the population) to the politically ascendant Malays (50 per cent of the population) and the ambigu-ously-situated Indians (11 per cent).

There is, inevitably, considerable debate as to the credit that the Malaysian state can claim for the rapid growth that the economy enjoyed after 1970. However, what has particularly attracted the ANC is the way in which the NEP set and pursued targets for the increased employment, education and owner-ship for the disadvantaged Malays and other indigenous peoples over a 20-year period, in order to ensure that employment at all levels and in all sectors should come to reflect the racial composition of the population. Likewise, the NEP also prescribed that these *bumiputera* (sons of the soil) should come to own 30 per cent of total commercial and industrial enterprises over the same time span. Although these targets were not uniformly met, they have accounted for a major transformation in employment and ownership patterns in favour of Malays, and in particular given rise to the substantial growth of the Malay middle class. Given also that by 1990 the share of *bumiputera* equity holdings amounted to over 20 per cent of the total, the attractions of the Malaysian model to the ANC are obvious (Southall 1997).

Of course, there are major differences between the historical and temporal locations of the South African and Malaysian developmental experiences. Indeed, there are strong grounds for believing that today's ANC is far less in control of the possibilities for economic growth than was UMNO at the time it launched the NEP (Southall 1997). Nonetheless, there can be no doubting the attraction that the Malaysian model holds for the ANC, not least because it provides a template for its present more vigorous assertion of broad-based black economic empowerment.

The proposition that the ANC is in the throes of shifting from GEAR to a more interventionist, developmental state needs to be treated cautiously. At this stage, it is more a working hypothesis than an unambiguously asserted conclusion. Nonetheless, it does make more sense than competing explanations that changes in economic policy since the start of the present century amount either to an adoption of social democracy on the one hand, or represent merely pragmatic adjustments to policy on the other. As with any government, the ANC is always forced to grapple with immediate and short-term considerations. However, it is also a liberation movement which has embarked upon a long-term project. What recent developments suggest is that short-term policy changes are increasingly being influenced by long-term thinking, and that at the outset of his final term as President, Thabo Mbeki is determined to make his mark on history. But if this is true, what are the foreseeable difficulties and problems which this vision is likely to encounter?

Problems along the way

Whether or not the Mbeki government is on the way to refashioning itself into a developmental state, it is going to encounter three sets of problems in its bid to boost growth and development in South Africa. These relate to first, *state capacity*; second, *the global and African environment*; and third, *democratic accountability*.

State capacity

Peter Evans (1995), a theorist who has made extensive studies of the state in the Third World, has drawn a distinction between predatory, intermediate and developmental states:

- The *predatory state*, which is controlled by a small political elite and often an authoritarian leader, is characterised by an incoherent and inefficient administration. The political elite use their power to plunder resources, and as a result the state has very little capacity to promote development. There are no shortages of examples from post-independence Africa of such states, the most spectacular being Mobutu's Zaire, Nigeria under a succession of military rulers and, of course, Zimbabwe today.
- The *developmental state* is characterised by a coherent bureaucracy with an homogeneous administrative culture which has the capacity to perform the functions assigned to it. Importantly, this bureaucracy has a considerable degree of autonomy *vis á vis* both political and economic elites, even though it has many and close connections with private interest groups, especially large corporations. Nonetheless there is a clear division of labour: the political elite dominates long-term strategic decision-making; implementation is carried out by the bureaucracy; and economic activity is left to corporations, which although enjoying free-dom in their day-to-day operations, function within broad parameters laid down by the state. South Korea is regarded as the major example.
- *Intermediate states*, exemplified by Brazil, are located between the two extremes. They possess considerable administrative capacity, and in some respects enjoy independence from both political and economic elites, although they often face challenges of internal coherence and stability.[2]

Chalmers Johnson (2001), another theorist, has endorsed the basic outline of Evans's theory, but stresses in addition that the developmental state enjoys political stability, that its bureaucracy is insulated from direct political influ-ence so that it can operate technocratically, and that it engages in extensive investment in education as well as pursuing concerted action to ensure the equitable distribution of opportunities and wealth. In addition, 'the capitalist developmental state pursues market-conforming interventions, rather than market repressing or replacing interventions' (Martinussen 1999:239).

Even this brief review indicates that, for the Mbeki government, the developmental state is more reference group than reality. To be sure, and thankfully so, South Africa under the ANC is far distant from the predatory model, against which Mbeki – albeit diplomatically – has declared battle via his strong personal commitment to the African Peer Review Mechanism, which constitutes an essential aspect of Nepad. However, apart from the questionable issue of the extent to which the government is prepared to risk loss of investor confidence by the adoption of a less conservative fiscal policy, there are arguably (at least) two major obstacles in the way of South Africa's progressing towards the status of a development state.

The first is the limited technical capacity of the public service, which blends with deficiencies in human resource development more generally. Andre Kraak, writing in the Human Sciences Research Council's recent *Human Resources Development Review 2003* (Kraak 2003) has elaborated with impressive authority what is generally recognised: that South Africa does not possess highly skilled labour in sufficient quantities to supply a rapidly modernising economy and that the shortages of training and scientific achievement are most acute amongst the black majority, and are made more acute by the emigration of professionals. Significantly, Kraak recommends (and commends existing moves towards) 'joined-up' policymaking oriented towards the medium and long term and pursuit of priorities across the breadth of government (notably key line departments), alongside the determined pursuit of industrial policy objectives (including research and development) and the 'implementation of a multi-layered economic growth, employment and skills formation strategy that will simultaneously build upon the country's low-, intermediate- and high-skill bases' (Kraak 2003:25). This issue is also explored by Vino Naidoo in a chapter in the politics section of this volume.

The racial disjunction is, of course, one of the most notorious outcomes of apartheid, and its elimination constitutes one of the government's most pressing priorities. Inevitably, too, it has had a major impact upon the labour market, one of whose most defining characteristics is the enormous demographic over-representation of whites in management. Hence, according to one account, although white male representation in management had declined since 1994, white males still held 63 per cent of managerial jobs in 2000, whilst blacks represented merely 20 per cent (Horwitz & Bowmaker-Falconer 2003:616–20). In this context, although private industry is increasingly subject to 'equity' demands to employ more blacks, it is to increased employment of blacks in the public sector that the government has looked to correct the global imbalance (and to satisfy the demands of its political constituency). However, whilst this is a necessary and welcome development, the rapid transformation of the public service has had to be carried through in the face of glaring training and skills deficiencies amongst blacks, with the inevitable result that many government departments are severely under-capacitated. Although, as Naidoo indicates in his chapter, there has been a concerted shift towards modern managerial systems to improve efficiency and effectiveness, it is the failings of the civil service which continue to provide much of the stuff of media reportage and urban legend. In this context, however much the Office of the Presidency and other high-level bodies may devise ambitious long-term plans, severe problems of implementation are likely to remain over at least the medium term – and certainly for the duration of Mbeki's second term.

The second major obstacle to South Africa moving towards the status of a development state is that of a lack of national coherence. The country's democratic transition was famously erected upon a basis of reconciliation between oppressors and oppressed, black and white, in a land where race had historically been the primary criterion for allocating wealth, power and life-chances. However, although it is generally acknowledged that considerable progress towards a common–sense of citizenship and nationhood has been made since 1994, fault lines based upon race continue to shape opportunity and attitudes. For instance, a recent survey conducted by the HSRC indicates consistently that, within an overall context in which less than half of respondents (45.8 per cent) indicated that they were satisfied with democracy, whites were consistently more negative in their attitudes towards the state of the nation and its prospects than Africans (who constitute a 70 per cent demographic majority). Thirty-eight per cent of Africans thought that life had improved since 1999, but only 13 per cent of whites; and whereas 62 per cent of Africans recorded trust in national government, the corresponding figure for whites was only 25 per cent (Daniel & Southall forthcoming). There is scarcely need to elaborate that white perceptions of diminishing opportunity attendant upon equity pressures, BEE and a less than satisfactory rate of economic growth may easily lead to declining commitment to democratic South Africa, whilst black impatience with continuing white privilege (even if the latter is based upon the possession of valuable skills) may equally likely translate into racial tensions. To be sure, these tensions may be mitigated by the growth of a black middle class and the resultant overall decline in economic inequality between black and white. Against this, class tensions (which will be interlaced with those of race) may simultaneously be increased by the currently growing *overall* level of inequality within South Africa, one of whose major characteristics is the divide between those employed in the formal, core economy and a large underclass, which is condemned to struggling for survival in an expanding informal economy.

In a context as peculiarly complex as that of post-apartheid South Africa, the challenges posed by race and class are formidable, and undermine the desirability of the country as a site for investment. For example, AngloGold's Chief Executive, Bobby Godsell, recently reported that UK fund managers regard investment in South Africa as more risky than in Russia or China, largely because of uncertainties regarding black empowerment (*Business Day* 25.05.04).

How the government manages these challenges and markets this management to international investors will clearly be an important factor in determining South Africa's development status.

The global and African environment

Democratic South Africa is engaging in its bid for development in considerably less propitious circumstances than those which faced the East and South-East Asian development states. They were able to take advantage of a major shift in the international division of labour, which in the post-Second World War era saw western corporations taking advantage of new technologies in communications and production to move many of their operations from high-labour-cost industrialised countries to low-cost, non-industrialised countries. Some, like South Korea and Taiwan, were also to be direct beneficiaries of their strategic significance to the West in the Cold War, and were to become major recipients of US and multilateral aid. The contemporary world is very different, and is one in which the end of the Cold War has enabled the transnational production process to become truly globalised, with China – in particular – having entered the reckoning as a site of production with inexhaustible supplies of cheap labour subject to despotic control by a market-oriented communist party overseer. The outcome is a highly globalised production system in which the capacity of individual states – especially those which are weak and poor – to steer their own economic fortunes has been substantially eroded as they are compelled to compete against each other for scarce supplies of foreign investment. Hence, whilst international political goodwill and an unwillingness to undermine the democratic transition may have provided South Africa with a degree of preferential market access during its first ten years of democracy, the country is likely to become just one more competitor as the memory of its achievement fades.

As noted earlier, the South African government's adoption of GEAR and its bid to deregulate the economy were designed to render the latter more able to compete internationally. It has been rewarded with considerable successes, as various sectors of South African industry have conquered new export markets. A case in point is the motor industry, which has boosted its exports from 5 per cent with a value of less than R4 billion in 1995 to 35 per cent with a value of more than R40 billion in 2004 (*Financial Mail* 21.05.04).

However, the major problem for South Africa, as for other countries of the South, is that the neo-liberal policies which favour and structure globalisation are increasing inequalities both within and between countries. 'Global inequality has increased sharply since the 1980s, in a clear rupture with the pattern over previous decades. The growth of extreme poverty coincides with an explosion of wealth over the same time period' (Pieterse 2002:1024). Within this context, the opportunities for poorer countries from the South to emulate the East Asian miracle are increasingly limited, especially given the migration of capital and production to post-communist Russia and Eastern Europe. Improvement of state and human resource capacities may serve to improve competitiveness, but prospects of making significant strides up the global ladder are minimal, and in any case likely to accrue only to the more advantaged within each country. 'While East and South-East Asian countries as a whole deviate from the pattern of increasing global inequality, inequality *within* these societies has increased' (Pieterse 2002:1029).

One major bright spot for South Africa is its growing trading and industrial presence in Africa (Daniel, Naidoo & Naidu 2003). However, it is not for nothing that Africa is sometimes described as the forgotten continent. According to the World Trade Organisation (WTO), Africa's share of world exports dropped from a dismal 3.1 per cent in 1990 to an even more catastrophic 2.2 per cent in 2002, whilst imports dropped from 2.8 to 2.1 per cent over the same period. This is against a background of the decline of Africa's share of world trade from 4 to 2 per cent in the 1980s. This truly appalling record clearly sets limits to any idea of South Africa staging a major development process on the back of its ease of access to the continent. Equally, it underlines the importance which President Mbeki attaches to Nepad as a platform for attracting higher levels of foreign investment in Africa as a boost to growth. In Africa's miserable condition, even marginal improvements would be welcome. Yet if, as critics suggest, Nepad is merely GEAR writ large for the continent, there are limited prospects for growth save for bonanzas linked to resource exploitation (notably oil), whose benefits will accrue largely to foreign oil companies and local elites and will do little to change the continent's role in the chain of global production. These issues are also touched upon in the chapter by Daniel, Lutchman and Naidu in the last section of this volume.

The indications that the South African government is rethinking aspects of GEAR and contemplating a more assertive role for the state in development suggest that it may become more willing to challenge the rules of the global economic game as they are dictated by multilateral institutions such as the International Monetary Fund, World Bank and WTO. Hence the importance of its linking up with other southern powers such as Brazil and India to challenge neo-liberal shibboleths. Much is made of the commitments to good governance in Nepad. However, it is only a revolution in governance globally, entailing a political choice to overcome global poverty, which is likely to alter the patterns of global inequality which are so sharply replicated within South Africa.

Democratic accountability and development

Stephen Friedman is among those who see the delivery targets established in the President's second 'State of the Nation' speech as providing a tool for opposition parties and civil society to hold government accountable (*Business Day* 2.06.04). He welcomes this as providing for the possibility of a dialogue which involves ordinary people in the realisation of development goals, at the same time as it keeps government in touch with ordinary people's wants and needs.

Friedman is not alone in regarding Mbeki's commitment to hard goals, which may open the government up to sharp criticism if it fails to achieve them, as commendable. However, whilst the prevailing wisdom today is very much that development is promoted by democracy, developmental states have often leaned strongly towards authoritarianism.

Malaysia, the country to which the ANC looks in such admiration, is a case in point. Formally it is a democracy, but the challenges posed by combining inter-ethnic redistribution with development have led to severe restrictions of civil liberty. Discussion of sensitive issues has been curtailed, the press has often been restricted, interest groups curbed, and the judiciary subject to political pres-sures. Furthermore, notably under the long prime ministership (1981–2003) of Mahathir bin Mohamed, the autonomy of the federal states was reined in, and the ruling party as well as the bureaucracy subjected to his highly personalised authority. But as in South Africa, the opposition parties were fragmented and unable to pose a challenge to UMNO, which wins recurrent elections. These are free of gross fraud, and parties and interest groups are allowed to organise, but they are subject to various restrictions, and ultimately 'the government keeps them so weak that they cannot mobilize a broad following and, in the end, wield little influence' (Neher & Marlay 1995:105).

It is scarcely surprising that Malaysia has been described by some analysts as a 'façade democracy'. Yet it is widely regarded as a qualified success because, for all its flaws, Malaysians have enjoyed a rate of economic growth that has been achieved by few other developing nations. In particular, the ruling party has attracted the support of the large middle class, which has been willing to trade its civil liberties for the benefits of prosperity (Kahn 1996).

UMNO has presided over the Malaysian development experience as a domi-nant party, in much the same way as the ANC has established its hegemony over the South African political arena since 1994. Most notably, it has become the vehicle of a new, largely Malay bourgeoisie, which has been largely empowered through *bumiputerisation* and privatisation. However, this class has become overwhelmingly dependent upon government favours and is widely regarded as pursuing rent-seeking rather than profit-making goals. In other words, the inter-ethnic redistribution project may have weakened what might have been a greater growth effort, as it is widely believed that the ethnic Malay-dominated government has actually favoured industrialisation under foreign transnational auspices in preference to the likely alternative of ethnic Chinese dominance (Southall 1997).

The low inflow of foreign investment into South Africa suggests that an equivalent trade-off may not be possible, and that if black empowerment initiatives are to promote development at the same time as effecting redistribution, they will have to work in harmony with and not at the cost of domestic white capital. This suggests the need for greater stress upon good corporate governance in South Africa than has historically obtained in Malaysia in order to constrain the tendencies towards 'crony capitalism' which can so easily be encouraged by the centrality of the allocation of government contracts to the promotion of BEE. In turn, this will require of the ANC that it rises above the temptation to inhibit democratic accountability, which is an inevitable accompaniment of its status as a dominant party.

Looking beyond tomorrow

It is easier to criticise than to govern. Any recitation of problems facing the post-apartheid government is likely to be both daunting and depressing and any examination of the dilemmas facing the development process will reinforce convictions that there is no easy road ahead, whatever strategies are adopted. However, what such considerations do suggest is that any government in Pretoria requires a long-term vision of South Africa's development as much as the ability to cope with the multiple, often conflicting, demands of the short term. During the first ten years of democracy, the ANC-led government was challenged by the immediacy of working a new Constitution, extending its control over the state, and renovating an economy which had been run down by decades of apartheid.

At the beginning of the second decade, there are indications that there is a shift towards the taking of a long-term view, a perspective not unfamiliar to a liberation movement which struggled for 82 years to come to power. This does not render Mbeki's South Africa a developmental state, for numerous contradictions remain at the heart of government policy and numerous questions abound about whether the experiences of the likes of Malaysia can be replicated.

However, it does suggest that during Mbeki's second presidential term he is determined to push hard to open the golden door.

Most of the contributions to this second *State of the Nation* volume were written before President Mbeki's second 'State of the Nation' speech of this year was delivered.

In his 'State of the Nation' speech in 2001, President Mbeki identified 43 delivery targets. A team at Stellenbosch University, under the economist, Willie Esterhuyse, analysed their implementation and reported that in an 11-month period '65 per cent of these have either been achieved or are credibly in progress' (Mbeki 2002), while only 16 per cent had not been attained. On the rest there was insufficient information, the team reported, on which to make a judgement. If just 70 per cent of the targets laid out in this address are achieved, then the country will have moved beyond the cusp and be deeply immersed in a transformation project of major proportions.

In its editorial comment after the second speech, *ThisDay* (24.04.04) noted that this was 'not an address by a politician sinking into complacency after an overwhelming electoral victory. Deadlines are a sure way to ensure accountability ... there was ... no fumbling around. Mbeki knows what he wants'. Target mapping will clearly have to form a central part of future annual editions of the *State of the Nation* volume. We will be checking to see if the President is getting what he wants and what the ANC believes the country needs. We will, in short, be watching to see if the golden door is finally opening.

Notes

1 The 'first economy' refers essentially to the modern, capitalist economy while the 'second ecomomy' refers broadly to those outside, or on the fringes of, the modern sector; that is, those in the informal, illicit and subsistence sectors.

2 This section is drawn from Martinussen (1997:238–39).

References

Amsden A (1989) *Asia's next giant: South Korea and late industrialization.*
New York: OUP.

Blair T (1998) *The third way: New politics for the new century.* London: Fabian Society.

Daniel J, Naidoo V & Naidu S (2003) The South Africans have arrived: Post-apartheid
corporate expansion into Africa. In J Daniel, A Habib & R Southall (eds.) *The State
of the Nation: South Africa 2003–04.* Cape Town: Human Sciences Research Council
(HSRC).

Daniel J & Southall R (forthcoming) Issues of politics, democracy, governance, the
Constitution and the citizen: South African social and political attitudes.
In B Roberts (ed.) *South African social attitudes survey (SASAS 1) 2003.*
Cape Town: HSRC.

Department of Social Development (South Africa) (2002) *Transforming the present –
protecting the future: Report of the Committee of Inquiry into a comprehensive system
of social security.* Pretoria: DoSD.

Evans P (1995) *Embedded autonomy: States and industrial transformations.* Princeton:
Princeton University Press.

Giddens A (1998) *The third way: The renewal of social democracy.* Cambridge: Polity.

Horwitz F & Bowmaker-Falconer A (2003) Managers. In HSRC *Human resources
development: Education, employment and skills in South Africa.* Cape Town: HSRC.

Johnson C (2001) *Japan: The rise of the developmental state.* New York: WW Norton.

Kahn J (1996) Growth, economic transformation, culture and the middle classes in
Malaysia. In R Robison & D Goodman (eds.) *The new rich in Asia: Mobile phones,
McDonalds and the middle class revolution.* London: Routledge.

Kraak A (2003) HRD and 'joined-up' policy. In HSRC *Human resources development:
Education, employment and skills in South Africa.* Cape Town: HSRC.

Martinussen J (1999) *Society, state and market: A guide to competing theories of
development.* Cape Town: HSRC.

Mbeki T (2002) State of the Nation address to the joint sitting of the Houses of
Parliament. Cape Town, 8.02.02.

Mbeki T (2004a) The State of the Nation Address at the opening of Parliament.
Cape Town, 5.02.04.

Mbeki T (2004b) Address of the President of South Africa, Thabo Mbeki, to the first joint sitting of the third democratic Parliament. Cape Town, 21.05.04.

Neher C & Marlay R (1995) *Democracy and development in Southeastern Asia: The winds of change.* Boulder, Colorado: Westview.

PCAS (Presidency Policy Co-ordination and Advisory Services, South Africa) (2003) *Towards a ten year review: Synthesis report on implementation of government programmes.* Pretoria: Government Communications and Information Systems (GCIS).

Pieterse J (2002) Global inequality: Bringing politics back in, *Third World Quarterly: Journal of Emerging Areas* 23:1023–46.

SAIRR (South African Institute of Race Relations) (2001) *South Africa survey 2000–01.* Johannesburg: SAIRR.

SARB (South African Reserve Bank) (2003) *Annual economic report 2003.*

Southall R (1997) Party dominance and development: South Africa's prospects in the light of Malaysia's experience, *Journal of Commonwealth & Comparative Politics* 35:1–27.

Stats SA (Statistics South Africa) (2000) *Measuring poverty in South Africa.* Pretoria: Stats SA.

UNDP (United Nations Development Programme) (2003) *South Africa human development report 2003: The challenge of sustainable development in South Africa – unlocking people's creativity.* Oxford: OUP.

Wade R (1990) *Governing the market: Economic theory and the role of the government in East Asian industrialization.* Princeton, New Jersey: Princeton University Press.

Part I: Politics

Politics: introduction

John Daniel, Roger Southall and Jessica Lutchman

In 2004, South Africa has not only celebrated a decade of democracy but has conducted its third democratic election. Not surprisingly, the country has been awash with self-examination, seeking to measure both the substance and solidity of the new democratic order and the impact that it has made on ordinary citizens' lives. Pride and pleasure in achievement have been counterbalanced by critique and contestation of the nature of the country's post-apartheid experience. In her paper, Erasmus reminds us of Zapiro's lovely cartoon in which, contrasting the relative uneventfulness of the 2004 election with violent horrors occurring in countries elsewhere, he admonishes us that it is 'sometimes better to be boring'! This after all is the great triumph of South Africa, and for which it is today justly renowned: from a country on the verge of implosion and civil war in the early 1990s, it is now one of constitutionalised normality. Yet debate remains vigorous, and no more so than about the impact upon democracy of the dominance of the African National Congress (ANC) in the political arena.

Southall and Daniel, in their article, do not question that the ANC's dominance results from its overall popularity amongst the electorate. However, they point to pre-electoral concerns that the guaranteed nature of the ANC's return to power might lead to declining electoral participation, in part because of popular disillusion with aspects of government 'delivery'. In the event, of course, the turnout of registered voters (75 per cent) – albeit lower than 1999 – was high by international standards, and South Africans again demonstrated their impressive commitment to the ballot box, even if – as they point out – we need to remind ourselves that some few million people remained unregistered or declined to vote. Yet do such non-voters form a pool of disaffected citizens who might provide the electoral basis for a new opposition capable of challenging ANC hegemony? After a review of the various parties' campaigns and the electoral outcome (which saw the ANC obtaining nearly 70 per cent of the vote, the New National Party [NNP] collapsing, the

Inkatha Freedom Party [IFP] being reduced to a minority in KwaZulu-Natal, the Democratic Alliance [DA] failing to make significant inroads amongst black voters, and no other party performing noticeably well), Southall and Daniel caution against any easy suggestion that the non-participating voters will easily translate into a social-movement-aligned party of opposition. Instead, they conclude that the ANC has increased its electoral dominance, and that the opposition remains as divided as ever.

Vino Naidoo, in his article, examines how transformation of the post-apartheid public service has entailed wide-ranging political and cultural change alongside massive reform at the technical and administrative levels. Only by an apposite combination of these dimensions, he suggests, can historical inequities be corrected alongside an advance in efficiency and effectiveness. Naidoo stresses the enormity of the challenge posed to the public service post-apartheid. An essential structural overhaul entailed the amalgamation of a pre-1994 system comprising 15 administrations serving 11 different governments, including four 'independent' states and six self-governing ('ethnic') territories. Integration has required the redress of a historically unequal distribution of decision-making power based on race preference. A fully inclusive political system has required a shift away from race domination to one of dual accountability to the public and political office-bearers. And whereas under apartheid the central state needed to dominate the periphery in order to police race relations, after 1994 the new provincial administrations have come to compose the largest segment of the public service. Yet as Naidoo also stresses, these transformations have been accomplished within the context of a slimmed-down public service, with most job losses being recorded amongst less skilled and part-time workers. At the same time, whilst the departure of many old-order civil servants has assisted the normative reorientation of the state machinery, the latter remains challenged by a severe dearth of senior management talent, notably in the provinces. Against this background of inherent and inherited complexity, Naidoo warns against sweeping and ill-considered judgement of the performance of the public service.

Naidoo's indication that the public service is – in numerical terms – primarily based in the provinces, reminds us that many millions of especially poor South Africans live in the areas of the former bantustans. As Lungisile

Ntsebeza points out in his paper, they are subject to a system of rural governance whose contours have been a subject of major contestations between a post-1994 thrust towards democratisation and a sustained rearguard action by traditional leaders who under apartheid enjoyed unaccountable authority under the aegis of the state. In his chapter, he demonstrates what is surely one of the most truly disturbing developments in recent times: how after years of ambivalence, the ANC-led government has recently passed two Acts, the Traditional Leadership and Governance Framework Act and the Communal Land Rights Act that make concessions to traditional authorities which effectively resuscitate the powers they enjoyed under the notorious Bantu Authorities Act of 1951.

Ntsebeza notes how, in following the provisions of the 1996 Constitution of South Africa, the government – in its attempts to democratise local governance – sought to separate the functions of local government and land administration, thus undoing a major legacy of apartheid which combined these in tribal authorities. Reforms in local governance sought to realise democratic intentions by establishing structures which would render traditional authorities more representative and accountable to their communities, only to be met by determined resistance by the traditional leaders themselves. Ntsebeza notes how the recently passed Acts have succumbed to this pressure, according traditional leaders a status which – against the weight of historical evidence – deems them representative of their people. In short, recent legislation has provided for the recognition of traditional councils, which will be dominated by unelected traditional leaders, in areas which premiers recognise as constituting 'traditional communities'. Furthermore, these councils will enjoy land allocation and administration powers and functions in communal areas. These councils, argues Ntsebeza, will enjoy 'unprecedented powers' which will provide for a rejuvenation of colonial-style, and largely unaccountable, traditional authority.

Ntsebeza attributes the ANC's remarkable turnabout to its own historical ambiguity towards the institution of chieftaincy, its constant need to find an accommodation with the IFP to avoid violence in KwaZulu-Natal, and the erosion of rural spending brought about by its commitment to conservative fiscal policies. What he does not state explicitly, but would also seem to be the case, is that the ANC was keen to confirm the allegiance of the traditional leaders in the run-up to the 2004 election. Whatever the reasons, land activists and concerned observers are hugely worried that the ANC has exchanged short-term political gain for the long-term subjection of huge swathes of the rural population to a continuation of rural despotism, and that the burden will fall particularly heavily upon the shoulders of rural women. They fear that this development represents one of the heaviest defeats for the democratic project since 1994.

Alongside Ntsebeza, Sam Sole similarly illuminates one of the darker aspects of South African democracy. His nuanced message stresses that the government's efforts to roll back corruption have been 'deeply impressive'. He warns nonetheless that a drift towards a general level of immunity in the political sphere risks the undoing of all the progress that has been made. Arguing that, apart from its inherent immorality, corruption is economically inefficient and likely to undermine the legitimacy of the political system, he notes that, although South Africa is by international standards a country of only moderate levels of corruption, there are no grounds for complacency. There is an apartheid heritage of patronage and rent-seeking that needs to be rooted out of the public service; affirmative action and black economic empowerment, whilst justified to counter decades-long discrimination, could transmute into the reorientation of the state towards the enrichment of a new elite; and the ANC's own internal heritage has a tendency to prioritise loyalty networks over internal pluralism and accountability.

Sole adopts a questioning attitude to perceptions that corruption is getting worse. However, his concern emerges through his analysis of the ANC's espousal of a new black capitalist class which, he suggests, encourages rent-seeking and cronyism. He contends that a leadership cult created around President Mbeki and intolerance of criticism have also increased a personalisation of competition for networks of patronage which have taken South Africa nearer to the crony capitalism of South-East Asia. He concludes: 'The success of the ANC's hegemonic project may, in time, become the most significant threat to the country's democratic one.'

In her chapter in this section, Zimitri Erasmus considers the state of race and identities at the end of the first decade of democracy. She has three dimensions to her subtle argument.

First, she stresses that race has no inherently biological or cultural basis. Instead, she argues it is socially constructed and intersects with other areas of inequality and identity. She notes that being white no longer automatically conveys race privilege, yet most whites continue to benefit from the legacy of race privilege. Meanwhile, although the new black elite have been able to escape race discrimination, poor black Africans continue to be subjected to it.

Second, Erasmus argues that even after the implementation of legislation intended to end exclusionary practices based on race, race continues to be a site of division and exclusion amongst South Africans. However, whereas racial divisions were previously legally and socially enforced, today they appear to be self-imposed, while racial exclusions are often hard to recognise and identify. Evidence of this is provided from the classroom, where even in integrated institutions pupils of the same colour tend to group together, and where black learners are very often expected to assimilate into dominant institutional cultures. Meanwhile, a growing phenomenon is that of xenophobia, whereby South Africans (black and white) use race to exclude black Africans from elsewhere on the continent from their rights and to violate their humanity.

Third, Erasmus points to the limits of various ways in which officialdom has responded to racial inequities of the past. Anti-discrimination, equity and black economic empowerment measures are all well intended, yet can have unintended consequences. One is that whilst they tend to benefit wealthy blacks, they fail to deal with the racialised structural inequalities among the working class and the poor. Another is that they do not always address racialised divisions that are based on unspoken racial antagonisms, which often come to the surface when people who have not previously talked to each other suddenly have to engage each other. Finally, and most complicatedly, they perpetuate race categories and 'race thinking'. She proceeds to pose complex questions about South African political discourse, hitting out as much at proponents of 'colour-blindness' (whose views tend to entrench existing hierarchies) as at black analysts who wish to strip individual black people of their agency by imposing approved 'black' views and 'proper' behaviours upon them.

Erasmus concludes that to overcome race thinking, we have to recognise that – even in 'non-racial South Africa' – racialised scripts of reality and behaviour are norms rather than exceptions, and that it is hence incumbent upon us to acknowledge our complicity with the past whilst simultaneously attempting not to repeat it.

1 Race and identity in the nation

Zimitri Erasmus

At the end of the first decade of democracy in South Africa, we are faced with three questions about race. First, does race continue to shape economic inequality? Second, does it remain a political fault line and a basis for exclusion and mobilisation in South Africa? And third, what are the limits of the hegemonic ways in which South Africans work with race?[1]

In this chapter, I draw on secondary sources to argue first that, although the relationship between race and economic inequality is not the same as during apartheid, it now manifests in more complex forms, making race a factor that continues to shape such inequality in South Africa today. Second, I draw on both primary and secondary sources to argue that race remains a source of division, mobilisation and exclusion. Third, by noting their limits and un-intended consequences, I point out that the hegemonic ways in which this continued presence of the legacy of race is negotiated are inadequate for con-structively working with this legacy. I argue that the common idea that racism is a disease to be cured and/or an evil to be eradicated locks into a discourse of legal and bureaucratic remedies on the one hand, and into a moralising discourse dividing 'good' and 'bad' South Africans on the other. I close with some suggestions for different ways of working with race and racism(s).

Race and racism(s)

It is appropriate at this point to outline my own conceptualisation of the con-cepts of race and racism. For the purposes of this chapter, race is understood as a socio-historical and political construct. This challenges the idea that race has any biological and/or cultural basis. In other words, race is not a fixed and tangible thing we can find in our blood or DNA; nor is it something we are born with because of our culture. Instead, race understood as a social con-struct draws our attention to the meanings we attach to real and/or imagined biological and/or cultural markers. We learn these meanings and teach them to our children. Consequently, we can – although apparently not easily – unlearn them, and teach our children differently. Furthermore, when understood in this way, one is able to recognise the hierarchies of power and privilege embedded within racialised structures of meaning.

That race is not biologically real does not make it an illusion. Racial meanings have real effects on people's lives. Hence, when I use the terms black(ness) and white(ness) in this chapter, I do not refer to skin colour. Instead, I refer to the ways in which hierarchical structures of meaning attached to skin colour have shaped people's material lives as well as their perceptions of themselves, of others, and of the world around them. It is important to bear in mind that these meanings are not fixed. Rather, people struggle over these meanings and they change over time and from one context to another. For example, in the context of apartheid, being white meant that white people were guaranteed certain privileges by virtue of being white. Although most white South Africans today continue to benefit from the legacy of this race privilege, being white no longer automatically grants one race privilege. Furthermore, struggles over who is to be considered black in South Africa today are struggles over what it means to be black and about who imagines themselves to have control over these meanings.

Understanding race as a social construct also challenges the notion that racism is about the prejudices of particular individuals. On the contrary, in this view, racism is understood as discourse that permeates the culture of our society. This implies racist practices and ideas that race is fixed are not exceptions to the norm. These are the norm. This conceptualisation allows one to move away from the accusatory question – 'Are particular black and/or white people racist?' – toward a more useful question – 'What are the ways in which people work with race, and what are the implications of these ways of working with race?' When we ask this question, we learn that both black and white people can work with race in ways that perpetuate inequality and violence, and promote understandings of race as fixed. Finally, race intersects with other axes of inequality and identity such as class, gender, sexuality, culture, nationality, ethnicity and religion. For example, as illustrated further on, when race intersects with class, its impact on the lives of poor black people in South Africa is different from that on wealthier black people, producing different experiences of race among black people.[2] Similarly, with the demise of white supremacist ideology and practice, the loss of race privilege is likely to have a different impact on the lives of poor white people in South Africa than it would on their wealthier counterparts. Also illustrated further on are the different outcomes for citizens and non-citizens when race intersects with nationality.

Race and economic inequality

Seekings and Nattrass (2002) show that the relationship between race and class has changed radically. They argue social and economic transformation has substantially eroded the correlation between race and class in post-apartheid South Africa. They assert, 'high levels of inequality are increasingly based on intra-racial not inter-racial inequalities' (2002:2). Drawing on Whiteford and Seventer (2000 cited in Seekings & Nattrass 2002:11), they provide statistical evidence for this argument and note that 'incomes of the richest ten per cent of African households rose by 17 per cent, whilst the incomes of the poorest 40 per cent of these households fell by 21 per cent'. They further argue already better-off African households were key bene-ficiaries of the total rise in income between 1991 and 1996, as 40 per cent of this income went to the richest 10 per cent of African people, and a total of 62.5 per cent went to the richest 40 per cent of this group of people. On the basis of this evidence, Seekings and Nattrass argue the most significant change in South African society since the 1990s has been the increasing and rapid growth of what is generally referred to as the black or African middle class. These authors conclude that while there was a clear overlap between race and class during apartheid, 'inequality is increasingly a function of class, rather than race ... [making race] a less adequate proxy for disadvantage' (2002:25). In other words, in South Africa today one cannot assume that blackness necessarily means disadvantage. This does not, however, mean that race is irrelevant as a factor shaping inequality. Two recent studies indicate poor black people in South Africa continue to be victims of race discrimination.

De Swardt's (2003) study draws on primary data based on both quantitative and qualitative research conducted in three different areas of the Eastern and Western Cape provinces: Mount Frere district, characterised by rural sub-sistence livelihoods; black African and coloured townships in Ceres, a town characterised by rural commercial farming; and Khayelitsha and Nyanga, two black African urban communities in Cape Town. Significantly, this study found that in Ceres, twice as many coloured workers (32 per cent) as black African workers (16 per cent) were likely to have permanent employment. In addition, compared to coloured residents with paid employment (66 per cent), black African residents in Ceres were less likely to have paid work (44 per cent) (de Swardt 2003:18–19). Furthermore, while level of education (between one and 12 years of education) made little difference to possibilities for employment among residents of Mount Frere, Khayelitsha and Nyanga, this study found that for coloured residents in Ceres there was a positive correlation between level of education and the likelihood of finding paid employment. Black Africans in Ceres with Grades 8 to 10 had a 43.7 per cent chance of finding paid work, while coloured residents with the same education had a 71.7 per cent chance. Similarly, black Africans in Ceres with Grades 11 and 12 had a 45 per cent chance of finding paid work as opposed to coloured residents with the same education who had an 80.6 per cent chance (de Swardt 2003:20–21).

This evidence shows marked differences between the access to paid employment of black African and historically classified coloured people with similar levels of education. This suggests while the new black African elite may have been able to escape race discrimination, poor black Africans remain its victim. This evidence indicates apartheid race categories continue to shape economic disadvantage in South Africa today, particularly among poor, work-seeking black people in South Africa. Although a simplistic two-nations-type mapping of class inequality onto race is inaccurate, we still need to explain why race continues to be a barrier to opportunity among the poor when all other factors seem to be equal.

A second study by Bezuidenhout (2003) provides further evidence of race as a factor shaping economic disadvantage among the working class. His is a regional comparative study based on qualitative interviews with workers and managers at factories in a sector of the engineering industry. Bezuidenhout argues that in South African factories, trade unions hoped job grading would, firstly, accredit and provide appropriate financial reward to black African workers, particularly those with skills not recognised under apartheid; and secondly, that it would provide these workers with incentives to acquire skills. Instead, workers he interviewed reported that job grading was often implemented in ways that replicated what von Holdt (2000 cited in Bezuidenhout 2003) called the 'apartheid workplace regime' by linking job grades to levels of payments with what Bezuidenhout calls 'a racial sub-text' (2003:7) based on apartheid racial categories. South African workers in Bezuidenhout's study reported that workers classified white, Indian, coloured and black under apartheid would often have the same job grade with unequal rates of payment per hour, organised along the lines of apartheid racial hierarchies. On the basis of this research, Bezuidenhout argues, alongside new legislation such as the Employment Equity Act of 1998, there is a 'competing logic ... that still operates in the workplace [namely,] the "informal wage colour bar"' (2003:5–8). In addition, he argues there is evidence that what Burawoy (1972 cited in Bezuidenhout 2003) defined as the 'upward floating colour bar' operates in these factories in the engineering sector in South Africa. This refers to evidence that although black African people are promoted to supervisory and managerial positions they often do not have access to the same benefits as white or historically classified coloured or Indian supervisors and managers. In addition, their counterparts, some of whom regard themselves as racially superior, often undermine their authority (Bezuidenhout 2003).

If, as the work of de Swardt (2003) and Bezuidenhout (2003) indicates, race continues to shape economic disadvantage among poor and working-class black people in South Africa, how does it function in the economic lives of poor white people who might not be benefiting from what Bezuidenhout calls 'informal wage colour bars'? Seekings & Nattrass (2002) point out 'relatively poor white households saw a big absolute decline in their incomes' (2002:11). However, they do not explain this decline. Is this phenomenon simply related to the general increase in poverty in post-apartheid South Africa? Or might it be that white households that were relatively poor during apartheid have now become even poorer *partly because they are white* and no longer benefit from race privilege, and partly because they do not have the economic power that such privilege accrued to wealthier white people? This is but one of the more complex questions we need to ask when considering ways in which race might or might not continue to shape economic disadvantage ten years after the introduction of democracy.

The work of de Swardt (2003) and Bezuidenhout (2003) points to complex ways in which race intersects with class to produce particular racialised patterns of inequality. Wealthy black and white people in South Africa are able to use their economic and related social power as protection against material manifestations of race discrimination. Poor black and white people in South Africa do not have access to such power. Having addressed my first question,

I proceed to consider whether race remains a site of division and exclusion among South Africans.

Race: discomfort, antagonisms and exclusions

Recent studies indicate that ten years after the introduction of democracy and the implementation of legislation against exclusionary practices based on race, race continues to be a site of division and exclusion among South Africans. While such divisions and exclusions were legally and socially enforced during apartheid, today the divisions appear to be almost self-imposed, while exclusions are so subtle they are often very hard to recognise and identify.

Studies by Erasmus with de Wet (2003) and Steyn and van Zyl (2001) in the higher education sector show learners (black and white) tend to group around race and often around apartheid race categories, making interaction across race among learners limited. The predominant reason learners provided was that they felt most comfortable with people from their own racialised experiences, suggesting continuity with life under apartheid. This is no surprise considering that growing up and living under apartheid has meant that in many ways South Africans of different racialised experiences find themselves both estranged from and antagonistic towards one another. Erasmus with de Wet (2003) found that racially homogeneous settings were the norm of comfort for most learners while several reported discomfort with racially heterogeneous contexts, for various reasons, one being their experience of marginality in a white dominant learning environment.

Several studies about the dynamics of race have pointed to similar experiences of marginality. The work of Vally and Dalamba (1999), Carrim and Soudien (1999) and Steyn and van Zyl (2001) provides further evidence of this marginality in historically white secondary and tertiary educational institutions. Luhabe (2002) points to similar experiences among black managers in the corporate sector. Erasmus (2000) notes similar experiences in the public sector. These studies reveal various subtle ways in which race remains a basis for division, exclusion and the preservation of privilege.

The most common finding noted in these studies is that historically white (and also coloured and Indian) institutions tend to assume that black, and particularly black African, learners and managers will assimilate into the existing dominant institutional cultures. This assimilationist paradigm is often accompanied by a multicultural approach that tends to regard culture and cultural differences as fixed and all-determining (Carrim & Soudien 1999; Vally & Dalamba 1999). These approaches often go hand in hand with covert,[3] not easily recognisable, often unintentional, exclusionary practices based on race. Examples from Erasmus with de Wet's (2003) study of some learners' experiences and perceptions of race and racism at the University of Cape Town (UCT) illustrate such practices. First, when educators consider only white learners as worthy of being spoken to in the learning environment they assume (consciously or unconsciously) that, intellectually, black learners have nothing to contribute and that their inclusion in the white classroom means they are there simply to observe, listen to and learn from white learners and staff. Such assumptions reinforce notions that whiteness carries intellectual authority in the learning environment. Second, when white educators give black learners exaggerated attention they highlight their presence as an exception to the norm. A third example is found in evidence that a discourse of deficit operates in these learning environments. The real effects of this discourse are to devalue black learners' contributions and emphasise their failures while, simultaneously, affirming the contributions of white learners and remaining silent about *their* failures (Erasmus with de Wet 2003).

Among the consequences of these practices is that black learners end up carrying the burden of race, leaving their white counterparts free of responsibility for its effects. In other words, they constantly have to prove themselves worthy of a place at these institutions, and they are expected to leave their identities outside the school gates in order to fit in, and to be extraordinary in order to be recognised. Luhabe (2002) and Erasmus (2000) note similar patterns in the corporate and public sectors respectively. These are some covert ways in which race privilege continues to be preserved in historically white (and coloured and Indian) institutions.

Xenophobia: the new racism of post-apartheid South Africa

I have sketched some ways in which race remains a factor shaping economic inequality, social division and exclusion among South Africans. Here, drawing on secondary resources, I show that South Africans (black and white) use race not only to exclude black Africans from elsewhere on the continent from access to certain rights, but also to violate their humanity. This indicates while racial discrimination continues in more complex forms along familiar apartheid divisions, new racial divisions are emerging as race intersects with nationality and citizenship rights, giving rise to xenophobia.

It is difficult to provide data of the actual number of non-nationals in South Africa. Although Landau (2004) suggests real figures are likely to be higher, he cites the 2001 census figure of 345 161 documented non-South African Africans and Crush and Williams's (2001 cited in Landau 2004) estimate of between 500 000 and 850 000 documented and undocumented foreign migrants. These estimates leave us with between approximately 155 000 and 505 000 undocumented migrants. Beyond these numbers, however, the literature suggests South Africans hold negative perceptions particularly of black African migrants.

Xenophobia is defined as a 'fear and hatred of strangers or foreigners or of anything that is strange or foreign' (Webster's New Collegiate Dictionary). This definition does not, however, account for the racialised and gendered aspects of xenophobia highlighted by several recent studies on this phenomenon in South Africa (*Agenda* No. 55 2003; Harris 2002; Landau 2004; Peberdy 2001; Valji 2003; Warner & Finchilescu 2003).

Peberdy (2001) notes citizens and state officials often identify migrant black Africans using racialised physical markers. These include skin colour (foreign black Africans are seen as darker than South Africans) and cultural markers such as ritualised scarification, dress, and language. In addition, Landau (2004) reports that many South Africans perceive non-South African Africans as the cause of unemployment, disease, inequality and crime. Here he cites a finding of a national survey by the South African Migration Project (SAMP) that 48 per cent of South Africans felt foreigners were a criminal threat (Crush & Williams 2003 cited in Landau 2004:6). This finding is confirmed by a more recent survey limited to central Johannesburg in which 70 per cent of South Africans thought crime was increasing and three-quarters of these respondents said immigrants were the main cause of increased crime (Landau & Jacobsen 2004:45 cited in Landau 2004:6). We are further reminded of news reports in September 1998 of two Senegalese and a Mozambican worker killed when thrown off a train in Pretoria by a group of individuals returning from a rally organised by the Unemployed Masses of South Africa. They blamed foreigners for high unemployment, crime and the spread of HIV/AIDS in attempts to justify this violence (Valji 2003). These biological and cultural markers, the negative meanings attached to them, and the violence perpetrated on the basis of these meanings, are painfully familiar.

Furthermore, Landau (2004) notes, although more women are migrating (Posel 2003 cited in Landau 2004) the majority of both domestic and international migrants are men. In addition, Warner and Finchilescu (2003) suggest gendered differences in the experiences of refugees, asylum seekers and economic migrants. They suggest black African male migrants are more prone to aggressive xenophobic responses from black South African men – these migrants are suspected of 'stealing' both jobs and women.

Despite most South Africans' perceptions of black African migrants as impoverished illegal parasites, research conducted by the SAMP revealed 93 per cent of their sample population were in South Africa legally; 49 per cent had partners; more than a third were heads of households; more than 90 per cent owned their home; 78 per cent were in paid employment; and 73 per cent had some secondary school education (McDonald, Mashike et al. 2000 cited in Valji 2003:18). Harris (2002), Landau (2004) and Peberdy (2001) argue that South Africa's Department of Home Affairs (DoHA), other state officials and the media are partly responsible for constructing negative images of African migrants.

Xenophobic practices are not unique to South Africa. What then is specific about such practices in South Africa? Crush and Pendleton (2004) compare perceptions among South African citizens with those of other countries in the southern African region and their findings suggest that among the harshest anti-foreign sentiments are found among South Africans. Furthermore, they suggest such sentiments are pervasive and expressed across divisions of class, race, gender, political persuasion and access to paid employment. This pattern, they argue, is significantly different from that in countries reflecting greater acceptance of foreigners where socio-economic factors shape xenophobic sentiments, with the economically most vulnerable exhibiting more negative sentiments. Valji (2003) notes a further factor specific to South Africa, namely, that black people from elsewhere in Africa are the exclusive targets of xenophobia. She further notes what makes this racism new is that while South Africans from all walks of life have xenophobic perceptions, most violent xenophobic practices have been perpetrated by *black* South Africans. This is particularly disturbing considering that until recently black South Africans were themselves the victims of similar violence under apartheid. The most striking similarity is that between apartheid pass laws and identity checks during which migrants' legal documents are often destroyed. Such checks are often followed by arrests, detention and deportation without any recourse to justice.

A reflective review of recent literature suggests it is important to consider the interplay between several historical and contemporary factors and processes when trying to understand and explain this violent new racism in South Africa. Among these are, first, South Africa's history of racialised violence as a common, accepted and legitimised means of dealing with difference and conflict (Harris 2002). In addition, violence is a common means by which South African masculinities were and continue to be made. This in turn shapes the gendered violence embedded in xenophobic practices. Second, the abrupt shift from apartheid to a racially inclusive democracy engendered high hopes, especially among poor and black South Africans who were deprived of basic economic and human rights for generations, and now perceive migrant Africans as their competitors for these rights. Third, in the light of these hopes, it is important to note increased poverty and unemployment since 1994 and the disillusionment this might mean for the majority of South Africans. Fourth, although black Africans from southern Africa formed part of apartheid South Africa's migrant labour force, some authors suggest migration to South Africa has increased since 1990 (Valji 2003). Fifth, South Africa's racist and draconian immigration policy, as well as the racism and violence of its DoHA, plays a significant role in setting the tone for popular perceptions and treatment of non-nationals (Landau 2004; Peberdy 2001). Finally, like all processes of nation building, post-apartheid South Africa's nation-building project is by definition exclusionary. In light of its history of divisions, post-apartheid South African nationalism focuses particularly on building a unified South African national identity. Data suggests this unity constitutes the creation of a right-less foreign African 'Other' (Harris 2002; Peberdy 2001; Valji 2003). For example, 85 per cent of South African citizens feel undocumented migrants should have no rights to freedom of speech and movement, while 60 to 65 per cent feel they should not enjoy police protection or access to social services (Crush 2001).

While it is important to contextualise the rise of xenophobia in post-apartheid South Africa, such discriminatory practices should not be left unchallenged. Xenophobia and related violence undermine South Africa's commitment to a non-racial democracy, a culture of human rights and to regional and continental co-operation. One of the challenges is to recognise the contributions black African migrants make to its economy and polity. Jacobsen (2002) suggests resources such as human capital (in the form of skills, labour, and entrepreneurship), trade and relief supplies, among others, that accompany refugee and migrant communities can improve the welfare of host communities as well as build state capacity and accountability. More specifically, the challenge facing South Africa's DoHA is to shift its focus and resources away from apartheid-type control, exclusion and demonisation of black African migrants towards embracing these migrants as people with the capacity to contribute to South Africa's economy and polity.

Limits of hegemonic ways of dealing with race

The evidence discussed points to some of the limits of the hegemonic ways in which the continued presence of race is negotiated in this country.

Race as quota and proxy

One of the predominant ways in which South Africa has responded to inherited racial inequities is by introducing quotas. Over the past ten years the new legal framework created to counteract apartheid race laws has focused on anti-discrimination measures, equity and black economic empowerment by emphasising change in the demographic composition of private and public institutions. This shift is particularly visible in the education and government sectors. Some young South Africans of various class backgrounds now have access to tuition in classrooms with both black and white learners. Schools, universities, businesses, government departments and a myriad of workplaces have been concerned with recruiting the correct number of black people to meet equity targets in line with the requirements of the Employment Equity Act of 1998. While equity quotas attempt to protect the rights of black South African citizens, the evidence provided earlier strongly suggests South Africans use race as a proxy to exclude migrants and deny them rights.

Furthermore, while equity policies often provide (or are supposed to provide) opportunities for training and capacity building in an attempt to address structural inequalities based on access to education, the implementation of such policies is often limited to achieving the correct quotas for a representative workforce. Today the degree of transformation of an institution continues to be judged often primarily in terms of these targets and quotas. Equity policies, targets and quotas are a necessary component for challenging continued institutionalised racial discrimination. However, it is important to be aware of the limitations and unintended consequences of such policies in their current form. Here I point to three such limitations.

Seekings and Nattrass (2002) help one to see where equity policies in their current form have effected change, while de Swardt (2003) and Bezuidenhout (2003) show us where such policies have failed. These authors illustrate one limitation of these policies, namely, while they benefit wealthy black people in South Africa, they cannot deal with the effects of racialised structural inequalities among the working class and the poor. This points to the need for more sophisticated measures of historical disadvantage that capture the impact of, rather than obscure, intersections of inequalities such as class, race, gender, sexuality and physical ability, among others.

Furthermore, the work of Erasmus with de Wet (2003), Vally and Dalamba (1999), Carrim and Soudien (1999), Steyn and van Zyl (2001), Luhabe (2002) and Erasmus (2000) indicates a second limitation: achieving equity targets as ends in themselves does not address underlying racialised divisions and exclusions often based on unspoken racial antagonisms. On the contrary, once implemented, such policies allow these antagonisms to surface often in heightened form. The recently well-publicised case of racial violence at Edgemead High in Cape Town is testimony to this (*Cape Argus* November, December 2003). Increased racial heterogeneity in everyday life has not necessarily meant the disappearance of racial antagonisms and exclusionary practices based on race in post-apartheid South Africa. This is a sign that, when it comes to race, democratisation is not simply about getting the numbers right. The real difficulty only begins once people who have, in some cases, never spoken to one another before, and who have learnt to engage with one another only within the parameters of hierarchical relationships of race, have to learn to engage with one another across, and in defiance of, these hierarchies.

A third limitation of equity policies in their current form is that they perpetuate apartheid race categories and race thinking. Maré (2001) argues while non-racialism seems to be their vision for South Africa, academics, activists and government officials continue to work with race – understood as apartheid race categories and/or as fixed – as a building block for their thinking and actions. He questions the use of apartheid race categories by the current government, and argues that race thinking as common sense persists in post-apartheid programmes for affirmative action, equity, and black empowerment and in the national census.

It might be tempting to dismiss Maré's arguments as yet another suggestion to ignore race. However, in her comparative study of the history of racial and colour categories in North American and Brazilian censuses, Nobles notes that 'far from merely counting race … census[es] … help … to create race … and sustain racial discourse … [by] register[ing] the evident existence of race (2000:1740–1741). She concludes: 'Racial categories in censuses do not merely capture demographic realities, but rather reflect and help to create political realities and ways of thinking and seeing' (2000:1745).

Nobles' (2000) and Maré's (2001) concerns are shared by medical professionals in South Africa who are debating various perspectives on the value of race as a proxy in medical research and practice. Ellison, de Wet, Ijsselmuiden and Richter (1996) argue against the use of race – understood as population groups – in health research because of the historical use of these categories under apartheid. In response, Walker, Sitas, Cleaton-Jones, Vorster and Whittaker (1997) argue for the use of race, understood as a biological factor that explains racial differences in disease. In a series of seminars on the subject of 'The use of race in medical research' in October 2003, local medical researchers and practitioners at UCT noted that North American arguments to maintain race – understood as population groups based on genetic pools – as a factor determining disease (Burchard, Ziv, Coyle, Gomez, Tang, Karter, Mountain, Pérez-Stable, Sheppard & Risch 2003; Wade 2003) needed to be challenged. Some participants at the seminars suggested class, rather than race, should be used as a factor to explain disease patterns. Others raised questions about the impact of intersections of race with class in shaping disease. Some noted race might be an important factor, not for understanding biological or genetic factors causing disease, but for understanding the consequences of racism on people's health. These are signs that some South Africans are engaging critically with established common sense ways of working with race.

Race as armour

The other predominant way in which South Africans negotiate its continued presence in their lives is to use race as a defence to protect privilege on the one hand, and as armour against criticism, intra-racial and national difference on the other. The former use of race is based on the idea that race is best forgotten, the past must be left behind and we need to focus on our future. The latter use of race often draws on essentialist[4] understandings of the term and on racialised conceptions of national identity.

FORGET ABOUT RACE

Race is used as a defence to protect privilege by those who regard mere recognition of it as an act of racism. This approach is generally referred to as colour-blindness. Goldberg (2004) helps one conceptualise colour-blind ways of working with race and their political implications. He distinguishes between being against *every* (my addition and emphasis at all times in the paper) use of the concept of race and of racial categories, and being against the conditions of living and being that continue to be shaped by this concept and the categories based on it. He notes when we lose sight of this distinction we collapse these two political agendas. In the process the political challenge to end racism and race thinking is reduced to being against *every* use of the concept of race, thus emptying this challenge of its substantive anti-racist political content. This, he argues, leaves residues of race thinking and racist order unaddressed.

This conceptualisation is valuable in two important ways. First, it highlights the limits and dangers of being against *every* use of the concept of race as an end in itself. Second, it posits that naming race, in order to challenge its real effects on people's lives, is necessary when working towards anti-racism. Goldberg argues, 'we are being asked to give up on race before and without addressing the legacy, the roots, the scars of racisms' histories, the weights of race. We are being asked to give up on the word, the concept, the category, at most the categorising. But not, pointedly not, the conditions for which those terms stand' (2004:19). I have shown earlier that these conditions include continued economic disadvantage, particularly among the poor in South Africa, and other forms of disadvantage resulting from informal and subtle exclusionary practices.

The Democratic Alliance (DA), the official opposition party, uses race as a defence to protect privilege. For example, soon after the debate on race in Parliament between President Thabo Mbeki and the DA's Tony Leon in June of last year, on 9 July 2003 the *Cape Times* reported:

> The DA is not opposed to affirmative action as such ... however ... it believes government policies have raised racial consciousness and led to the re-racialisation of South Africa ... that compliance with the requirements of the Employment Equity Act ... necessitates racial-headcounting and race-labelling and, consequently, the reclassification of South Africans according to race.

Thus, for the DA, any acknowledgement of the continued significance of race amounts to a return to apartheid. This ahistorical approach to race does not take cognisance of ways in which the legacy of apartheid continues to shape conditions of living and being in the present.

Members of the general public often express similar sentiments. For example, in response to Michelle Booth's attempt to problematise whiteness in her recent photographic exhibition entitled 'Seeing White', one observer's comment sums up 20 per cent of responses to the Cape Town leg of the exhibition. She identifies herself as white. In the visitors' book at the exhibition she writes to the artist:

> I fear you have fallen into a trap of racism yourself. Why demerit a group of people based on their skin colour? Surely this is not moving forward (which we are supposedly all working so hard to achieve) but returning to past discriminations and the society we have tried to abolish? ... You appear to want to lay guilt on every white S[outh] African without realising this means regression and not progress. And here I was thinking the new SA stood for equality.

For this observer, naming the importance of race (in this case whiteness) is in itself an act of racism. Race is reduced to skin colour with little awareness of the hierarchies of power and privilege within structures of racial meaning. Furthermore, for her, naming race marks a return to a past that should be abolished in favour of equality. For her, moving forward means forgetting about race and apartheid while remembering race and the real effects of apartheid amounts to regression.

There are various permutations of this discourse. Proponents of this colour-blind approach often pay lip service to affirmative action. But this is about as far as they would go in their support of arguments for transformation. The inclusion of black people in institutions previously reserved for whites (schools, universities, workplaces) is, in their view, a sufficient measure challenging racially exclusionary practices, as long as such inclusion is based on merit. Anyone who argues that racially exclusionary practices continue, as shown earlier, despite increasing numbers of black people in such institutions, is seen as playing the race card.

One of the limits of this way of working with race is that it leaves racialised inequalities untouched. Furthermore, it suggests a complete rupture with the past and fails to deal with racial divisions, antagonisms and exclusions shaped by this past. While colour-blindness loudly resists every use of the concept, it silently reserves the right to continue using race as a defence to protect privilege.

HOLD ONTO RACE, DON'T BE A 'SELL-OUT'

The common alternative view to forgetting and ignoring race in South Africa is to treat it as though it determines everything we do and all that we are, and as if it limits what is available to us. This approach sometimes translates into living with racialised identities as though they were prisons that limit all possibility, or scripts that prescribe behaviour. It assumes one can read someone's politics and belonging from the colour of their skin. Goldberg helps one understand this way of working with race. Goldberg (2004:5) refers to 'an abstract presumption of familialism'– namely, that I share characteristics with those I perceive to be like me (racially and/or nationally) – which forms the basis for 'an abstract familiarity' – that we share these characteristics implies that we share others, too. Consequently, 'I can presume to know you [politically] because [of] your somehow looking like me ...' biologically and/or culturally. For Goldberg, this presumed familialism and familiarity carries and exposes the stigma of race. In other words, such presumptions are based on race thinking – ideas that race and racialised identities are fixed and definitive.

Working with race in this way is central to the racialised xenophobia displayed by most South Africans. Their fabricated national familiarity produces the unfamiliar, racially-marked non-citizen who has become the target of this new South African racism. This way of working with race is also used by black

South Africans against black South Africans. Consider, for example, political analyst Nhlanhla Ndebele's recent construction of black people who voted for the DA. Ndebele is reported to believe that most black people who voted for the DA are 'rural, illiterate and not psychologically free' and they 'still see a white man like Leon as a saviour' (*ThisDay* 2.04.04). In contrast, reporter Charles Molele found black people who voted for this party did so for reasons such as the DA's provision of anti-retroviral drugs in certain provinces and the need for a party to oppose some of the ANC's views (*ThisDay* 2.04.04). But for Ndebele, the act of voting is defined and determined by race. Ndebele assumes that because they are black, these voters should be like other voters politically, and since they are not, there must be something wrong with them. In this view black people are only 'truly' black when their voting choices reflect hegemonic ideas of what constitutes a politically correct 'black' vote. The underlying assumption is when a black person votes for a party led by and/or supported by white people, that person, his/her blackness and his/her vote are flawed. Moreover, this flaw is often described as 'white' and/or associated with whiteness. This thinking not only strips black people of their agency, it ignores the possibility that people might vote according to their interests, and that different black people might and do have different political interests and views.

Such racialised constructions of voting behaviour and political choices are not new. Major political parties have used the race thinking behind such constructions in their campaigns. Davis (2003) provides substantial evidence for this in his overview of campaigning strategies among major political parties – including the African National Congress (ANC) and the DA during the 1999 election – and of interpretations of voting patterns at that time. He shows the ANC, DA and New National Party (NNP) used both implicit and explicit appeals to race as a resource for political gain during the 1999 elections. Although Davis is uncritical of the ANC's simultaneous stance of non-racialism and its use of race for this purpose, the evidence he provides points to what Gilroy (2001:43) refers to as the 'double standards' adhered to by self-proclaimed non-racialists who justify – by virtue of having been victims of racism – their 'invocation of absolute race' as different from the same invocation by their oppressors. Although media reports suggest key parties used race less as a resource for mobilisation before the 2004 elections (*ThisDay* 2.03.04; *Cape Times* 11.02.04), the question remains whether this was simply their official public stance, and whether this time around, the same practices used in the 1999 election were simply reserved for more localised and off-the-record campaigning strategies within communities. For example, the NNP's (2004) campaign supplement distributed in the mail uses race as a resource for mobilisation.

It is indeed not uncommon for black intellectuals, analysts and state officials repeatedly to respond to non-hegemonic political views and choices among black people by either discounting their blackness, as Ndebele does, or by using race as a defence against criticism. President Mbeki's use of race as a defence against criticisms of the government's stance on HIV/AIDS and on corruption is an example of such practice. For example, at the height of the debate about whether HIV causes AIDS and whether the government should provide anti-retroviral medication, President Mbeki suggested a distinction between his supporters and opponents in this matter. In his address at the ZK Matthews lecture, he seemed to equate his supporters with what he calls educated Africans (those with Afrocentric political ideas who have 'their people's' interests at heart), and his opponents with mis-educated Africans (those with Eurocentric political ideas who hold contempt for 'their own people'). President Mbeki referred to his opponents as follows:

> Others who consider themselves to be our leaders take to the streets carrying their placards, to demand that because we are germ carriers, and human beings of a lower order that cannot subject our passions to reason, we must perforce adopt strange opinions, to save a depraved and diseased people from perishing from self-inflicted disease. (Mbeki 2001)

In defence of the government's controversial position on HIV/AIDS and its initial reluctance to provide anti-retroviral medication, President Mbeki accuses activists protesting in favour of such medication of racist assumptions about black Africans. Similarly, analyst Devan Pillay notes President Mbeki's response to criticisms of the arms deal uses race as a defence when he calls his critics 'fishers of corrupt men' who believe that Africans are inherently 'corrupt, given to telling lies, prone to theft and self-enrichment by immoral means; a people that is otherwise contemptible in the eyes of the "civilised"' (*Sunday Times* 29.06.03).

In both examples quoted above, President Mbeki works with race in a way that suggests anyone who holds views alternative to and critical of the government, by implication, holds Eurocentric racist views of black Africans. It is important to remember and recognise the historical legacies of race and white supremacy and their influence on the present. However, it is equally important to move away from holding onto race as a form of cultural and political armour without necessarily negating the history of black suffering.

The examples given earlier are not of the same order. However, they are based on the same flawed understanding that racialised identities are fixed ways of being that should determine one's political actions and right to belong. This implies, in the cases discussed, that blackness is an essence to be policed and defended in terms of a particular moral and behavioural code. This essentialist way of working with race is at play in the new division arising among South Africa's youth: apartheid's children *versus* democracy's children. Many young black people in South Africa use a racially dichotomous language in which those who are seen as not 'truly' black are referred to as 'coconuts' – black youth, most likely from Model C schools, who are seen to speak, dress and act like white people; while those seen to inhabit a 'backward blackness' – rural ways of being and/or black youth seen to be stuck in 'old struggle politics' – are called 'dusty-crusties'. This language reveals the resilience of essentialist understandings of race that keep us locked into equating particular ways of being with race. This is race thinking.

Approaches that work with race as all determining often present blackness and whiteness as polar opposites equating the 'Self' with suffering, authenticity and innocence, and the 'Other'[5] with oppression, in-authenticity and guilt. For example, during the first decade of democracy many white South Africans complained that they had become victims of reverse discrimination. These complainants often lost sight of the privileges they already had, the possibilities these presented, and the new possibilities for living with whiteness in South Africa. Instead, many chose to leave South Africa, often in search of continued protection of their race privilege. Furthermore, the common idea that those historically classified coloured were not white enough to benefit from apartheid, and, today, are not black enough to benefit from the new dispensation, is a further example of using race as armour and positioning particular communities as victims.

Gilroy (2001) prompts one to ask an important question: When the DoHA, analysts like Ndebele, political parties like the ANC, and young, often educated, black people in South Africa invoke race in this impalpable way, why is it any different from white people invoking race in the same way? Gilroy (2000, 2001) emphasises the importance of being against *particular* uses of the concept race and of racial identities in our attempts to challenge racism and race thinking. More specifically, he argues against an uncritical acceptance of race as given, definitive, all-determining and part of common sense. Gilroy (2000) cautions against the use of racialised identities as defences against oppression or as means to protect privilege and notes that such mobilisation of identities further reinforces race thinking as common sense.

His judgement of the state of race and commitment to non-racialism in South Africa is that 'we are certain of what we are against but cannot say what we are for with the same degrees of clarity' (Gilroy 2000:41). It seems to me most South Africans are clear about being against apartheid and racism. Most seem to be as clear about what it *should* mean to be black and white, and about which black people belong in South Africa today. The problem lies with this second position as it presumes fixed, prescribed ways of being that can be policed by those who imagine themselves to have the power to define these ways of being. It also re-racialises citizenship in South Africa. The problem, as I have shown, is that South Africans who are ready to prevent others from using race as a political resource for their own gain, all too often preserve their own right to do the very same. This leaves us with an important question: are South Africans clear about what they want in place of a society based on race thinking?

Towards a different understanding of racism(s)

For most South Africans racism is understood as a disease to be cured and/or an evil practice to be eradicated. This view is articulated by the South African Human Rights Commission. In his opening address to the First National Conference on Racism, Dr Barney Pityana asserted 'we cannot afford to be ... complicit in the evil of racism' and 'we will eradicate racism from our midst'(2000:56–57). It is also the view of President Thabo Mbeki. In his 2002 'State of the Nation' address, he said, 'we are progressing towards ... the eradication of ... racism'. In response to Tony Leon, he said, 'nobody ... is going to stop us from confronting the cancer of racism' (*Mail & Guardian* 19.06.03).

This thinking remains stuck in a moralising discourse that divides 'good' South Africans, assumed not to be racist, and 'bad' South Africans defined as racist. It comfortably (dis) places acts of, and complicities with, racism and/or race thinking outside of everyday life. It places such acts and complicities at the feet of the 'Other' and constructs government and associated institutions, assumed to be immune to such practices and thinking, as the key agent responsible for punishing and/or correcting the 'Other'.

This thinking assumes a complete rupture with the past. It also assumes racism is a problem that can be fixed. This assumption produces responses such as racial quotas, forgetting, and holding onto race as possible ways of fixing the problem. I have pointed out some of the limitations and unintended consequences of these responses. Moreover, these responses inhibit any constructive engagement about race, limiting debates about race to patterns of accusations and counter-accusations.

There is a more constructive way of working with race. It is premised on the acknowledgement that racialised scripts of reality and for behaviour are norms in our society rather than odd exceptions. Maré (2001) shows that such scripts underlie legal and bureaucratic attempts to achieve equity in South Africa. Davis (2003) shows that they underlie ways in which political parties mobilise citizens. The literature on xenophobia in South Africa highlights that such scripts permeate the social fabric. Bezuidenhout (2003) points out that the continued presence of race as a factor shaping disadvantage in South African everyday life is a reminder that the apartheid state and its politicians were not solely responsible for maintaining exclusionary practices based on race. Instead, ordinary South Africans reproduce these practices through simple everyday ways in which we work with our racialised identities and with race. So, although one cannot afford to be complicit, if not with overt racism but with race thinking, by virtue of one's history as a member of this society one is likely to find oneself complicit with racism and/or race thinking.

We do not have to view such complicity as sinful. Nor do we have to condone it. But we do need to acknowledge complicity with racism and race thinking. This implies that we need to engage critically with the continued presence of patterns of race thinking both in our own structures of thought and feeling, and in the public sphere. It implies being open to criticism and abandoning political correctness. It requires reflective political practice. We cannot be expected to throw away our histories, nor can we pretend to be untouched by them. But now that the laws and the context have changed, it is incumbent on us to work with our histories in ways that acknowledge our complicity with the past while at the same time attempt not to repeat it.

As we enter the second decade of democracy the euphoria of the first years of freedom has long worn off and the legal framework against racial discrimination is in place. The time has come for citizens to ask themselves: What do I do to make a difference to the way in which race works in this country? And more importantly, what do I do to keep race working in more or less the same way as it always has? The same questions need to be asked of the laws implemented thus far.

In this chapter I have shown that the dynamics of race in South Africa today are in a state where for some there remains a remarkable continuity with everyday life under apartheid, while alongside this there are daily struggles with ways of breaking away from this legacy. I have argued that our freedom demands that we be more vigilant about race thinking and learn new ways of working and living with our racialised identities and with race. The challenge before us is to find ways of recognising race and its continued effects on people's everyday lives, in an attempt to work against racial inequality, while at the same time working against practices that perpetuate race thinking.

Notes

1   I am indebted to Andries du Toit for valuable comments on several drafts of this chapter. Thanks also go to Michelle Booth for providing me with photocopies of the pages from the visitors' books at her exhibition, 'Seeing White', and to the University of Cape Town for funding towards my attendance at a conference in England where the ideas developed in this chapter were presented.

2   For the purposes of this chapter, 'black' refers to a transnational political category defining the experiences of people who have suffered and continue to suffer white domination. This includes those historically classified coloured, Indian and African/black in South Africa. Unlike black Africans, people historically classified coloured and Indian in apartheid South Africa suffered oppression at the same time as benefiting from selected privileges. In order to illustrate the continued effect of these divisions in South Africa today, these racialised divisions are named by referring to black Africans and coloured or historically classified coloured and Indian South Africans.

3   For Essed, 'overt racism refers to acts that openly express negative intentions' while
    with covert racist practices, 'negative intentions cannot be inferred from the acts
    themselves' (1991:46).

4   Essentialism is generally understood as a belief in the unchanging and trans-
    historical true essence of identities. This position advocates one way of being black,
    for example, with little regard for the various ways in which blackness is lived.

5   Processes of constructing an 'Other' are embedded in relations of social power. The
    consequences (whether intended or unintended) of 'Othering' entail representing the
    'Other' in a distorted fashion with the effect of maintaining power. Priority is given
    to the hegemonic view and experience as the standard or universal measure against
    which all other viewpoints and experiences are evaluated.

References

Agenda No. 55, 2003. Women: The invisible refugees.

Bezuidenhout A (2003) Post-colonial 'colour bars' in the South African engineering
    industry. Paper presented at the South African Sociological Association Conference,
    University of Natal, July.

Booth M (2003–04) 'Seeing White', photographic exhibition, visitors' books. Cape Town
    & Johannesburg.

Burchard EG, Ziv E, Coyle N, Gomez SL, Tang H, Karter AJ, Mountain JL, Pérez-Stable
    EJ, Sheppard D & Risch N (2003) The importance of race and ethnic background in
    biomedical research and clinical practice, *New England Journal of Medicine*
    348:1170–1175.

Carrim N & Soudien C (1999) Critical antiracism in South Africa. In S May (ed.)
    Critical multiculturalism. London: Falmer.

Cooper RS, Kaufman JS & Ward R (2003) Race and genomics, *New England Journal of
    Medicine* 348:1166–1170.

Crush J (2001) *Immigration, xenophobia and human rights in South Africa*. Southern
    African Migration Project (SAMP) & South African Human Rights Commission
    (SAHRC). Available at <http://www.queensu.ca/samp>.

Crush J & Pendleton W (2004) *Regionalising xenophobia? Citizen attitudes to immigration
    and refugee policy in Southern Africa*. SAMP. Available at
    <http://www.queensu.ca/samp>.

Davis G (2003) The electoral temptation of race in South Africa: Implications for the 2004 election, *Transformation* 53:4–28.

De Swardt C (2003) Unravelling chronic poverty in South Africa: Some food for thought. Paper presented at the conference 'Staying poor: Chronic poverty and development policy', University of Manchester, 7–9.04.03. Available at <http://www.chronicpoverty.org>.

Ellison GTH, de Wet T, Ijsselmuiden CB & Richter LM (1996) Desegregating health statistics and health research in South Africa, *South African Medical Journal* 86: 1257–1262.

Erasmus Z (2000) *Managing change and diversity in Cape Town's city government.* Research report. Institute for Intercultural and Diversity Studies in Southern Africa, UCT.

Erasmus Z with de Wet J (2003) *Not naming 'race': Some medical students' experiences and perceptions of 'race' and racism in the Health Sciences Faculty of the University of Cape Town.* Research report. Institute for Intercultural and Diversity Studies in Southern Africa, UCT.

Essed P (1991) *Understanding everyday racism.* London: Sage.

Gilroy P (2000) *Between camps: Nations, cultures and the allure of race.* London: Penguin.

Gilroy P (2001) After the great white error … the great black mirage, *Transformation* 47: 28–49.

Goldberg D (2004) Buried alive. In *The death of race.* London: Basil Blackwell.

Harris B (2002) Xenophobia: A new pathology for a new South Africa? In D Hook & G Eagle (eds.) *Psychopathology and social prejudice.* Cape Town: UCT Press.

Jacobsen K (2002) *African states and the politics of refugees: Refugee assistance as political resources.* Feinstein International Famine Center, Working Paper No. 6. Available at <http://www.famine.tufts.edu>.

Landau L (2004). The laws of (in)hospitality: Black Africans in South Africa. Paper prepared for Colloquium on 'The Promise of Freedom and its Practice: Global Perspectives on South Africa's Decade of Democracy', University of the Witwatersrand, Institute for Social and Economic Research, 17–21.07.04.

Luhabe W (2002) *Defining moments: Experiences of black executives in South Africa's workplace.* Pietermaritzburg: University of Natal Press.

Maré G (2001) Race counts in contemporary South Africa: 'An illusion of ordinariness', *Transformation* 47:75–93.

Mbeki T (2002) State of the Nation Address of the President of South Africa. Parliament, Cape Town, 8.02.02.

Mbeki T (2001) He wakened to his responsibilities. Address by President Thabo Mbeki at the inaugural ZK Matthews memorial lecture, University of Fort Hare, 12.10.01.

NNP (New National Party) (2004) *The Cape plan.* Supplement of the New National Party, March.

Nobles M (2000) History counts: A comparative analysis of racial/color categorisation in US and Brazilian censuses, *American Journal of Public Health* 90:1738–1745.

Peberdy S (2001) Imagining immigration: Inclusive identities and exclusive policies in post-1994 South Africa, *Africa Today* 48:15–32.

Pityana B (2000) Reinventing history for a new humanity: Confronting the challenge of racism in South Africa. Opening address, '1st National Conference on Racism', Johannesburg. National Conference on Racism, final report. SAHRC.

Seekings J & Nattrass N (2002) Class, distribution and redistribution in post-apartheid South Africa, *Transformation* 50:1–30.

Steyn M & van Zyl M (2001) *'Like that statue at Jammie stairs': Some student perceptions and experiences of institutional culture at the University of Cape Town in 1999.* Research report. Institute for Intercultural and Diversity Studies of Southern Africa, UCT.

Valji N (2003) *Creating the nation: The rise of violent xenophobia in the new South Africa.* A research report written for the Centre for the Study of Violence and Reconciliation. Available at <http://www.queensu.ca/samp/>.

Vally S & Dalamba Y (1999) Racism, racial integration and desegregation in South African public secondary schools. Report on a study by the SAHRC, Johannesburg.

Wade N (2003) Gene study identifies 5 main human populations, linking them to geography, *New York Times* 20.12.03.

Walker ARP, Sitas F, Cleaton-Jones PE, Vorster HH & Whittaker DE (1997) Letter to the editor in response to 'Desegregating health statistics and health research in South Africa', *South African Medical Journal* 87:329.

Warner C & Finchilescu G (2003) Living with prejudice – xenophobia and race, *Agenda* 55: 36–44.

2 The state of parties post-election 2004: ANC dominance and opposition enfeeblement

Roger Southall and John Daniel

For the foreseeable future, there is nothing in the current opposition ranks that poses a serious challenge to the ANC. The threat to
a future vibrant democratic system is not, as some may suggest, a
strong ANC. To say this is to punish success. After all, it is hardly
the job of the ANC to create and nurture opposition to itself.
Opposition parties must rather address the problem of lacklustre
and ineffective opposition. *Vincent Maphai, ThisDay 09.04.05*

The holding of the 2004 general elections against the backdrop of celebrations
of ten years of South African democracy ensured widespread reflection upon
the achievements and limitations of the post-apartheid order. This was in part
deliberately engineered. Whilst the government was engaged in a far-reaching
stocktaking of its stewardship since 1994, in the form of its ten-year review
exercise (PCAS 2003), it was simultaneously determined that the African
National Congress (ANC) should reap full electoral advantage from the presentation of its record (of which it is proud). In turn, this was combined with
a re-emphasis upon its status as the party which had liberated the oppressed
from apartheid. However, the concurrence of a decade of freedom with the
election also encouraged consideration of the quality of South Africa's democracy. It was this latter aspect which tended to structure comment upon the
election, notably with regard to the idea of ANC 'dominance'.

In the immediate sense, the idea of the ANC as a 'dominant' party is a product of its successive overwhelming majorities in the 1994 and 1999 elections.
More distantly, it is an outcome of political science thinking, rooted in the
work of Pempel (1990), who defines parties as 'dominant' which:

• establish electoral dominance for an uninterrupted and prolonged period;

- enjoy dominance in the formation and running of governments and which, consequentially;
- shape and dominate the public agenda, notably with regard to pursuit of a 'historical project'.

The concept of 'party dominance' was rapidly applied to South Africa after the first democratic election of 1994, most particularly in the work of Giliomee and Simkins (1999), and Giliomee, Myburgh & Schlemmer (2001). The argument that they proposed had various elements, but most notably that there is a fundamental tension between dominant-party rule and democracy, for whilst party dominance can pave the way to competitive democracy, it can also lead to façade democracy or barely concealed authoritarianism.

Allegations of party dominance have been rejected by the ANC on primarily political grounds, arguing that the concept of dominance is inherently conservative, and that even if it is not deployed in the interests of the Democratic Alliance (DA) directly, it serves as a cover for white interests which have an inherent distrust of black governance, and which are suggesting, at base, that the ANC is anti-democratic (for example, Mbeki 2004; Suttner in *ThisDay* 26.03.04). In contrast, academic criticism has replied that although Giliomee et al. have provided a valuable analytical platform, they are nonetheless guilty of excess. Hence, whilst the idea of the ANC having become a dominant party has been accepted by many commentators as common sense, they simultaneously propose that the ANC's dominance has been, and is, limited by constitutional counterweights (such as the democracy-promoting bodies in the form of the Human Rights and Gender Commissions), its relative incapacity to impose its authority upon society as a whole, and the ability of its at times unruly partners within the Tripartite Alliance to substitute for otherwise ineffective opposition parties by provoking important debates about major issues, such as the economy and HIV/AIDS (for example, Southall 2001, 2003).

In many respects, the ANC has a right to feel aggrieved at the negative aspersions cast at it over the fact of its dominance. First, it could point to the fact that single-party dominance is nothing new in South African politics. In fact, it has been its dominant characteristic since the 1960s when the National Party (NP), through manipulation and other forms of gerrymandering, managed to secure a monopoly control over white South African politics. Where were the doom-and-gloom white commentators then, it might well ask? But, and this is the second point, there is a huge and qualitative difference between the ANC's single-party dominance of the present and that of the NP's of old. That domination derived from an illegitimate electoral process which, in their first ten or so years in power, they frequently manipulated to their electoral advantage.[1] The ANC's domination is quite the opposite. It derives from a wholly legitimate electoral system and is the product of successive expressions of the democratic will of most South Africans. Is it fair then, the ANC can rightly ask, for it to be pilloried for its democratic successes?

Whatever the intricacies of this debate, prior to the election none doubted that the ANC was going to win, and this ensured that the queries about the durability of the ruling party's dominance framed pre-electoral speculation. In particular, would the ANC's continuing dominance be secured, yet in a context of declining electoral participation and disillusion with its record of delivery? Would the popular and emotional identification with the ANC as a liberation movement amongst the previously politically oppressed translate into a more instrumental notion of it as political party? Would the elections of 2004 see a consolidation of, or further fragmentation of, a hitherto divided opposition? Finally, what impact would recurrent ANC victories have upon the quality and future direction of South African democracy?

This analysis can offer only preliminary answers to these various questions. However, our working hypothesis is that, whilst the 2004 elections have for the moment extended ANC dominance electorally, there is some evidence of underlying change within the political system which could erode this in the years ahead.[2]

The electoral framework, the results and voter participation in 2004

In post-apartheid South Africa, the political parties compete electorally via a list system of proportional representation (PR). Hitherto, the separate elections for the National Assembly (composed of 400 seats) and the nine provinces (whose number of seats is determined according to their share of the population) have been held simultaneously. Under this system, parties present separate lists of candidates to the electorate. They either present a single list of candidates for the National Assembly, or two lists for that body – one a list of candidates for 200 national seats (referred to colloquially as 'national to national') and another for the 200 seats which represent the provinces ('provincial to national'). They may also present lists of candidates for the different provincial assemblies. In exercising their choice, voters have two votes, one for the national and one for the provincial elections. Seats are allocated to parties in the different assemblies according to their share of the vote, using the 'droop' quota, with surplus seats resulting from fractional shares of the vote distributed through the highest remainder method (Lodge 1999:19, 215–16). The elections are administered by the Independent Electoral Commission (IEC), which was established as a permanent body under the Electoral Commission Act of 1996.

Prior to the 2004 elections, there were widespread predictions that the level of voter participation would decline from the impressive heights achieved in 1994 (when 19 533 498 people voted, their eligibility prescribed merely by their valid possession of an identity book) and 1999 (when 15 892 367 valid votes, or 86.7 per cent of a registered electorate of 19 533 498 people, were cast). The reasons suggested as to why participation would be lowered revolved around notions that voter apathy or alienation would be increased by, *inter alia*, constraints or limitations imposed upon popular political participation by formal governmental institutions and/or the behaviour of politicians since 1994 (Hicks 2004; Southall 2004), dissatisfaction with the level of delivery by the government (Landsberg & Mackay 2004), a sense amongst opposition voters (in particular) that their votes would have little impact or efficacy (Roefs 2004), and importantly, the rapid depoliticisation of post-apartheid youth and the loss of impetus of 'struggle politics' (Daniel 2004). Meanwhile, it was also regularly predicted that a low turnout would increase the ANC's advantage relative to the parties of opposition. In the event, the outcome of the election for the National Assembly was to need some careful disaggregation.

The initial reaction to the 75 per cent turnout was one of self-congratulation by the media and politicians, whose overwhelming response was that South Africans had again demonstrated their commitment to democracy in enthusiastic fashion. Although voter turnout was down on 1999, it was argued by some that this was merely a reflection of growing democratic 'normalcy', and that in any case, the proportion of active voters continued to compare extremely well with considerably lower electoral participation rates in countries like the USA and Britain. And the ANC itself was triumphant: 70 per cent of the electorate had voted for the ANC and given it a decisive mandate,

Table 2.1 *Outcome of the national election, 1994, 1999 and 2004*

Party[a]	1994 Votes	%	seats	1999 Votes	%	seats	2004 Votes	%	seats
ANC	12 237 655	62.65	252	10 601 330	66.35	266	10 878 251	69.68	279
DP/DA	338 426	1.73	7	1 527 337	9.56	38	1 931 201	12.37	50
IFP	2 058 294	10.54	43	1 371 477	8.58	34	1 088 664	6.97	28
UDM	-	-		546 790	3.42	14	355 717	2.28	9
ID	-	-		-	-		269 765	1.73	7
NNP	3 983 690	20.39	82	1 089 215	6.87	28	257 824	1.65	7
ACDP	88 104	0.45	2	228 975	1.43	6	250 272	1.60	6
FF+	424 555	2.17	9	127 217	0.80	3	139 465	0.89	4
UCDP	-	-		125 280	0.78	3	117 792	0.75	3
PAC	243 478	1.25	7	113 125	0.71	3	113 512	0.73	3
Other parties	159 296	0.82	0	246 396	1.56	5	210 204	1.34	0
Total valid votes	19 533 498			15 977 142			15 612 667		
Registered electorate	-			18 335 224			20 674 926		
Percentage valid votes	-			87.1			75.5		

Source: All but one of the figures are derived from the website of the IEC (www.elections.org.za). The exception is the valid vote percentage figure of 75.5 per cent. The discrepancy is caused by the fact that IEC records electoral participation as including spoilt votes , arriving at a voter turnout rate of 76.6 per cent. We have chosen to exclude invalid votes, hence arriving at a lower participation rate of 75.5 per cent.

Note: a Abbreviations: Inkatha Freedom Party (IFP); United Democratic Movement (UDM); Independent Democrats (ID); New National Party (NNP); African Christian Democratic Party (ACDP); Freedom Front Plus (FF+); United Christian Democratic Party (UCDP); Pan-Africanist Congress (PAC)

Figure 2.1 *Comparison of 1994, 1999 and 2004 elections by votes*

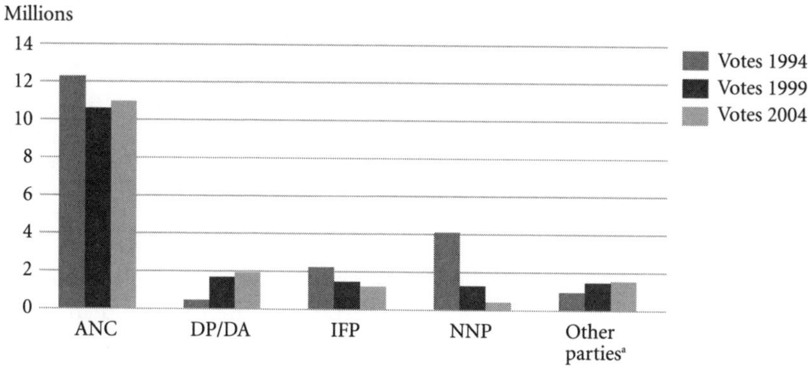

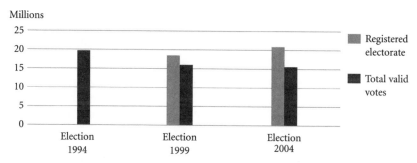

Source: IEC website (www.elections.org.za)

Note: a Other parties include: UDM, ID, ACDP, FF, UCDP, PAC, AZAPO and the Minority Front

Figure 2.2 *Voter registration and valid votes for 1994, 1999 and 2004 elections*

Source: IEC website (www.elections.org.za)

and the party had achieved overwhelming majorities of the same level or higher than in 1994 and 1999 (*ANC Today* 16–22.04.04). However, whilst it was only natural for the ANC to celebrate this 'outstanding victory' (*ANC Today*, 30.04–6.05.04), a more detailed analysis of participation rates suggests caution:

- Only 57 per cent (15 833 554) of all estimated eligible voters (27 438 897) cast ballots.
- 6.76 million eligible voters had inadvertently or deliberately remained unregistered.
- 5.06 million registered voters stayed away from the polls, or were for one or other reason prevented from voting.[3]
- Consequently, the nearly 70 per cent ANC popular majority translates into a 40 per cent minority of the entire eligible population.

At present, it is too early to say with confidence the reasons why over 40 per cent of the eligible population failed to participate in the election (although survey findings such as those of Afrobarometer indicate massive distrust of politicians).[4] However, what this level of non-involvement of the eligible voting population in the electoral process may suggest is a degree of political alienation which questions conventional analysis that democracy has taken firm root in South Africa. Dale McKinley (*Mail & Guardian* 14–20.05.04) has argued that:

> The lack of participation confirms the huge potential that exists for South Africa's social movements, alongside the rank-and-file of the organized working class, to fill the political vacuum and build a viable and radical people's power alternative to the ANC.

Such analysis will draw sustenance from indications of growing support for the formation of a party to the left of the ANC. For instance, a survey carried out by AC Nielsen found that one-third of all urban adults backed the idea of a workers' party being formed by the trade union movement (*Business Day* 1.03.04).

However, there is a need for caution here, for whilst analysis of continuing ANC dominance of the political arena needs to be informed by awareness of decreasing levels of commitment to the party amongst its historical constituency, and whilst there are clear limitations upon the extent to which existing opposition parties are able to generate support, it remains a moot point whether social movement activism can be translated into a sustained organisation which can challenge the ANC politically. Nonetheless, it is questions such as these which should lie behind any assessment of the ANC's triumph in the elections of 2004.

The ANC's victory

Embedded in pre-election concerns that the election would be characterised by voter apathy were numerous predictions that the ANC would experience a drop in support. Two main reasons were regularly cited. The first was its declining salience as the party of liberation. The second was that failures of delivery were likely to have eroded its constituency. Meanwhile, other factors, from Thabo Mbeki's alleged lack of magnetism through to the government's perceived flaws around job creation, HIV/AIDS and Zimbabwe, were all regularly thrown into the pot.

In the event, of course, as indicated earlier, the ANC's proportion of the vote increased from 62.65 per cent in 1994 and 66.35 per cent in 1999 to 69.68 per cent in 2004, presenting it with 279 out of the 400 seats in Parliament, and although its national vote of 10.9 million votes was down on its high of 12.2 million in the freedom election of 1994, it was some 277 000 votes above the more strictly comparable figure for 1999. Yet what gave the ANC particular pleasure was its performances in the provincial elections in the Western Cape and KwaZulu-Natal (KZN), where in the previous contests it had been out-smarted by the opposition. Although now failing to secure outright majorities in both, it was able to form ANC-led minority governments, and hence achieve its goal of establishing political control over all nine provinces.

Of course, the ANC had started its campaign from a strong base, as the historic standard-bearer of democracy, and as the party of the racially-oppressed black majority, of the working class and of the wider poor. Yet these were all advantages that might have been imperiled by various aspects of its performance in government since 1994. For instance, various commentators had accused the ANC of misusing its dominance to secure unjustified party advantage during the last Parliament (as through its introduction of floor-crossing legislation which seduced opposition members into its own ranks and enabled it to unseat the DA as government of the Western Cape). It had also been accused at various times of using the 'race card' at cost to its commitment to non-racialism, whilst its black empowerment strategies appeared to have received a mixed welcome amongst coloureds and Indians, some of whom claim to be newly disadvantaged relative to Africans. Meanwhile, throughout the last Parliament, there had been numerous tensions between the ANC and the Congress of South African Trade Unions (Cosatu), its most powerful partner in the Tripartite Alliance, largely around the government's commitment to macroeconomic policies which trade unionists and leftists claimed were responsible for the destruction of jobs and the growth of unemployment. Finally, as the party of power, it had increasingly found itself facing charges – even from within its own constituency of impoverished citizens – of multiple failings of delivery of water, electricity, housing, healthcare and welfare. In any case, said the analysts, the legacy of apartheid in terms of social deficits was so great that no government which had been in power for ten years could hope to face an electorate impatient for improvements without some unavoidable costs.

In the event, the ANC met these and other challenges head-on by a remarkable feat of organisation and electoral mobilisation. Their election campaign had three major elements.

A highly organised and united campaign

Long-term governments often lose power because of internal divisions and loss of energy. In contrast, the ANC presented a united face and mounted a vigorous and effective campaign. Despite denials of lack of solidarity, differences between the ANC and its Tripartite Alliance partners, Cosatu and the South African Communist Party (SACP), had caused significant policy rifts and bitter arguments during the last Parliament (Southall 2003). These rifts were reflective of criticism that, in office, the ANC had abandoned the promises of liberation, and in adopting market-driven policies it had become the vehicle for a self-serving elite, and the alliance a machine for political management and patronage (*Sunday Times* 11.04.04). Further, critics argued that its dominance had been transformed into political arrogance (*Financial Mail* 9.04.04) and that it was ignoring – and indeed, suppressing – criticism from new social movement organisations, such as the Treatment Action Campaign and local 'crisis groups' (*Sunday Independent* 16.05.04).

As instanced by McKinley's post-election judgement cited earlier, various observers saw these divisions within the ANC family as potentially productive of a new opposition initiative to the ANC's left. However, whatever the longer-term accuracy of these predictions, the ANC dealt with them with skill and aplomb during the 2004 election campaign. Months before the election it had moved closer to the Cosatu and SACP leaderships, hinting at a shift towards a more redistributive economic strategy. Differences were either buried or resolved, and Cosatu threw its undivided weight behind the party. Meanwhile, the ANC brushed aside all that the social movement organisations could throw at it, labelling such bodies as the Landless People's Movement (which called for a boycott of the election) irrelevant and irresponsible (*ThisDay* 5.03.04) and, allegedly, not hesitating to find legal obstructions to their right to demonstrate (*Sunday Independent* 16.05.04).

Undistracted by internal divisions, the ANC played its trump card of membership in depth to trounce the opposition. Prior to the poll, it had revitalised its branches, which are spread throughout the land. During much of 2003 the nation had been treated to the spectacle of open conflict between factions of the party hierarchy who had lined up behind one or other of Deputy President Jacob Zuma (who was rebutting suggestions that he had accepted a bribe to facilitate the notorious arms deal) and Director of Public Prosecutions, Bulelani Ngcuka (who was accused by Zuma of having been a spy for the apartheid regime). The rift was papered over by President Mbeki's referring the spying allegations to a Commission, chaired by Judge Theo Hefer. Reporting in January, this had found the allegations against Ncguka unproven, whilst having meanwhile spared Zuma from having to testify in person.

Although the extended spat was regarded by many as critical to the survival of Zuma's presumed ambitions to succeed Mbeki as President in 2009, its referral to a Commission was interpreted as having moved a potentially damaging political battle away from the party rank-and-file in the lead up to the election (*Financial Mail* 19.12.03). As a result, it did not impinge directly upon the selection process for the party's lists, even though this was to confirm Zuma's immense popularity amongst the party faithful. In the event, the ANC's party lists' nomination process (which worked its way up through branch, provincial and national level conferences) went smoothly, with remarkably few disputes, as the party successfully accommodated something of a circulation of its elites (notably the inclusion at high level on the national list of two premiers whose terms of office, as such, had constitutionally expired) alongside its attainment of required levels of gender and racial representivity (Kotze 2004). Even the exclusion of Winnie Madikizela-Mandela from the party's lists was accomplished without any discernible protest from the grassroots.

An unexpected aspect of the listing process was Mbeki's declining to confirm that those candidates who topped the provincial lists were the party's nominations for the provincial premiership positions. Although strongly criticised by observers and opposition parties as obscuring transparency and denying voters an informed choice, the move was deemed as inhibiting internal party factionalism during the election whilst adding to the centralised authority of the President after it (Cherry 2004). Ultimately, whatever the motivations, the various presidential machinations worked in uniting the party during an energetic drive for votes, which saw ministers, Members of Parliament (MPs) and provincial legislators all deployed alongside ordinary 'cadres' in a house-to-house campaign which reached deep into the townships and countryside.

Importantly, the ANC also repackaged Thabo Mbeki. Before and after he had become President, Mbeki had come over to the voters as a well-meaning but austere and intellectual leader, who, in contrast to the universally-loved Madiba, lacked the popular appeal which could touch the hearts of ordinary voters. However, during this campaign, Mbeki's image was deliberately transformed. Building on the earlier success of presidential *imbizos* (gatherings), the President now joined the house-to-house campaigning in carefully orchestrated visits to ordinary people from diverse communities, showing a humility and concern which belied his previous lofty image. In particular, as well as visiting the homes of families from the ANC's established constituency, he also made carefully stage-managed descents upon white, coloured and Indian families to, in essence, make ANC inroads into opposition support (*Mail & Guardian* 23–29.01.04). Importantly, too, the ANC deliberately disaggregated these communities, Mbeki meeting with, *inter alia*, representatives of Greek, Italian, Portuguese and Tamil groups (*Mail & Guardian* 2–7.04.04). Overall, Mbeki was presented highly effectively as a caring and responsive 'man of the people'. Some said this was a campaign device forced upon the ANC by a relative lack of campaign finance (*Sowetan* 8.01.04), in part resulting from corporate diffidence about party funding attendant upon a concurrent challenge being made to the High Court by the Institute for Democracy in South Africa (Idasa) demanding that political parties make public the names of all their donors granting them more than R50 000. If this was so, then it was a fortunate impoverishment, for the emergence of 'the new Mbeki' proved a masterstroke which perhaps even the ANC itself had not anticipated.

The vigorous defence and sale of its record

Before the election, the government was deemed to be vulnerable, particularly around issues of slow economic growth, the increase in unemployment, and the lack of improvement in living standards for many amongst the poor. The ANC's response combined intellectual riposte with populist appeal. Its manifesto, entitled the 'People's contract to create work and fight poverty', proclaimed the government's triumphs and contested criticisms. Its main tenets were that growth – although modest – had been consistently positive since 1994, the economy had become more internationally competitive, and although many jobs in 'old' industries had been lost, two million new employment opportunities had been created in 'new' industries such as services, industrial technology and finance. Meanwhile, workers' rights had been protected, the social security net had been vastly extended, R50 billion in assets had been transferred to the poor through housing and land reform, and the economy was becoming increasingly deracialised. The ANC, proclaimed party spokesperson, Smuts Ngonyama, was a 'reliable and able steward' (*ThisDay* 13.04.04). This message was taken to the middle classes largely via the media. More importantly, it was sold to the working class and the poor via the ANC's more popular campaigning with Mbeki taking the lead. His consistent theme was to acknowledge that high levels of poverty and unemployment remained, but to promise that the ANC was absolutely committed to their relief. Cosatu was also prominent in throwing its weight behind the government with its President, Willie Madisha, quoted as saying that, 'Any threat to an ANC victory is a threat to political stability and the creation of legitimate political institutions' (*Mail & Guardian* 8–15.04.04).

For all the positive spin applied to its message, equally important was the ANC's negative argument that, for all the limitations of its record, there was no other party so devoted to the interests of the poor.

The exploitation of the opposition's vulnerabilities

The opposition parties were all fair game for the ANC's hunting pack. The major problem for the parties that could be said to really matter – the DA, NNP, IFP and UDM – was that they combined an inability to launch a convincing attack upon the government's policies, notably upon the economy, with their appeal to only limited segments of the population. All the major parties' economic platforms were, in essence, so similar, that the opposition was simply reduced to saying, and saying unconvincingly, that 'we could do better'. Where they differed significantly, as for instance with the DA's demands for an increased pace of privatisation, criticisms of ANC policy on Zimbabwe and Mbeki's support for President Aristide of Haiti (who had been controversially ejected from office by rioters apparently backed by the US), they ran against anti-colonial sentiment that remains deeply entrenched amongst black voters. In addition, they were confronted by the particular ANC tactic of ignoring them as individual entities, to the particular frustration of the DA, which was determined to differentiate itself as a potential alternative government. However, the tactic did not always run smoothly, as instanced by the sharp criticism which President Mbeki received from the women's lobby when he was reported as jesting that he would beat his sister if she were to marry ACDP leader Kenneth Meshoe (*Mail & Guardian* 2–7.04.04).

By the time voting came, the ANC had chipped away at the opposition parties' constituencies, and rendered the reasons for voting for them – or the NNP, IFP and UDM in particular – far less convincing.

The opposition's weakness

The task facing the opposition parties in this election was always unenviable. With the ANC's hegemony guaranteed, the problem was how to convince voters of their relevance. As ever, the PR system encouraged a wide array of hopefuls to throw their hats into the ring, although in the national elections it was only Patricia de Lille's ID party that was thought likely to make its way into Parliament to join the DA, NNP, IFP, UDM, ACDP, FF+, UCDP and PAC on the opposition benches. Of this raft of aspirants, the ACDP, UCDP and FF+ were all looking to expand very narrow constituencies on grounds of values or identity, but none failed to break out of their chains. The UDM, the most virile newcomer in the 1999 elections, had had its locks shorn during the previous Parliament – by internal dissidence, the loss of seats during the floor-crossing saga, and the ANC's largely successful wooing of the chiefs – and as a result had lost significant ground. The PAC, never happier than when engaged in internal ideological battles of supreme insignificance to the electorate, had so divided its already-minute constituency pool (perhaps pond would be a better word) that it did remarkably well to hang on to its miserable quota of just three seats.

Amongst this constellation of losers, the only 'winner' was the ID. Formed by Patricia de Lille after she had taken the gap provided by the 2004 floor-crossing saga to exit the PAC, the ID secured a creditable 1.73 per cent of the national poll. This was largely, however, a racial vote in that the party performed best in the Western and Northern Cape provinces, home to significant numbers of coloureds. Five of its six provincial seats were won in those two provinces; the other was in Gauteng. Interestingly, anecdotal evidence suggests that the ID attracted at least the national vote of white left-wing voters alienated from the ANC by its steady post-1994 drift to the centre. In 1999, much of this tiny fraction had voted for the Green Party but this time around it was not on the national ballot.

The demise of the NNP and the ANC's capture of the Western Cape

For much of the twentieth century, the NP dominated South African politics. In its heyday in the 1960s and 1970s, its image was that of a monolith, grimly and determinedly pursuing an ideological vision, mirage-like though that was. In its efforts it was prepared to brook no serious opposition, willing to sacrifice the rule of law and international respectability in its attempts to crush the forces of African nationalism. And for a brief period in the late 1960s and 1970s it seemed it would prevail. Even as seemingly astute an analyst as US National Security adviser, Henry Kissinger, was convinced. In 1969 his National Security Council had adopted a position on southern Africa – the so-called 'Tar baby' option – which reasoned that white and minority rule would prevail far into the foreseeable future. Five years later, Portugal's African empire collapsed, and five further years on, the white minority in Southern Rhodesia ceded power to the African majority.

Despite these events, in 1990 few could have anticipated the pitiful spectacle, 14 years on, of the party of Malan, Verwoerd and Vorster clinging to the boot-straps of the organisation it had spent so much time and so many lives on trying to destroy. The suggestion that the NNP would haemorrhage support had been widespread, but few predicted that its collapse would be so comprehensive. In 1994, the former ruling party had secured 20.4 per cent of the vote, and had served in the Government of National Unity (GNU). Following its withdrawal from the GNU in 1996, and the subsequent resignation from its leadership of former president FW de Klerk, it was always struggling to keep hold of its constituency, which apart from its appeal to minority rights had long been glued together by its position in government. After the 1999 election, its new and largely untried leader, Marthinus van Schalkwyk, proceeded to engage in what now looks like a dance with death.

First he teamed the party up with the then DP, in the DA, only to find that he and his ilk were unable to stomach playing second fiddle to the more cerebral and feisty Tony Leon. Then he took his party out of the DA to join up with the ruling party once again in a loose coalition which enabled the ANC and NNP together to seize control of the Western Cape and the City of Cape Town as a result of the floor-crossing saga of 2002–03 (Southall 2003). Yet when it came to elections 2004, van Schalkwyk – nicknamed 'Kortbroek' or 'Short pants' for his lack of political weight and experience – found, to his wholly predictable cost, that it was the ANC which was wearing the trousers.

The disadvantage faced by the NNP was that, 90 years after its formation, its supporters no longer really knew what it stood for. Led by the thick-skinned and feisty Tony Leon, the DA evinced no doubts about its mission as an unabashed critic of government. In contrast, 'Kortbroek' had taken the NNP into a corner where it had nothing really to sell. His principal message was that the NNP was committed to 'constructive opposition, reconciliation and consensus politics': it differed from the ANC on a number of aspects (for instance, it was tougher on crime and critical of its handling of Zimbabwe), yet its presence in government gave important leverage to whites and coloureds in the corridors of power. However, this was a message which was as confusing as it was unconvincing. Was it in opposition? Or was it in government? If in government, did it really have influence? Van Schalkwyk might be premier of the Western Cape, but was this by sanction of the ANC or at the behest of his own voters? Or was he there by dint of self-seeking, constitutional manipulation? Yet most damaging of all for the NNP in election 2004 was the DA's cruelly pointed barb: a vote for the NNP was in reality a vote for the ANC, and those of its supporters who wanted to vote for an opposition should vote for the real thing. By the end of the campaign, van Schalkwyk's pants were distinctly threadbare, utterly unable to hide his political impotence.

It was evident to all but the NNP leadership that the ANC had the former ruling party precisely where it wanted it. What van Schalkwyk had never realised was that the ANC had courted the NNP out of political convenience and contempt. If the renewed links between the ANC and the NNP were a marriage, then it was a blatant case of a cynical, up-and-coming bridegroom marrying a vainglorious elderly widow for her tawdry wealth. The ANC had long pined for control of the Western Cape, where in 1999 it had won over large numbers of coloured votes from the NNP to emerge as the single largest party, only to be denied control of the province by a post-election coalescence of the DP and NNP. From its own perspective, the Western Cape remained unliberated, and a brutal affront to the spirit of South Africa's new democracy. Hence it was that, during the floor-crossing saga, the ANC had played to the NNP's susceptibilities: van Schalkwyk's personal ambition for office, his party's lack of commitment to principled opposition, and its lingering lust for power. The ANC's hug of alliance with the NNP was therefore that of the bear, and its smile was that of the crocodile. It was scarcely surprising that the NNP's disgruntled voters were to be greedily gobbled up in a ruthless feeding frenzy of ambitious competitors.

Meanwhile, the NNP's dizzying flight from government to opposition and back again, and its overwhelming preoccupation with the Western Cape, had comprehensively undermined its status as a party of national significance. Voters scurried away like rats from a sinking ship, conservatives (especially whites) to the right in the form of the DA, others to the left in the form of the ANC. Many of the latter – coloureds in particular, and especially in the Western Cape (albeit somewhat less so in the provincial than the national election)[5] – were to decamp to the ID.

The failure of the DA to consolidate the opposition

Leon's vision as a political leader has always been consistent. It has been to defy the odds by turning a minority, white, liberal political tradition into an electable, centre-right, multiracial voting bloc. His strategy in the first instance was to appeal to minorities through vigorous opposition to the ANC. This was termed 'fighting back' in 1999, and was dramatically successful, increasing the DP vote from 1.7 per cent in 1994 to 9.6 per cent in 1999, the latter result earning his party the mantle of official opposition. His next step, the construction of the DA, was dressed up as merger, yet designed to absorb the NNP, a bid so blatant that it soon sent van Schalkwyk (although by no means all of his followers) scuttling into the arms of the ANC. Bloodied, but by no means unbowed, Leon thereafter cranked up efforts to repudiate ANC claims that the DA was polarising the electorate on racial grounds. He took its campaign to the townships, whilst also seeking to secure an African partnership by striking up a working relationship with the IFP, whose always-awkward coalition with the ANC in the GNU was, by the 2004 election campaign, becoming manifestly unstuck.

The DA's campaigning was far from unimpressive. Leon himself, an articulate and forceful speaker, was unapologetically bold and abrasive, typified by his challenges to Mbeki to unequivocally state that he would not undermine the Constitution by seeking to run for a third term as president in 2009. He was stylishly packaged as an alternative president, the unquestioned leader of the leaders of opposition. Although his bid for pre-eminent status was foiled by Mbeki's refusal to take him on head-to-head in a US-style, televised debate, his campaigning in the townships had razzmatazz, colour and the aura of a party on the move. Black supporters wearing DA T-shirts and waving party flags were his constant companions as he trawled for African votes and paid less attention than previously to the party's traditional support base in the green and leafy suburbs. ANC praise-singing attacks upon the DA as a party which was racially divisive and reactionary (*Sowetan* 8.03.04) only served to firm conviction that Leon was its principal enemy (*Sowetan* 4.03.04). Yet the DA undermined its own good work by other facets of its strategy.

Its principal error was that it proclaimed contradictory messages to the different segments of its support. On the one hand, it adopted an unconvincing, somewhat populist platform to attract blacks (*ThisDay* 22.04.04). Whilst it proclaimed its backing for a basic income grant (deemed unaffordable by the ANC) as an approach to addressing poverty, it simultaneously campaigned against black economic empowerment, affirmative action, and minimum wages and in favour of a largely unrestricted free market and more flexible labour laws. Meanwhile, its efforts to attract black candidates had met with only extremely limited success, and those that it did attract were reported as at times being nervous of showing their faces. On the other hand, whilst seeking to convince blacks of its good intentions, the DA simultaneously played to the white vote by attacking Mbeki over his welcome to Aristide, his policy on Zimbabwe, and other issues which, whilst always overtly referring to important human rights concerns, embodied a subterranean appeal to anti-black senti-ment. Nor was Leon's reputation for integrity enhanced by his mid-campaign, opportunistic U-turn on capital punishment, which he now hailed as a poten-tial antidote to crime. This was a crude and clumsy appeal to the conservative vote (albeit across racial divisions), yet it deeply offended the DA's traditional constituency on a cardinal point of liberal principle. Furthermore, his entering the alliance of convenience with the IFP, dubbed the 'Coalition for change', likewise linked the DA with a party which many liberals regarded as an apartheid collaborator, and ethnically chauvinist to boot. Finally, Leon's unmanly assaults on the ID as a one-woman party identified it as a threat to the DA's monopoly of vigorous opposition, and reminded the electorate of Verwoerd's similar derogatory assaults upon Helen Suzman – who, for her part, was not slow to condemn Leon on his about-turn on the death penalty.

The DA had projected, early in the campaign, that the 'Coalition for change' was heading for 30 per cent of the national vote. However, when the chips were down, it secured only 12.4 per cent, which, together with the reduced 6.97 per cent of the IFP, fell far short of the target. Although the DA put on a brave face, and correctly noted that it had gained over 400 000 votes over its 1999 tally, in private it must have been bitterly disappointed. Its increased votes appeared to have come very largely from whites and coloureds who had abandoned the NNP and opted for the DA as the conservative alternative to the ID; far, far fewer Africans than it had hoped for had chosen to abandon the ANC and a slim but significant slice of its traditional white supporters had jumped ship in favour of de Lille. Yet what was predictable, and raised a major question about Leon's political acumen, was that after the election, the IFP – earmarked as a future partner in opposition – demonstrated its acute reluc-tance to relinquish its faltering grasp on power.

The ANC's capture of KwaZulu-Natal and the regionalisation of the IFP

In 1994, the IFP had imperiled the democratic transition by threatening to boycott the election. Against a background of more than a decade of violent conflict between the ANC and IFP throughout KZN, the threat was a serious one, only averted by a last-minute deal. An uneasy peace was secured by a notoriously negotiated election result, whereby – although a final count of the votes might have pointed otherwise – the IFP was awarded a narrow majority of the vote in the KZN provincial election, and hence allowed to assume control of the government. This was much to the dismay of the provincial ANC, which was admitted into the provincial government only as a junior partner. Meanwhile, from 1994, IFP leader Mangosuthu Buthelezi and other party heavyweights had served in the national government, whilst also claiming to be a party of opposition.

A war-weary population in KZN subsequently enjoyed the benefits of peace and some evidence of delivery by mainly ANC-led departments. However, the wind-down in conflict eroded control of the rural areas by IFP chiefs and warlords. Hence, in 1999 the party's slip was showing, as support began to drain away. Its vote in the second provincial election dropped to 41.9 per cent, ANC support increasing from 32.3 per cent to 39.4 per cent. A hair's breadth separated the parties, even though the IFP again retained the premiership. Subsequently, the ANC's crude attempt to seize control of the province by wooing floor-crossers in 2003 was only foiled by the IFP's threatening a return to mayhem if it was to be rudely tricked out of power. However, by election 2004, Buthelezi and the IFP knew very well that their long-established dominance of their own backyard was under serious threat.

Buthelezi's political tightrope dance since 1994 had seen him simultaneously basking in glory as Minister of Home Affairs and sulking in public because of the ANC's disrespectful treatment of him in Cabinet. By 2004, mounting tensions had seen personal and political relations between himself and Mbeki reaching breaking point. Given the looming situation in KZN, he therefore bid to broaden the IFP's options by forging the 'Coalition for change' with the DA, a linkage which had its origins in the floor-crossing drama whereby the latter saw potential to substitute itself for the ANC as the IFP's partner in the provincial government. The coalition also claimed continuity with the old Progressive Party's espousal of Buthelezi as an African leader of peace, a relationship which was as doubtfully founded as Leon's latter-day embrace of Buthelezi as a principled democrat. However, what Leon reckoned without was the IFP's umbilical attachment to the politics of patronage, which – as for the NNP – constitutes its lifeblood.

During the 2004 election, the ANC moved in for the kill. Symbolically, it launched its national campaign at King's Park stadium in Durban, taking its fight deep into the heart of enemy territory. Buthelezi, the old lion, was visibly weakening. IFP rumbles of war were subdued by the widespread deployment of security forces. For the first time, the ANC was enabled to position its party agents at every voting station in the province, which it believed was a major deterrent to fraud. The combination of security forces and party agents persuaded enough rural-based ANC supporters to come out and vote for their party of choice. The result was that in the IFP heartland of northern Natal the ANC improved its 1 per cent share of the 1999 vote to 10 per cent. The IFP vote also suffered from the fact that since 1994 there had been a demographic shift of population from rural to urban areas which had the effect of eroding the IFP's foundations in the countryside. Additionally, white conservatives who had thrown in their lot with Inkatha since 1994, now condemned it as tribalist, and were otherwise alienated by the costly absurdity of splitting the provincial administration between the isolated royal outpost of Ulundi and the more practical urban seat of Pietermaritzburg. In short, history was pulling the rug from under the feet of the IFP, and there seemed little that it could do about it.

The voters confirmed these trends with a 47 per cent vote for the ANC in the provincial election. It was not a majority, but it was ahead of even the combined vote of the IFP (36.8 per cent) and the DA (8.4 per cent) (a significant proportion of whose national voters opted for the IFP rather than the ANC at the provincial level).[6] If push came to shove, it was clear that the ANC could cobble together a majority with the support of the Minority Front and the UDM, with the ACDP standing on the sidelines proclaiming it would cast its vote in line with Christian principles.

The IFP – active in government since the 1970s – was facing ejection from power. Its quandary was whether to retain access to influence and resources by playing humble supplicant to the ANC, or striking out boldly into the wilderness of opposition. For its part, the ANC matched strength with conciliation. It offered to continue its provincial partnership with the IFP, yet Mbeki appointed his party's provincial leader, Sibusiso Ndebele, as premier, without consulting Buthelezi. The new premier, in turn, appointed three senior IFP members to his Cabinet, again without consulting the IFP leadership. The party reacted by withdrawing its appointees from the provincial Cabinet. As negotiations continued, Mbeki offered two national deputy-ministerial posts to IFP members Musa Zondi and Vincent Ngema. However, whilst keen to accept, they were ordered to delay taking their oaths of office as Buthelezi himself was regarding his own exclusion from the Cabinet as a calculated insult. Mbeki lost patience and made alternative offers, leaving the IFP's foothold as junior partner in the KZN Cabinet as its sole remaining stake in government.

The ANC: more dominant

Whether or not its leaders choose to contest the epithet, there can be little doubt that the ANC has emerged from the 2004 election as, in the immediate future, more rather than less dominant. It has claimed a higher proportion of electoral support than ever before, it has a two-thirds national majority which would enable it to change the Constitution, and it is now in charge of all nine provinces. Furthermore, it would seem to have made major inroads into support amongst coloureds and Indians, whilst the demise of the NNP and the decline of the IFP have already raised the prospects of their future merger into the ruling party.

Meanwhile, the DA seems as distant as ever from breaking down racial barriers, whilst the recent inflow of large numbers of white refugees from the NNP could well tilt it towards a deeper conservatism that is unappealing to the black majority. Furthermore, although many have trumpeted the ID's success in propelling seven members into Parliament, the reality is that the party obtained a miniscule proportion of the vote, most of which was drawn from Patricia de Lille's own coloured community. Although three smaller parties (the FF+, ACDP and PAC) all increased the levels of their support, their gains were infinitesimal, and in all three cases expansion runs up against self-defined racial or religious boundaries, whilst the UDM and UCDP represent little more than highly specific, former-homeland interests. In short, even though there is widespread acknowledgement of the case for mergers and coalitions to overcome the fragmentation of the opposition, the individual parties remain as divided as ever by the ambitions of their leaderships and their diverse constituencies.

All this suggests the greater ability of the ANC to shape the public agenda and President Mbeki's post-election 'State of the Nation' address leaves no doubt as to his and the ANC's determination to tackle the crippling scourge of poverty head-on. The President's selection of provincial premiers (in some cases over the heads of candidates said to enjoy more local support) suggests a greater degree of central control over especially poorly-performing provinces so as not to jeopardise the delivery crusade. Combined with greater assertiveness concerning black empowerment and indications of a more developmental role for public enterprises, the 2004 election could well prove to have been as watershed an event as the 1994 poll in that it turned out to be a launch pad for more rapid economic growth in South Africa and for a dramatic extension of the safety net of public welfare to that vast army of South Africans dubbed by Desai (2002) as 'the poors'.

Notes

1   Examples of such manipulation in 1949 involved extending parliamentary representation in the South African Parliament to the white voters of the then South West Africa (Namibia), even though it was, in international law, not South African territory but a UN Trust territory. This gave the NP five additional seats in the 1953 and all subsequent elections. In 1955, it abolished the direct representation of coloured voters in Parliament by white MPs. They had consistently voted for opposition MPs. It also abolished the indirect representation system for African voters. Introduced in 1936, the indirect voting system by which seven white representatives (four in the lower house and three in the Senate) were chosen had consistently resulted, after 1948, in the 'election' of left-wing and communist MPs like Sam Kahn, Brian Bunting, Ray Alexander, Fred Carneson, and Len Lee-Warden, amongst others.

2   The analysis that follows draws heavily upon media coverage. Specific references for events, facts or opinions are given only when they are controversial or deemed necessary for reasons of confirmation.

3   We have knowledge of voters who were turned away from polling stations for various reasons. For instance, in some cases presiding officers incorrectly told voters they could only vote at the polling station where they had originally registered – this appears to have happened on a large scale in KwaZulu-Natal. In other cases, women who had registered under their original surnames, and who had since the last election married but retained their original last names, found that the IEC had unilaterally changed their registrations to reflect the names of their husbands. Finally, we know of a case where a 94-year-old registered voter who had voted in 1994 and 1999 found that he had been deregistered when he turned up to vote in 2004 because, according to an official at the station, the IEC 'must have assumed he had died'.

4   According to Afrobarometer (*Mail & Guardian* 13–19.12.02) only one in ten South Africans believe that their elected representatives act in their best interests or listen to them most of the time.

5   All the major parties, including the ID, received fewer votes in the Western Cape provincial election than in the national election, except the NNP, whose provincial election vote was 19 000 votes larger.

6   The DA vote in the KZN provincial election was 47 572 less than in the national election. The majority of these votes appeared to have been transferred to the IFP, whose provincial election vote was 45 166 more than its national result.

References

Cherry J (2004) Elections 2004: The party lists and issues of identity, *ElectionSynopsis* 1(3):6–9.

Daniel J (2004) The South African elections of 1994, 1999 and 2004: The (non)issues then and now, *ElectionSynopsis* 1(1):12–14.

Desai A (2002) *We are the poors: Community struggles in post-apartheid South Africa.* New York: Monthly Review.

Giliomee H & Simkins C (eds.) (1999) *The awkward embrace: One party domination and democracy.* Cape Town: Tafelberg.

Giliomee H, Myburgh J & Schlemmer L (2001) Dominant party rule, opposition parties and minorities in South Africa. In R Southall (ed.) *Opposition and democracy in South Africa.* London: Frank Cass.

Hicks J (2004) Public participation beyond the election, *ElectionSynopsis* 1(1):8–12.

Kotze D (2004) The nomination processes of candidates on party lists, *Election Update 2* 16.02.04:2–7.

Landsberg C & Mackay S (2004) South Africa's decade of democracy, inequality and impoverishment, *ElectionSynopsis* 1(1):3–5.

Lodge T (1999) *Consolidating democracy: South Africa's second popular election.* Johannesburg: Witwatersrand University Press.

Mbeki T (2004) We salute all South Africans on a decade of freedom, *ANC Today* 4, 16, 23–29 April.

PCAS (Presidency Policy Co-ordination and Advisory Services, South Africa) (2003) *Towards a ten year review: Synthesis report on implementation of government programmes. Discussion document.* Pretoria: Government Communications and Information Systems.

Pempel TJ (1990) *Uncommon democracies: The one-party dominant regimes.* Ithaca, NY: Cornell University Press.

Roefs M (2004) One-party dominance, racial cleavages and decreasing voter turnout, *ElectionSynopsis* 1(1):17–19.

Southall R (2001) Conclusion: Emergent perspectives on opposition in South Africa. In R Southall (ed.) *Opposition and democracy in South Africa.* London: Frank Cass.

Southall R (2003) The state of party politics: Struggles within the Tripartite Alliance and the decline of opposition. In J Daniel, A Habib & R Southall *The State of the Nation: South Africa 2003–04.* Cape Town: HSRC Press.

Southall R (2004) Containing accountability, *ElectionSynopsis* 1(1):6–8.

3 Rural governance and citizenship in post-1994 South Africa: democracy compromised?

Lungisile Ntsebeza

Introduction

The post-1994 South African state has committed itself to the establishment of a democratic, representative and accountable form of governance through-out the country.[1] This is a most challenging task, especially given the authoritarian and despotic histories of colonialism and apartheid in this country. An area where these highly undemocratic practices and injustices of the past manifested themselves, and which forms the basis of this chapter, is the rural areas falling under the jurisdiction of traditional authorities.[2] The post-1994 state has inherited a system of administration in these areas that was based on the concentration of all power in these areas in the hands of unaccountable traditional authorities (chiefs and headmen).[3] Despite claims by the apartheid architects that this form of rule was based on pre-colonial African institutions, in reality, the 'institution of traditional leadership', in the form of apartheid-created tribal authorities, was incorporated into the structures of government as an extended arm. Tribal authorities were, in the mould of their apartheid creators, highly authoritarian and despotic. As a result they were discredited, hated and feared.

Soon after the advent of democracy in 1994, the African National Congress (ANC)-led government embarked on the all-important democratisation process. In the rural areas of the former bantustans, this included attempts to dismantle the concentration of powers in tribal authorities in the form of reforms in local government and land administration.[4] As will be seen further on, a new conception of developmental local government introduced the notion of elected local leadership and an emphasis on improving the quality of life of previously disadvantaged sectors. Attempts are also being made to democratise the system of land administration with a focus on including women in land administration structures.

However, in this chapter it is argued that this democratisation process risks serious compromise. After years of ambivalence and prevarication, the ANC-led government passed two Bills through Parliament – the Traditional Leadership and Governance Framework Act (the Framework Act) and the Communal Land Rights Bill (CLRB) – which make concessions to traditional authorities, effectively resuscitating the powers they enjoyed under the notorious Bantu Authorities Act of 1951. As will be seen, the Framework Act accepts tribal authorities as a foundation for establishing what it refers to as traditional councils, while the CLRB recognises these traditional councils as having the authority to administer and allocate land in the rural areas. This raises critical questions about citizenship and the nature of democracy in South Africa. Is liberal democracy as espoused in the South African Constitution compatible with traditional authorities who inherit their posts? To what extent is the granting of separate and different rights to rural and urban South Africans a continuation of colonial and apartheid divisions between the urban and the rural? Is the denial of the right to elect one's leaders compatible with democracy and full citizenship?

This chapter explores the manner in which the South African state has attempted to extend democracy to the rural areas falling under traditional authorities, with particular focus on the tension in the Constitution between enshrining democratic principles largely modelled along liberal democratic lines of representative government on the one hand, and recognising and giving wide-ranging powers to an inherently undemocratic hereditary institution of traditional leadership on the other. The role of traditional authorities will be investigated against the backdrop of the role they played during the colonial and apartheid periods. The discussion of the role of traditional authorities in post-1994 rural development will be explored through the prism of local government and land administration. The chapter is not an empirical examination of the problems of rural governance or an evaluation of the performance of post-1994 rural structures; the focus is on policy and its implications for democracy and citizenship for rural people. The cardinal issue here is whether rural residents must continue to be subjects under the rule of unelected traditional authorities, or whether they will enjoy the citizenship rights, including the right to elect leaders and representatives, that the South African Constitution confers on all South Africans, or both.

Conceptual and historical background

The main conceptual issue confronting the post-1994 state is whether it is possible to democratise rural local governance through enfranchising forms of rural authority, while at the same time recognising and giving powers to an unelected, hereditary institution of traditional leadership. This is a question that does not only affect South Africa, but many African countries that have hereditary traditional institutions. There seem to be two schools of thought on this matter, what I call a co-existence thesis and a common citizenship approach.

Mamdani is by far the foremost advocate of the common citizenship school. His thesis is that the colonial state in Africa was 'bifurcated', with different modes of rule for urban 'citizens' and rural 'subjects'. The colonial strategy of 'divide and rule' took two related forms: an enforced division of Africans along ethnic lines, and an enforced division between town and countryside. According to Mamdani, the African was 'containerised', not as a native or indigenous African, but as a 'tribesperson'. Colonialists justified 'indirect rule' on the basis that 'tradition' and 'custom' were indigenous forms of social organisation. But, they reinforced and used these identities to divide and manage rural Africans. In order to enforce their dual policy of 'ethnic pluralism' and urban-rural division, Mamdani asserts, colonialists exercised 'force to an unusual degree'. In this way, colonial despotism was highly decentralised (1996:22–4).

According to Mamdani, the chief was pivotal in the local state, the native authority. His authority was rooted in the fusion of various powers – judicial, legislative, executive and administrative – in his office, rather than the classic liberal democratic notion of a separation thereof. Mamdani uses the analogy of a 'clenched fist' to delineate this concentration of power. Native authorities, according to him, were protected from any external threat. Their officials were appointed from above and never elected. They had no term of office, and remained therein for as long as they enjoyed the confidence of their superiors.

Mamdani argues that the colonial legacy was reproduced after independence. However, no nationalist government was content to reproduce the colonial legacy uncritically. Each attempted to reform the colonial state, but in doing so reproduced a part of that legacy, thereby creating its own variety of despotism. Post-colonial African states, whether conservative or radical, deracialised the colonial state, but, according to Mamdani, did not democratise it. On democratic transformation, Mamdani proposes 'nothing less than dismantling' the 'bifurcated state'. This will entail 'an endeavour to link the urban and the rural – and thereby a series of related binary opposites such as rights and custom, representation and participation, centralization and decentralization, civil society and community – in ways that have yet to be done' (1996:34).

On their part, Bank and Southall (1996) have argued that democracy in post-colonial Africa would be compromised if traditional authorities were accorded an active role in politics. They doubt the capacity of traditional authorities in political administration. Drawing from the South African experience, Bank and Southall point out that a large number of traditional authorities became collaborators with the apartheid regime and were unaccountable and corrupt when they administered the former bantustans. They also argue that there is a conflict between the patriarchal values of traditional leadership and gender equality that is entrenched in the Constitution. For Bank and Southall, the role of traditional authorities should be confined to ceremonial functions. However, they do not elaborate on what these would be in concrete terms.

Ismail (1999:1–5), on the other hand, is critical of the manner in which post-colonial African states have addressed the role of traditional authorities. He accuses those who were engaged in the South African political negotiation process in the early 1990s of merely raising and making 'platitudinous statements regarding the future role of chiefs' without any concrete suggestions. According to him, the general trend 'has been dramatic marginalisation' of traditional authorities and their 'traditional roles' or 'a mere symbolic retention of the institution'. He suggests a model that he considers to be 'effective, yet realistic' that would engage traditional authorities 'and some aspects of indigenous governance in liberal democratic governance'. Ismail proposes strongly that 'indigenous governance' has its 'democratic elements' that 'can strengthen rather than weaken current efforts to build a democratic culture among the African people'. According to him, this kind of engagement could lead to the democratisation of the 'institution itself'.

The meaning of democracy has also been revisited in the context of the advent of multiparty democracy and decentralisation in the 1990s. According to Agrawal and Ribot (1999:478) 'political/democratic decentralization' is said to occur when powers and resources are transferred to authorities that are 'downwardly accountable to local populations'. Manor (2001) has elaborated on this notion and recently argued that studies of democratic decentralisation point out three essential conditions for democratic local government: substantial resources (especially financial resources) from higher levels of government; substantial powers to be devolved to local authorities; and mechanisms to ensure that bureaucrats are accountable to elected representatives, on the one hand, and that elected representatives are accountable to voters, on the other hand.

Apart from the conceptual and theoretical issues that the ANC-led government has to grapple with, it is important to take into account the legacy of traditional authorities. Indeed, the features of native authorities that Mamdani depicts in general terms, aptly capture those of tribal authorities in South Africa. These apartheid-era structures fitted Mamdani's notion of a 'clenched fist' in the sense that all power in the rural areas of the former bantustans, including local government and land administration, was concentrated or fused in them. They comprised of chiefs, headmen and councillors, and a tribal secretary.

Tribal authorities were imposed on resisting rural inhabitants and were an extended arm of the central state. A prime objective of the National Party (NP) when they came to power in 1948 was to resolve the question of 'native administration'; what Hendricks (1990) appropriately refers to as retribalisation. Chiefs and headmen were roped in and were given greater administrative powers than during the segregation period. Their main function, as Evans puts it, was 'to contain and discipline the reserve army of African labour: those Africans prevented by law from departing to the urban areas, the "idle or disorderly" evicted from the urban areas, and the "excess labour" skimmed off the white farming areas' (1997:260).[5] According to Hendricks, 'the state's policy was transformed from a stated commitment to "saving the soil" to an attempt to reinvigorate tribalism in the reserves as a cooptive device bringing African chiefs and headmen into the local machinery of government' (1990:122).[6] They were, not surprisingly, discredited, undemocratic, unaccountable, autocratic, and, in many instances, feared (Lodge 1983; Manona 1998; Mbeki 1984; Ntsebeza 1999, 2001).

The involvement of traditional authorities thoroughly discredited even those who may have enjoyed some degree of legitimacy during the segregation period prior to apartheid, by virtue of their marginalisation. Hammond-Tooke (1975) has argued that some traditional authorities gained legitimacy among their people for the simple reason that they were not identified with government policies.[7] Those that are often cited as having retained their legitimacy include Paramount Chiefs Sabata Dalindyebo of abaThembu and Morwamoche Sekhukhune in the Northern Transvaal, now Limpopo (Delius 1996; Lodge 1983). Van Kessel and Oomen have even made an unsubstantiated claim that Sabata 'headed the revolt in Tembuland' (1997:563). Some residents in western Thembuland in the Eastern Cape, and political activists such as Tsotsi (1989), also regarded Chief KD Matanzima as a progressive chief. However, with the introduction of the Bantu Authorities Act, there was little room left for this variation. As paid government agents, they were forced to comply.[8]

Having said this, traditional authorities did not all relate in the same way to the apartheid system. There were those, such as KD Matanzima, who shamelessly collaborated with the apartheid regime. Others, such as Sabata Dalindyebo, were reluctant participants in the apartheid game.[9] Yet chiefs such as Albert Luthuli and Nelson Mandela never collaborated with the apartheid system and Luthuli was even willing to renounce his chieftainship. However, both the latter were minor chiefs and it is as leaders of political organisations, and not as traditional authorities, that they won their recognition.

Tribal authorities were set up even in areas where there were no chiefs, a recognition on the part of the apartheid regime that rural areas were very uneven and not homogeneous. In these areas, community authorities were established, headed by headmen.[10] By making chiefs central in apartheid administration in the rural areas of the former bantustans, the Bantu Authorities Act thus represented one of the building blocks of apartheid policy of consolidating reserves/bantustans/homelands. These bantustans were later to become self-governing, and some became independent.[11]

Given its significance in the post-1994 period, it is worth noting that the powers of traditional authorities and their structures were, even when they were given greater powers during the apartheid period, subject to endorsement by magistrates, from the chief magistrate downwards to district commissioners. As Spiegel (1992) noted, magistrates were as concerned with administration of agriculture and roads, engineering, health, welfare and education, land allocation and tenure, and the collection of taxes, as they were with local administration of justice.

The allocation of land, one of the contentious issues in the current period of democracy in South Africa, provides an excellent example.

The process of allocating land started at a local, sub-headman area and was finalised with the issuing of a permit to occupy by the magistrate/district commissioner.[12] In theory, a person (usually a man) who wanted land, first identified the land and approached people in the neighbourhood to establish if there were other claimants and to solicit their support. If the land was available, the applicant approached the sub-headman of the ward in which the property was situated. The sub-headman then called a ward general assembly (*imbizo*) to offer people an opportunity to comment on the application. If there were no objections, the sub-headman submitted the application to the headman of the administrative area. The headman verbally verified that the general assembly was called, and that no objections had been lodged. In addition, the headman established whether the applicant was a married, registered taxpayer. In this regard, the sub-headman had to produce a receipt issued by the magistrate as proof. If the applicant could not produce a receipt, the headman would have to accompany the applicant to the magistrate's office to be registered. The applicant had to be accompanied by a headman or the chief to register.

Upon production of the receipt, the headman normally granted the application. This was seen as a formality. As one headman stated: 'As a headman, I accept and respect the decision of the sub-headman.' The headman then submitted the application to the tribal authority. This was also seen as a formality. The tribal authority completed the application form that was submitted to the district commissioner. The application form had to be signed by the chief, councillors and the secretary of the tribal authority. Only at this point was the applicant expected to pay an application fee to the tribal authority in order to augment the funds of the latter. This was the only fee that the applicant was supposed to pay.

In practice, though, the system of land allocation was complex and often did not adhere to the letter of the law. The main problem was how to monitor the system and make those charged with authority accountable. In the majority of cases, traditional authorities were upwardly accountable to the government, rather than to rural residents. This was made possible by the fact that the apartheid and bantustan regimes gave traditional authorities such powers that they were feared, rather than respected, by their communities (Ntsebeza 1999). This made it extremely difficult for ordinary, elderly rural residents to hold traditional authorities accountable.

Traditional authorities exploited the lack of checks and balances. There were basically two forms of violations: allocating land without going through the procedure, and illegal taxation. Traditional authorities abused their power by charging unauthorised fees, in the name of the 'rights of the great place' (*iimfanelo zakomkhulu*), to applicants. These included alcohol, poultry, sheep, and even an ox. This practice reached its zenith in the early 1990s when, for instance, some cottage sites were illegally allocated to some whites along the Wild Coast in the old Transkei. These sites were dubbed 'brandy sites', as it was imperative that applications were accompanied by a bottle of brandy. It was standard practice in some parts that ordinary rural residents present the sub-headman with a bottle of brandy (or some suitable gift) (de Wet & McAllister 1983). Further, in a number of cases, traditional authorities allocated land to rural residents, bypassing the district commissioner. These rural residents were consequently not issued with a permit to occupy.

Dealing with the legacy of 'decentralised despotism'

The framework for developing a policy on rural local governance in South Africa is provided in the 1996 Constitution of South Africa. As indicated, it is contradictory in the sense that, while providing a basis for dismantling the 'clenched fist' of tribal authorities by means of democratically elected representatives, the Constitution also recognises a role for the hereditary institution of traditional leadership. The Constitution itself is silent on the specific roles, functions and powers of the institution of traditional authorities in a democracy. It only provides guidelines for legislative processes that will clarify the roles, functions and powers. For almost ten years, the ANC-led government has been attempting to introduce the necessary legislation that would bring some degree of clarity on these matters – the Framework Act and the CLRB have gone a long way in this regard. Earlier legislation, as will be seen, seemed to avoid defining roles for traditional authorities.

A significant step that the ANC-led government took in its attempts to democratise rural local governance was to separate the functions of local government and land administration, thus undoing a major legacy of apartheid of concentrating and fusing power in one authority, the tribal authority. With regard to local government, the division between the rural and the urban was abolished in the sense that municipalities made up of elected councillors were extended to all parts of the country, including rural areas under traditional authorities where municipalities did not exist before. At the same time, various attempts were made to phase out tribal authorities as the land administration and allocation authority.

Rural local government reform, democratising land administration and traditional authorities

The Constitution of the Republic of South Africa establishes three distinct, interdependent and interrelated spheres of government, namely, national, provincial and local government (Section 40[1]). The local sphere of government is made up of municipalities which, as already indicated, must be established throughout the country, including rural areas (Section 151[1]). The Constitution and the 1998 *White Paper on local government* define post-1994 local government as 'developmental' local government, involving integrated development planning. This requires municipalities to co-ordinate all development activities within their areas of jurisdiction (Pycroft 1998). Developmental local government thus seeks not only to democratise local government, by introducing the notion of elected representatives even in rural areas, but also to transform local governance, with a new focus on improving the standard of living and quality of life of previously disadvantaged sectors of the community (Pycroft 1998). In addition, developmental local government requires that citizens should actively participate in development initiatives in their areas (see Section 152[1][e] of the Constitution; also, ANC 1994; Ntsebeza 1999, 2001).

Local government in post-1994 South Africa went through two phases: a transition phase between 1995 and 2000, followed by the establishment of fully-fledged municipalities in December 2000. The 1993 Transitional Local Government Act was amended in 1995 in order to define local government in rural areas. The amendment provided for a district council model for these areas, establishing a two-level structure, consisting of a district council at a sub-regional level, and a range of possible structures at local (primary) level.[13] Unlike in urban areas, where municipal transitional structures were accorded the powers of a fully-fledged local authority, structures in many rural areas were seen as fulfilling representative and brokering functions, and as bodies that would eventually evolve into effective and democratic local authorities.[14] In practice, however, at the end of the transitional period in 2000 these structures had not evolved into local authorities. The urban bias was also shown in the electoral system. Whereas in the urban areas the system was based on a combination of the constituency and proportional representation, the system that was adopted for rural areas was proportional representation. This meant that rural people voted only for political parties, rather than political parties and independent candidates.

Following the demarcation of municipal boundaries in 2000, new municipalities were established. A model amalgamating several urban and rural municipalities was adopted. This resulted in the creation of fewer and geographically larger municipalities. The number of municipalities was drastically reduced from 834 to 284 between 1995 and 2000. The number of councillors was also reduced, meaning that fewer councillors would be responsible for larger municipalities. The electoral system combining constituency and proportional representation that applied to urban areas was extended to all municipalities with wards.

Attempts to empower rural residents by involving them in decision-making processes on land issues were given a boost with the launch of the *White Paper on South African land policy* in April 1997. The White Paper provided a guide for the legislative process that would define the land tenure rights of rural people and a system of land administration. By the beginning of 1998, the Department of Land Affairs (DLA) had developed principles to guide its legislative and implementation framework. The principles emphasised that where land rights 'to be confirmed exist on a group basis, the rights holders must have a choice about the system of land administration, which will manage their land rights on a day-to-day basis'. In addition, 'the basic human rights of all members must be protected, including the right to democratic decision-making processes and equality. Government must have access to members of group-held systems in order to ascertain their views and wishes in respect of proposed development projects and other matters pertaining to their land rights' (Thomas, Sibanda & Claassens 1998:528).

It seems quite clear that both the Departments of Provincial and Local Government and Land Affairs intended to subject traditional authorities to a system that would make them more representative and accountable to their communities. The notion of developmental local government sits well with the views of Agrawal and Ribot (1999) and Manor (2001) on democratic decentralisation outlined earlier. The Local Government Act of 1993, as amended in 1995, provided an extremely limited, if not vague, role for traditional authorities in local government. Defining them as an interest group, along with women and farm workers, the Act gave traditional authorities not more than 10 per cent representation in an *ex officio* capacity. However, the main challenge was how these principles would translate into concrete practice. In fact, as it turned out, it would take the two departments, and indeed, the ANC-led government, almost ten years from the advent of democracy to come up with laws that reasonably clarify the role of traditional authorities in rural areas.

Part of the delay was the attitude of traditional authorities towards the emerging policies and laws. Moves by the ANC-led government towards democratising rural local governance drew fierce criticism and resistance even from the Congress of Traditional Leaders of South Africa (Contralesa), an organisation that is made up of traditional authorities who collaborated with the ANC in the pre-1994 period. In fact, the ANC had been instrumental in setting up this organisation in the late 1980s (van Kessel & Oomen 1997). By 1994, traditional authorities in South Africa were divided broadly between those who were members of Contralesa and those owing allegiance to the Inkatha Freedom Party (IFP) of Chief Mangosuthu Buthelezi. The latter was violently opposed to the ANC. However, post-1994 government policies and laws have almost closed the ideological gap between members of Contralesa and those traditional authorities who are sympathetic to the IFP (Ntsebeza 2002, 2004). While the initial collaboration was around local government, it is quite clear that the main issue that brings traditional authorities together is their opposition to the notion of introducing new democratic structures. They would be happy to be the only primary structure in rural areas and insist on preserving the concentration of functions they enjoyed under apartheid, in particular land administration.

Government's reaction up to 2002

Government seems to have succumbed to the pressure exerted by traditional authorities. As we have seen, in the immediate post-1994 period, policy and legislation seemed, on the whole, to have been driven by a commitment to extending participatory and representative notions of democracy to rural areas. An expression of this radicalism was the 1997 promulgation of the Regulation of Development in Rural Areas Act by the Eastern Cape Legislature. This Act sought to divest traditional authorities of all their development functions and transfer these to elected councillors. This, of course, was in line with new functions of local government. However, since the end of 1997, the pendulum seems to have swung in favour of traditional authorities (Ntsebeza 2002, 2004). The *White Paper on local government* published in March 1998 makes broad and sweeping statements about the possible role that traditional authorities can play. Traditional 'leadership' is assigned 'a role closest to the people'. On the issue of development, a task that has been added to local government by the Constitution, the White Paper boldly asserts: 'There is no doubt that the important role that traditional leaders have played in the development of their communities should be continued' (1998:77).

The recommendation in the White Paper that the institution of traditional leadership should 'play a role closest to the people', flies in the face of the recommendation of the 1994 ANC election manifesto, the Reconstruction and Development Programme (RDP). The RDP was emphatic that democratically elected local government structures should play this role. The White Paper thus marks a major shift in government policy, and has grave consequences for the possibility of democracy in rural areas. Similarly, the Constitution has explicitly added development functions to democratically elected local government structures. Yet, the White Paper recommends that traditional authorities should continue performing these tasks. Moreover, the statement that traditional authorities played an important role in development among their communities must be viewed with suspicion. No evidence is adduced to support this statement. Existing evidence shows that traditional authorities were never directly involved in development projects. These projects were implemented by government line-departments. Where traditional authorities acted as a link between government departments and their communities, research has shown that they have often been corrupt. An example is the illegal taxes imposed by traditional authorities in the process of land allocation as outlined earlier (see also Ntsebeza 1999, 2004).

The issue of the role of traditional authorities was the subject of much discussion and negotiation in the run-up to the second democratic local government election in December 2000, and was instrumental in causing the postponement of announcing the date for the election. The position of the government was still ambivalent in the run-up to the election. After a series of meetings between government and traditional authorities, the government made some concessions. The first significant concession was the amendment of the Municipal Structures Act that was successfully rushed through Parliament just before the local government elections. The amendment increased the representation of traditional authorities from 10 per cent to 20 per cent of the total number of councillors. Further, traditional authorities would not only be represented at a local government level, but also at a district and, in the case of KwaZulu-Natal, metropolitan level. Traditional authorities, though, would not have the right to vote.

This concession seemed to have encouraged traditional authorities to ask for more. They rejected the 20 per cent increase. They wanted nothing short of amending the Constitution and legislation flowing from it regarding municipalities in rural areas in the former bantustans. They wanted municipalities to be scrapped in these areas in favour of apartheid-era tribal authorities as the primary local government structures. Traditional authorities have claimed that the President had promised them, in word and in writing, that their powers would not be tampered with. If anything, they would be increased.[15] On his part, the President has neither denied nor endorsed this claim.

The response of government was, for the second time in as many months, to present a Bill to Parliament to amend the Municipal Structures Act. The Bill did not address the central demand of traditional authorities, the scrapping of municipalities in rural areas in favour of tribal authorities. The Bill merely sought to give local government powers to delegate certain powers and functions to traditional authorities. In addition, a range of peripheral duties would be assigned to traditional authorities. Predictably, traditional authorities rejected the Bill and threatened to boycott the 2000 local government election. They also threatened that there would be violence in their areas if their demands were not met. The Bill was subsequently withdrawn on a technicality. It would seem that the President made some undertakings, given that traditional authorities eventually participated in the election.

The manner in which this vexed issue of the role of traditional authorities in a democratic South Africa has been handled and negotiated is intriguing. Insofar as local government issues are concerned, traditional authorities fall under the Department of Provincial and Local Government (DPLG). In practice, though, traditional authorities did not seem to recognise this Department, preferring to deal with the President and Deputy President. For example, traditional authorities have submitted almost all their requests to the Office of the President. They seem to think that the Minister of Provincial and Local Government is not as favourably disposed towards them as the President. Alternatively, this might be a deliberate strategy to pit the President against the Minister.

With regard to land administration, similar shifts in favour of traditional authorities were taking place. We have seen that the guiding principle of the DLA towards land administration was that where land was held on a group basis, the land rights holders would have a choice about the system of land administration. However, when Thoko Didiza replaced Derrick Hanekom as Minister of Land Affairs, after disbanding the drafting team of the Land Rights Bill she had inherited from Hanekom, she unveiled her strategic objectives regarding land tenure and administration in rural areas in February 2000. With regard to land administration, she committed herself to building on 'the existing local institutions and structures, both to reduce costs to the government and to ensure local commitment and popular support' (Lahiff 2000:63).

This statement raises a number of issues. In the first place, there is no necessary connection between reducing costs and ensuring 'local commitment and popular support'. If anything, I would contend that, given the legacy of colonialism and apartheid, including the effects of bantu education, the task of ensuring that effective governance structures are created in rural areas would not be a cheap exercise. In the second instance, this principle makes dangerous assumptions about 'local institutions and structures' that clearly demonstrate poor knowledge and understanding of conditions in the rural areas. Given existing conditions in rural areas, the Minister's statement raises various questions, for example: What if local institutions and structures are dysfunctional? What if they are unpopular and corrupt? What about situations where there is contestation between or within various structures? Is building on existing structures necessarily a cheap option?

By August 2002, there was no clarity as to how the question of land adminis-tration in rural areas would be resolved. Neither was it clear how the issue of the role of traditional authorities in local government would be handled. The promised amendment to the Municipal Structures Act had not been finalised. A draft amendment published for public comment on 20 November 2000 seemed to propose a trade-off, rather than amending the Constitution. The draft amendment gave traditional authorities control over the allocation of land in so-called 'communal' areas. According to Section 81(1)(a) of the Municipal Structures Second Amendment Bill:

> Despite anything contained in any other law, a traditional auth-ority observing a system of customary law continues to exist and to exercise powers and perform functions conferred upon it in terms of indigenous law, customs and statutory law, which powers and functions include – (a) the right to administer communal land …

It is not clear what happened to this draft amendment. The promulgation of the Framework Act and the Cabinet approval of the CLRB in 2003 seem to have rendered the amendment no longer relevant.

The Traditional Leadership and Governance Framework Act, the Communal Land Rights Bill and traditional authorities

One of the problems facing government was that, despite the fact that an attempt was made to separate the various powers that were concentrated in tribal authorities and to allocate them to various departments (the Departments of Provincial and Local Government and Land Affairs), there was very little communication between these departments. For example, interviews with some senior DLA officials suggest that the DPLG did not consult these officials when proposing the amendment to the Municipal Structures Act regarding giving traditional authorities powers to allocate land. Yet, the task of deciding who should allocate land in rural areas is the competency of the DLA. Under the circumstances, a trade-off of the nature proposed by the DPLG was not going to be easy to negotiate. A significant feature of the 2003 legislative process involving the two departments is that once co-operation took place it was possible to clinch the trade-off, as will be shown below.

The Traditional Leadership and Governance Framework Act

An objective of the 2003 Framework Act that is pertinent for the purposes of this chapter is the provision for the establishment and recognition of traditional councils. According to Section 3(1), a traditional council will be established in an area which has been recognised by the premier as a traditional community. This would take place, in terms of the preamble, within the context of transforming 'the institution of traditional leadership, in line with constitutional imperatives ... so that democratic governance and the values of an open and democratic society may be promoted'. The Act provides for a role for traditional leadership, not only in the local government sphere, but in all three spheres of government. It does not specify a role for traditional authorities in land administration. This is dealt with in the CLRB.

The introduction of the Act again raised the question of the meaning of democracy and citizenship in rural areas. How should we understand notions such as transforming the institution of traditional leadership, democratic governance and the values of an open and democratic society in the preamble? These questions become all the more pressing considering that the Act recognises existing tribal authorities which were established in the apartheid era, and in terms of the 1951 Bantu Authorities Act, traditional councils. Although a four-year transition period is allowed for their transformation (whatever this means), there is no provision for sanctions in the event that the tribal authorities have not been transformed.[16]

The traditional councils are undemocratic in their nature, resembling the tribal authorities they are meant to replace. Although there is provision for a minimum of 30 per cent representation of women in the councils, the major-ity of the members are not popularly elected. Initially, there was a recommen-dation that a mere 25 per cent of members should be elected. After strong protests from non-governmental and other civil society organisations, this number was increased to 40 per cent. This, however, still gives unelected tra-ditional authorities and their appointees a majority.

On the question of the incompatibility of traditional leadership and democ-racy, a report by the Portfolio Committee on Provincial and Local Government (2003) stated that 'traditional leadership … is certainly reconcil-able with the basic principles and values of our Constitution including democracy and gender equality'. The Committee further reminded: 'After all, the institution of traditional leadership is provided for in the Constitution.' However, the Committee did not spell out the type of democracy they had in mind that was reconcilable with an unelected institution of traditional leadership. They would surely not be referring to representative democracy inscribed in the Constitution, which requires that leaders should be popularly elected. Moreover, the fact that the institution of traditional leader-ship is provided for in the Constitution does not nullify the significance of the question.

It seems clear from discussions in the Portfolio Committee that establishing traditional councils dominated by traditional authorities and their appointees was a trade-off to persuade traditional authorities not to push for a constitutional amendment. Members of the Committee agreed that a constitutional amendment could be made after the finalisation of the Framework Bill and if there was 'significant consensus between the tradi-tional leaders, South African Local Government Association and other key stakeholders' (Portfolio Committee 2003). In the same report the Committee suggested that 'transformation in the areas of custom and tradition has to be phased in appropriately' and that 'all stakeholders should be prepared to compromise in this phase'.

The Communal Land Rights Bill

A last-minute Cabinet amendment to the CLRB on 8 October 2003, at about the same time that the Framework Bill was being considered, seems to have resolved the thorny issue of the role of traditional authorities in local governance for the moment. The amendment provided that the traditional councils established in terms of the Framework Act will have land allocation and administration powers and functions in communal areas. This gives enormous powers to a structure with a majority of unelected members. According to a report in the *Cape Times* of 28 January 2004, the amendment was made shortly after a meeting involving Deputy President Zuma, King Zwelithini and IFP's Chief Buthelezi, leading to speculation that the amendment was a deal.

It is worth noting that this was an amendment to a draft CLRB which was gazetted on 14 August 2002. This draft Bill proposed the transfer of registrable land rights to individuals, families and communities. On land administration, it divested traditional authorities of their land administration functions, including land allocation, in favour of democratically elected administrative structures. Where applicable, legitimate traditional authorities were accorded *ex officio* representation not exceeding 25 per cent. The draft Bill clearly attempted to strike a balance between the constitutional obligation to extend democracy to all parts of the country, including rural areas, and accommodating the institution of traditional leadership, which is recognised in the Constitution. What was not clear in the draft, however, was the meaning of a 'legitimate traditional authority'. Did it refer to a traditional authority that is born from the correct lineage, as opposed to colonial- and apartheid-appointed traditional authorities or did it mean one that has the support of the community?

Traditional authorities rejected this draft Bill. According to reports in the *Sunday Times* and *City Press* of 25 August 2002, Chiefs Holomisa (of Contralesa) and Mzimela (of the National House of Traditional Leaders) indicated that they were going to oppose the envisaged legislation and would take up the issue with the President, as they had in the past. A report in the *Daily Dispatch* of 2 November 2002 alleged that some traditional authorities had threatened bloodshed. The paper also quoted Chief Holomisa as saying:

> In 2000, we (traditional leaders) held three meetings with him (Mbeki), where he categorically stated that in no way would the power of traditional leaders be reduced or diminished by his government. We asked him to put it in writing, and he took exception, saying it looked as though we doubted his word.

The amended and Cabinet-approved version of the CLRB gives traditional authorities unprecedented powers, particularly with regard to the allocation of land. The amended draft of the CLRB drew criticism from a range of civil society organisations, gender and land rights activists, organised under the auspices of the University of Western Cape-based Programme for Land and Agrarian Studies (PLAAS) and the National Land Committee (NLC). It was also criticised by some ANC Members of Parliament.[17] The criticism was based on the view that traditional councils are a retreat from democracy and an attempt to revive a defunct apartheid institution which, among other things, was deeply discriminatory of women. In an article in the *Mail & Guardian* of 31 October 2003, Cousins and Claassens argued that under 'customary law' women will be dependent on men, and vulnerable to loss of their land and other property on divorce or the death of their husbands. Despite the protest, the controversial Bill was bulldozed through and passed unanimously by Parliament on 27 January 2004.[18]

The response by traditional authorities

For the first time in more than ten years traditional authorities gave their overwhelming support for the CLRB.[19] The chairperson of the National House of Traditional Authorities, Chief Mpiyezintombi Mzimela, stated that: 'The Communal Land Right Bill aims to restore to rural communities ownership of the remnants that they occupy of land that the colonial and apartheid government took from them by force – giving the communities registered title, so that it cannot happen again' (*Business Day* 2.12.03).

However, Mzimela indicated that the push for a constitutional amendment may not be over, saying, 'Our communities wish to govern their own areas and want traditional communities to constitute the local government, not a fourth tier, but part of the third tier.' He averred that the institution of traditional leadership is the 'only institution that does not have its powers and duties set out in the Constitution', an 'omission', he urged, that should be 'rectified'.

The Framework Act avoided the constitutional amendment and recognised municipalities made up of elected councillors as the primary form of local government in rural areas. But the establishment of traditional councils has arguably given traditional authorities more powers than elected councillors.

Why is the ANC-led government making these concessions?

Shifts in ANC thinking regarding traditional authorities should be seen against the backdrop of a wider conservative shift in the ANC, particularly after the Cold War in the late 1980s and early 1990s and the compromises made in the political negotiation process of the early 1990s. Some of these shifts were already evident in the 1994 ANC election manifesto, the Reconstruction and Development Programme. On the question of land, for example, the RDP committed the ANC, albeit cautiously, to a market-led land reform programme. (This was a sharp reversal of the position, expressed in the Freedom Charter, that land and other major sectors of the economy would be nationalised.) Two years later, the ANC-led government formally embraced conservative, neo-liberal economic policies in the form of GEAR (Growth, Employment and Redistribution Strategy) (see Bond 2000; Fine & Padayachee 2001; Marais 1998).

The shift is often justified in terms of there being no alternative to global capitalism. But, as analysts such as Marais have commented, this marked a victory for the more conservative, capitalist-inclined forces within the ANC, thus suggesting that the ANC itself and its Alliance partners, the South African Communist Party and the Congress of South African Trade Unions, are not unanimous on this issue. The ANC is also not unanimous on the issue of the role of traditional authorities in a democracy. Historically, the ANC has been divided on this question between pro- and anti-chief factions. Former President Nelson Mandela, who is pro-chief, and Govan Mbeki, the father of President Thabo Mbeki and a strong critic of chieftainship, epitomise this division (Ntsebeza 2002). It seems clear that the pro-chief lobby won the debate in 2003.

Another reason could be that government was concerned to avoid a repetition of the bloody conflict in rural KwaZulu-Natal in the 1980s and 1990s. Lodge has argued that government accommodation of traditional authorities was:

> a compromise to avert a threatened boycott of the first general elections by the Inkatha Freedom Party if the institution was not recognised and protected in the Constitution. If it was not for the pressure from the IFP, the institution would have been destroyed by now ... Rather than abolishing it, the ANC is creating

legislative conditions through local government that will allow for the gradual phasing out of the institution … to avoid resistance from traditionalists … [T]he ANC has become more tactful and has recognised that abolishing the institution will cause serious political conflict in the country. (Quoted in Dladla 2000:15)

Given the passing of the two pieces of legislation in 2003 and 2004 discussed earlier, it is difficult to see how these laws are creating legislative conditions for the gradual phasing out of the institution and its incumbents. Traditional authorities have been recognised in the Constitution, their existence legitimised in the provincial Houses of Traditional Leaders, they are handsomely remunerated and have been given power to allocate land. This contrasts sharply with the minimal support given to rural elected councillors. It could be that its macroeconomic policies substantially constrain the government from setting up and monitoring new democratic structures of government in rural areas. As Hart has lamented: 'GEAR sits uneasily astride the emancipatory promises of the liberation struggle, as well as the material hopes, aspirations, and rights of the large majority of South Africans' (2002:7). In addition, it has not always been clear how, in wooing traditional authorities, the ANC would dismantle tribalism and the reserves. Indeed, tribalism is inherent in the recognition of separate chieftaincies (Hendricks & Ntsebeza 1999).

There is also the view that some traditional authorities are popular and legitimate and that alienating them would make the ANC lose the rural vote. Analysts such as Cousins and Claassens make sweeping claims that in some areas 'traditional leaders do enjoy support and have legitimacy' (*Mail & Guardian* 31.10–6.11.03). But it is not clear how this support and legitimacy are determined, especially as these analysts seem to agree that 'the right to choose one's leaders is the fundamental principle of democracy'. The institution of traditional leadership can potentially be democratic in one important respect: the involvement of rural residents in decision-making processes. This was indeed the hallmark of governance in most southern African societies at the advent of colonialism.[20] However, there is a critical sense in which the institution in South Africa cannot be democratic. In so far as so-called traditional leadership is based on ascribed hereditary rule, the possibility of rural residents having the freedom to choose which institution and/or individuals should rule them is automatically excluded. Yet, it is precisely this right upon which the South African Constitution is based.

With regard to the claim that elected representatives may be as corrupt as unelected traditional authorities, my argument is that elected representatives are more accountable in the sense that they can always be replaced, and no such mechanism is available under the rule of hereditary traditional authorities.

Lastly, but equally important, rural civil society is still relatively weak and unorganised. Although there are signs of a resurgence of rural organisation and mobilisation – the formation of the Landless People's Movement in 2001 being the most significant development – it is perhaps too early to judge how resilient rural civic organisation structures are.[21] More research needs to be done on these emerging structures. Without a strong and organised voice, rural inhabitants are going to find it hard to influence government. By contrast, traditional authorities are much more organised and consistently apply pressure on government. Ironically, they are made strong by the state resources they have at their disposal, from the salaries they draw, to institutions such as the Houses of Traditional Leaders. None of these resources are available to rural residents.

Conclusion

For almost ten years since the birth of South Africa's democracy there was ambivalence on the precise role, functions and powers of unelected traditional authorities in local government and land administration in particular, but also in a democracy modelled along liberal values of representative government in general. The passing through Parliament in 2003 and 2004 of two controversial pieces of legislation, the Framework Act and the CLRB, brings a greater degree of clarity about the role of traditional authorities in local government and land administration. Whereas the position of traditional authorities in local government remains that of having a 20 per cent *ex officio* capacity, the CLRB gives them unprecedented powers in the critical area of land allocation. This means that in one respect, namely, local government, rural residents enjoy the same citizenship rights that are enjoyed by their urban counterparts, in the sense that they elect their councillors. However, on the vital issue of land allocation, rural people become subjects in the sense that decisions are taken by traditional councils which are dominated by unelected traditional authorities and their appointees.

This raises critical questions about citizenship and the nature of democracy in South Africa. Mamdani has proposed that 'dismantling' the 'clenched fist' of tribal authorities entails 'an endeavour to link the urban and the rural – and thereby a series of related binary opposites such as rights and custom, representation and participation, centralization and decentralization, civil society and community – in ways that have yet to be done' (1996:34). To what extent has post-1994 South Africa succeeded in dismantling the apartheid-created 'clenched fist' of unaccountable tribal authorities? As indicated in this chapter, while some traditional authorities may choose to promote local participation, the fact that these authorities are hereditary limits the possibility of rural residents to elect or reject their leaders over questions of land administration and allocation. This compromises a fundamental, though not the only, principle of democracy and full citizenship.

Notes

1 See the 1996 South African Constitution on the Bill of Rights and Local Government.

2 The term 'traditional authorities' is used in this chapter as an all-encompassing term to refer to chiefs of various ranks. It is thus used to refer to *people*, and not structures such as tribal authorities. Since the 1990s, the use of the term 'chiefs' has increasingly been viewed by traditional authorities, government officials and some analysts as derogatory. A range of names is thus used, the most popular being 'traditional leaders'. The extent to which traditional authorities/leaders are legitimate leaders is highly disputed. This partly explains the range of terminology.

3 See Mamdani (1996) and his notion of a 'clenched fist' leading to a 'decentralised despotism'.

4 Bantustans/homelands/reserves are areas which colonialists put aside for African occupation as early as the nineteenth century. The size of this land comprised about 13 per cent of the South African land. It is in the rural areas of these bantustans that traditional authorities were given wide-ranging powers. After the 1994 democratic elections, these areas were formally reincorporated in South Africa.

5   See also Hendricks 1990. To ensure that unemployed Africans were restricted to the reserves, the NP adopted the Unemployment Labour Preference Policy. This policy was meant to serve both as a measure to curb African urbanisation and at the same time act as a social and political control over the youth problem (Posel 1991).

6   See Mafeje 1963:7.

7   It is important to bear in mind, though, that the Native Administration Act of 1927 had already undermined the independence of chiefs. For example, the Act provided that the chief or headman carry out orders given through the Bantu Affairs Commissioner or any other officer of the government, on pain of summary dismissal.

8   For details and examples see Ntsebeza 2002, 2004.

9   Dalindyebo was eventually stripped of his power as Paramount Chief, prosecuted, and finally hounded out of the country by KD Matanzima. He joined the ANC in exile, where he died in 1985. For details of the power struggle between Sabata and Matanzima, see Ntsebeza 2002, chapter 6.

10 It should be noted that with time, the term 'tribal authority' was used as a general term.

11 None of the bantustans was recognised as an independent country except by the apartheid regime and other bantustans.

12 This account is based on interviews with various rural residents, sub-headmen, headmen, chiefs and government officials.

13 See Ntsebeza 2003a for details.

14 The rationale for a district councils model is based on attempts to move towards equity and redistribution in terms of which the wealthier urban councils will be amalgamated with poorer neighbouring communities, and so extend basic services to the latter. This argument, though, does not address the widespread problem in the former bantustans: here the towns that are surrounded by large poverty-stricken rural communities are themselves small, poorly run, and lack a strong revenue base.

15 I have not been in a position to get a copy of this statement by the President.

16 See Cousins & Claassens, Looming land disaster, in *Mail & Guardian*, 31.10–6.11.2003.

17 This is based on my own observation and participation in some of the meetings.

18 For the Bill to become law, it has to be considered, *inter alia*, by the various provinces with traditional authorities. This process has been delayed by the April 2004 election.

19 Disagreements between traditional authorities and government about their role in a democracy go back to the period of political negotiation in the early 1990s.

20 It should be pointed out, though, that only men participated in these gatherings (*iimbizo/pitso/kgotla*). Further, these systems differed, and some were more autocratic than others (Ntsebeza 1999).

21 Stephen Greenberg is currently doing an assessment of the Landless People's Movement in the Gauteng area. We are eagerly looking forward to his findings.

References

Agrawal A & Ribot J (1999) Accountability in decentralisation: A framework with South Asian and West African cases, *The Journal of Developing Areas* 33, 473–502.

ANC (African National Congress) (1994) *The Reconstruction and Development Programme: A policy framework.* Johannesburg: Umanyano.

Bank L & Southall R (1996) Traditional leaders in South Africa's new democracy, *Journal of Legal Pluralism and Unofficial Law* 37–38:407–430.

Bond P (2000) *Elite transition: From apartheid to neoliberalism in South Africa.* Pietermaritzburg: University of Natal Press.

Delius P (1996) *A lion amongst the cattle: Reconstruction and resistance in the Northern Transvaal.* Johannesburg: Ravan.

De Wet CJ & McAllister PA (1983) *Rural communities in transition: A study of the socio-economic and agricultural implications of agricultural betterment and development.* Working Paper No. 16, Department of Anthropology in collaboration with the Institute of Social and Economic Research, Rhodes University, Grahamstown.

DLA (Department of Land Affairs, South Africa) (1997) *White Paper on South African land policy.* Pretoria: DLA.

Dladla S (2000) Slow fall of the house of chiefs, *Land & Rural Digest* 11:6–12.

DPLG (Department of Provincial and Local Government, South Africa) (1998) *White Paper on local government.* Pretoria: DPLG.

Evans IT (1997) *Bureaucracy and race: Native administration in South Africa*. California: University of California Press.

Fine B & Padayachee V (2001) A sustainable macroeconomic growth path for South Africa? In JK Coetzee, J Graaff, F Hendricks & G Wood (eds.) *Development: Theory, policy and practice*. Oxford: Oxford University Press.

Hammond-Tooke WD (1975) *Command and consensus: The development of Transkei local government*. Cape Town: David Philip.

Hart G (2002) *Disabling globalization: Place of power in post-apartheid South Africa*. Pietermaritzburg: University of Natal Press.

Hendricks FT (1990) *The pillars of apartheid: Land tenure, rural planning and the chieftaincy*. Uppsalla: Acta University, Studia Sociologica Upsaliensa.

Hendricks F & Ntsebeza L (1999) Chiefs and rural local government in post-apartheid South Africa, *African Journal of Political Science: New Series* 4: 99–126.

Ismail N (1999) Integrating indigenous and contemporary local governance: Issues surrounding traditional leadership and considerations for post-apartheid South Africa. Unpublished Doctor of Administration thesis, University of the Western Cape, Bellville.

Lahiff E (2000) Land tenure in South Africa's communal areas: A case study of the Arabie-Olifant's scheme, *African Studies* 59: 45–69.

Lodge T (1983) *Black politics in South Africa since 1945*. Johannesburg: Ravan.

Mafeje A (1963) Leadership and change: A study of two South African peasant communities. Unpublished MA thesis, University of Cape Town, Cape Town.

Mamdani M (1996) *Citizen and subject: Contemporary Africa and the legacy of late colonialism*. Cape Town: David Philip.

Manona C (1998) The collapse of the 'tribal authority' system and the rise of civic associations. In C de Wet & M Whisson (eds.) *From reserves to region: Apartheid and social change in the Kieskamahoek district of (former) Ciskei, 1950–1960*. Grahamstown: Institute of Social and Economic Research, Rhodes University.

Manor J (2001) *Local government in South Africa: Potential disaster despite genuine promise*. Sussex: Institute for Development Studies.

Marais H (1998) *South Africa, limits to change: The political economy of transformation*. London: Zed.

Mbeki G (1984) *South Africa: The peasants' revolt*. London: International Defence and Aid Fund.

Ntsebeza L (1999) *Land tenure reform, traditional authorities and rural local government in post-apartheid South Africa: Case studies from the Eastern Cape*. Research Report No. 3. Bellville: Programme for Land and Agrarian Studies.

Ntsebeza L (2001) Traditional authorities and rural development. In JK Coetzee, J Graaff, F Hendricks & G Wood (eds.) *Development: Theory, policy and practice*. Oxford: Oxford University Press.

Ntsebeza L (2002) Structures and struggles of rural local government in South Africa: The case of traditional authorities in the Eastern Cape. Unpublished Doctor of Philosophy degree, Rhodes University, Grahamstown.

Ntsebeza L (2003a) *Local government, power and natural resources: A perspective from the rural areas of South Africa's former bantustans*. Environmental Governance in Africa Working Paper No. 14, Washington, DC: World Resources Institute.

Ntsebeza L (2003b) Land rights and democratisation: Rural tenure reform in South Africa's former bantustans, *Transformation* 52: 68–95.

Ntsebeza L (2004) Democratic decentralisation and traditional authority: Dilemmas of land administration in rural South Africa, *European Journal of Development Research* 16: 71–89.

Portfolio Committee on Provincial and Local Government (2003) Report on Traditional Leadership and Governance Framework Bill to the National Assembly, 28 October.

Posel D (1991) *The making of apartheid 1948–1961*. Oxford: Clarendon.

Pycroft C (1998) Integrated development planning or strategic paralysis? Municipal development during the local government transition and beyond, *Development Southern Africa* 15: 151–163.

Spiegel A (1992) A trilogy of tyranny and tribulations: Village politics and administrative intervention in Matatiele during the early 1980s, *Journal of Contemporary African Studies* 11: 37–42.

Thomas G, Sibanda S & Claassens A (1998) Current developments in South Africa's land tenure policy. In *Proceedings of the International Conference on Land Tenure in the Developing World with a focus on Southern Africa*. University of Cape Town, 27–29 January 1998.

Tsotsi WM (1989) Out of court: The memoirs of a black lawyer in apartheid South Africa, 1950–1960. Unpublished manuscript.

Van Kessel I & Oomen B (1997) 'One chief, one vote': The revival of traditional authorities in post-apartheid South Africa, *African Affairs* 96:561–585.

4 The state of corruption and accountability

Sam Sole

> Corruption and maladministration are inconsistent with the rule of law and the fundamental values of our Constitution. They undermine the constitutional commitment to human dignity, the achievement of equality and the advancement of human rights and freedoms. They are the antithesis of the open, accountable, democratic government required by the Constitution. If allowed to go unchecked and unpunished they will pose a serious threat to our democratic state. *President of the SA Constitutional Court, Judge Arthur Chaskalson*[1]

Introduction

It is appropriate that a review of corruption in contemporary South Africa is tied to an assessment of accountability. While the relationship between a lack of accountability and corruption may not be immediate or direct, it seems self-evident that an absence of pre-emptive monitoring of – or disciplinary consequences for – corrupt behaviour, will tend to lead to greater abuse over time.

Indeed, this paper will argue that, while South Africa's efforts to contain and roll back corruption have been significant, and while the framework of individual accountability has been tightened up considerably, a drift towards a general level of institutional 'immunity' in the political sphere risks, in the long run, undoing the progress that has been made.

Neither corruption nor accountability is simple to define or measure. Corruption may vary from the clearly illegal – such as fraud – to more subtle forms of unethical rent-seeking, patronage and abuses of power that may be just as damaging to the social fabric of a nation.

I would like to suggest the following definition: corruption is the wilful subversion (or attempted subversion) of a due decision-making process with regard to the allocation of any benefit.

The subversion may take place via inducement, or by the exercise of patronage or other forms of solidarity, or by dint of ideological conviction. The essential feature is an intervention in bad faith. To take a currently notorious case: the decision by the South African Cabinet to remove cost as a factor in the middle of the adjudication of bids for one of the weapons systems – the jet trainers – purchased as part of the country's controversial Strategic Defence Procurement programme. Such a decision – which resulted in a different bidder being preferred – was arguably corrupt, not because it was necessarily taken as a result of graft, but because it wilfully subverted the due process. It is hard to imagine any other reason for this intervention than to rig the adjudication; whether this was done for sound strategic reasons or not is immaterial.

Accountability also covers a huge of range of phenomena, from the formal legal framework and criminal justice system, to the oversight of Parliament, independent statutory institutions, the media and civil society watchdogs, all the way through to more intangible factors such as the prevalent kind of business and political culture, the social bedrock of ethical standards and norms. Levels of social self-discipline and cohesion are likely to be key indicators as to whether corruption grows more widespread, or remains limited. Formal accountability may be extensive on paper, but may be rendered weak by a lack of enforcement, or be bypassed by strong informal codes of secrecy and solidarity, and a certain social approval or cachet being attached to 'beating the system'.

Accountability failure does not necessarily mean corruption, but it does suggest a trend, at the very least a warning of the likelihood of trouble being stored up for the future. There are of course major disincentives for the exposure of corruption, particularly when it involves powerful individuals or interests. Typically, companies may let a corrupt executive resign quietly, rather than expose themselves to public reputational damage. Thus accountability failure also has a nastier cousin, the cover-up, which forms a kind of 'accessory' to corruption. Evidence of a cover-up invites the suspicion of corruption and suggests accountability failure of a more systematic nature.

Finally, in modern politics, where media-generated perceptions are a powerful factor, the public exposure of corruption – a 'scandal' in popular terminology – is an important terrain of political contest (and, via the deliberate leak, also an important tool), serving to undermine the reputation of political opponents. This has also been a significant feature in South African post-apartheid politics. Loud and frequent accusations of corruption and mismanagement from government's opponents have been met with counter-accusations of racism and wanting the democratic state to fail.

A further brief exploration of theoretical concepts is necessary prior to a review of corruption and accountability in South Africa. This is, firstly, because the notion of corruption is politically highly contested, as described earlier, and secondly, because it will assist us in identifying some ways in which we can answer the questions: how bad is corruption in South Africa, what kind of corruption do we have here and what forces will shape it in the future?

Two concepts are crucial to any discussion of corruption: rent-seeking and patronage. Together they form the largely unseen mass of the corruption iceberg, of which publicly reported fraud and influence-peddling are merely the visible tip. I am indebted to a paper by Johnathan Hyslop for a valuable analytical framework as well as the following definitions of 'rent' and 'patronage':

> In defining rent, I follow the analysis of Khan and Jomo (2000:5), where a rent is characterised as 'an income which is higher than the minimum which a firm or an individual would have accepted given alternative opportunities ... Rents include not just monopoly profits, but also subsidies and transfers organised through the political mechanism: illegal transfers organised by private mafias, short-term super-profits made by innovators before competitors imitate their innovations, and so on'. Rents may thus be legal or illegal. (Hyslop 2004:3)

Rents, which I would argue include licences that grant preferred access to limited resources, are important markers because they are 'something for nothing' areas of commercial exchange (or, more usually, 'more for less'), and therefore are nodes around which competition for 'easy money' will occur. If the rents are sufficiently high, it is likely that rent-seeking activity will spill over into corrupt behaviour.

Hyslop discusses patronage as follows:

> Khan and Jomo (2000:10) usefully define patron-client relation-
> ships as 'repeated relationships of exchange between specific
> patrons and their clients'. Such relationships are further charac-
> terised by a personalised pattern of identifiable patrons and
> clients; and by significant differences in the status, power, or
> other characteristics of patrons and of clients. The existence of
> patron-client networks is seldom illegal in itself, and a patron
> may often be able to help a client in ways – personal donations
> or recommendations for instance – that do not involve violating
> rules or procedures. But in contexts of fierce conflicts over scarce
> resources, it is unlikely that a patron who is unwilling or unable
> to break the law will retain his or her client base. What types of
> relations constitute patronage is perhaps open to debate ... A
> number of other social scientists, particularly in the modern-
> isation school, while accepting that patronage relationships are
> not always literally familial, argue that in societies where the idea
> of the family has a particular power and prestige, patronage
> relations are likely to be stronger than in those social orders
> which emphasise individualism (Lipset & Lenz 2000). But it is
> surely also the case that some highly modern forms of organisa-
> tion contain patronage networks based not so much on familial
> links or thinking, as on ideological or institutional loyalties.
> (Hyslop 2004:3)

Hyslop's latter point will be significant in my discussion of the South African
situation and the nature of the ruling party, the African National Congress
(ANC).

Does corruption matter?

Another basic question that must be answered is: what's wrong with corruption anyway? A certain kind of free-market fundamentalism suggests that a
modicum of corruption 'oils the wheels' and can bypass an inefficient and
obstructive bureaucracy.

In answer: firstly, rents are by definition economically inefficient. Secondly, corruption and patronage disrupt and distort rational decision-making and selection, with consequences that may vary from simple inefficiency – getting the job done, but more expensively than necessary – to making choices that run entirely contrary to public interest policy and may have significant unforeseen consequences.

Thirdly, a key problem is that corruption does not remain isolated – it infects the system. Most competitive social transactions are not 'one-off' – they continue or are repeated over time. Therefore if the transaction is once infected by corruption, it is likely that the perceived rules are affected for other competitors. If the playing fields are tilted, other players face the choice of leaving the game or of adopting the stance of 'if you can't beat them, join them'. When resources and opportunities are scarce, the pressure to join in is that much greater. Typically, the transaction also involves an imbalance of power, and therefore the risks attached to whistle-blowing are significant: the small business tendering for a large company or government department risks being blacklisted or punished in other ways if it rocks the boat about demands for bribes and favours.

Fourthly, the more perceived unfairness in the system as a result of corruption, the less legitimacy it will enjoy, with a resultant decline in voluntary compliance or the buy-in necessary for more complex forms of social co-operation, for instance across ethnic or class divisions.

It is perhaps useful to view corruption as a virus that is doing constant battle with a society's corrective immune system. If the infection is allowed to get too severe, the virus starts to overwhelm the body-politic. It can devastate first the integrity and then the functioning of state institutions.

Corruption in Africa

As Hyslop (2004:6) points out, there is some evidence that in certain East Asian cases corruption seems indeed to have 'lubricated the wheels of rusty political systems', but in Africa, corruption has generally caused growth and development to 'seize up'.

He suggests two main reasons for the different outcomes. Firstly, the state and its institutions in Africa are often weak, sometimes little more than an 'empty shell'. In such a state, he argues: 'The real business of politics is conducted informally, outside the official realm. There is little institutionalisation and hence conventional notions of corruption, which rely on a clear delineation of private and public spheres, have little relevance' (Hyslop 2004:6) In this situation, local warlords and mafias are readily able to exploit the power vacuum. The second difference, he argues, relates to the prevalence in Africa of vertical social networks that distribute patronage far more widely and dissipate its proceeds. Together such circumstances lead to high levels of corruption and low levels of growth.

By contrast, Hyslop describes what he characterises as 'high growth/high corruption' societies, such as some of the East Asian Tiger economies, where corruption is mainly horizontal – among the same elite stratum – and where its legitimisation is limited. As we shall see, South Africa shares some features with these states.

South Africa: a world (of corruption) in one country

South Africa cannot in any way be described as a failed or 'empty-shell' state. A successful transition from white minority rule to a functioning multi-ethnic democracy was accomplished without the destruction of core bureaucratic competencies. Since the first democratic election in 1994, a plethora of new laws and institutions – considered in more detail further on – have generally bolstered both the legitimacy and the effectiveness of the state.

Even by the imprecise measurement of perception, which tends to exaggerate corruption, South Africa is a country of moderate corruption, coming in at number 48 of 133 countries measured in the Transparency International corruption perception index (TI 2003),[2] grouped together with such countries as Greece, Jordan and South Korea, and faring considerably better than, for instance, Brazil, China, Egypt, India and Turkey.

Nevertheless, notwithstanding its relatively high levels of urbanisation and modernisation, it would be foolish to ignore the reality that South Africa retains strong elements of traditional African vertical social networks and therefore the patronage risks associated with them.

To take an anecdotal example: the country's Deputy President, Jacob Zuma, remains embroiled in controversy surrounding claims that he accepted or solicited significant amounts of money (or, at best for him, loans) from private business interests. Popular wisdom accepts that Zuma, who does not have an obviously ostentatious lifestyle, simply could not keep up with the financial demands of an extensive network of family responsibilities.

And while the South African state is not in crisis, neither are the institutions of accountability so entrenched that we can be complacent. The trajectory of Zimbabwe, which at independence was relatively wealthy with low levels of official corruption, suggests that, notwithstanding our much larger economy and more developed institutions, the distance from successful state to empty shell may be shorter than we might like to think.

The crucial questions therefore seem to me to be: are we getting better or worse, to what extent is the state winning or losing the battle against corruption or itself becoming subverted, and what are the key factors that can influence this path?

Corruption and accountability: the apartheid inheritance

It makes little sense to compare levels of corruption in pre- and post-1994 South Africa. While contemporary South Africa is a constitutional democracy with guaranteed liberal freedoms, the apartheid state was in a sense built on entrenched racial and ethnic (Afrikaner) patronage. The state system was itself a form of institutionalised grand corruption, kept in place and (at least initially) in check by an authoritarian minority regime. However, it would also be unfair to ignore the legacy of apartheid rule for any assessment of current corruption, or the (sometimes uncomfortable) parallels and continuities that exist between the apartheid and democratic eras.

As others have pointed out, the maintenance of an unjust and undemocratic system took its toll on apartheid state institutions. Policing was for decades directed less at crime fighting than keeping blacks out of so-called 'white' areas, and latterly towards combating the liberation movements. Apartheid laws, restricting the movement and opportunities open to 'non-whites', created fertile ground for thousands of petty officials to extort bribes from those trying to navigate their way through and around the system. The attempt to give some sort of reality to grand apartheid necessitated the creation of spatial areas – the bantustans – that existed mostly in a zone of economic irrationality and political illegitimacy and therefore had to be built largely on the basis of subsidies (or rents) of every kind. This naturally attracted a leadership and bureaucracy drawn to the large opportunities for patronage and rent-seeking – and which remained largely in place after the advent of democratic rule.

At the same time, the very success of the main patronage project in producing a class of wealthy, worldly Afrikaners contained within it the seeds of a fatal corruption. This influential elite no longer had the inclination or discipline to maintain a hegemonic project like apartheid and began reorienting the state in its own interests, both via a pressure for liberalisation, and via a more cynical pursuit of self-enrichment. As Hyslop notes:

> The ethos of the National Party leadership almost visibly shifted from one of service to the *volk* to one of the establishment of Swiss bank accounts. (Hyslop 2004:12)

This outcome may contain some lessons for the programme of institutional black advancement adopted by the post-1994 government – styled as affirmative action and black economic empowerment – as part of a necessary bid to counter decades of anti-black discrimination.

The final years of crisis for apartheid also saw a massive shift towards the secret extra-legal use of state power to prop up the regime and attack its foes – and thus towards subverting the elements of state accountability that still existed in the white Parliament, the courts, and other civil institutions such as the media. The rise of death squads and other loosely-controlled special forces, the covert funding of militias, the illegal exploitation of natural resources, the establishment and funding of thousands of covert projects, the involvement of the state and private companies in sanctions-busting, the integration of state agents into smuggling networks and other criminal mafias – all these factors contributed to creating the skills, networks and culture that allowed corruption to thrive and survive to pose a challenge to the post-apartheid order.

This is also true of corporate morality – as can be seen, for instance, in the recent exposé of alleged massive illegal capital export and tax fraud on the part of South African Breweries (now SAB-Miller) in issue 51 of the investigative magazine *Noseweek*.

There is one other point to make about the legacy of the pre-1994 era: its impact on the nature and culture of the main liberation movement, the ANC. The war situation the ANC found itself in up to the 1990s understandably led to a secretive, 'need-to-know' culture in which trust and loyalty were prized above other qualities. As Hyslop points out, such loyalty networks can easily transmute into networks of patronage. The ANC's long association with Marxist thought and Soviet support and training also contributed to a hegemonic, corporatist approach to political organisation and accountability, rather than a more pluralist outlook.

Corruption and accountability in the post-1994 era

Constitutional reform

The first and most significant achievement was the adoption of a new Constitution which reconfigured South Africa as a constitutional state, governed by the rule of law, in which the Constitution, rather than the elected executive, existed as the ultimate authority for governance. The Constitution and the new state, at least initially, enjoyed wide legitimacy – even among the white minority – as did the joint ANC-National Party Government of National Unity. There was also support across the political spectrum for the government's mildly redistributive economic and social blueprint, the Reconstruction and Development Programme.

The Constitution dramatically improved the formal framework of social transparency and accountability, providing that all executive organs of state must be accountable to the National Assembly, and directing that mechanisms be established for the Assembly to carry out an oversight function. Parliamentary portfolio committees were established in terms of this directive, including a Standing Committee on Public Accounts (Scopa) to oversee government spending, which followed the convention of other liberal democracies in appointing an opposition Member of Parliament to sit as Committee chair. The Constitution also established the so-called Chapter 9 independent institutions of oversight – including the office of the Auditor General, the Public Protector and the South African Human Rights Commission – and entrenched the freedom of the media and the rights of citizens to have access to information needed to protect their rights.

New laws, new corruption busters

In the last ten years the ANC government has introduced a wide range of legislation and institutions that have transformed the country's governance landscape, and which have generally followed international best practice.

Key among the new laws have been:
- The Public Finance Management Act, which rigorously sets out the fiduciary responsibilities of public-sector managers, including making provision for them to be held personally liable for governance failures.
- The Financial Intelligence Act, which obliges banks to keep better records about their customers and report suspicious transactions, especially with regard to identifying money-laundering activities.
- Legislation making provision for the seizure of assets that are the proceeds of crime (via the Asset Forfeiture Unit) and for the investigation and civil recovery of losses suffered by government as a result of fraud and theft (via the Special Investigation Unit [SIU]).
- The Promotion of Access to Information Act, South Africa's freedom of information law and the Protected Disclosures Act, designed to offer whistle-blowers statutory protection if they follow the stipulated procedures.
- The new Prevention and Combating of Corrupt Activities Act passed in late 2003 makes it an offence to offer or receive gratification that has not been earned, either in the private or public sector. The offence carries much stiffer sentences, including a maximum of life imprisonment. The Act also places a duty on individuals holding a position of authority to report corrupt activity. Failure to do so carries a maximum penalty of ten years' imprisonment.
- Government has also established a Public Service Anti-Corruption Strategy that sets out a number of goals for improving and co-ordinating anti-corruption measures across departments. The passing of the Corrupt Activities Act is the first major milestone for this strategy.

Apart from those already mentioned – the Asset Forfeiture Unit, the SIU, the Public Protector, the Auditor General (AG) and the South African Human Rights Commission – new institutions of accountability include:
- The centralisation of the prosecuting authority under a National Director of Public Prosecutions (NDPP) and, under President Thabo

Mbeki, the establishment of a specialised directorate combining intelligence, investigation and prosecuting capabilities (the so-called 'Scorpions') which reports to the NDPP.

- The establishment of an Independent Complaints Directorate to investigate complaints against the police service.
- A restructured South African Revenue Service (SARS), in particular its removal from public-sector bargaining structures, allowing SARS to establish its own more attractive but more stringent employment conditions. Improved efficiency (perceived and real) has led to a broadening and deepening of tax revenues and compliance.
- The Public Service Commission, which sets standards for and monitors the performance of the civil service.
- Provisions for an Inspector General of Intelligence.
- The establishment of various independent boards, with their own charters, to manage and exercise oversight over key public institutions. These include the then South African Telecommunications Regulatory Authority and the Independent Broadcasting Authority – now merged as the Independent Communications Authority of SA – and the board of the South African Broadcasting Corporation.
- The Competition Commission and Tribunal, which scrutinises all major mergers and acquisitions, as well as complaints of uncompetitive corporate behaviour.

The private sector

In general, the private sector has got off relatively lightly, with guidelines on reporting and disclosure set out in the two King reports. The first (1994) and second (2002) King reports, compiled by former judge Mervyn King, set out guidelines for improved corporate governance by South African companies and directors. They have been incorporated in the requirements for companies listed on the Johannesburg Securities Exchange. The migration of several of South Africa's largest companies to primary listings offshore, where reporting requirements are more stringent, has added to the impetus for improved disclosure. A number of local and international accounting scandals (for instance, Enron, and locally, the collapse of the Health & Racquet Club) have also placed greater pressure on auditors to improve accounting ethics. The popularisation of business news has also led to a greater degree of business scrutiny by the media. The more open use made of existing legislation for probing company failure – the so-called 'Section 417 inquiries', which generally used to be held in secret, but are now typically made public – has also contributed to a more stringent level of oversight.

In sum, the new edifice of accountability is deeply impressive. The evidence on implementation and results, however, is more mixed.

A corruption snapshot

As there is no commonly accepted definition, corruption is hard to measure. Legally it cuts across a number of defined offences, such as theft and fraud, which may have nothing to do with what is generally understood to be corruption, making bald crime statistics of limited value. Assessments tend therefore to be perception-based or largely anecdotal.

The most comprehensive effort to measure the phenomenon in South Africa was via the *Country corruption assessment report* prepared as a result of a joint effort by the government of South Africa and the United Nations Office on Drugs and Crime (UNODC 2003). The report found that there were no consolidated statistics of corruption incidents or of the internal or external legal (civil, criminal and administrative) responses to such incidents. To try to fill this gap and establish a baseline, three surveys on perceptions and experiences of corruption were conducted: a household survey, a business survey, and a survey of the public service and its clients in the provincial offices of three government departments in two provinces (KwaZulu-Natal and Gauteng).

Perceptions

The UNODC found that South Africans perceive that there is a lot of corruption, and that it is one of the most important problems facing the country (41 per cent), while just a few less (39 per cent) contend that although there is a lot of corruption it is not the most pressing issue. The business sector (62 per cent), in particular, believed that corruption had become a serious issue in business and for business. Although it is not seen as an overriding factor in deciding on investment, some 12 per cent claimed they had refrained from making a major investment because of corruption.

In the two provinces, KwaZulu-Natal and Gauteng, clients of public services (health, police and home affairs) estimated that between 15 and 30 per cent of public officials in these locations were corrupt, and 10 per cent indicated that public officials expected some form of extra payment for services rendered. Public officials themselves perceived clients to be corrupt in a sense of constantly seeking 'back-door' solutions to their problems. The managers interviewed held quite a negative view of corruption within their own departments, some claiming that even 75 per cent of staff are untrustworthy and involved in low-level corruption in the form of bribery.

Reality

In contrast to their perceptions, the UNODC found the actual experience of corruption by private citizens, businesses and public officials was much lower. For example, a 1998 national victim survey carried out by Statistics South Africa found that only 2 per cent of individuals experienced corruption, while the 2001 UNODC household survey revealed that some 11 per cent of entire families/households had a direct experience with corruption.

The business survey showed that 15 per cent were approached to pay a bribe, while 7 per cent had to pay a bribe and a further 4 per cent had to pay extortion. More than one-third of public officials in KwaZulu-Natal and Gauteng admitted to having been approached by a client wanting to give them a gift in exchange for a service provided. Slightly more than one in ten public officials admitted to accepting such a gift.

Using the worldwide International Crime Victim Survey (ICVS), UNODC also suggests that South Africans (surveys in Johannesburg in 1993, 1996 and 2000) experienced lower levels of corruption than those in Lusaka (Zambia), Maseru (Lesotho), Mbabane (Swaziland), and Maputo (Mozambique) but still higher than their counterparts in Gaborone (Botswana) and Windhoek (Namibia).

The UNODC (2003) study found that:
- South African citizens appear to view the most common areas of corruption to be in relation to seeking employment and the provision of utilities such as water, electricity, and housing. Public-service managers also identified nepotism in job seeking, promotions and in the provision of entitlements.

- The business community identified clearance of goods through customs, procurement of goods for government, police investigation and obtaining of business licences and permits, work and residence permits as the most corruption-prone activities.
- The public servants most associated with corruption, both for the citizens and businesses, appear to be the police. All surveys indicate that police officers are the most vulnerable to corruption, followed by customs, local government, home affairs and court officials. To this list, businesses added the managers and/or employees from companies other than their own.

Corruption trends

The corruption snapshot tells us little about whether corruption is getting better or worse. In Johannesburg the rates for victimisation were increasing over time, from 6.7 per cent in 1992, to 7.6 per cent in 1996 and 13.3 per cent in 2000. A new national crime victim survey by the Institute for Security Studies[3] also shows a significant increase in corruption experienced by members of the public. The incidence of experienced corruption was up from 2 per cent in 1998 to 5.6 per cent in 2003, though the questions in this survey were also more clearly articulated and detailed than in the previous sample, which may explain some of the increase. Nevertheless, corruption now represents the second most common category of experienced crime, after housebreaking. Traffic officers, followed by police officers, topped the list of alleged offenders.

This statistical trend is supported by the Transparency International corruption perception index where South Africa's rating has also dropped significantly over time, from 5.68 (out of a possible 10) in 1996 to 4.4 in 2003.

What are the reasons for this trend, given the obvious improvement in the formal anti-corruption infrastructure? Part of the answer may lie in the reaction to a general relaxation of restraints that has been observed in other societies moving out of a period of authoritarian rule. The crime rate in general has increased dramatically since 1990, though it has stabilised and some categories have dropped in the last two years. Corruption may simply be part of this trend.

A further explanation might lie in the gap between policy, capacity and practice. The UNODC study found:

> serious weaknesses and shortcomings in the capacity and will of public sector bodies to implement and to comply with the laws. For example, certain public bodies view some of the legislation (e.g. Access to Information) as too demanding of resources.

But, equally, social attitudes to corruption and the example of leaders in society may also play a role. In focus group interviews conducted during the UNODC (2003) study, respondents indicated they believed corruption had become part of the national psyche:

> Members of Parliament, who are aware of corruption within the ranks, feel that they are supposed to act but, all too often, when a corrupt official is exposed, party discipline is imposed.

> Trade unionists said that any meaningful reform 'needs to start from the top', and that lower level workers will only think twice about corruption when the people they look up to set the right example. They tended to blame government officials more than anyone else for setting a bad example.

> 'If you don't deal with it from the top, it's no use even trying to deal with it.'

One problem with the statistical analysis is that it provides very little qualitative information. The impact of corruption is likely to be more severe the higher the value of the benefit that is being sought or offered and, arguably, the power and status of the parties involved is also of significance. General surveys, by their nature, are mostly likely to reveal corruption of a petty nature. Corruption among the powerful, including political corruption, will have to rely on a more anecdotal, analytical assessment.

Corruption and the politics of elite privilege

Any survey of the South African media reveals a seemingly inexhaustible litany of examples of officials and politicians, particularly at the local and provincial level, abusing their positions for personal gain. Generally they are joined by partners or beneficiaries in the private sector.[4]

Perhaps the nadir of this rush to 'cash in' was the case of the black ex-mayor and his white partner, an ex-member of the extreme right-wing *Afrikaner Weerstands Beweging*, who teamed up in a scheme to defraud the Kokstad municipality.[5]

But blaming public corruption on a general decline in moral standards, as experts surveyed by the Institute for Security Studies (Camerer 2001) did, appears to add little explanatory value. Then Deputy-President Thabo Mbeki offered a more trenchant analysis in his keynote address to a government anti-corruption conference in 1998:

> May it not be that after all is said and done, apartheid can be recorded not only as a crime against humanity and also as an ideology of moral corruption – an instrument of oppression used, among other things, to help its victims imbibe its very immoral mores and foundations, even unwittingly so. Consider the matter of legitimacy. Years of resistance to the state apparatus constituted the fibre of struggle for most South Africans – as the object of making the country ungovernable before 1994 became one of the strategic objectives of the struggle. Transplanted overnight into a new democratic order, requiring a different moral ethos and outlook, the citizenry has laboured and lingered in redirecting their loyalties and hierarchy of responsibilities. (Mbeki 1998)

But Mbeki's speech went further to identify the influence of global capitalist ideology in promoting a selfish individualism that, he argued, provided fertile ground for corruption:

> In the macro-context of world values where the private accumulation of material wealth has unleashed a total onslaught on every other determining value possible, mental conditioning remains captive to the triumph of the stronger glow of success measured as personal prosperity. That we, as South Africans in all spheres of life, have been overtaken by material self-seeking should therefore come as no surprise, even if it is contrary to public interest, and is at public expense. (Mbeki 1998)

Given this understanding, it is ironic that the ANC, and Mbeki himself, have emerged as the chief architects of a racialised capitalist project that has promoted the very ethos Mbeki once warned of – to the extent that one of his ministers, Phumzile Mlambo-Ngcuka, famously once told a gathering of black businessmen they should not be ashamed of wanting to be 'filthy rich' (quoted in Adam, Slabbert & Moodley 1997:201).

Hyslop (2004) argues that attitudes towards corruption in the post-1994 political leadership were certainly affected by the ANC's 180-degree shift in ethos, from advocacy of an austere socialism in the mid-1980s, to celebration of the self-enrichment of a new black elite by the mid-1990s.

The trappings of power adopted by the ANC leadership have eschewed an effort at conscious frugality in favour of a certain ostentatious materialism – from fancy cars and designer clothes, to the President's R500 million state jet.

The shift is more than simply an example of the caricatured descent of African elites into the realm of the *Wabenzi*. I would argue that it is a by-product of a deliberate political project under Mbeki to foster a powerful new black capitalist class, which is also, not coincidentally, tied to his own political interests. Mbeki himself underlined the importance of this project in a speech to the Black Management Forum in late 1999:

> As part of the realisation of the aim to eradicate racism in our country, we must strive to create and strengthen a black capitalist class. A critical part to create a non-racial society is the deracialisation of the ownership of productive property. (Mbeki 1999)

According to Gumede, 'He went so far as to equate the failure of black economic empowerment with the ANC failing to achieve its historic mission, namely to eradicate racism' (2002:207).

The potential moral hazards of this approach are evident. As Hyslop notes:

> Under Mandela, and even more, under Mbeki, government policy encouraged rent-seeking activity by black entrepreneurs through the economic preferences they were given through a whole gamut of policies, especially those relating to the awarding of state contracting and corporate ownership. The tendency of such policies was to create a climate in which the line between legal forms of rent-seeking and outright corruption and cronyism became

increasingly blurred. Senior ANC figures became increasingly comfortable with seeking material rewards for their past political contributions and old 'struggle' networks provided political connections which could be parlayed into economic leverage. (2004:17)

In a stinging critique of what she calls 'Mbekism', Ryklief concludes that Mbeki's project has seen:

the rise of a nascent black middle and ruling class, numerically small but ideologically cohesive, inextricably tied to white capital and Mbeki's government and policies, and willing and able to act as a consolidated and conspiratorial force in order to maintain itself. (2002:119)

This description echoes the threat of the development of a crony capitalism detailed elsewhere in this volume by Roger Southall in his discussion of black economic empowerment (BEE).

Mbeki has chosen, via the formation of a powerful black capitalist class, to emphasise the deracialisation of inequality, rather than to diminish it absolutely. This strategy can be a powerful political tool, as the example of Malaysia shows. According to Case:

The rise of Malay business elites, far from exacerbating the disparities that trigger social grievances, inspired a broader sense of 'group worth' among the Malays, hence aiding the community in its collective rivalry with the Chinese. (2003:6)

Schlemmer (2004) has also identified the very strong stabilising influence of what he calls the ANC's effective 'symbolic populism', combined with not insignificant social spending to deliver a social wage.

But the perception of massive corruption among the elite – of crony capitalism – can also undermine this strategy. In his study of Malaysia's economic transformation, Case (2003) argues that the perceived disproportionate subsidisation of the Malaysian elite in the wake of the Asian economic crisis contributed to the outbreak of street protests in Kuala Lumpur during late 1998.

It is important to stress that my critique is not intended to suggest that BEE, affirmative procurement and other forms of state-sanctioned rents or subsidies, should not form part of the South African transformation agenda, but merely to note that they will attract dubious forms of rent-seeking – such as bribery and white fronting – and may provide camouflage for patronage.

Such subsidies are not free but should be weighed up in terms of cost and benefit against other forms of transfer, such as land reform and the suggested Basic Income Grant (BIG). In this regard it is worth noting the conclusions in the paper in this volume by Stephen Gelb on the state of the South African economy, that BEE has not succeeded in establishing a 'positive feedback' of productive investment and growth that could 'pay' for redistribution – notwithstanding an initial euphoria over what the 'democracy dividend' might deliver. As a result, debt-funded equity transfers have proved risky to lenders and beneficiaries alike. Big business has been reluctant to assume the cost of redistribution and has begun to mount a campaign (via the Oppenheimer family's Brenthurst Initiative[6]) for empowerment to be backed with tax breaks that will transfer at least some of the cost to taxpayers. Newer empowerment models greatly increase the impetus for dubious rent-seeking by transferring the cost to the empowered, who are supposed to deliver new business to pay for their shares over time.

In general, I would argue, BEE is likely to accelerate the stratification of black society, such as has already taken place in the trade union movement (von Holdt 2003). More optimistic observers (see Adam, Slabbert & Moodley 1997; Lodge 2003) have suggested that the ANC – as a dominant but well-functioning ruling party – will help keep such centripetal forces at bay and, combined with other constitutional and practical checks and balances in the society, will hold corruption at acceptable levels. However, there are several counterarguments. As Schlemmer notes:

> For dominant party systems in recent history, 'historic projects'
> like transformation, by shaping the national agenda, produce a
> cycle of dominance or hegemony. (2004:16)

In addition, I would argue that the leadership cult created around Mbeki, and the intolerance of criticism that has been a hallmark of his presidency, has led to a reduction of political competition and the increased personalisation of competition for networks of patronage in a way that takes us closer to the crony-capital systems of East Asia.[7] The contradictions between this hegemonic project and our liberal Constitution and its institutions are obvious, and were always likely to lead to a showdown between party solidarity and constitutional accountability.

Accountability failure

The most drastic challenge to the democratic government's commitment to accountability emerged in the wake of the 1998 Cabinet decision to purchase some R30 billion worth of new defence equipment – backed by foreign loans and the promise of guaranteed counter-trade or 'offset' investments and export support. What became known as 'the arms deal scandal' enjoyed sustained media attention and led to the testing and, arguably, the failure of a string of institutions of oversight and accountability.

The real test of such institutions is when the going gets tough – and the investigation of the arms deal was a fearsome challenge: placing contracts worth billions of Rands at stake, dealing with an industry that is highly technical and secretive at the best of times, and pitting the oversight agencies against the highest reaches of the Executive.

The initial impetus for the investigation came from within the ANC itself, initially via allegations raised by disaffected ANC intelligence people, and later via the concerns of members of Scopa, including, prominently, its ANC members. Thus the probe of the arms deal was also a test of the ANC's internal democracy, an important asset in a state so dominated by one party.

In early 2000 Scopa had supported a request by the AG's office for a preliminary performance audit into the deal, approved by Cabinet in November 1998. The AG subsequently tabled a preliminary report indicating some key areas of concern around possible conflicts of interest and irregularities in the way in which contracts were awarded. He recommended a full forensic audit. Scopa – led by its chair, the Inkatha Freedom Party's Gavin Woods, and supported by the ANC's Andrew Feinstein – delivered its own swingeingly critical report, and recommended a multi-agency probe of the arms deal, suggesting the inclusion of the AG, the Public Protector, the NDPP and the SIU, led at the time by Judge Willem Heath. The report was tabled on the last day of the legislative sitting and (apparently while the Executive wasn't paying attention) it was accepted by Parliament. When the Executive woke up to the implications of this muscular experiment in accountability, all hell broke loose.

Scandal

Before we relate what happened next, it is worth pausing to examine why a big corruption scandal is so instructive. As Hyslop notes: 'A scandal exposes the hidden geological strata of politics and hidden linkages and connections of which we would otherwise be unaware' (2004:2) This scandal, the biggest to hit post-apartheid South Africa, exposed the tensions and battles within the ANC – and also the ruling party's limits in regard to tolerance of accountability.

The issue emerged at a particular point in our political history, when the Mbeki presidency began to be seriously contested and questioned by persons in the ANC and the wider political landscape, including the media. It should also be noted that, at that time, the President's dissident views on AIDS had begun to emerge, but what had also become clear is that there was very little room for public debate or disagreement over AIDS within the party. Thus the arms deal became an area where there was an outlet for dissent, legitimised and protected, at least initially, by the constitutional provisions for oversight.

A peep at the hegemonic wolf in the sheep's clothing of liberal democracy

The Executive launched a furious attack on Scopa, initially weighing in with a press conference of three ministerial heavyweights who told the committee it did not know what it was talking about.

For the Executive, the first key to managing the crisis was to exclude Judge Heath from the investigation that had now been irreversibly mandated. Judge Heath, regarded by government as abrasively independent if not hostile, represented a major threat because the special legislation under which his SIU operated could be used to attack the main arms contracts.

By good fortune, Heath was facing a bid for his removal by the Association of Personal Accident Lawyers, who objected to his bid to recover excessive fees charged to road accident victims. When the Constitutional Court ruled that a judge should not act as an investigator, government leapt on this opportunity to exclude the SIU from the investigation, though Heath had offered to resign as a judge and nothing in the judgement precluded his unit from continuing its work.

President Mbeki went so far as to place his credibility on the line by delivering a special national address in which he claimed he had obtained legal advice that the SIU should not be included in the probe. He was swiftly contradicted by the senior legal officers involved who had provided the advice.

Party heavies were deployed to lay down the party line in Scopa, thus destroying the tradition of non-partisanship the committee had built up. First Feinstein, and then Woods, resigned their positions in the face of this interference. Two key members of the AG's audit team also stepped aside.

The three remaining investigating agencies proceeded with the probe and delivered a verdict that also severely compromised their credibility. They signed off on a conclusion that government was not implicated in any wrongdoing (despite clear evidence of abuse by Defence Minister Joe Modise – by then retired) and nor was government's contracting position compromised, despite evidence of irregularities on nearly every page of the body of the report (see Woods 2002).

I would argue that what government's overall response demonstrated was that accountability would be shut down when there appeared to be any real risk to the ANC. What emerged at this point of crisis was a consensus among the ruling elite that prioritised the survival of the ANC's hegemonic project over the more abstract demands of liberal accountability.

The decision not to prosecute Deputy President Jacob Zuma over his untoward relationship with businessman Schabir Shaik, while legally defensible, was arguably also informed by the same strategic assessment of the risk of such a prosecution.

Given the ruling party's avowed intention of extending its control over the transformation project to all strategic areas of society, the likelihood exists of future damaging accountability challenges. Up to now, the party has kept its response to those challenges within reasonable bounds, but a matter of real concern about the ANC's response to events in Zimbabwe is that it appears to identify with the basic legitimacy of Mugabe's own hegemonic project and accept almost any abuses in the name of protecting that hegemony.

The arms deal also exposed the problematic nature of some of the economic relations set up by Mbeki's emphasis on elite empowerment. One arms deal investigator acknowledged in a personal communication that the investigation was faced with a grey area that flowed from a political process in which ANC cadres were consciously deployed by the party to wrest control of areas of the economy that were considered strategic – like the arms industry. In that process, 'mistakes' were made.

Thus, the very 'mistakes' for which Zuma was being investigated flowed from the attempt politically to manage and control the transfer of economic power – or at least strategic elements of it – from the alliance of the *Broederbond* (or, more broadly, Afrikaner nationalism) and big capital, to an alliance of the ANC and big capital. So, although Zuma may (or may not) have overstepped the line, that line is in fact a very wide and dirty smudge, within whose boundaries fall a myriad empowerment deals – and the funding of the ANC itself, as well as of its pet projects and competing factions.

In the course of the past year, the *Mail & Guardian* newspaper has investigated a handful of these cases that, for one reason or another, have risen close enough to the surface to glimpse what lies beneath. They range from the funding of research into the supposed AIDS cure, Virodene, to an inexplicable oil deal with Nigeria – promoted by President Mbeki but benefiting a mysterious offshore company. They demonstrate the same basic outline: the involvement of ANC 'fronts' or personalities connected to the ANC's treasury department, often combined with irregularities in the awarding of contracts. There is every reason to suspect that the arms deal suffered from the same intentional confusion of national, party and personal interests.

With regard to businessman Schabir Shaik, the overlap between representing private and party interests – and indeed the active blurring of the boundary between the two – was built in from the start. His company, Nkobi Holdings, was named after the ANC's late Treasurer General, and Shaik was recently explicitly acknowledged by Zuma as having played a role in raising and managing funds for the ANC. In fact, it is arguable that all Shaik did was devise a business plan based on unwritten rules of the game – rules which in effect institutionalise corruption on the basis of both funding the party and extending its control from the political sphere to the economic.

It is important to note that this is not an African disease. France, to take but one example, has long run its politics this way – and the level of corruption under the apartheid regime was less visible simply because it was more neatly integrated into the fabric and institutions of power. In France, too, the establishment of a deeply corrupt intelligence, business and political oligarchy was based on the veneer of a nationalist project – that of promoting and projecting the 'French way' as an international 'third way' between the Anglo-American axis and the Soviet Empire.

Here we have our own national project – whether cloaked in the garb of empowerment or of the national democratic revolution – which similarly can hide a multitude of sins against the Constitution and good governance.

Conclusion

In conclusion, the picture is mixed. The corporatisation of patronage embodied in the empowerment project is nothing new to capitalist accumulation in South Africa and, arguably, it represents a positive step up from the mafia-style competition embedded in more primitive black business networks such as the taxi industry. Although there has been no systematic effort to measure the cost and benefits of BEE as it actually manifests itself, judging from the broad macroeconomic indicators, it does not appear to have had a significantly negative impact and appears at least sustainable, if not necessarily broadly and deeply beneficial. However, any significant financial shock or world economic slump may raise and change the stakes for BEE.

But the risk remains of building an influential yet parasitic elite that will vigorously resist being weaned from the advantages it enjoys, and will even lobby to increase state support for its interests. The policing of this redistribution project remains the responsibility of the oversight institutions. A problem for such institutions remains the ruling ANC's deliberate policy of deploying cadres to institutions in a manner in which they retain a party loyalty that may undermine or even trump the new independent institutional loyalty. The ability of such institutions to impose accountability in situations where the political cost is significant is likely to be limited, as critics argued was the case in the probe of the arms deal.

The ANC's increasing monopoly of political and state power – the party captured nearly 70 per cent of the vote in the 2004 elections – is likely to increase the scope for such conflicts of interest as the party and its cadres become more and more influential, including in business. With such influence will come increased pressure – already evident in the Zuma case – to keep the management of such conflicts within the ambit of the ANC's own political and disciplinary structures. In this atmosphere there will be a tendency to use information around corruption for internal political bargaining, rather than throwing it open to the proper public accountability process.

As analyst Adam Habib has noted, what keeps parties honest is uncertainty, the fear that too much abuse might persuade voters to give someone else a chance (*Sunday Times* 4.04.04).

Such uncertainty is also important for the civil service and the oversight institutions: they too will be aware of the possibility that in a few years time a new administration may uncover the skeletons of any cover-up. South Africa's hegemonic political reality negates such uncertainty. Although the ANC's internal disciplinary processes (which are mostly informal) remain strong, the liberation ideal and its disciplines have already been replaced to a remarkable degree by a brash materialism. Inevitably the ANC's ability and willingness to police itself will be compromised. The success of the ANC's hegemonic project may, in time, become the most significant threat to the country's democratic one.

Notes

1 Extract from a judgement in the Constitutional Court (Case CCT 27/00) in the matter between South African Association of Personal Injury Lawyers (Appellant) v. Heath, Willem Hendrik (First Respondent), the Special Investigating Unit (Second Respondent), the President of the Republic of South Africa (Third Respondent) and the Minister of Justice (Fourth Respondent) – heard on 7.09.00, decided on 28.11.00.

2 See www.transparency.org.

3 Personal communication, Institute for Security Studies researcher, Hennie van Vuuren.

4 For a useful archive of recent corruption reports, see '*Umqol' Uphandle – SA Corruption Briefing*, published monthly on the ISS website, www.iss.co.za.

5 *Sunday Times*, 23.11.03.

6 Published in July 2003 by South Africa's most powerful mining dynasty, the Brenthurst Initiative was the Oppenheimer family's contribution to the debate on BEE. It suggested a package of tax incentives and other measures to encourage companies to commit themselves to 'broad-based' empowerment.

7 Note, for example, the apology forced on ANC executive committee member, Jeremy Cronin, for relatively mild and academic public criticism of the ruling party and the plot allegations aired against perceived political opponents of Mbeki in May 2001.

References

Adam H, Slabbert F & Moodley K (1997) *Comrades in business*. Cape Town: Tafelberg.

Camerer L (2001) *Corruption in South Africa: Results of an expert panel survey*. Institute of Security Studies Monograph No. 65.

Case W (2003) *Malaysia: New reforms, old continuities, tense ambiguities*. South East Asia Research Centre Working Papers Series, No. 51.

Hyslop J (2004) Political corruption: Before and after apartheid. Revised version of paper presented at Conference on State and Society in South Africa, Witwatersrand University, July 2003.

King M (1994) *King report on corporate governance for South Africa (King 1)*. Johannesburg: Institute of Directors in SA.

King M (2002) *King report on corporate governance for South Africa (King 2)*. Johannesburg: Institute of Directors in SA.

Khan MH & Jomo KS (2000) Introduction. In MH Khan & KS Jomo *Rents, rent seeking and economic development: Theory and evidence in Asia*. Cambridge: Cambridge University Press.

Lodge T (2003) The ANC and the development of political party politics in modern South Africa. Seminar paper presented at Conference on State and Society in South Africa, Witwatersrand University, July 2003.

Mbeki, T (1998) Statement at the Anti-Corruption Summit Conference, Cape Town, 10.11.98.

Mbeki T (1999) Speech at the annual national conference of the Black Management Forum, Kempton Park, 20.11.99.

Ryklief S (2002) Does the Emperor really have no clothes? In S Jacobs & R Calland (eds.) *Thabo Mbeki's world*. Scottsville: University of Natal Press.

Schlemmer L (2004) The ANC's dominance not written in stone. *Focus, Journal of the Helen Suzman Foundation* No.33.

UNODC (United Nations Office on Drugs and Crime) (2003) *Country corruption assessment report (South Africa)*. United Nations Office on Drugs and Crime. Available at <http://www.info.gov.za/reports/2003/corruption.pdf>.

Von Holdt K (2003) *Transition from below*. Scottsville: University of Natal Press.

Woods G (2002) *A critique of the JIT report*. Available at <http://www.armsdeal-vpo.co.za/special_items/ reports/accountability_failure.html>.

5 The state of the public service

Vino Naidoo

Introduction

The transformation of the public service in South Africa is an all-encompassing project corresponding to the complexities of wider political and socio-economic change. Despite these complexities, there appear to be interrelated yet discernible dimensions in the post-apartheid evolution of the public service, which require comment. One dimension emphasises practical-administrative capacity for improving the processes of executing public policy. Another dimension emphasises historical-political factors of culture change, which forces a consideration of the normative basis of transformation itself, and the influence of such factors on evaluating the effectiveness of measures to enhance practical administrative capacity.

It often appears that, in urgently responding to severe socio-economic disparities and deprivation, calls to strengthen practical-administrative capacity risk sterility in underplaying historical-political factors associated with wider public service transformation. This chapter follows from this observation, and debates the substance of practical administrative improvement in the public service, referred to in recent presidential 'State of the Nation' speeches, against the background of historical and political factors inherited from the pre-liberation period.

Public service transformation and the apartheid environment

Dynamism and flux have characterised the South African public service since the country's first democratic elections in 1994. The public service, officially comprising national departments and provincial administrations (excluding municipal government) under the Public Service Act (No. 103 of 1994), has undergone a major structural overhaul, reflecting the political negotiations prior to the 1994 elections. The principal aim of this transition has emphasised integration, which, in the case of the public service, has involved the amalgamation of a scattered pre-1994 system comprising 15 administrations serving 11 different governments, including four 'independent' states and six self-governing territories (Adler 2000). Integration has also necessitated a more appropriately weighted representation of the country's population in the public service to redress a historically unequal distribution of decision-making power based on race preference. The role of the public service in policy development and implementation has also had to adapt to the demands of inclusiveness and transparency within the democratic process. Finally, the progressive shift to inclusive and socially-geared legislation after 1994 also places greater demands on public servants to utilise discretion, flexibility, interpretation and adeptness in the implementation of corresponding public policy.

Setting aside the scale of these structural changes for the moment, the true measure of growth in the post-apartheid public service will be less about how effectively the new machinery functions, and more about the kind of ethos supplanting that which existed prior to 1994 in relation to rehabilitating what Mokgoro refers to as its 'dual accountability' (1996:268) to the public and to political office-bearers. The complexity of evaluating public service accountability from this viewpoint is further compounded by its administrative structure which, Mokgoro (2000) reminds us, comprises a complex system composed of many interdependent and interrelated sub-systems. Analysis therefore cannot divorce the administrative responsibility of the public service from the impact of politics and policy orientations of political office-bearers. Assessments of the efficiency and effectiveness of the public service therefore must go beyond technical explanations, to include the historical, political and philosophical foundations underpinning this.

It should be noted that the apartheid and post-apartheid governments both articulated with conviction and clarity, philosophically-laden visions of the make-up of society, and the state's role in bringing this about. For pre-liberation governments, this comprised a gradually more complex and interventionist agenda, based on an authoritarian and unrepresentative unevenness and inequity in the administration and regulation of services and, in effect, of people, grounded in a racial classification framework articulated on the basis of ethnic self-determination.[1] Moreover, although the interplay between state power and public accountability was, in principle, democratic for a minority of the population – prompting van den Berghe to characterise South Africa as a 'herrenvolk democracy'[2] (quoted in Marger 1994:402) – it in fact represented a negation of the freedom even for apartheid's intended beneficiaries, due to the restrictive and authoritarian measures taken by the state to maintain separate development.

The structure and accountability of the public service during the apartheid years was therefore closely entwined and dependent on the capacity of the ruling National Party (NP) to implement policy measures through the creation of a state that was sufficiently large, powerful and centrally co-ordinated to manage and police race relations in the country (Posel 2000). Seegers (1994) infuses this view through her analysis of disaggregated statistics on the growth of the public service as a whole between 1920 and 1980, and in particular, accelerated growth from about 1950. It should be noted from her analysis that central authority departments comprised the largest segment of the total, as compared with provincial authorities, a situation that has been reversed in the democratic period. The rationale for this earlier configuration appears consistent then with the imperative under apartheid of reinforcing central co-ordination in order to maintain control over the government's separate development programme.[3]

Table 5.1 *Public service growth in personnel (including apartheid period)*

Year	Total state employment	Central	Provincial	Local	Homeland
1920	150 718				
1930	227 408	140 042			
1940	321 403	177 392			
1950	481 518	280 310			
1960	798 545	454 692	130 477	151 459	
1975		509 424	220 248	232 000	132 926
1970	1 105 295	549 865	185 361	191 294	
1980	1 601 158	665 965	248 703	244 600	191 309

Source: Adapted from statistics presented in Seegers 1994:40–43

An analysis of the growth of the public service during apartheid also reveals the marginalisation of black public servants from senior decision-making roles, for example Cloete's (1995) reference to the central public service using the most recent data available to him at the time (see Figure 5.1). One should add to this picture arguments that, despite the Public Services Act of 1957 barring public servants from participating in party politics, the law was completely ignored in practice and that a tacit affirmative action policy represented a strategy of patronage by the NP, resulting in tremendous pressure being exerted on public servants to comply and conform with political objectives (Posel 2000).

Figure 5.1 *Comparative racial representation within central public service*

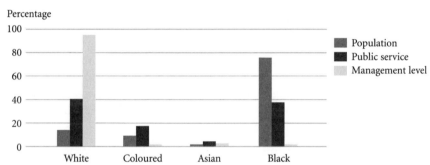

Source: Adapted from Cloete 1995:194

Evans (1997) provides an insider's view of the impact of apartheid within the public service by his discussion of the gradual expansion of the authority of the Department of Native Affairs. He observes that apartheid authoritarianism was not just about the general circumscription of liberties for blacks, but also favoured a particular concentration of authority within the state itself, and in particular towards state entities whose business was most tightly connected to the suppression and regulation of blacks.

Pines (1979) gives an account of the lack of success of many development initiatives managed by the apartheid public service in black homeland territories, arguing that the most prominent feature of community development was its 'system-maintaining' (1979:5) properties, which resulted in government officials, by initiating self-help schemes, being unlikely to promote social-political processes outside of, but parallel to, the established political structure.[4] Jeppe and van Baalen (1995) further add that an economic growth approach to development under bureaucratic direction and control characterised the development policies in homeland territories, through a project method that was subjected, as Moerdijk points out, to the discretion of racial politics:

> The new development corporations ... are all headed by Afrikaner members of the Afrikaner establishment ... The same can be said for the entire senior management ... The few token 'homeland' representatives wield no real power ... They are called upon to develop peripheral regions of a centralised economic system, and not national economic entities. (1981:87)

Community development therefore had a peculiar meaning prior to 1994. Moreover, this meaning must take into consideration the limitations exerted on it by an overriding agenda to maintain strict political and social boundaries, as well as how this agenda shaped and influenced the economic possibilities for black development considering the comparative environment in which it took place (see Table 5.2).

The credibility of community development initiatives is also questionable, given evidence that homelands were housing the greatest concentration of South Africa's poor[5] (Reynolds cited in Muller 1984), coupled with the observation that they were also not generating sustained development opportunities, while white urban areas inside the Republic of South Africa had a high absorption demand for black labour[6] (cited in Morast 1975).

The objective of this cursory review of the pressures exerted on the public service during apartheid is to establish the relevant backdrop for evaluating public sector transformation after 1994. It also illustrates the utility of examining public service transformation from a 'cultural-institutional' theoretical approach, inquiring into the gradual production of informal norms and values growing out of what remains a formal institutional framework, which surely then must take into account historical and sociological factors (Christensen 2003). This framework can be useful in providing a more nuanced complexion to evaluating otherwise technical measures to improve efficiency and effectiveness, as well as providing greater insight into

Table 5.2 *Comparative economic figures for white areas and black homelands, 1985*

Region	Area	Arable land	Population[a]	Absent workers[b]	GDP	GNP
	(000 km²)	(hectares)	(000s)	(000s)	(Rm)	(Rm)
Bophuthatswana	40.5	400	1 721	362	1 163	2 640
Ciskei	7.8	75	750	108	397	825
Gazankulu	6.6	65	620	75	230	530
KaNgwane	3.8	36	448	109	108	485
KwaNdebele	0.9	24	286	92	52	411
KwaZulu	31.0	565	4 382	770	1 062	4 044
Lebowa	21.8	347	2 157	283	540	1 604
Qwaqwa	0.6	7	209	60	110	363
Transkei	42.0	754	3 000	412	1 359	2 909
Venda	6.9	65	460	51	245	446
Total homelands	**161.9**	**2 338**	**14 033**	**2 322**	**5 266**	**14 257**
White areas	10 059.2	12 260	19 477		104 338	89 992
South Africa	**1 221.1**	**14 598**	**33 510**		**109 604**	**104 249**

Notes: a Migrant workers are included in total for white areas. Other citizens of the homelands permanently resident in white areas are included in the figures for white areas rather than for homelands. Absent workers are the sum of migrant workers in white areas and those who live in the homelands and commute daily or weekly to white areas for employment.

b The Bureau for Economic Research (1976:72) illustrated the economic importance of absentee worker income contributions to homelands by noting that it represented on average the largest proportion of homeland gross national income.

Source: Lewis 1990:43

the factors that facilitate or constrain the dual accountability role of the public service that Mokgoro introduced earlier.

Developments in the public service since 1994

The immediate task following democratic transition in 1994 was to dismantle the administrative framework for separate development and adapt the knowledge and systems housed within this framework to the new political geography defined by a single public service comprising central departments and nine provincial administrations. According to the Department of Public Service and Administration's (DPSA 1999) *Report on service and skills audits,* the public service as a whole contracted between 1994 and 1999 (150 000 positions or 13 per cent). Currently the public service employs just over a million people (PSC 2004). Job losses were greatest amongst less-skilled and part-time workers and defence force members. Job losses in these categories were, however, partly offset by substantial growth in relatively skilled occupations, such as educators and nurses (DPSA 1999). Figure 5.2, for example, illustrates the retention of emphasis from the apartheid period on education and health personnel in provincial administrations (the smaller yet no less important social development/welfare services have also been added), with the important footnote that these are no longer distinguished by a racialisation of services rendered – especially white education versus bantu education and so on (see Standish 1984).

Figure 5.2 *Profile of public service, 2003*

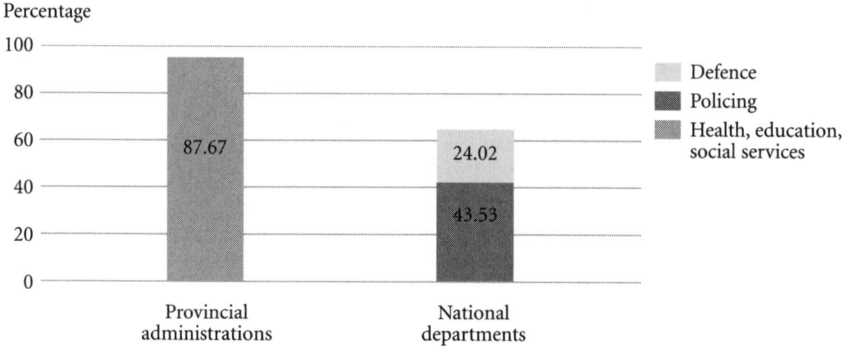

Percentage

Source: Modified from absolute numbers presented in PSC 2004

Figure 5.3 illustrates the current racial composition of the South African public service, which needs to be read along with Figure 5.4, depicting the more significant shift in the distribution of senior posts. Although the ratio of white to black senior management demonstrates a sizeable shift in reversing senior management marginalisation of black public servants under apartheid, the problem of management capacity remains. The DPSA's *Policy statement on the establishment of a senior management service in the public service* revealed persistent problems in management capacity, including poor levels of performance and skills among some senior staff, underdevelopment of core

Figure 5.3 *Racial composition of the South African public service, 2003*

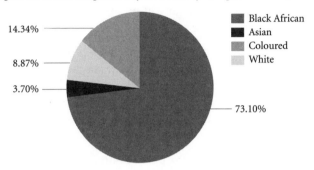

Source: Modified from absolute numbers presented in PSC 2004

Figure 5.4 *Senior managers by race and salary level*

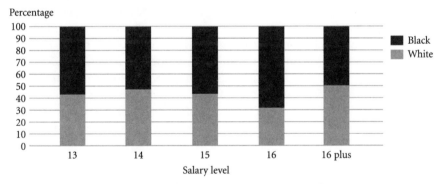

Source: Modified from DPSA 2000

leadership/managerial competencies and little horizontal mobility due to rigidities in the employment framework (DPSA 2000).

These difficulties should not, however, be overemphasised in a post-apartheid context if we consider Posel's (2000) observation that a bloated state, increasingly ambitious in its social engineering efforts, coupled with prolonged and chronic staff shortages (particularly from 1944–68), had devastating effects on labour productivity and efficiency during apartheid. This appeared to have exacerbated a pre-existing problem with insufficient training of new recruits. Although this led some to question the quality of new public service recruits, the bigger problem appeared more ironic as Posel describes:

> Whites were streaming into better paying jobs in the private sector with little competition from blacks. Yet the very same job reservation policies prevented the state from training black people in sufficiently large numbers for the civil service positions which the available white labour supply was too small to fill. (2000:47–48)

The problem of management capacity in the post-1994 public service, which, although not a new phenomenon, is in danger of being worsened by a dearth of senior management in provincial administrations as compared to the comparatively smaller-staffed national departments (DPSA 2000) (see Figure 5.5). This is particularly problematic for provinces that have incorporated former homeland administrations in being able to provide general management co-ordination and oversight to an administrative agenda composed primarily of policy implementation (DPSA 1999). Furthermore, skills in strategic and change management would be considered vital for these provinces where, according to the DPSA (1999), provinces that inherited homeland administrations were characterised, amongst other things, as having low employment in high-level planning and administrative functions (finance, economic affairs and planning). Finally, Moerdijk's (1981) earlier point regarding Afrikaner senior management control over homeland development corporations must also be factored into this discussion, as it relates to the character of development planning.

The context for evaluating contemporary expectations of the public service

Recent presidential 'State of the Nation' addresses (2002–04) have referred to the public service primarily in practical language, including references to improving skills levels, professional competency and efficiency for enhancing the quality of service delivery. In the most recent address in 2004, these improvements were linked to the public service having a 'clear understanding of the developmental tasks of a democratic state'. While this is clearly pertinent to post-apartheid public service accountability, it nonetheless requires constant scrutiny of the extent

Figure 5.5 *Senior managers by provincial administration and national departments*

Number

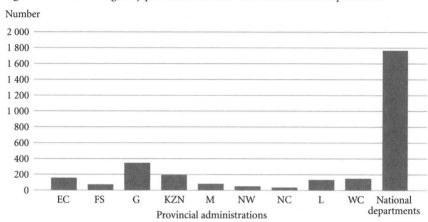

Source: Modified from DPSA (2000)

Note: Eastern Cape (EC), Free State (FS), Gauteng (G), KwaZulu-Natal (KZN), Limpopo (L), Mpumalanga (M), North West (NW), Northern Cape (NC), Western Cape (WC)

to which there is consistency with the expectations of democracy and development among political elites, public servants, and the citizenry.

Let us first consider the message of service delivery in the post-apartheid period – the prevailing circumstances clearly require public servants to actively contribute to the public's material and psychological development, where needs are both wider in scope (as compared with neglected or differential services under apartheid) and depth (in many cases dealing with previously underserviced areas). Although *service delivery* has become the most pressing issue on the public service agenda, the present cadre of public servants are in reality expected to do more than deliver services efficiently and effectively. They are expected to continuously examine and respond to circumstances that constrain the utilisation of and access to services. This goes beyond simply redressing material imbalances. In effect it involves a kind of psychological rehabilitation of the relationship between the public service and the public, progressively retarded by years of alienation climaxing in apartheid. The demands of this therefore require going beyond a minimalist provision of services where black takes preference over white.

Latib (1995) reminds us of the dynamics of public service accountability under apartheid, where he argues that performance was evaluated within tightly controlled hierarchical and secretive public policy decision-making between bureaucrats reporting to their political heads. The task therefore was highly prescriptive, regulatory, and geared towards what Latib calls 'procedural accountability', to the exclusion of 'ethical values and standards' (1995:11–13). Since then, accountability (in form) under democracy has become more transparent and diversified, including extra-governmental processes comprising such provisions as a broad-based Bill of Rights, a constitutionally mandated group of government oversight institutions including the Public Protector, a reoriented Public Service Commission (PSC), the South African Human Rights Commission, legislation such as the Promotion of Access to Information Act (No. 2 of 2000), and specific provisions in the *White Paper on the transformation of service delivery* (1997) prescribing public consultation to determine service standards and the subsequent publication of these standards.

Although these gains in formal democratic procedures represent a broadening of the space for accountability, they do not in themselves guarantee a corresponding shift in the behaviour of the public service. The various accountability mechanisms outlined above are formal, procedural in their compliance, and represent expectations and responsibilities externally directed at the bureaucracy. Within this context, these are subject to certain limitations such as the willingness of public service entities to co-operate, how these responsibilities are interpreted and formulated by entities to the satisfaction of external parties involved in the democratic process – Parliament, judiciary, oversight institutions – and the extent of information shared and the quality thereof.

Something that has not changed since apartheid is that the public service remains an institution separate from the public, to whom it is responsible for providing a range of administrative and regulatory services. Regardless of how one characterises the balance between procedural accountability and ethical values and standards, it cannot be assumed that new slate of legislation, strategies and mechanisms will itself prompt a corresponding response from the public service.

Interestingly, the subject of political influence on the bureaucracy appears undecided nearly a decade after political liberation. Johnson, for example, argues that the Mbeki administration 'restricts civil society organisations' role to that of mobilization and implementing directives from above' (2002:9), the latter formulated by government and governing party experts. Oldfield makes a more measured and analytical, yet no less critical point, recognising that 'the state is a product of political compromise, and a site and agent in post-apartheid struggles for resources and power, its relationships with organs of civil society are complex and uneven' (2000:35).

She further adds that state structures encompass multiple sites of power (and contestation) at various levels, and that the level of determination and co-ordination of priorities, as well as perspectives, of recipients impacts on the shape, pace and implementation of initiatives. Mokgoro illustrates this complexity by pointing out that we should 'consider the fact that each province has about 11 departments, which in turn means that there are about 90 approaches to management in government' (2000:2). Although these observations do not constitute satisfactory explanations concerning the extent of the accountability shift of the politico-bureaucratic complex, they do at least outline its size and complexity, which must be taken into account when evaluating technical performance.

Mokgoro (2000:3–5) provides insight into the complexity of interpreting public service 'capacity', describing as 'inadequate' a limited emphasis on training initiatives alone. He advocates for a greater focus on the process of public servants steering themselves through the complex of structures and relationships defining the public service, which both he and Oldfield have described earlier. Van der Waldt (2001) suggests an interesting administrative construct that attempts to address the shortfall in a narrower conception of capacity, through a 'management by projects' approach. The approach advocates for public servants having a wider departmental conscientiousness in the execution of their designated responsibilities. Given the scale and enormity of the public service mandate, it is necessary for public service entities to have clearly defined, demarcated, and specialised units. It is also necessary that these more confined responsibility designations do not limit the scope and ability of public servants to understand, respond and contribute to public policy issues that may not fall strictly within the ambit of their designated areas.

Van der Waldt appears then to be stressing management as a skill, and not just that attached to specific task designations, implying (or one could say requiring) effective general management (Stacey 1993 cited in van der Waldt 2001:301). This perspective is all the more persuasive considering the multiplicity of tasks expected of today's development-minded public servant, which include, among others, programme and project management, involvement in the design of new activities, negotiating the terms and use of resources with partners, and ensuring that activities that contribute to wider entity objectives and goals are planned and implemented.

Van der Waldt effectively raises our expectations of public servants as transcending their ability to implement a project, or two or three. An aspect of his paper that requires further elaboration is his recommendation of a project-based management structure, which outlines a preferred management by project operational set-up. In short, van der Waldt suggests teaming up specifically designated officials into project teams where officials collaborate on a specific cross-functional project or activity, thereby bringing together a wider mix and sharing of experiences and expertise to a particular problem. An advantage of this approach is that it forces public servants to think beyond the limitations of their designated areas of responsibility.

Although van der Waldt's proposal is to be commended for constructing a model whose intent is to promote collaboration among designated officials, we ought to be careful that this does not end up as project management in a larger form. This is a cautionary note with policy implications stemming from Kotzé's criticism of the limited confines of the project method configuration containing 'strains' (2004:23) of the self-help schemes Pines referred to under apartheid. She further argues that, in essence, this has translated into an expectation that the poor take greater responsibility for uplifting themselves in a situation marked by minimal social expenditure.

Structurally, Kotzé's concern remains as relevant today as it has been in our repudiations of apartheid 'development' methodologies, insofar as the project framework for development interventions continues to dominate development discourse in South Africa. Although the development-co-operation regime has been legitimised post-1994, comprising public servants, donor agencies, consultants, researchers and non-governmental organisations, questions remain about the relative effectiveness of the project and empowerment (self-help) framework significantly reducing social and economic disparities. In particular, it is debatable to what extent this framework structurally limits and constrains development thinking to interventions that are not dealing more directly with the underlying causes of poverty and inequality (Kotzé 2004).

At one level Kotzé's critique relates to the appropriateness and orientation of social and economic policy, which defines the agenda of what is possible for even the most efficient of projects to respond to social and economic upliftment. At another level, that of project planning and implementation, her critique forces us to re-examine the ability of these interventions to operate according to a sharing of support and responsibility that dispenses with past approaches. Contemporary problems towards this end could include the beneficiaries of development projects trying to interpret public accountability to the public servant versus that to a service provider under project implementation strategies, the consistency of expectations between beneficiaries and members of the project regime with regards to the appropriate design of the intervention, and the subjectification of project beneficiaries as participant subjects (in participatory methods), where this might end up merely justifying project technique. Finally, there is concern with the character and depth of engagement with beneficiaries being pre-empted by project managers and intermediaries objectifying development as an intervention rather than viewing the intervention itself as a means to understand development as a condition.

Public service accountability and intergovernmental relations

The 2003 'State of the Nation' presidential address introduced the idea of deploying community development workers to improve the government's interaction with the public. However, what does this proposed deployment imply about the effectiveness of existing modes of interaction between the government and the public? The much anticipated *Towards a ten year review: Synthesis report on implementation of government programmes* (PCAS 2003) observed that, although the government had put in place many inter-organisational forums to enhance the effectiveness of policy formulation and service delivery, greater involvement by the recipients of these services was needed. It specifically cited research showing that the poor in particular lacked 'formal organisational power' to engage and that where civil society organisations participated 'more fully', service-delivery gaps were better identified

(PCAS 2003:14). It would, however, be unfair to say that the poor simply lack 'formal organisational power', given the plethora of small-scale, informal community-based organisations in South Africa.[7]

What seems more appropriate is to question the quality and effectiveness of government engagement with the poor, and indeed with all members of the public, through the public service. Moreover, it ought not be taken for granted that the existence of inter-organisational and indeed *inter-governmental* structures and forums represents sufficient indicators of accountability between the public service and the citizenry.

Although not afforded as much prominence in previous presidential 'State of the Nation' addresses, intergovernmental relations, it must be noted, are pivotal factor in the movement away from authoritarian and overly centralised decision-making processes. This is not, however, simply a matter of decentralising administration closer to the public, but the extent to which the reconfiguration of the system promotes a two-way democratic conversation that moves away from the ineffectual development approaches of the past.

A key intergovernmental structural challenge confronting post-apartheid governments is that the public service does not officially incorporate local or municipal government as per the Public Service Act (No. 103 of 1994). This legislative technicality is constitutionally catered for by the expectation that national and provincial governments provide capacity support to local government.[8] The government's ten year review report in fact remarked on capacity shortages in provincial and local governments, which have constrained delivery and forced the national sphere to consider intervening (PCAS 2003).

The challenge of co-ordinating the various administrations representing the state is often remarked upon. This includes the PSC's submission to Parliament's Public Services and Administration Portfolio Committee on the release of its *State of the public service report 2002*. In this submission the PSC described the making and implementing of policy as being hampered by a lack of 'unison' between national and provincial governments and the public service, where the link between these agents was 'difficult to understand'. The PSC added that co-ordination and integration of service delivery efforts was also problematic (PMG 2003). Inadequate co-ordination and integration are frequently cited as challenges by public servants, which is understandable given the complex organisational system Mokgoro referred to earlier. The problem can also be interpreted in at least two ways. The first relates to the PSC's statement to the Portfolio Committee that there is 'uneven alignment' of policymakers and implementers, which could be read as primarily a technical issue requiring logistical and organisational consistency in executing policy positions. Secondly, there are also situations where policy approaches may differ according to the fiscal and strategic circumstances of provincial administrations. This may have less to do with the misalignment of policy and implementation and more to do with how priorities are planned.

Because the structure of intergovernmental administration is complex, the corresponding challenge of co-operative government could be said to largely follow suit. The solution then tends to be simpler than one can imagine, where this could entail simply improving communication and ultimately co-ordination. The deployment of community development workers needs to be reflected on within this context. Do they represent necessary supplementary resources reaching areas and depths not able to be penetrated by existing public servants, or is their deployment simply papering over the neglect in public servant outreach, depth of engagement and communication with the public?

This is an important question to ponder if we fall back on problems of co-ordination and alignment disrupting the reach and depth of administrative services, because we may be in danger of playing to a public perception not far removed from apartheid experience. Moerdijk (1981), for example, pointed to the administrative complexity of the structure governing homelands, including a mix of homeland, central government and agency entities, with specific powers flowing to each, all falling under the ultimate authority of the then Prime Minister and Cabinet of the Republic of South Africa. The post-1994 government system has continued with a decentralised unitary political structure with a great deal of authority residing in the President and Cabinet.[9] This system has also suffered setbacks, including: imprecision about the sharing of powers and functions between the three spheres of government, which is being dealt with now; occasions where severe provincial underperformance (Eastern Cape provincial administration) has resulted in direct central government intervention; and finally, instances of poor administrative engagement with the public that have even been compared by members of the public with apartheid-period treatment.[10]

The point is not that decentralisation and complexity are necessarily negative. Rather, it rests on the extent to which the decentralisation and complexity of the post-apartheid government reaches and engages with people in a fundamentally different way than in the past. Clearly the allegiance of the post-1994 administrative dispensation is to a non-racial democratic society. However, to what degree will neglect on the part of administrative entities to consistently reach and communicate with the public in a radically different way result in significantly increasing the public's confidence that a democratic government is not simply the same old complex structures, but only this time with blacks and women replacing whites (Mokgoro 1996).

Some could then question the reconstitution of the public service, as described in the PSC's submission to Parliament, as a:

> network of delivery-oriented public service providers, each responsible for their own management according to national norms and standards, rather than the standardised rigid procedures that characterised the previous system. This has created a foundation for success, although major challenges remain in the areas of implementation, co-ordination and integration of services to end-users. (PMG 2003)

Is the reconstitution of the public service as a network of delivery-oriented service providers sufficient? In expediting delivery to the public in response to historical neglect and pressing socio-economic needs, are public servants failing to fashion their responses more carefully and widely to also take into account those factors that can impinge on the public's utilisation of these services? For example, the public service is composed of sector-oriented bureaux conducting regulatory, dispensary, and facilitation services. These are designated by a variety of posts and job descriptions, with varying degrees and types of interaction with the public. In some cases, such as with dispensary services (for example, the Department of Home Affairs' processing of identity-related documentation, and the Department of Social Development's processing of social assistance applications), interaction with the public is subject to greater standardisation and governed by a set of strict procedures. In other cases, such as with facilitation-type services including the design, implementation and monitoring of programmes, projects, and ad hoc initiatives, there is a variety of less 'routine' and more flexible forms of interacting with the public. These may include dealing with disasters, instituting and evolving various types of state support to promote economic development, assisting the poor, improving public health and so on.

There is no fundamental difference in the various ways the public service responds to its diverse mandate – be it at the dispensary level or at the facilitation level, the task is still based on service to the public. Although this is not the sole responsibility of less-developed countries, but most certainly more greatly felt in these, it ought to go beyond a minimalist technocratic understanding of the task to a kind of postmodern view of how formal bureaucratic institutions discourse with those whom they represent (Fox & Miller 1995). For example, is not the dispensing of identity documents more than just a routine paper-based transaction, when at the counter-level the purpose and utilities of this document ought to be explained and clarified to its recipient? The dispensing of social assistance also cannot be reduced to the efficiency of a paper-based service, when it could be said to also include constant monitoring (and related advisory services) of the conditions and extent of public need. For example, is there not a need to assist the public by explaining other instruments of support that they may not be aware of, as well as advising them on how they can otherwise improve their socio-economic conditions? If financial and technical planning were determined on the basis of these actions, it may produce greater credibility for development.

It should be reiterated that post-apartheid public servants are in reality expected to do more than deliver services efficiently and effectively. They are expected to continuously examine and respond to circumstances that constrain the utilisation of and access to services. This represents a fundamental break with the notion of accountability experienced in the past and could engender real credibility amongst the public about transformation. Finally, this issue is relevant to Adler's discussion of the sensitivity around debates about 'right-sizing' or rationalising the public service whilst taking into account 'service delivery requirements' (2000:19). The issue here is not that the negotiation between the government and public servant representatives simply agree to a quantifiably acceptable compromise (in terms of job retentions, retrenchments and redeployments), but is fundamentally about the extent and content of the normative discussion underpinning how service delivery requirements are defined, including what public service actors think the public requires versus what the public thinks, which will ultimately influence how service delivery is shaped and resourced.

Conclusion

Public service transformation has much to reflect and learn from apartheid-period public administration. This is precisely because the process of transformation by definition incorporates a pre-existing system requiring multi-dimensional analysis. Despite the gains made in restructuring the public service since, there is still a great deal of inherited complexity that requires greater reflection before reducing and narrowing the emphasis to practical efficiency and effectiveness. Perhaps in this vein we should not be too quick to criticise the performance of the current public service without more insight and serious reflection on the system that was inherited. However, we also need to be mindful of the public service having not just repudiated the structures of the old system, but whether it is succeeding in substantially rehabilitating its credibility amongst the public.

Notes

1 Speaking during the introduction of the Bantu Self-Government Bill in 1959, Minister de Wet Nel stated: 'It is our deep conviction that the personal and national ideals of every ethnic group can be best developed within its own national community ... This is the philosophical basis of the policy of apartheid.' See No Sizwe (Neville Alexander) (1979) *One Azania, one nation: The national question in South Africa.* London: Zed:12.

2 Refers to a state that provides most democratic features of political rule to whites, while ruling blacks dictatorially.

3 The NP government also presided over an increase in the number of central authority departments from 26 to between 38 and 41 by 1970 (the figure of 38 is quoted in Seegers 1994:40; the figure of 41 indicated by Roux is quoted in Posel 2000:43).

4 Pines referred to such organs of government as the Department of Community Development, established in 1964, and the Department of Plural Relations and Development. He pointed out that in establishing the former, the Prime Minister of South Africa stated as its responsibilities: providing for and assisting in the proper

settlement and housing of all population groups, the development of 'sound' communities, and the removal of poor conditions impeding proper community development. The latter department's more technical descriptions of its tasks included to support planning and co-ordination of community development in 'black states' and urban areas, the training of blacks and whites in the theory and practice of community development, guidance in the implementation of community development, project evaluation, co-ordination for development and research. As much as one can criticise the overriding state of unequal access to resources that characterised South African-homeland relations, and more precisely white-black relations, one cannot ignore or disregard the fact that development planning and implementation was carried out by apartheid-era administrations.

5   Reynolds estimated that 71 per cent of absolutely poor people in South Africa resided in homelands.

6   Morast pointed to research by the University of Stellenbosch's Bureau of Economic Research (BER) that showed 150 000 Africans entering the South African labour market annually, while only 89 000 jobs had been created in 'decentralised' or homeland areas between 1960 and 1973.

7   According to a 1999 Johns Hopkins University study (Swilling & Russel 2002:20) 53 per cent of the over 98 000 non-profit organisations in South Africa were classified as informal and community-based.

8   See Section 154 (1), The Constitution of the Republic of South Africa, 1996, and in particular the general principle of 'co-operative government'.

9   The Department of Provincial and Local Government recently commissioned a study reviewing the powers and functions shared between provincial and local government in South Africa (2003).

10 Referring to the reported manner in which the removal of Alexandra township residents was carried out in 2001 (*Mail & Guardian* 22.06.01).

References

Adler G (2000) The neglected role of labour relations in the South African public service. In G Adler (ed.) *Public service labour relations in a democratic South Africa.* Johannesburg: Witwatersrand University Press.

Bureau for Economic Research (1976) *Black development in South Africa: The economic development of the black peoples in the homelands of the Republic of South Africa.* Pretoria: Benbo.

Christensen T (2003) Organisation theory and public administration. In BG Peters & J Pierre (eds.) *Handbook of public administration.* London: Sage.

Cloete F (1995) Summary and conclusions: Towards a strategic framework for public sector transformation. In F Cloete & J Mokgoro (eds.) *Policies for public service transformation.* Cape Town: Juta.

DPSA (Department of Public Service and Administration, South Africa) (1999) *Report on service and skills audits.* Available at <http://www.dpsa.gov.za/DocumentsAlll/DocumenrsAll.html>. Accessed on 20.04.04.

DPSA (2000) *Policy statement on the establishment of a senior managment service in the public service.* Available at <http://www.dpsa.gov.za>. Accessed on 20.04.04.

Evans I (1997) *Bureaucracy and race: Native administration in South Africa.* Berkley: University of California Press.

Fox CJ & Miller HT (1995) *Postmodern public administration: Towards discourse.* Thousand Oaks: Sage.

Jeppe J & Van Baalen J (1995) Sustainable development. In F Cloete & J Mokgoro (eds.) *Policies for public service transformation.* Cape Town: Juta.

Johnson K (2002) State and civil society in contemporary South Africa: Redefining the rules of the game. Available at <http://www.rci.rutgers.edu/~waltonj/330_sa/Mbekichapter%20Krista.doc>. Accessed on 1.08.03

Kotzé H (2004) Responding to the growing socio-economic crisis? A review of civil society in South Africa, *Development Update* 4:1–32.

Latib S (1995) Accountability. In F Cloete & J Mokgoro (eds.) *Policies for public service transformation.* Cape Town: Juta.

Lewis SR (1990) *The economics of apartheid.* New York: Council on Foreign Relations Press.

Marger MN (1994) *Race and ethnic relations: American and global perspectives,* 3rd edition. Belmont, California: Wadsworth.

Moerdijk D (1981) *Anti-development: South Africa and its bantustans.* Paris: Unesco.

Mokgoro J (1996) Implementing affirmative action and culture change in the public service. In B Nzimande & M Sikhosana (eds.) *Affirmative action and transformation.* Durban: Indicator.

Mokgoro J (2000) *Transforming the public service, Policy Forum No. 9.* Johannesburg: Centre for Policy Studies.

Morast B (1975) The 'policy of separate development': An assessment of its function and effects, *Africanus Liaison,* Journal of the Department of Development Administration and Politics, University of South Africa, 5:20–25.

Müller JJ (1997) *Civil service systems in comparative perspective. South Africa: A country Study.* Available at <http://www.indiana.edu/~csrc/muller1.html>. Accessed on 5.01.04

Muller N (1984) The dynamics of rural poverty in the Transkei, *Africanus Liaison,* Journal of the Department of Development Administration and Politics, University of South Africa, 14:53–64.

Oldfield SE (2000) *State restructuring and urban transformation in South Africa: A negotiation of race, place and poverty.* PhD thesis, University of Minnesota.

PCAS (Presidency Policy Co-ordination and Advisory Services, South Africa) (2003) *Towards a ten year review synthesis report on implementation of government programmes: Discussion document.* Pretoria: Government Communications and Information Systems.

Pines NJ (1979) A political perspective on community development, *Africanus Liaison,* Journal of the Department of Development Administration and Politics, University of South Africa, 9:1–12.

PMG (Parliamentary Monitoring Group) (2003) *Public services and Administration Portfolio Committee 26 February 2003 State of the public service report 2002: Briefing by Public Service Commission.* Available at <http://www.img.org.za/docs/2003/ viewminute.php?id=2458>. Accessed on 28.01.04

Posel D (2000) Labour relations and the politics of patronage: A case study of the apartheid civil service. In G Adler (ed.) *Public service labour relations in a democratic South Africa.* Johannesburg: Witwatersrand University Press.

PSC (Public Service Commission, South Africa) (2002) *State of the public service report 2002*. Pretoria: PSC.

PSC (2004) *State of the public service report 2004*. Pretoria: PSC.

Russell B & Swilling M (2002) *The size and scope of the non-profit sector in South Africa*. Johannesburg & Durban: School of Public & Development Management and the Centre for Civil Society.

Seegers A (1994) The head of government and the executive. In R Schrire (ed.) *Malan to de Klerk: Leadership in the apartheid state*. London: Hurst.

Standish JB (1984) *State employment in South Africa*. MA thesis, University of Cape Town.

Van der Waldt G (2001) Establishing a management by projects approach for service delivery, *Journal of Public Administration* 36:296–311.

Part II: Society

Society: introduction

John Daniel, Roger Southall and Jessica Lutchman

Under the broad rubric of 'society', the previous *State of the Nation* volume dealt with civil society, families, curriculum reform in education, higher education, HIV/AIDS policymaking and the land question. All these important topics could valuably be aired again. However, with the exception of the particularly pressing issue of HIV/AIDS, the editors have postponed revisiting them in favour of topics which have similarly pressing claims for attention: an analysis of crime and policing, the defence force, the state of our schools and of women, Islam, and of the arts and our archives. Equally good cases could be made for the examination of, say, the state of science, research and development, of the delivery of health services (in general), and of social grants to the poor, of human rights, of the media, and of our small arms control. However, even if our selection of topics is inevitably somewhat arbitrary, few are going to quibble at the salience of all our present contributions.

There are few topics which loom so large in popular debate as crime. In his chapter on crime and policing, Ted Leggett offers an exemplary critique of many of the shibboleths of both policy and opinion which shape discussion on how South Africa can be rendered a safer society, noting that whilst it is demanded that the police reduce the level of crime, it is unclear how they are expected to do it.

Leggett argues that the confusion around the extent to which the South African Police Service (SAPS) can control crime has muddled two endeavours: the national efforts to reform the police and those to prevent crime. Whilst the reform of SAPS is about making the police more efficient and democratically accountable, the prevention of crime is about addressing the causes of crime via interventions which often lie well beyond police expertise. However, both politicians and the public are impatient, and have demanded instant successes from the police in reducing crime. The result has been that the SAPS has been forced into adopting some apartheid-era strategies of policing that run counter to the values of democracy.

Well-thought-out reform strategies for the police have been subordinated to the more immediate political demands that they be seen 'to be doing something'. Yet the apartheid heritage of the police is formidable. Not only did the SAPS have to incorporate the inefficient, corrupt and brutal forces of the former homelands, but it also had to absorb the various municipal auxiliary forces, such as the notorious *kitskonstabels* (instant police), which the former regime had created to deal with urban protest. In effect, the police force – already suffering from an acute lack of staff with basic skills – has become 'a dumping ground for unwanted men with guns'. They undertake a dangerous job, yet are badly underpaid according to a totally inappropriate pay structure which links pay to rank, and thus encourages rank inflation. Hence, although much has been done to reorient the police, much remains to be done.

Leggett concludes by arguing the case for a strategy of social law enforcement, which would see the police actually enforcing rules which presently exist but whose non-enforcement allows crime to flourish. This would entail a more active, regulatory role for municipalities, and would significantly reduce the space that is at present so readily made available for illegal and antisocial activities.

In contrast to the police, the South African National Defence Force (SANDF) has been substantially transformed. Len le Roux and Henri Boshoff discuss how, following the integration of the former homeland and liberation armies into the former apartheid force, policy came to envisage the need for an affordable and representative force which was primarily oriented towards the defence of the state (rather than, as under the previous regime, towards the crushing of dissent and the export of violent counter-revolution to neighbouring states). This transformation has entailed considerable downsizing, including the reduction of reserve and commando forces. Yet personnel costs remain extremely high relative to the resources that have been made available for equipment, much of which is obsolescent.

Contrary to critics of the arms deal, the authors argue that the equipment ordered by the government after 1994 is necessary for the SANDF to fulfil its obligations. However, they also propose that the reorientation of the defence force towards conventional operations has been at cost to the vision of a more flexible and mobile force capable of undertaking peace missions in Africa. Budgetary restrictions impinge particularly upon the army, which has not trained operationally at brigade level for several years; the air force has too few transport aircraft, fighters and helicopters to support ground troops; the navy lacks the capacity to defend South Africa's maritime environment; and the present conventional reserves would be of little help in any crisis or combat situation. Despite this, the SANDF is doing well to carry out peace-making operations in Burundi and the Democratic Republic of Congo. However, it remains severely overstretched, and difficult decisions will have to be made if the SANDF is to be enabled to undertake its functions effectively and to avoid gradual disintegration.

A similarly mixed picture is provided by Linda Chisholm of the state of South Africa's schools. There have been major accomplishments since 1994. The racial disparities that divided the school system under apartheid have been formally abolished, and educational budgets have been redesigned to achieve equitable outcomes; curricula have been revamped through Curriculum 2005 (which Chisholm addressed in last year's volume); and new forms of assessment, qualification and certification have been introduced. Yet the translation of aspirations into practical reality has been complex and contested. Numerous inequalities remain; many who need and deserve good school education are under-served; and overall the educational gap between urban and rural areas remains vast. The right of public schools to set fees (enabling them to provide extra resources and hire extra staff) redounds largely to the benefit of the more privileged; schools in poorer provinces and rural areas have a higher proportion of poorly qualified staff; and despite the formal deracialisation of education, the majority of schools remain uni- or mono-racial. Furthermore, there are numerous linguistic, class and cultural imbalances which work against genuine equality.

Much has changed, and many momentous initiatives have been undertaken to redress the inequalities and injustices of the past, but improvements remain unevenly spread, and the provinces that suffered greatest neglect in the apartheid period are still those showing the greatest difficulties in overcoming the legacy of apartheid.

In last year's volume, Mandisa Mbali concluded that the development of a national HIV/AIDS policy had been hampered by denial in the upper reaches of the African National Congress (ANC) and foot-dragging in implementation. A year later, Tim Quinlan and Samantha Willan have arrived at a similar conclusion. They recognise that the ANC has now announced the 'roll-out' of anti-retroviral drugs. Yet they note that this was in a context of an election campaign during which promises had to be made but that ambiguities and ambivalences on HIV/AIDS policy remain in statements made by both President Mbeki and the Minister of Health. It is certainly true that considerably increased funding is now being provided to deal with HIV/AIDS from the national Budget, yet the authors worry that this is happening at the cost of other components of national healthcare. It is also true that the elements of an integrated policy to combat HIV/AIDS are in place, but the President and the Minister of Health either imply that this is not yet the case, or argue about the difficulties of its implementation. Meanwhile, policy has to confront the inertia of bureaucracy, and worse, emerging tension between the Departments of Health and Social Development. The authors conclude that there is still a failure of leadership from the top, and considerable reasons for remaining sceptical that the government will make adequate progress towards containing the pandemic.

An absence of political will is similarly identified by Lynn Maree as underlying a failure by government adequately to implement transformation of the arts. Under apartheid, only white artists were subsidised by the state and only western artistic activity seen to be of value. Yet artists of all backgrounds played a prominent role in the struggle against apartheid, and all saw the arrival of democracy as heralding a period of transformation in which previously marginalised and suppressed art forms would be officially encouraged, resource allocation would be equalised, and the arts would flourish.

Ten years on, white privilege in the arts has correctly been abandoned, and a general shift accomplished towards more popular, African and community-based activities. A new Department of Arts, Culture, Science and Technology (DACST) was created in 1994 with a remit to propose new arts and culture policies for South Africa; an exciting White Paper was produced in 1996; a new National Arts Council was appointed in 1997; and in 2002, a Department of Arts and Culture (DAC) was carved out of DACST, and went on to outline a major strategic programme for the support, sustainability and promotion of the arts. However, policy aspirations remain largely unrealised through failures of implementation. Many put this down to a low status accorded to arts and culture by government, and most certainly by certain provincial governments. Moreover, whilst funding is now more evenly spread, artists remain financially insecure, without a career path, and training of new talent has been hampered by official inertia.

Of course, this tale of official woe is accompanied by many exciting initiatives and South Africa's creative output remains remarkable. However, more commitment by government is badly needed if the arts are going to be fully enabled to contribute to the defining and repairing of the nation. It is hence with some anticipation that Maree notes that President Mbeki acknowledged an official neglect of the arts in his first 'State of the Nation' speech in early 2004. It may also be added that the appointment to the new, post-election Cabinet of Dr Pallo Jordan as Minister of Arts has been widely greeted with enthusiasm.

Many people will think a focus upon South Africa's archives is obscure, but as Seán Morrow and Luvuyo Wotshela point out, a society without archives is like a person without memory. The peculiar importance of the topic is that the archives in far too many countries in Africa are in a state of appalling neglect or disrepair, and much valuable information about African societies is being lost forever, and sometimes is being actively destroyed. Morrow and Wotshela observe that South Africa is fortunate in having a relatively well-functioning national archives. However, the situation at provincial and local government level is far less satisfactory, with particular problems arising in those provinces which have absorbed the former homelands. Their particular case study is of the Eastern Cape, where the archives of the former Transkei and Ciskei are presently housed in wholly unsuitable structures, and have been rendered largely inaccessible to researchers. The story is a familiar one of limited resources, wasteful spending, inadequate skills and low official commitment. Archives, the authors conclude, are always problematic. They are always incomplete, and they often reflect the stories of the powerful. Yet they are simultaneously vital for unravelling past and present oppressions, and play an intrinsic role in any society's struggle for freedom of information.

Two papers in this section deal with the state of the Muslim community and women respectively. The first of these, by Goolam Vahed and Shamil Jeppie, provides a fascinating review of the complexity of Islamic communities. Muslims, who constitute just 1.5 per cent of the population, are customarily viewed as a monolith, yet the authors demonstrate with lively authority how they constitute 'multiple communities'. Indians and Malays, based largely in

KwaZulu-Natal and the Western Cape respectively, still make up the majority of South Africa's Muslims, yet Africans constitute the fastest growing, and poorest, segment – their numbers swelled by refugees and migrants from Africa rather than by local converts. This development is not without its tensions, with many African Muslims feeling marginalised by both more established Muslim communities and other Africans, who often query their commitment to an 'Indian' religion. Yet Muslim identity is more widely contested than that. In the Western Cape, for instance, it has revolved variously around notions of being 'Malay', 'coloured', 'Cape Muslim' or 'black', and Muslim cultural politics in the 1990s were to become even more compli-cated by their involvement with Pagad (People Against Gangsterism and Drugs), which from its hesitant birth on the streets of the Cape Flats was to evolve into a powerful entity that seriously challenged the values of the fledgling non-racial democracy.

Meanwhile, partly in response to global challenges to Muslim communities posed by Palestine and the American-led 'war on terror', contradictory impulses towards a revival of piety – often versed in conservative forms – vie with more modernist trends, notably towards the attainment of equality for women. Whilst both the longer history of the liberation struggle and these latest global assaults work to strengthen the political identification of Muslims with the ANC, the authors stress that the Islamic resurgence presently taking place is less one of political emancipation than of preserving and deepening religio-cultural identity in a highly diverse society.

The issue of equality for women is dealt with in-depth by Shireen Hassim, who notes that South Africa's transition to democracy is often seen as having encapsulated a 'virtuous political circle' in which women's participation in politics is rewarded with shifts in the allocation of public resources to address women's needs.

South Africa has been so favourably viewed because of the commitment in the Constitution to gender equality, the state's pursuit of gender equitable poli-cies, and the ANC's adoption of a quota (30 per cent) of women to be attained amongst its representatives in elected bodies. These are all vital, yet limited, indicators of a 'virtuous political circle', an idea which has three 'drivers' – participation, representation and equality. After comparing formal with effec-tive participation, processes of representation versus effective representation (with quotas being viewed as politically affordable in a party-list, dominant party system), and formal versus substantive equality, Hassim reviews the real gains which have been delivered to women in the form of several pieces of far-reaching legislation.

The passage of these laws was in considerable measure due to the pressure of women within Parliament, yet equally women Members of Parliament (MPs) also ran up against party machines for which gender equality was not a high priority. Many gains were therefore only registered with the addition of external pressure upon Parliament by women's advocacy groups. The struggle is a continuing one, and Hassim highlights the widely felt concern that the pre-election passage of the Communal Land Rights Act favours the interests of traditional leaders (whose support the ANC has been keen to solicit) over the rights of rural women. The latter have historically always been poorly organised, and their plight merely confirms for Hassim that the representation of women is most effective when accompanied by strong forms of political participation and a clear vision of what kinds of gender equality are desirable.

6 The state of crime and policing

Ted Leggett

This chapter discusses two distinct issues generally conflated in the minds of both the public and policymakers: crime and policing. This confusion is understandable. The police are the largest and most visible government body assigned to deal with crime, and we expect them to protect us from it. If anyone is responsible for reducing our risk of becoming a victim of crime, it seems logical that it should be the police.

But studies that look at what the police actually do with their time illustrate that most of their activity has little to do with crime, much less the ambitious project of preventing crime before it happens (Criminal Justice Commission 1996; Dadds & Scheide 2000; Leggett 2002). Rather, they spend most of their time on the challenging task of maintaining social order. The police deal with our traffic problems, they guard our public buildings and events, they sort out our civil disputes, and they arrive whenever we have a crisis that needs immediate state intervention.

When this crisis does involve a crime, much of what they do is reactive and administrative – they help us sort out the consequences, rather than the causes, of crime. They minimise the harm caused by a criminal incident by authoritatively taking control of the situation, assuring that the human rights of all concerned are protected, and proceeding according to the rule of law. As a result, one of their most important functions is the prevention of mob justice and vigilantism. The police take ownership of the crime and treat it as an offence against society, rather than a personal matter to be resolved through feuds of vengeance. While few would want to live in a society without the police, they are generally kept so busy dealing with our emergencies that they have little time to work on projects aimed at reducing risk.

Indeed, the literature supports the counter-intuitive position that most normal police activity, such as patrolling the streets and responding to calls for assistance, has little impact on the level of crime at all (Bayley 1994). Surprisingly, research has shown that the intensity of police patrols in an area is not correlated with crime reduction (Kelling, Pate, Dieckman & Brown 1974). This is difficult for most people to grasp at first, since we generally think of the police as though they are units of anti-crime serum being pumped into the body of society – the more cops, the less crime. But it would seem that their work in providing a visible deterrent and in incapacitating individual criminals does not have nearly as great an impact on crime levels as most people think.[1] In performing their core functions, they act more like aspirin than antibiotics, dealing with the symptoms, rather than the causes, of crime.

Of course, it is possible for the police to contribute to efforts to address the core causes of crime, but this is generally not what they are trained to do. The police are trained in applying the law, handling firearms, taking statements, gathering physical evidence, and defusing tense situations – not in social engineering. They may lack the aptitude or even the interest to engage in the types of activities that address underlying social conditions. And before they can aspire to the additional task of changing the world in which they work, they first need to be competent to perform the basic reactive functions of the job.

Unfortunately, crime prevention is the first of the duties assigned to the South African Police Service (SAPS) in the national Constitution. We continue to hold the police accountable for crime, as manifest in the official crime statistics: when the number of crimes recorded by the police goes up, we accuse them of failing to do their jobs, regardless of how well they deal with the crimes we report or the other services they provide. In essence, we have demanded that the police reduce the crime figures quickly and dramatically, without being terribly clear on how we expect them to do this, and without reducing the workload of other duties we expect them to perform.

This confusion around the extent to which the SAPS can control the number of crimes reported has muddled two related but separate endeavours: the national efforts to reform the police on the one hand, and to prevent crime on the other. Police reform is about making the SAPS more effective, efficient, and equitable as a democratic law-enforcement body; it is about strengthening the police as an organisation for performing its core reactive function. Crime prevention is about addressing the causes of crime via a wide range of interventions, many of which lie outside the expertise of the police.

The distinction between these two processes has been blurred in the way crime prevention has been discussed in South Africa. The 1998 *White Paper on safety and security* defines crime prevention as:

> all activities which reduce, deter, or prevent the occurrence of specific crimes, firstly, by altering the environment in which they occur, secondly by changing the conditions that are thought to cause them, and thirdly by providing a strong deterrent in the form of an effective Justice System.

As is explained in the document, this definition encompasses two distinct types of crime prevention: crime prevention through effective criminal justice, and social crime prevention. The former embraces not only police work but also the rehabilitation of criminals and the empowerment of victims. But it allows the perpetuation of the myth that routine policing can reduce crime levels, and it allows resources that could be used to address social conditions to be diverted to what has been called 'proactive' law enforcement. This is essentially an oxymoron, because in order for the law to be enforced, a crime must be committed. The proactive work of the SAPS is thus largely about treating those unfortunate enough to live in high-crime areas as though they were criminals, an abuse of which the South African public has been amazingly tolerant. But this practice is inimical to the democratic values the state is trying to infuse in the police; it is contrary to the goals of police reform.

Thus, as a result of the pressure to produce lower crime statistics, it is arguable that neither of the broad objectives of the state in this area – the reform of the police or the prevention of crime – has been satisfactorily addressed. In our efforts to compel the police to correct situations they have little ability to control, we may have neglected to ensure their competence to provide other equally important services that they should be delivering. And we may have forced them into forms of policing that run counter to the values of democracy.

This chapter argues that, at present, it is likely that the SAPS lacks the capacity to engage in crime prevention of the type described in the White Paper, due to a lack of police reform. Each station does have a uniformed unit called 'crime prevention', but the kinds of activities it tends to engage in – roadblocks, building searches, visible patrols – are precisely the kinds of routine police activities which have been found to be ineffective in addressing the causes of crime. The present operational strategy of the police – the National Crime Combating Strategy (NCCS) – conducts these activities with furious intensity and military back-up in small geographic areas, harkening back to the authoritarian police practices of the apartheid era.

In 2004, the next phase of the NCCS was entered, in which the technique of 'sector policing' is being used to 'normalise' crime levels. This approach does hold the potential to promote social crime prevention, but it is doubtful that the SAPS as presently comprised has the capacity to implement this challenging approach to police work nationally. To engage in this complex approach to policing, progress must be first made in reforming the SAPS.

This chapter attempts to briefly summarise the changes in crime and the state's response to it since 1994. Clearly, this is an ambitious exercise, and there are, of necessity, many gross omissions. In particular, emphasis is placed on the work of the police rather than on the work of justice and corrections officials, or social development departments. In short, this summary replicates the error bemoaned at the opening of this chapter – the conflation of crime and the police. The intent is simply to give, in a short space, an overview of where we have come from and some speculation about where we might be going in these two interrelated fields. In conclusion, it suggests an alternative to the crime prevention practised by the SAPS and the oversimplified conceptions of social crime prevention that prevail in South Africa, a set of interventions I have dubbed 'social law enforcement'.

Fear of crime

President Mbeki is generally tidy in his 'State of the Nation' speeches, assigning a discrete section of his talk to discussion of crime and justice issues. Between 2001 and 2003, he assigned about the same share of words to the topic, six to nine per cent of the total word count, not far off the share demanded by the criminal justice system from the national Budget. In 2004, he departed from his usual form in his celebration of ten years of democracy. But there can be no doubt that, being election year, the topic was close to his mind, and it was paramount in the campaigns of the opposition parties.

In the Social Attitudes Survey undertaken biannually by the Human Sciences Research Council (HSRC), South Africans have consistently identified two issues that they feel the government needs to pay more attention to: job creation and crime prevention (wa Kivilu 2002). Surveys undertaken by the Institute for Security Studies (ISS) have unpacked this issue further by asking what respondents feel the state needs to do to reduce crime. In one large survey of court sites, most respondents (82 per cent) felt that job creation is the key to eradicating crime (ISS 2002). Thus, the prevention of crime may also be one of the reasons why South Africans are so concerned about creating jobs.

There is reason for concern. South Africa does have a remarkable crime problem. A country of some 44 million, it experiences at least 22 000 murders a year, which is about 25 per cent more than the United States, a violent country with over six and a half times the population. While the number of South Africans murdered each year is much less today than it was at the time of the democratic transition, it is still far more than could be considered 'normal' by international standards.

Why this massive body count? A laundry list of reasons has been generated, all of which have some validity, and none of which can be discussed comprehensively here. South Africa has an extremely violent past, due to the nature of the political struggle, and these cycles of violence still reverberate today. Due to this history, violence has become somewhat normalised in some segments of South African society, and this culture of violence as a means of resolving disputes is highly resilient and contagious. South Africa, like the rest of the continent, has a very youthful population, and internationally, young males are more likely to be involved in crime and violence – simply put, we have a disproportionately large potential offender pool. South Africa has one of the highest levels of income inequality in the world, and one of the most robust quantifiable correlates of homicide levels is income inequality, the theory being that violent acquisitive crime and 'frustration violence' are more closely tied to a sense of unjust distribution of wealth than with absolute deprivation. High levels of alcohol abuse in some communities seem to be tied to assaults that inadvertently become murders, as does the availability of firearms. The list goes on, with considerable variation in relevance depending on the community or population segment being observed.

Statistics on other crime types are less reliable than the murder figures, as will be discussed later. Despite their dubious validity, these figures have been emphasised by both the police and the public, to the point that the present national policing strategy is explicitly focused on reducing crime statistics. This is not entirely illogical: these figures are arguably as responsible for the fear of crime experienced by the public as is the real crime situation. The impression these figures generate is one of chaos and lawlessness, a national image that is blamed for deterring foreign direct investment, domestic investment, and tourism, as well as fuelling the emigration of skilled workers (the so-called 'brain drain'). For those who believe the solution to crime is social development through economic growth, a vicious cycle is created: crime retards growth; lack of growth feeds crime. Or, perhaps more accurately, crime statistics sap public confidence and lack of confidence impacts on our bottom-line ability to do anything about the problem. Reversing this momentum is as much about addressing public perceptions as it is about crime fighting.

Changes in crime since 1994

The crime statistics are key to understanding the national obsession with crime. These figures are presented as though they give a straightforward and objective assessment of the level of disorder in the society; in fact, as is the case in all countries, they are deeply flawed and subject to manipulation. Since the police have been tasked with preventing crime, the crime statistics have become their primary performance indicator. As will be explained later in this chapter, this is a serious mistake, because it has led the police to adopt strategies motivated by the desire to reduce crime statistics, rather than focusing on vital internal reform.

A spike in the crime figures was seen in 1994, due to the inclusion of the ten bantustans in the crime counts. These areas did not keep accurate counts of crime figures, so comparing pre- and post-election crime statistics is nearly impossible. But looking at trends in crime rates over time, it is clear that the rates for most of the country had been increasing since at least the mid-1980s (Schönteich & Louw 2001). Those who try to associate the rising crime figures with policy under democracy, black leadership, or excessive emphasis on human rights, must explain this trend. These figures also seem to indicate that it is in the area of violent crime, rather than property crime, that South Africa is most remarkable.

When asked how crime has changed since 1994, a slight majority of South Africans surveyed in the most recent national victimisation survey (53 per cent) say they feel it has increased (Burton, Leggett, Louw & Mistry 2004). According to the official statistics, however, the crime in several categories is down since 1994, including a strong decrease in recorded murders. Remarkably, the crime figures that show the largest decreases are also the most reliable.

Official crime statistics everywhere in the world need to be treated with great caution. In most cases, in order for a crime to be recorded by the police, a member of the public must make the effort to report it, and the police must consider the report reliable enough to record it. This means official crime statistics tend to contrast dramatically with the experiences of the public, as revealed, for example, in victimisation surveys. The level of under-reporting varies depending on crime type, with people more likely to report crimes such as murder (where a corpse must be accounted for) and certain types of theft of property, especially where that property is either insured or where there are good prospects for recovery. People are far less likely to report crimes of an extremely traumatic and interpersonal nature (such as rape and domestic violence) and crimes where the hopes of a positive outcome are outweighed by the effort involved in reporting (such as robbery or minor thefts). Likelihood of reporting also depends on who you are: whether you have the time, resources, and inclination to engage in a civic duty where the chances of positive returns may be small.

The more accessible the police are, and the better their reputation for positive outcomes and sensitive treatment of victims, the more likely people are to report crime. This is the reason why some of the most developed countries in the world (including Norway, Denmark, Canada, and the United Kingdom) have the world's highest rates of overall recorded crime (Interpol 1999). Internationally, a minority of survey respondents in developing countries around the world who say they were victims of crime say they reported the incident to the police (Zvekic 1995). In South Africa, two national victim surveys have indicated that less than half of all thefts, assaults, and robberies are reported (Burton et al. 2004; Stats SA 1998). If the government is success-ful in further reforming the police, this situation should improve. This would be bad news for those who argue that police performance has improved, based on declining crime statistics, because increased reporting would create the appearance that crime levels are going up.

Figure 6.1 *Percentage change in crime rates between 1994–95 and 2002–03*

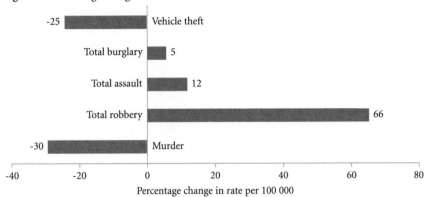

Keeping these caveats in mind, a review of the official crime figures suggests that while the numbers are up in many categories, much of serious crime may have decreased since 1994. Looking specifically at the crimes most likely to be reported (such as murder and vehicular theft), strong declines can be seen. Increases are seen in crime categories where under-reporting is traditionally high, such as robbery and assault (Figure 6.1). Indeed, looking at victim survey data, the most under-reported crime listed above is robbery (78 per cent unreported according to the 2003 victim survey), which shows the largest increase in the official figures, followed by assault (62 per cent), burglary (44 per cent) vehicular theft (3 per cent) and murder (less than 1 per cent). In fact, the more under-reported the crime, according to the victim surveys, the greater the increase in the official crime statistics after 1994.

This phenomenon should have been expected. Prior to 1994, it is likely the majority of the population would have been reluctant to report crime to the police, since the security forces were associated with repression rather than service. With all the effort spent on making the police more accessible under democracy, an increase in the rate of reporting was inevitable. An increase in reporting is indistinguishable from an increase in real incidence as far as the crime statistics are concerned: both show up as more recorded crimes to count.

Perhaps the best demonstration of the effects of changes in the reporting rate is the increase in attempted murders reported during the same period that murder itself has decreased. Attempted murder is oftentimes indistinguishable from other forms of serious assault on its face: the differentiation only comes with a finding of intent by a law enforcement official. While most murders are recorded by the police, many attempted murders, like other forms of assault, are not. Thus, attempted murder is likely to have been more under-reported in the past than it is today. The massive increase in attempted murders – up 34 per cent since 1994–95 – may be a reporting phenomenon. The alternative is to believe that South Africans have become less effective killers, since the murder 'success rate' (the ratio of completed murders to all attempts) has declined from 49 per cent in 1994–95 to 38 per cent in 2002–03. This is especially unlikely given that the share of murders committed by firearm has gone up, which indicates that South Africans are using more lethal weapons to kill one another, and so should be successful more of the time.

Similarly, it is difficult to explain why vehicular theft is down so strongly, while more property crime of other sorts is being reported. While it could be argued that fewer cars are stolen by stealth due to improvements in vehicle security, the ratio of vehicles taken by force (that is, hijacked) to those taken by stealth (simply stolen) has remained constant over time: about 19 per cent. Other trends support the idea that the increase in property crimes is a reporting phenomenon. For example, commercial burglaries have remained fairly steady since 1994, while residential burglaries have skyrocketed. This may be due to the fact that commercial premises are generally insured, so reporting rates have always been high. But as more South Africans have access to household insurance, the reporting rates are bound to increase. Sceptics of this theory would be compelled to explain why homes, rather than businesses, have suddenly become more attractive to the country's burglars.

So is crime in South Africa increasing or decreasing? It is difficult to say for certain.[2] It is likely that the location of crime shifted during the political transition, and it shifted to areas where both reporting and access to the media are likely to be much higher: that is to say, white areas. White people may indeed be experiencing more crime than they did in the days when the poor and marginal were kept boxed in reserves, and they reflect this experience back to the broader public through the media. The decline in the murder figures suggests that increases in other violent crimes, such as attempted murders and serious assaults, may be a product of increased reporting due to improved accessibility and relations with the police across communities, as well as increased consciousness of the wrongfulness of crimes like domestic violence.

Regardless of whether the real crime situation is getting better or worse, it is difficult to ascribe this trend to police action or lack thereof. The real crime trends are most likely part of broader social trends, and are thus mostly beyond the control of the state. While the purpose of the state is to try to generate a healthy society, the first order of business must be ensuring that it functions effectively and efficiently as an organisation. Expecting positive social outcomes to emerge from a poorly functioning organisation is simply illogical, and placing political pressure on this organisation to achieve the impossible is an invitation to deception.

So is the SAPS, as an organisation, up to the task of mending the tattered social fabric? A quick look at the challenges faced by the organisation at its inception leaves one wondering how it functions at all. The SAPS is a key part of the miracle of South Africa's transition, but it may be that we are paying for this miracle on the instalment plan.

The state response

The transformation of the state's response to crime after the democratic elections has been remarkable. In a short space of time, several progressive policy documents and numerous innovative pieces of legislation have been passed.[3] In many respects, South Africa is a world leader in criminal justice policy, as one of the few industrialised nations that has recently had an excuse for comprehensively revamping the system. Unfortunately, problems with implementation and concessions made, and the public pressure for instant impact, have left the state with rather mixed results in terms of delivery.

The move to democracy in the early 1990s brought two distinct but related issues to the fore with regard to safety and security:
- the reform of the SAPS from an authoritarian to a democratic police force; and
- the belief that, as is the case in many countries in political transition, crime was on the rise.

In order to enhance the reform of the police service, several measures were taken to instil civilian oversight of the police, including: the promotion of community police forums, which, among other things, allowed the public to voice complaints; the creation of a civilian Independent Complaints

Directorate (ICD) to investigate police misconduct; and the creation of a civilian Secretariat for Safety and Security. While these changes were in line with international best practice, it is likely they were also fuelled by an understandable lack of trust by the new politicians for their former oppressors.

None of these measures has managed to achieve its full potential. The fate of the community policing forums is discussed further later on. The founding of the ICD was of great symbolic value, but while it has produced some remarkable work, it has failed to live up to its initial promise. This is chiefly due to underfunding – the ICD is kept quite busy simply investigating deaths in custody, and many other misconduct issues, including claims of brutality and corruption, cannot be fully pursued due to lack of resources. This means that the ICD is often focused on resolving individual cases, particularly deaths, and cannot deal with the larger problems.

But of all these innovations, the most important was the Secretariat, reporting directly to the Minister, on a par with the National Police Commissioner. The intent, at least in the eyes of civilians, was that the Secretariat would set policy, while the SAPS would deal with the details of operationalising it (Rauch 2000). The focus of much of the policy work of the Secretariat was on crime prevention.

This arrangement arguably led to the creation of two separate policymaking streams, one that dealt primarily with crime prevention (a topic best approached interdepartmentally) and one that dealt with the operational strategies of the police. The Secretariat produced the National Crime Prevention Strategy (NCPS) of 1996 and the *White Paper on safety and security* of 1998, while the SAPS produced the Community Safety Plan of 1995, and the National Crime Combating Strategy of 2000. The relationship between these two sets of policies is unclear, and, in the end, the police-led strategies have won out.

The turning point for crime prevention was the 1999 elections. South Africa's first democratic administration, under Nelson Mandela, had Sidney Mufamadi as Minister of Safety and Security and George Fivas as National Police Commissioner. This was a period of reform, and of coping with the costs of transition. The progress made in this regard was remarkable, although the project of reforming the police was incomplete at the time of the next round of national elections.

But a number of incidents changed the orientation of the government toward democratic policing and shifted the emphasis from reform to crime combating. According to Shaw (2002), the bomb attacks in the Western Cape between 1998 and 2001 caused the former 'terrorists' in power to revisit the tactics used against them in the apartheid past, including considering a return to detention without trial and banning of organisations. Attacks on farms and smallholdings during the same period also created fears of political instability and a demand for hard line intervention. These issues, teamed with popular perceptions about out-of-control crime rates, compelled South Africa's second President – Thabo Mbeki – to appoint a 'get tough' team in 1999: Minister Steve Tshwete and National Commissioner Jackie Selebi. Both in their rhetoric and in the kind of policing they promoted, these two adopted an approach to law enforcement that had more in common with the practices of the apartheid era than the progressive talk of the early democracy. After the untimely death of Tshwete, Charles Nqakula was appointed to replace him, and there has been little evidence of a shift in orientation since that time. Indeed, the post-Tshwete era seems to have been dominated by a desire to de-emphasise the crime issue in preparation for the 2004 elections, and both the Minister and the National Commissioner cut back on the sabre rattling.

While the government continues to pay homage to the crime prevention paradigm and the NCPS, in practice social crime prevention was dramatically de-prioritised after 1999. One possible pivotal misstep was the recommendation in the *White Paper on safety and security* of 1998 that the Secretary for Safety and Security be made the financial reporting officer for the SAPS, a move that, if implemented, would mean placing the purse strings in the hands of civilians. This overstep may be partly responsible for the dramatic downscaling of social crime prevention and civilian oversight in the new administration. The position of Secretary for Safety and Security was downgraded to the level of Deputy Director General, although the office still appears on a par with the National Commissioner on the organisational charts. And, ironically, while the pre-1999 Secretary was allowed to be the accounting officer for the Secretariat, the National Commissioner has now assumed this responsibility.

Today crime prevention for the police has largely meant reverting to what they know best: large-scale militaristic policing. This reversion has implications for both the reform of the police and the prevention of crime.

Police reform

The reform of the South African Police (SAP) began long before the democratic elections. The unbanning of the African National Congress (ANC) by President de Klerk in February 1990, and the subsequent release of Nelson Mandela, began preparations for a future democratic government in many government circles, including the SAP. For some members of the SAP, this meant a hasty retirement; for those who remained, it meant the SAP Strategic Plan of 1991, which centred around the concept of 'community-supported policing'. According to Rauch (1993), the drive for reform was largely defensive, instigated as a measure to insulate the force from radical restructuring under new leadership.

The newly-elected government faced a daunting challenge in 1994. It inherited a criminal justice system that had not been dedicated to justice for many decades. The new rulers of the country had until recently been considered criminals, persecuted by the very people they now commanded, whose loyalty was necessarily suspect. Taking what had been, essentially, an army of occupation and turning it into a democratic police service, was no mean feat.

Clearly, decommissioning the entire force and starting from scratch was not an option. For starters, it was prevented by the Convention for a Democratic South Africa agreements, which ensured a place for the old civil service in the new democracy. But on a more practical level, policing is a skill largely learned by experience, and national training facilities could only produce a few thousand new recruits a year. Retrenchment packages were offered to those who felt they could not serve under the new administration or who saw greener pastures elsewhere, like in the private security industry. But the core of staff was retained, in the hopes that they would adapt to the massive paradigm shift. In addition, the police forces of the ten former homelands were amalgamated, and masses of semi-trained law enforcement adjuncts were integrated into the new SAPS. These transfers were especially problematic, for reasons that are explained next.

Amalgamation

The base force into which all other units were amalgamated was far from perfect, but there were some things the SAP did well. As members of the democratic resistance can testify, the SAP was a formidable opponent. Years of political policing had made it adept at controlling crowds and securing public spaces, skills that the SAPS continues to use to the benefit of the public today, albeit with substantial modification of technique. There was also significant expertise in combating criminal organisations. Technical skills, such as handling dogs and forensic testing, are very usable in the democratic context, with some adaptation. The skills of SAP detectives who opted to stay with the service can be applied, to some extent, to present efforts against organised crime. Of course, information-gathering techniques such as torture are no longer permissible, so a learning curve should have been anticipated as detectives beefed up their democratic investigation skills. Much brainpower was lost to the private sector during the transition, but much was also retained. There is little evidence to suggest that old SAP members remaining with the service have acted to undermine organisational performance.

Under the National States Constitution Act of 1971, the homelands were allowed to establish their own police forces. The core staff of these units was drawn largely from SAP members of appropriate ethnicity, as well as seconded white members. While these individuals, and the forces they built, received basic training from the SAP, their extremely rapid promotion and lack of in-service training (including management training) meant that many were not completely competent to hold the positions they filled. And while the policies and procedures were modelled closely on those of the SAP, policing in the homelands was often characterised by corruption, nepotism, and political interference (Marais 1992). At the time of amalgamation in 1995, the combined homelands forces comprised just over 20 per cent of SAPS force strength.

Outside the homelands, as the political struggle became more violent in the 1980s, the SAP was facing a losing battle. The community councils created to control the black townships were failing, and many councillors were driven from their homes or killed by angry mobs. In a diabolically brilliant attempt to strengthen these structures and generate more uniforms on the streets, two new types of law enforcement personnel were created: the *kitskonstabels* and the municipal police.

The *kitskonstabels* were instant constables, trained in six weeks, granted full police powers (but not full police membership), and cut loose on the townships. While some of these people were simply poor job seekers, a few even having finished school, many were recruited from those who had reacted against the excesses of overzealous comrades – conservative vigilantes, and other local strongmen. Many were illiterate, so their training and examinations were conducted orally. The abuse they heaped on communities is well documented, as the SAP was reluctant to take legal action against them, and they were notorious for drunkenness, corruption, and a brutality beyond even that of the white security forces (CIIR 1988).

While their training and education standards were later raised, they were never intended to become full police members. They were integrated just before the national elections, and were required to do additional training. Those who were designated 'untrainable' were given the option of undergoing adult basic education at least as late as 1996. The exact number of *kitskonstabels* integrated is difficult to determine, but Cawthra (1993) estimates that they constituted 10 per cent of SAP strength. The municipal police were a slight variant, being slightly better trained and placed directly at the command of the puppet black local authorities. They were fully incorporated into the SAP in 1989, at which time they numbered 10 000 members, or about 12 per cent of the entire force.

While this incorporation went a long way toward improving the overall ethnic representivity of the SAPS, it also impacted on the mean skills level of the police, including basic skills such as functional literacy and the ability to drive a car. Subsequent waves of integration, including the demands for inclusion of members of the notorious self-defence units and self-protection units,[4] exacerbated this effect. The new politicians brought with them their personal bodyguards, who were never trained as police, yet were made full SAPS members. Later, staff hired by the SAPS as security guards managed to be converted into police members through union pressure, despite the fact that they had not been hired or trained with this in mind. And even today, continued talks about the transfer of surplus staff from the military to the SAPS threaten to maintain the status of the service as a dumping ground for unwanted men with guns.

The impact of these troops has grown as they have followed the natural trail of promotion. Up to the rank of inspector, the highest non-commissioned and the senior field supervisory rank, promotion over time is somewhat obligatory, as it is linked to pay increases. At the beginning of 2003, the SAPS had five times as many inspectors as it had constables. This 'rank inflation' has seriously undermined field accountability, because no one on the streets is senior to anyone else (Leggett 2002).

Thus, while incorporating the various armed forces into the SAPS may have been a political and practical necessity, it left the service with a tremendous skills deficit and with personnel whose interest in democratic police work may have been limited. This would seem to place the project of police reform, and all the retraining and monitoring that goes with such a project, at the top of the agenda. Before the amalgamated SAPS could be expected to engage in complex activities like working with communities to solve crime problems, some basic housekeeping was in order. While efforts were made in this regard, the political sensitivities and pressures for delivery of crime reduction seem to have forced the SAPS to make do with the skills and talents their personnel possess. And in many cases, these skills are pretty basic, similar to those of the common infantry. This has forced a reversion to the old tactics – those of pre-democratic policing.

Democratisation

Democratisation of the police is the process of turning an army of occupation into a modern public service. It is about making the police subject to the public, instead of the other way around. In addition to a range of cosmetic measures taken to demilitarise the police (change of ranks, uniforms, vehicle colours and so on), the policy thrust of the democratisation process was based on the notions of community-oriented policing (COP). COP is a broad conceptual framework assigned to a wide range of practices internationally. It emerged initially in the United States, in response to the increasingly reactive nature of police work, with the advent of radio-dispatched vehicles and the consequent decline of foot patrols. The central idea is that the police should not be present only during times of crisis, but that they should be visible and in contact with community members on a daily basis. The informal links this presence creates between the police and the public are thought to aid in both the prevention and detection of crime, as well as improving the community's sense of safety.

In the South African context, this idea had appeal for several reasons. It was hoped that enhanced community contact would both sensitise the police to the concerns of the public they were serving, and enhance the confidence of the community in the humanity of the police. By better understanding the public, it was hoped that the police would come up with interventions that could address the core causes of crime. By winning the confidence and co-operation of the public, it was hoped that crime reporting and witness participation would be improved. In short, COP was intended to both reform the police and to make them more effective at preventing crime.

The primary concrete manifestation of this policy, however, was the constitutionally mandated creation of community police forums (CPFs) in every station area in the country. According to the 1993 Interim Constitution, the CPFs were intended to provide accountability, monitoring, and evaluation of the police. Later, other ideas emerged about their utility,[5] and the policy began to suffer from a lack of clear focus, with considerable variation in emphasis between areas.

The success of the CPFs has not been even, with the best examples emerging in well-resourced areas, where people have the time and resources to empower the police, and where there is more commonality in community interests. In poorer, more conflicted areas, these bodies have been accused of becoming politicised or even tools of criminal syndicates (Mbhele 1998). On the whole, public knowledge of, and participation in, the CPFs has not been good, with several studies showing that only a minority of South Africans polled know what a CPF is (Pelser, Schnetler & Louw 2002).

Setting aside the relative success of the CPFs, what is more problematic is the way that COP was compartmentalised into these bodies and the officers assigned to head them. While the concept of COP is vague and needs concrete manifestation in order to have any meaning, it surely encompasses more than can be accomplished in a monthly meeting between a police representative or two and a self-appointed body of community members. Ideally, the philosophy of COP should inform everything police members at station level do, from their patrol patterns to their performance indicators. In the SAPS, COP is often seen as the responsibility of the staff members assigned to attend the CPF meetings.

Despite this shortcoming, the language of COP seems to have had a subtle but profound impact on police attitudes in general, and there can be no doubt that the character of the SAPS is very different from that of the SAP (Pelser et al. 2002). In addition, the SAPS does seem to have managed to win the hearts of the majority of South Africans in its first decade of existence. In the most recent national victim survey, over half of those polled felt the police were doing a good job in their area, including 54 per cent of the black respondents (Burton et al. 2004). This would indicate that one important objective of COP policy – the legitimisation of police authority – is being accomplished. Whether this has made the police more effective in ensuring public safety is a matter for debate.

But in order for COP to promote crime prevention, station commissioners need to be able to adapt to local responses based on public inputs. This would require some decentralisation of authority in an organisation that has always been highly centralised. With a sizeable share of total staff assigned to the head office in Pretoria, several layers of administrative management (station, area, province, and national), and a great fear of fragmentation, the SAPS would have to overcome considerable organisational inertia in order to bring the authority to make real decisions closer to the people. At present, station commissioners do not control their own budgets and cannot even discipline their own staff members. Recent changes in the organisational structure, such as the consolidation of the specialised detective units that had proliferated across the country in response to local issues, have tended to promote even greater centralisation of authority.

Human rights

Democratisation implies an enhanced concern for the rights of the public, and there can be no denying that great strides have been made in this regard. But there is a parallel discourse among both the police and the public that portrays human rights as an impediment to law enforcement. In addition to the anti-terrorism legislation discussed earlier, perhaps the best example of this is the furore around the legislation that changed the standard of force allowed in making an arrest. The Judicial Matters Second Amendment Act (No. 122 of 1998)[6] simply required the presence of a real threat before lethal force was allowed, while the law had previously tolerated killing a fleeing suspect that could not be apprehended otherwise. Both the Minister and the National Commissioner denounced this legislation, and the President failed to promulgate the Act for five years after it was passed by Parliament, a delay of questionable constitutionality.

Both the Minister and the Commissioner claimed the change in force standards would result in more police members being killed, and their fears were justifiable if confusion over when to shoot caused police in the field to err on the side of caution, failing to take appropriate action to protect themselves. The remedy, of course, is training: a complete retraining on use of force for every armed member of the Service. And this is probably the core of the issue. Bullets cost money, and there is no way to train the police on something that must be as instinctive as the use of force without repetitive drilling. An extremely expensive exercise, but this is the cost of police reform. The police justifiably fear progressive legislation if it is not accompanied by the training they need to apply it effectively in the field.

In short, the SAPS has come a long way in democratising since the early 1990s. If nothing else, the persistence of democratic rhetoric has changed the mindset of the service. But in the end, as will be discussed next, the project of police reform is incomplete, its importance eclipsed by public concern over crime figures.

Crime prevention

From the beginning, the South African crime policy debate has involved a basic philosophic tension between two polarised perspectives on the best approach to crime: the law enforcement approach and the crime prevention approach. This debate is not unique to South Africa, and is essentially about whether money spent on crime prevention should go to the criminal justice system or to social programmes.

The law enforcement approach is premised on the idea that the best way to reduce crime is by jailing criminals. This incapacitates the problematic individuals, at least for the period of their incarceration, and supposedly provides a deterrent to others who wish to avoid a similar fate. Within this paradigm, the purpose of the prison system is often muddled in the minds of both policymakers and the public alike. On the one hand, it is about retribution, and some degree of hardship is expected. On the other, it is about rehabilitation, and thus should provide opportunities and incentives for reform. In a society with the kind of poverty seen in South Africa, however, these opportunities are not generally available to the law-abiding public, and so would negate, to some extent, the punitive nature of incarceration.

The crime prevention approach is based on the notion that crime is caused by social conditions, and only by rectifying these problems can crime be addressed. Unfortunately, the causes of crime are often cast in the broad terms of poverty and inequality, an approach that blurs the line between crime prevention and the broader project of social justice. As a result, it is often seen as a long-term policy, and one that is foreign to the mindsets of those most clearly charged with sorting out crime: the police.

The simplest, and perhaps the best, solution to this dilemma is to pursue both paths simultaneously, and this is the tack the government has nominally taken. But prioritisation is inevitable in a climate of scarce resources, and money often follows the path of least resistance. The ambitious, long-range social reform programmes have disappeared into the black hole of inter-departmental co-operation, while those programmes that supported what the police already understood and wished to pursue, drained the available resources.

The 1996 National Crime Prevention Strategy

The key South African government document on crime prevention is the 1996 NCPS. It was one of the most important outputs of the Secretariat, and was intended to be the guiding framework for a wide range of interdepartmental programmes aimed at increasing safety. A draft version submitted to officials was returned with a request for more short-range programmes, one of the first indications that the government was feeling public pressure for results in the war on crime. At the peak of its powers, the NCPS was seen as one of six pillars of the National Growth and Development Strategy, a far-sighted move that recognised the vital role safety plays in development. But in the end, short-range thinking won out, the Growth and Development Strategy was shelved in favour of the Growth, Employment, and Redistribution strategy (GEAR), and, with the possible exception of victim support, most of the social programmes envisaged by the NCPS never came to fruition. The document is still cited as though it is active policy, but it requires considerable imagination to see the connection between current police practice and the ideas advanced in the NCPS.[7]

The *White Paper on safety and security* of 1998 has already been briefly discussed. It was squarely positioned within the NCPS paradigm, and teased out some of the implications of this stance for the SAPS. It was explicitly a time-bound policy document expiring in 2003, and it is expected that the next White Paper will be developed in line with a scheduled review of the Police Act this year. Like the NCPS, many of its provisions were never realised.

The change of administration in 1999 was the beginning of the end for the NCPS. Comparing pre- and post-1999 organograms in the SAPS annual reports, the Secretariat literally disappeared off the SAPS charts. The NCPS, which had at one stage denoted both a policy document and a funded organisation in place to implement it, with a figure no less impressive than former Reconstruction and Development (RDP) head Bernie Fanaroff at the helm, was finally reduced to little more than a footnote to far less progressive approaches to public safety.

The National Crime Combating Strategy

The NCCS differs from the NCPS by one word and an ocean of ideology. Despite some claims to the contrary,[8] the NCCS can hardly be considered an outshoot of the NCPS. It is true that the priority crimes of the NCCS are similar to those of the NCPS,[9] but this is not saying much: in both cases, the only serious crimes not prioritised are burglary and theft. Simply looking at the titles, however, gives some sense of how the two differ: 'prevention' calls to mind a public health approach; 'combating' has distinct military undertones.

In keeping with this orientation, the NCPS was a document that was produced by an inter-departmental committee and published for public scrutiny, while the NCCS was produced in-house by the SAPS and has never been issued as a public document. Of course, the NCPS was, in theory, an inter-departmental policy, and the NCCS is explicitly a security cluster matter. Or so it would seem, based on what information is publicly available.

The NCCS is broken into two phases: the stabilisation phase (2000–03) and the normalisation phase (2004–09). In April 2000, the first phase was launched.

Phase one

The NCCS is 'a multi-disciplinary approach that focuses managerial, human and logistical resources on "hot spot" areas where crime is disproportionately high' (National Treasury 2001). It is often equated with 'Operation Crackdown' by many, including the Presidency (PCAS 2004), though technically 'crackdown' only refers to one phase of the geographic approach of its operational strategy. The SAPS identified 140 or so stations (about one station out of ten) that account for more than 50 per cent of serious crime, and these stations are subjected to saturation policing by both the SAPS and the military. In addition to this, ad hoc crackdowns may be applied to emerging crime problems and hot spots. The detectives also need something to do, so they are to engage in intelligence-driven operations against organised crime, which sounds suspiciously like what many of them should be doing anyway. The goal is to stabilise recorded crime in the 140 station areas by 2004.

The strategy is explicitly about controlling crime statistics. The targeted station areas were identified by crime statistics. The goal is to stabilise crime statistics in the chosen areas. Since these areas generate 50 per cent of the country's crime statistics, this should result in a stabilisation of crime statistics in the country as a whole.

To achieve this remarkable goal, the SAPS has resorted to traditional, albeit targeted, authoritarian policing. The police and the military show up in force. They make themselves visible. They wake everyone up at three a.m. and search their sugar bowls, without specific probable cause. They arrest people who arouse their suspicions if they cannot provide the appropriate identification documents or paperwork. They seize lots of undocumented people and guns, as well as drugs and suspected stolen property. They add any incidental arrests to their statistics. They throw up roadblocks and cordon-and-search operations to accomplish the same thing on the roads and sidewalks. What year is this again?

This return to militaristic policing should surprise no one. To a man with a hammer, everything looks like a nail. Organisations do what they know how to do, and they cannot do otherwise when they have not been trained to do otherwise. Given the masses of members who have little capacity for more reflective police work, the herding of bodies into mass operations may be the optimal use of available resources. Whether it is the route to a safer South Africa is another question.

The statistics moratorium

The NCCS was launched in April 2000. A moratorium was placed on the crime statistics, and explicitly the station-level crime statistics, in June 2000. It is highly unlikely that these two events were unrelated. By changing the rules around the way crime figures are collected, it is theoretically improper to compare pre- and post-moratorium statistics. Since the strategy is to stabilise crime statistics via crackdown operations, the success of the strategy cannot be evaluated.

While the general statistics moratorium was lifted at the end of 2001, the station-level statistics remain a state secret. This makes it even more difficult to evaluate the NCCS on its own terms. The stated goal of the NCCS is to stabilise crime in the priority areas. In order to evaluate whether this has been done, whether the changes are lasting, and whether there are displacement effects (pushing the crime into adjoining areas), station-level statistics are necessary. They are denied to the public.

We are asked to take the Minister's word for it when he claims that crime has been stabilised in 100 of the 145 crackdown areas (Tshwete 2002). We must also accept SAPS assurances that there is no displacement of crime to adjoining station areas, and that the changes are maintained after the removal of saturation patrols. And we mustn't be alarmed when the SAPS stops commenting on the targeted station areas altogether, making reference only to the aggregated national statistics when making claims of stabilisation.

But if we want crime figures to tell us where in the country it is safest to move our families or start a business, we are out of luck. If we want to be aware when new crime trends emerge in our neighbourhoods so we can take appropriate measures to protect ourselves, the information is denied to us. If we want to compare the crime situation in our area to that in areas with more police resources, as a device for lobbying for more money for our neighbourhoods, we are left to our own devices.

The denial of basic information vital to public safety is perhaps the strongest indication of the need for further police reform, and it comes from the very top. As under apartheid, the state has paternalistically decided that what we don't know won't hurt us. This is antithetical to democratic policing, and clearly illustrates the reactionary tack the organisation has taken in this regard since 1999.

Prospects

At the opening of 2004, we theoretically entered phase two of the NCCS: normalisation. During this phase, the SAPS intends to go beyond crime stabilisation, to crime reduction. The SAPS acknowledges that this process will require social crime prevention, and it plans to deliver it via the technique of sector policing.

Sector policing is an approach to policing that was, until recently, in vogue in the United Kingdom. It is a slight variation on COP, with a geographic focus. Station areas are divided into smaller sectors, each with a police member or team of members assigned to it. These members are expected to consult with the communities they serve to identify crime problems and their solutions. Instead of CPFs, we have sector police forums.

Crime prevention and police forums? It may sound like we have come full circle, but this is probably a good thing. The SAPS has had the courage to revisit the concepts that were fumbled earlier on. The question is whether it has the capacity to deliver on these strategies, without further police reform.

Recognising that doing sector policing properly would require much more staff than is currently available, the SAPS has requested, and been awarded, funds to hire and train 37 200 new police officers between April 2002 and March 2007. In 1996, after the amalgamations, there was a hiring freeze in the SAPS. In 2002, management woke up to the reality of declining police numbers, and a massive hiring campaign was launched. In order to accommodate the large number of new recruits promised, the academy time of the trainees was reduced, though the training division insists that this has not cut down on quality.

What will be the impact of this mass of new recruits on SAPS operations? The quality of the new hires appears to be good, with a median age of 27 and all high-school graduates. But it is clear that many will be shipped to the most understaffed station areas in the country, which are often the most troubled. This will mean that these hot spots will be policed by very 'green' troops, and that these 'green' troops will be exposed to difficult conditions. They may be shunted straight from the academy into extremely responsible roles, including sector policing and detective work on serious crimes. There are also concerns that there are not sufficient field training officers or vehicles in the receiving station areas. Finally, they will be supervised by the old staff, with all its capacity challenges.

Hiring new staff does not necessarily mean that sector policing, or police capacity in general, will be enabled in the short term. Rather, the new hires will require supervision from more experienced members, and this should mean less personnel available for innovative strategies for some time. Giving the recruits too much responsibility too soon is a sure way to burn them out, and they are bound to make mistakes more seasoned members would not. If the SAPS is hinging its hopes for sector policing on incoming personnel, it may be making a serious mistake.

A third way: social law enforcement

South Africa has a crime problem, and it has a policing problem. This chapter has argued that the latter has been neglected due to pressure to deal with the former. This is largely due to the view that crime prevention through law enforcement has been seen as a short-term response, while social crime prevention is necessarily a long-term project, and the public demands immediate gains in the war on crime.

I believe these basic premises to be faulty. Social crime prevention is about changing the social conditions that generate crime, rather than simply trying to lock up all the criminals and expect this to scare potential criminals into submission to the law. Social crime prevention does not have to be a long-term project. It is possible to change social conditions *now*, by changing and enforcing the rules under which society operates. The rules in question are most often local and usually have nothing to do with crime *per se*. They are the by-laws that regulate the way citizens conduct their businesses, manage their property, and live their daily lives.

For example, any urban street cop will tell you that the majority of calls for assistance in their duty areas come from a limited number of premises. These 'bad buildings' may be residences or businesses, but they have one thing in common – they are essentially unregulated. These properties are also owned by someone; someone who is not taking responsibility for the activity that takes place on his premises, and someone who has something to lose: his property. By-law enforcement can force these landlords to take responsibility for the crime problems their properties are generating, or lose the property if they fail to comply.

Some rental blocks in this country, such as residential hotels, are crime generators. This is because people are allowed to live there anonymously, without long-term commitments. The owners of these properties don't know who lives in their buildings or how they pay their rent, and frankly, they don't care. They could be illegal immigrants or they could be wanted criminals. And they could be up to just about anything, housed in a building where nobody asks too many questions.

The solution is to force building owners to control who lives in their properties and who has access to them. They should be required to keep copies of the identity documents or passports with valid visas of all residents and visitors. Since we cannot control our borders, we need to ensure that illegal immigrants receive a cold reception when they arrive at their destination: not the other side of some line in the sand, but the inner-city areas where so many seek their fortunes. The best way to do this is to limit housing opportunities, with the goal of producing a deterrent to entry in the first place. While some groups may opt for the informal settlements, other groups much prefer formal urban housing, as the masses of illegal immigrants in places like Hillbrow attest. Removing these options should take some of the glitter off El Dorado.

This is not to suggest that South Africa attempt to shirk its international responsibilities to receive legitimate political refugees, but the present system, which allows asylum seekers to reside in the country but forbids them to work, is a sure recipe for generating a socially-excluded criminal underclass with little investment in the country. South Africa needs to come to terms with its immigration issues, and one of the first steps in doing this is to reassert sovereignty in areas that have been allowed to fester with neglect.

Buildings should be subject to spot inspections to ensure they are in compliance with resident documentation by-laws. Failure to have the required documentation should result in escalating fines, and ultimately property forfeiture. To avoid litigation, forfeiture could be accomplished indirectly through very large fines, with attachment of the premises in settlement.

Of course, this scheme requires agents to enforce it, but we already have these, at least in the major metro areas: the municipal police. Their primary mandate is by-law enforcement, but unfortunately they have not been utilised very creatively. Instead, they spend most of their time on petty offences and traffic enforcement, often simply acting as a force multiplier to the SAPS. There is scope for much more. And they could be assisted in making spot inspections by civilian city employees, who are cheaper and easier to train. The offenders could be tried in municipal courts, and thus avoid burdening the already overstretched national court system.

In addition to controlling who resides in a building, other social conditions should also be regulated. Consistent patterns of criminal activity on a premise, such as drug sales, can be dealt with under existing asset forfeiture laws, but by-laws can create a scheme of fines that may force a clean-up before such action is necessary.

Compliance with basic health and safety requirements is not being pursued presently with the vigour it deserves, largely because these are seen as minor issues in comparison to the crime problem. In fact, these conditions are key to the crime problem. For example, South Africa's inner-city areas are notorious for horrific population density, with stacks of residents occupying tiny living spaces. This kind of crowding is well-established to be correlated with criminality, and the solution is as simple as enforcing residential capacity laws.

The ultimate result of this activity will be displacement of criminals, but it may also involve the displacement of law-abiding citizens, and this must be taken into account. Luckily, enforcement should result in municipalities taking ownership of lots of residential property. This could be converted into social housing, in which ordinary South Africans are allowed to buy a flat with their land reallocation grants. Since the building was free, this money could be used to refurbish the properties and to provide building management. This would stabilise the population and give residents an interest in protecting their new investments.

This is but one example of the way social conditions can be changed in the short term. It is clearly focused on urban areas, but similar interventions could be designed by those knowledgeable about the causes of rural crime. While space does not allow for the example to be fully discussed, it does illustrate a simple fact: social crime prevention need not be about ensuring that everyone is educated, employed, and equal before we can expect the violence to stop. By creating and enforcing local laws that regulate social conditions, the environments in which crime thrives can be radically transformed.

Other examples where local regulation can have an impact are in the areas of guns and alcohol, two elements that aggravate, if not cause, crime. While these matters may be formally controlled at the national level, it should be permitted for local authorities to regulate their availability according to local conditions. For example, municipalities should be allowed to zone in such a way that liquor licences are distributed appropriately throughout the city. This may result ultimately in vendors having a licence but no premise in which to sell, at least within their chosen municipality, but it may have a positive impact on the availability of alcohol. As with smoking legislation, the idea is not to prohibit consumption, but to make it inconvenient enough that total consumption is reduced.

Similarly, while the national government issues firearm licences, certain types of firearm conduct, such as carrying a weapon on the city streets, should be locally controlled. The national government gives you the right to own a gun, but cities should be allowed to determine where you can take it within their jurisdictions. This should reduce the number of times petty street squabbles become homicides, without impinging on anyone's right to protect their home.

By overcoming the conceptual impasse between law enforcement and crime prevention, progress could be made in both reducing the risk of victimisation and in making the South African police more capable of performing their jobs. South Africans need not give up their hard-won civil liberties in order to feel secure. There is no inherent contradiction between being safe and being free.

Notes

1   For example, much crime occurs indoors, where street presence is of small importance, and a lot of it is committed in the heat of the moment, often under the influence of alcohol or drugs, so that the participants are not rationally weighing the risk of arrest. Further, there is a whole class of criminals for whom the threat of imprisonment is not much of a deterrent – those whose whole identity is tied up with fighting the police, like some street gangsters.

2   National victim surveys conducted along similar methodological lines by Statistics South Africa in 1998 and the Institute for Security Studies in 2003 suggest an overall decline in victimisation of about 2 per cent.

3   These include the 1994 *Green Paper on safety and security*, the 1995 Police Act, the
     1996 National Crime Prevention Strategy, the 1996 Proceeds of Crime Act, the 1997
     Criminal Procedure Second Amendment Act (tighter bail), the 1998 National
     Prosecuting Authority Act, the 1998 *White Paper on safety and security*, the 1998
     Prevention of Organised Crime Act, the 1998 Judicial Matters Second Amendment
     Act (use of force), the 1998 South African Police Service Second Amendment Act
     (municipal police), the 1998 Magistrates Court Amendment Act, the 1998 Domestic
     Violence Act, the 2000 Firearms Control Act, and the 2000 (unpublished) National
     Crime Combating Strategy, just to name a few.

4   The self-defence units were ANC-aligned vigilante groups formed to maintain order in
     township areas neglected by the police. The self-protection units were the Inkatha
     Freedom Party (IFP) version. Clashes between rival factions of these groups comprised
     much of the organised 'black on black' violence during the transition period.

5   This concept was expanded in the 1995 Police Act, where the functions of CPFs were
     articulated to include the creation of public/police partnerships; the promotion of
     communication and co-operation concerning the needs of the public; the
     improvement of overall service levels, as well as the transparency and accountability
     of the police; and joint police/public problem-solving.

6   The Judicial Matters Second Amendment Act 122 of 1998 replaced Section 49 of the
     Criminal Procedure Act 51 of 1977.

7   The NCPS has four 'pillars':
     •   Re-engineering the criminal justice system;
     •   Reducing crime through environmental design;
     •   Community values and education;
     •   Transnational crime.

     The first pillar – re-engineering the criminal justice system – came to be dominated
     by a programme called the Integrated Justice System (IJS). The IJS is, essentially, an
     attempt to apply sound business principles to the criminal justice process, and as
     such, the involvement of Business Against Crime has been essential. The IJS has
     gobbled up much of the NCPS funding, as well as masses of partnership funding,
     and remains one of the few remaining active programmes of any consequence that
     can be directly traced to the NCPS. This 'success' can be attributed to the fact that its
     goal – improving organisational efficiency – is one that is clearly understood, and
     one for which there is a great deal of existing expertise. Rather than the grand task
     of social engineering, the IJS was simply about oiling the machine.

Despite the massive resources applied to the subject, however, the outputs of these efforts have been unclear. Very basic conflicts between the methods and strategies of the criminal justice system departments remain; their operations remain very much 'unintegrated'.

For example, the current police strategy emphasises making massive numbers of arrests. The current prosecutorial strategy emphasises cutting down on case backlogs and achieving more convictions. In 2001–02, the National Prosecuting Authority faced a whopping 1.1 million new cases coming to court, over 30 per cent more than the previous year. Despite processing more cases and achieving more convictions than ever before, backlogs grew (Leggett 2003). Of course, the prisons system is on the receiving end of all this, with the number of awaiting-trial prisoners increasing as case backlogs grow, and more sentenced prisoners as convictions increase. This makes their stated goal – rehabilitation – a cruel joke.

If the three criminal justice departments remain at odds with one another on a basic managerial issue like performance indicators, one wonders what all the IJS money has been spent on. In fairness, the IJS seems to have settled for more modest goals than truly synchronising criminal justice operations, and has largely been reduced to an information technology exercise, the outputs of which are also, unfortunately, yet to be delivered.

The second pillar – crime prevention through environmental design – seems to have gone nowhere. While a little creative thinking could link the ideas of this pillar to the much broader project of urban renewal, it does not appear that crime prevention has been key in town planning since 1996, not even in government housing projects. Most urban renewal operations appear to be driven at the level of the municipality, which is probably where they belong.

The third pillar – community values and education – could be obliquely linked to the Moral Regeneration Campaign housed in the Deputy President's office, another project whose outcomes, if any, are unclear. Of course, it would difficult to determine whether anyone has been morally regenerated as a result of this or any campaign, and it is probably unfair to expect any government effort to have this effect. Even on the output level, however, the Campaign seems to have stalled in the barracks.

The fourth – fighting organised crime – is already being energetically pursued by the police in any case. It would appear that most of the designated NCPS funding assigned to this pillar went to strengthening border control. While border control is an important matter, it is also an exercise doomed to failure. The United States has spent billions of dollars attempting to keep illegal Latin Americans and drugs out of the United States, and despite making massive seizures of each, one need look no further than the state of California to know that, at the very least, equal quantities managed to find their way through. The key to stopping undesired elements entering a geographic area would seem to be rooted in controlling demand for these elements, rather than drawing lines in the sand. This point is discussed in the conclusion of this chapter.

8   See, for example, the rather bizarre evolutionary chart to the contrary published in *Towards a ten year review* (PCAS 2004).

9   The NCCS identifies four key strategic priorities. First, to combat organised crime, focusing on crimes relating to drugs, firearms trafficking, vehicle theft and hijacking, corrupt public officials and organised commercial crime. This parallels pillar four of the NCPS. Second, to reduce the country's 'unacceptably high levels of *serious and violent crimes*'. With this in mind, the Department seeks to develop strategies to counter the proliferation of firearms, which fuels high levels of violent crime; improve safety and security in high-crime areas; combat specific crime generators, such as taxi and gang violence, and faction fighting; and maintain security at major public events. Many of these crime problems were also mentioned in the NCPS. Third, to develop strategies to reduce the incidence of crimes against women and children, while also improving the investigation thereof. These groups were identified for special attention in the NCPS. Fourth, to improve service delivery at police stations. This could be linked to programmes described under pillar one of the NCPS.

References

Bayley D (1994) *Police for the future.* New York: OUP.

Burton P, Leggett T, Louw A & Mistry D (2004) *National victims of crime survey: South Africa 2003.* Pretoria: Institute for Security Studies.

Cawthra G (1993) *Policing South Africa: The SAP and the transition from apartheid.* London: Zed.

CIIR (Catholic Institute for International Relations) (1988) *Now everyone is afraid: The changing face of policing in South Africa.* London: CIIR.

Criminal Justice Commission (1996) *The nature of general police work.* Research Paper Series, Vol. 3 No. 2. Brisbane: Kingswood Press.

Dadds V & Scheide T (2000) *Police performance and activity measurement.* Trends and Issues in Crime and Criminal Justice No. 180. Canberra: Australian Institute of Criminology.

Department of Safety and Security (South Africa) (1998) *White Paper on safety and security.* Available at <http://www.info.gov.za/whitepaper/1998/safety.htm>.

Interpol (International Criminal Police Organisation) (1999) *International crime statistics.* Lyon: Interpol.

ISS (Institute for Security Studies) (2002) National court site survey. Unpublished report.

Kelling G, Pate T, Dieckman D & Brown C (1974) *The Kansas City preventative patrol experiment: A summary report.* Washington DC: Police Foundation.

Leggett T (2002) *What do the police do? Performance measurement and the SAPS.* ISS Paper No. 66. Pretoria: ISS.

Leggett T (2003) *The sieve effect: South Africa's conviction rates in perspective.* SA Crime Quarterly No. 5. Pretoria: ISS. Available at <http://www.iss.co.za/CJM/pdf/sieve.pdf>.

Marais E (1992) Policing the periphery: Police and society in South Africa's 'homelands'. Paper presented at the 22nd Congress of the South African Sociological Association, Pretoria, 30 June. Available at <http://www.csvr.org.za/papers/papolpem.htm>.

Mbhele W (1998) Community police forums: Why aren't they working? *Crime and Conflict* 14:9–13.

National Treasury, South Africa (2001) *Estimates of national expenditure.* Pretoria: Government Printers.

PCAS (Presidency Policy Co-ordination and Advisory Services, South Africa) (2004) *Towards a ten year review: Synthesis report on implementation of government programmes.* Pretoria: Government Communications and Information Systems.

Pelser E, Schnetler J & Louw A (2002) *Not everybody's business: Community policing in South Africa's priority areas.* ISS Monograph No. 71. Pretoria: ISS.

Rauch J (1993) State, civil society, and police reform in South Africa. Paper presented at the International Society of Criminology Conference, Budapest, August 1993. Available at <http://www.csvr.org.za/papers/papstate.htm.

Rauch J (2000) Police reform and South Africa's transition. Paper presented at the South African Institute for International Affairs Conference, Johannesburg, 7–8.06.00. Available at <http://www.csvr.org.za/papers/papsaiia.htm>.

Rauch J (2002) Changing step: Crime prevention policy in South Africa. In E Pelser (ed.) *Crime prevention partnerships: Lessons from practice*. Pretoria: ISS.

Schönteich M & Louw A (2001) *Crime in South Africa: A country and cities profile*. Occasional Paper No. 49. Pretoria: ISS.

Shaw M (2002) *Crime and policing in post-apartheid South Africa: Transforming under fire*. Bloomington: Indiana University Press.

Stats SA (Statistics South Africa) (1998) *The national victims of crime survey*. Pretoria: Government Printers.

Tshwete S (2002) Parliamentary media briefing, 11 February. Available at <http://www.pmg.org.za/briefings/feb2002/020211justice.htm>.

wa Kivilu M (2002) National priorities. In Human Sciences Research Council (HSRC) *Public attitudes in contemporary South Africa: Insights from an HSRC survey*. Pretoria: HSRC.

Zvekic U (1995) *Criminal victimisation in the developing world*. Rome: United Nations Interregional Crime and Justice Research Institute.

7 The state of the military

Len le Roux and Henri Boshoff

Introduction

Since 1994, the defence function in South Africa has been substantially transformed. This transformation has focused on making defence matters more accountable to civil authority and more transparent to civil society, making the Department of Defence (DoD) more representative of South Africa's demographic profile, redefining the roles, posture and composition of the South African National Defence Force (SANDF), ensuring its greater efficiency and aligning the norms and standards of defence with the Constitution, international law and national values. Today, ten years on from the ending of apartheid, the SANDF is deployed in Burundi and the Democratic Republic of Congo (DRC) in international peace-support operations, as well as internally in support of the South African Police Service (SAPS). The SANDF is also involved in a process of renewing its conventional capabilities. These activities pose challenges to the Department to ensure the efficient and sustainable development of the SANDF into a force that can meet future challenges and national requirements.

The South African Defence Force pre-1994

The South African Defence Force (SADF) had its origins in the Union Defence Force, established in 1912. The SADF of the apartheid era consisted of the Army, the Air Force, the Navy and the Military Health Service. It was organised along the lines of a conventional force and a territorial or counter-insurgency force. The conventional force, both regular and part-time, was responsible for external operations and operated extensively in Namibia and Angola in operations against the South West African Peoples' Organisation (Swapo) and in support of the National Union for the Total Independence of Angola (Unita) against the armed forces of Angola (Fapla), which were supported by Cuba and the USSR. The counter-insurgency forces operated in the Republic, opposing the liberation struggle of the African National Congress (ANC) and its armed wing, Umkhonto We Sizwe (MK), as well as other groups.

The SADF in the 1970s and 1980s was a significant military power in southern Africa and could field three army divisions supported by strong and sophisti-cated air and naval power. These forces relied heavily on conscript soldiers (white male national service conscripts who served for an initial period of two years and then joined the part-time force for another ten years). The two-year obligation totalled, at its peak, 100 000 conscripts. This system allowed for the rapid expansion of the SADF if and when required. The counter-insurgency strategy of the SADF was based on a pre-emptive, operationally offensive doc-trine of counter-revolutionary warfare, and the operational structure of the force was designed to meet the requirements of this doctrine. Central to the doctrine, the fundamental principle was that any and all threats to national security should, where possible, be confronted beyond South Africa's borders by highly mobile forces with high firepower and strategic reach.

The SADF's budget reached a peak of around 4.4 per cent of gross domestic product (GDP) in the early 1980s. This imposed a huge strain on an embat-tled South African siege economy, which in time became a significant factor in contributing to the initiatives for a negotiated settlement of the region's political problems and the ending of armed conflict. In the latter part of the 1980s and early 1990s, as the peace process gained momentum and the SADF started its withdrawal from Angola and Namibia, the defence budget was pro-gressively reduced to reach 2.2 per cent of GDP in 1993. However, the combi-nation of the high defence costs of the pre-emptive interventionist strategy of the 1970s and 1980s, coupled with the impact of the arms embargo and United Nations-imposed sanctions, meant that the SADF could not replace ageing equipment and led to the creeping obsolescence of main equipment, especially in the SA Navy and certain conventional army formations, by 1994.

The creation of the South African National Defence Force

The present South African DoD, consisting of the Defence Secretariat and the SANDF, came into being on 27 April 1994 with the establishment of the new democratic order in South Africa. At its inception, the SANDF was comprised of an amalgam of the former SADF's forces, the defence forces of the former 'independent states'/homelands of Bophuthatswana, Ciskei, Transkei and Venda, MK and the Pan Africanist Congress's armed wing, the Azanian Peoples' Liberation Army (Apla), as well as the KwaZulu Self-Protection Forces of the Inkatha Freedom Party (IFP).

This integration of forces into a new defence force was preceded, in the period 1990–94, by negotiations for an Interim Constitution and the establishment of a Government of National Unity. Around these key issues other critical questions were addressed. One was the restructuring of the defence force and the reformulation of defence policy. It was in this period that the groundwork was done upon which future defence policies were to be developed, and the size and shape of the armed forces established.

The Interim Constitution of the Republic of South Africa (Act 200 of 1993) established the SANDF as the 'only defence force for the Republic' and provided that 'the SANDF would be a balanced, modern and technologically advanced military force'.[1] It also provided for the integration of forces into the new military entity and laid out the fundamental policy framework on which further developments were to be based. Central to this framework was the ensuring of civilian control over the military by the establishment of a Parliamentary Joint Standing Committee on Defence, and the provision that the Minister responsible for defence would be accountable to Parliament for all matters pertaining to the SANDF.[2]

Right from the outset in 1994, a considerable effort was devoted to crafting a new defence policy through the elaboration of a *White Paper on defence* and a subsequent *South African defence review*. This involved a redefinition of the SANDF's defence posture and strategy, its roles and tasks, required defence capabilities, human resource policies, its management structures, defence acquisition processes and a review of the military's legal system. In the course of the development of policy governing these tasks, a needs-driven but cost-constrained approach was used. This entailed an analysis of present and future security environments, the definition of probable future defence contingencies and associated risks, and the evaluation of required capabilities to confront these contingencies. This was then costed and debated with the parliamentary defence committees and various civil society groups. After nine regional and three national consultative conferences, Parliament decided on what was considered to be an affordable core force, namely, a balanced and sustainable nucleus maintaining capabilities and expertise for immediate requirements, with a capacity for expansion should this be required. Parliament also accepted the risks that this entailed. Present defence policy is therefore based on an analysis of possible future defence contingencies and the risks that are entailed, as well as the economic realities and priorities of South Africa. The processes used in the development of this new defence policy were open and consultative and the DoD has earned high praise for the manner in which the whole review process was conducted.

Since the completion of the review back in 1998, it has become clear that, as a result of security developments on the African continent, as well as various internal factors, the attainment of the envisaged force design cannot be achieved and that some adaptations are required. At present this matter is under consideration in the DoD and will probably come up for consultation with Cabinet and Parliament in the near future.

Description of the South African Department of Defence

Organisation and structure

The DoD comprises: (1) the Defence Secretariat headed by the Secretary for Defence; and (2) the SANDF headed by the Chief of the South African National Defence Force (CSANDF). The Secretary for Defence is the head of department and the accounting officer and he/she is the principal advisor to the Minister of Defence (MoD) regarding defence policy. The CSANDF executes defence policy, directs the work of defence headquarters and manages the overall functioning and operations of the SANDF. He/she is also the principal advisor to the MoD on military, operational and administrative matters within his/her competence.

The SANDF is structured much like the former SADF, with the four former services of old (Army, Air Force, Navy and Military Health), as well as staff divisions that report primarily to the CSANDF. These are the Corporate Staff, Joint Operations, Joint Support, and Defence Intelligence divisions. Five other divisions report primarily to the Secretary for Defence – the Policy and Planning, Finance, and Acquisition divisions, as well as the Defence

Inspectorate and the Equal Opportunities Directorate. The structure of the DoD is shown in Figure 7.1.

Figure 7.1 *Structure of the Department of Defence*

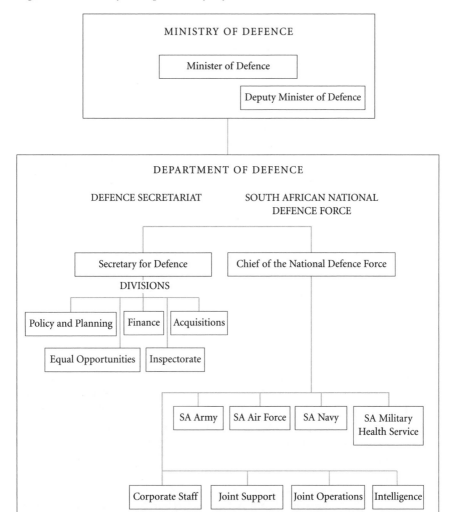

Source: DoD 2003

The SA Army force design consists of: armour and armoured reconnaissance; mechanised, parachute, motorised, light and specialist infantry; artillery and air defence artillery; intelligence; logistic and engineer support capabilities. The personnel strength of the Army on 15 January 2003 was 34 265 members (DoD 2003:56).

The SA Air Force force design consists of: air combat and reconnaissance squadrons; helicopters, transport and maritime air squadrons; command and control units; operational support; and intelligence capabilities. The personnel strength of the Air Force on 15 January 2003 was 10 616 members (DoD 2003:56).

The SA Navy force design consists of: surface warfare; submarine warfare; mine-countermeasures; operational and tactical logistic support capabilities. The personnel strength of the Navy on 15 January 2003 was 6 581 members (DoD 2003:56).

The South African Military Health Service force design consists of: deployable medical units; military and specialist health services and facilities; logistic support; operational and medical product support capabilities. The personnel strength of the Military Health Service on 15 January 2003 was 7 100 members (DoD 2003:56).

The total personnel strength of the DoD (including all supporting services) on 15 January 2003 was 75 318 (DoD 2003:56).

Functions and tasks

The Constitution of the Republic of South Africa (Act 108 of 1996) determines that the 'primary object of the defence force is to defend and protect the Republic, its territorial integrity and its people in accordance with the Constitution and the principles of international law regulating the use of force'.[3] The Constitution provides that the SANDF may be employed in the following functions:

- for service in the defence of the Republic, for the protection of its sovereignty and territorial integrity;
- for service in compliance with the international obligations of the Republic with regard to international bodies and other states;
- for service in the preservation of life, health or property;

- for service in the provision or maintenance of essential services;
- for service in the upholding of law and order in the Republic in co-operation with the SAPS under circumstances set out in law where the police service is unable to maintain law and order on its own; and
- for service in support of any department of state for the purpose of socio-economic upliftment.[4]

In interpreting these constitutional functions, the *White Paper on defence* took the rather narrow view that: 'It is the policy of government that the above functions do not carry equal weight. The primary function of the SANDF is to defend South Africa against external military aggression. The other functions are secondary'(1996:16). This interpretation received support from both the SANDF, then dominated by ex-SADF members, and other ANC-aligned policymakers. Underlying this was the desire of the military to renew the wherewithal of the ageing conventional force and the desire of political decision-makers to forge a fully professional defence force, and not one like the SADF of old which, under PW Botha and Magnus Malan, became deeply enmeshed in internal political affairs. This view has skewed the eventual force design of the SANDF towards conventional operations at the cost of more flexible, light and mobile forces for peace missions into Africa. The consequences of this are currently being experienced by the SANDF. This will be discussed later in the paper.

The defence budget

The DoD's expenditure estimates for the medium-term expenditure framework (MTEF), as well as a summarised output for each programme, are reflected in Table 7.1. Table 7.2 reflects this estimate of expenditure in item form.

The major challenges facing the DoD in relation to this MTEF budget forecast are:

- The high percentage expenditure on personnel. This is largely a result of the inability of the DoD to rightsize and rationalise, which in turn has been a product of a lack of an employer-initiated severance mechanism. Due to the imperatives of the initial integration programme, the DoD's personnel numbers expanded rapidly and well beyond its requirements. The DoD also 'aged' rapidly as many of the

Table 7.1 *Expenditure estimates and summarised outputs for DoD programmes for the medium-term expenditure framework 2004–07 (R thousands)*

Programme	2004–05	2005–06	2006–07	Output
Administration	719 700	756 891	778 983	Overall management of the DoD
Landward Defence	3 325 508	3 454 090	4 486 624	Provision and deployment of combat-ready Army forces
Air Defence	2 222 296	2 329 256	2 456 151	Provision and deployment of combat-ready Air forces
Maritime Defence	1 092 571	1 149 406	1 219 771	Provision and deployment of combat-ready Navy forces
Military Health Support	1 305 559	1 378 318	1 454 694	Provision of medical support to the DoD
Defence Intelligence	145 820	153 996	162 794	Provision of intelligence and counter-intelligence
Joint Support	2 303 398	2 294 040	2 422 588	Provision of common support to the Services
Command and Control	1 218 866	1 021 755	1 052 403	Provision of operational direction to combat forces
Special Defence Account	7 923 608	9 585 865	9 326 721	Acquisition of defence equipment and strategic armaments
TOTAL	20 257 326	22 123 617	22 360 684	

Source: Defence Vote (Vote 22), available at <http://www.treasury.gov.za:585>

Table 7.2 *Itemised expenditure for DoD, MTEF 2004–07 (R thousands)*

Item	2004–05	2005–06	2006–07
Compensation of employees	7 770 087	7 880 786	7 972 650
Goods and services	4 187 685	4 245 346	4 626 453
Transfers and subsidies	8 232 641	9 927 282	9 687 516
Payment for capital assets	66 913	70 203	74 065
TOTAL	20 257 326	22 123 617	22 360 684

Source: Defence Vote (Vote 22), available at <http://www.treasury.gov.za:585>

new intake did not qualify for promotion and remained in the lower ranks. This has led to the DoD carrying some 15 000 members over and above requirement for some years. The expenditure on these surplus members has amounted to more than R5 000 million since 1998.[5] Until very recently, personnel expenditure has constituted as much as 57 per cent of the overall budget, well over the ideal target of 40 per cent. This has been substantially rectified in the 2004–05 MTEF cycle, but mostly due to the high expenditure on the Special Defence Account for the Strategic Defence Packages.

- The threat of obsolescence of much of the SANDF's major equipment. This is not just a product of current spending priorities and demands. It stems from the lack of capital expenditure in the late 1980s and throughout the 1990s. This is currently being partly rectified by the so-called Strategic Defence Packages being acquired principally from the UK, Sweden, Germany and Italy. The low expenditure on capital equipment during the 'lean years' has now caused a situation where currently-needed acquisitions are eating into other defence expenditure. Despite this, many needs, such as those for maritime patrol and long-range transport aircraft, new anti-aircraft systems, new generation infantry equipment and modern command-and-control systems, are not being addressed.

- The additional demands made on the SANDF since 1994 to assist the SAPS internally and conduct peace-support operations in Burundi and the DRC. Large parts of these deployments are being funded from the defence budget and only in the case of the DRC operation, is there a chance for reimbursement. This is because that is a UN-mandated operation.

The above factors have led to a reduction in the operating budget (goods and services) of the SANDF to 21 per cent of the budget (up to the 2004–05 cycle of the MTEF this was below 20 per cent). Operating expenditure represents the portion of the DoD budget spent on day-to-day running of the defence force, maintaining equipment and infrastructure, developing and preparing personnel, and administering the force. This includes, amongst others, spares and tools, fuel and lubricants, training munitions, uniforms, rations, communications, information technology and stationery. This figure should not include the cost of actual operations, as this should be covered from National Treasury contingent funds. Unfortunately a significant proportion of SANDF operations is also funded from this part of the Budget. The benchmark figure for operating expenditure (excluding actual operational deployments) is 30 per cent, well above the current DoD level. This has led to restrictions in the maintenance of infrastructure and equipment, training and force preparation and general support to the force.

Integration and transformation: issues of race and gender equity

The integration process described earlier began almost immediately after the elections in 1994. It aimed at integrating into the SANDF all personnel whose names appeared on the certified personnel registers of the statutory and non-statutory forces identified in the Constitution (with the subsequent inclusion of Apla), as well as the education and training of all members of the SANDF to meet international standards of competence and professionalism.

The process was neither easy nor trouble-free. Numerous problems and grievances emerged and, at times, gave rise to serious tensions. Many of these difficulties were inevitable, given the political and logistical complexities of merging forces. One of the complaints was that the integration process was simply a matter of absorption of the other forces by the SADF. To manage these tensions, a Ministerial Integration Oversight Committee was established to monitor the process and, particularly, adherence to policy. The Committee included members of the SANDF, the Defence Secretariat and the Joint Standing Committee on Defence. A British Military Advisory and Training Team (BMATT) was incorporated into the process to ensure its fairness. A Parliamentary Integration Oversight Committee of the Joint Parliamentary Standing Committee for Defence was created and was regularly briefed by the DoD on the integration process. It also visited units of the SANDF to monitor progress.

In regard to whether this was a true integration process or simply a matter of absorption, elements of both were present. The size of the SADF element (see Table 7.3) and its institutional capacity, made it inevitable that it would numerically and technically dominate the process. On the other hand, the political leverage of MK and the control and oversight provided by the Defence Ministry and the Parliamentary Oversight Committees, ensured the political dominance of the decision-making process. BMATT also played an important role in ensuring fairness and objectivity and their contribution was largely responsible for the ultimate credibility of the integration process. It is our view that, despite the difficulties and the setbacks experienced, the integration process was largely successful and has contributed significantly towards the present stability and success of the SANDF in its internal and external operations.

Table 7.3 *Numbers of members of forces integrated into SANDF*

Force	Anticipated	1998
SADF	90 000	57 053
MK	22 000	11 738
Apla	6 000	3 713
TBVC[a]	11 000	7 243
KZP[b]		1 788
SANDF		10 600
Total	129 000	93 324

Source: DoD 1998:70

Notes: a TBVC refers to forces in the former 'independent' homelands; b KZP refers to the former KwaZulu Police

The most critical area of transformation for the SANDF was that of ensuring equity in racial and gender representation. The predominantly white and male character of the apartheid defence force had rapidly to be eliminated, or at least ameliorated. However, due to the imbalances in the sizes of the integrating forces, the initial composition of the SANDF did not reflect positively on this imperative. This led to the need for concerted rationalisation strategies, through affirmative action and fast-tracking on the one hand, and the institution of voluntary severance packages on the other. Significant advances have been made in this regard, albeit far more in relation to race than gender (see Tables 7.4 and 7.5).

While a degree of progress is clear, the major challenge currently lies in the fact that, although top management is representative and aligned with national demographics, middle management is still biased towards white ex-SADF members (around 65 per cent). At the same time, the SANDF is not attracting whites at the lower levels, causing that level to be predominantly black. Asians are also still under-represented in the SANDF. In terms of gender representivity, the figure of 21 per cent for females in the DoD is obviously low, yet good by international and especially African standards.

Table 7.4 *Racial composition of the SANDF, 1994, 1998, 2003*

Race	1994	1998	2003
African	38%	57%	62%
Asian	1%	1%	1%
Coloured	16%	12%	12%
White	45%	30%	25%

Source: DoD 1998:71; DoD 2002–03 *Annual Report*:23

Table 7.5 *Gender composition of the SANDF, 1994, 1998, 2003*

Gender	1994	1998	2003
Female	20	19	21
Male	80	81	79

Source: DoD 1998:71; DoD 2002–03 *Annual Report*:23

All in all, it is our view that the present situation in the SANDF, regarding both integration in general, and racial and gender representation in particular, is satisfactory and that remaining problems will be addressed successfully by the recently approved DoD Human Resources Strategy 2010.

Transparency and accountability

The legislative framework for the governance and management of the DoD and SANDF is contained in the Constitution, the Defence Act (Act No. 42, 2002), the Public Service Act (Act No. 103 of 1994) and the Public Finance Management Act (Act No. 1 of 1999). The internal management responsibilities and respective roles of the Secretary for Defence and the CSANDF were described earlier.

Substantial mechanisms, forums and procedures exist to ensure political oversight and executive control over defence. This is to ensure that both the executive and the national legislature accept responsibility for defence policy, its plans and budget, as well as the execution of the defence plan. These bodies are to ensure that policy priorities are linked to departmental spending plans and the delivery of service. The key role players in this process of political oversight and executive control over defence are discussed next.

The MoD is the political head of the DoD. He/she is designated as the Executive Authority for defence by the Public Service and Public Finance Management Acts. As such, the Minister has the primary responsibility for political oversight of defence including the defence budget. He/she is responsible for ensuring that political priorities are linked to departmental spending plans, the delivery of service and determining departmental priorities. The Executive Authority is responsible for ensuring that the Department performs its statutory functions within the limits of the funds authorised for the relevant vote. The Minister executes these functions primarily through the statutory Council of Defence consisting of the Minister, the Deputy Minister, the Secretary for Defence and the CSANDF.

The Portfolio Committee of Parliament on Defence (PCPD) is a committee of the National Assembly, with membership open to all parties represented in the legislature. It ensures parliamentary oversight over defence. According to Rule 201 of the National Assembly the PCPD is mandated, amongst other things, to:

- 'deal with Bills and other matters falling within its portfolio as are referred to in terms of the Constitution, these Rules, the Joint Rules or by resolutions of the Assembly'; and
- 'monitor, investigate, enquire into and make recommendations concerning any such executive organ of state, constitutional institution or other body or institution, including the legislative program, budget, rationalisation, restructuring, functioning, organization, structure, staff and policies of such organ of state, institution or other body or institution.'[6]

Parliament is the highest authority for the approval of defence policy, legislation, the deployment of the SANDF and approval of the defence budget.

The National Treasury plays a key technical role in the national budgetary process and guides the budgeting process of all departments. The National Treasury is responsible for:

- identifying the overall level of spending that can be afforded within government's macroeconomic and fiscal framework;
- evaluating departmental policy options and budget planning submissions;
- presenting comments and views on proposed departmental options;
- developing a MTEF;
- negotiating allocations, reprioritisation and funding levels of programmes/activities including possible savings;

- making recommendations to the Medium Term Expenditure Committee; and
- presenting the national MTEF to the Ministers' Committee on the Budget.

External auditing of the DoD is done by the Auditor General. He/she reports to the Parliamentary Standing Committee on Public Accounts.

The principles of civil-military relations and the fact of parliamentary oversight of defence, have special reference to Defence Intelligence. For that reason a National Intelligence Act (Act No. 39 of 1994) was enacted to provide for control in respect of all intelligence agencies. Defence Intelligence structures are furthermore subject to scrutiny by the Inspector General of the DoD, the National Intelligence Co-ordinating Committee, the Inspector General for Intelligence and the Joint Standing Committee on Intelligence of Parliament.

With the SANDF becoming more involved in peace-support operations in Africa, the Defence Intelligence Division is accordingly co-operating more closely with the intelligence structures of the SADC region. The main emphasis is on 'producing intelligence in support of operations in the region (and) developing strategic partnerships with member countries of Southern African Development Community (SADC)'.[7] This is a positive development as intelligence co-operation is an important confidence- and security-building measure amongst regional states.

In terms of accountability, the SANDF is under democratic civil control. Indicative of this is the fact that 13 meetings of the Joint Standing Committee on Defence and 18 of the Portfolio Committee were convened in 2003. These meetings covered a range of issues, from a human resource strategy to the defence budget, the defence strategic plan and the Armscor Bill. Much the same is true of the transparency issue.[8]

There is, however, some dissatisfaction on the part of most non-governmental organisations and in the media over access to the DoD itself. It is difficult to acquire any information requested and there is little proactive engagement of the DoD with broader civil society. This is a reverse of the consultative posture of the DoD during the 1994–98 period and is a cause for concern. The DoD should return to the more consultative and inclusive approach it adopted at the time of the defence review exercise. The benefits are simply better policies, a better understanding of defence by the public and greater support for the cause of defence. A study by the Institute for Democracy in South Africa on 'Budget transparency and participation' rates South Africa as good in terms of the legal framework and moderate in terms of transparency and participation. In relation to the latter it states, 'If the participation dimension was not included in the horizontal axis (of the table), a score of good/good would have been arguably correct' (Folscher 2002:13). Although this does not refer specifically to the military, but to the state in general, it is the opinion of the authors that it certainly applies to the military planning and budgeting process in South Africa today.

Preparedness

South Africa's defence capabilities

This is an area of some concern. The current approved force design of the SANDF is set out in the *South African Defence review* (DoD 1998). It was developed as a planning document covering a forward period of 'the next decade or longer', although it was acknowledged that 'the continuously changing strategic environment' (1998:47) will influence the realisation of the design and might necessitate changes. The design is reflected in Table 7.6.

Currently, six years on from its conceptualisation, the SANDF does not measure up to the force design. The most serious shortcomings are in the sphere of maritime defence where most of the Navy's main equipment (submarines and strike craft in particular) needs replacement, and where maritime air capability (medium- to long-range maritime patrol aircraft) is nearly non-existent. Things are little better with regard to the Air Force where its fighter aircraft are fast reaching obsolescence, and the transport aircraft fleet lacks long-range transport capability. The SA Army has been put under particular stress in regard to its force levels due to budget pressures and the priority given to naval and air systems in the Strategic Defence Package – the arms deal which has been the subject of so much controversy. One of the Army's major areas of concern is the low level of availability and readiness of its conventional reserve component. Due to budgetary restrictions, the non-availability of equipment and the priority of the execution of internal and external operations, the training and development of this element of the Army's force design has been seriously neglected since 1994.

Table 7.6 *Approved force design of SANDF*

Arm of service and element		Quantity
SA Army		
Mobile Division		1
Mechanised Brigade (Rapid Deployment Force)		1
Parachute Brigade (Rapid Deployment Force)		1
Special Forces Brigade		1
Territorial Forces:	Group Headquarters	27
	Light Infantry Battalions	14
	Territorial/Motorised Infantry Battalions	12
	Area Protection Units	183
SA Air Force		
Fighters:	Light fighters	16
	Medium fighters	32
Reconnaissance aircraft:	Light reconnaissance aircraft	16
	Long-range maritime patrol aircraft	6
	Short-range maritime patrol aircraft	10
	Remotely piloted squadrons	1
Helicopters:	Combat support helicopters	12
	Maritime helicopters	5
	Transport helicopters	96
Transport aircraft:	Transport aircraft	44
	VIP service	9
	Voluntary squadrons	9
In-flight refuelling/electronic warfare aircraft		5
Airspace control:	Radar squadrons	3.5
	Mobile ground signals intelligence teams	3
SA Navy		
Submarines		4
Corvettes		4
Strike craft		6
Combat support ships		1
Minesweeper/hunter		8
Inshore patrol vessels		2
Harbour patrol boats		39
SA Military Health Service		
CB Defensive Programmes		1
Medical Battalion Groups (full-time component)		1
Medical Battalion Groups (part-time component)		1.5

Source: DoD 1998:47–8

The process of modernising the major weapon systems of the SANDF began when Cabinet approved the Strategic Armaments Procurement Programme, more commonly known as the Strategic Defence Package (SDP), in September 1999. The SDP, which was handled as a single package to obtain maximum commercial leverage, constitutes the largest armaments deal ever concluded in South Africa. It provides for the acquisition of four corvettes, three submarines, 30 light-utility helicopters, 24 lead-in fighter trainer aircraft, and 28 fighter aircraft. While this package will help meet some of the shortcomings cited earlier, it must be remembered that these systems will be phased into the SANDF force design over an eight-year period beginning in 2004. The total cost of the package is projected to be about R48.7 billion, of which the largest annual projected expenditure is R7 billion in 2005–06. In order to ensure full operational capability of the corvettes, approval was obtained in 2002–03 to procure four additional maritime helicopters. The first of the corvettes arrived in Simon's Town in November 2003. The process of fitting the vessel with combat systems will take about 18 months. The remaining corvettes were delivered in September 2004. The light-utility helicopters (Augusta 109) will be delivered between 2004 and 2006. Delivery of the submarines is scheduled for the period 2005 to 2007, while delivery of the lead-in fighter trainer aircraft (Hawk) is scheduled for between 2005 and 2006. The delivery of the Gripen fighter aircraft is scheduled to take place between 2008 and 2011.[9]

These acquisitions will help fill the gaps in the maritime and air defence capabilities of the SANDF. The corvettes will provide a so-called 'blue-water' capability that has been absent for many years. Together with the existing combat support ships and the maritime helicopters, these systems will allow the SANDF to supply much-needed maritime capabilities for the protection of the subcontinent's maritime defence and marine protection requirements. The *Military balance 2002–2003*, referring to the threat of piracy and the illegal exploitation of marine resources in sub-Saharan Africa, stated that, 'No country, not even South Africa, has the resources to patrol its territorial waters or exclusive economic zone against this challenge' (IISS 2002:195). The naval acquisitions are correcting this strategic gap in the SANDF force design to some degree. The absence of any real maritime air-patrol and reconnaissance capability still remains an area of concern in South Africa's (and the region's) maritime defence capabilities. The Navy is also scrapping the current strike-craft force and there is no indication that they will be replaced in the near future. This leaves a significant gap in the force design of the Navy as approved in the *Defence review*.

The acquisition of light-utility helicopters, the lead-in fighter trainer aircraft and the Gripen fighters will greatly address the problems of the Air Force regarding the ageing of its current main systems. The first two of these systems will respectively replace the very old Alouette helicopters and Impala fighter trainers, which are already difficult and expensive to maintain and operate. The Air Force is also acquiring the 12 combat-support helicopters (*Rooivalk*) approved in the *Defence review*. This will enhance the capacity of the Air Force for close air support to land forces. The other existing capabilities of the Air Force, although in places below the force design, are probably sufficient for the country's short- to medium-term requirements.

No provision is made for the South African Army in the current arms deal, leaving the Army to struggle with the problem of ageing equipment and the obsolescence of many of its major systems. Furthermore, the second component of the existing reservist force – the Army Territorial Reserve Force or Commandos – is being phased out, with no apparent plan for its replacement. This, along with the aforementioned low level of preparedness of the conventional Reserve Force, leaves the Army well below the required *Defence review* force design, and under some stress to perform all its expected functions. Currently, its Casspir armoured personnel carriers are being upgraded and a new portable ground-to-air missile system is being developed. Armament acquisition projects for the Army completed during 2002–03 included heavy-recovery vehicles, parachute-deployable Gecho vehicles and trailers, the SS77 machine gun, the Mamba armoured personnel carrier, and a number of five-axle trailers for transporting battle tanks, G6 mobile artillery and *Rooikat* armoured cars.[10]

Force preparation

Force preparation refers to the SANDF's training processes for the execution of military operations. It excludes basic and administrative types of training. It is done at unit level, in larger 'all-arms' exercises, in joint exercises incorporating all services, and in combined exercises where forces of different countries are involved. Due to budgetary restrictions, fewer joint and combined exercises are taking place than required to maintain a high level of preparedness in the SANDF. The major shortcoming in the SANDF's force preparation during recent years has been the lack of conventional training at brigade and higher level for both the regular and reserve forces. On the other hand, the SANDF participated in three combined multinational exercises during 2003–04. These were:

- 'Exercise Rainbow Trek' held at Richards Bay. This was a command post and Field Firing Exercise between the SANDF and French forces and included beach landing and evacuation exercises.
- 'Exercise Flintlock' held in July 2003 at Bloemfontein and the Army Battle School between SANDF and US forces and focusing on parachute training and military support during humanitarian disasters.
- 'Exercise African Shield' held at the SA National War College. This was a command post exercise between SANDF and British forces focusing on a Chapter 3-type UN operation.

Force employment

In recent years, the SANDF has been deployed operationally internally and externally. Due to budgetary restrictions and the provisions of the *White Paper on defence* and the *Defence review*, planning is under way to withdraw the SANDF from internal operations as well as its ongoing support to the SAPS. Even so, in 2003 the SANDF was involved in two major and ongoing internal operations in support of civil society, namely:[11]

- 'Operation Intexo' (border-line control) – aimed at combating transnational crime. The SANDF's role included the air and maritime operations along the coast and within South Africa's exclusive economic zone.
- 'Operation Stipper', in terms of which the SANDF supplied specialist equipment to the SAPS in its operation to safeguard the rural arena and in particular the farm sector. This involved efforts to curb cattle rustling, the illegal entry of foreign migrants, the growing of dagga, and the smuggling of mandrax, weapons, and stolen vehicles.

Instability and continuing conflict in Africa has led to an ever-increasing role for the SANDF in support of South Africa's foreign policy objectives. In 2003–04, observers and staff officers were posted to various UN and African Union peace missions in the Comores, Eritrea, Ethiopia, and Liberia.

However, the SANDF's ongoing two largest external operations are in Burundi and the DRC. 'Operation Fibre' involves the deployment of a 700-strong South African Protection Support Detachment to Burundi. The aim of the deployment changed in 2002–03 from protection of VIPs to ensuring the establishment of a climate for free and fair elections. This change resulted in an increase of personnel deployed to approximately 1 600 as part of the African Union Mission in Burundi, which also involves forces from Ethiopia and Mozambique. In terms of 'Operation Mistra', the SANDF contributes 1 500 servicemen and women to the UN mission in the DRC.

The preparedness status of the SANDF: a summary

The discrepancy between defence policy and the defence budget has led to the SANDF being unable to maintain and develop its conventional capabilities. The Army has not trained operationally at brigade level for several years; in fact, it probably could not fully even staff all the elements of a brigade group; it lacks air-transportable equipment that would facilitate an effective rapid response and it lacks modern anti-aircraft weapons. The current plans to reduce the strength of the Army further will aggravate this problem. The fact is that the Army will increasingly be under pressure to execute its functions unless these shortcomings are urgently addressed.

The SA Air Force has too few transport aircraft to rapidly deploy even a small ground force, let alone support a larger force; its Cheetah C fighters are few and difficult to support far from base, and its 12 *Rooivalk* combat helicopters on order will not be sufficient to enable it to give the SA Army the close support it needs operationally.

In the maritime environment, the Navy does not have adequate sealift capability, its strike craft lack the endurance to support a ground force, and the Air Force does not have long- or medium-range maritime aircraft to provide reconnaissance and surveillance support.

The conventional reserves would be of little help in any crisis or combat situation. They have few fully trained troops, have a grossly over-age leadership corps and have not participated in large-scale field training exercises in many years. There is, however, still a core around which an effective or more efficient reserve force could be rebuilt, but as things stand now, there is no viable reserve force to back up the regular force. The one exception is the Territorial Reserve, the former Commandos, which still has reasonable strength levels and proficiency, but which is not trained for a conventional role and is in any event being phased out.

Looking at the operational capabilities of the SANDF as opposed to the DoD management and headquarter structures, there are also grounds for concern about the so-called 'tooth-to-tail' ratio of the DoD. The SANDF's current ratio of total soldiers to general-officers of around 300:1 is way too low in terms of international benchmarks. The comparative figure for the US military is around 1650:1.

Despite all of the above, the SANDF can execute its present obligations regarding peace missions, support to the SAPS and to civil society in cases of emergency. It has a core capability out of which it could build a more capable force, although the present overextension and imbalance between policy expectations and funding will make that more difficult and more costly as time passes.

Another area of concern is the level of HIV/AIDS within the SANDF. This figure is set at around 23 per cent (Heinecken 2003). As pointed out by General Charles Wald, Deputy Chief of the US European Command, this could detrimentally influence the role that the SANDF can play in peace-support operations in Africa. If not contained, it will also push up the defence budget significantly and render the SANDF even less capable of executing its mission. The DoD Human Resource Strategy 2010 recognises that this problem constitutes the biggest single threat to the deployment potential and operational effectiveness of the SANDF. A national HIV/AIDS strategy is therefore an imperative.

Revisiting the Defence review

Despite the problems and shortcomings cited earlier, and when one considers the immensity of the transformational challenges that the SANDF has faced over the last ten years, the organisation deserves credit for what it has achieved. It has taken an instrument which lay at the core of the late apartheid order, and transformed it to be aligned with our new democracy, achieving successes in the areas of civil-military relations, integration, reconciliation and the crafting of a force that represents the interests of the whole South African nation. The SANDF does, however, still face significant challenges in aligning defence policy with the defence budget and improving operational preparedness and efficiency.

The ending of apartheid brought with it a vision of peace and stability in Africa. Nationally the focus was on the Reconstruction and Development Programme that would produce internal stability and growth. For this reason, the White Paper and *Defence review* argued that South Africa could significantly reduce defence spending and concentrate on the establishment of a small (core) conventional regular force and a large part-time force, which could be mobilised when required. It was anticipated that the SANDF would progressively withdraw from the internal policing function and that a force of about 1 000 soldiers, with air, maritime and medical support units, would be sufficient for the country's international and regional peace support obligations.

These planning assumptions, combined with budgetary restrictions, led to the decision to aim at creating a defence force of some 55 000 uniformed regular soldiers focused on the maintenance of a core conventional capability. This figure encompassed all four services and was inclusive of all uniformed support and headquarters personnel. With civilians, the total strength of the DoD was set at 70 000. The regular force was to be backed by a sufficiently large part-time component to ensure expansion capability when required.

At present the SANDF has about 2 000 soldiers employed internally and 3 000 soldiers deployed in conflict areas in Africa but with a demand for more. This brings the present SANDF deployment (nationally and elsewhere) to some 5 000 men and women, the majority being infantry soldiers – significantly more than the number envisioned by the *Defence review*. To maintain these force levels requires, at the very least, three times as many mission-ready soldiers to allow for rotation, contingency reserves, training and force preparation, home duty and leave. Even such a figure will mean a very high percentage of time spent on operations away from home and will make long-term deployments impossible to sustain. This is putting a large burden on the SANDF and eroding the ability to develop, maintain and prepare the conventional force.

There is therefore a lack of coherence between policy and practice and this suggests to us a need for a review of defence policy. Government policy on defence, and its guidance to and funding thereof, needs to be brought in line with present reality and practice.

Conclusion

This evaluation of the SANDF has highlighted the achievements of the SANDF over the last ten years, as well as its current major challenges. Our conclusion is that in the course of the last decade the South African military has undergone deep-rooted fundamental change, but this has left the SANDF only relatively well-positioned to execute its constitutional mission and secondary tasks. In terms of civil-military relations and racial and gender representation, the DoD has progressed well and has achieved stated policy objectives. The new weapons acquisitions in the pipeline, although not necessarily focused on the right priorities, will nonetheless enhance the operational capability of the SANDF.

Despite this, there are four major challenges that face the military. First, the DoD needs to address the inconsistency between defence policy and the defence budget. Currently the SANDF is overextended in terms of budget realities and this is leading to a general running down of capabilities. In doing so, the DoD must revisit the definition of its primary function and broaden this to include peace missions in Africa as an essential element of the South African defence strategy. Second, the DoD must address its internal inefficiencies. The size of the support structures and the rank inflation are disproportionate to the operational capabilities of the SANDF. Third, the DoD must reinvigorate the part-time force to ensure sustainability and affordability in the defence function in South Africa. Finally, the DoD, along with the rest of the nation, must boldly address the AIDS pandemic if it is to prevent the gradual disintegration of the defence force and the crippling of its capacity to undertake its defence functions.

Notes

1 Interim Constitution of the Republic of South Africa, 1993 (Act No. 200 of 1993), (Republic of South Africa, Government Gazette Vol. 343 No. 15466, Cape Town, 28.01.94), Section 224(1):146 & 226(4):148.

2   Interim Constitution of the Republic of South Africa, 1993 (Act No. 200 of 1993), (Republic of South Africa, Government Gazette Vol. 343 No. 15466, Cape Town, 28.01.94), Section 225:146, Section 227(1)& (2):148, and Section 228(3):150.

3   Constitution of the Republic of South Africa, 1996 (Act No. 108 of 1996), (Republic of South Africa, Government Gazette Vol. 378 No. 17678, Cape Town, 18.12.96), Section 200(2):88.

4   Constitution of the Republic of South Africa, 1996 (Act No. 108 of 1996), (Republic of South Africa, Government Gazette Vol. 378 No. 17678, Cape Town, 18.12.96), Section 200(2):88.

5   See <http://www.pmg.org.za>. Report on Adjustments Budget requirements for financial year 2003–04 as presented by the DoD to the Defence Portfolio Committee, 16.09.03.

6   Rules of the National Assembly, Chapter 12: Committee System, Rule 201(1). Available at <http://www.parliament.gov.za>.

7   Defence vote (Vote 22). Available at <http://www.treasury.gov.za/:599>.

8   The defence strategic plan can be seen on the DoD website at <http://www.mil.za>, the budget on <http://www.treasury.gov.za>, and the minutes of nearly all committee meetings are available at <http://www.pmg.org.za>.

9   Defence vote (Vote 22). Available at <http://www.treasury.gov.za/:582 & 583>.

10 Defence vote (Vote 22). Available at <http://www.treasury.gov.za/:606>.

11 Defence vote (Vote 22). Available at <http://www.treasury.gov.za/:584 & 604>.

References

DoD (Department of Defence, South Africa) (1998) *White Paper on defence.* DoD.

DoD (1996) *South African defence review.* DoD.

DoD (2003) *South African Department of Defence strategic business plan 2003/04 to 2005/06.* Cape Town: Government Printers.

Folscher A (ed.) (2002) *Budget transparency and participation: Five case studies.* Cape Town: Idasa.

Heinecken L (2003) Facing a merciless enemy: HIV/AIDS and the South African armed forces, *Armed Forces and Society* 29: 281–300.

IISS (International Institute for Strategic Studies) (2002) *The military balance 2002–2003.* London: Oxford Press.

The state of South Africa's schools

Linda Chisholm

Introduction

Much has changed for South Africa's schools in this post-apartheid era in which HIV/AIDS has emerged as the deadly, unspoken and silent scourge of liberation, casting its shadow over every statement, initiative and intervention. For education, it was a decade in which the institutionalised injustices of apartheid were expunged and new directions were charted for a 12 million-strong cohort of learners and approximately 350 000 teachers spread across nine provinces in a largely public school sector.[1] The majority is concentrated in provinces that are predominantly rural and now include the former home-lands.[2] South Africa is now set on a new course. But there are diverging views on whether it is on the right track or not.

There can be few, if any, areas of education that have been left untouched by the drive since 1994 to overcome the legacy of apartheid. And yet there is a powerful perception that not much has changed and that things may even have become worse. This is exemplified in the heated debate over matric results in early 2004, conducted in the context of rising election fever. Newspaper headlines provide a sense of the passions invoked for and against the view that the results were credible. Sparking the debate was Jonathan Jansen's broadside against the overall positive picture painted by a 73.1 per cent pass, 'Matric quick fixes miss the mark' (*Sunday Times* 4.01.04). This was rapidly followed by rebuttals and countercharges: 'Top marks for matric fair-ness,' wrote *The Star* (5.01.04), 'Matrics assured marks were not manipulated,' said *ThisDay* (7.01.04) and 'Matric successes worth celebrating' opined *Business Day* (9.01.04). But the attack continued, with the *Mail & Guardian* leading the charge in pieces titled 'Classrooms versus classy acts', 'A house of bright colours' (9–15.01.04) and 'Fiddling marks' (30.01–5.02.04). Its criticisms were echoed by the *Citizen*, which maintained that 'Eastern Cape matric results (were) slanted' (13.01.04) and the *Financial Mail* that predicted that the 'New matric exam spells class war' (16.01.04). By now, voices of moderation were also beginning to enter the debate. Columnists in the *Sunday Times* (11.01.04), *ThisDay* (12.01.04), the *Sowetan* (15.01.04) and *HSRC Review* (March 2004) were concerned that critics were missing the key issues – that 'it's wrong to judge the entire system by the matric results', that 'matric critics (were) bluster(ing) about old problems', that 'quality of education is key' and that 'the public debate lacks information and analysis'.

In this debate, as in discussions over the state of South Africa's schools ten years after the transition to democracy, it is important to distinguish between the initiatives taken to address the apartheid legacy, the actual changes, and the explanations for the overall emerging pattern. It is also important to bear in mind the enormous diversity and heterogeneity of schools in South Africa. Every generalisation can be countered by specific examples that challenge the general argument.

There are generally three kinds of explanations for continuing inequalities and failures to shift the system – there are those that focus on the individual responsibility of Ministers of Education, those that argue that change has been mainly symbolic and linked to the political character of change (Jansen 2000), and those that identify the root of continuing inequality in a combination of the 1994-compromise, neo-liberal policies pursued since 1994, the nature of the post-1994 state and bureaucracy and limited capacity at provincial level to implement policies (Chisholm, Motala & Vally 2003; Fleisch 2002; Kallaway 2002; Motala & Pampallis 2001; Nzimande & Mathieson 2000).

The debate about what is to be done focuses on a slightly different set of issues. Here, too, three approaches can be identified (van der Berg 2001; van der Berg, Wood & le Roux 2002; and Vally, Porteus, Carrim & Tshoane in Chisholm, Motala & Vally 2003). Underlying all three are assumptions about what matters: schools or contexts. In practice, differences are essentially a matter of emphasis. There are few analysts that do not see a link between contexts and the quality of schooling. The first argues for more and better facilities and resources. The second says that these do not make much difference to schooling outcomes. What matters is the management of resources, on the one hand, and the uses made of resources in the teaching and learning process, on the other. Thus, regardless of how many resources are put into schools, what matters is how districts and principals manage them and what teachers do with them. The third approach is more concerned with the values that are embraced by, taught and embodied in the pedagogy and practice of schools. From different perspectives, this was equally important to the Minister of Education and his critics, all of whom were, and are, interested in promoting a rights-based culture in schools.

There are major changes in the state of South Africa's schools, but there are also deep continuities with the past. It is no accident that the poorest provinces with the poorest schools are those that incorporate former home-lands: the current state of schools in these provinces is closely intertwined with the twists and turns of a history more than two centuries old. But it is also linked to present dynamics and social forces unleashed by the democra-tisation of South African society, as well as the nature of education itself, a system that is slow to change and so embedded in the tensions, stresses and strains of the society itself that there is a continuous contradiction between its intentions and outcomes. This combination of history, contemporary dynamism and the character of the system itself must go some way towards explaining both success and failure.

This chapter uses a combination of primary and secondary information to explore the impacts and shortfalls of these changes. The collection of educa-tional statistics has both changed and improved since 1994 but there are still gaps because data collection systems are still developing. Reliability of educa-tional statistics is always open to question because of the way in which such statistics are gathered. They are also always collected in terms of officially determined parameters. As such, the statistics available reflect the priorities of governments and the ways in which education is organised for administrative purposes. The collection of statistics assists in the ordering of the population, but also in the evaluation of inequalities and the implementation of govern-ment programmes aimed, for example, at poverty reduction. As government created a new system of education, so too did its data-gathering system and categories of data collection change. Whereas statistics were previously gath-ered by race, and very inadequately in the previous homelands, they are now gathered principally by province and in terms of the new divisions of educa-tion: General Education and Training band (GET), Further Education and Training band (FET), Adult Basic Education and Training (ABET), Early Childhood Department (ECD), Education for Learners with Special Needs

(ELSEN) and Higher Education (HE). Differences and variations in the questions asked between different provinces mean that it takes time for the necessary adjustments to be made for information to be immediately available. The most recent educational statistics made available by the Department of Education's (DoE's) Education Management Information System (EMIS) thus exist for 2001. The chapter will begin with a brief analysis of the issues on which there was unanimity at the dawn of 1994. Information on such issues will thus be supplemented by other sources and use will be made of recent research that is not only based on the official statistics.

What impact have the changes that were effected between 1994 and 2004, and sketched at the beginning of this chapter, had on inequalities between urban and rural areas? Have conditions improved in the majority of South Africa's schools? In order to make this assessment, it is necessary to examine the legacy of apartheid.

Legacy of apartheid

The state of South Africa's schools in 1994 can only be described as parlous. Beset by conflict for well over two decades, the majority of black schools suffered not only from state-imposed deprivations, but also from what many observers referred to as the collapse of a culture of teaching and learning.

Assessments of the legacy of apartheid at the end of apartheid highlighted major inequalities between white and black and urban and rural areas and departments of education. Overlain by an ideology of white superiority and black inferiority, apartheid education divided educational privilege and achievement by race. Inequalities were apparent in differential spending which had an impact on access to, and the quantity and quality of education on offer to black and white. Typical indicators were literacy levels, school completion rates, pupil–teacher ratios, number, quality and qualifications of teachers and availability of different types of resources. On all indicators, the poorest off were Africans living in the previous homelands, and on farms and in townships.

Literacy rates followed this pattern. A 1994 study showed that while 80 per cent of black South Africans were unable to read passages written at a Standard 5 (Grade 7) level, about 40 per cent of all white South Africans failed to read and compute at this level. Indians were on average more literate than whites, with coloured literacy between that of whites and blacks. While black females on average stayed in school half a year longer than black males, female literacy was lower. The study drew attention to deep and continuing inter-racial inequalities and to the fact that black children suffer from the lowest quality schools. It argued that although enrolments had expanded in the 1980s, this was not matched by improvements in literacy levels, pointing to a contradiction between expanding schooling and educational quality (Fuller, Pillay & Sirur 1995; see also *Business Day* 1.06.95, *Weekly Mail* 2.06.95, *Sowetan* 2.06.95).

The Reconstruction and Development Programme (RDP) of 1994 traced this 'destruction, distortion or neglect of the human potential of our country' to a system 'fragmented along racial and ethnic lines' (RSA 1994:58). To address this legacy, the RDP promoted the integration of the education and training system at all levels, the introduction of ten years compulsory general schooling in which classes do not exceed 40 students, special attention to the education of girls and women, and the development of ECD, ABET and special education as an integral part of the education system. It argued for the transformation of the structure, curricula and certification of the system and their realignment with a new qualifications system. It argued for the improvement of school buildings, proper attention to farm schools, provision of opportunities for students learning within formal institutions, workers in industry, out-of-school youth and adults in community learning centres, the restructuring of higher education and the expectations of teachers. HIV/AIDS was not yet as present in the consciousness of people as it has since become. The RDP recommendations on education made no mention of the pandemic.

Post-apartheid initiatives

There can be little doubt that there have been major changes since 1994. In the first two years after 1994, 18 racially-divided departments were restructured into one national and nine provincial departments and the National Education Policy Act (1995) was introduced, establishing the foundations for an integrated system of education based on an outcomes-based rather than a Christian National Education philosophy. Education budgets began to be designed in principle to achieve equitable outcomes and overcome the racial disparities that marked apartheid budget allocations. Funding for school building programmes and school meals was made available. Schools, colleges, technikons and universities were opened to all races. The South African

Schools Act of 1996 provided for the establishment of public and independent schools and decentralised educational control through the establishment of school governing bodies. Curricula, their review and design, were revamped through the introduction of Curriculum 2005. New forms of assessment, qualification and certification were introduced.

Higher education was rationalised and reorganised. New expectations were expressed of teachers, and in the immediate aftermath of 1994, an ambitious exercise was undertaken to redistribute teachers from urban to rural and white to black schools. Numerous poor-quality teacher education colleges located by apartheid governments in the former homelands were closed and some were incorporated into higher education. A new multilingual language policy was articulated for schools. Skills levies and sector education training authorities were brought into being to provide training for workers.

But in many respects change has not been as simple and clear-cut as originally imagined. The unfolding and translation of aspirations into practical reality has been a complex and often tortuously contested affair. In terms of the RDP aspirations described earlier, the system is now racially integrated, but the attempt to integrate education and training has been less successful. South Africa has introduced nine and not ten years of compulsory schooling.[3] On average, classes do not exceed 40 students per teacher, but there are still schools with as many as 80 learners in one class. The structure, curricula and certification of the system have been overhauled and aligned with a new qualifications system. The education of workers in industry is high on the agenda. There have been improvements in school buildings, higher education, teacher expectations and other areas highlighted by the RDP. But the education of girls and women, early childhood development, adult and special education, and opportunities for out-of-school youth remain under-served. And overall, the educational gap between urban and rural areas and between different social classes remains vast.

Facilities and infrastructure, basic services and adult education

Inequalities between urban and rural schools are visible in the facilities and resources available to them. Continuing backlogs and inequalities are very unevenly spread across the provinces. There are differences between provinces, between schools in the same locality and even within the same school grounds. A rural school might have new toilets, but no water and the rest of the school buildings will have collapsing ceilings and broken windows. In rural areas where sanitation is inadequate, children still use dongas or forests or dams, sharing valuable water resources with animals (EPC 2004).

These inequalities are documented most clearly and comprehensively in the School Register of Needs Survey (SRNS), first conducted in 1996 and then again in 2000. It collects information from every school in the country on its exact geographic location, physical facilities, condition of school buildings, services provided, and equipment and resources available. The SRNS conducted in 2000 reported some improvements: less overcrowding, improvements in the educator to learner ratio, basic facilities and access for learners who are physically disabled. For the rest, provincial variations were striking. There was an increase in the number of schools that reported weak and very weak buildings, and a significant percentage of schools reported on criminal incidents in schools.

None of this gives any idea, however, of the interrelated sets of hardships imposed on poor rural communities by poverty, unemployment, inadequate access to basic services such as water, good roads and electricity, and lack of education and skills. There are numerous communities that have had the benefit of initial service delivery, in the form, for example, of water taps, pumps and dams, but whose basic lack of skills and communication networks means that they are easily defrauded, and unable to fix or maintain new installations, leaving them there as symbols of failed development. Broken taps and pumps, telephone poles without electricity, dams with no means of getting water to the land – these litter the landscape in too many ruralcommunities and draw attention to the dire need for linking improved service delivery with adult education (EPC 2004). Schools are embedded in these contexts and both reflect and reproduce patterns of poverty, unemployment and illiteracy that pre-date 1994. Increased educational spending can be only part of the answer for this comprehensive challenge.

Equitable spending is not equal to equity and quality

Contemporary budgets look very different from apartheid budgets. Budgeting is no longer on the basis of race. Between 1994 and 1999, budgeting priorities fell on reorganising rather than expanding the existing budget. As a percentage of gross domestic product, South Africa spent 7.3 per cent on education in 1991–92. Between 2001 and 2004, it spent an average of 5.5 per cent. Despite major wage increases for teachers in 1996, there was a decline in public school budgets between 1997 and 2001 at an annual rate of 1.5 per cent (Wildeman 2003). After this rough start, expenditure is expected to grow at an average 2.7 per cent in real terms over the next medium-term expenditure framework (MTEF). At 36.7 per cent of total provincial spending, education makes up the largest proportion of provincial spending. Up to 1998, the greater part of this was committed to personnel expenditure (salaries), leaving very little for capital expenditure or learning support materials. These aspects of the budget are, however, expected to grow by 35.7 per cent over the next MTEF (RSA 2003:52). Spending on education as a share of provincial expenditure is highest in Limpopo (40 per cent), Mpumulanga (40.4 per cent), Eastern Cape (38.6 per cent) and North West (38.2 per cent). According to the *Inter-governmental Fiscal Review*, 'this may reflect budget choices and preferences, (but) it does also have a structural and historical basis. Provinces which amalgamated multiple administrations tend to have bigger staff numbers, with duplication in a number of functions and positions' (RSA 2003:53).

Table 8.1 shows how provincial budgets are structured and that public ordinary school education makes up the biggest percentage of provincial education expenditure.

Under apartheid, per capita expenditure was determined by race. Spending patterns are now visible per province. Spending patterns show that although there has been an increase in per capita expenditure, there is still a large gap between provinces. The *Intergovernmental Fiscal Review* (RSA 2003:54) points out, for example, that despite having the biggest education budget of R10.4 billion, and notwithstanding the highest growth in total spending of 12.4 per cent a year between 1999–2000 and 2002–03, KwaZulu-Natal still has the lowest per learner expenditure.

Much of the initial reorganisation of education was conducted in the context of a commitment by the new state to fiscal discipline and belt-tightening. In the period between 1994 and 1999, these parameters of change jostled uncomfortably with imperatives for social justice. The need for state inter-vention sat equally uncomfortably with the global emphasis on extending markets to education, which found resonance amongst some quarters in

Table 8.1 *Provincial education expenditure per programme (R million)*

	1999–2000 Actual	2000–01 Actual	2001–02 Actual	2002–03 Estimate	2003–4	2004–5	2005–6
					Medium-term estimates		
Administration	2 644	2 472	3 479	3 780	4 328	4 574	4 832
Public ordinary school education	33 653	36 966	39 213	44 306	48 804	52 702	56 083
of which: primary schools	20 322	22 200	23 709	24 526	27 121	28 920	30 807
of which: secondary schools	12 493	13 695	14 703	18 970	20 802	22 825	24 293
Other	838	1 071	801	811	881	957	982
Independent school subsidies	176	206	187	196	235	245	253
Public special school education	1 116	1 134	1 356	1 446	1 595	1 665	1 764
FET	754	827	869	1 082	1 201	1 276	1 360
ABET	362	410	401	512	551	595	637
ECD	199	197	248	449	510	538	591
Auxiliary and associated services	657	653	844	1 111	1 519	1 701	1 784
Other programmes	266	359	293	132	154	151	161
Total expenditure	**39 828**	**43 223**	**46 889**	**53 102**	**58 897**	**63 447**	**67 465**
Economic classification							
Current expenditure	39 369	42 551	45 507	51 251	55 730	59 958	63 792
of which: personnel	36 221	39 308	41 531	46 046	49 322	52 718	55 813
Capital expenditure	459	672	1 382	1 851	3 167	3 489	3 672

Source: RSA 2003:55

Table 8.2 *Expenditure per learner by province (Rand)*

	1999–2000 Actual	2000–01 Actual	2001–02 Actual	2002–03 Estimate
EC	2 846	3 362	3 866	4 466
FS	3 570	3 910	4 433	5 155
G	4 021	4 384	4 655	5 077
KZN	2 633	3 069	3 432	3 762
L	3 211	3 452	3 674	4 015
M	3 019	3 287	3 685	4 321
NC	4 438	4 858	5 139	5 805
NW	3 602	4 065	4 447	4 727
WC	3 987	4 391	4 721	5 081
Average	3 234	3 631	3 995	4 437

Source: RSA 2003:54

Note: Eastern Cape (EC), Free State (FS), Gauteng (G), KwaZulu-Natal (KZN), Limpopo (L), Mpumalanga (M), North West (NW), Northern Cape (NC), Western Cape (WC)

South Africa. Even as new legislation was sweeping away apartheid-era relics, and spending patterns were revised in the direction of greater equity, the commitment to fiscal discipline resulted in conflict and changes in the cultures of institutions (Jansen 2004).

Keeping the budget within limits was one challenge. Improving both equity and quality within the context of constrained resources was another. In the first few years after 1994, the intention was to achieve both by redistributing teachers (the highest cost in the budget) from better-resourced, white and mainly urban schools to poorer-resourced, black and mainly rural schools and by shifting part of the burden for costs onto parents through school fees. I will deal with the impact and unintended consequences of each in turn.

According to the *Intergovernmental Fiscal Review*:

> After 1999, the budgeting process was stabilised, and the emphasis fell on targeted pro-poor funding mechanisms as well as a stronger emphasis on social justice and human rights pro-grammes. Fees have not however been abolished. In 2000, the Department introduced the National Norms and Standards for School Funding, the aim of which is to focus non-personnel expenditure on those schools with the greatest need. All schools are assessed in terms of their physical conditions and poverty levels of the community in which they are located. Resources are now targeted at those schools … Items such as water and electricity, teaching equipment and supplies, and learner support materials are distributed according to the resource targeting list. Government has recognised some weaknesses in this system of resource targeting. One of the most important challenges involves the capacity to implement it. (RSA 2003:65)

School fees

Despite major changes in spending patterns, there is still considerable discomfort about the use of school fees as a dimension of policy. School governing bodies have the right to set fees. These vary enormously, depending on the wealth of the supporting community. Fiske and Ladd (2004) argue that it is the consequence of advice offered by consultants and adopted by the African National Congress (ANC) in the transition to democracy. The basis of their argument was that it would ensure that the system remained a public one as it would keep the middle classes within the public school system, a necessity for the overall health of the system.

On the one hand, as Fiske and Ladd argue, it is certainly true that the system has remained a public one and that fees have not limited access. The DoE itself claims universal access at primary level. And a recent analysis of changes in access to schooling and the efficiency of the system confirms this by observing that 'there has been an extraordinary increase in the provision of schooling over the last two and a half decades ... with gross enrolment ratios of 99 per cent in the primary phase and in the secondary phase just below 87 per cent' (Perry & Arends 2003:304). This growth has been mainly amongst African learners. Primary school enrolments reached a peak in the mid-1990s and slowed down thereafter, whereas secondary school enrolment doubled in each decade from 1975, beginning to slow down only after 1997.

But there have been unintended consequences. The result of South Africa's fee-paying policy has been that richer public schools have been able to retain their privilege and edge over poor schools by employing additional teachers and improved resources to ensure better quality teaching. Poorer schools, on the other hand, have not charged high fees but are often unable to extract even their low fees from impoverished parents. Poor parents are exempt from fees, and pro-poor funding mechanisms have been instituted, but are virtually unknown in rural areas. Unscrupulous and not-so-unscrupulous principals who require income additional to that provided by the Department, often fail to inform or are unable to implement fee-exemption policies. In urban areas, access to former white, Indian and coloured schools is limited by the high fees they set. The rapid growth of informal settlements, and lack of schools in them, means that families here rely on access to neighbouring schools – but are often excluded by the inability to pay fees. The shame and humiliation imposed by the inability to pay even meagre school fees is a pervasive feature of the lives of the poor.

Universal access also does not mean that all children are in school all of the time and flow smoothly through it. Enrolment figures hide the high numbers of over-age learners in classes, and high levels of repetition and dropout, especially in rural areas. Perry and Arends (2003) suggest that more than 50 per cent of appropriately aged learners were either outside the school system or held back in primary grades. High enrolments obscure the fact that learners are not necessarily enrolled in the proper grades. In 1997, for example, 77 per cent of learners aged 14 to 18 years were enrolled at school, but 20 per cent of this age group were still in primary school. The drop-out rates in the secondary grades climb steadily to Grade 11, with 14.1 per cent of learners dropping out at the end of Grade 11. Such enrolment rates also hide the 'mainstreaming by default' of disabled learners.

In addition to school fees, there are other burdens that the poor have to carry that inhibit full participation in schooling. A 2003 departmental review of the financing, resourcing and costs of education in public schools (DoE 2003a) revealed that despite budget reforms to ensure equality in per-learner expenditure, poorer schools need assistance in procurement of goods and services and asset management and also continue to suffer from expensive textbooks and an inefficiently managed ordering process, high school uniform and transport costs, as well as poor management of school nutrition programmes.

In conclusion, then, spending has become targeted on the poor, but the relative wealth or poverty of communities that schools serve determines the extent to which schools are able to provide quality education.

Teachers

The quality of teachers and teacher to pupil ratios in classrooms are amongst the most critical resources for making an impact on teaching and learning in schools. The new government inherited large disparities between teachers on the basis of their qualifications, class sizes and teacher to pupil ratios. These were manifested racially and between provinces. In 1996, the DoE introduced a policy of rationalisation and redeployment of teachers based on Resolution 3 of the Education Labour Relations Council which anticipated phasing in a learner to educator ratio of 40:1 in all primary schools and 35:1 in all secondary schools (Crouch & Perry 2003:480). The racial dynamics of South African society determined the way in which the rationalisation and redeployment policy of 1996 actually took effect. More expensive teachers in the system were offered voluntary severance packages. Teachers in the better-resourced parts of the system did not move to the poorer-resourced parts of the system. Instead, poorer provinces employed new teachers, many of whom were poorly qualified.

There has been a huge increase in the number of teachers employed by school governing bodies (Perry & Arends 2003). In order to retain their previous small pupil to teacher ratios, formerly privileged schools with low pupil to teacher ratios used the powers given to them under the South African Schools Act to set fees that would enable the employment of additional teachers, who have become known as 'governing body teachers' – teachers, in other words, who are not employed by the Departments but by the school.

There is conflicting evidence on whether the number of unqualified teachers has risen or dropped. The *Intergovernmental fiscal review* (RSA 2003:63) argues that intensive teacher education initiatives have contributed to a drop in the number of educators without suitable qualifications. It cites the case of KwaZulu-Natal where the number of educators without matric was reduced from 1 757 in 1997 to none in 2002. It acknowledges that nationally there are still 68 000 educators who do not have this minimum qualification.

Research by the DoE and the Human Sciences Research Council (HSRC) reveals a different picture. According to Crouch and Perry (2003:481), the number of unqualified teachers in the system (less than matric plus a diploma or degree) has risen over time, rather than decreased. In 2000, the percentage of underqualified or unqualified teachers in the system was higher than in 1975. In 1975, 11 per cent of educators were unqualified or under-qualified. In 1985, this increased to 17 per cent, and in 1994 to 36 per cent. By 2000, it had decreased to 22 per cent, still an unacceptably high percentage.

The incorporation of teacher education colleges into universities has significant implications for improving the quality of teacher education in South Africa. Since many institutions are still grappling with the changes at an institutional level, these implications will probably take some time to become visible.

In the short term, teachers who are upgrading are doing so through distance education. In 2001, of the 107 922 students enrolled at universities, 20 321 were enrolled full-time at contact institutions. Table 8.3 shows that the large major-ity of students enrolled in educator training at universities and technikons in 2000 and 2001 were enrolled in distance education. Distance education programmes for upgrading qualifications are generally public-private partnerships. They generate sizeable subsidies for their respective institutions but, as suggested earlier, the DoE has concerns about the extent to which universities are monitoring the quality of these distance programmes.

Table 8.3 *Enrolment in educator training at universities and technikons, 2000 and 2001*

Year	Universities				Technikons			
	Distance at contact institutions	Unisa	Contact only	Total	Distance at contact institutions	Technikon SA	Technikon Contact only	Total
2000	60 486	12 241	17 451	90 178	11 280	183	1 819	13 282
2001	63 999	23 602	20 321	107 922	8 498	253	2 929	1 680

Source: DoE (2000, 2001a) as represented in Crouch & Perry 2003:482
Notes:
Data for 2001 are missing for the University of North West, Border Technikon and Eastern Cape Technikon.
Data for 2001 are provisional.

Almost all teachers (97 per cent) are unionised (Govender 2004). They are distributed across three main union bodies, the South African Democratic Teachers' Unions (Sadtu), National Association of Professional Teachers' Associations of South Africa (Naptosa) and the Suid-Afrikaanse Onderwysersunie (SAOU). The vast majority are in Sadtu, followed by Naptosa and SAOU. Table 8.4 shows changing union membership since 1999.

Table 8.4 *Changing union membership, 1999–2002*

Union	1999	2000	2001	2002
Sadtu	218 878	214 247	211 480	210 235
Naptosa	84 841	91 375	90 157	95 988
SAOU	46 920	43 878	42 800	41 315

Source: Drawn from Govender 2004

The impact of HIV/AIDS on schools and teachers is a major public issue (see Chisholm et al. 2003). Some have argued that 'the gains of education for all are being undone by the AIDS pandemic' (Coombe 2000). Others are more sceptical, arguing that the empirical and statistical basis of these claims is inflated and that teachers in particular are a low-risk category of people (Bennell 2003). Anecdotal and documented evidence of, amongst other things, the kinds of relationships many teachers engage in with learners suggests otherwise. Recently, the Education and Labour Relations Council commissioned the HSRC to study HIV prevalence rates amongst teachers. This is a comprehensive study that intends to look, along with other things, at the relationship of HIV/AIDS to workload, absenteeism, knowledge about, and impact of, HIV/AIDS amongst teachers.

How to address HIV/AIDS in education is partly a question of values. Despite policy commitments, campaigns and programmes to promote peace and democracy, anti-racism and anti-sexism, violence in schools remains a major issue, as does racism and sexism. Rape of schoolgirls, sexual violence and abuse, often by teachers, have been a marked feature of the schooling experience of many girls as well as boys. The connections of sexual and other violence, and teenage pregnancy, with access to schooling and drop-out rates are key. The connections between sexual violence, HIV/AIDS and gender identity are complex and vital to understanding social action as some recent work shows (Epstein, Morrell, Moletsane & Unterhalter 2004; Moletsane, Morrell, Unterhalter & Epstein 2002; Morrell, Unterhalter, Moletsane & Epstein 2001). The role of teachers in all this is central. Unions and the DoE have, to some extent, undertaken programmes and initiatives to turn teachers into change agents in this regard, but there is still a great deal of work that needs to be done. Much depends on the combined effort of the Department, teacher education initiatives, communities and unions.

In conclusion, there is still cause for concern about the numbers of unqualified teachers in the system and the quality of teacher education on offer. Hopefully, new teacher education programmes at universities will start kicking in to improve the overall quality of teachers, teacher unions will continue to use their muscle to strengthen teachers' professional commitments and communities, and the Department will support and recognise teachers in their efforts to improve schools.

Deracialisation and racial integration

1994 provided the opportunity for the wholesale dismantling of an edifice of schooling founded on race. If race separation was the defining feature of schools in the apartheid era, race integration became a defining feature in the post-apartheid era. 1994 also provided the opportunity for South Africa to experiment, explore and innovate in this area. The Constitution forbade all forms of discrimination and the South African Schools Act of 1996 provided the basis for the reconstruction of schools in the image of non-racialism. Provisions were made for the integration of schools, the rewriting of curricula and textbooks, the renovation of institutions dedicated to the training and education of teachers, and renewal of support structures in the management of education. In the meantime, the doors of previously white, Indian and coloured schools had opened also to the wider world and new and different ways of seeing race and racism, segregation and integration, were emerging and beginning to confront traditional and received ways of seeing these issues in South Africa.

The production of a new curriculum, which places citizenship and rights at its centre, as well as a National Action Plan to Combat Racism, raises a series of new questions about integration policies and practices in schools: on what kind of terrain in schools and teacher education institutions does the revised curriculum, as well as the National Action Plan, build? What are the national patterns in terms of integration?

Many school principals, espousing 'colour blindness', claim not to keep track of the colour of their learners or to keep statistics on a racial basis. Information for the EMIS of the national DoE is collected on a racial basis, but this information has not been analysed as yet, and there are concerns about the validity of such analysis related to questions about race.

Evidence from recent studies suggests, however, that despite desegregation of white, Indian, and coloured schools, and significant demographic movements of people over the last decade and large numbers of children being bussed from townships to suburban schools, the large majority of schools in South Africa remain uni- or mono-racial. This emerges most clearly in the tracking of trends in Gauteng between 1996 and 2002. Sujee (2004) shows that, in 2002, 74 per cent of learners in Gauteng were African, 18 per cent white, 4.9 per cent coloured and 2.7 per cent Indian. Only 0.2 per cent were non-South African. The number of Indian and white learners decreased in their former departments over the period 1996 to 2000. The former white, Indian and coloured schools increased their enrolment of African learners substantially. The greatest increase was shown in former Indian schools, where African learners now constitute the majority of learners. According to Sujee (2004), 25 per cent of African learners have shifted from the former township schools to other departments since 1996, but only 7 per cent of these are in former white schools. An even higher proportion of Indian and coloured learners has moved to formerly white schools. The percentage of Indian learners in Indian schools dropped from 78 per cent in 1996 to 40 per cent in 2002. The majority of white learners (86 per cent) are in former white schools, but their number has decreased since 1996 as some have moved to independent or private schools. The percentage of white learners in independent schools overall has increased from 8 per cent in 1996 to 13.5 per cent in 2002. This does not mean that all schools have integrated equally or that township schools have emptied of learners; Sujee is emphatic that this is not the case.

But what happens once learners are integrated into these schools? Anecdotal evidence suggests that many schools, particularly those on the *platteland*, stream children – officially on the grounds of language, but unofficially on the basis of race and class. Others exercise a more benign form of assimilation but nonetheless expect children to adapt to the cultural norms and practices of the schools – established under apartheid. The assumption here is that if children want to come to these schools, they must abide by their rules and regulations. These rules and regulations often include hidden forms of discrimination against children who do not share the school's linguistic, class and/or cultural norms (Dolby 2001). Soudien (2004) argues that this is the dominant model in South Africa, and that there are in fact few genuinely anti-racist classrooms or teachers who are sensitive to the differences amongst learners at school.

Despite reconciliation at national level and integration at school level, racism persists and is evident in both continuing manifestations of racial conflict and numerous forms of re-segregation inside schools. In the 1990s, several cases caught the attention of the national media. The South African Human Rights Commission was inundated with cases of school racism to such an extent that it commissioned a report that demonstrated the continuing, widespread character of race and racism in schools. This report and other research highlighted the deep continuities with the apartheid era (Vally & Dalamba 1999).

The consequence has been the development of a two-tier system in which social class is a major factor in determining who is included and who is excluded. Ultimately, formerly white, Indian and coloured schools are only a minority of schools. The majority of schools in South Africa are in townships, on farms, in informal settlements, and the former homelands. They are largely uni-racial and poor.

Changing classrooms

The issues discussed in the preceding two sections raise questions about what it is inside schools to which learners have access: while more learners might be enrolled, albeit at the wrong levels, and many teachers may be unqualified, what is the curriculum to which they are exposed, what is the quality of resources and how relevant is the learning that occurs? How does it manifest, reproduce or change inequalities? How does it address and challenge new issues of diversity and rights inside classrooms? And finally, what meaning does the context of HIV/AIDS give to classroom practice?

The main initiative since 1994 has been the introduction of outcomes-based education and Curriculum 2005 in 1997. At the heart of Curriculum 2005 is a set of values linked to social justice, human rights, equity and development, as well as a learner-centred approach to teaching and learning. In 2000 this curriculum was reviewed and revised. It will be implemented through the Revised National Curriculum Statements for Schools from 1994 (Chisholm 2003; DoE 2002).

The revision was undertaken partly in response to studies which showed that despite the new curriculum and pedagogy which it mandated, 'learners' scores are far below what is expected at all levels of the schooling system, both in relation to other countries (including other developing countries) and in relation to the expectations of the South African curriculum' (Taylor, Muller & Vinjevold 2003:41). One of their most significant conclusions is, however, that 'pupils who attend classes conducted in a language which is not their first language are at a significant disadvantage' and that 'this disadvantage is accentuated when the language of teaching and learning is not the first language of the teacher'(Taylor et al. 2003:65). A sample survey by the Southern African Consortium for Monitoring Educational Quality of Grade 6 learners in 2000 confirmed this picture. It showed that South African learners in Grade 6 achieve a level of reading and mathematics proficiency that is better than that in neighbouring Lesotho and Namibia, but lower than that for almost all other countries in the region. This is despite South Africa's much higher expenditure per learner than in any other country in the region, with the exception of Botswana. Thus, although Tanzania spends about half as much as South Africa in terms of expenditure over GNP, scores measuring reading skills amongst Tanzanian learners are about 50 per cent higher than South Africa's scores (DoE 2003b:101).

Why are achievements so low? Common explanations hinge on physical resources and infrastructure, curriculum, the language of instruction, texts and teachers.[4] These all play their part. The introduction of a revised curriculum with expanded budgets for learning support materials should support improvements, but in impoverished contexts there are the additional consequences and effects of poverty. Research conducted in 2003 for a Nelson Mandela Foundation study on rural education (EPC 2004) provides evidence that patterns of daily life in rural areas have a major impact on attendance and concentration. This is what a high school learner from Mnqagaye, in KwaZulu-Natal, had to say when asked about the problems that he experiences with school:

> As you can see, I start the day by going out to sell wood so that I can get money with which to buy a bus coupon. This is because there is no high school nearby; they are all far away ...

> I sell my own wood to buy the coupon and the candle, which I use to study. My mother sells her own wood to buy food for the family ... And the issue of distance is very serious. I have to wake up at 04:00 and only get back home at 16:00. I am normally dead tired and very hungry on my return and there is no time to study.[5]

The problem affects primary school learners as well. Children perform household, childcare and agricultural duties at home before school and they also do maintenance chores at school. These are part of the expectations of families and teachers. Both boys and girls in rural schools spend time cleaning classrooms, toilets and the schoolyard and fetching water. Teachers often send children on errands, which take them out of the school. A Grade 6 schoolgirl described her day as follows:

> After school at home I'm bound to do all the household tasks because I am the firstborn at home. I travel long distances and go through the bush to fetch water at Magesheni, but it's not a fearful place, therefore I'm not afraid to go there. From there I clean the house until it shines ... After that I clean the family yard. By the time I finish it is already late therefore I don't get time to play.

A schoolteacher in KwaZulu-Natal explained a not uncommon situation of impaired attention in class when she said that:

> Children come to school hungry, become dull in morning
> sessions, they are sleepy, they are cold when it is cold, they do
> not wear warm clothes, they stay with grandparents who depend
> on a government grant that is not adequate, their parents are
> in Durban and some of the parents have passed away.

In these contexts school meals play a vitally important role. But not all schools have them, let alone clinics to attend to the numerous everyday ailments such as poor eyesight, and diseases such as cholera, that afflict children. The stigma and taboos that surround HIV/AIDS compound the difficulties of dealing with and treating orphans and vulnerable children at school.

Performance in school is less important in some approaches than democracy and social relations in schools. Who participates in school decision-making processes, and with what effect, has long been seen as critical to democratic schools. So too are pedagogies that maximise learner involvement and partic- ipation. Decentralisation through school governing bodies is one aspect of the equation. The other is learner-centred education. The decentralisation of decision-making to school governing bodies, composed of parents, teachers and learners in high schools, has had greatly varied effects. In the main, they have entrenched existing inequalities. Schools in better-resourced communi- ties have, on the whole, been able to use the powers granted them under the 1996 South African Schools Act to better effect than schools in rural commu- nities (Grant-Lewis & Motala 2004). In both urban and rural communities, local elites play a significant role in schools. Learner-centred educational pedagogies show a similar pattern, working well in the better-resourced schools, and less well in poorer rural schools (Harley & Wedekind 2004).

The major inequalities inherited from the apartheid past have softened but have not been overcome and are still extremely harsh in many areas. There remain significant social class differences that are manifested in schooling. This is also evident when one considers the issues examined earlier in relation to schools that have historically served the minority of the population – formerly white, Indian and coloured schools. The changes in these schools are a mirror of the broader social changes that have shaped the overall character of the education system.

The evidence on what has happened, and is happening, in formerly white, Indian and coloured schools is unambiguous. The defining feature of South

African schools and schooling is arguably the politics of race and racism. It is one of the central fault lines of South African society, intersecting in complex ways with class, gender and ethnicity. Race is historically inscribed into the functioning of everyday life through those institutions in which the majority of children spend the greater part of their lives: schools. Seen as one of the principal generators, justifiers and vehicles of racialised thoughts, actions and identities, the challenge has been, and continues to be, whether and how the roles, rules, social character and functioning of schools can change to challenge the retrograde aspects of such formation and stimulate new and diverse identities and forms of acknowledgement and social practice.

Although a rights-based discourse suffuses official statements of both the DoE and non-governmental organisations, the meaning and real conflicts over values play out far from the public eye: in many racially integated schools where an assimilationist model denies the identities of those who do not belong to the dominant culture, and in many rural schools, where both parents and teachers continue to believe in the value of corporal punishment despite its prohibition. Expressing the tension between the patriarchal authority of elders in rural communities and the authority of the new state embodied in the Constitution, at a meeting called by researchers on the project for the Nelson Mandela Foundation, one community member in Limpopo said: 'In the rights-bound South Africa, we find it hard to discipline children since they are aware of their rights. They always talk child abuse and threaten to take us to court. Educators as well are trapped in the same kind of helpless situation' (NMF 2004).

Conclusion

Over the first decade of democracy, much has changed and many momentous initiatives have been undertaken to redress the inequalities and injustices of the past. But the system is complex, uneven and diverse, and the consequences of policy have been ambiguous and contradictory. Access and physical infrastructure have improved in many schools, pupil to teacher ratios have been reduced and the introduction of school governing bodies has enabled local decision-making. Schools have stabilised and the impact of democracy must be felt in innumerable invisible and immeasurable ways. But the quality of schooling overall, and in rural areas particularly, still leaves much to be desired. The high percentage of un- and under-qualified teachers in the system is a cause for concern. The persistent and unresolved language issues that continue to hamper learning also require decisive action. High dropouts and repetition rates compromise the claimed achievements of universal access.

Improvements are highly unevenly spread, and the provinces that suffered greatest neglect in the apartheid period still show the greatest difficulties in overcoming the legacy of apartheid. They are the provinces that incorporated the previous homelands, namely Limpopo, Eastern Cape and KwaZulu-Natal. The system remains broadly unequal, with previously middle-class schools – and many previously white, Indian and coloured schools – able to charge fees and employ additional teachers to ensure adequate levels of resourcing and a better quality education. These schools have desegregated in different ways, assimilating African students into their dominant ethos. Poverty, race and gender inequality remain deeply etched into the fabric of daily school life. This is the challenge for the next decade. In this context, renewed commitments to poverty eradication at national level are a vital complement to initiatives in education, such as pro-poor funding, Curriculum 2005, new emphases on the professional development of teachers and sustained attention to how HIV/AIDS can be addressed in and through schools.

Acknowledgement

Information in this chapter was first presented in April 2004 by Linda Chisholm in a paper commissioned by Unesco's *Education for All Global Monitoring Report* titled, 'The quality of primary education in South Africa'.

Notes

1   Private schools currently comprise only about 2.1 per cent of South Africa's schooling sector (Fiske & Ladd 2004).

2   Table 8.5 *Number of teachers in schools, per province*

Province	Primary	Secondary	Combined	Inter-mediate & middle	F %	M %	Total
EC	627	397	1 002	0	51	49	2 027
FS	344	208	43	107	50	50	703
G	858	488	98	0	50	50	1 444
KZN	1 663	851	146	0	50	50	2 661
L	1 136	639	17	0	50	50	1 793
M	494	286	112	0	50	50	894
NC	96	45	22	29	50	50	194
NW	494	235	13	139	50	50	883
WC	504	285	21	77	51	49	888
National	6 222	3 438	1 478	353	50	50	11 492

Source: SNAP Survey 2001, District Development and Support Project 2003

3   It can be argued that with Grade R, the reception year, there are ten years of schooling; in practice too few schools actually have a Grade R to count it as part of a ten-year structure of schooling.

4   Taylor, Muller and Vinjevold (2003) argue for intensive instruction in the language of teaching and learning in teacher education, home practice in the official language of the school and a conscious focus on the importance of language at the school level, as well as explicit policies and programmes to develop proficiency amongst staff, pupils and parents in the official language of the school.

5   The interviews here are drawn from research conducted in the course of a Nelson Mandela Foundation study on rural education conducted between May and August 2004 in specific villages of Limpopo, Eastern Cape and KwaZulu-Natal.

References

Bennell P (2003) The impact of the AIDS epidemic on schooling in sub-Saharan Africa. Background paper for the Biennial Meeting of the Association for Development in Africa.

Chisholm L (2003) The state of curriculum reform in South Africa: The issue of Curriculum 2005. In J Daniel, A Habib & R Southall (eds.) *State of the Nation: South Africa 2003–2004*. Cape Town: HSRC Press.

Chisholm L, Motala S & Vally S (2003) *South African education policy review 1993–2000*. Johannesburg: Heinemann.

Coombe C (2000) Numbers and the AIDS effect in Southern Africa, *Norrag News* 26, April.

Crouch L & Perry H (2003) Educators. In HSRC, *Human resources development review 2003: Education, employment and skills in South Africa*. Cape Town: HSRC Press.

DoE (Department of Education, South Africa) (2000) *A South African curriculum for the twenty-first century: Report of the Review Committee on Curriculum 2005*. Presented to the Minister of Education, Prof. Kader Asmal, Pretoria, 31.05.00.

DoE (2002) *Revised national curriculum statement Grades R–9 (schools)*. Pretoria: DoE.

DoE (2003a) *Education statistics in South Africa at a glance in 2001*. Pretoria: DoE.

DoE (2003b) *Report to the Minister: Review of the financing, resourcing and costs of education in public schools: Free education for the poor*. Pretoria: DoE.

Dolby N (2001) *Constructing race: Youth, identity, and popular culture in South Africa*. Albany: State University of New York Press.

EPC (Education Policy Consortium) (2004) *Participatory data: Description, analysis and presentation*. Nelson Mandela Foundation Rural Schools Project, Volume A–B.

Epstein D, Morrell R, Moletsane R & Unterhalter E (2004) Gender and HIV/AIDS in Africa south of the Sahara: Interventions, activism and identities, *Transformation* 54.

Fiske E & Ladd H (2004) Balancing public and private resources for basic education: School fees in post-apartheid South Africa. In L Chisholm (ed.) *Changing class: Education and social change in post-apartheid South Africa*. Pretoria: HSRC.

Fleisch BD (2002) *Managing educational change: The state and school reform in South Africa*. Johannesburg: Heinemann.

Fuller B, Pillay P & Sirur N (1995) Literacy trends in South Africa: Expanding education while reinforcing unequal achievement. Harvard University & University of Cape Town, 31.05.95.

Govender L (2004) Teacher unions, policy struggles and educational change 1994–2004. In L Chisholm (ed.) *Changing class: Education and social change in post-apartheid South Africa*. Pretoria: HSRC Press.

Grant-Lewis S & Motala S (2004) Education decentralisation and the quest for equality, quality and democracy. In L Chisholm (ed.) *Changing class: Education and social change in post-apartheid South Africa*. Pretoria: HSRC Press.

Harley K & Wedekind V (2004) Political change, curriculum change and social formation 1990–2004. In L Chisholm (ed.) *Changing class: Education and social change in post-apartheid South Africa*. Pretoria: HSRC Press.

Jansen J (2000) Rethinking education policymaking in South Africa: Symbols of change, signals of conflict. In A Kraak & M Young (eds.) *Education in retrospect*. Pretoria: HSRC.

Jansen J (2004) Changes and continuities in South Africa's higher education system 1990–2004. In L Chisholm (ed.) *Changing class: Education and social change in post-apartheid South Africa*. Pretoria: HSRC Press.

Kallaway P (2002) *The history of education under apartheid 1948–1994: The doors of learning and culture shall be opened*. Cape Town: Pearson Education.

Moletsane R, Morrell R, Unterhalter E & Epstein D (2002) Instituting gender equality in schools: Working in an HIV environment, *Perspectives in Education* 20:37–53.

Morrell R, Unterhalter E, Moletsane R & Epstein D (2001) HIV/AIDS, policies, schools, and gender identities, *Indicator South Africa* 18:51–57.

Motala E & Pampallis J (2001) *Education & equity: The impact of state policies on South African education*. Johannesburg: Heinemann.

NMF (Nelson Mandela Foundation) (2004) *Emerging voices: A report on rural education in South Africa*. Cape Town: HSRC Press.

Nzimande B & Mathieson S (2000) Educational transformation in South Africa's transition to democracy. In T Mebrahtu, M Crossley & D Johnson (eds.) *Globalisation, educational transformation and societies in transition*. Oxford: Symposium Books.

Perry H & Arends F (2003) Public schooling. In HSRC *Human resources development review 2003: Education, employment and skills in South Africa*. Cape Town: HSRC Press.

RSA (Republic of South Africa) (1994) *White Paper on reconstruction and development*. Vol. 353, No. 16085, 23.11.94.

RSA (National Treasury) (2003) *Intergovernmental fiscal review*. Pretoria: National Treasury.

Soudien C (2004) 'Constituting the class': An analysis of the process of 'integration' in South African schools. In L Chisholm (ed.) *Changing class: Education and social change in post-apartheid South Africa*. Pretoria: HSRC Press.

Sujee M (2004) Deracialisation of schools in Gauteng. In M Nkomo, C McKinney & L Chisholm (eds.) *Reflections on school integration: Colloquium Proceedings*. Cape Town: HSRC Publishers.

Taylor N, Muller J & Vinjevold P (2003) *Getting schools working: Research and systemic school reform in South Africa*. Cape Town: Pearson Education.

Vally S & Dalamba Y (1999) *Racism, 'racial integration' and desegregation in South African public secondary schools. A report on a study by the South African Human Rights Commission (SAHRC)*. Johannesburg: SAHRC.

Van der Berg S (2001) Resource shifts in South African schools after the political transition, *Development Southern Africa* 18:309–325.

Van der Berg S, Wood L & le Roux N (2002) Differentiation in black education, *Development Southern Africa* 19:289–306.

Wildeman R (2003) Public expenditure on education. In HSRC *Human resources development review 2003: Education, employment and skills in South Africa*. Cape Town: HSRC Press.

9 HIV/AIDS: finding ways to contain the pandemic

Tim Quinlan and Samantha Willan

Introduction

This chapter shows that the South African government is beginning to confront the challenge of actually containing the HIV/AIDS epidemic, but its efforts are still constrained by lack of leadership from the President and the Minister of Health. The net effect is that the spread of HIV and the deterioration of the population's health and welfare continue.

We include discussion on the politics of HIV/AIDS because of changes within government policy in 2003, the persistent pressure from civil society that has forced changes to date to government policy, and the continuing use of HIV/AIDS for party political interests, particularly in the run-up to the general elections on 14 April 2004.[1] Late in 2003, the government promised to implement a treatment plan which included provision of anti-retroviral treatment (ART). The promise of ART marked an about-turn in treatment policy to date. We consider why and how the changes occurred, because of their bearing on the politics of HIV/AIDS after the elections.

On the one hand, the African National Congress (ANC)-led government is set to win the country's third democratic election, but, in an emerging democracy, this is a difficult phase: the glory of the initial transition has faded, the electorate has started to ask substantive questions about delivery and accountability, and the ruling party has to work harder to convince the electorate of its right to govern. Notably, the ANC election campaign highlighted the government's actions on AIDS – an issue which was nowhere on the ANC's agenda six months ago. Other political parties have used HIV/AIDS to attack the ANC in areas that it has neglected. A Democratic Alliance (DA) election poster proclaimed 'Free AIDS drugs', for example, while Patricia de Lille, head of the newly formed Independent Democrats (ID), proclaimed the government's lack of action on AIDS.

On the other hand, if the ANC's announcement to 'roll out' ART was simply an electioneering tool, there is cause for concern about actual implementation and sustainability of the plan. What will happen after the general elections? Will the government's HIV/AIDS policy be driven once again by pressure from civil society and people living with AIDS? Put differently, the emphasis on HIV/AIDS care and treatment in party manifestos suggests that the elected government has a social contract with the populace to deal with HIV/AIDS, but, as we outline shortly, this has not happened, except for a brief period before and after 1994.

We also discuss the sound plans to confront the epidemic that the government has put in place; indeed, a number of government departments, at national, provincial and local levels, have been elaborating plans and programmes for several years in order to deal with the threat of HIV/AIDS to society at large. The Minster of Finance, for example, has allocated extensive funds for the delivery of treatment in 2004, adding to substantive AIDS funding provided in the 2003 national Budget. The secretary for the Treatment Action Campaign (TAC), which has been at the centre of civil society campaigns for improvement and speedier implementation of government policies, has commended the Minister of Finance's 2004 Budget allocations. Indeed, in 2003, the TAC suspended a civil disobedience campaign on the basis of promises from the Deputy President of imminent implementation of a national ART programme.

This discussion is essential to contextualise the politics of HIV/AIDS. We indicate that the professional staff of various ministries have given due consideration to the challenges facing the government, and that the national executive has this knowledge. However, we argue that the ambiguities and ambivalence on HIV/AIDS in major policy speeches of the President, as well as statements by the Minister of Health, indicate a lack of decisiveness about how to use that knowledge.

This chapter thus describes the curious state of the country's efforts to control the HIV/AIDS epidemic. Public sector AIDS policies and programmes provide a foundation for a comprehensive confrontation against HIV/AIDS. However, there is still good cause to ask: will there be meaningful change for the lives of those infected with, and those affected by, HIV/AIDS – together, the vast majority of the country's population? In sum, we are sceptical about the progress that the government will make in 2004 in confronting the epidemic. Nonetheless, we acknowledge increasing momentum in the government's interventions. This leads us to perceive an opportunity for a definitive social contract between the national executive and the populace.

A brief background

The process of formulating the first post-apartheid structural response to AIDS began in 1992. Substantive consultation between the ANC, the National Party government and civil organisations in South Africa led to the launch of the National AIDS Committee of South Africa (Nacosa) in 1992, and a national AIDS plan in 1994 (Schneider 1998). Government policy has evolved since, including formulation of the HIV/AIDS and Sexually Transmitted Disease (STD) Programme in 1996, establishment of the South African National AIDS Council (Sanac) in 2000, and compilation of the country's comprehensive National HIV/AIDS and STI Strategic Plan for 2000–2005, in the same year. The latter plan has four pillars: prevention; treatment, care and support; human and legal rights; and monitoring, research and surveillance.[2]

Since the late 1990s, however, the TAC has been challenging the government on the lack of practical, national ART programmes. The challenge culminated in April 2002, when the TAC took the matter to the Constitutional Court. The court decreed that the government had to provide ART to all HIV-positive pregnant women in order to prevent transmission of the virus to their babies (PMTCT – prevention of mother-to-child transmission). Subsequently, the Cabinet released a statement that government policy would henceforth be based on the *assumption* that HIV causes AIDS, and that post-exposure prophylaxis (PEP) would also be made available to individuals who had been sexually assaulted (Willan 2004).

In October 2002, the Cabinet announced the formation of a task team to investigate the costs and benefits of providing ART to all HIV-positive individuals. However, the study findings were embargoed until 8 August 2003, and at the same time the Minister of Health released a cautious and vaguely worded statement:

The Department of Health has been asked (by the Cabinet) as a matter of urgency to develop a detailed operational plan on an antiretroviral treatment plan. (Cabinet 2003)

The operational plan was submitted to the Minister of Health on 30 September 2003. In November 2003, the Minister revealed the plan that was to be implemented in phases – the first phase aiming to provide ART to 53 000 people by the end of March 2004 (DoH 2003a). In a newspaper report, the Minister denied that this was ever the target (*New York Times* 20.02.04). On 13 February 2004, the government began to solicit proposals from pharmaceutical companies to supply the drugs, with delivery in June. In other words, it was evident that the government would neither adhere to its stated schedule nor achieve the objective of Phase I, which it set for itself prior to the general elections. Accordingly, there is cause to doubt the proclaimed intent and the process of implementing the plan.

This doubt arises from the ambivalence of the President and the Minister of Health about public concern over HIV/AIDS (Nattrass 2003b; Willan 2004). The root of this doubt lies in the seeming inability of the national executive to resolve the need for innovative social welfare policy in view of the country's socio-economic problems. We refer to the marked economic inequality and poverty indicated in the high levels of unemployment and burgeoning informal sector, now exacerbated by the HIV/AIDS epidemic. We also refer to the long-standing debate within and beyond government, since the mid 1990s, over the principles and content of social welfare programmes, which has coalesced around the question of whether the country should institute a basic income grant (BIG) (Makino 2003).

It is not difficult to perceive continuing ambivalence on HIV/AIDS and social welfare policies. The mid-1990s saw the government moving away from its proclaimed 'people-centred approach', espoused in the Reconstruction and Development Programme(RDP) policy, to a 'top-down approach', espoused in the Growth, Employment and Redistribution (Gear) policy.[3] Similarly, the formulation of a national AIDS policy changed from the inclusive approach of the early-to-mid 1990s, to the autocratic approach since then, reflected in the President's and the Health Minister's oft-expressed irritation with civil society input and critique.

However, South Africa has recently heard a revival of RDP language (see the introduction to this volume by Southall, Daniel and Lutchman). ANC election posters, for example, proclaimed 'A people's contract to create work and fight poverty'. Likewise, the weekly 'Letter from the President' (Mbeki 2004b) of 20 February 2004 made repeated references to meeting needs as expressed in the RDP, and in being 'united in a people's contract to fight poverty and create jobs'. The President's 2004 'State of the Nation' address, in particular, emphasised the government's social spending record and valid achievements. His speech was wrapped in rhetoric such as the regular holding of *imbizo* (public meetings) and reassertion of statements in his 1999 'State of the Nation' speech about the government's efforts to mobilise 'the whole nation into united people's action, into a partnership with government for progressive change and a better life for all' (Mbeki 2004a:8–9).

Nonetheless, there were substantive caveats in the President's speech to forestall any reading of a genuine turnaround in government policy on HIV/AIDS and, more broadly, social welfare. He stated, 'We do not foresee that there will be any need for new and major policy initiative' (Mbeki 2004a:10). He also noted:

> We will have to focus on the implementation of the measures we have identified to ensure that we achieve better value for money spent on social delivery. Among other things, our successes with regard to both the first and second economies *must create the conditions for us to reduce the number of our people dependent on social grants.* (Mbeki 2004a:12, emphasis added)

References to the 'first' and 'second' economies were synonyms for the formal and informal sectors and, presumably, allusion to his well known 'two-nation' thesis to characterise South Africa's racial and wealth inequalities. The caveat lies in the highlighted phrase, for this section of the speech was preceded by statements indicating an orthodox, contemporary perspective on social welfare issues[4] and on economic development.[5]

The Minister of Finance subsequently affirmed this perspective in his 2004 Budget speech:

> Given the challenges we face, we have made these choices. But in the longer term, it seems clear that we will need to seek a better balance between growth in welfare spending and our investments

in education and infrastructure development. In this Budget, we take several steps in this direction – an expanded public works programme through increased allocations to provincial and municipal infrastructure, a renewed focus on learner support materials and facilities at disadvantaged schools, further allocations for restructuring of higher education institutions. (Manuel 2004:9)

In sum, recent major policy speeches do nothing to inspire confidence in the President's leadership on the issue of HIV/AIDS.

The current situation

The government is implementing its national HIV/AIDS strategic plan set out in 2000 (Government of South Africa 2000). Leaving aside for now the questions of why and how, principal components of that strategy are coming to the fore. An integrated approach that recognises that the epidemic is not simply a health issue has been proclaimed formally and, more loosely, in the term 'mainstreaming'. Mainstreaming means sound understanding of the links between socio-economic and biophysical drivers of HIV/AIDS and, in turn, substantive reformulation of sector and organisational activities to develop and elaborate effective interventions. This approach is rooted in the existence of Sanac, in similar provincial bodies located in premiers' offices, and in the posts of 'HIV/AIDS co-ordinators' in municipal government offices. A multi-sectoral response, in the form of partnerships between the public and private sector, is evolving; for example, the Tripartite Summit on HIV/AIDS of 2003 between the government, mining companies and trade unions. There is an emphasis on prevention, treatment, care and support – key elements of the national strategy – evident in a diverse range of government-backed initiatives, from financial support of the loveLife campaigns to initiation of the national ART programmes.[6]

This is supported by increased funding – substantive absolute amounts – for HIV/AIDS interventions in the 2003 and 2004 national Budgets. Table 9.1 illustrates this increase for the three departments that are centrally involved in the government's intervention efforts – Health, Social Development and Education (Hickey 2004).

Again, leaving aside questions of why and how, the 2003 Budget aimed at combining health, welfare and education agendas and sought to mitigate

Table 9.1 *Summary of HIV/AIDS-specific allocations in the national budget*

R million	2001–02	2002–03	2003–04	2004–05	2005–06	2006–07	MTEF
DoH: HIV/AIDS Directorate (including conditional grant, ARV funds)	265.84	459.95	766.29	1 212.17	1 545.34	2 008.37	4 765.88
DoSD: HIV and AIDS programme (including conditional grant)	14.954	51.153	70.388	78.29	85.153	89.402	252.85
DoE: HIV and AIDS conditional grant	62.896	133.458	131.621	128.579	136.293	144.471	409.34
Total	343.69	644.56	968.30	1 419.04	1 766.79	2 242.24	5 428.07
Real terms	395.83	674.86	968.30	1 346.33	1 588.88	1 916.79	4 852.00
Real growth rate	49%	70%	43%	39%	18%	21%	

Source: 2004 Division of Revenue Bill. 2003 Estimates of National Expenditure. Real terms calculated based on gross domestic product (GDP) inflation, with 2003–04 as the base year.

poverty, at the same time as improving capacity to manage HIV/AIDS directly. Funds, albeit relatively small amounts, were made available for improving nutrition programmes, basic services of municipalities, child support grants and pensions. The national government provided funds directly to improve infrastructure (for example, hospital refurbishment), with the aim of freeing up more of the provincial governments' own discretionary funding for HIV/AIDS interventions. An additional R1 billion was made available to enable provincial governments to focus on confronting the epidemic.

The 2004 Budget has gone further. The allocation to the Department of Social Development (DoSD) has increased to 16 per cent of the total Budget, and pensions, disability and child support grants are expected to increase on average at a rate of 13.6 per cent a year over the remaining two years of this medium-term expenditure framework (MTEF) (Government of South Africa 2004). R1.9 billion has been set aside in the medium term for ART, and 60 per cent of the R4 billion in tax cuts went primarily to the working class, as did the reduction in property taxes. However, direct funding to the Department of Health (DoH) appears to be declining (Portfolio Committee 2004). The Department received 11 per cent of the 2004 Budget[7] (Government of South Africa 2004), but a substantive portion was for implementing the comprehensive treatment plan. Even with inclusion of funding for ART, the Department's budget is projected to increase by an average of only 8.4 per cent a year over the remaining two years of this MTEF (Government of South Africa 2004). Nhlanhla Ndlovu from the Institute for Democracy in South Africa (Idasa) has observed that 'when the HIV/AIDS allocation is taken out the health budget drops, compared to other sectors' (*Mail & Guardian* 20–26.02.04). In short, it seems that funding for HIV/AIDS intervention is being provided at a cost to other components of public healthcare.

Nonetheless, new initiatives have been made public in the light of the proposed national ART programme and, it must be noted, shortly before the general elections. Early in March 2004, the Gauteng provincial government announced that it would roll out its ART programme in five hospitals from 1 April. The National Treasury revealed in its study on 17 March, that a comprehensive national ART programme would significantly reduce the impact of HIV/AIDS on economic growth (*ThisDay* 18.03.04).

In summary, government initiatives are increasing in pace and scope. There is greater capacity than before for co-ordinated intervention and, to all appearances, a coherent and constructive agenda. The reality is different. This is not to say that the opposite holds true. If we are to understand where South Africa is now – a country confronted with the challenges of actually containing the epidemic – then we need to see what is missing from the equation of evident capacity and a sophisticated set of principles, strategies and plans.[8] In other words, how is it that a country that has so much has yet to harness its resources effectively?

In the first instance, the evident capacity and general intent are the basis on which government executives and spokespersons are able to counter criticisms, indeed, to question the integrity of critics and cast doubt in the minds of the populace about their disquiet. But the disquiet is well-founded, even if we discount the litany of provocative statements and actions of the President and Health Minister that gave rise to it. There are glaring gaps in the implementation of policy and plans described earlier.

Starting at the top, and to give an apt illustration, in March 2004, the TAC threatened to sue the Minister of Health yet again over her apparent reluctance to speed up the procurement of anti-retroviral drugs (TAC 2004b). The TAC case was based on the premise that there were procedures in place that allowed government to purchase an urgent interim supply of anti-retroviral medicines while awaiting completion of the procurement process. The TAC gave the Minister of Health notice to reply by close of business on 17 March or it would proceed with legal action. The Minister stated that she would reply by 24 March. On 25 March, the Minister agreed to the TAC's demands.

Sanac, like all national AIDS councils, is supposed to show the national government's commitment to combating HIV/AIDS. Chaired by the country's Deputy President, it is supposed to be a forum that provides direction, gets strategic demands through to the national executive and, equally, facilitates implementation of decisions. In short, its role is to co-ordinate action. This has not happened. Sanac has yet to be seen to play any constructive role. The Deputy President's most notable act as chair of the council has been to negotiate with the TAC to suspend its civil disobedience campaign in 2003. Alarmingly, lack of progress has been evident in equivalent councils at lower levels of government. For instance, the eThekweni (Durban) city AIDS council was launched in 2002, but it has not been evidently active since then.

With regard to financial planning, the National Treasury provided substantive support in 2003, but masked its commitment, seemingly for political reasons to do with tensions in the Cabinet – notably the President's ambivalence about the significance of HIV/AIDS. HIV/AIDS funding was hidden within poverty-alleviation line items. The direct funding to refurbish hospitals and clinics cleverly gave provincial governments an opportunity to use funding that would otherwise have to be allocated for this task to HIV/AIDS programmes. Budgetary provisions to provide more scope for strategic interventions, however, have faltered. For instance, efforts within the KwaZulu-Natal (KZN) Premier's office to 'mainstream' HIV/AIDS into the province's poverty relief and development programmes have faltered under the difficulties of getting co-operation from other provincial departments.[9] HIV co-ordinators in local government often move on, following promotion or redeployment, leaving initiatives to be picked up or modified by new appointees. This is testimony to common problems with mainstreaming efforts in the public sector. The idea has been interpreted often as simply including HIV/AIDS prevention activities in sector plans, and/or adding responsibility for HIV/AIDS to a person's job description, rather than restructuring programmes and work procedures to ensure integration into departmental activities (Stover & Johnston 1999).

The difficulties of harnessing public sector resources reflect both a universal problem of governments and its particular manifestation in South Africa. The universal problem is bureaucratic inertia; notably, the difficulty of changing procedures and practices, of transforming institutions, to address new ideas of governance and new challenges in a changing world. Concerns about the 'silo' nature of government structures – coupled with calls for co-ordination, integration and sustainability – have been voiced in relation to other challenges and roles of government, not just with regard to HIV/AIDS. The damning fact in the case of HIV/AIDS is that the President and current Minister of Health have encouraged that inertia. Cases in point are the former's emphasis on the need to address poverty and the latter's emphasis on the need to promote sound nutrition.[10] These postulations have been widely seen as obstructive; correctly so because they say nothing new.

While they highlight critically important issues that need to be addressed in HIV/AIDS programmes, the issues are presented simplistically: on the one hand (poverty), seemingly though ambiguously as a direct cause of HIV/AIDS and, on the other hand (nutrition), as an alternative to ART. The net effect is that the President and the Minister contradict themselves. They voice either the need for an integrated approach, despite the existence of a strategy and structures conceived on that basis, or the difficulties of implementing this approach. If difficulties of implementing policy are their true concern, then one must wonder why there has been no recourse to the lessons learned by the Department of Water Affairs and Forestry (DWAF) and the Department of Environmental Affairs and Tourism (DEAT). These Departments and their Ministers have actively pushed implementation of the same principles and associated strategies in their fields of responsibility and, notably, have achieved successes.

The particularity of bureaucratic inertia in the case of South Africa lies in the ongoing tension between commitment to integration and co-ordination on the one hand, and, on the other, the dominant position of the Ministry of Health in public sector campaigns against the epidemic. In other words, the DoH has retained its position of power as the arbiter of policy and strategy despite long-standing and wide acknowledgement that HIV/AIDS is not only a health issue, but also a social issue. Furthermore, as we indicate shortly, in holding onto the reins of the country's efforts to contain the HIV/AIDS epidemic, the Department has been drawn into contesting any insurrection of its position. The net effect is to restrict scope for co-ordination of government actions, let alone mainstreaming as defined earlier.

This is a deeply embedded problem. Schneider (1998) and Nattrass (2003b) have suggested how the gap between practice and intent began in 1994, with the appointment of a national AIDS director to implement a national AIDS plan. They argue that the problem lay in appointing a person from the DoH. For Nattrass, it would have been more appropriate to locate the position in the President's office, given that the entire programme was a 'presidential-lead project', meaning that it had preferential access to funds. For Schneider, the allocation of responsibility to a line department (health) rather than a co-ordinating unit (including the RDP office at the time she wrote) was not necessarily problematic, because of the short-lived existence of the RDP in particular. However, she questioned the effect of placing AIDS intervention planning within a biomedical framework. Nattrass later summarised this problem in noting how the provincial governments also located HIV/AIDS programmes in their respective health ministries, thereby 'recasting AIDS as a health (rather than social) problem, and limiting the potential for a multi-sectoral, co-ordinated response' (2003b:44).

The disjunction intimated in these assessments is that the national plan of 1994 had the hallmarks of an integrated methodology, but there was no requirement that the DoH transform itself to accommodate the plan. This critique leads us to reconsider the government's revised strategic plan, the National HIV/AIDS Strategy 2000–2005. The multi-sector programmes and broad-based interventions give the appearance of an integrated approach. What is missing, however, is substantive transformation of the Department's procedures and activities. Accordingly, we suggest that this is an underlying reason for the conflict between civic organisations such as the TAC and the government. Institutional transformation is part of the social contract of any organisation that proclaims an integrated approach. In moving away from fulfilling that contract (which had been espoused in the early-to-mid 1990s' formulation of HIV/AIDS policy), the DoH made itself vulnerable to challenges from civil society, and the courts inevitably became the means.

Related to the above disjunctions is the emerging tension between the DoH and the DoSD. Shortly before presentation of the 2004 Budget, the DoH (2003b) released evidence of a decline in real levels of funding. The political significance here is that the DoSD has garnered significant Budget allocations very rapidly in the space of two years, largely through nominal raises in pensions and other social grants.

The DoSD, however, is itself struggling to formulate an integrated approach. For instance, since mid-2003 it has been trying to finalise a proposed National Action Committee for Children Infected and Affected by HIV/AIDS (NACCA) as an umbrella body, consisting of representatives from other departments, non-governmental organisations (NGOs), provincial governments and donors, to oversee programmes to co-ordinate HIV/AIDS interventions (DoSD 2002; NACCA 2002).[11] This effort follows somewhat belatedly upon its Call for Co-ordinated Action Conference held in 2002. In recent months, it has been holding workshops in the provinces to reach a conclusion on how best to structure a co-ordinated action framework in relation to other agencies in the field of social welfare. The national Department is attempting to find a solution to the practical problems posed by this agenda. For instance, the Department recognises the danger of duplicating structures and initiatives and that the NACCA, while representative, is a very large body that is difficult to convene and may not be workable. Currently, it is encouraging provincial departments to find their own answers within the broader proposed framework.[12]

The DoH's concern about its budget is bringing into the open a contest over health and welfarist ideologies in government planning. In 2002 the Taylor Committee of Inquiry (2002) on social security issues produced its report, highlighting the need for South Africa to define an approach to social spending. In particular, the Committee found wanting the approach of developmental social welfare adopted in 1996, that emphasised employment generation and skills training and reduction of cash transfers (Makino 2003). The Committee proposed an innovation, 'comprehensive social protection', which emphasised the need for grants to deal with the immediate problem of minimal income amongst much of the population before implementing development-oriented social programmes. Makino recorded misgivings expressed by members of the Cabinet about the Committee's findings, and their affirmation by the ANC. However, in 2003, the Cabinet held a *bosberaad* (a retreat), which reportedly was a scenario-planning exercise that revealed the need for the government to adopt a more interventionist role in future.

More broadly, the internal debate is occurring in the context of broader contests over how governments should respond to the HIV/AIDS pandemic (United Nations 2000; van der Walle 1995; WB-IMF 2000; World Bank 2000). These contests reflect the growth of global social movements, such as the World Social Forum, which are protesting against increasing socio-economic inequalities across the world, including a general trend of governments away from welfarist policies, particularly social spending on pensions and grants.

The social policies, plans and government budgets in South Africa highlight these challenges, and the lack of any resolution in the foreseeable future (Hickey, Ndlovu & Guthrie 2003). The nub of the matter is that lack of decisive leadership on the challenge of HIV/AIDS means there has yet to be coherent linking of general social spending with efforts to combat HIV/AIDS. Even though budgets for pensions, disability grants and child support grants have increased, there is no clear policy rationale of how that funding is related to, let alone expected to contain, the HIV/AIDS epidemic (Nattrass 2003a). In other words, there is no clear outline of how the money is expected to reach particular targets, nor what system will improve access of individuals to the money, and how the amount of money, the targeting and access system are expected to contain the transmission of HIV/AIDS and reduce poverty.

These limitations underlie widespread criticism of the President's leadership. Over the past few years, the President has expressed his 'denialist' opinions on HIV/AIDS repeatedly; indeed, he has never publicly denounced them. He has publicly withdrawn from the debates, but has continued to make ill-conceived statements. For instance, in September 2003, he stated, 'Personally I don't know anyone who has died of AIDS. I really honestly don't' (*Washington Post* 25.11.03). There was a passing reference to HIV/AIDS in his 2004 'State of the Nation' speech, and his comments in a nationwide interview on 8 February revealed disregard for the scale of affliction. When asked why he did not display a greater sense of compassion for people living with AIDS, he replied that the AIDS campaign was led by Deputy President Jacob Zuma and that tuberculosis and diabetes were also reaching epidemic proportions (*Pretoria News* 9.02.04).

In sum, the President has refused to provide leadership in this matter. Likewise, his public rhetoric on government social spending has been misleading and, as with HIV/AIDS, has avoided engagement with the challenges.

Effects of the epidemic and government's responses

The convolutions discussed earlier show that HIV/AIDS is a highly politicised issue in South Africa. While there is considerable effort to contain the epidemic, the singularly important fact is that to date the country has few results to show.

National statistics suggest that between 11 and 25 per cent of South Africans two years and older are infected with the virus. The figures vary, depending on the data source and method of extrapolation. Tables 9.2 and 9.3 present the provincial estimates from a relatively recent national household survey (HSRC 2002) and the Department of Health's national antenatal clinic survey data compiled annually (DoH 2002).

Table 9.2 *Overall HIV prevalence (extrapolated from study sample) by province, South Africa 2002*

Province	N	HIV + (%)	95% CI
Total	8 428	11.4	10.0 – 12.7
WC	1 267	10.7	6.4 – 15.0
EC	1 221	6.6	4.5 – 8.7
NC	694	8.4	5.0 – 11.7
FS	540	14.9	9.5 – 20.3
KZN	1 579	11.7	8.2 – 15.2
NW	626	10.3	6.8 – 13.8
G	1 272	14.7	11.3 – 18.1
M	550	14.1	9.7 – 18.5
L	679	9.8	5.9 – 13.7

Source: HSRC 2002

Note: For this and other tables in this chapter, Eastern Cape (EC), Free State (FS), Gauteng (G),
KwaZulu-Natal (KZN), Limpopo (formerly Northern Province) (L), Mpumalanga (M),
North West (NW), Northern Cape (NC), Western Cape (WC)

Table 9.4 summarises figures commonly cited, which are drawn from the antenatal clinic data. The fact that many are not infected emphasises the importance of prevention efforts, but the large number of infected individuals means that everyone is affected in one way or another.

Table 9.3 *Provincial HIV prevalence, antenatal clinic attendees, South Africa 1994–2002*

Province	Estimated HIV-positive (%)								
	1994	1995	1996	1997	1998	1999	2000	2001	2002
KZN	14.4	18.2	19.9	26.8	32.5	32.5	36.2	33.5	36.5
M	12.1	18.3	15.8	22.6	30.0	27.3	29.7	29.2	28.6
G	6.4	12.0	15.5	17.1	22.5	23.9	29.4	29.8	31.6
FS	9.2	11.0	17.5	19.6	22.8	27.9	27.9	30.1	28.8
NW	6.7	8.3	25.1	18.1	21.3	23.0	22.9	25.2	26.2
EC	4.5	6.0	8.1	12.6	15.9	18.0	20.2	21.7	23.6
L	3.0	4.9	7.9	8.2	11.5	11.4	13.2	14.5	15.6
NC	1.8	5.3	6.6	8.6	9.9	10.1	11.2	15.9	15.1
WC	1.2	1.7	3.09	6.3	5.2	7.1	8.7	8.6	12.4

Source: DoH 2002

Table 9.4 *Extrapolation of HIV prevalence amongst antenatal clinic attendees to the general population, 2000–02*

Gender	Age grouping	2000 Number of HIV+ individuals	2002 Number of HIV+ individuals
Female	15 – 49 years	2.5 million	2.95 million
Male	15 – 49 years	2.2 million	2.3 million
Babies		106 109	91 271
Total		4.7 million	5.3 million

Source: DoH 2002

The large number of people who are infected, and how this affects the lives of many others, is the major source of concern and frustration about South Africa's efforts to date to contain the epidemic. In early 2004, there were reportedly 40 000 people receiving ART treatment in South Africa, and the vast majority had to find their own means to pay for it. The public health services provided ART treatment for 1 500 people only. The limited scope of ART provision in relation to the numbers infected is itself cause for concern, as are the indications that other developing countries with fewer public resources than South Africa are achieving more. Brazil, for instance, reportedly has been providing treatment for over 100 000 individuals; Botswana, 15 000; and Cameroon, 7 000 (TAC 2004a).

The stresses of the epidemic pervade the daily lives of the majority of the country's population. Stigma and discrimination are widespread. Impoverishment of families as a result of the cost of caring for sick members is widespread (Booysen, van Rensburg, Bachmann, O'Brien & Steyn 2002; Hosegood, Herbst & Timaeus 2003). The burden of care in homes and communities is stretching the emotional and physical resources of individuals and institutions (Akintola 2004; Steinberg, Johnson, Schierhout, Ndegwa, Hall, Russell & Morgan 2002). The burden of funeral costs puts pressure on the extended family (universally, the traditional social security net), and on business of all kinds (for example, increasing demand for compassionate leave, increased costs of recruitment and training to replace deceased employees). Inequality and poverty exacerbate socially destructive behaviours and conditions, ranging from risky sexual relationships to entrenchment of abuse and discrimination against women (Human Rights Watch 2003).

The broader economic effects of the epidemic have become discernible (Bell, Devarajan & Gersbach 2003; Quattek 2000). South Africa has a formal social safety net in the form of child grants and pensions, but millions of South Africans still face increasing misery, along with many others throughout southern Africa (Floyd, Crampin, Glynn, Madise, Nyondo, Khondowe, Njoka, Kanyongoloka, Ngwira, Zaba & Fine 2003; Mushati, Gregson, Mlilo, Lewis & Zvidzai 2003; Yamano & Jayne 2003). Furthermore, even though the effects of HIV/AIDS on people's existing vulnerability to various threats, like drought and war, are not well understood, starvation is a reality (de Waal & Whiteside 2003).

Turning to the effects on companies, Table 9.5 shows the costs of HIV infection within the workforce of three companies in different sectors in KZN during different years. The costs may not seem significant, but they represent an additional burden, the significance of which lies in its cumulative effect.

In the first instance, companies do incur an absolute financial cost. Morris, Burdge and Cheevers (2000), for example, looked at the impact of HIV infection on male sugar mill workers in KZN from 1991–98. A prevalence survey indicated that 26 per cent of the workforce were HIV-positive in 1999. Of these HIV-positive workers, 93.6 per cent were in the lowest two payroll bands

Table 9.5 *Cost of HIV to three companies in KwaZulu-Natal, South Africa*

	Company 1	Company 2	Company 3
Study year	1999	2001	2001
Sector	Agribusiness	Mining	Retail
Workforce size	5 000–10 000	500–1 000	<500
Estimated HIV prevalence in study year			
Company average	23.7%	23.6%	10.5%
Unskilled workers	26.7%	34.5%	12.9%
Skilled workers	22.7%	18.55%	2.5%
Supervisors/managers	8.2%	6.23%	2.3%
Non-permanent	31.2%	n.a.	17.6%
Cost of HIV infections as a % of wages	1.8%	1.9%	0.4%

Source: Adapted from Rosen et al. 2003

– primarily unskilled or semi-skilled workers. For each of the HIV-positive employees taking ill-health retirement status, costs amounted to R8 463.73 (1999 South African Rand values) over each of the last two years of employment. On average, a total of 27.73 days were lost due to illness per year over this period.

Secondly, mitigating the impacts of HIV/AIDS on businesses cannot be done by replacing those workers affected by the epidemic. South Africa's high unemployment rate might suggest that this is an option. However, the costs associated with worker absenteeism, loss and replacement can result in labour becoming more expensive, and even deter foreign investment in industries that depend on low-cost or unskilled labour. In turn, diminishment of foreign investment or capacity for companies to compete is likely to affect the country's general economic growth and development (Rosen et al. 2003). A cause for concern is that the private sector in South Africa as a whole has yet to confront the epidemic. A recent survey has shown that only around 50 per cent of companies have an HIV/AIDS policy in place and that 75 per cent of smaller companies do not even conduct education and awareness in the workplace (SABCOHA 2003).

Similarly, the rising prevalence amongst skilled and highly skilled workers in South Africa, presented in Figure 9.1, indicates a substantive threat: loss of skilled labour can lead to a decrease in demand for unskilled labour (Arndt & Lewis 2001). For instance, illness and death of a skilled individual as a result of HIV/AIDS has the same consequences as emigration of skilled individuals from South Africa: the inevitable loss of employment for those who depended directly and indirectly on those individuals.

Figure 9.1 *HIV prevalence rate by skill level in South Africa*

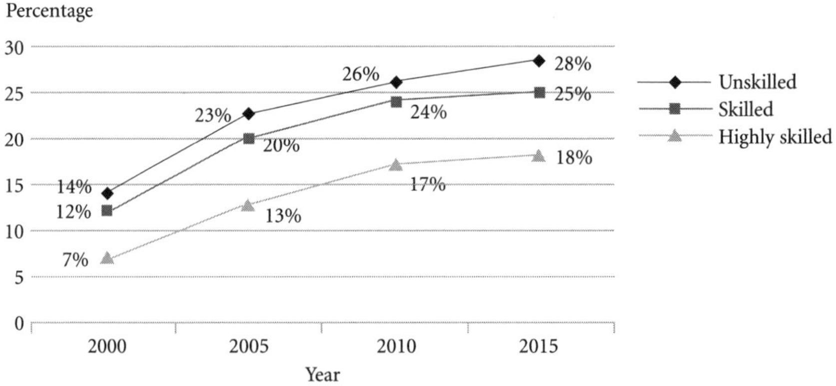

Percentage

Source: Bureau for Economic Research, cited in Vass (2003)

The scale of the problems outlined has already become evident in the country's public sector. Research in the education sector of KZN, for example, has revealed a 50 per cent increase in teacher deaths due to illness and natural causes between 1998 and 2001. Calculation of the financial costs shows that it would cost approximately R170 million to replace the 1 700 teachers in KZN under the age of 49 years who died of illness (Badcock-Walters, Desmond, Wilson & Heard 2003). A recently released national study of health workers showed that 13 per cent of deaths of staff between 1997 and 2001 were attributable to HIV/AIDS (Shisana 2003). A micro-level study of health workers, at Hlabisa hospital in KZN indicated some of the economic effects (Unger, Welz & Haran 2002). This study found that staff turnover due to death increased from 0.3 per cent to 2 per cent between 1995 and 2001. The same study also found that the mean number of days taken off work amongst staff was 41.8 days in 1998, and 57.7 days in 2001, indicating use of more than the stipulated annual (22 days) and sick leave (approximately 15 days) benefits.

In short, the poor are getting poorer, the country is getting poorer and the virus is still spreading.

Conclusion

We began this review by saying that the South African government was *beginning* to confront the challenge of containing the HIV/AIDS epidemic. Our purpose was to intimate a change in the government's thinking and action; not to deny past and current efforts to find solutions. We went on to illustrate this – emphasising the challenge of developing a new approach to social spending that lies behind the decision to institute a national ART programme and the revival of populist rhetoric about reconstruction and development. In sum, we have suggested the immanence of a new disposition as a result of many interventions and increasing pressure to find answers in the last few years.

We also based our review on the argument that the efforts of the government are *still* constrained by lack of leadership from the President and the Minister of Health. Our purpose was not simply to reiterate popular criticism; it was to indicate that their views and actions remain a significant factor in any assessment of South Africa's past and current efforts to contain the epidemic. We went on to show how the President has not only refused to recognise the particular significance of HIV/AIDS, but has also avoided engaging substantively with the social spending challenge. On reflection, we realise that our critique of the Minister of Health has been more implicit than overt. In looking beyond the obvious criticisms that could be made – notably her provocative and defensive statements about treatment options – we have intimated that she has not grasped the structural implications of implementing an integrated approach to public health management. In sum, we have shown why there is reason to be sceptical about the progress that the government will make in 2004 towards containing the epidemic.

Our discussion of the politics and context of HIV/AIDS is really an attempt to pose and answer a key question – namely, why is South Africa struggling to harness effectively its relatively abundant resources (the wealth of infrastructure, skills, expertise and finances)? Nattrass's (2003b) recent book drew to a close debate in South Africa about the cost of dealing with the epidemic. In short, the country cannot afford not to deal with it. We have argued that the issue now is really one of exploring ways to use the country's resources effectively and efficiently, which have been outlined in principle but not yet implemented fully. Sanac, for example, provides intent and form, but it has yet to give direction on transformation of government institutions.

In other words, we see within a diversity of events – ranging from the activities of the TAC, to the report of the Taylor Committee, to the many practical programmes within and beyond government (that we have not described) – effort to elaborate a comprehensive approach to containing the epidemic. These interventions reflect a common perspective, namely, that the country has the resources to contain the epidemic. The decision to roll out ART was an admission that the country has the means. The TAC's intervention in March, showing the Minister of Health how procurement of anti-retroviral medicines could be obtained to enable speedy implementation of the ART programme, indicated how resources could be deployed efficiently and effectively. The Treasury's report in the same month on how national ART programmes could reduce the impact of HIV/AIDS on the growth rate of the economy, showed the potential indirect benefits of ART. As importantly, it revealed the value of seeking a holistic view with regard to containing the epidemic.

In contrast, the thought and actions of the President and Minister of Health reflect bedazzlement with the scale of the problem, and failure to see the imperative to elaborate a comprehensive approach. Juxtaposing elements of the problem, be it in terms of poverty or nutrition, refer to ways of planning and acting that others, in and outside government, have gone beyond in the quest to find ways of containing the epidemic.

Notes

1   The penultimate draft of this article was written in March 2004 and the final draft by the end of April. The ANC won the general elections with a 69.68 per cent majority (Independent Electoral Commission www.elections.org.za/elections 2004). In the immediate aftermath of the general elections, the reappointment of the incumbent Minister of Health, and no mention of HIV/AIDS in President Mbeki's inaugural speech, affirm the content and form of this chapter's critique.

2   There are other policies which focus on HIV/AIDS, but they refine the principal policy reflected in the 2000–2005 National Strategic Plan. See the South African government and DoH websites specifically at www.doh.gov.za/docs/policy-f.html.

3   The RDP programme was abandoned in favour of the GEAR economic policy in 1996. For more discussion see Manning (2001).

4   '... expanded public works programmes, the expansion of micro-credit and small enterprises, the provision of adult basic education and modern skills, and the development of the social and economic infrastructure' (Mbeki 2004b:12).

5   'We must continue to focus on the growth, development and modernisation of the First Economy ... to confront the challenges of the Second ... This is going to require ... infrastructure investments, skills development, scientific and technological research, development and expansion of the knowledge economy, growth and modernisation of the manufacturing and service sectors, deeper penetration of the global markets by our products, increasing our savings levels, black economic empowerment and the further expansion of small and medium enterprises' (Mbeki 2004a:12).

6   loveLife is an extensive national awareness campaign funded partly by the South African government as well as by donor organisations.

7   In the 2004 budget the Department of Education received 20 per cent and protection services received 16 per cent.

8   This review is informed by a simple, unelaborated historical framework. We perceive a process of 'assessing impact' (identifying, understanding and acknowledging the scale of the problem), 'containing' (interventions to control the spread of the epidemic) and 'managing' (routine implementation of effective and tested systems and procedures for prevention, treatment, care and support; categorisation of HIV/AIDS as a chronic illness). Our implicit contention is that South Africa has a long way to go before it actually 'manages' HIV/AIDS.

9   Several collaborative ventures between provincial departments and the Health Economics and HIV/AIDS Research Division (HEARD) and other research units at the University of KwaZulu-Natal were delayed and/or faltered in 2003 because of the need for, coupled with the associated difficulties of, obtaining support and co-ordination of input from different provincial departments.

10 During February 2004, amidst activity to implement the national ART plan, the Health Minister stated that 'traditional remedies might replace traditional drugs' (*New York Times* 20.02.04).

11   The proposal includes broader operational structures such as a national AIDS and children task team, with equivalents of it and NACCA at provincial and local levels of government.

12   Discussion at KwaZulu-Natal DoSD workshop, Illovo, 13.02.04.

References

Akintola O (2004) *Home-based care: A gendered analysis of informal caregiving for people living with HIV/AIDS in a semi-rural South African setting.* PhD thesis, University of KwaZulu-Natal, Durban.

Arndt C & Lewis J (2001) The HIV/AIDS pandemic in South Africa: Sectoral impacts and unemployment, *Journal of International Development* 13:427–449.

Badcock-Walters P, Desmond C, Wilson D & Heard W (2003) *Educator mortality in-service in KwaZulu Natal: A consolidated study of HIV/AIDS impact and trends.* Durban: University of Natal.

Bell C, Devarajan S & Gersbach H (2003) *The long-run economic costs of AIDS: Theory and an application to South Africa.* Washington: World Bank.

Booysen F le R, van Rensburg H, Bachmann M, O'Brien M & Steyn F (2002) *The socio-economic impact of HIV/AIDS on households in South Africa: Pilot study in Welkom and Qwaqwa, Free State Province.* Bloemfontein: University of the Free State.

Cabinet (South Africa) (2003) *Statement on special Cabinet meeting: Enhanced programme against HIV and AIDS,* 8.08.03. Available at <http:// www.gov.za/speeches>.

De Waal A & Whiteside A (2003) New variant famine: AIDS and food crisis in southern Africa, *The Lancet* 362:1234–1237.

DoH (Department of Health) (2002)
Year 2000 – <http://196.36.153.56/doh/docs/reports/2000/hivreport.html>.
Year 2001 – <http://196.36.153.56/doh/docs/sum-report.html>.
Year 2002 – <http://196.36.153.56/doh/docs/reports/2002/hiv-syphilis.pdf>.

DoH (2003a) *Operational plan for comprehensive HIV and AIDS care, management and treatment for South Africa.* Pretoria: DoH.

DoH (2003b) *Essential health care for all South Africans: An investigation into the adequacy of public health financing and the equity of provincial health resource distribution.* Pretoria: DoH.

DoSD (Department of Social Development, South Africa) (2002) A call to co-ordinated action for children affected by HIV/AIDS. Conference Report, Pretoria, 2–5.06.02.

DoSD (n.d.) Co-ordinated Action Framework. Pretoria: DoSA.

Floyd S, Crampin A, Glynn J, Madise J, Nyondo A, Khondowe M, Njoka C, Kanyongoloka H, Ngwira B, Zaba B & Fine P (2003) The impact of HIV on households structure in rural Malawi. Paper presented at the Conference on Empirical Evidence for the Demographic and Socio-Economic Impacts of AIDS, Durban, 26–28.03.03.

Government of South Africa (2000) *National HIV/AIDS/STD strategy for South Africa 2000 –2005*. Pretoria: Government Printers.

Government of South Africa (2004) *2004 Budget highlights*. Available at <http://www.treasury.gov.za>.

Hickey A (2004) *HIV/AIDS Budget brief 2004* (forthcoming). Cape Town: Idasa.

Hickey A, Ndlovu N & Guthrie T (2003) *Budgeting for HIV/AIDS in South Africa: Report on intergovernmental funding flows for an integrated response in the social sector*. Cape Town: Idasa.

Hosegood V, Herbst K & Timaeus I (2003) The impact of adult AIDS deaths on household structure and living arrangements in rural South Africa. Paper presented at the Conference on Empirical Evidence for the Demographic and Socio-Economic Impacts of AIDS, Durban, 26–28.03.03.

HSRC (Human Sciences Research Council) (2002) *Nelson Mandela/HSRC study of HIV/AIDS South African national HIV prevalence, behavioural risks and mass media household survey*. Pretoria: HSRC.

Human Rights Watch (2003) *Policy paralysis: A call for action on HIV/AIDS –related human rights abuses against women and girls in Africa*. Available at <http://www.hrw.org/doc/?t=hivaids_pub>.

Makino K (2003) *Social security policy reform in post-apartheid South Africa. A focus on the Basic Income Grant*. Centre for Civil Society Research Working Paper No. 11, University of Natal.

Manning R (2001) *Noble intentions, harsh realities: The politics of AIDS policy in South Africa*. MA thesis, Princeton University.

Manuel T (2004) *Budget Speech*, 18.02.04. Pretoria: Communication Directorate, National Treasury, South Africa.

Mbeki T (2004a) State of the Nation Address of the President of South Africa, Thabo Mbeki. Parliament, Cape Town, 6.02.04. Available at <http://www.gov.za>.

Mbeki T (2004b) Letter from the President, *ANC Today* 47.

Morris S, Burdge D & Cheevers E (2000) Economic impact of HIV infection in a cohort of male sugar mill workers in South Africa, *The South African Journal of Economics* 68:933–946.

Mushati P, Gregson S, Mlilo M, Lewis J & Zvidzai C (2003) Adult mortality and erosion of households viability in towns, estates and villages in eastern Zimbabwe. Paper presented at the Conference on Empirical Evidence for the Demographic and Socio-Economic Impacts of AIDS, Durban, 26–28.03.03.

NACCA (National Action Committee for Children Infected and Affected by HIV/AIDS) (2002) Report of NACCA Workshop, 6–7.08.02.

Nattrass N (2003a) *Unemployment and AIDS: The social-democratic challenge for South Africa*. Centre for Civil Society Research Working Paper No. 43, University of Natal.

Nattrass N (2003b) *The moral economy of AIDS in South Africa*. Cambridge: Cambridge Univerity Press.

Portfolio Committee (Portfolio Committee on Finance Hearings on the Budget, South Africa) (2004) *Submission to Parliament on the Division of Revenue Bill 2004/5*. Cape Town: Portfolio Committee on Finance Hearings on the Budget.

Quattek K (2000) *The economic impact of AIDS in South Africa: A dark cloud on the horizon*. Report commissioned by ING Barings.

Rosen S, Vincent J, MacLeod W, Fox M, Thea D & Simon J (2003) *The cost of HIV/AIDS to businesses in Africa*. Boston: Center for International Health and Development, Boston University School of Public Health.

SABCOHA (South African Business Coalition on HIV/AIDS) (2003) *Rapid assessment of the private sector response to HIV/AIDS in South Africa*. SABCOHA & Deloitte and Touche Human Capital Corporation. Available at <http://www.eldis.org/static/DOC11766.htm>.

Schneider H (1998) The politics behind AIDS: The case of South Africa. Paper presented to the 12th World AIDS Conference, Geneva, 28.06–3.07.98.

Shisana 0 (2003) *The impact of HIV/AIDS on the health sector: National survey of health personnel, ambulatory and hospitalised patients and health facilities, 2002*. Report prepared for the South African Department of Health.

Steinberg M, Johnson S, Schierhout G, Ndegwa D, Hall K, Russell B & Morgan J (2002) *Hitting home. How households cope with the impact of the HIV/AIDS epidemic. A survey of households affected by HIV/AIDS in South Africa*. Johannesburg: Health Systems Trust & The Kaiser Family Foundation.

Stover J & Johnston A (1999) *The art of policy formulation: Experiences from Africa in developing national HIV/AIDS policies.* Washington DC: USAID.

TAC (Treatment Action Campaign)(2004a) *President Mbeki misrepresents facts and once again causes confusion on HIV/AIDS,* 11.02.04. Available at <http://www.tac.org.za>.

TAC (2004b) *Letter to Minister of Health,* News Service, 10.03.04. Available at <http://www.tac.org.za>.

Taylor Committee (2002) *Transforming the present – Protecting the future.* Report of the Committee of Inquiry into a Comprehensive System of Social Security for South Africa, Pretoria.

Unger A, Welz T & Haran D (2002) *The impact of HIV/AIDS on health care staff at a rural South African hospital, 1990–2001.* Available at <http://ari.ucsf.edu/pdf/Posters/barcelona/unger1.pdf>.

United Nations (2000) *Enhancing social protection and reducing vulnerability in a globalising world: Report of the Secretary-General,* 39th session of the Commission for Social Development, New York, 13.02.00.

Van der Walle D (1995) *Public spending and the poor: What we know, what we need to know.* World Bank Policy Research Working Paper, Washington.

Vass J (2003) *The relationship between labour market dynamics and HIV/AIDS prevalence: A literature review.* Paper presented to Methodological Workshop, HSRC 30.04.03.

WB-IMF (World Bank-International Monetary Fund) (2000) *Social protection programs in poor countries – costs, trade-offs and implications for a Poverty Reduction Strategy.* WB-IMF Forum on Supporting Comprehensive and Country-led Poverty Reduction Strategies, Washington DC, 24–25.04.00.

Willan S (2004) Briefing: Recent changes in the South African government's HIV/AIDS policy and its implementation, *African Affairs* 103:109–117.

World Bank (2000) *Dynamic risk management and the poor: Developing a social protection strategy for Africa.* Washington: Africa Region Human Development Group.

Yamano T & Jayne T (2003) Measuring the impacts of prime-age adult death on rural households in Kenya. Paper presented at the Conference on Empirical Evidence for the Demographic and Socio-Economic Impacts of AIDS, Durban, 26–28.03.03.

10 Multiple communities: Muslims in post-apartheid South Africa

Goolam Vahed and Shamil Jeppie

In letters to newspapers and call-in programmes on radio stations, and also among many journalists and political commentators, South Africa's Muslims are largely viewed as a monolith, whether they live in the working-class townships of Phoenix in KwaZulu-Natal (KZN), the Cape Flats in the Western Cape, or Soweto in Gauteng; or the plush suburbs of Houghton in Gauteng or Westville in KZN. That they turn daily towards Makkah in prayer seems to be sufficient to conclude that Muslims constitute a unitary bloc. This, of course, is not the case, as we argue in this paper. We explore change and continuity, conflict and harmony, both among Muslims, and between them and the wider society, as well as the competing voices of authority among Muslims, and the multiple narratives of what it means to be a Muslim, in the context of rapid social, political and economic changes during the past decade. This paper is divided into three parts. The first section profiles South Africa's Muslim population; the middle section provides a historical and contemporary perspective on Malay, Indian, and black African Muslims; while the final part focuses on significant developments affecting Muslims during the past ten years, national and global, and how they have responded to these challenges. Throughout, we underscore the role of race, class, ethnicity, politics and gender in fashioning and re-fashioning Muslim identities.

Census 2002: markers of differentiation

Islam is a minority religion in South Africa. Muslims, numbering 654 064, comprised just 1.46 per cent of South Africa's population of 44.8 million in 2001. Even among coloureds and Indians, Muslims are a minority, constituting a quarter of the Indian population and eight per cent of the coloured population.[1] But as Tayob has observed, statistics do not reflect the qualitative experience of being Muslim in South Africa. Residential concentration of

Indian and coloured Muslims in racially segregated urban areas has meant that many of them live in proximity to mosques and madrasahs, and have a strong sense of being Muslim (Tayob 1996).

Table 10.1 *Muslim population per province and race*

	African	White	Indian	Coloured	Total
EC	3 601	630	5 866	9 575	19 672
FS	1 798	108	1 847	284	4 037
G	24 597	2 967	98 823	23 695	150 082
KZN	2 987	1 036	117 424	6 143	142 460
L	3 760	90	6 242	195	10 287
M	9 429	227	6 680	500	16 836
NC	738	65	1 015	2 833	4 651
NW	4 717	221	7 234	961	13 133
WC	8 204	3 065	29 800	251 837	292 906
Total	74 701	8 409	274 931	296 023	654 064
Percentage	11.42	1.28	42.04	45.26	100.00

Note: Eastern Cape (EC), Free State (FS), Gauteng (G), KwaZulu-Natal (KZN), Limpopo (L), Mpumalanga (M), North West (NW), Northern Cape (NC), Western Cape (WC)

Table 10.1 reflects the perception that Islam is a 'foreign' religion. However, while Indians and Malays make up the bulk of South Africa's Muslims, Africans constitute the fastest growing segment, having increased by 52.3 per cent since 1991, when they numbered 11 986. The proportion of Muslims who are African increased from 3.5 to 11.42 per cent during this period. There are many markers of differentiation besides race. Class differences are stark. The average per capita income of Indian Muslims was R2 163 per month, Malays R1 262, and Africans R935. Among Indian Muslims, per capita monthly income differed regionally – R2 794 in Gauteng, R2 396 in the Western Cape, and R1 656 in KZN, reflecting the predominantly trader origins of Indian Muslims in Gauteng and the Western Cape, while most Indian Muslims in KZN have indentured roots.

Class differences are due to discrepancies in education levels, unemployment, and income levels of the employed. A sample of Muslim males in the 18–65 age group reflects that of 80 238 Malays in the Western Cape, 39.52 per cent were paid employees, 55.76 per cent were 'not working', and only 4.72 per cent were self-employed; among the 36 500 Indians in Gauteng, 45.38 per cent were paid employees, 19.87 per cent were self-employed, while 34.75 per cent were 'not working'. In KZN, 44.92 per cent of 39 845 Indians were paid employees, 14.83 per cent were self-employed, and 40.25 per cent were 'not working'. Work status is influenced by level of education. Africans were at a huge disadvantage. In the 20+ age group, 13.9 per cent of Africans had no schooling, as against 5.23 per cent of Indians, and 2.29 per cent of Malays. While 35.94 per cent of Indians completed Grade 12, only 24.67 per cent of Africans and 24.17 per cent of of Malays did likewise. The percentage with university degrees was 7.72 per cent of Indians, 3.09 per cent of Africans and 2.07 per cent of Malays. Language is another marker of differentiation. While 92.7 per cent of Indians regarded English as their first language, among coloureds the divide is roughly equal between English and Afrikaans, with Afrikaans predominating in the Western Cape; among Africans, English (18.61 per cent) and isiZulu (28.62 per cent) predominate with isiXhosa, Sepedi, Setswana and SiSwati also represented. Given the importance of English in the economy, proficiency in this regard has given Indians an important advantage. Given these profound differences, Kramer's observations are germane. Islam and Muslims, she contends, should not be seen as a:

> distinct and homogeneous entity that is essentially defined by
> normative texts, i.e. the Qur'an as divine word and the Sunnah,
> or tradition of the Prophet Muhammad. For the unreformed
> orientalist, Muslims are sufficiently defined by their being
> Muslim … They are overdetermined by Islam. (2000:57)

Regional/'racial' developments

Western Cape

'IMAGINED COMMUNITY?' CONTINGENCY OF MALAYNESS

The notion of being Malay is heavily contested. In the South African context 'Malay' refers to coloureds of the Muslim faith who, until the twentieth century, were referred to as 'Mohammedan', 'Malay', 'Mussulman 'or 'Coloured Muslims' in official records. Malay ethnic identity was constituted from the 1920s, largely as a result of folklorist Izak du Plessis, whose book, *The Cape Malays* (1944), formally isolated coloured Muslims from the broader coloured community by presenting them almost as a distinct Malay race (Jeppie 2001).

Adhikari (1989) has shown that 'Malay' identity was open, and embraced individuals from diverse cultural and racial categories, including descendants of slaves from South and South-East Asia and Mozambique, Arabs, and Khoisan. The Population Registration Act of 1950 formally divided South Africans into four race groups, whites, Indians, Africans, and coloureds, who were defined as 'not a white person or a native', and sub-divided into 'Cape Malay', 'other coloureds' and Khoisan.

The hardening of apartheid during the 1960s and 1970s, and the emergence of a political climate in which there was widespread support for internal and external liberation movements, resulted in coloureds and their sub-categories attaching 'so-called' to their ethnic labels. Politically, younger coloured Muslims opted for the label 'black', while the religious label of choice was Muslim (Haron 2001). Social historian and radio presenter Achmat Davids (1938–98) exemplified the contingency of identity. Davids influenced a generation to use the term 'Cape Muslim' rather than Malay, which he saw as filled with racial bigotry (Davids 1980:12). But as the political situation became fluid in the early 1990s, Davids reverted to the nomenclatures 'Malay' and 'Indonesian' instead of 'Cape Muslim', began wearing Malaysian headgear, and in 1994, visited Indonesia (Jeppie 1998–99). Assertion of 'Malayness' during the post-apartheid period must be seen in the context of the 'rainbow nation' concept put forward by former president Nelson Mandela, which encouraged people to seek their own identities. Ward (1996) locates the resurgence of 'Malay ethnicity' post-1990 within the framework of globalisation and political change in South Africa, which fragmented identities.

Since reconnection between South-East Asian and Cape Muslims through a seminar in April 1993 on 'Evolving Muslim identity at the Cape', there has been a flurry of activity between the regions, and the formation of organisations like the Cape Malay Chamber of Commerce, the South African Malay Cultural Society, and the Forum for Malay Culture in South Africa. These groups defended their use of 'Malay' and have vied to attract moral and economic support from the Department of Arts, Culture and Technology in South Africa, as well as similar government departments in South-East Asia, even though there are 'particularities to Malaysian Islam which are quite different from what has been constructed as "Malay" in Cape Town' (Pillay 2003: 296). The project to reinvent Malay identity has been opposed in many quarters. Jeppie, for example, warned that, 'If representatives of the new-found (re-newed?) ethnicity, with its wealthy connections, contribute to the type of isolation, insularity and belligerent communalism rampant elsewhere in the world ... they ought to be scorned and rejected by South Africa and its Muslim population' (2001:3).

PEOPLE AGAINST GANGSTERISM AND DRUGS

The cultural politics around identities in the Western Cape in the immediate aftermath of non-racial democracy gave way to more urgent questions of gangs and drugs. This gave birth to a movement that attracted tremendous international attention, but faded after a relatively short but forceful campaign. From its hesitant birth on the streets of the Cape Flats in mid-1996, People Against Gangsterism and Drugs (Pagad) evolved into a powerful entity that seriously challenged the fledgling non-racial democracy. It drew on elements in Islamic religious sources such as the Quran and practices of the Prophet Muhammad (*sunnah*), without regard to historic context, to emphasise the believer's imperative to take direct action to achieve a morally just society. Pagad roused Muslims into action and castigated those who questioned its methods. While Pagad's approach attracted 'reformed' drug addicts and ex-gang members, its tactics provoked the opposition of many, including Muslims, who were branded 'hypocrites' (*munafiqun*), a severe accusation in Islamic ethics, or 'religious gangsters' (*Cape Argus* 22.09.98).

The abolition of the death penalty, tighter rules governing police behaviour, and perceived corruption in police services in post-1994 South Africa contributed to the perception among ordinary South Africans that crime was soaring. In 1996 a loose grouping of Muslims marched, alongside other activists, on Parliament and the house of the then Minister of Justice, the late (Ab)dullah Omar, a resident of the Cape Flats. Chanting 'Who are we? We are People Against Gangsterism and Drugs', they called on government to show its commitment to the masses by putting an end to gangs and drugs, the scourge of the people (Jeppie 1996a:15). Pagad achieved international publicity when notorious gang leader Rashaad Staggie was pulled from his luxury 4x4 vehicle in August 1996, shot, and set alight in full view of dozens of policemen and the public. The gruesome public murder was captured on television and shown throughout the world. The Staggie twins, Rashaad and Rashied, controlled the Hard Livings gang from their tavern *Die Hok* in Manenberg. When they were released from jail in the late 1980s, they moved beyond the localised drug dealing of Manenberg to control drug-trafficking networks across the Western Cape (*Mail & Guardian* 2.08.02). The murder of Rashaad Staggie propelled Pagad, and the issues that it was raising, to the front pages of newspapers, not only in the Western Cape, but throughout South Africa.

Pagad's novelty lay in its tactic of direct action, which included spectacular public performances and militant rhetoric. The first few marches attracted around a thousand protesters. Organisers held mass meetings at a mosque, prayed collectively to prepare marchers psychologically, and then marched to the homes of alleged drug dealers, displaying an array of firearms. Pagad gained Muslim support by embracing Islamic slogans, dress and rhetoric. It evolved from mass public protest to reliance on small, secretive cells once police curtailed public protest because of safety issues. Small cells of activists, called the G-Force (G purportedly standing for 'guard'), protected the leadership and, it is alleged, carried out attacks on drug dealers. According to journalist Mark Gevisser, the G-Force, consisting of 'armed *keffiyeh*-clad *mujahedin* brought to the Flats an intifada image calculated to instil both fear and romance' (*Mail & Guardian* 16.08.96). Firebombs and armed attacks on the homes of alleged drug peddlers and opponents became the norm.

Due to its Muslim face, the police and media sought explanations for Pagad's rise in global Islamic fundamentalism, portraying it as an extension of militant Middle East groups like Hamas and Hezbollah, or an agent of Libya and Iran (Tayob 2002). One reason for this association was the presence of seasoned Qibla members within Pagad. Qibla, formed in 1981 by Achmat Cassiem, shortly after the Iranian Revolution, is a fringe but vociferous Muslim political grouping originally allied to the Pan Africanist Congress (PAC). Cassiem advocated 'international Islamism', which sought a worldwide Islamic revolution (Pillay 2003:298). Although Qibla exerted internal pressure on Pagad leaders, and it was said that Ali Parker, Mansoor Jaffer, and 'Commander' Aslam Toefy resigned because of such pressure (*Mail & Guardian* 5.12.97), support for Pagad was the product of local social and economic problems. Pagad waged war on drug lords and gangsterism, which were of concern to Muslims and non-Muslims alike. The estimated 137 gangs in the Cape Peninsula, with their approximately 100 000 members, are responsible for around 60 per cent of violent crime, and a large proportion of muggings, break-ins to houses and cars, and theft from warehouses. A *Mail & Guardian* report concluded that 'gangs have largely replaced council authority and filled the vacuum left by the lack of jobs, social services and recreation facilities. Being part of a gang brings a sense of belonging, power and material goods' (2.08.02). Pillay (2003) argues that the impulses that led to the formation of Pagad date back to the mid-1980s with the formation of anti-drug community organisations in Salt River, Bo-Kaap, Surrey Estate, Athlone, and Wynberg.

Pagad spawned unprecedented levels of violence on the Cape Flats. Bombings and shootings became common, as gang members retaliated by embarking on a systematic programme of killing Muslim businessmen and professionals who supported Pagad, while petrol bombs were hurled at mosques in Kensington and Mountview during 1996 and 1997 (Jeppie 1998). A popular slogan among gang members was 'one shopkeeper, one bullet' (Pillay 2003:301). Ordinary people normally outside the regular circuits of gang violence were drawn into the conflict. Pagad altered the texture of social life and civil society in the Western Cape. While it emerged within civil society, and mobilised across class and religious lines, Pagad's tactics undermined public life by destabilising civil society. While exploiting the new democratic civic space to mobilise support, Pagad increasingly employed anti-democratic measures against its opponents. A reign of fear impoverished civil society as Muslims and non-Muslims alike were silenced. Pagad did not enjoy universal support among Muslims. In particular, it had a troubled relationship with the Muslim Judicial Council (MJC), Imams like Rashied Omar of Claremont Mosque and Shaykh Moerat of Muir Street Mosque, as well as academics like Ebrahim Moosa of the University of Cape Town, who were critical of its *modus operandi* (Baderoon 2003). There was a grenade attack on Sheikh Nazeem Moahmed of the MJC, death threats against Imam Sadullah Khan, and a pipe bomb attack on the home of Ebrahim Moosa. Khan and Moosa subsequently emigrated to the USA.

The police were ambivalent when killings were confined to gang members, but actively pursued Pagad when from 1998 its pipe-bombing campaign targeted restaurants, police stations and courts in white Cape Town. In the first ten months of 1998 there were 80 pipe bomb explosions in the Western Cape, which killed 11 people, a further 165 incidents of urban violence attributed to Pagad, and 437 incidents blamed on gangs (Pillay 2003:308). The bombing of Planet Hollywood restaurant in 1998 received widespread international publicity, and impacted negatively on the Cape as a holiday destination. Despite the state's determination to crack down, the police were largely ineffective.

There were 600 cases of unsolved urban terrorism by 1999. The courts routinely dismissed cases because of lack of evidence or seriously flawed investigations (*Cape Times* 12.04.99). Anti-crime campaigns such as 'Operation Recoil' during 1996 and 1997, and 'Operation Good Hope' from 1998 to 2000, received massive funding, and involved both police and soldiers, but the violence continued unabated.

The police changed strategy in 2000. They focused on neutralising Pagad by arresting its key leaders. This had the desired effect as the movement unravelled over the next two years. The first sign of trouble was the resignation of Pagad's Chief Commander, Aslam Toefy, in November 1997. Pagad leader Abdus-Salaam Ebrahim, former spiritual leader Abdurazak Ebrahim, and member Moegsien Mohammed, were acquitted of murder in the Rashaad Staggie trial, but marginalised in March 2002 when they were found guilty of the lesser charge of public violence (*Mail & Guardian* 8.03.02). The state relentlessly pursued the leadership through legal channels. Pagad was exhausted through these lengthy and expensive court cases. Key figures were apprehended, and eventually a number of them were found guilty and incarcerated. The movement was neutered in this way. Pagad's was a bold, if reckless, attempt to address a problem with deep roots in the Cape Flats. Its methods created ambivalence among the rank and file, which prevented it from developing a genuinely multi-religious, cross-class, ethnically mixed support base. The response of the state, to target the leadership without necessarily eliminating Pagad, was successful. The arrest of leaders stalled Pagad's momentum, and thwarted its ability to carry through campaigns of civil disobedience.

There are intermittent signs of Pagad organising an event, but these are negligible. The effective demise of Pagad gave space for the ordinary and everyday life of the Muslim community of the Cape to continue without much drama. The two Muslim radio stations, Voice of the Cape and 786, continued their programming, and have remained at the core of the search of many households for Islamic education, information about the broader Islamic world, and a platform for ordinary Muslims to have their voices heard through various call-in programmes. Apart from the monthly newspaper *Muslim Views*, print media have largely disappeared among Muslim organisations in the Cape. With the demise of Pagad, other trends have been building up – the growth and influence of neo-Sufi groupings throughout the Cape, such as the Alawi and Tijanniyya, and stronger emphasis on religious education for children as well as adults, as reflected in the growth of private Muslim schools, and after-school and weekend religious classes. Even a few former whites-only schools offer after-school Islamic classes.

This brief overview of developments within Islam in the Western Cape during the past decade will conclude by alluding to several intellectuals who attempted to provide an alternative narrative of Islam and what it means to be a Muslim in contemporary South Africa. Ebrahim Rasool, Ebrahim Moosa, Farid Esack, Rashied Omar, and Abdulkader Tayob, all based in the Cape, espoused what they called a 'democratic' Islam, one that was willing to participate within secular groups and was 'forward-looking', in contrast to the *Ulama* who were seen as representing 'traditional Islam'. These intellectuals saw democratic Islam as nationalist, while traditional Islam, with its gaze towards an international *ummah*, was seen as 'utopian, un-South African' and out of touch with South African social, economic and political realities. Democratic Islam respected diversity and accepted that Islamic values were among a number of value systems that coexisted in a politically plural dispensation (see Esak 1997). Rashied Omar, Imam of the Claremont mosque, broke new ground by accommodating women during communal prayers and even allowed a woman to give the sermon during the Friday prayer. However, Tayob has since moved to Leiden, Esack has served on the Gender Commission and spent time on sabbatical in the USA, while Moosa moved to Duke University shortly after his house was bombed in July 1998, allegedly by Pagad because he had criticised it (Pillay 2003).

'Turning to the core': Indian Islam in KwaZulu-Natal

Historical background

The majority of Indians arrived between 1860 and 1911, either as contract indentured workers or traders who came of their own accord from Gujarat on the western coast of India. Aside from obvious differences of class, traders and indentured migrants were divided by religious tradition, caste, language, ethnicity and culture, as they were drawn from a range of ecologies and modes of production (see Vahed 2001a, 2001b, 2002). Many traders made their way to the Transvaal and the Cape from the early 1880s, where they remain the predominant element among Indian Muslims. Traders did not attempt to forge a broad Muslim community on the basis of Islam, but formed class alliances with Hindu traders to protect their economic and political rights. The most important identity in the political realm was race because the emergent white state separated Indians legislatively into a discrete racial category. Use of the appellation 'Indians' inferred that the attribute 'Indianness' united them as a collectivity against whites and Africans (Bhana 1997:100).

The coming to power of the National Party (NP) in 1948 had paradoxical consequences. Segregation intensified, but in 1961, Indians were finally recognised as permanent citizens. The expansion of educational opportunities and economic mobility from the 1960s had important consequences. Younger, better-educated Muslims challenged traditional conceptions of Islam at the same time that conservative *Ulama* began to emerge as an influential factor shaping local Muslim communities (Vahed 2000b). Residential clustering through the Group Areas Act allowed Muslims to practise Islam in a value-friendly environment (Vahed 2000b). Free and compulsory education from the 1960s transformed Indian society. The number of candidates who wrote the final year secondary school examination increased from 2 623 in 1968 to 10 449 in 1984 (Naidoo 1989:116). Coupled with the opening of the University of Durban-Westville (1963) and expansion of the ML Sultan Technical College, mass education led to economic mobility, and helped reshape conceptions of self and religion. It gave Muslims direct access to the printed word, and cultivated debate and formulation of clear statements of belief that illuminated sectarian distinctions. Differences became cemented as Islam became a subject to be explained and understood rather than assumed (see Eickelman 1992).

Islamic revivalism manifested itself among all sectors of Muslim society in Durban from the 1960s. Three broad traditions emerged – modernist, Deobandi and Sunni. Younger Muslims drew inspiration from thinkers like Muhammad Iqbal (d. 1938) and Sayyad Qutb (d. 1966) who attempted to marry Islamic and secular knowledge. Organisations like the Muslim Youth Movement (MYM) promoted an intellectual approach in order to make Islam meaningful in the day-to-day lives of Muslims. They enjoyed support among students and some professionals (Jeppie, forthcoming). The Muslim masses, however, embraced conservative tendencies that came to be termed 'Deobandi' and 'Sunni'[2] (Vahed 2000b).

Post-apartheid period

Non-racial democracy resulted in massive social, political and economic change. The new African National Congress (ANC) government did not support an Islamic world view, but legalised abortion, prostitution, and pornography. This was compounded by affirmative action policies, the African Renaissance agenda of the ANC, and the impact of globalisation. These changes triggered important behaviour modification among large numbers of Muslims. The most striking transformation has been the growth of personal piety and growing tolerance between the Deobandi and Sunni traditions. There is a staggering increase, for example, in the numbers of women who cover their faces with a veil; there is greater concern with observing dietary regulations; televisions have been rooted out from many Muslim homes; and there has been a dramatic growth in Muslim schools. Theological debate is virtually absent. Truth has become synonymous with the *Ulama* and to question the *Ulama* means questioning the truth. Another conspicuous feature of the new Islam is self-reformation. An increasing number of Muslims are becoming attached to *Shaykhs* (spiritual mentors) in their search for personal stability and guidance (Vahed 2000a).

The last decade has also been witness to the arrival of economic migrants from South Asia. They are visible as chicken vendors, or running cellphone shops and other small businesses in places like Durban and Lenasia. Anti-immigrant discourse among Indians has given rise to xenophobia and stereotypes, particularly against those from Pakistan, who are seen as dishonest, as living in overcrowded apartments, undercutting local traders, and engaging in false marriages to obtain passports (including marriage to African women). It remains to be seen whether these are marriages of convenience or whether they mark the beginnings of a breakdown in race barriers. Themba Ndebele of Home Affairs in Pretoria was certain that 'most of these men – after getting South African citizenship – go back home to collect their lawful wives, leaving the local ones miserable' (*Pretoria News* 23.10.03).

Black African Muslims

The number of African Muslims has increased from 9 048 in 1980 to 74 701 by 2001. They now make up almost 12 per cent of South Africa's Muslims as opposed to 2.5 per cent in 1980, and yet they 'remain on the margins of

Muslim community life' (Sitoto 2002:44). This increase is due to factors such as the conscious decision of many township youth to embrace Islam during the 1980s; students going into exile in Malawi and Mozambique after 1976, where they came into contact with Islam; and the involvement of organisations like the Islamic Propagation Centre International (IPCI) in townships. IPCI president Ahmed Deedat translated the Quran into isiZulu (Fakude 2002). In contrast to other parts of Africa where migrant Arab traders were instrumental in locals embracing Islam, in South Africa, Indians have largely remained isolated from Africans, who have historically viewed Islam as an Indian, and exploitative, religion because of its close association with traders (Vawda 1993).

The arrival of 112 freed slaves from Zanzibar in 1873 laid the foundation of African Islam in Natal. In local parlance they came to be known as 'Zanzibaris', a term applied generally to all African Muslims. Officially they have been transformed by successive white governments from 'freed slaves' to 'Bantu', 'Coloureds', and finally 'Other Asians'. They settled around the King's Rest mosque on Bluffs Road. After the NP came to power in 1948, Bluff was declared a white area and Zanzibaris, who distinguished themselves from non-Muslim Africans, were categorised as 'Other Asian' and placed in a separate section of the newly-built Indian township of Chatsworth (Oosthuizen 1982).

Since the early 1990s, refugees – mainly political exiles from the Democratic Republic of Congo (DRC), Burundi, Rwanda and Malawi – have augmented the African Muslim population in Durban. Concerned about the economic plight of migrants, a Refugee Relief Programme was instituted by local Muslims in 1996 to provide food and shelter. Kathrada (2001) reported that most of the refugees were between ages 20 and 30, educated, overwhelmingly male, and many had spouses in their home countries. He found that 94 per cent of refugees felt well treated by Indian Muslims; their major complaint was that they were not considered 'true Muslims' even though they were fluent in Arabic and several had trained as Imams.

Islam's presence in Soweto strengthened from the late 1970s with the arrival of economic migrants from Malawi and Mozambique. Soweto's first mosque was built in Dlamini, which remains the heart of Soweto Muslim community life. It was the scene of the first blast when right-wing extremists rocked

Soweto with nine bombs on 29 October 2002 (*Mail & Guardian* 30.10.02). In Soweto, too, there is a negative association between Islam and Indians. Salama Motsoatose, a Sotho woman who embraced Islam in 1971, told reporter Emeka Nwandiko that there was a perception that Islam was an exclusively 'coolie thing … It is difficult to be a Muslim because people think we've been colonised by Indians'. Her son Abdulazeez added that 'most blacks don't like Indians. As employers they do not treat blacks fairly. Blacks wonder why we are following an Indian church' (*Mail & Guardian* 5.03.99).

In Johannesburg, relations between refugee and Indian Muslims are tense. The Africa Muslim Agency (AMA), which was assisting refugees with food parcels, suspended its aid in January 1997. Somali refugees claimed that Indians were racist and showed a bias towards Tunisians and Algerians. Aid organisations, on the other hand, cited limited resources and the greed of refugees as causes of the tension. AMA spokesperson Yusuf Seedat said that, between 1994 and 1996, the food relief budget had escalated from R6 000 per month to R40 000 per month, which was beyond the capacity of his organisation. An AMA aid worker added, 'We go up in Africa and find people who don't have flesh on their bones, and here we are abused by Somali fat cats' (*al-Qalam* February 1997).

Islam spread in the Western Cape through the pioneering work of Imam Abdullah Haroon who broke the law by entering townships during the 1960s. One of the highest profile individuals to accept Islam was Hasa Gila, a founding member of the PAC (MMC 2002). The 1980s and 1990s were marked by careful expansion, with the opening of Islamic schools and the Jihad Centre in Guguletu, controlled by the youth organisation Al-Jihad; study circles in Khayelitsha by Hadji S Bayat and Mrs Faika Kriel; and a Shia centre in Phillipi (MMC 2002). The training of locals in Islamic theology raised the quality of Islamic teaching in townships and reduced their dependency on Indian and Malay teachers and theologians. Abdullah Nonyana was the first African to study abroad when he went to Kuwait in 1981, while Ismail Gqamane and Shaykh Jamiel Kobus graduated from Madinah University in 1997 (MMC 2002). An umbrella body, the Masakhane Muslim Community (MMC) – *Masakhane* meaning 'building one another' in isiXhosa – was formed in 1997 to unite township Muslims, provide 'coherent leadership and direction, arbitrate disputes and provide quality education'. In 1999 Cassiem Gqamane was appointed president (*Amir*), while Abdullah Quick, Director of the Da'wah Department of the

MJC, was appointed 'special advisor' to any Muslim in the township (MMC 2002:51). The dual role of Abdullah Quick in the MJC and MMC suggests formal co-operation.

African Muslims are debating the relationship between what has variously been referred to as 'developing Islam' and 'established Islam' (Fakude 2002:47); 'the emerging and unorganised African Muslim sector' and 'established sector' (Sitoto 2002: 43); or 'historically imported' and 'historically indigenous' Muslims (Rafudeen 2002: 59). It irks many Muslims in townships that, while their economic and social needs have not been met, there is swift reaction to the plight of Muslims elsewhere in the world. Aid, in the form of cash, food and medical supplies, has been provided to Bosnia (1997), Gujarat (2002), Palestine (2001), Algeria (2003), Afghanistan (2002), and Iraq (2003).

An example of this tension was the plan by the mainly-Indian Muslims of Houghton, an affluent suburb north of Johannesburg, to build the King Fahd Grand Mosque at a cost of $15 million. 'Uncle Sid' Sadrudeen of Soweto led a campaign against the Mosque in 1999, arguing that instead of building extravagant facilities for the rich, the money should be used to equip poorer areas like Soweto where worshippers had to be bussed to Dlamini Mosque from Klipspruit, Rockville and Meadowlands. Sadrudeen branded this 'financial apartheid'. The project was put on hold even though the foundation stone had been laid by Saudi Crown Prince Abdullah bin Abdel-Aziz during a state visit to South Africa in 1999 (*Mail & Guardian* 8.10.99).

For their part, the Islamic Dawah Movement, IPCI, African Muslim Agency, Al-Ansaar Foundation, and other Muslim organisations point to the many projects they are involved in across townships in South Africa. The problem, however, centres around ownership – those in townships want to implement projects relevant to them, rather than leave the decision-making to others. One respondent described how dependency forced African Muslims to constantly change their Islamic identity:

> We are the have-nots. They are the haves, they support us with food yearly, pay our electricity, and all that … On Tuesdays you have to be a Tablighi and wear a long kurta and speak about the Hadith. Why? Because you need something from that guy. Then the following day you have to change from Tablighism to Sunnism

because they are giving something. On Sunday, then you have to go to Soofie Sahib to ask for dholl and other things. If you are not a Soofie, he won't give you … It's a push. (Vawda 1993:61).

There remain problems in townships – the most significant being the lack of facilities, mosques, and madrasahs, in a climate of poverty and un-employment. As racial tensions developed, some African Muslims boy-cotted 'Indian' mosques, while a group marched to the Union Buildings, and submitted a letter of complaint to President Thabo Mbeki in 2002. Their grievances included racism, exploitation, and unfair distribution of charity (*zakaat*) collected from Muslims during the fasting month of *Ramadaan* (Fakude 2002).

Seeking an indigenous voice: black African Muslims

African Muslims are wrestling with the notion of being African and Muslim. Recently arrived refugees constitute a nascent grouping; others like Advocate Dawood Ngwane of the IPCI and Cassim Modise of the Islamic Dawah Movement are working through existing organisations to bridge the gulf between Muslims in the 'centre' and those on the 'periphery'; a third and growing tendency has shunned the paternalism of existing organisations, and is seeking to forge an independent identity rooted in Africa. Sitoto has noted that South Africa is the only country in Africa where Islam is not 'in concert with the socio-cultural experience of the African Muslims, in tune with the local environment' (2002:47). He feels strongly that African Muslims should not be regarded as a charity case. Those living in poverty in townships, he said, are like millions of township dwellers across the country for whom poverty is the norm. Sitoto rejected 'condescending discourse' about African Muslims and called for a 'Muslim identity that has its home in Africa rather than seek shelter in a misplaced pan-Islamic rhetoric' (Sitoto 2002:45–46). Amir Yusuf Jakubeni, of the Katlehong Islamic Foundation, told *Pace* magazine (June 1997) that, 'for too long leadership has been monopolised … we want to develop our own values and own interpretation'. Nceba Salamntu deprecated the Indian influence on African Islam:

Indian Muslims have built mosques, assisted financially and materially, and through their monopoly of Muslim educational institutions have managed to impose an Indian expression of

Islam on others ... It is cultural imperialism. Indian people are proud of their culture and identity even in the diaspora, why can't we be so in our motherland? (*Al-Qalam* February 1997)

The Organisation of African Muslim Unity (OAMU) was formed in KZN in 1997, to achieve 'self-empowerment and assist African Muslims to become organised and focused' (*Muslim Views* July 1997). Vice-Rector of the Islamic College of South Africa, Auwais Rafudeen (2002:58–59), called for Islam 'to be Africanised'. He wanted Muslims to 'be thoroughly aware of African history and traditional African culture'. He said that Muslims existed in particular cultural milieus, and while they should shed those beliefs considered 'un-Islamic', the cultural aspects of identity should be maintained. A pristine 'Muslimhood' remains elusive. To 'Africanise' Islamic identity did not mean wearing Madiba shirts, but changing mindsets to understand African culture and world view, and incorporating it where there was no contradiction with Islamic law. Rafudeen wanted Islamic schools to teach African languages and culture. He called on the *Ulama* to circulate pamphlets, arrange lectures, and circulate information campaigns that underscored Islam's abhorrence of racism.

Some organisations and individuals are addressing this problem. During the latter half of 2003, for example, the KZN *Jamiat* published articles such as 'Combating the monster of racism', 'Islam and racism', 'Smashing the idol of racism', and 'Racial equality' on its website. The Anti-Racism Forum has conducted workshops to educate Muslims. In December 2003, the MYM held an anti-racism education workshop, while in January 2004 the KZN *Jamiat* held a similar workshop. On 19 March 2004, as part of Human Rights Day celebrations, mosques across KZN focused on anti-racist education during their friday *Khutbahs* (lectures) (*Al-Qalam* December 2003).

'Liberated zones'

Many Muslims have made use of South Africa's new political freedoms and its liberal Constitution to pursue their distinctive rights. For many, this is part of a broader programme of introducing tighter Islamic codes in public and private domains. Roy refers to this as the creation of 'liberated zones', that is, forming spaces where the ideals of a future society can be implemented, but where 'no counterpower is established, no counterstate' (1996:80). The creation of 'liberated zones' does not imply animosity to the state nor is there a serious proselytising aspect to it.

One example is *shariah*-based Muslim Personal Law (MPL), which is arguably the most important development over the past decade, particularly with regard to the rights of women. The Constitution recognised 'personal or family law' provided it was in accord with other provisions of the Constitution. The South African Law Commission (SALC) project committee, headed by Supreme Court Judge Mohamed Navsa, released a draft Bill on Islamic marriages in December 2001. Journalist Khadija Magardie described the draft Bill as 'a progressive step towards resolving the mismatch between Muslim personal law and the Bill of Rights ... While it is good news for some, its contents are likely to have some quarters sighing into their three-fists long beards' (*Mail & Guardian* 7.12.01). Magardie was referring to the fact that aspects of the Bill, such as the requirement that a man wanting to marry a second time had to obtain the permission of a civil court, were rejected by Muslim judicial bodies. Muslims are deeply divided over the Bill. Some have welcomed its commitment to gender equality, others accept that aspects of it are problematic but are willing to work from within to effect change, and yet others have rejected it totally because they believe that the Law of God supersedes laws created by human beings. *Al-Haq* of Port Elizabeth, for example, claimed that a committee 'consisting of modernists, liberals, and females has assumed the responsibility to impose on the Muslim community a measure which the majority of *Ulama* have outrightly rejected as being in conflict with *Shariah*' (February 2004). MPL is heavily contested among Muslims.

Finance and investment is another area in which Muslims have attempted to introduce Islam into their personal lives. Most Muslims try to avoid participating in interest-related economic activities. *Ulama* who prohibit participation in pension funds, insurance, medical aid and unit trusts and so forth, realise that substitutes have to be provided for Muslims to participate in the modern economy, and are pioneering efforts in *shariah*-compliant finance. The Albaraka Bank, started in 1989 by South African investors and the Saudi-based Dallah Albaraka Bank, has developed a range of *shariah*-compliant investment and financial products. Albaraka does not invest in the shares of companies involved in gambling, non-halaal food, alcohol, or interest transactions. The rules governing fund investments and banking principles were established by a *Shariah* Supervisory Board comprised of

Islamic legal scholars from throughout the world (Joosub 2003). Albaraka's growth has been exceptional; at the end of 2003 its assets stood at R700 million. However, stringent criteria governing loan arrangements, which are more onerous than most commercial banks, mean that it is mainly the affluent who are able to take advantage of Albaraka's services. The Cape Town-based Muslim financial services company, Oasis, is Albaraka's major competitor. For example, when Albaraka Equity Fund won three 'Raging Bull Awards' for being the top performing general equity fund for the three years ending December 2003, the awards ceremony had to be postponed because Oasis objected that Albaraka contravened the rules by moving away from its original investment mandate when it became *shariah*-compliant (*Independent on Saturday* 17.01.04). Though the Association of Collective Investments overruled the objection, this incident shows that being Muslim does not diminish competition (*Independent on Saturday* 31.01.04).

Islamic media – radio, magazines, websites, books and newspapers – have mushroomed over the past decade. Monthly newspapers like *Majlis, Al-Haq, Al-Ummah, Muslim Views, Al-Jamiat,* and *Al-Qalam* reflect different, and contested, shades of opinion among Muslims. Muslim magazines like *KZN Islam* and *The Muslim Woman* provide alternatives to mainstream women's magazines, and project images of the ideal Muslim woman. Islamic story-books are freely available for children, as are tape cassettes and CDs of Islamic songs. These include nursery rhymes and songs for younger children, as well as songs dealing with current international events. Songs are not accompanied by music, which is considered *haraam* (forbidden) by many Muslims. Virtually every Islamic organisation, including theological institutes, has set up websites that cover the latest developments in the Islamic world, as well as theological issues. Many of the websites are interactive, and the Muslim public is free to communicate online for *fatwahs* (religious decrees) or advice. Radio stations have grown from strength to strength. Some target local and regional markets, such as *Al-Ansaar* in Durban, Radio 786 in the Cape, and Radio Islam in Johannesburg. The Johannesburg-based Channel Islam International (CII), which started broadcasting in October 2000, is an international station broadcast to over 60 countries across Africa, the United Kingdom and Europe. Its aim, shared by much of the new Islamic media, is 'to bring Muslims around the world into the information age, to use the fruits of the twenty-first century to provide high quality Islamic content designed to sow the seeds of religious education and growth as tools for upliftment and empowerment'.[3] CII is managed by professionals with expertise in information technology, marketing, law, and finance, but the overall content is supervised by Islamic scholars. The 'new media' is playing a crucial role in forging and reaffirming a broader Muslim identity internationally across the boundaries of sectarian and national divisions through, for example, the live broadcast of the funeral of Hamas founder Sheik Ahmed Yassin, who was murdered by the Israeli government in March 2004, interviews with Muslims subjected to harassment in the West, and other such coverage. This re-imagining of identity is not neutral. The 'new' Muslim media is controlled by hegemonic groups among Muslims, usually conservative and monied, who are playing a key role in implanting a common perspective consistent with their normative outlook.

Gender: making space for women

There have been contradictory tendencies regarding the position of women. On the one hand, far more women are fully veiled and wear loose-fitting black garments, even though Muslim jurists disagree over whether Islam requires women to cover their faces. The position of the KZN *Jamiat* is that 'due to the immorality of the times and weakness of resistance, it is compulsory for a female to cover her face which is the focus of her beauty' (*Al-Mahmood* July 1999). By 'veil', *Ulama* mean the total seclusion of women from public spaces and not merely the covering of their faces. The story of the Johannesburg-based Radio Islam is illustrative. It was granted a licence to broadcast for one month during January 1999. Contrary to the Broadcasting Act, which makes it mandatory for women to comprise one-third of management, the station excluded women from its management and did not allow female voices to be heard over the air. Members of the public lodged a complaint with the Independent Broadcasting Authority (IBA). The hearing to consider the renewal of Radio Islam's licence was attended by several hundred Muslim women, fully covered from head to toe, presenting a very powerful image. Radio Islam management remained adamant that to allow women to speak on radio would be a violation of Islamic beliefs and practices, but in order to renew its licence, the station was forced to allow women access to the air for four hours each day (*Sunday Independent* 7.02.99).

The attitude of many parents towards education, particularly in KZN and Gauteng, has changed as part of a gender counter-revolution. These parents no longer consider it desirable for girls to receive secular education beyond a certain age, if at all. Secular education, according to the KZN *Jamiat,* was placing pitfalls in the pathway of 'sincere Muslim women, wanting to follow the pure and pristine Islam of the last 1 400 years. Our young Muslim sisters at schools, colleges, and universities are exposed to dangers all the time. A Muslim lady needs to acquaint herself much more with the correct teachings of Islam than ever before' (*Al-Jamiat* December 1998). Girls are either sent to Muslim schools, which combine secular and religious education, or Islamic schools, where the syllabus comprises Arabic, Urdu, and Islamic jurisprudence, supplemented by English and mathematics to Grade 7.

A countervailing tendency has been that of some Muslims challenging the authority of traditional *Ulama,* debating issues relating to women's rights in Islam, including MPL and attendance at mosques. One of the leading activists was Shamima Shaikh, who was national co-ordinator of the Muslim Youth Movement's Gender Desk (1993–98), editor of the progressive Muslim monthly *Al-Qalam* (1996–97), chairperson of the Muslim Community Broadcasting Trust in Johannesburg (1995–98), and founder of The Voice radio station. Together with her husband, Naeem Jinnah, she authored *Journey of discovery: A South African Hajj,* a personal story of their pilgrimage (*Hajj*) to Makkah. The book examines issues of gender and power in Islam, and the attempt to reconcile social activism with traditional faith. Sadly, Shamima Shaikh died of cancer in January 1998.

Another recent example of the division around women's rights was the 'Family Eidgah', a prayer meeting held on an open field at the Durban beachfront in November 2003 during the festival of Eid. On 29 October, the KZN *Jamiat* informed the organiser that women should not attend because it would be impossible to meet stringent conditions such as the complete separation (*purdah*) of men and women, and women abstaining from the use of perfume in the presence of men. The *Jamiat* had no doubt that if the Prophet had 'seen the condition of women today, he would have prevented them from attending'. The organiser responded by challenging the *Jamiat* to a 'public debate once and for all on this issue'. He cited Islamic sources to argue that women were permitted to participate in prayer at mosques and accused the *Ulama* of 'attempting to enforce your oppressive Indo-Pak, male-dominated, cultural norms on the Muslim community under the guise of theological legality'. Though, clearly, elements among Muslims are willing to challenge the authority of traditional *Ulama*, the birth of the 'new' Muslim woman and the end of patriarchal ideology are not in immediate sight.

9/11, the 'war of terror' and conflict in Palestine

Although most Muslim organisations condemned the attacks on the World Trade Centre and the Pentagon on 11 September 2001, in certain quarters local Muslims were deemed culpable. Shortly after the attacks, journalist Marianne Merten (*Mail & Guardian* 21.09.01) wrote that 'Muslim "harassment" was linked to rising Islamophobia'. The MJC in Cape Town was subjected to very abusive calls and an arson attack, while Muslim organisations, community radio stations and newspapers across the country received hate mail. While Sheikh Achmat Sedick, secretary general of the MJC, said that his organisation would overlook the abuse 'to avoid the confrontation some appear to be wanting', fringe groups like the Islamic Unity Conference (IUC) propagated conspiracy theories about who might have caused the attacks or blamed American foreign policy for triggering the attacks (Tayob 2002:22). While South African *Ulama* agree that Islam forbids suicide bombings, speaking on Channel Islam on 11 September 2003, Imam Quick and Mufti AK Hoosen explained that random suicide bombings were prohibited, but that *Ulama* internationally distinguished between random bombings like 9/11 and the conflict in Palestine. Palestinians were regarded as victims of Israeli aggression and their actions were branded legitimate martyrdom operations under occupation and warlike conditions.

Sympathy for the USA over 9/11 dissipated when it attacked Afghanistan on 7 October 2001. Together with the Congress of South African Trade Unions (Cosatu) and the Western Cape Council of Churches, the MJC organised a peace march of around 5 000 people on 11 October 2001. However, in response to calls by fringe groups, like Abduraghman Khan's little-known Muslims Against Illegitimate Leaders, for a *jihad* against the 'infidel', main-stream bodies like the MJC, as well as those regarded as 'pro-Taliban', urged Muslims to respect South African law, which prohibited military assistance to any foreign country unless authorised by the state (*Mail & Guardian* 12.10.01).

Like the 'war on terror', the Palestinian *intifada* spawned important debates. According to Naeem Jeenah, MYM president and member of the Palestinian Solidarity Committee, the participation of the South African Communist Party (SACP), Cosatu, as well as non-governmental organisations like the Anti-Privatisation Forum in pro-Palestinian protests strengthened interfaith solidarity, and dispelled the myth that the struggle of the Palestinians was a Muslim cause. Jeenah felt that participation in multi-faith protests broadened Muslim concerns to include the problems of the landless and the negative impact of privatisation in South Africa (*Mail & Guardian* 12.04.02). In the Cape, the MJC supported the *intifada*. In March 2002, Secretary General Ighsaan Hendricks said that the MJC recognised Palestinian groups 'as legitimate freedom fighters. We view them in the same light as people view the role of the ANC and PAC in the liberation struggle of this country' (*Cape Argus* 14.03.02). Qibla was more defiant. A march to the American Consulate on 28 November 2002 was led by two young boys dressed as suicide bombers, wearing Hezbollah headbands and dressed in black with cardboard dynamite sticks strapped to their chests. Marchers shouted slogans like 'death to America, death to Israel' and 'one American tourist, one bullet'. The MJC branded the use of children 'irresponsible' (*Cape Argus* 29.11.02).

In Durban, the impetus for response to events in the Middle East was led by the Palestinian Solidarity Committee. There were tensions from the outset because the committee was home to individuals from a variety of backgrounds, including academics Fazel Khan and Lubna Nadvi from the University of KZN, radio presenter and media personality Abie Dawjee, Zulekha Mayat of the Women's Cultural Group, as well as Mawlana's Walid and Essa. Areas of tension included the *moulana's* insistence that men and women march separately, which did not sit well with activists; certain members opposed public protest and advocated face-to-face meetings with the US consul-general; and Muslim-owned businesses that stocked American products opposed consumer boycotts. An exasperated member exclaimed: 'We could put people on the streets, get media coverage, embarrass the government, but we could not build a movement.' Post-9/11 saw the erosion of Palestinian Solidarity Committee gains, as non-Muslim progressives who had supported the organisation did not support mobilisation against the US war in Afghanistan because of the nature of the Taliban. Afghani and Palestinian mobilisations had a different meaning and support base.[4]

The war on Iraq revived tensions. On 15 February 2003, South Africans joined millions of demonstrators in approximately 600 cities worldwide to protest against the impending war. Cosatu, the New Unity Movement, the Socialist League, and the MJC, as well as politicians Kader Asmal, Pallo Jordan and Ebrahim Rasool of the ANC, took part in an anti-war march in Cape Town; 3 000 people formed a human chain outside the US consul-general's office in Johannesburg; and around 1 000 marched in Durban. As many, if not more, non-Muslims participated than Muslims. During a programme on CII on 20 February 2003, many callers considered it shameful that, while millions of non-Muslims worldwide were marching for a Muslim country, South African Muslims were conspicuous by their absence. Mainstream *Ulama* in KZN and Gauteng generally discouraged Muslim participation in marches. They attribute the weak position of Muslims to spiritual shortcomings rather than western military superiority. Muslims were being punished by God because of their transgressions, they explained. When all Muslims acted according to a literal interpretation of the Quran and *shariah*, this would lead to the transformation of the Muslim world, to a just and perfect society, and Islamic civilisation would regain lost ground in relation to the West. Public demonstrations were regarded as counterproductive as they led to the transgression of Islamic norms, such as the separation of sexes.

Thirty-two South African housewives, students, professionals, and activists – men and women, Muslims and non-Muslims[5] – volunteered as human shields in Iraq. They were organised by Abie Dawjee, national co-ordinator of the Iraq Action Committee, and positioned themselves at civilian structures like schools, hospitals and water filtration plants. The human shields left on 18 March and reached Iraq around the time of the first attack on Baghdad. They provided first-hand reports in daily newspapers as well as live interviews on CII, giving graphic accounts of the suffering of ordinary Iraqis. Once bombing began, families pressured volunteers to return as they could not stop the war, and most returned to a heroes welcome on 1 April 2003 (*Natal Mercury* 2.04.03).

Whether they choose to protest publicly or not, most Muslims are convinced that George Bush is leading a global war against Islam. In an attempt to improve America's image among Muslims, US consulates invited prominent Muslims for lunch during the Eid festival in November 2003. Predictably, the invitations were declined because they were seen as a ploy to get local Muslims to reject anti-American sentiments. The ongoing imprisonment of Muslims at Guantanemo Bay and attacks on the civil liberties of Muslims in the West, such as the headscarf ban in France, heighten the sense of injustice among Muslims.

Although the reaction of Muslims to international events is complex, the perceived 'Islamic threat' is given prominence in the local media. Journalist Max du Preez made unsubstantiated allegations of Muslim complicity in the attack on the Israeli-run Paradise Mombasa Hotel in Kenya on 27 November 2002, and questioned the loyalty of Muslim citizens to South Africa (*Star* 5.12.02). Martin Schonteich, senior researcher at the Institute of Security Studies in Pretoria, told the Crime Writers' Club that, while the white right wing was too divided and demoralised to constitute a threat, Muslim resentment against the USA and Israel constituted a great danger in South Africa: 'The threat of Islamic terrorism is linked directly to the rising fundamentalist sympathy in the Muslim community. Polarisation will see more radical sections within that community come to the fore, with even traditionally moderate Muslim leaders becoming increasingly outspoken' (*Citizen* 13.02.03). He also suggested links between 'Islamic fundamentalists' and organised crime. The MJC took umbrage with Schonteich's 'unsubstantiated and unwarranted' attack:

> It is with total disgust that the MJC read the blatant, irresponsible and misleading statements about Muslims by Schonteich. For his own reasons Schonteich makes a very poor attempt at clearing the criminal intent of the Afrikaner right-wing elements and at the same time tarnishing the name of Islam and its followers. (*Cape Argus* 19.02.03)

Durban-based Mawlana Rafique Shah said that Schonteich was spreading 'rubbish' that was creating divisions between South Africans. 'No Muslim has any intention of taking over the state. We do not want power. Understand that. The white right wing wants to take over the state. They have a motive. Muslims do not have such intentions' (*Daily News* 18.02.03).

There is little to support the typecasting of Muslims as 'extremists', 'fundamentalists' and 'terrorists' in the South African context. While the religious commitment of Muslims is ever deepening, Islamic resurgence is not a movement of political emancipation but one aimed at preserving and deepening religious-cultural identity. However, because of what is happening in the 'radical' face of Islam, there is a tendency to treat this assertion of Islamic identity with suspicion, misgivings, anxiety and fear (Ali 2000).

South Africa has not entirely escaped Islamophobia. Anti-Muslim discourse, however, should not be homogenised. As a result of political opposition to US hegemony, many South Africans, including large numbers of non-Muslims, have strongly opposed American actions through trade unions, civic organisations and tertiary institutions. Anti-Muslim sentiments in the press, for example, are dominated by white respondents, as well as non-Muslim Indians, perhaps reflecting current Muslim-Hindu tensions in India.

One area of concern for Muslims was the Anti-Terrorism Bill. Organisations such as the Islamic Medical Association, *Jamiatul Ulama* (KZN), MJC, *Sunni Jamiatul Ulama* (SA), MYM, Media Review Network, Association of Muslim Accountants and Lawyers, South African National Zakaah Fund, Africa Muslim Agency, and the Palestinian Solidary Committee, urged President Thabo Mbeki not to pass the Bill: 'If the Anti-Terrorism Bill is passed here, no South African will be able to support in *any* way *any* of the liberation struggles presently being waged in many parts of the world. This is hugely ironical because virtually the entire world supported the South African freedom struggle.' Their letter, dated 11 November 2003, emphasised that groups like Pagad and the *Boeremag* had been apprehended without the Bill, on the basis of good police work and existing criminal laws. While conceding that the present Members of Parliament were sensitive to the struggles of oppressed people in places like Palestine, the danger was that:

> years ahead from now, new people at the helm of government may
> not have this awareness. They will only see the letter of the law
> and may also succumb to outside pressure … The Anti-Terrorism
> Bill in other countries, especially the United States and Britain has
> terrorised innocent people, the vast majority of victims being
> Muslim. We are deeply dismayed and disappointed that our
> government could even contemplate such legislation. Mr President
> we urge you, sir, please do not take us back to the dark days of
> fear, suspicion and injustice. Please scrap the Bill.

Muslims, politics, and the ANC

Muslims have long debated whether to embrace the broader democratic movement or constitute an independent force. The Port Elizabeth-based *Majlis* (Voice of Islam) condemned co-operation with non-Muslims in anti-apartheid structures during the 1980s, because it meant working with 'poly-theist priests and godless communists' (quoted in Moosa 1989:76). This was not the majority view. In the Cape, the Call of Islam's Moulana Faried Essack and Ebrahim Rassool were senior members of the United Democratic Front, and encouraged Muslim co-operation and participation in anti-apartheid organisations. Pressure from these activists resulted in the MJC declaring participation in the 1984 tricameral election juridically forbidden. The Natal *Jamiat* also called for a boycott of the election while the Transvaal *Jamiat* remained silent. The latter, in fact, never made anti-state political statements (Moosa 1989).

The debate over Muslim participation in the political process resurfaced during democratic elections in 1994 and 1999. The IUC, under Achmat Cassiem, which claimed to represent 600 Islamic organisations, called for Muslims to boycott the 1999 election. Cassiem argued that to vote in an un-Islamic state would make Muslims partners to legalised abortion, gay rights, prostitution, and other un-Islamic practices (*Daily News* 20.05.99). However, the majority feeling – articulated by mainstream Muslim organisations such as the *Jamiat*, the MJC, the United Ulama Council of South Africa and the MYM – was that Muslims should vote in the elections for a party of their choice (*Al-Qalam* May 1999). Both the Africa Muslim Party in 1994 and the Africa Moral Party, purporting to represent Muslims, failed to gain representation in Parliament in 1999 as Muslims voted for predominantly non-Muslim parties (*Al-Qalam* May 1999).

Muslims, whether practising or nominal, have featured strongly in representative institutions since 1994, far out of proportion to their numbers. Past Members of Parliament (MPs) have included Kader Asmal, Valli Moosa, and Dullah Omar; Essop Pahad is a key member of President Thabo Mbeki's office; Naledi Pandor was Speaker of the Council of Provinces until she replaced Kader Asmal as Minister of Education in 2004; her deputy is Enver Surti; Ebrahim Rassool was leader of the ANC in the Western Cape from 1994 to 2004, and appointed Western Cape Premier in 2004. In June 2004, ANC MP

Ismail Vadi was elected chairperson of the 17-member multiparty committee formed to consider Public Protector Lawrence Mushwana's report into his investigation of Deputy President Jacob Zuma's complaint against Bulelani Ngcuka and the National Prosecuting Authority relating to their corruption investigation against him; Dr RAM Saloojee and the late Ismail Meer featured at provincial levels; the late Justice Ismail Mohammed occupied the most senior legal position in the country, while Ms Gadija Khan was head of all magistrates in the Western Cape.

This was not matched by support for the ANC in 1994 and 1999. Voting patterns among Indians and coloureds suggest that many voted against the ANC despite the long history of oppression. The NP in 1994, and Democratic Alliance (DA) in 1999, exploited minority fears of the consequences of affirmative action and escalating crime to gain conservative support. The ANC failed to win elections in KZN and the Western Cape, provinces with significant numbers of Indians and coloureds respectively. Habib and Naidu attribute this to class rather than racial 'electoral homogeneity'. While affluent Indians and coloureds supported the ANC, lower-income individuals voted against the ANC because of economic 'rather than racial considerations. Since these classes constitute the largest single bloc within these communities, the class divide has the potential of manifesting itself as a racial divide' (Habib & Naidu 1999:198).

The 2004 election was marked by three important developments: the absence of debate about whether Muslims were permitted to participate in the democratic process; for the first time there was no Muslim party; and Muslims voted in large numbers for the ANC. This was connected both to local and global events. Locally, largely because of the stability of the past decade and economic prosperity of the middle and upper strata, Indian and coloured minorities are generally optimistic about the future. Globally, events since 9/11 have given rise to Islamophobia in many parts of the world. Across the mosques in South Africa, *Ulama* regularly acknowledge the absence of such Islamophobia locally, and also recognise with pride that South Africa takes an independent line on world issues. As a result, religious leaders have, openly and subtly, advocated support for the ANC. A panel discussion on Channel Islam shortly after the election date was announced, chaired by Moulana Essa of West Street Mosque and Rafick Hassen of the IPCI, urged Muslims to vote. While panellists said that it would be wrong to tell Muslims who to vote for, they reminded Muslim voters that the DA was pro-Israel, and that in several instances DA councillors objected to mosques and madrasahs being built in predominantly white areas.

In the lead-up to the elections, the KZN-based *Sunni Jamiatul Ulama* placed an advert in a local newspaper disowning Moulana Rafeek Shah who had joined the DA; the *Sunni Jamiat*, with ten other Muslim organisations, also placed an advert calling on Muslims not to vote for the DA: 'Tony Leon of the DA has failed to condemn the murder of Sheik Ahmed Yassin, the war on Iraq, the war on Afghanistan, and the occupation of Palestine' (*Tribune Herald* 18.04.04). In the Cape the MJC provided guidelines on how Muslims should choose a party, which left Muslims with just one choice, the ANC (*Al-Qalam* April 2004). In areas where Muslims live in significant numbers, there was an overwhelming victory for the ANC: from Bo-Kaap to Landsdowne in the Cape; Lenasia and Laudium in Gauteng; and in Phoenix, Chatsworth, Reservoir Hills, Umzinto, Overport and other urban centres in KZN. Ebrahim Rassool became the first Muslim provincial head when he was appointed Western Cape Premier by President Thabo Mbeki. According to a delighted Rassool, 'the fact that the President of this country could elect a Muslim as Premier even though most people in South Africa are not Muslims, says a lot for the respect Islam has in this country' (*Al-Qalam* April 2004). This statement very succinctly captures the feelings of the majority of Muslims in present-day South Africa.

Conclusion

This paper has argued that South Africa's Muslims are 'complex and sociologically diverse' (Roy 1996:vii). They are divided along lines of race, class, gender, ethnicity, language and beliefs, and it is highly simplistic to collapse them into a monolith on the basis of their being Muslim. There are multiple Islamic voices, traditions and identities. As Wasserman and Jacobs point out:

> The challenge is to speak about Islam without reverting to binary thought ... [Islam] is made up of a diverse range of competing elements. Amongst these elements are contested meanings of Islam, its role in a plural society, party-political legitimacy ... Islamic narratives are being constructed using global and local symbols, which produce specific and hybridised Muslim identities.

They are intimately connected to the 'routes' of these symbols
produced within colonialism, globalisation and the post-apartheid
period. It presents us with an assemblage of tensions that are
intensely internal and local, while at the same time being external
and global. (2003:26)

Muslims in the Western Cape often have more in common with non-Muslims
than Muslims elsewhere in the country. Working-class Muslims in the
economically depressed Cape Flats, for example, share common experiences
with their Christian neighbours around issues of poverty, drugs, and gangs,
which differ from those of wealthier Muslims in the north of the country, or
indeed in the upmarket parts of the Cape southern suburbs.

Indian Muslims mostly lived as Indians under apartheid, where race was
central in defining existence. Uncertainties created by majority rule in 1994,
the far-reaching impact of globalisation and the 'war on terror' have resulted
in many Muslims retreating into an imagined, essentialised Islamic identity in
their private and communal lives. Boundaries are being constructed between
men and women, Muslims and non-Muslims, Islam and secularism.
Identification with Muslims internationally is deepening as a result of new
media, particularly the Internet and radio stations. These are forging Muslim
identity at the expense of 'Indian-ness'. While the growth of personal piety
features across class lines, it is mainly the affluent who are able to fully
embrace most aspects of the 'liberated zones'. The turn to religious conservatism is of concern to some Muslim commentators. Jaffer, for example, fears
that a Muslim retreat from the wider society and its institutions will have
negative consequences:

If we consider the array of outstanding individuals spread
across the country … then we have to conclude that we occupy
a respected and solid presence, astounding for so small a
community. There is however a very real threat to this trend …
We could potentially move towards closing off from broader
national life … The setting in of a greater conservatism, could
lead to isolation. (2001:24)

Black African Muslims show the fastest growth in numbers, though they face
many difficulties as a result of their geographical dispersion and lack of
resources. It is expected that over the next two decades they will constitute the

largest segment of the Muslim population. It remains to be seen to what extent they will be successful in re-imagining an indigenous Islam. The nascent refugee Muslim communities may have an important role to play in fashioning an indigenous voice because many speak Arabic and a few are formally trained in Islamic theology. Notwithstanding efforts to bridge the racial divide, there remains a strong perception among black Africans that Islam is the religion of 'foreigners', of rich Indian traders in KZN and Gauteng, and less affluent but nevertheless 'foreign' Malays in the Western Cape. Given the widespread problems of poverty and unemployment, there are many unwelcome stereotypes about Malay and Indian Muslims: they are rich and affluent, drive expensive cars, live in beautiful mansions, spend excessively on lavish mosques, are inward-looking and racist. The challenge for Indian and Malay Muslims is to bridge the race and class divide. If they fail to do this, Muslims will remain peripheral, which might be dangerous as stereotypes and envy intensify in a climate of poverty and struggle over scarce resources. Indian and Malay Muslims need to take a leaf out of President Thabo Mbeki's book and have their own *iimbizo* across the townships to forge a spirit of genuine partnership, what Mbeki calls 'the spirit of *vuk'unzenzele*', between the Muslim 'centre' and 'periphery'.[6]

Notes

1   The terms used in this paper are problematic to the authors, who hold that the division of people into biological groups differentiated by colour ('race'), to which we can attribute specific features, has no scientific validity or explanatory value in social science. However, the categorisation of South Africans according to race is a legal and social fact, even in post-apartheid South Africa. Census 2001, for example, categorised South Africans as either 'white', 'coloured', 'Asian' or 'black African'. Further, these categories are in continuous use in everyday life, whether one is applying for a job, an identity document, a research grant, or filling in government documentation pertaining to skills training or employment equity. For this reason, the authors have, in most cases, not placed these terms in inverted commas. To avoid confusion, and despite our deep reservations, we will adhere broadly to the terms used in the Census and generally in public discourse. Thus 'Indian' is used to describe Muslims whose ancestors arrived from South Asia over a century ago; 'African' is used to describe individuals whose mother tongue is a language indigenous to Africa, and who are described in Census 2001 as 'black African';

while 'Malay', a heavily contested term, will refer to those of the Muslim faith who are part of the category 'coloured' in the Census. There is urgent need for South Africans to begin to engage with the notion of African identity. We regard all the latter categories as African, though this is not the classification employed in this essay. We also contend, with Modood, Berthoud and Nazroo, that 'the act of studying them ["race" groups] does not "construct" them: they are part of the basic facts of British [read South African] society and their study is a well-established activity. They are "given" to us by British [read South African] society and an ongoing research stream' (2002:43).

2   Deobandi Islam took root in India when Muhammad Nanautawi and Rashid Gangohi opened a madrasah in Deoband in 1867 after their defeat by the British in the 1857 uprising. They remained aloof from political activity and attended to Muslim educational and religious needs to create a cohesive cultural community. Their concern was that compromises with Hinduism had resulted in syncretistic developments and they targeted practices considered to stem from Hindu culture, such as visitation to tombs and belief in the intercessionary role of saints. The gap between 'ideal' and 'actual' Islam was attributed to 'incomplete conversion' and they sought to acquaint Muslims with 'pure and unalloyed Islam' (Metcalf 1982). Deobandi Islam was popular among the Gujarati trading class. According to Robinson, reformist Islam required Muslims to be literate, and most who embraced reformism were located within the middle class and engaged in aspects of the modern economy (Robinson 1997).

The Sunni tradition has its origins in the work of Ahmad Raza Khan (1856–1922) of Bareilly, Uttar Pradesh, India, who sought to maintain the status quo (Sanyal 1996). In South Africa this tradition found expression mainly among descendants of indentured Muslims. Differences between Deobandis and Sunnis are due to class (trader against indentured), regional origins (western India against North and South), ethnicity (Gujarati against mainly Urdu), as well as differences in belief and practice. As descendants of indentured Muslims acquired education and economic mobility from the 1970s, they challenged trader hegemony, leading to numerous altercations, even violence, which was particularly marked during the 1970s and 1980s (Vahed 2002).

3   http://www.channelislam.com/welcome.htm.

4   Interview, Ashwin Desai 20.04.03.

5   For example, Chris Pitsi, a 32-year-old Pretoria-based human resources company owner; senior advocate of the Durban Bar, Reggie Reddy; and Mduduzi Manana,

the 19-year-old son of Mpumalanga Health Member of the Executive Council (MEC) Sibongile Manana (*Sunday Independent* 16.03.03).

6   *Iimbizo* refers to a gathering of leaders, while *vuk'unzenzele* refers to a partnership across class, race, and gender lines to work for the upliftment of humanity.

References

Adhikari M (1989) Identity and assimilation in the Malay community of 19th century Cape Town. Unpublished paper, History Workshop, University of Cape Town (UCT).

Ali A (2000) Islamism: Emancipation, protest and identity, *Journal of Muslim Minority Affairs* 20:13–27.

Baderoon G (2003) Covering the East – veils and masks: Orientalism in South African media. In H Wasserman & S Jacobs *Shifting selves. Post-apartheid essays on mass media, culture and identity*. Cape Town: Kwela.

Bhana S (1997) Indianness reconfigured, 1944–1960: The Natal Indian Congress in South Africa, *Comparative Studies of South Asia, Africa and the Middle East* XVII:100–107.

Bradlow F & Cairns M (1978) *The early Cape Muslims*. Cape Town: Balkema.

Davids A (1980) *The mosques of the Bo-Kaap*. Cape Town: South African Institute of Islamic and Arabic Research.

Du Plessis ID (1944) *The Cape Malays*. Cape Town: Maskew Miller.

Eickelman DF (1992) Mass education and the religious imagination in contemporary Arab societies, *American Ethnologist* 19:643–655.

Erasmus Z (2001) *Coloured by history, shaped by place: New perspectives on Coloured identities in Cape Town*. Cape Town: Kwela & SA History Online.

Esak F (1997) *On being a Muslim: Finding a religious path today*. Oxford: OneWorld.

Fakude E (2002) Muslims in the townships of South Africa. In *Annual Review of Islam in South Africa* 5:47–49.

Habib A & Naidu S (1999) Was there a 'Coloured' and 'Indian' vote? *Politikon* November.

Haron M (2001) Conflict of identities: The case of South Africa's Cape Malays. Paper presented at the Malay World Conference, Kuala Lumpur, 12–14.10.01.

Jaffer Z (2001) Recent political development and Muslims in South Africa. In *Annual Review of Islam in South Africa* 3:21–25.

Jeppie S (1987) *Historical process and the constitution of subjects: ID du Plessis and the reinvention of the Malay*. BA Hons. thesis, UCT.

Jeppie S (1996a) Introduction. In R Galant & F Gamieldien (eds.) *Drugs, gangs and people's power: Exploring the Pagad phenomenon*. Cape Town: Claremont Main Road Masjid.

Jeppie S (1996b) Commemorations and identities: The 1994 centenary of Islam in South Africa. In T Sonn (ed.) *The question of Muslim minorities*. Atlanta: Scholars Press.

Jeppie S (1998) People Against Gangsterism and Drugs. In *Annual Review of Islam in South Africa* 1. Available at <http://web.uct.ac.za/depts/religion/IE/index.html>.

Jeppie S (1998–99) Achmat Davids, 1939–1998, *Journal for Islamic Studies*.

Jeppie S (2001) Reclassifications: Coloured, Malay, Muslim. In Z Erasmus *Coloured by history, shaped by place: New perspectives on Coloured identities in Cape Town*. Cape Town: Kwela & SA History Online.

Jeppie S (forthcoming) *History of the Arabic study circle of South Africa*. Durban: Institute for Black Research Press.

Joosub S (2003) *Unit trusts. The Shariah perspective with specific reference to the Futuregrowth Albaraka Equity Fund*. Durban: Financial Services Authority.

Kathrada Y (2001) *African Muslim refugees in the Durban area 1994–2001*. BA Hons. thesis, University of Durban-Westville (UDW).

Kramer G (2000) On difference and understanding: The use and abuse of the study of Islam, *Allgemeine Themen* XII:57-60.

Mahida EM (1993) *History of Muslims in South Africa: A chronology*. Durban: Arabic Study Circle.

Metcalf BD (1982) *Islamic revival in British India: Deoband, 1860–1900*. New Jersey: Princeton University Press.

MMC (Masakhane Muslim Community) (2002) Islam in the African townships of the Cape. In *Annual Review of Islam in South Africa* 5: 50–51.

Modood T, Berthoud R & Nazroo J (2002) 'Race', racism and ethnicity: A response to Ken Smith, *Sociology* 36:419-27.

Moosa E (1989) Muslim conservatism in South Africa, *Journal of Theology for Southern Africa* December:73–81.

Naidoo M (1989) Education. In AJ Arkin (ed.) *The Indian South Africans: A contemporary profile*. Durban: Owen Burgess.

Oosthuizen GC (1982) *The Muslim Zanzibaris of South Africa*. Durban: UDW.

Pillay S (2003) Experts, terrorists, gangsters: Problematising public discourse on a post-apartheid showdown. In H Wasserman & S Jacobs *Shifting selves. Post-apartheid essays on mass media, culture and identity*. Cape Town: Kwela.

Rafudeen A (2002) Towards forging an 'African' Muslim identity. In *Annual Review of Islam in South Africa* 5: 57–59.

Robinson F (1983) Islam and Muslim society in South Asia, *Contributions to Indian Sociology* 17:185–203.

Robinson F (1997) Religious change and the self in Muslim South Asia since 1800, *South Asia* XX:1–15.

Roy O (1996) *The failure of political Islam*. Harvard: Harvard University Press.

Sanyal U (1996) *Devotional Islam and politics in British India. Ahmed Riza Khan and his movement, 1870–1920*. Delhi: Oxford.

Sitoto TF (2002) Imam Essa al-Seppe and 'the emerging and unorganized African Muslim sector: A contextual analysis'. In *Annual Review of Islam in South Africa* 5. Cape Town: Centre for Contemporary Islam, UCT.

Tayob AK (1996) Counting Muslims in South Africa. In *Annual Review of Islam in South Africa*. Cape Town: Centre for Contemporary Islam, UCT.

Tayob A (2002) The South African Muslim communities response to September 11th. In *Annual Review of Islam in South Africa* 5. Cape Town: Centre for Contemporary Islam, UCT.

Vahed G (2000a) Indian Islam and the meaning of South African citizenship – a question of identities, *Transformation* 43:25–51.

Vahed G (2000b) Indian Muslims in South Africa: Continuity, change and disjuncture, 1860–2000, *Alternation* 2:67–98.

Vahed G (2001a) Uprooting, rerooting: Culture, religion and community amongst indentured Muslim migrants in colonial Natal, 1860–1911, *South African Historical Journal* 45:191–222.

Vahed G (2001b) Mosques, Mawlana's and Muharram: Establishing Indian Islam in colonial Natal, 1860–1910, *Journal of Religion in Africa* XXXI:3–29.

Vahed G (2002) Constructions of community and identity Among Indians in colonial Natal, 1860–1910: The role of the Muharram Festival, *Journal of African History* 43:77–93.

Vawda S (1993) The emerging of Islam in an African township, *al-Ilm* 13:45–62.

Ward K (1996) The 300 years: The making of Cape Muslim culture exhibition, Cape Town April 1994: Liberating the Castle? *Social Dynamics* 21:96–131.

Wasserman H & Jacobs S (2003) Introduction. In H Wasserman & S Jacobs *Shifting selves. Post-apartheid essays on mass media, culture and identity*. Cape Town: Kwela.

11 *The state of the art(s)*

Lynn Maree

Artists played a prominent role in 'the struggle' that led eventually to the new South Africa. Among them were Athol Fugard, Nadine Gordimer, Gibson Kente, Miriam Makeba, Hugh Masekela, Mbuyiseni Mtshali, John Muafangejo, Mbongeni Ngema, Mongane Wally Serote, Barney Simon and Pieter-Dirk Uys – whose work resonated around the world, telling their stories of oppression with vitality, talent, humour and wisdom. As artists are wont to do, these stories proclaimed their expectations, hopes and visions of the new South Africa.

Ten years on, has their new world dawned?

It could be argued that ten years is too short a time to make any conclusive judgement, but this paper will posit that, while for some the dawn of democracy heralded freedom of expression and the possibility of artists being able to flourish freely, for others it signalled the start of a battle for redress, transformation of cultural icons, and job creation in the arts.[1] Ten years on, that contest, plus an absence of will on the part of government, had, by the time of the April general election, destroyed more than it had built. Even the presidential inauguration concert did not seem to celebrate the last ten years, but appeared stuck in a time warp.

A brief overview: privilege and prejudice

Under apartheid, only white artists received subsidies from the state and only western artistic activity was seen to be of value. The National Party (NP) government provided subsidies to performing arts councils in the four provinces. Those councils, operating in the two official languages, were mandated to support the performing arts and, in every case, this was interpreted as operating their own performing arts companies, with rehearsal and performance venues.

White boards and white administrators employed white artists. They ran theatre companies, ballet companies and opera companies, employed singers, and often produced musical theatre. They operated sophisticated costume wardrobes, and workshops in which they built fine sets. The nature of the work performed could be described as western and white, and elite rather than popular. Company members were paid salaries, offered pensions, medical benefits and housing loans, and large numbers of administrators were employed. Many of the artists employed were from abroad so that the 'best' orchestral musicians or ballet dancers could be placed in front of white South African audiences. This elevation of an elite western arts practice even extended to institutions like the Durban Art Gallery, one of the oldest in the country, which, until well into the 1980s, had a paid agent in Europe seeking artwork to acquire for the gallery.

Alongside these imposing institutions, smaller arts organisations, or arts centres emerged, sometimes in the city centres, sometimes in the townships, like Fuba and Funda, Dorkay House and, later, Moving into Dance in Johannesburg, the Community Arts Project (CAP) in Cape Town, and the Stable Theatre in Durban, where plays were produced, artists painted, potters potted, dancers danced and, occasionally, training was offered. For the most part, these were funded from abroad (if they received funding at all) with what was often referred to as 'struggle money'. It came from organisations and foreign governments opposed to apartheid and interested in helping to offset some of its effects and bring about change – political change even more than artistic change, because the arts were seen as a safer way of offering money, and of indirectly empowering artists and audiences.

In some cases these 'artistic spaces' were multiracial, like The Space in Cape Town, where Athol Fugard and Yvonne Bryceland worked, or The Market Laboratory in Johannesburg, where Barney Simon, Mbongeni Ngema and Winston Ntshona worked. No one had any money, no one considered job security: making art, and art that often could be seen by the ruling powers as subversive, stimulated creativity, while the sense of community it gave provided purpose enough. *Isicathimiya* singing competitions were held all over what was then Natal, and dance performances took place in rural villages and migrant worker hostels. South Africans of all races painted, made pots, decorated their homes, sang in choirs, wrote poetry; Todd Matshikisa produced 'King Kong'; *'Ipi Tombi'* toured Europe; Mbongeni Ngema wrote and directed 'Sarafina'. In the townships, playwrights went from door to door issuing invitations to attend their performances – 'watch for free, pay if you like it' – and all of this was achieved without state support.

Over all of this a fierce censorship was enforced: novels and plays were banned, and the Dutch Reformed Church feared the sexuality of dance. Television was only introduced in 1976, when the NP government was sure it could control what was broadcast. A cultural hegemony existed, allowing some people to feel that they came from civilised and artistically rich cultures, and that others were barbaric or lacking in any culture.

The beginnings of change: the 1990s

Once it was known that the government of South Africa was to change, the African National Congress (ANC) set up an Arts and Culture Desk to start to consider what needed to be put in place. At the same time the National Arts Initiative (later known as the National Arts Coalition) – a civic organisation made up of artists and growing out of the United Democratic Front – also began to envisage what was needed to enable artists to flourish and make their contribution in a democracy where there was freedom of expression.

By 1994 shifts had begun to take place in both employment patterns and what was produced at the performing arts councils, as a result of pressure from arts activists, and the easing up on the enforcement of apartheid laws. White visual artists still talk with excitement of the 1985 exhibition 'Tributaries', funded by BMW, which brought together, for the first time, work by self-taught, rural artists (usually black) and western-trained and 'sophisticated' artists (usually white), paired many of the exhibits, and provided an opportunity for discussion and debate. Many of the 'newly discovered' artists went on to exhibit internationally and to sell quite widely.

Even before the April 1994 election, the performing arts councils – some of them under new boards – had made their own changes. For example, the Natal Performing Arts Council, now known as The Playhouse Company, had established an education and development department, offering training in the performing arts, arts administration, performance opportunities for community groups and outreach work – particularly to schools – by the Playhouse's resident companies. It also began to scale down its ballet company to establish a creative and African-oriented dance training programme, which paid trainees who had talent but no formal training. The training programme grew into Siwela Sonke Dance Theatre and was officially launched in April 1997, by which time it had already given many public performances, toured KwaZulu-Natal with several programmes for schools, and visited Germany. In all instances, the composition of the staff and the artists employed, as well as the nature of the work produced, had become more African in orientation.

Structures

In May 1994 the Government of National Unity created the Ministry of Arts, Culture, Science and Technology, and Dr Ben Ngubane was appointed as minister. In October 1994, he appointed a national committee, the Arts and Culture Task Group (Actag), to research and propose new arts and culture policies for South Africa. This culminated in a national conference of the arts and culture community at which Actag's recommendations were debated and received overwhelming support, ultimately evolving into the White Paper on which legislation was based. Those artists who were at the conference – and they came from all spheres – felt that another part of 'the struggle' was over and their government was set on the right course. Their only concern was that they wanted to see arts and culture higher on the new government's agenda, a concern mirrored by artists all over the world.

In June 1996, the *White Paper on arts, culture and heritage* was published, and in September of that same year it was adopted as official government policy. In the White Paper 'the arts' are defined as all forms and traditions of dance, drama, music, theatre, visual arts, crafts, design, written and oral literature, all of which serve as a means for individual and collective creativity and expression through performance, execution, presentation, exhibition, transmission and study (DACST 1996). This definition of the arts is the one on which this paper is premised, so it will only touch on culture at those margins where there is overlap with the arts, as opposed to culture's wider remit, which includes heritage, beliefs and value systems.

The Department of Arts, Culture, Science and Technology (DACST) set about enacting legislation to establish the organisations that would give shape to the policies contained in the White Paper. The performing arts councils were told that their budgets were to be cut over the next three years, they were to devolve their performing arts companies, and to open their spaces to all. The new department moved swiftly: the new National Arts Council (NAC) met in April 1997 and distributed its first grants in late 1997. Before this, the department had made its own funding decisions; the new landscape was created through the cutting of the size of the grants made to the old structures and new disbursements of grants made to new organisations and for new purposes. The NAC funds dance, drama, literature, visual arts, music and crafts. Initially it was set up to operate on the 'arm's-length' principle by which members of the arts community are appointed to make funding recommendations in their fields of expertise, and the government does not interfere in artistic decisions, though it requires strict accounting practices for this use of taxpayers' money. Systems are in place to prevent advisors from making decisions that favour either themselves or their organisations, and they are chosen for their fair-mindedness and commitment to the development of their art form. Board members are chosen after interviews from a list of nominations generated from the general public. A board member chairs each of the advisory panels. In the initial legislation, the board was to elect its own chairperson.

In 2002 the DACST was split so that the Department of Arts and Culture (DAC) had its own director-general and staff, although still under one minister. The DAC had its own funds and saw its role as wider than the funding of the arts in response to applications from artists. It has signed many bilateral agreements with other governments, which it manages itself, has been given funds from other sources, such as the Poverty Relief Fund, and on occasion instigates and co-operates with other government departments such as the Department of Trade and Industry. In 2002–03 it spent R495 million. Its Strategic Plan for 2003–06 includes in its arts and culture programme provisions ensuring the sustainability of the six playhouses as cultural institutions, the funding or part-funding of three orchestras, support for grassroots communities, community arts centres and ten festivals, and financial support to the NAC to distribute funds equitably.

The arts have been affected by changes in other sectors, theoretically in extremely positive ways. Chapter 4 (clauses 30 and 31) of the White Paper committed the Arts and Culture Ministry to:

> actively promote the Constitutional right of every learner in the General Education and Training (GET) Phase to access equitable,

appropriate life-long education and training in art, culture and heritage to develop individual talents and skills … (this should) embrace opportunities for making, performing and presenting as well as appreciating the many expressions of South African cultural heritage to realise the right of all South Africans to participate fully in, contribute to, and benefit from an all-inclusive South African culture. (DACST 1996)

So arts and culture became a learning area in the GET-level of the Revised National Curriculum, paving the way for huge changes in the way that the arts are viewed. All schools are now meant to teach the arts until the end of Grade 9, and in such a way that the White Paper principles of equality, reclamation and exposure of all to all are promoted. The aim is to overcome imbalances in opportunity by using schools and community centres to find and nurture the talented.

The establishment of the South African Qualifications Authority (SAQA) as the body mandated to establish and manage the National Vocational Qualification (NVQ) was welcomed by the arts world as a way of upgrading the qualifications of many people with arts expertise and experience, but no formal training and no paper certificates. In a globalised world this matters. A Culture and Arts National Standards Body was established and this included a subset of standards generating bodies (SGBs) for dance, three for music, art, craft and design and technical production services, and more recently a performing arts SGB, as well as a working committee drawn from these for creating qualifications in cultural management. And because the arts and culture sector is not profit-producing, preventing the skills levy imposed on all industries from generating sufficient funds in the cultural sector, the DAC established and funded CreateSA. This body is tasked with providing training in what has become known as the cultural industries. The DAC is particularly interested, at least initially, in those seen as having the potential to create employment and alleviate poverty: craft, music, film and video, and the printing industry. Audits have been carried out, proposals made for the music industry, and learnerships established, most notably in craft and music.

It was hoped – in fact enacted – that there would be continuity and connection between national, provincial and local government. This was particularly the case in the areas of the infrastructure of the performing arts councils, the funding and support of the community arts centres, and the setting up of provincial arts and culture councils, responding to applications and plugging gaps in provision at the provincial level, in a loose partnership with the NAC. This has not worked as was hoped. In a newspaper interview, Dr Ngubane said: 'The provincial arts councils are not providing money from the provincial coffers' (*Sunday Independent* 16.11.03). In many provinces little attention is paid to existing arts and culture organisations. Suspicion seems to exist between artists who need funding and the bodies empowered to fund them. So this part of the post-1994 plan has not functioned, and its dysfunction has led to strains and distortions on the rest of the system.

There are other additions to the range of funding possibilities, including the Arts and Culture Trust, funded partially by the Arts Card available at Nedbank, whose normal ceiling on funding for any particular organisation is R30 000, and the National Lotteries Distribution Fund, capable of giving very large sums but without the fixed percentage for the arts that had been recommended in the White Paper. This makes it the favourite funder for artists, but also the one most capable of inconsistency, and difficult to rely on. Finally, Business and the Arts (BASA) was established in 1997, offering a way for South African businesses to be involved in supporting the arts and raising their company's profile through this support, and trying to encourage private philanthropy. BASA lobbies government for tax breaks for arts sponsorship. So, for an artist there are sources of funding inside South Africa and, where intergovernmental cultural agreements exist, outside South Africa – for example, Mmino for music and music education, housed with the NAC and funded by Norway.

Stabilisation, refinement, disillusion, contestation

Government

The early hopes for an artist-led dispensation for the arts received some setbacks in 2003. Explanations for these changes are contested: some attribute this to the low status of arts and culture in government priorities; others to the fact that Minister Ngubane was a member of the Inkatha Freedom Party; others to high staff turnover in the department, understaffing, lack of capacity, desire to do too much and to delegate too little, and the nature of bureaucracy; others to a defensiveness and resistance to criticism; and others, particularly those closer to the department, put it down to a perception within the DAC that the outside arts world seems determined to give them no credit, never acknowledges their efforts and their successes, and does not appreciate the difficulties they face. As Dr Ngubane said in a radio broadcast on SAFM in October 2003: 'The artists can go to hell'.

Before 1994 the National Arts Coalition had grown out of the United Democratic Front, and had organised for a new dispensation for artists. With 'the struggle' over, artists thought that they could get on with their art-making. And yet, in 2001, the Performing Arts Network of South Africa (Pansa) was launched 'against a background of a major decline in the infra-structure underpinning the performing arts'.[2] There was a significant loss of morale and flight of skills from the sector, with many performing artists leaving the industry or the country. Pansa's mission is to ensure that there is a viable, sustainable performing arts industry in the country:

> To achieve this, we have to lobby decision-makers in government and elsewhere, initiate projects that service our members' needs, undertake research and make policy recommendations where necessary, and build our organisation so that it is an influential force within the sector.[3]

In 2003, the Network for Arts and Culture in South Africa (Nacsa) was formed. Speaking at the launch, Mike van Graan said:

> The Network for Arts and Culture is about fighting for and defending democratic spaces for creative practice. It is about empowering and defending the right of individuals to exercise their constitutional rights. It is about pushing back the barriers to freedom, engaging the high priests of new censorship, about ensuring that there is the political space, the funding resources and the will to promote and defend freedom of creative expres-sion. For when we are silent, when we allow anti-democratic actions to flourish, we participate in our own disempowerment, we encourage reactionary processes and we allow others to mould our democracy in their self-serving image. (van Graan 2003:3)

These were brave words, uttered before turbulence engulfed the NAC and, with hindsight, they sound prophetic.

Performing arts councils

By 1999, the performing arts councils had ceased funding all of their performing arts companies and these companies disbanded or found other ways of continuing. In most cases the 'divorce' was not as gentle as the White Paper had indicated that it should be. In the process of disbandment, much of value was lost, notwithstanding contestation over what is of value: workshop, wardrobe, production and administrative expertise; training sites; mentoring possibilities; even the mounting of locally produced, large-scale musical theatre. Some of the performing and rehearsing spaces are 'dark', so resources are being underutilised. Artists no longer know the luxury of being employed by a performing arts council – well or badly paid, but with some job security and support, a housing bond, medical aid and access to a pension fund. Although the funding cake is spread more fairly, and the profile of the kinds of artistic endeavour supported with public money is radically different – in particular the funding of art forms other than the performing arts – the lack of security and prospects of a career path still need to be remedied if South African artists are to stay at home.

Arts and culture centres

The Reconstruction and Development community arts centres, now renamed arts and culture centres, are to be strengthened with poverty alleviation funds administered by the DAC. Research was commissioned from the Human Sciences Research Council (HSRC), and a member of the HSRC staff was seconded to the DAC. An audit was carried out, recommendations made, and some of the funds from the Flemish government, raised in a bilateral agreement set up by the DAC, are now being used to offer training and support over three years. However, many independent community arts centres, such as CAP in Cape Town, the Bat Centre and the eKhaya Multi-Arts Centre in the eThekwini municipality, which have experienced, committed staff and an infrastructure, are left to find their own funding. The new recommendations include using these to mentor and network with the DAC's arts and culture centres in future.

Arts and culture in the education system

The new school curriculum, Curriculum 2005 (and its revision, the National Curriculum Statement), includes arts and culture as a learning area at the level of general education. Arts and culture embraces music, dance, drama and the visual arts; what is missing are trained teachers, artists in residence and teaching materials to ensure that, even in uni-cultural schools, the cultural diversity of our land is made apparent and accorded time and respect. Implementation strategies need to be put in place to achieve an 'integrated developmental approach leading to innovative creative and critical thinking, (as well as) a sense of pride in our diverse cultural heritage' (DACST 1996) – at this point, in most parts of the country, these are merely words on paper. Until 2011, there will be a major mismatch between what learners have covered at the GET level and what is available to study at the level of further education and training (FET).

Some initiatives and proposals exist to address this in the short term. One such initiative is a partnership between the Curriculum Development Project, a non-governmental organisation (NGO), and the University of the Witwatersrand School of the Arts, with the support of the Flemish government and the DAC. This concentrates on using visual artists and craftspeople as artists-in-schools, after they are equipped with teaching skills by the programme. While some individual teachers and teachers' organisations, and a few universities, are trying to implement this learning area seriously, in the main, both in schools and in initial teacher training, the working group that wrote the curriculum for the learning area feels that it is a waste of time and that 'if it continues to be done as badly as it is being done, there will be very few learners equipped to specialise in any of the arts subjects at FET level, so that the only young people who will qualify to study the arts at the tertiary level will be those whose parents could afford to let them study the piano outside of school. We will have weakened the arts, switched most learners off them, and failed to equip anyone even to appreciate them'.[4] Some ex-model C schools do not teach arts and culture, nor welcome arts and culture student teachers into their schools.

Training and qualifications

The same determination, resources and a delivery programme are needed in the training of artists and technicians. SAQA is the body charged with the establishment of qualifications structures for all education and training. It has been joined by CreateSA[5] to ensure that all 'cultural industries' and their attached technical and management needs have registered outcomes-based unit standards that can be used by training institutions, accredited NGOs and work-based learnerships. Some SGBs are almost at take-off point in terms of accreditation of the prior learning of those artists who are already experienced teachers and practitioners but have no formal qualifications, and in the provision of short courses to fill in any gaps. But there is an inertia at the heart of SAQA, and a failure by the Departments of Labour and Education to agree on moving forward the integration of education and training. This is a major blow for the arts sector since SAQA was seen as the route to recognition, accreditation and redress.

However, not all training is failing: the beginnings of a rural success story can be seen in the Greater St Lucia Wetland Park Authority in KwaZulu-Natal, where links between the upgrading of craft design and production, and the enhancement of the performing arts skills of local people are seen as likely to increase tourism and tourism spend in the area. In 2003, CreateSA ran two pilot learnerships in the area: a cultural programme and a craft programme, helping learners to understand the value chain, with a continuing mentorship by qualified artists. The aim was to introduce quality and development into an area where there is a danger that the making of 'heritage' art for tourists could freeze and exoticise the art forms. There is a tension that must be acknowledged between providing people with skills so that they can earn a living, and empowering them so that they can be creative and knowledgeable about the art form or artefact they are working with, respecting tradition and designing it for a market. The National Qualifications Network (NQF) is meant to provide for both.

Apart from subsidy and government initiatives, what voices have been found?

In contrast to the lack of delivery by provincial government, some of the larger cities are embarking on exciting development initiatives that include arts and culture, recognising the possibilities of using the arts in public ways to increase tourism and international city status. In Durban, the intention is to create an 'African' city. In Johannesburg, where a Director of Arts, Culture and Heritage was appointed early in 2004, the regeneration of the inner city is being matched – and complemented and influenced – by the Cultural Arc, an extraordinary cultural rebirth centred on cultural projects linking Constitution Hill through Braamfontein to Wits University's new cultural precinct, across the Nelson Mandela bridge to a Newtown precinct beginning to realise some of its immense potential. The artistic achievements of the past ten years were celebrated with a month-long festival in Newtown in April 2004. The Cultural Arc is currently providing creative employment for architects and visual and conceptual artists, and has the potential to place the arts in a dynamic relationship with the public. The Constitutional Court on Constitution Hill not only houses works of art, but commissioned artists to design and make doors and carpets so that the aesthetic is inherent in the fabric of the building – and it is a powerfully South African aesthetic. The reasoning behind these developments is varied: in some cases to attract tourists; in others, as in the inner city of Durban, to train and empower locals to give them a sense of ownership and pride in a part of the city they have made their own, and in which they find means of surviving.

Government policies and funding cater for only a small section of the arts in any country, and most arts activity is unsubsidised. One such unsubsidised and expanding area is that of South African soap operas on television – a growing output has broken the American stranglehold prevalent until 1994, and South African audiences of all language groups get to watch South African stories. While not always offering the most challenging of roles, the work is well paid, and sometimes allows those actors to take time out to take part in more risky productions.

Television and video, often documentary, can provide the base for a new film industry. The National Film and Video Foundation has funded some creative activities and provided training opportunities, in addition to entering into potentially hugely lucrative funding partnerships with foreign governments and private business for feature films. South Africa has become a popular location for the filming of foreign-funded and foreign-directed movies. Anant Singh of VideoVision has begun work on Dream World, a major studio in Cape Town, and has recently bought a building on Durban's beachfront to house more studios. South Africans have won major prizes at international film festivals, while indigenous festivals – such as Sithengi in Cape Town, the Festival of African Films in the refurbished Art Deco Apollo cinema in

Victoria West, the Durban International Film Festival run by the Centre for Creative Arts at the University of KwaZulu-Natal – have brought an end to isolation. All of these festivals run training workshops and work at using new venues. In 2003, the Durban International Film Festival held several screenings at eKhaya Multi-Arts Centre, and attracted an audience from across the city of Durban to the sprawling township of KwaMashu.

There has been a drastic cut in cultural programmes, especially drama, on radio so that there is now a severe limit on the availability of stimulating, thought-provoking plays, which could deal with current issues and controversies. This seems a missed opportunity in a society where more people listen to the radio than watch television or read the newspaper – a society in the early stages of becoming a participating citizenry, still struggling with an inadequate education system that continues to bear the scars of the apartheid years.

Music, on the other hand, has benefited: there are more radio stations and the percentages for the broadcasting of local music have been increased, creating new opportunities for musicians, especially the youth market. Although local musicians still want to see the percentages raised, there is always tension between the demands of musicians, music production companies and audiences/listeners. After the isolation of the cultural boycott before 1994, it is also important that both artists and audiences are able to enjoy artistic products from the rest of Africa, as well as the rest of the world.

In the clubs of urban Gauteng, there is a vibrant music culture around the hip-hop and electronic dance scene. Some of these artists are melding popular pulsating dance rhythms with traditional sounds, stories, and instruments; some of them, like Lebogang Moshile of Feela Sista, speak their microphone poetry that draws on rap, intelligent hip-hop and the heritage captured in the wisdom of the ancients, to create poems of great power and beauty that express the beginnings of a new South African artwork that represents us and speaks to the world. School choirs participate with intensity in countrywide competitions. The Field Band Foundation uses brass bands and dance to bring life skills and hope to thousands of young people, and the Buskaid Soweto String Ensemble offers music training to young people.

Contemporary dance is often hailed as the major success story in creating a new language for the South African celebration of what the body can say. The First National Bank Dance Umbrella in Johannesburg in March 2004 showcased a wealth of choreographic talent, complete with social comment, and at the same time, a souped-up tribal/kwaito show was performed at the São Paulo Carnival in Brazil. Many choreographers spend more time out of the country than in, and the dancers live from hand to mouth. It is difficult to sustain freshness and creativity when appreciation seems to have to be self-inspired.

Theatre is in even more trouble. There is limited funding for scriptwriting, the basis of contemporary theatre, and the absence of full-time companies has forced many actors into television and industrial theatre, or out of the country. Perhaps self-censorship too plays a part both in what theatre companies feel able to produce and venue managers to book. An examination of current locally-produced theatre productions, as well as conversations with actors and theatre directors, shows that the initiative and drive of theatre people mean that work is still produced, and notwithstanding the disenchantment that those private conversations indicate, 'the show must go on' vigour is what the audience is given.

The proliferation of festivals, music, film and the performing arts in general has had a positive effect on the public profile of the arts, although they do very little for the pockets of the artists. The Grahamstown Festival, begun by the 1820 Settlers' Association as a high arts festival of music and some theatre, has been transformed into a major South African and international arts festival, with associated jazz, visual arts, poetry and literature programmes, and a large fringe and street theatre component. Unfortunately, some muddles with the NAC, including the late appointment of its new board in 2003 and its prolonged 'pause' in 2004, have prevented and will prevent South African work from all parts of the country from being seen in Grahamstown. The country's only literature and literacy festival, WordFest, which has run for many years at the Grahamstown Festival, did not get funding in time for 2004 and so did not take place. But, funding problems and caveats notwithstanding, the Grahamstown Festival has survived and thrived in a decade of change.

The District Six Museum, an arts and culture centre deeply rooted in and connected to the destroyed community it aims to commemorate and make a living memorial, is showing the way and attracting visitors from all over the world. The museum has had marked success in raising funds and winning prizes, and forms part of Cape Town's tourist network. The 'coon carnival', once an opportunity for slaves to dream of freedom, then an actual celebration of freedom from 1834 through the 1950s, during which time it evolved into a fiercely contested competition with judges and prizes, declining under apartheid into a shell of itself, is 'now surely ... in the next major phase of evolution – ascension' (Harris 2004:88–90). Cape Town city authorities have included the carnival as one of its Cape of Great Events – the only concern is the sanitisation that comes with turning a community activity into a tourist attraction.

There are new opportunities for visual artists: funding from the NAC (when it functions); city developments; corporate commissions; arts prizes; the opening up of international markets and circuits; and open admissions to tertiary institutions. Galleries are starting to open up – a notable initiative is that of Red Eye, hosted by the Durban Art Gallery, that has turned an ostensibly impersonal municipal location into a welcoming and relevant space for youth of all race groups. The celebration of ten years of democracy in 2004 has provided an opportunity for creative stocktaking and curating – for instance, over 150 artists have work on exhibition at the South African National Gallery in Cape Town, entitled 'A decade of democracy'. The exhibition both celebrates where South Africa is now, and critiques some of those achievements – mind and heart combine intelligently. However, some opportunities that arose with the ending of South Africa's isolation in the late 1980s and early 1990s have closed down again – for example, the re-marginalisation of the rural artist and the self-taught artist, and the shrinking of budgets for gallery acquisitions.

The writers and poets of the country are in a singular space: freed to write what they like in a country where the majority of the population do not read; a country which has 11 official languages, yet where writing in a mother tongue that is not mainstream means the death of these books; where we have a very high rate of value added tax on books, even pushing up the price of set text books; and where writers such as Mandla Langa and Njabulo Ndebele are committed to high-powered jobs that leave them little time for writing, and the country's newest winner of the Nobel Prize for Literature leaves the country. The establishment of more libraries, the constant acquisition of books and improvement of existing libraries: these have slipped down on the priority lists of municipalities. There are fewer independent publishers and booksellers today than in 'struggle' days, when remarkable publishers evaded censorship lists and provided readers with the challenges of protest literature. Nonetheless, for those who do read, a wealth of thoughtful work published in the past ten years has made an important contribution to nation-building – honest works like Njabulo Ndebele's, *The cry of Winnie Mandela*, Antjie Krog's, *A change of tongue*, and Aziz Hassim's, *The lotus people*.

Globalisation

South African artists want to travel the world, to be free to perform anywhere and to try to find work in other parts of the world. But because of our skewed education system, because many of the old inequalities of opportunity and training have yet to be overcome and because of the many years of technical isolation, there is a skills deficit that needs to be remedied over time. At the same time, the Growth, Employment, and Redistribution strategy and the free-trade agreements entered into by the South African government mean that performers and technicians from elsewhere can obtain employment easily in South Africa. This causes resentment among those who feel that, at least for a while, South African artists should experience some protection.

South Africa has signed up to join two international organisations that have emerged in a bid to protect local cultures from the cultural hegemony of America: the International Network for Cultural Policy (INCP) is a grouping of cultural ministries from around the world, signed up to by the DAC; and the International Network for Cultural Diversity (INCD) is an NGO network with similar intentions, signed up to by Pansa and Nacsa. Both organisations are currently involved in a move to hold an international convention on cultural diversity.

Increasingly, South Africa is taking its place in the artistic community of the continent. The Pan-African Society for Musical Arts Education exists for music educators on the continent. The Centre for Creative Arts at the University of KwaZulu-Natal in Durban hosts annual festivals for writers, poets, contemporary dance and film, and their 'Time of the writer' festival held in March 2004 consisted entirely of writers from Africa. Links with theatres, festivals, arts centres and performing artists are being forged across the continent through the cultural organisations and networks of *Operateurs Culturels et Reseaux*,[6] where the *lingua franca* is at least as much French as it is English. The stronger South Africa's artistic culture, the more it can seek partnerships from a basis of strength. The alternative – for example if we strive for American production values in our film-making – is that our landscape will be used by foreign film-makers, who bring in their celebrity actors, and sometimes even their technical staff and crew, and pay them more than they pay local actors and technicians. Our stories will be told by others and we will be sucked dry.

Where to now?

In South Africa, the discrepancy between the rich and the poor is one of the greatest on Earth, and unemployment and poverty are massive problems. The arts are sometimes seen as a potential creator of jobs, a sector of the economy that is labour-intensive and, with its connections to tourism, a growth area. This market mentality has led many artists to emphasise the contribution that the arts can make to the economy, viewing this as a potential argument to strengthen the case for subsidy and training. But the arts have additional contributions to make to society. The arts can make us think and question so that we become more aware of what it means to be a person; the arts relate us to each other and the complexity of living with each other, to our history, our country, our environment, the world – they enrich our lives and help us to dream. These starting principles and values are at least as important as the label on the jeans we wear, the make of car we drive, or the number of CDs we buy.

To realise and reach their potential, artists need talent, commitment, application, time, an appreciative audience, something to say, and the freedom to say it. To work without hardship, artists need and want resources, support, a sense of an artistic community and recognition. Our society ranks sport and possessions higher than the arts, and artists often lack resources and do not feel valued. But artists do now have the freedom to express themselves, whether that is in creating something beautiful or something that expresses indignation; the funding cake is spread more fairly, cultural values are more open to choice, and there is a sense of a democratic nationhood struggling to be born. 'Liberation is consciousness of self, not the closing of a door to communication but a never-ending process of "discovery and encouragement" leading to true national self-liberation and to universalism' (Said: 1993:330).

What was embarked on in 1994 was an exercise in trying to undo a great wrong with the least possible breaking of eggs. In some areas of national life the objectives are simple and clear, such as access to water and electricity for everyone.

The only problems are affordability and delivery – there are no arguments over what sort of water, what kind of electrification, and certainly not what sports are played in international competition. But arts and culture are about identity, about who we are and what we value, and, in a multicultural nation, repairing or setting right the damage done by the denigration of customs and rituals and finding ways to promote our national pride. Building the new includes everyone having to give up something vital, to being persuaded that the new is not only politically and morally correct, but actually enriching!

From 1994, with the launch of Actag and the White Paper, some of the anger was put aside, some of the hurts papered over, and there was a recognition of what was necessary for the greater good. Boards of impeccable representivity were appointed, but there was still scope for misunderstandings and arrogance. Black publicists get bookings abroad, white arts publicists get bookings in schools in South Africa. Perhaps the emollience of John Kani, when he chaired the NAC – a man who had spent much time in England – was a source of irritation to those who wanted something saltier, something that jolted white liberals who seemed to think they could smoothly change gear.

In my own experience as a current member of the Dance Advisory Panel of the NAC, it is clear that all members of the panel want to fund those applications that set the nation on a pathway of equity and redress. There has been a marked development in dance, with some very fine dancers and choreographers shaping new traditions and directions for a truly South African creative dance, using and celebrating what they know. But still the panel rejects most of the applications it receives. There are several problems: in some cases projects are too small and local for the NAC to fund, which would not be a problem if provincial and local levels were functioning as they should; in other cases, although the NAC's countrywide workshops have helped applicants to understand how to fill in application forms, supply constitutions and references, the applications do not indicate a strong enough dance content to win the panel's approval. For this to improve, the NAC needs more and experienced staff, and outreach staff to advise, guide, and develop the initiators of projects. Sometimes the budgets include all the necessary information, but their presentation makes one doubt that anyone involved would know how to manage those budgets. For this to improve, training and mentoring is needed, and perhaps the oversight of a more established organisation. Public money must be accounted for. The problem is much larger than just the panel and the nature of its deliberations.

Since November 2003 there has been a breakdown of trust on the part of the NAC board, for which the chief executive officer has been held responsible. During her suspension, the chairperson of the board overturned a recommendation of the NAC Theatre Advisory Panel on the grounds that the play to be funded to tour 'only deals with one culture'. In this case, the play, 'At her feet', by Nadia Davids, deals with a Muslim girl growing up in multicultural South Africa, and has been acclaimed by audiences of all race groups. Perhaps this is an aberrant decision portending nothing, or perhaps it is a forerunner of things to come. Objections to this ruling include: a great deal of what is funded only deals with one culture, and there is no such requirement in NAC policy; and such action is outside the remit of the chairperson as only applications above R100 000 are meant to be reconsidered by the board, and the sum requested was below that. While this decision may seem insignificant, it underlines the need for vigilance in protecting newly-won freedoms. However much the situation with regard to the arts may have improved since 1994, new dragons still arise to be battled.

Why the conflict? Is there hope?

The research for this chapter was begun late in 2003 in a mood of cautious optimism. The feeling was that the high hopes of 1994 and the heady freedom of the Actag consultancy period – while somewhat dashed by delivery problems and some unnecessarily stringent destructions – were returning. While there had been teething problems at take-off and some turbulence thereafter, the arts were making steady and elevated progress. But that mood has been overtaken by events. Struggles within the NAC have left it rudderless, with arts organisations suffering and even perishing from collateral damage. At the time of the April general election, the arts dangled in a dangerously unsupported position, a situation which had been exacerbated by the sudden departure in February of Minister Ben Ngubane. Once the new Cabinet was announced, a sigh of relief and anticipation flooded the arts world: a separate Ministry of Arts and Culture; a president who acknowledged that the area had been neglected over the past ten years; and the appointment as minister of an ANC heavyweight, the intellectual Pallo Jordan.

The Lotteries Fund stipulated a new last minute deadline in August 2004, before pronouncing on the previous round of applications, thus hindering preparation and causing stress to applicants. Within eThekwini Municipality, Durban Arts, the arts body inherited from the old regime and subsequently transformed, has been allowed to die with a whimper, leaving arts organisations that had come to rely on it stranded. Its arts magazine, *D'Arts*, which has won national prizes and provided a space to publicise all the arts activities of the region at every level, was unable to print its March 2004 issue, and is limping on from month to month with private trust funding. The KwaZulu-Natal Arts and Culture Council took eight months to decide on applications received in June 2003 for the financial year 2003–04. If this were not sufficient cause for alarm, there was no mention of arts or culture in the discussion document *Towards a ten-year review (PCAS 2003)* emanating from the Office of the Presidency in October 2003, while the government's glossy insert in national newspapers, *Report to the nation*, in February 2004, was equally silent on the subject. Hence the President's acknowledgement of neglect in late April brought relief and the hope that funding would become more secure for those whom their peers judge worthy, and that creativity would be given a boost through challenges, artist-led workshops/residencies, off-the-wall training opportunities and writing fellowships.

Racism and racially-structured thinking still affect the arts deeply. Apartheid taught that white culture was superior, and that white inventions, including works of art, were the ones of worth. Whites were allowed to lay claim to the achievements of Greeks, Germans, English and the Dutch, while insisting that the Xhosa, Zulu, Venda and Shangaan people and their cultures were each different. Even in 2002, an Indian dance event at The Playhouse in Durban was described by a white arts journalist on SAFM as 'different'. So there are those who feel that redress can only be implemented by not funding anything 'white'. Apartheid and racism taught us to think of culture and arts as belonging to certain groups – ballet was/is white, opera was/is white, *isicathimiya* is Zulu – and so there is tension between those who want there to be no ballet on our stages, and those who want to make ballet more South African and to encourage young black people who want to study it.

Sometimes black people in positions of power are pressured into thinking 'black' – black employees, black cultural performing groups or exhibiting artists, black cultural traditions. Some white people with useful skills or expertise and experience are lost; some black people, feeling that their turn has now come, are unwilling to take time to learn the ropes. In addition there is a sense that sectarianism and cronyism sometimes operate when appointments are made, not on the basis of expertise, but on the basis of political affiliations and friendships. And so the race card is played, and whenever it is played, for the most historically understandable reasons, it mires us in potential discriminations, and in possibly constitutionally questionable decisions.

Today there is a risk that those rigidities will be used to foster divisions, this time for the seemingly valid reason of reclaiming the status and respect that was denied by apartheid. But it keeps us in our boxes and it divides us when the chapter on 'Underlying values' in the *White Paper on arts, culture and heritage* that forms the basis of policy in these areas states: 'Culture should not be used as a mechanism of exclusion, a barrier between people, nor should cultural practices be reduced to ethnic or religious chauvinism' (DACST 1996).[7]

Employment equity can only be implemented where there is restructuring or expansion or when posts become vacant. And so there are cultural institutions and organisations in which there is frustration at 'glass ceilings'. Among artists and administrators the most frequently mentioned frustration in which race played a part was that of white women in senior positions who are sometimes viewed as unreconstructed in their mindsets about excellence and display, even when they consider themselves to be deeply committed to the new South Africa.

In some instances, white board members feel silenced by their whiteness. Given our past this is sometimes an understandable feeling, but it is not helpful to anyone when there are issues that need debate. The National Action Plan and Strategy to Combat Racism by the South African Human Rights Commission contains recommendations for arts and culture, including that:

- We agree to share a culture: bits of it do not 'belong' to bits of our society.
- We *value* the 'ways of life' of all – not tolerate, not even merely respect, real value.
- We encourage borrowing and innovation, but from a sense of equality. Art forms and traditions, unlike sacred relics, necessarily evolve, borrow from what's around them, and are creatively improvised. We let the arts

massage the cultures to allow for flexibility. There are two forms of the new: one is that of creative artists making something different, the other is the introduction of something recognisable to one group and quite new to another. The cognitive extension that comes to us all on finding new ways of seeing is something we may all come to share.

- The vision in the White Paper on arts and culture needs to be implemented in order to give a shape to the funding policies and strategies adopted for the arts: what must be provided at national level, what mechanisms must be put in place for touring, for infrastructure across the country, and for training in the arts and in arts management at all levels.
- We introduce anti-racism and anti-sexism workshops at all levels and structures in the arts sector, from the DAC down to the smallest arts group to be in receipt of funding.
- We learn to find the words and the tone and context for the words that allow us all to be critical in a constructive way, so that we can hear each other. (SAHRC 2002)

In a newspaper article in the *Sunday Times* of 15 October 2000, Judge Albie Sachs, who sits on the bench of the Constitutional Court and played an active role in the design of its new building in Johannesburg, defined the situation succinctly:

> We are in a strange position. No group is in charge; no section exercises cultural hegemony. The old establishment has lost its hauteur, but no confident and powerful new establishment has emerged to replace it … what we lack is confidence, organisation, focus and leadership … we have to learn to enjoy and be invigorated by the multiplicity of our cultural forms, and to get used to being as we are, even while we are changing.

Notes

1 Research for this paper included interviews with many role players in the arts sector (see list of acknowledgements).

2 www.artslink.co.za/pansa: Keeping the dream alive, towards a vision and plan for the performing arts in South Africa.

3 Available at www.artslink.co.za/pansa.

4   Jenny van Papendorp, interview, 6.02.04.

5   CreateSA is responsible for the development and implementation of learnerships (work-based training programmes) that lead to the achievement of qualifications registered on the NQF through SAQA. So while CreateSA is involved in the delivery side, SAQA is involved in the design. However, CreateSA does get involved in supporting the work of SAQA's SGBs so that the qualifications upon which learnerships are constructed are developed. This is because there is a legislated requirement that learnerships should lead to NQF-registered qualifications – in order to register a learnership with the Department of Labour (DoL), CreateSA has to provide the DoL with proof that the qualification is registered with SAQA.

6   Approximately 70 cultural organisations, festival directors and artists from 20 African countries met in Durban for the second OCRE Encounters Cultural Conference from 23–27.09.02. The OCRE – *Operateurs Culturels et Reseaux* (cultural organisations and networks) – Encounters, hosted by the Centre for Creative Arts, University of KwaZulu-Natal, was organised by the French Association for Artistic Action, a branch of the French Foreign Ministry, as part of its *Afrique en creation* programme.

7   Chapter 1, Clause 13.

Acknowledgements

Ahmed, Junaid	Film-maker
Baduza, Utando	Researcher in the Social Cohesion and Integration Research Programme, HSRC
Brown, Carol	Director, Durban Art Gallery
Callinicos, Luli	Chairperson, National Heritage Council
Constant, Michelle	Radio journalist
Chorn, Anriette	Director, Mmino Music Education Project
Cronje, Riaan	Programme Manager, Art and Design/Interior Decorating, Cape College, Cape Town
Danby, Nicola	Director, BASA
Dobson, Richard	Joint leader of the iTRUMP Project for the regeneration of the inner city of Durban
Du Plessis, Nicky	Independent arts consultant
Gaylard, Joseph	Chairperson of National Standards Body for Culture and Arts, researcher and project manager

Greig, Robert	Theatre critic, journalist
Herbst, Anri	Senior lecturer, Music Education, SA College of Music, University of Cape Town
Hobbs, Stephen	Visual artist: The Trinity Session
James, Bronwyn	SEED Programme Director, Greater St Lucia Wetland Park Authority
Krog, Antjie	Writer, poet
Loots, Lliane	Dance lecturer, Drama and Performance Studies Programme, University of KwaZulu-Natal (Durban Campus)
Malanga, Nise	Director, BAT Centre
Martin, Marilyn	Director, Art Collections, Iziko Museums of Cape Town
May, Ivan	Independent consultant
Mbalo, Eddie	Director, National Film and Video Council
Mbeki, Moeletsi	Deputy Chairperson, SA Institute of International Affairs
Mhlongo, Edmund	Director, eKhaya Multi-Arts Centre, KwaMashu
Mhlophe, Gcina	Writer, storyteller
Minty, Zayd	Deputy Director, District Six Museum
Ngema, Mbongeni	Musical Theatre Director
Nteta, Doreen	CEO, National Arts Council
Oliphant, Andries	Chair of Nacsa, Chair of South African Writers' Association
Pather, Jay	Director, Siwela Sonke Dance Theatre
Prosalendis, Sandra	Deputy Director, Arts and Culture, Social Cohesion and Integration Research Programme, HSRC
Sack, Steven	ex-Chief Director, Cultural Development, Department of Arts and Culture, now Director of Arts and Culture for the City of Johannesburg
Sichel, Adrienne	Theatre critic
Singh, Lorraine	Head of Discipline, Drama Education, School of Education, University of KwaZulu-Natal
Stark, Peter	Arts consultant
Tembe, Bongani	CEO and Artistic Director, KZNPO
Van Graan, Mike	General Secretary, Pansa
Van Papendorp, Jenny	Senior Curriculum Planner, Dance, Arts & Culture, Western Cape Education Department
Verster, Andrew	Artist, designer

References and sources

Abrahams R (2003) *Spinning around: The South African music industry in transition.* Cape Town: Human Sciences Research Council (HSRC).

Business and the Arts South Africa (BASA), the National Arts Council (NAC) and Arts and Culture Trust (2001) *The adult arts and culture and arts and culture sponsorship market in South Africa.* Commissioned research.

Chidester D, Dexter P & James W (2003) *Whatholdsustogether: Social cohesion in South Africa.* Pretoria: HSRC.

CreateSA (2003) *Training and developing the creative industries, national skills and resource audit.* Available at <http://www.createsa.org.za/index2.html>.

Curriculum Development Project and the University of the Witwatersrand School of the Arts (2003) *Artists in schools and community art centres project.* Briefing document compiled jointly with the support of the Flemish government and the Department of Arts and Culture.

DAC (Department of Arts and Culture, South Africa) (undated) *Investing in culture: A poverty alleviation project.*

DAC *Strategic Plan 1 April 2003 – 31 March 2004.* Available at <http://www.dac.gov.za>.

DACST (Department of Arts, Culture, Science and Technology, South Africa) (1996) *White Paper on arts, culture and heritage.* Pretoria: DACST.

Deacon H, Mngqolo S & Prosalendis S (2003) *Protecting our cultural capital: A research plan for the heritage sector.* Cape Town: HSRC.

Departments of Education and Labour (2003) NQF (National Qualifications Framework) consultative document.

Durban Art Gallery (undated publication) *Umbukiso.*

Gostner K (2004) *Kwaito nation: An industry analysis.* Johannesburg: YFM.

Gostner K (2004) The South African music industry: Trends, analysis and questions. Unpublished paper, commissioned for the South African Cultural Observatory, DAC. Pretoria.

Hadland A (2004) Shape of the print media industry. Unpublished paper, commissioned for the South African Cultural Observatory, DAC.

Hagg G & Selepe S (2002) *Towards optimally functioning community arts centres in South Africa.* Report on a national audit of community arts centres compiled jointly by the HSRC and the Department of Arts and Culture Council.

Harris I (2004) Ol' Skool: The carnival of dreams, *Rootz magazine* 8.

NAC (National Arts Council) (2001) *Annual report 2000–2001* NAC.

NAC (2002a) Strategy and policy meeting of the board at Aloe Ridge, Johannesburg 12–14 September. Internal document.

NAC (2002b) Mmino, South African-Norwegian Education and Music Programme. Annual Progress Report, January–December 2002. Internal document.

NAC (2002c) *Annual report 2002.* NAC.

NAC (2003a) *Annual report 2003.* NAC.

NAC (2003b) *Report to the Minister: National Arts Council of South Africa 1997–2003,* NAC.

Pansa (Performing Arts Network of South Africa) (2002) *Keeping the dream alive: Towards a vision and a plan for the performing arts in South Africa. Draft discussion document.* Available at <http://www.artslink.co.za/pansa>.

PCAS (Presidency Policy Co-ordination and Advisory Service, South Africa) (2003) *Towards a ten-year review: synthesis report on implementation of government programmes: Discussion document.* Pretoria: Government Communications and Information Systems.

SAHRC (South African Human Rights Commission) (2002) *Arts, culture, heritage and racism, draft national action plan and strategy to combat racism.*

Said EW (1993) *Culture and imperialism.* London: Chatto & Windus.

Spivak GC (1990) *The post-colonial critic: Interviews, strategies, dialogues.* New York: Routledge.

The State Theatre Advisory Board and Implementation Committee Report (2001).

Van Graan M (2003) *Speech for launch of Nacsa.* Available at <http://www.artslink.co.za/nacsa>.

Van Graan M & du Plessis N (1998) *The South African handbook on arts and culture.* Cape Town: Creda.

Van Papendorp J (2003) Discussion document to support a proposal for a strategic policy intervention in, and re-interpretation of, the senior phase in the learning area: Arts and culture. Compiled in consultation with the Western Cape Education Department Arts and Culture Curriculum Planners and Curriculum Advisers.

12 The state of the archives and access to information

Seán Morrow and Luvuyo Wotshela

Why should citizens concern themselves with the records of the past? They should do so because such records are the collective memory of government, business, civil society, and individuals, and because a society with inadequate archives is like a person who has lost his/her memory. Without them there can be no effective collective action, and activities will take place in a fog of ignorance, limited by the fallibility of individual recollection. In particular, archives can contribute powerfully to forming and maintaining a state whose political and administrative functionaries have the opportunity to be aware of the past and can therefore hope to avoid continually stumbling down the same culs-de-sac.

Archives are also about history. The authors of this chapter are historians, with a professional interest in archives. We believe, however, that a historical view, and the accompanying concern with archives, is of vital interest beyond this discipline. History does not belong to professional historians, and a sense of history is crucial to South African democracy. Archives are about maintaining, and even recovering, memory of a complex and often troubled past. They are about the creation of new materials for and ways of seeing this past, and of enabling obscured and ignored social actors to come to the centre of the historical and contemporary stage. They are about redress of past injustices and about establishing markers that may help to reduce the likelihood of future ones. They are about maintaining memory in a world where technology accelerates communication and multiplies records to the point where their very mass threatens to make them incomprehensible, and where potentially unstable electronic material can be altered, deleted or cease to be readable.

In outline, what is the contemporary state of South African archives? A well-functioning but circumscribed official archives system that concentrated on the records of the apartheid state has now been given a wider remit. This has put the system under strain, but the National Archives of South Africa (NASA) remains one of the most efficient official archives in Africa. At provincial and local government levels the situation is often unsatisfactory, with insufficient skilled personnel and, as this chapter demonstrates, sometimes highly inappropriate storage conditions. Archives everywhere are shaped by their provenance, and they generally reflect structures of authority. South African archives follow the fault lines of the country's divided history, with those inherited from the dominant elements in the previous regime remaining relatively well organised, and those generated by homelands, township administrations and the like less so. Previously, all government records were totally embargoed for 20 years. Now, at least in theory, individuals can view particular recent documents if they submit a good case for doing so.

It is difficult to generalise about the huge area of non-governmental records. These are highly diverse and, being private papers, are not always in the public domain, though recent legislation has enabled people to apply to examine even non-governmental records if they can demonstrate the need to do so. As with all record-keeping, much is and must be destroyed, but companies, churches, universities, trade unions, non-governmental organisations (NGOs), and many other civil bodies, as well as individuals, have generated and continue to generate great quantities of material that is in different states of preservation and organisation.

In emphasising the importance of archives, this chapter stresses two areas. Firstly, it emphasises the vulnerability of some provincial records. There is a particular focus on current problems with the management of the records of the Eastern Cape, where there have been attempts to organise the records from the different administrations into which the province was previously divided. Secondly, the chapter stresses the importance of archives in the context of contemporary politics, and the ways in which this importance has been demonstrated in recent times.

Why history matters

In the immediate aftermath of the third democratic election, there are reminders everywhere that South Africa's future will be marked by the past. As his speeches commonly are, the President's inauguration speech was saturated with references to history and its impact on the present.[1] In his 'State of the

Nation' address on 6 February 2004, he undertook to support Freedom Park, being developed on a hill near Pretoria, to challenge 'traditional narratives' on the South African past,[2] and 'other legacy projects that celebrate our humanity, our commitment to the all-round emancipation of all human beings, and human dignity'. This, surely, is a commitment to the past, and to the institutions that enable us to look at it seriously and analytically.

Ironically, given the grounding of the liberation struggle in a historical view, and the marginalising of the majority of the population in history as studied and taught under apartheid, there was a period in the aftermath of the first democratic election when history appeared to be in danger of disappearing from the educational system. It was, for instance, substantially downgraded in the school curriculum (Morrow 2000). A superficial view of the usefulness of history, combined with the apparent fragility of the South African political settlement and an interpretation of the need for political and social reconciliation that confused amnesia with understanding, seemed to make it difficult to adopt a historical perspective.

However, attempts to take a 'blank page' approach, like downgrading history in the school curriculum, appear to have been reversed, and history is back, if at times in the anodyne form of 'heritage'. Professor Kader Asmal, until recently Minister of Education, has spoken frequently and enthusiastically about the importance of history in schools, and for society as a whole, and launched the South African History Project under the aegis of the Department of Education to revitalise and reform school history. 'Historical research,' he recently reminded his listeners, 'demands the highest standards of integrity in the use of evidence; it requires skill in the critical analysis of sources and their interpretation; and it depends upon a talent for making connections and developing explanations that will enable us to make sense out of events and processes of the past.'[3] At universities, though it is difficult to generalise, the fortunes of history, which dipped disastrously in the period after 1994, seem at least in some cases to have partially revived.[4] As publicity for the launch of the History Project put it, 'You thought that history was dead and gone? You are wrong!!!!'[5]

What are 'archives' and why are they important?

Archives are the incomplete, partial, and often deliberately or unintentionally misleading records of this history, always reflecting the limitations of the environment in which they were accumulated. Their definition is potentially very wide. However, here we take a relatively restricted definition: we see archives as material from the past, including the very recent past, written, oral or pictorial, often collected with the purpose of facilitating the contemporary functioning of government, business or other organisations, and/or enabling contemporaries, 'historians' in the broadest sense, to retrieve a sense, or senses, of this past and reflect upon it.

There are vigorous debates, in South Africa and elsewhere, concerning archives, revolving around a postmodernist 'refiguring' (Hamilton, Harris, Taylor, Pickover, Reid & Saleh 2002). Such approaches tend to stress the often arbitrary nature of documentary survival, and to encourage a critical approach to archives. Archival collections, the argument goes, are, in themselves, constructions of systems of power, never neutral, always contested, and sometimes tendentious. While this argument does indeed need to be constantly reiterated, it is an approach based more on a reading of philosophers such as Jacques Derrida, than on the actual struggles of often sceptical historians with documents that they have long learned to treat as mere approximations to 'truth'. It is an approach that sometimes claims as novel that which many historians have long taken for granted. As early as 1962, in a classic study, the historian and journalist EH Carr (1962) argued that historical sources are necessarily subject to a whole range of questions surrounding interpretation, representation and narrative.

Though in South Africa, as elsewhere, 'the struggle of man against power is the struggle of memory against forgetting' (Kundera 1982:3), this memory is necessarily selective and people do forget, as well as being encouraged to forget. But at least citizens should be enabled to do their own remembering and forgetting, directly or through access to a wide range of evidence-based arguments about their society, rather than having someone else wield the airbrush on their behalf or, less culpably but often causing equal damage, simply losing or mismanaging records. As we will see, these are precisely the contemporary points of tension in this area, with forces pulling in both directions.

The state and its records

State documents are only a part, though a vital one, of archival records. In the context of the state of the nation, however, they are of particular significance:

they certainly do not give a complete picture of the nation, but they do have the potential to indicate the interaction of the state with its citizens, the internal workings of the state, and its interaction with other states.

As with most departing autocracies, the transition from the South African racial tyranny to the contemporary democracy was accompanied by an 'orgy of paper-shredding' (Frankel 2001:248). Only where the collapse of authority was particularly rapid, as in the German Democratic Republic, did reasonably full records of the more sensitive proceedings of the old regime tend to survive. As Simpson put it, 'in the process of the collapse of East German communism, through popular action, the entire Stasi archive was effectively "captured" before it could be destroyed' (1994:3).

South Africa's archival record is complex and moulded by its history. It is far larger and generally in better condition than other African archives. Also, because of the particular way in which colonialism and white settlement impacted on the country, more of it is retained within the national borders than in many other African countries. Some state archives are well tended elsewhere in Africa, but many range from slow deterioration to complete destruction, as in Guinea-Bissau in 1998.[6]

The National Archives of South Africa

NASA is a key institution, repository of official documentation, and, increasingly, of documents from non-official sources, including visual and oral material. Its role has been extended from that of its predecessor, the State Archives Service, of simply storing records of state, and it now has the remit of gathering material from previously marginalised sections of the population, and of proactively publicising and making available records to citizens. At the same time, some functions have been transferred to provincial archives. NASA was established in 1997 in terms of the National Archives Act of South Africa. Placed under the Department of Arts, Culture, Science and Technology (DACST) – and, recently, under the now-separated Department of Arts and Culture (DAC) – its public records mandate covers all governmental bodies at central level, including statutory bodies. NASA also has professional control over the records of the South African National Defence Force (SANDF), previously autonomous in this sphere, even though this institution retains its custodial responsibility.[7]

Provincial archives: the case of the Eastern Cape

The 1996 Act also provided for the establishment of provincial archives whose services were to incorporate those of the former homelands, as well as the components of the former State Archives services located in the provinces (Harris 2000). Some provinces have created or are creating archives services; others have not done so, and are using the services of the regional NASA depots. The condition of provincial facilities ranges from reasonable to appalling. On the whole, this follows predictable lines, in that records of the more privileged areas are relatively well-resourced and preserved, and those which contained ex-homelands are least so. With the exception of Transkei, which had an archives service, the homelands, whether 'independent' or self-governing, had resource centres at places like Ulundi, Mmabatho, Zwelitsha and Thohoyandou where documents were simply stored. It appears, for instance, that the records of the KwaZulu homeland remain in Ulundi where they always were, with no reference to the NASA depots in Pietermaritzburg and Durban. By 1999, the provinces of Mpumalanga and Free State had passed archives Acts. Recently, North West province has made moves to upgrade the resource centre that kept the Bophuthatswana records. It will be interesting to see how this process unfolds.

The Eastern Cape illustrates the position at its worst, yet the archives of this province are of exceptional significance. The Eastern Cape, a key area of conflict and interaction between colonisers and colonised in South Africa, from the nineteenth century became a focus for the development of African Christianity and education. It was at the heart of new political movements, particularly African nationalism. Under apartheid, the Transkei became the lynchpin of the government's homeland policy, and the model was later extended to neighbouring Ciskei. The new Eastern Cape province has now absorbed these entities, with the official records that they generated, or perhaps, since the bulk of the population lives in them, the ex-homelands have semi-absorbed the Eastern Cape. These records are of particular concern in that they deal with the most underprivileged people in one of the poorest parts of the country – the very kind of people and type of area said to be a vital concern of the new democracy.

In 2001, the Eastern Cape provincial government drafted a Provincial Archives and Records Service Bill that set the legislative framework for the Archives and Records Management Service under the provincial Department of Sport, Arts and Culture (DSAC). Already in 1997 this Department had been rationalised to incorporate the directorates of sports and recreation, arts and culture, museums and heritage resources, and libraries and archives.

The Libraries and Archives Directorate had the task of managing the new Eastern Cape archives depot set up at King William's Town, just outside the legislative capital, Bisho. While there remained a plethora of church, university, business, NGO and civic archives in various parts of the Eastern Cape, the King William's Town depot initially focused strictly on state records.

The location as well as the administration of government archival records in the Eastern Cape before 1997 reflected the legacy of apartheid. Before the King William's Town depot was established, there were two distinct 'official' archival depots in the province. Firstly, there was the Port Elizabeth repository, established in the 1970s, that served as a provincial depot with services linked to those of the Central Archives and Cape Archives depots in Pretoria and Cape Town.[8] In Port Elizabeth, official records going as far back as before the formation of the Union of South Africa could be accessed. The depot also facilitated access to many records generated within the departmental structures of the central South African government under National Party rule. By the early 1990s, its records, like those of the Central Archives and Cape Archives, were linked to a computerised database of manuscript collections kept in all South African archives depots.[9]

Secondly, Transkei's acceptance of a spurious 'independence' in 1976 resulted in the establishment of a separate Transkei repository in the *Bunga*, or Parliament, in Umtata. This was placed under the homeland's Department of Education and Culture, and kept most of the records generated during the period of administration by the *Bunga* under the Union government. It also kept the records of the Transkei Territorial and Bantu Authority systems from the early 1960s to the mid-1970s, as well as records generated during Transkei's independence from 1976 to 1994. Records were catalogued and the depot had its own published guide. Files could be accessed manually, but were not linked to a computerised database of manuscript collections, as were the records of the Central Archives and South African Provincial Depots (Wotshela 2003).

The new King William's Town depot initially focused on archiving Ciskei government records. During its equally questionable independence, Ciskei never had a fully-fledged archival repository. Departments kept their respective records and occasionally, after an undefined period, they were transferred to and kept in the Ciskei Department of Education, that in turn transferred them to the Central Archives depot in Pretoria. This system was fraught with problems, particularly the failure of departments to transfer their records. From its early administrative centre in Zone 6 Zwelitsha (1968–80), to its new capital in Bisho (1981–94), stacks of files proliferated along office walls. Some were dumped in foyers and basements of government buildings (Wotshela 2003).

In its initial phase of operation (1997–2001) the Directorate of Libraries and Archives facilitated the transfer to King William's Town of most of the early Ciskei archival records generated by departmental offices when the administrative centre was still in Zwelitsha. These were first housed in a privately owned building, previously Radue Milling Company, for a monthly fixed rent. Parts of the building were converted for office use, accommodating staff members of the four directorates of the DSAC. A large section of the building was refurbished and provided with temperature-regulated strongrooms with shelves for storage of archival material.

Archiving became difficult because the Directorate of Archives and Libraries was understaffed. This meant that the pre-1981 official Ciskei records, initially housed in Zwelitsha, would take longer to process. Moreover, the staff at the King William's Town repository still had to collect and collate the records generated during this homeland's period of 'independence' from 1981 to 1994. In addition, the new Eastern Cape provincial government retained Bisho as its legislative headquarters. Bisho absorbed much of the former Ciskei and Transkei bureaucracy so that most of the official records that were generated within the homeland structure remained in place, and indeed were added to further.

Like any other bureaucracy, the new Eastern Cape government generated its own records. New and old bureaucrats kept what they wanted and disposed of what they deemed useless. Some experienced civil servants made use of the upheavals to ensure that records of some of their activities disappeared. Files changed hands, and even moved from location to location too rapidly and confusingly for the Libraries and Archives staff to contend with. Again, it became almost impossible for some government departments to make space to store their records. By 1995, overcrowding in Bisho had led to the expansion of departmental offices, such as education, health, welfare, transport and public works, to areas such as King William's Town, Zwelitsha, and even to the airport building in Bulembu, near King William's Town, where some personnel records from these departments were moved to a semi-derelict warehouse. By 2001, some were yet to be collected from their originating departments. At a stroke, the provincial government of the Eastern Cape had lost the records of its professional civil servants (Wotshela 2003).

Interdepartmental competition proliferated during the African national Congress's (ANC) second term in office. The provincial DSAC embarked on its programme of resuscitating African heritage and creating official museums in African areas. This was tied to tourism, regarded as indispensable to growth and local development in the Eastern Cape. Directorates within the Department tussled for funds and for prestigious outcomes. In the process, the Libraries and Archives Directorate was further submerged. By 2000–01, the Bunga building that held the Transkei repository had to be renovated and prepared for the Mandela Museum. There were initial talks of removing the Transkei archives to King William's Town, or even to the Port Elizabeth repository, but mounting pressure from the Transkei users, as well as distance and the logistics of relocation, meant that they had to be retained in Umtata. There was, however, no space available for them, and in the initial stage of their relocation the files were dumped in the basement of what was now the Mandela Museum building. They were later moved to an adjoining building that was subsequently vandalised. 'Windows were broken and doors were looted and there was even talk of records and leaflets being eaten by mice and some blowing around the town centre.'[10] The deteriorating situation prompted the intervention of the national archivist in Pretoria late in 2001 and it was resolved to return the archival material under special guidance to the basement of the Museum building.[11]

From late 2001, the Libraries and Archives Directorate had no choice but to agitate for the renovation of the building adjoining the Museum so that it could be used to store the Transkei archives. While this was still under discussion, the provincial government revoked the DSAC's use of the privately-owned building in King William's Town. The fixed monthly rent was a grossly exaggerated R400 000 – an agreement locked in by a ten-year contract.[12] After some four to five years, and having paid rent of some R20 million, the provincial government finally realised that it could not carry the costs. This meant that the depot in

King William's Town had to be closed and the archival material and departmental staff relocated. In a hastily arranged removal, the relocated personnel were squeezed into some of the already congested Bisho offices. There was, however, no alternative storage space in Bisho for the material that had been stored in the King William's Town depot, even though the Bisho politicians had given ambitious promises in the pre-relocation discussions:

> We were informed that the provincial government would provide
> its own repository by May 2002. We understood that the Bisho
> Pick 'n Pay building would be cleared and certain sections would
> be converted into offices and strongrooms [archival storage]
> for the repository to operate there. But this never happened and
> up to now nothing has happened [*akukabikho nto yenzekileyo
> nangoku*].[13]

From July 2001 the archives that had been in the King William's Town depot were locked in a private container arranged by a removal company, Biddulphs, at a rental fee of about R75 000 per month. This material is not easily accessible to the public and, at times, not even to the staff of the Libraries and Archives Directorate. When rent is paid, access is facilitated. Conversely, 'no rental fee payment effectively means no access to the storage, as well as a possibility of prosecution for default payment'.[14] The Libraries and Archives Directorate could not and cannot acquire outstanding or new records while the only available storage is a privately-owned container. Likewise, the processing of records already acquired cannot be completed. 'We cannot work from a storage room that is too full even to fit in desks and no space to move around and sort out files.'[15]

In the meantime government departments continue to keep records internally and some have makeshift in-house records storage facilities. For example, the provincial departments of Agriculture and Land Affairs, and Local Government and Housing, have absorbed most of the Ciskei records on land use, settlement planning and administration. The former Ciskei and Transkei departments of Agriculture were particularly pivotal in rural planning, possessing technical services with planning divisions as early as the mid-1970s. These divisions administered surveys, planned settlements, ran irrigation schemes and even facilitated land allocation. They also administered and managed land use with the assistance of tribal authorities in most former Ciskei and Transkei rural villages.[16] These records were kept in the Land Use Unit of the Department of Agriculture and Land Affairs in late 2003. Some records regarding the administration and profiles of previous tribal authority areas of the Ciskei and Transkei were moved to the Local Government and Housing Department on the eve of the 2000 local government elections, and they remain there. Records such as these are of great administrative, political and historical significance. Yet at the beginning of 2004 there was, and still is, no functioning depot in the Eastern Cape other than the one in Port Elizabeth that largely remains unchanged from its pre-1994 structure.

Meanwhile the 2001 draft Bill has provided a framework for the future of archives in the Eastern Cape. It provides for the establishment of provincial archives and for the promotion of proper management and care of the records of provincial and local government bodies. It also provides for the preservation and use of the broader provincial archival heritage.[17] For most of 2003–04 the staff of the directorates of Libraries and Archives and of Museums and Heritage Resources have campaigned for various local government offices and government departments to transfer their records to their offices in Bisho, even though there is no depot in place. Public hearings on the 2001 Bill were held throughout the province in the latter part of 2003 (Wotshela 2003).

Despite the problems regarding the setting up of a depot in King William's Town, valuable archives remain in place, though there is not yet a complete guide to them. The archives of the former Ciskei's Department of Foreign Affairs from 1982 to 1994, which were already processed, were transferred from the Central Archives depot. These deal with resettlement on trust land, tribal affairs, transfer of land to Ciskei and such matters, and contain correspondence between South African and Ciskeian officials. Because different individuals moved in and out of government positions, filing chronology is haphazard.

Other records transferred from the Central Archives depot include those of the Eastern Cape Chief Bantu Commissioner (or Chief Native Commissioner). These contain correspondence between district bantu commissioners on aspects of African settlement in the 'white areas' of Cathcart, Stutterheim and Queenstown outside Ciskei and Transkei. They cover the period 1966 to 1988.

Records of pre-1981 Ciskei that were brought to the King William's Town repository in 1998 were processed before the depot was closed in 2001. These records, particularly those of the Ciskei Territorial Authority (CTA) that became a semi-legislative body in 1968, are from 1968 to 1980. From this period, CTA incorporated seven government departments: Interior, Works, Chief Minister and Finance, Health, Education and Justice, Agriculture and Forestry. The archived records reflect the wide range of government departmental activities. The following categories, not in chronological order, indicate what has been archived for this period. There are records on Ciskei afforestation; soil erosion and soil conservation programmes in the Ciskei; planning of irrigation schemes and water conservation programmes in the Ciskei; Ciskei livestock, Ciskei farmers co-operatives and dairy schemes; urban planning and urban management boards; Ciskei African townships and urban areas of Mdantsane and Zwelitsha; African labour, labour bureaux and tribal authorities; health institutions and health administration in the Ciskei; bantu/regional authorities and the CTA; bantu education, its organisation, control, financial assistance and bursaries; rural trading and business sites in the Ciskei; African extension assistance, African clerks – recorders and interpreters, and regulations for unsurveyed locations in certain districts of the Ciskei.[18]

The fate of these archives, and those in Umtata, remains uncertain. One cannot overemphasise their precarious situation while they remain in makeshift storage. There is a danger of records covering some four decades of South African, and particularly Eastern Cape, history being lost completely. This is not just of academic concern but relates to contemporary and often controversial questions such as landholding, rural development, and the position of traditional leaders. Though the input from the 2001 draft Bill is likely to reinforce the provincial government's determination to institute an archives depot, it has to be asked how such a repository is to be provided and managed. So far the provincial government has shown itself incapable of setting up and managing the King William's Town depot. It utilised large sums of public money (approximately R24 million) for some five years (1997–2001) in leasing space for departmental offices and a repository. For the subsequent leasing period from August 2001, at R75 000 per month, the government has continued to pay substantial sums.

Yet, despite such expenditure, there remains no repository in either Bisho or King William's Town. While this problem continues, the proper preservation of records generated within Ciskei and Transkei government departments and, subsequently, from within the provincial government of the Eastern Cape from 1994 onwards, is unlikely.

Non-official archives

There are numerous private archives in South Africa. A 1999 survey by NASA lists 90, but there are far more than that.[19] Some are dedicated to the records of a particular business, church or other institution. Some, especially at universities and museums, are multifaceted collections drawn from many sources. Examples are the papers in the William Cullen Library at the University of the Witwatersrand, Johannesburg,[20] the papers in the Cory Library for Historical Research at Rhodes University, Grahamstown, specialising in records of the Eastern Cape,[21] and the archives of the Institute for Contemporary History at the University of the Free State, Bloemfontein, a collection relating mostly to the Afrikaner tradition in South African politics.[22] Collections such as these are in good condition; others are less so, often influenced by the same factors that affect government collections.[23] Because of a lack of awareness, resources and skilled archival personnel, the loss of important collections of documents from private sources continues.

Since 1994, there have been moves to create archives, generally of oral provenance, that are often designed to rectify previous neglect and marginalisation. Examples are the ANC Oral History Project being carried out in collaboration with the University of Connecticut,[24] the South African Democracy Education Trust[25] (SADET) and the NASA National Oral History Programme.[26]

These are all worthwhile projects. SADET, for example, is not just accumulating oral testimonies, but is also organising and publishing studies of the South African struggle for freedom. However, there is a tendency for such projects to place politics in the foreground, albeit resistance politics. Ironically, in the best-funded and most officially favoured spheres of historical and social research, the democratic revolution has been accompanied by a privileging of politics above agrarian, labour, cultural, gender and other areas of social life. Alternative archives are in danger of creating a new narrative that remains overwhelmingly political. There are spheres where this is not the case. To take some varied examples, the Gay and Lesbian Archives,[27] the District Six Museum, the collections of which include archival material,[28] and The Employment Bureau of Africa,[29] are involved in interesting initiatives that are making possible the exploration of alternative sexualities, local communities and the life of migrant labourers in South Africa and in the southern African region.

New technology and South African archives

All over the world, archives are facing the challenge of the increasing immateriality of records.[30] More and more records are in electronic form, and rapidly changing technology means that even those that are preserved are sometimes difficult to access since the equipment to do so is no longer manufactured and records may not have been converted to currently accessible forms. Ironically, the records of a paper-based administration or business may be more reliably preserved and more accessible than those using electronic means of storage and access.

However, the impact of new technology is unpredictable. It provides opportunities but it also has dangers. Digitisation in particular offers the opportunity to release archives from their site-bound existence, given its potential to separate access to the record from its physical location. This is a revolutionary phenomenon that has had exciting yet disturbing consequences for South African archives. It can be seen in the context of debates about globalisation, of which this is one aspect.

A number of recent schemes to digitise South African archival material, involving United States (US) universities and foundations, have been understood by some as a form of neo-imperial information grab. Amongst the issues that arise are ownership of copyright to digitised material and the physical location of servers. For example, the site of the Mayibuye Archives, an important collection of material dealing particularly with the South African freedom struggle, is now hosted at Michigan State University. Others have dealt rather differently with these issues. The Digital Imaging Project of South Africa (DISA), a South African initiative based at the Killie Campbell Library and funded by the Andrew W Mellon Foundation, set about digitising difficult-to-obtain liberation periodicals from 1960 to 1994, in many cases creating complete virtual runs where none in hard copy actually exist.[31] The intention is to expand this initiative through collaboration with the Aluka Project, which hopes to foster and further expand DISA through links with the resources of large North American foundations.

These examples seem to show that while there may be dangers of the takeover of material by well-resourced First World institutions, South Africa has the expertise to use overseas resources and skills without being overwhelmed by them. There is another side to this, which indeed reflects the debates on globalisation of which it can be seen as a part. It would be a mistake, as Williams and Wallach (2001) imply, to retreat into a 'nationalist' approach that sees archives as a local possession, even a symbol of a unique and closely guarded individuality, rather than as a universal resource to be shared with the international community, as South Africans would in turn hope to share the intellectual resources of other communities and cultures.

The contemporary politics of archives

Politics is the mode in which people engage with their society, and the language in which they discuss it. While records have an importance that relates to deeper social currents than is normally the case with day-to-day political engagement, it is important that in that engagement the long-term interests of preservation and access are maintained. South Africa comes from a situation where freedoms of all kinds were circumscribed and denied, including freedom of information. The gains in this area, while remarkable, have a short history, and should not be assumed to be irreversible.

Archives are closely linked to questions of access to information. The Freedom of Information Act in the US goes back to the 1960s. Internationally, particularly since the end of the Cold War, there has been a move towards increasing freedom of access to information in many democratic states, and towards making contemporary records available to the public for examination. The effects of such availability on what is actually allowed to enter the record is difficult to estimate, given that those recording know that they may be open to scrutiny. It remains also to be seen what the impact of the 'War on Terror' and its accompanying security concerns will be on such policies of ready access in countries like the US.

The South African legislative framework on such access is extremely liberal. The Promotion of Access to Information Act of 2000 goes further than similar legislation in most other countries in that it applies to the private as well as the public sector. Private commercial companies, for example, cannot deny access to their records for *bona fide* enquiries under the terms of the Act. The

Act sets in place mechanisms to assist in utilising it. For example, the South African Human Rights Commission is given various tasks, such as publicising the Act, providing information as to how it can be used, and assisting people to use it. Even where there are restrictions, as in obtaining material concerning defence and security, there is provision for overriding these restrictions when it is considered to be in the public interest. Clearly, this legislation hinges on questions of access to archival material.[32]

However, there are cross-currents flowing in this area which seem to represent differences of ideological emphasis within the ANC, as well as the abiding concerns of power and authority when faced with potential questioning of their roles and actions. Governments tend to limit access to documents that it is thought might endanger state security. It is not easy to define with certainty what is or is not a danger to the security of the state, and such decisions have to be seen in relation to the interests of those who have something to lose or gain. Those who might have something to hide are not likely to be impartial in deciding on access to information that might be discreditable to themselves. Politicians and functionaries may thus try to impede those with legitimate questions from getting answers, using the argument, difficult to challenge by those outside the magic circle of security and intelligence, of interests of state.

These questions have been raised in several ways, in relation, for instance, to documents of the Truth and Reconciliation Commission (TRC) and to the events surrounding the accusations of spying for the apartheid government made against Bulelani Ngcuka, until recently Director of Public Prosecutions. However, a good indication of the dilemmas and contradictions in this area is that of access to the archives of the external wing of the ANC itself.

The decision was taken in the early 1990s to deposit the archives of the ANC-in-exile at the University of Fort Hare in the Eastern Cape. The first consignment of documents, those concerning the ANC settlements of Mazimbu and Dakawa, and especially the ANC school at Mazimbu, came straight from Tanzania. The documents and artefacts arrived, unprocessed and unsorted, at the university in September 1992 and once there, the task of ordering and archiving this large collection began. Though secrecy in some areas had been an essential part of operating in exile, in the changing but still unpredictable environment of the early 1990s, the ANC was remarkably open in making available an important part of its records for scholarly examination.[33] Subsequently, the records of the ANC's various overseas offices began to arrive in South Africa. They no longer went straight to the University of Fort Hare, but rather to Shell House, now Luthuli House, where it appears sensitive documents are removed, hopefully to be kept safely for a future when it will be deemed possible to release them for scrutiny. This process continues to the present.

The records of a political movement or party are not the same as those of government. Neither is the removal of sensitive documents necessarily in itself a dubious procedure. There may well be medical and other personal records that should not be in the public domain, though even here it can be argued that what is excluded should be identified, so as to give an idea of the dimensions of what is missing. However, this episode does reveal a shift in balance within the governing party, with a moment of openness between exile and office, a utopian pause between the old regime and the new realities, regrettably if predictably giving way to a more secretive mode. It would be wrong to oversimplify – there was plenty of secrecy and suspicion in exile, and the Promotion of Access to Information Act itself indicates that the more open and libertarian tendency within the ANC has by no means disappeared – but it would appear that, as everywhere, civil society, journalists, scholars and the public cannot assume that they will gain easy access to sensitive material. They will have to struggle to achieve and maintain it. To its credit, the government has, in the Promotion of Access to Information Act, created a powerful tool for citizens to do just that. Nevertheless – and this represents a dichotomy within the ANC itself – there appears to be a pervasive suspicion of those who wish to assert the right of citizens to information. To assert these rights costs money and time, and private individuals may be blocked from information by the very difficulty and expense of obtaining it, even if in theory it should be theirs by right.

The South African History Archive, an NGO based at the University of the Witwatersrand, as well as itself creating an archive for material that might not otherwise find a home in one of the established repositories, has assumed the task of testing the parameters of access under the Promotion of Access to Information Act.[34] The most celebrated instance is the long-running contest with government, which still continues, about the fate of 34 boxes of 'sensitive' TRC documents (see the *Sunday Independent* 18.01.04). This raises many issues, including the ethics of releasing information that might conceivably destabilise South Africa's carefully crafted status quo, the right of government to determine the status of TRC documents, and the role of the various ministries and agencies – the Justice and Intelligence ministries, the National Intelligence Agency, the National Archives and the Classification and Declassification Review Committee – that have played pass the parcel with the issue, and even, it would appear, with the actual documents (see *ThisDay* 2.03.04).

Similar issues arose in relation to the accusations of spying against Bulelani Ngcuka. The cross-examination of the protagonists during the Hefer Commission that followed the accusations was, fundamentally, an argument about evidence and records. The accusations were shown to be hollow when his accusers could not produce convincing documentary evidence to support their charges.[35]

Again, sensitive issues about the holding of quasi-official records by private individuals and the use by the state of privileged information were raised. Moe Shaik, one of Ngcuka's accusers, produced, and subsequently surrendered to the state, what he claimed was a list of apartheid-era spies that he possessed from his time in ANC intelligence.

Also, the question arose as to why the President, who can be assumed to have access to all the intelligence resources of the state, including its records, could not have short-circuited the political-cum-judicial process and pronounced *ex cathedra* on the veracity or otherwise of the accusations.

There thus appears to be a probably unstable balance in relation to access to information. There is a favourable legislative environment where, for example, the names of more than 7 000 opponents of apartheid whose files escaped the shredders have been released, enabling them, or others, to apply to the National Archives to examine them (see *ThisDay* 1–4.12.03). On the other hand, the release of information seems to be resisted, through fighting the release of documents, through the courts, or through an apparent inertia that may stem from a shortage of the expertise needed to handle the situation or may be due to a more deliberate obstruction. In the words of Dumisa Ntsebeza, the TRC's chief investigator, the practical difficulties of getting information, in spite of the enabling legislation, make the public's right of access to information 'a chimera, an ephemeral right' (quoted in *ThisDay* 1.12.03). If this is the case, South African citizens have reason to be very concerned.

Conclusion

Archives are always an incomplete record. Nonetheless, they are crucial, not just for the efficient functioning of government, but also for citizens who wish to participate intelligently in the life of their society. Not many of these are themselves going to search in the archives – though some will, and they should be encouraged and facilitated – but archives provide researchers with the material to fuel well-informed public debate. In South Africa, because of the complexity of its history, there are numerous official and unofficial archives, but they are particularly uneven in their reach. This reflects the influence of earlier class and racial discrimination with, for example, persisting neglect and mismanagement of homeland archives. On another level, the technically more competent system that has its origins in the pre-1994 white administrations is opening itself to more public involvement, and attempting to extend its range currently and retrospectively to encompass the wider population as more than simply the subjects of government. Various non-governmental agencies are involved in similar enterprises.

Archives are an intrinsic part of debates over freedom of information. The tensions between secrecy and openness, control and emancipation, persist. They are embedded in the fabric of government itself, with measures to promote the free flow of information, and yet resistance to the very freedoms that flow from that policy. These issues are working themselves out in a number of prominent specific cases. Behind these lie principles and conflicts that are universal, and can never be finally resolved. However, the balance and maturity of a society is indicated by how judiciously it deals with these issues.

Notes

1 See <http://iweb.hsrc.ac.za/virtualLibrary/governmentPublications/mediaBriefings/addressThaboMbekiInauguration.pdf>. Accessed on 29.04.04.

2 See <http://www.freedompark.org.za/index.html>. Accessed on 12.05.04.

3 Address by Professor Kader Asmal, Centre for the Book, Cape Town, 31.03.04. See <http://education.pwv.gov.za/index.asp?src=mvie&xsrc=355>. Accessed on 30.04.04.

4 As, for instance, through a focus on oral history at the University of Cape Town: Bickford-Smith, Field & Glaser (2001); or on public history, memory and identity, as at the University of the Western Cape: <http://www.uwc.ac.za/arts/history/>. Accessed on 10.05.04.

5   See <http://education.pwv.gov.za/sahp/history/sa_history_brochure%202.htm>. Accessed on 29.04.04.

6   In the discussion group H-AfrArts on 24 September 1998, Claude Ardouin reported that the Guinea-Bissau archives were being used as military dormitories. Documents 'are scattered, shredded and exposed to rain and dirt. Hundreds of audio cassettes which record the history of the national liberation struggle, as told by its actors and witnesses, cannot be found. Hundreds … which record the oral history of the different regions of the country have disappeared. Photographs and films from the Audiovisual Archives are found dispersed and lying in the mud outside. In other words, entire pages of the history of Guinea-Bissau risk being irredeemably blank or illegible'. See <http://h-net.msu.edu/cgi-bin/logbrowse.pl?trx=vx&list=h-afrarts&month=9809&week=d&msg=kYFEFmogqQeLuSFwDc0NYg&user=&pw=>. Accessed on 29.04.04.

7   The founding charter of the new archival service is the National Archives and Records Service of South Africa Act (No. 43 of 1996). See *Government Gazette* 17471, 2.10.96.

8   The key legislation for the establishment and direction of government archives depots in South Africa was the Archives Act (No. 6 of 1962). This was amended four times before 1980 (in 1964, 1969, 1977 and 1979). Most of these amendments dealt with the regulation and establishment of provincial depots.

9   Interview with Messrs van Zyl and de Villiers, Port Elizabeth, 24.08.99. At the time of the interview they worked in the Port Elizabeth and King William's Town depots respectively.

10   Interview with Spikes (pseudonym), at Bisho, 22.07.03. In most cases names of informants and the respective government departments to which they are attached have been withheld for their security. Where appropriate, pseudonyms have been provided. Pseudonyms do not necessarily indicate a particular race and/or the sex of informants.

11   Interview with Fana (pseudonym), at Bisho, 22.07.03, and Spikes (pseudonym), at Bisho, 22.07.03; Wotshela 2003:4–8.

12   Interview with Fana (pseudonym), at Bisho, 22.07.03, and Spikes (pseudonym), at Bisho, 22.07.03.

13   Interview with Spikes (pseudonym), at Bisho, 22.07.03.

14   Interview with Fana (pseudonym), at Bisho, 22.07.03, and Spikes (pseudonym), at Bisho, 22.07.03.

15 Interview with Spikes (pseudonym), at Bisho, 22.07.03.

16 The Ciskeian Agricultural Development Act (No. 5 of 1973) gave the Department overall powers to regulate residential land, livestock and access to grazing land, as well as managing agricultural land; Wotshela 2001:1–30.

17 See the Preamble to the Provincial Archives and Records Service Bill, 2001 (Eastern Cape):2.

18 See the preliminary draft guide for the archives held under the Directorate of Libraries and Archives, Department of Sport, Arts and Culture in the Eastern Cape Province.

19 See http://www.national.archives.gov.za/dir_repository1999.htm>. Accessed on 8.01.04.

20 See http://www.wits.ac.za/library/campuslib/cullen.html#hlpapers>. Accessed on 13.05.04.

21 See <http://www.rhodes.ac.za/library/cory/index.html>. Accessed on 13.05.04.

22 See <http://www.uovs.ac.za/support/library/E_library_arca.php>. Accessed on 13.05.04.

23 The neglect of valuable records that go back to the early twentieth century is illustrated in Morrow & Gxabalashe (2000).

24 See <http://www.sp.uconn.edu/~wwwanc/index.html>. Accessed on 29.04.04.

25 South African Democracy Education Trust (2004) is largely based on these oral records.

26 See <http://www.national.archives.gov.za/>. Accessed on 29.04.04.

27 See <http://www.wits.ac.za/gala/archives.htm>. Accessed on 29.04.04.

28 See <http://www.districtsix.co.za/frames.htm>. Accessed on 29.04.04.

29 See <http://www.teba.co.za/>. Also telephone conversation with Mr Kevin Cottrell, Regional Manager Gold and Coal, 14.05.04.

30 There is a large literature. The website of the International Council on Archives, <http://www.ica.org/>. Accessed on 14.05.04, indicates the preoccupation of professional archivists worldwide with the authenticity, preservation and management of electronic records.

31 See <http://disa.nu.ac.za/>. Accessed on 29.04.04. For a South African commercial initiative to digitise pictorial images, see *ThisDay*, 9.03.04.

32 See, for example, Currie & Klaaren (2002) and Klaaren, *Access to information and national security in South Africa*. Available on <http://www.law.wits.ac.za/rula/klaaren.pdf>. Accessed on 30.11.03.

33 This enabled a corresponding openness in the literature that emerged: see Morrow 1998; Morrow, Maaba & Pulumani 2004. For reflections on exile, secrecy and records see Morrow, Maaba & Pulumani 2002.

34 See <http://www.wits.ac.za/saha/>. Accessed on 10.05.04.

35 The Hefer report can be read at <http://www.gov.za/reports/2004/heferreport.pdf>. Accessed on 13.05.04.

References

Bickford-Smith V, Field S & Glaser C (2001) The Western Cape Oral History Project: *The 1990s, African Studies* 60:5–23.

Carr EH (1962) *What is history?* London: Macmillan.

Currie J & Klaaren J (2002) *The Promotion of Access to Information Act commentary*. Cape Town: SiberInk Publishers.

Frankel P (2001) *An ordinary atrocity*. Johannesburg: Witwatersrand University Press.

Hamilton C, Harris V, Taylor J, Pickover M, Reid G & Saleh R (eds.) (2002) *Refiguring the archive*. Cape Town: David Philip.

Harris V (2000) *Exploring archives: An introduction to archival ideas and practice in South Africa*. Pretoria: National Archives of South Africa (NASA).

Kundera M (1982) *The book of laughter and forgetting*. London: Faber & Faber.

Mbeki T (1994) *State of the Nation Address of the President of South Africa*. Parliament, Cape Town, 6.02.04.

Morrow S (1998) Dakawa Development Centre: An African National Congress settlement in Tanzania, *African Affairs* 97:497–522.

Morrow S (2000) An argument for history, *South African Journal of Higher Education* 14:32–37.

Morrow S & Gxabalashe K (2000) The records of the University of Fort Hare, *History in Africa* 27:481–497.

Morrow S, Maaba B & Pulumani L (2002) Revolutionary schooling? The Solomon Mahlangu Freedom College, the African National Congress liberation school in Tanzania, 1978 to 1992, *World Studies in Education* 3:23–37.

Morrow S, Maaba B & Pulumani L (2004) *Education in exile: SOMAFCO, the ANC School in Tanzania, 1978–1992*. Cape Town: HSRC Press.

Simpson G (1994) 'Truth recovery or McCarthyism revisited': An evaluation of the Stasi Records Act with reference to the South African experience. Research paper for the Centre for the Study of Violence and Reconciliation. Available at <http://www.csvr.org.za/papers/papstasi.htm>. Accessed on 29.04.04.

South African Democracy Education Trust (2004) *The road to democracy in South Africa, Volume 1 (1960–1970)*. Cape Town: Zebra Press.

Williams B & Wallach W (2001) Documenting South Africa's liberation movement: Engaging the archives at the University of Fort Hare, *Comma: International Journal on Archives* 1/2:45–67.

Wotshela L (2001) Homeland consolidation, resettlement and local politics in the Border and the Ciskei region of the Eastern Cape, South Africa, 1960 to 1996. Unpublished D.Phil. thesis, University of Oxford.

Wotshela L (2003) Archiving without a repository – The current nature and status of the Eastern Cape archives in Bisho/King William's Town. Paper presented at the Eastern Cape Historical Legacies and New Challenges Conference, 27–30.08.03.

13 A virtuous circle? Gender equality and representation in South Africa

Shireen Hassim

Introduction

In the ten years since the formal end of apartheid, South Africa has attracted enormous interest internationally. One of the most noted features of the new democracy is the acceptance of gender equality as a core value in constitutional and policy terms, and the creation of special institutions for advancing women's interests in the state. In this respect, South Africa is regarded as an example of a successful transition from authoritarianism to democracy, where women's organised struggles have led to tangible gains – what I would call a 'virtuous political circle', in which women's participation is rewarded with shifts in the allocation of public resources to address women's needs. While most of sub-Saharan Africa languishes at the bottom of the Gender and Development Index scale, South Africa appears to offer hope that, if properly constituted, African democracies can overcome the historical legacies of women's subordination and that a virtuous circle will be instituted. For this reason, among others, feminists working with Southern African Development Community (SADC) structures and in association with international organisations, have begun a campaign for increased, even equal, representation of women within legislative bodies in the southern African region. The South African version of the 50–50 campaign was launched in 2002, and activism around this campaign intensified with the third general election. The 50–50 campaign is firmly on the side of quotas as a mechanism through which increased representation can be secured.

In this chapter I explore the model of a virtuous circle of representation by examining recent experiences of legislative and policy reform in South Africa.[1]

South Africa is a good case study on which to base a critical analysis of representational strategies because it contains many of the features which are seen to facilitate women's struggles for equity, as well as those which are seen as key obstacles. It sits at the intersection of Third-World democracies which struggle with weak institutions, poor resources and resistant civil society, and First-World democracies in which state institutions are strong, formal attention to gender equality is a matter of course, and the economic ability to deliver sometimes expensive gender-equitable policies (such as paid maternity leave, state-subsidised childcare and so on) is much greater. South African processes of democratisation challenge assumptions of many Third-World women's movements that the state and political parties are 'empty shells' and that rights are unlikely to impact on the systemic inequalities of gender. In South Africa, perhaps more than in any other country on the African continent, feminists have engaged political parties as serious actors (Goetz & Hassim 2003). This engagement has resulted in significant victories, and the constitutional commitments to gender equality and the socio-economic rights clause are both regarded as vital resources by feminist activists. They argue that rather than seeing rights as limited to the formal political sphere, rights-based strategies have the potential to transform the conditions of people's lives.

This review of the state of the nation, coming ten years after the inception of democracy, is also a good point historically to review the impact of increased representation of women in the state. Apart from the global 50–50 campaign, the advent of a third set of elections denotes a new phase in South Africa's democracy. Although it is difficult to denote a 'moment' which marks the maturation of a democracy, or even an 'end' to the transition, political party rhetoric has moved from a focus on institution building and the development of policy and legal frameworks to a phase of consolidating democracy through policy implementation and service delivery. Although processes of identity formation are an important part of groups' abilities to make claims on the state, quota demands in themselves are a relatively superficial way of developing collective identity. In the context of policy implementation, the challenges centre much more firmly on questions of *how* interests are articulated, on *what* interests are being represented and by whom, and on the relationship between representatives and the represented.

Participation, representation and equality: understanding the terms of the debate

Turning particularly to the idea of a virtuous political circle of representation, each of the 'drivers' – participation, representation and equality – deserves closer interrogation. What forms of *participation*, underpinned by what kinds of ideologies and in which arenas, are most likely to facilitate a gender equity agenda? How can effective *representation* be secured in the context of considerable institutional bias against women's presence in the public sphere? And finally, what kinds of policy *outcomes* are desirable from the point of view of different constituencies of women?

Increasing women's participation in decision-making is a key part of the model. However, there are differing views on what constitutes participation. The thinnest definition (which is often evident in discussions of quotas) is that the mere presence of women in parliaments shifts 'the patriarchal demeanour of political institutions'[2] and forces institutions to recognise women. Anne Marie Goetz and I (Goetz & Hassim 2003) have distinguished this from effective participation, where the emphasis is on more effective interest articulation and representation – that is, to make the 'voice' of women louder. However, as Goetz points out, we should be careful not to assume that amplified voice 'will automatically strengthen the moral and social claims of the powerless on the powerful and produce better accountability to that group' (2003:34). Institutional norms and procedures, and the nature of processes of deliberation, can undermine the extent and impact of women's voice in the public sphere. As Fraser (1997) has pointed out, even though the formal blockages to women's participation in parties and Parliament may be removed, it is much harder to deal with the subtle patterns of deliberation that uphold particular power relations. Drawing on Mansbridge, she argues that 'deliberation can mask domination' as 'social inequalities can infect deliberation, even in the absence of any formal exclusions' (Fraser 1997:79).

Similarly, the nature of representation is a matter of considerable debate. Mahon and Jenson (1993) have pointed to two forms of representation. The first form is the 'representation of self to others via the creation of a collective identity' (Mahon & Jenson 1993:78). The second form is interest representation through parties and civil society organisations. Both forms are important because they involve 'the power to give meaning and visibility to social relations, and thereby the power to represent and dispute interests' (Mahon & Jenson 1993:78). Quota demands tend to emphasise the creation of collective identity; they rest on the successful articulation of women's group-based interest in entering arenas of power. This strategy derives from the marginal status most women occupy in society, and entails a collective demand for recognition that can win support across class, race and ideological lines. Interest representation, on the other hand, may shatter the notion of women as a homogeneous group as the resource claims of some women based on their class and/or race disadvantages may come into conflict with the interests of other women, or require privileging the building of alliances with other social actors. In the South African experience, these forms of representation have not been seen as contradictory, but rather as being in creative tension.

The tension between identity formation and interest articulation is also addressed in Fraser's formulation of the differences between struggles for recognition and struggles for redistribution. For Fraser, gender is a 'bivalent mode of collectivity' (1997:20), having the face of cultural devaluation as well as being economically rooted. Women's struggles for justice thus encompass both struggles for recognition as well as struggles for redistribution. Recognition entails the constitution of women as a group, while redistributive struggles demand the deconstruction of women as a group and the articulation of poor and working-class women's claims in alliance with other social forces. Seeing representation through the recognition-redistribution lens offers new ways to think about the possibilities and limits of South African struggles for gender equality. Clearly the formation of women's collective identity was bolstered in the last ten years; women were 'recognised' in official discourses in ways that were barely imaginable in 1994. However, it is not so evident that women were able to use this recognition effectively as a lever to ensure that inequalities based on gender in the economy and in society were addressed. I will address this question more directly in the discussion of the politics of the Communal Land Rights Bill (CLRB).

A central problem with the ways in which representation is debated is that, increasingly, the issues have become limited to pro- or anti-quota arguments. Although it is generally accepted in feminist literature that a combination of factors is responsible for women's increased access to political office – the nature of the political system and the organisation of political competition, the nature of civil society and especially of the feminist lobby within it, and the nature and power of the state – all too often actual political strategies are collapsed into a demand for a quota. This is not surprising; it is without doubt more difficult to reshape the nature of the political system except, as the South African case demonstrates, during periods of major transition. Quotas are seen as a fast-track mechanism to cut through more intractable institutional blockages, to at least get 'a foot in the door' of the political system. Quotas are also politically cheap in political systems where there is a single dominant party; extending a quota to women does mean that some men will not get onto party lists, but with sufficient power a dominant party can in any case deploy men to other important positions in the state and in parastatal organisations. Advancing women into prominent positions is also relatively costless electorally when you have the combination of an electoral system of proportional representation (PR) with list and a dominant party. The form of the quota adopted in South Africa is in fact its weakest and simplest version: voluntary party quotas are a long way off from the legislated quotas that operate in Argentina, for instance.

Processes of representation also matter from the perspective of effective representation. Electoral systems play a key role in determining the nature of the relationship between elected representatives, political parties and constituencies. The PR system, which has had such distinct advantages for women in pushing recognition claims, may have a different impact on redistributive demands. The PR system privileges power brokerage within political parties over constituency formation and representation. The result is that what happens within political parties – the struggles within parties to make gender equality part of the policy programmes – has an important bearing on policy outcomes. The ability of women representatives to mobilise within their parties, and their willingness to challenge party hierarchies, is an important determinant of the extent to which women will be effectively represented.

Looking finally at the nature of policy outcomes, there has been surprisingly little debate since 1994 about what gender equality would entail. In the apartheid era, a clear line was drawn between struggles for formal equality and those for substantive equality. Formal equality – the achievement of equal rights and opportunities – was regarded as an inadequate conceptualisation of liberation. What was needed was substantive equality, understood as the transformation of the economic conditions which produce gender equality.[3] The Women's Charter for Effective Equality, adopted by the Women's National

Coalition in 1994, articulates a notion of equality which is closer to the vision of substantive equality, with a very clear emphasis on the structural and systemic underpinnings of women's subordinate status. I would argue that a strong notion of equality, one that would provide some guidance about appropriate policy choices, would rest on the degree to which women have autonomy and are able to make choices free of the constraints of care work within families and communities, as well as free of the pressure to remain in oppressive and violent relationships (Orloff 1993).[4] This notion of equality has specific implications for social policy, as it would require that resources be directed in such a way that they serve not only to address the needs of the poorest women, but also become part of an incremental process of enhancing women's autonomy.

In sum, while increasing women's representation is important at the broad political system level, it is also important to examine critically the processes of representation, as well as the ways in which women's interests are conceptualised. We need to examine how different groups of women are 'constructed' for the purposes of policymaking, particularly in relation to other claimants on public resources, the ways in which the needs of different groups of women (in alliance with other social formations) can be articulated, and what implications this has for what can be claimed as a social policy entitlement.

Attributing gender equality gains

The first five years of democracy (1994–99) was a period which was dominated by the need to elaborate the rules, procedures and norms of the new institutions, policies and laws. This period saw an intense preoccupation with outlining policy frameworks and creating enabling legislation in a vast number of areas. The most prominent gain for the women's movement was the African National Congress's (ANC) eventual acceptance of an internal quota, and the well-known effects this engendered in putting a 'critical mass' of women into Parliament (Ballington 1998; Fick, Meintjes & Simons 2002; Mtintso 1999). Several far-reaching pieces of legislation were passed in the first term. The Termination of Pregnancy Act of 1996 provides women with access to abortion under broader and more favourable conditions than previously. The Domestic Violence Act of 1998 provides protection against abuse for people who are in domestic relationships, regardless of the specific nature of the relationship (that is, whether marital, homosexual or family relationships). It is a highly significant piece of legislation in that it entails a recognition that the 'private' sphere of the family is not inviolate from the democratic norms established by the Constitution, and that women are entitled to state protection of their rights even in the private sphere. The Maintenance Act of 1998 substantially improves the position of mothers dependent on maintenance from former partners. The Recognition of Customary Marriages Act of 1998 abolished the minority status of women married under customary law, and legalised customary marriages. In addition, a number of policy programmes were introduced, such as free healthcare for pregnant women and children.

During this period, there were also significant gains in embedding gender equality concerns in the broad frameworks of law and policy, which have been well-documented (Albertyn 1999; Gouws 2004 [forthcoming]; Hassim 2003). A number of areas of legislative discrimination against women remain intact, and there are other areas in which legislation is needed to enable the freedom of women. While discussion of these is beyond the scope of this paper, it is important to examine the strategic routes through which legislative gains were achieved, and the conceptual underpinnings of key policies. In the next section I examine, firstly, the politics of achieving legislative change, and secondly, what kinds of assumptions about gender are embedded in new legislation and policy.

Representation and legislative change

Several researchers have found that it was initially difficult for women Members of Parliament (MPs) to define strategies for legislative intervention (Britton 1997; CASE 1999; Mtintso 1999). Their immediate challenges in 1994 were to understand how Parliament itself worked, and to address the culture and working conditions in Parliament so that their participation would be facilitated. The differences between women also emerged very quickly as the 'critical mass' of women came to grips with the real differences in legislative and policy priorities between different political parties. The establishment of a multiparty women's caucus (the Parliamentary Women's Group) failed to provide either a support structure or a lobbying point for women MPs. The ANC Women's Caucus, by contrast, acted as the key pressure point within Parliament, even within the multiparty Joint Monitoring Committee on the Improvement of the Quality of Life and Status of Women (hereafter referred to as JMC). The most notable example of the tension this engendered was the process surrounding the introduction of employment equity legislation. ANC women MPs worked extremely hard to ensure that women were recognised as a disadvantaged group in the new laws. However, Democratic Party (DP) women MPs voted against the legislation because the party as a whole was opposed to the imposition of strong labour market regulation. The JMC – under the chair of experienced gender activist Pregs Govender[5] – established in part as a consequence of the new government's signing of the United Nations Convention on the Elimination of All Forms of Discrimination Against Women (CEDAW), provided an important institutional forum within which to identify a set of legislative priorities and begin to lobby for policy changes. Indeed, this committee demonstrated the most significant positive impact of representational strategies. Working closely with civil society through a series of public hearings and expert submissions, this committee arrived at an independent assessment of the nature and scale of the HIV/AIDS crisis, for instance, and called on Parliament to make eradicating the disease and dealing with its effects the number one priority. Despite ANC and presidential pressures, ANC members of this committee, led by Govender, stood firm on the need for anti-retrovirals. The committee was also the only parliamentary committee to openly oppose the arms deal. At the opening of Parliament in 2003, Govender joined the Treatment Action Campaign (TAC) outside Parliament, rather than take her seat in the house. Addressing Mbeki directly, she said, 'It is time for my President to say no to so much unnecessary death, to so much grief, to so many wars.' This is an important indication of the willingness of a few MPs to challenge the party in the face of contestations between different interests. It is not insignificant, however, that Govender resigned from Parliament at the end of the 2002 session.

Looking more closely at the legislative gains made in the first five years, it is important to analyse how changes were introduced, and whether the impact of women in Parliament is sustainable, and not dependent on exceptional MPs such as Pregs Govender (who would probably have been on the ANC list without a quota). What is notable about the processes of bringing in new legislation was that the linkages that existed between gender activists in civil society and the ANC, in particular (though importantly not solely) ANC women MPs, was crucial. In the first years of the new Parliament, gender equality was not prioritised as an area for legislative attention, despite the formal commitments. Legislation dealing with women's inequality was only placed on the parliamentary calendar in 1998, towards the end of the first term of Parliament, and only after high-level lobbying by the ANC Women's Caucus, with the support of progressive male MPs, including, by some accounts, President Mbeki. The legislation then had to be fast-tracked through the National Assembly so that the first Parliament would be seen to be concerned with gender equality as a substantive issue. The key advocates for the legislation were women MPs who would in all likelihood have been on the ANC list regardless of the quota, and male MPs who had a commitment to gender equality. Pressure to push the legislation through before the end of the first term came from gender activists outside the state. In the case of the Termination of Pregnancy Act, the proposed legislation was consistent with the ANC's health policy and with its electoral platform (the Reconstruction and Development Programme), which included reproductive rights. This pressure had been exerted within the ANC before quotas were introduced. The key interventions here related to processes of democratisation within the party, supported by constitutional commitments (notably also achieved through internal party pressure and constituency building rather than a politics of presence).

External pressure on Parliament was particularly evident in putting a Termination of Pregnancy Bill before Parliament. Pressure was exerted by the Reproductive Rights Alliance, which had been formed in 1995, in part to advocate for progressive pro-choice abortion legislation (Albertyn 1999). In 1996, the Reproductive Rights Alliance appointed a lobbyist to work in Parliament for the duration of the law reform process. Women's health and legal advocacy groups used the parliamentary hearings to push forward a pro-choice agenda. Albertyn comments that, 'the Committee hearings provided an opportunity for progressive organisations to develop and rekindle working relationships with former health and women's rights activists now in Parliament' (1999:71). Indeed, rather than interventions of women MPs *per se*, Albertyn's account of the politics surrounding this legislation suggests that it was the historical relationship of trust between activists outside government and the ANC that facilitated the passage of legislation.

While the reproductive rights example points to the value of the relationship between women activists in civil society and women in Parliament, the political process surrounding the Domestic Violence Act (1998) identifies the support of senior members of the ruling party as the critical lever. As with reproductive rights, violence against women was an area that had been highly organised prior to 1994. Meintjes (1999:137) points out that by 1995, links had been made between the 'violence lobby' and key people in government, especially the Minister of Welfare and Population Development Geraldine Fraser-Moleketi and the Deputy Minister of Justice Dr Manto Tshabalala-Msimang, both of whom were gender activists in the ANC. Advocates of legal reform were greatly assisted by the fact that the government had ratified CEDAW in December 1995, three months after the Beijing Conference. In line with CEDAW and the Beijing Platform for Action, the government was required to ensure that steps would be taken to eradicate violence against women. The government entered into a partnership programme with civil society organisations, resulting in the National Network on Violence Against Women, which included government departments and non-governmental organisations (NGOs). By early 1998, however, no Bill had been tabled before Parliament; nor did it seem likely that the Law Commission, responsible for overseeing the legislation, would be able to prepare a Bill before the end of the first government. The ANC Women's Caucus was able to secure the support of the (male) Minister of Justice and the (male) Chairperson of the Justice Portfolio Committee to expedite the production of a draft Bill (Meintjes 1999).

Although an array of institutions, known collectively as the national gender machinery, was created to give women access to decisio-making, in the first five years of democracy these were not influential in setting the policy agenda for gender equality. In terms of the legislative changes, Meintjes argued in regard to the Domestic Violence Act, that both the Commission on Gender Equality (CGE) and the Office of the Status of Women (OSW) were 'conspicuously ineffective' (1999:144). Lack of resources, institutional resistance and, not least, the reluctance of the leadership in the OSW to openly challenge the ruling party, undermined the effectiveness of the government machinery. However, the anti-political tendencies in the bureaucratic sphere were countered by the strong core of feminists in Parliament and in civil society, which in many cases bypassed the machinery to ensure legislative and policy change. As Albertyn, Goldblatt, Hassim, Mbatha and Meintjes argue, '"gender sensitive" women and men holding diverse positions of power and influence in state institutions were far more important in ensuring that gender issues were placed on the policy agenda' (1999:149). In particular, they found that the ability of feminist politicians to lobby successfully within the ruling party, and their networking capacities outside of government, outweighed the role of structures such as the OSW.

What of the CGE, the institutional centrepiece of the new national machinery? Set up with extensive statutory powers, the CGE 'appeared to offer remarkable promise for feminist intervention' (Seidman 2003:551). However, as Seidman (2003) has argued, for several years the CGE battled to define how the organisation should represent women, and on what issues they should be represented. Seidman argues that the CGE vacillated between a mobilising role and a representative role, neither of which in fact accurately captured the remit of its constitutional mandate to act as an oversight and accountability mechanism in relation to progress towards gender equality. CGE submissions on key policy issues were often poorly drafted; in High Court and Constitutional Court cases the CGE played a secondary role to NGOs. Appointments to the CGE have not always been based on the best available gender expertise. Rather, they seem to be driven by considerations of party loyalty and mobility as much as by a track record in gender activism.

In more recent years, however, there have been significant changes in the ways in which the national machinery works, spurred in part by heavy criticism at the National Gender Summit in 2001 and by women's organisations in civil society, and in part by new commissioners in the CGE and greater openness in the OSW. New decision-making procedures were put in place and a system for co-ordinated action around legislative and policy intervention appears to be working quite well.[6] As the discussion of the CLRB later on demonstrates, the CGE has also developed its 'voice' in relation to legislative and policy processes, and took the lead in challenging the Bill.

Conceptualising gender equality in key legislation

At a conceptual level, the extent to which gender-sensitive legislation and policies significantly advance equality, if this is understood as increasing women's choice and autonomy, is uneven. A number of 'victories' have been limited to women's rather than gender concerns. There have been gains in areas where women have clear and definable gender needs that do not impinge on (or impinge positively on) men's needs and interests (for example, maternal health), while areas in which attention to women's gender needs might challenge the power of some groups of men (for example, land rights) have been slower to change, or have not changed. Many of the gains that have been made in advancing gender equality are made on the basis of addressing 'family failures' and children's needs, rather than on directly empowering women. Thus, for example, free healthcare for women has been supported because maternal health is seen to be crucial (in an ironic twist, HIV-positive pregnant women get anti-retrovirals in doses large enough to protect the new-born baby but too small to be effective for the mother). Similarly, the Maintenance Act, which empowers the state to hold defaulting parents (mainly fathers) accountable for debts, has won support in government not least because it entrenches the notion of privatised responsibility for children. Discourses of violence against women can also easily fall back on notions of women's vulnerability and on the idea that the role of the state is to protect women and children when families fail.

Yet, despite these problematic assumptions underlying policy, the legislation has been claimed by women's organisations as a significant example of the benefits of increased representation. This is understandable in the context of the strong maternalist tradition in women's movement politics, in which women have been politically mobilised on the basis of their familial ideologies. There is indeed a consistency in the group-based difference strategy of quotas and the strategy of addressing women's group-based needs. In policy terms, this has translated into a demand for women's caring work to be validated as socially useful and as a legitimate basis for policy. However, as comparative welfare state literature shows, this kind of politics can have contradictory outcomes. Bolstered by feminist lobbies, the recognition for care work can lead to the introduction of state-sponsored or subsidised crèches and old people's homes, and for extensive maternity leave privileges (as in Britain, Norway and more recently Sweden) (Giullari & Lewis 2003). As Kathryn Sklar (1993) has noted, policies in relation to children's welfare, although often driven by women on the basis of a maternalist politics, can become 'an entering wedge for the extension of state responsibility to other groups' (1993:50). On the other hand, when these policies are supported by relatively conservative governments, as in the US, they lead to grants directed at children which do not shift ideologies of privatised and gendered caring.

In South Africa, a strong maternalist emphasis is particularly evident in social welfare policy. The *White Paper on social welfare*, gazetted in February 1996 and adopted in 1997, is an interesting example. In yoking the cultural concept of *'ubuntu'* (humanity) the White Paper signals the importance of cultural norms and values, particularly the principles of caring and mutual inter-dependence. However, the emphasis on the *cultural value* of caring is not accompanied by a recognition of the *work* of caring. This could be seen as loading the dice against women, who bear the practical burdens of care work within families and communities. As Lund, Ardington and Harber note, 'a double equation is at work which assumes that community care is equal to care by families which is equal to unpaid care by mostly women' (1996:115). Walker makes a similar point in relation to the ways in which community is conceptualised in land reform processes. She notes that, 'there are no clearly sexed (and sexual) beings in land reform. Instead there are "communities", within which the normative being is male, appended to which there is (from time to time) "gender" which refers, dimly, to women' (Walker 2003:127). The discussion of the CLRB later on demonstrates the extent to which an emphasis on community can deny the rights of women.

Obscuring women's specific burdens under the content-less rubric of gender has real consequences for how effectively the state is able to address those burdens, as well as for the extent to which social policy expenditures begin to shift relations of power between women and men. Women's caring burdens have, for example, increased dramatically as the HIV/AIDS infection rates have assumed pandemic proportions. The shift away from the language of rights and entitlements in the *White Paper on social welfare* would seem to dilute the particular (and greater) responsibility of the state in meeting social security needs through the redistribution of public resources. Since the adop-tion of the White Paper, moral discourses continue to infect social security provision, with criticisms that the child support grant is responsible for increasing teenage pregnancy (girls getting pregnant in order to access cash), that women are spending the money on 'clothing and lipstick' and that it has fostered a culture of dependency on handouts from the state. Newspaper reports castigate 'runaway mothers' who 'claim the child support grant meant to feed their offspring' (*Sunday Times* 23.02.03). Even the chairperson of the CGE had to be gently reminded by feminist activists not to fall into the trap of stereotyping women receiving the child support grants as undeserving.

These examples highlight the importance of recognising that state institutions and actors are embedded in social relations. The ideologies that derive from the organisation of gender relations in the family and community shape the ways in which policies are drafted and the assumptions, often hidden, which underlie particular policy paths. There is an interesting disarticulation between the assumptions of the gendered nature of care work in the *White Paper on social welfare* and the emphasis in the Constitution on women's autonomy. Care work is certainly 'recognised' in the White Paper, but that recognition is not presented as an opportunity to shift the burdens away from women. The caring model, while ostensibly valuing collective social responsibility, does not value the importance of women's autonomy from the expectations of family and community. Collective social responsibility is in effect privatised rather than made a responsibility of the state, and the opportunity to create the conditions for women to exercise their agency in a variety of social and economic arenas is lost.

The Communal Land Rights Bill

The real test of whether the representation model would work is to consider what would happen if women's organisations were to push for legislative changes that would directly challenge entrenched patriarchal interests – that is, to demand changes on the basis of their gender interests rather than women's needs. The contestations over the CLRB are an instructive case study in this regard, for a number of reasons. The contestation between women's organisations and traditional leaders dates to the Constitution-making period, when the principle of gender equality was opposed by some traditional leaders, setting the stage for a protracted conflict. The Constitution itself validated both equality and cultural autonomy, while placing equality as the 'trump' criterion in cases where both came into conflict. In the proposed new legislation in 2003 (the Traditional Leadership and Governance Framework Bill [hereafter referred to as 'the Framework Bill'], championed by the Portfolio Committee on Provincial and Local Government, and the CLRB, supported by the Portfolio Committee on Land and Agriculture), concerns about gender equality once again came up squarely against those of traditional leaders. At issue in this particular contest was the extent of traditional leaders' formal authority over land allocation in rural areas. The CLRB was set to become the biggest test of the extent to which a constituency of (rural) women could successfully defend their policy claims against other powerful interests.

Fairly soon after the first democratic elections, the new Minister of Land Affairs, Derek Hanekom, proposed the introduction of legislation that would shift control of trust land, including a significant proportion of land in KwaZulu-Natal held under the Ingonyama Trust, back to central government. Although the proposed legislation would include a variety of different forms of land and property, traditional leaders treated this as a direct attack on their traditional authority. Inkatha Freedom Party (IFP) leader Mangosuthu Buthelezi went as far as to call it a 'severe provocation' to the Zulu nation (*Mail & Guardian* 13.10.95). The opposition of traditional leaders was strong enough that the ANC feared an electoral backlash, particularly in KwaZulu-Natal, and the proposed legislation was shelved. After the 1999 elections, the new Minister of Land Affairs, Thoko Didiza, announced that a Land Rights Bill would be introduced in April 2001. Again the Bill was not published, although Minister Didiza undertook to publish the Bill following discussions at a national conference on land rights held in Durban in November 2001.

Discussions of the new CLRB at the Durban conference provoked deep divisions, even within the ANC. The Bill recognised 'communities' as juridical persons and proposed to transfer state land to communities. ANC MP Lydia Kompe-Ngwenya, a veteran land rights activist, rejected this proposal, arguing that the land rights of individual users and occupiers needed to be recognised and protected in law, in accordance with the Freedom Charter. Her party colleague, and leader of the Congress of Traditional Leaders of South Africa, Nkosi Patekile Holomisa, on the other hand, argued that the legal title to communal land should be bestowed on the traditional authority. For the traditional leaders, the Bill did not go far enough in securing traditional authority, as communities would now have rights. For women, on the other hand, the emphasis on communities reinstated the power of traditional leaders as they became the officially recognised representatives of community interests.

Traditional leaders vociferously opposed the eighth draft of the Bill, published in August 2002. This draft proposed the creation of land administration structures which would comprise community representatives as well as traditional leaders, although traditional leaders would only constitute 25 per cent of the council. Communities would be given discretion as to whether the land would be held by communal title or subdivided and registered in the names of individuals. The anger over this reallocation of land authority was so strong among some traditional leaders that many felt it would take violent forms.

The IFP Women's Brigade and Youth Brigade threatened retribution if the Bill went through Parliament. The *Sunday Times* (22.1.03) reported an Ulundi resident as saying, 'If the Bill is passed it will be understood that any tribe member who applies to own land can be killed or have their house burnt down. Many will be happy to strike the match.' Mbeki shifted from his conventional friendly tone to traditional leaders to warn that the government would not tolerate violence (*Mail & Guardian* 1.11.02).

Despite the President's firm warning, the threats of electoral retaliation and political violence in KwaZulu-Natal seemed to have an effect on legislators. In July 2003, an informal group of experts meeting in Pretoria warned that the government needed to prioritise land and agrarian reform to avoid political instability in South Africa (*Mail & Guardian* 31.7.03). At the same time, there was considerable pressure from civil-society actors to move ahead on finalising the Bill. In October that year a final draft of the Bill was published, this time containing last-minute alterations which provided that traditional councils, set up in line with the Framework Bill, would have powers of land administration, allocation, and ownership in communal areas. Cabinet endorsed the Bill and announced that it wanted the Bill enacted before the 2004 elections, leaving under a month for the Bill to pass through the appropriate parliamentary processes.

The issue of women's rights remained unresolved. The Framework Bill provided for 30 per cent representation of women in traditional councils. It also provided that, while 40 per cent of the members of the council were to be elected, the remaining 60 per cent 'must comprise traditional leaders and members of the traditional community selected by the principal traditional leaders concerned in terms of custom' (Section3[2][b]). The Bill also gave the Minister of Agriculture and Land Affairs discretionary powers to determine the nature and content of land rights, without their consultation or consent. This was in part a response to the concerns of women's organisations that gender equality issues might not be automatically taken into account, or might be overridden by the traditional councils. In these cases, the Minister would be able to confer rights to ownership or occupation on women. These changes were far from satisfactory for traditional leaders, who saw them as further eroding their authorities. Tensions – between the IFP and ANC in particular – escalated. Buthelezi claimed that the ANC had reneged on its agreements with the IFP before and after 1994, commenting that relations between the two parties 'have never been worse' (*Mail & Guardian* 15.11.03).

Despite the concessions to women's representation in the amendments to the Bill, reactions from women's organisations and land NGOs were equally vociferous, albeit without the threats of violence.[7] There is not the space in this chapter to detail the objections or to delineate the sometimes fine differences between various civil society groups. I will concentrate on the objections relating to women's rights. The key objections related to the failure of the Bill to protect the rights of rural women, the undemocratic nature of the traditional councils, and the entrenchment of the control of chiefs over key aspects of women's lives. Both the Programme for Land and Agricultural Studies (PLAAS) and the CGE, in their submissions in November 2003, argued that the Bill's aim to restore so-called 'old-order rights', which had become legally insecure as a result of apartheid laws, did not adequately address the demands of gender equality. Under customary law, as well as under apartheid law, women's rights in land were derivative and temporary. Women could not own land or occupy property in their own right, but were dependent on male spouses or customary partners. They lost these rights upon the death of the male spouse, in part also as a result of the principle of male primogeniture which required that property be passed to the nearest male relative. This principle was upheld as recently as 2000 by the Supreme Court of Appeal (Budlender 2003). PLAAS researchers found that most traditional leaders continue to refuse to allocate land to women. While earlier versions of the Bill had explicitly provided for the right to gender equality in respect of ownership, allocation, use of or access to land, this provision disappeared from the final version of the Bill. There was no longer any provision clearly banning discriminatory practices. Similarly, there is no injunction that the rules devised by communities to govern the administration of communal land must comply with the equality clause in the Bill of Rights, although earlier versions of the Bill did make such provisions (PLAAS 2003). Women's concerns were partially addressed by the Portfolio Committee: the proportion of women on the councils was raised, and the Minister's discretionary powers would include oversight with regard to gender discrimination.

However, the CGE and PLAAS opposed the discretionary power of the Minister in principle. The two concerns in this regard were, firstly, that gender equality, as an entrenched right, should not be subject to discretion, particularly in view of the many documented cases of male officials turning a blind eye to women's complaints (CGE submission), and secondly, that the discretionary power created the conditions for a potential abuse of power. Finally, a wide range of organisations opposed the proposal that traditional councils should be nominated rather than fully elected bodies. PLAAS (2003) pointed out that the Framework Bill 'gives tribal authorities perpetual life and the Communal Land Rights Bill gives them powers over land that surpass any that they previously enjoyed'. The organisation argued that 'it is very likely that the 30% quota will come from the royal family and be comprised of female relatives of the chief. Can women handpicked by chiefs really be relied on to represent the interests of ordinary rural women, and to address the legacy of gender discrimination against women practised under customary law?' (PLAAS 2003). The JMC pointed out that women would be a permanent minority on traditional councils, and requested that a quota of 50 per cent of seats be allocated. The CGE warned that the creation of non-elected bodies with decision-making power over women's access to key economic resources set up a form of secondary citizenship for black rural women, who would be discriminated against on the basis of both race and gender.

This rather truncated narrative of the debates around the CLRB raises crucial questions about the power of women's organisations and women's representatives in Parliament to successfully defend women's rights. Rural women have never been strongly organised in South Africa. In many instances, rural NGOs with dedicated feminist activists (such as the Association for Rural Advancement and the Transvaal Rural Action Committee [Trac]) spoke on behalf of rural women, and attempted to give profile to their specific concerns. However, there has been little independent organisation of women and in policy terms there was certainly not the kind of organisational base and resources that either the Reproductive Rights Alliance or the Network on Violence Against Women, for example, could draw on. In the late 1980s and early 1990s, the Rural Women's Movement (RWM) emerged, supported in the initial stages by TRAC. The RWM was able to make significant inputs to the Women's National Coalition and in the Constitution-making process, and acted as a national voice for rural women. However, by the time the Framework and Communal Land Rights Bills were introduced, the RWM was a virtually defunct organisation which had collapsed under the weight of financial and administrative problems. Local rural women's groups therefore lacked connection to urban-based policy debates. As Claassens and Ngubane (2003) point out, 'There are vibrant groups of rural women, keen and committed to supporting one another and organising around these issues. However, there are currently no resources available to enable rural women to come together on a regular basis to take these matters forward ... nor ... are there provincial or national rural women's organisations that can support and co-ordinate the process of organising rural women.'

Consultations with rural women over the Bills were facilitated by research organisations and NGOs such as Trac, PLAAS and the National Land Committee (NLC). This process was both enabling and problematic. It made it possible for rural women's concerns to be heard by the legislators in the absence of parliamentary hearings in rural areas. Rural women's concerns were thoroughly 'mainstreamed' in the PLAAS/NLC submission to Parliament. The CGE played a leading role in highlighting rural women's interests and concerns, testament to the more effective advocacy role it has adopted since 2002. However, the alliance with, and representation by, urban-based land rights NGOs also had drawbacks. Firstly, some of these NGOs were labelled by ANC MPs as 'ultra-left' critics and, while they had a strong voice, it was not always an influential voice. Various interviewees noted the subtle ways in which some NGO representatives were ignored and even belittled. Secondly, even with the best of intentions, NGOs did not always foreground issues of gender equality in their strategies. Finally, many of the urban-based activists were young, and age has emerged as an important issue in debates about customary law. Likhapha Mbatha, head of the Gender Research Project at the Centre for Applied Legal Studies (Cals), and presenter of the Cals submission to Parliament on the CLRB, points out that 'older people, rightly or not, perceived young activists as disrespectful. They didn't think young people had the right to talk to them in an angry way'.[8] This view was corroborated by other participants in the process, who pointed out that in pursuing changes in customary practices, strategies have to take into account issues of dress, tone and discourse very carefully.

Finally, what about the alliance with women inside Parliament? ANC women MPs did not appear to recognise the significance of the Bill until relatively late in the process. No objections were raised to the Bill in Cabinet and, of course, it was sponsored by a woman minister. However, when approached by the CGE and women's rights NGOs, the MPs did signal their concerns about the Bill. Naledi Pandor, chairperson of the National Council of Provinces, worked with women activists to facilitate debate about the Bill. The JMC made a submission to the Portfolio Committee on Land and Agricultural Affairs, laying out their objections to the Bill – a rare occurrence of one portfolio committee opposing another. The ANC Women's Caucus also voiced their objection to the Bill. However, when it came to voting in Parliament, there were no official abstentions among ANC women MPs. The Bill passed unanimously through the Portfolio Committee, Parliament and Cabinet. Several explanations have been offered for this degree of public support, despite the private reservations of ANC women MPs. The first is that there was little strategising in relation to the Bill early on in the process. The ANC Women's Caucus, which had been so effective in getting the controversial Termination of Pregnancy Act passed, did not take up the issue of rural women's rights in the CLRB. This might also have been a consequence of the poor organisation of women outside Parliament. Secondly, some have argued that women MPs had instructions 'from above' not to oppose the Bill. The finalisation of the Bill and its appearance before the National Assembly occurred while party electoral lists were being drawn up, and some activists have suggested that women MPs feared that they might be left off or pushed low down on the lists. One ANC MP argued that 'it didn't appear to be an opportune time to take on the party'. Ironically, some of the very factors that had assisted women activists with regard to the Termination of Pregnancy Act – the role of senior members of the Cabinet and the portfolio committees and the 'party line' of the ANC – now appeared to have worked against them. This has led one prominent feminist activist to question 'whether there is a strong anchor for gender activism in Parliament any more. We have lots of women in Parliament but I wonder how strongly they support women's interests when push comes to shove. Especially at election time the party is what matters'.

Women's organisations are currently debating whether to take the government to the Constitutional Court to challenge the legitimacy of the legislation. Legal opinions taken by the South African Human Rights Commission and the CGE both argue that the legislation violates the constitutional right to gender equality. Legal struggle is the only remaining avenue for those opposing the Bill.

Conclusion

The model of a virtuous circle of representation offers a helpful way to conceptualise the relationship between activism around gender equality at different sites in the state and civil society. However, South African experiences suggest that representation is most effective when there are strong forms of political participation and a clear vision of what kinds of gender equality are desirable.

If the gender laws in the first Parliament demonstrate the importance of the support of a strong political party for women's interests, the CLRB shows the cost that attaches to that factor. In this case, the party was subjected to conflicting pressures from a constituency hostile to women's interests, and moreover, it was a constituency that posed a perceived electoral threat. The women's vote, on the other hand, was relatively poorly mobilised, and in any case the party could rest on its track record of being the key promoter of gender equality. While women MPs might see themselves as organically linked to women's organisations in civil society, they placed considerable emphasis on intra-party debates and were aware of their need to survive within the party. The harsh lesson for women activists was that women MPs ultimately represent the party and are accountable to the party rather than directly to an electoral constituency.

The case of the CLRB highlights the importance of developing strong women's organisations in civil society. Without the pressure from outside, and without a strong articulation of the interests of different constituencies of women, the virtuous circle model is reduced to its thinnest form – that is, increased representation of women as a group without any concurrent representation of the policy interests of disadvantaged women.

Notes

1   I would like to thank Godfrey Chesang for his meticulous research assistance. This paper has also benefited from discussions with Catherine Albertyn, Likhapha Mbatha, Sheila Meintjes and Beth Goldblatt. The section of the chapter on the Communal Land Rights Bill (CLRB) also draws on interviews with a number of women activists and parliamentarians who do not wish to be quoted.

2   From the website of the Gender Advocacy Programme. Available at <http://www.gender.co.za/campaigns.htm>.

3   Elsewhere Catherine Albertyn and I have argued that even this conceptualisation of freedom is limited, as it fails to address the social and cultural dimensions of inequality (see Albertyn & Hassim 2003).

4   Orloff (1993:319) takes this argument much further in suggesting that social policies should aim at decommodification of gender relations by enabling women to form and maintain autonomous households. I am hesitant to apply this notion to women in the South African context, given the particular cultural attachments and support systems that women value within family and communities. It could also be argued that the high number of women-headed households in South Africa suggests that women are indeed free to form autonomous households, but this has patently not empowered women to become full and equal citizens.

5   Govender was the Project Manager of the Women's National Coalition and a leading union and women's organiser.

6   Commissioner Sheila Meintjes and Catherine Albertyn, personal communication.

7   The Landless People's Movement warned that it would encourage voters to boycott the 1994 elections if land redistribution processes were not speeded up.

8   Likhapha Mbatha, personal communication.

References

Albertyn C (1999) Reproductive health and the right to choose – policy and law reform on abortion. In C Albertyn et al. (eds.) *Engendering the political agenda: A South African case study*. Johannesburg: CALS & United Nations International Institute for Research and Training for the Advancement of Women.

Albertyn C, Goldblatt B, Hassim S, Mbatha L & Meintjes S (1999) *Engendering the political agenda: A South African case study*. Johannesburg: CALS & United Nations International Institute for Research and Training for the Advancement of Women.

Albertyn C & Hassim S (2003) The boundaries of democracy: Gender, HIV/AIDS and culture. In D Everatt & V Maphai (eds.) *The real state of the nation: South Africa after 1990*. Johannesburg: Interfund.

Ballington J (1998) Women's parliamentary representation: The effects of list PR, *Politikon* 25:7–93.

Britton H (1997) Preliminary report of participation: Challenges and strategies. Unpublished report. Syracuse University.

Budlender G (2003) Opinion on the Communal Land Rights Bill. Annexure to the Commission on Gender Equality, *Submission to the Portfolio Committee on Agriculture and Land Affairs*, 10.11.03.

CASE (Community Agency for Social Enquiry) (1999) *Synthesis report on the participation of women in Parliament researched for the European Union.* Braamfontein: CASE.

Claassens A & Ngubane S (2003) Rural women, land rights and the Communal Land Rights Bill. Draft paper presented at the Women's Legal Centre Advancing Women's Rights Conference, Cape Town, October.

Fick G, Meintjes S & Simons M (eds.) (2002) *One woman one vote.* Johannesburg: Electoral Institute of South Africa.

Fraser N (1997) *Justice Interruptus: Critical reflections on the 'postsocialist' condition.* New York: Routledge.

Giullari S & Lewis J (2003) The adult worker model family, gender equality and care: The search for new policy principles and the possibilities and problems of a capabilities approach. Unpublished paper prepared for UNRISD Project on Gender and Social Policy.

Goetz AM (2003) Women's political effectiveness: A conceptual framework. In AM Goetz and S Hassim (eds.) *No shortcuts to power: African women in politics and policymaking.* London: Zed.

Goetz AM & Hassim S (2003) Women in power in Uganda and South Africa. In AM Goetz and S Hassim (eds.) *No shortcuts to power: African women in politics and policymaking.* London: Zed.

Gouws A (ed.) (2004 forthcoming) *Unthinking citizenship.* Cape Town: UCT Press.

Hassim S (2003) The gender pact and democratic consolidation: Institutionalising gender equality in the South African state, *Feminist Studies* 29:505–528.

Lund F with Ardington S & Harber M (1996) Welfare. In D Budlender (ed.) *The Women's Budget.* Cape Town: Idasa.

Mahon R & Jenson J (1993) Representing solidarity: Class, gender and the crisis of social democratic Sweden, *New Left Review* 201:76–100.

Meintjes S (1999) The state, civil society and gender violence: A case study of the Domestic Violence Act. In C Albertyn et al. (eds.) *Engendering the political agenda: A South African case study.* Johannesburg: CALS & United Nations International Institute for Research and Training for the Advancement of Women.

Mtintso TE (1999) The contribution of women parliamentarians to gender equality. Unpublished MA thesis, University of the Witwatersrand.

Orloff AS (1993) Gender and the social rights of citizenship: The comparative analysis of gender relations and welfare states, *American Sociological Review* 58:303–328.

PLAAS (Programme for Land and Agrarian Studies) (2003) *Submission to the Portfolio Committee for Land and Agriculture.* Cape Town, 10.11.03.

Seidman G (2003) Institutional dilemmas: Representation versus mobilization in the South African Gender Commission, *Feminist Studies* 29:541–563.

Sklar K (1993) The historical foundations of women's power in the creation of the American welfare state, 1830–1930. In S Koven & S Michel (eds.) *Mothers of a new world: Maternalist politics and the origins of welfare states.* New York: Routledge.

Walker C (2003) Piety in the sky? Gender policy and land reform in South Africa, *Journal of Agrarian Change* 3:113–148.

Part III: Economy

Economy: introduction

John Daniel, Roger Southall and Jessica Lutchman

'It's the economy, stupid' is the slogan made famous by Bill Clinton during his first presidential campaign in 1991. What it conveyed was the fact that, whatever other issues were germane, the state of the national economy almost invariably determined the outcome of US elections. Did the electorate feel, or would they feel, better off under this Democratic or that Republican candidate? Even though elections in South Africa are not yet solely determined by issues economic, there can be no doubting that matters economic are central to political life in South Africa today. Indeed, there are those who suggest that the very success of the democratic transition hinges on whether the new order in South Africa can deliver a better life to enough South Africans to forestall a backlash from those who remain stuck in penury and without hope. It is for this reason that the editors determined on a more comprehensive economics section in this volume than that in the first volume.

The section begins with Stephen Gelb's overview of the economy's performance since the transition of May 1994. He opens by quoting the Presidency's own assessment of the economy's ten-year growth performance, which it described as 'mediocre' and 'unspectacular'. He shares this view, but locates it in an analysis of the immediate post-apartheid political economy and how that shaped and limited the new regime's policy choices. He argues that the negotiations process produced an 'implicit bargain' between (white) big business and the African National Congress (ANC), 'involving the ANC committing to macroeconomic stability and international openness and business agreeing to participate in "capital reform" to modify the racial structure of asset ownership'. This accommodation, Gelb suggests, laid the foundation for the two dominant features of South African economic life these last ten years – the embrace by the ANC of neo-liberal orthodoxy in the form of tight monetary and fiscal policies (from the Reconstruction and Development Programme [RDP] to the Growth, Employment and Redistribution [GEAR] strategy) and black economic empowerment (BEE). Both of these issues are also examined in detail in the contributions by Rumney and Southall.

Gelb explores some of the fallout from this accommodation with capital – the strains within the Tripartite Alliance and the sidelining of the labour movement, currency volatility and foreign-exchange crises. These difficulties notwithstanding, Gelb identifies South Africa's post-apartheid fiscal policies as a success, producing, *inter alia*, more effective financial planning and expenditure management, and increased levels of tax collection. The net effect has been a steady reduction of the inherited fiscal deficit. Gelb argues that this lowered debt level has, since 2001, enabled government to adopt a more expansionary fiscal stance in the form of increased levels of public expenditure and a reduction of interest rates and the tax burden.

Gelb is less flattering about South Africa's post-apartheid monetary and exchange policies, which he regards as having been inconsistent and initially over-ambitious, pursuing goals which were unattainable. Gelb tracks the inevitable policy shifts as government sought to achieve these goals, before moving on to a sectoral analysis of South Africa's macroeconomic performance. With average incomes growing since 1994 at only 0.44 per cent, he describes the economy as being trapped in a 'low-growth path' while levels of new foreign direct investment (FDI) in the same period have 'disappointed'. This slack in investment inflow, Gelb argues, has not been met either by public-sector contributions or by national savings, both of which have been at levels lower than those required. Given the at best moderate achievements of South Africa's monetary and exchange policies, Gelb suggests that the fact that South Africa ended its first decade of democratic rule with a current account which, since 1999, 'has been more or less in balance', and debt and interest levels lower than those of ten years ago, is a tribute to the success of its fiscal policies.

Reg Rumney's article examines ownership patterns in South Africa, analysing how and to what extent they have changed since 1994. At the outset, he poses the tantalising question as to 'who should own South Africa?' but leaves that to the reader to decide. The picture Rumney paints is a complex one in which he suggests that in some areas ownership patterns have changed significantly but little in others. The state – directly and through its parastatals – still owns some 20 to 25 per cent of South Africa's land, and state-owned enterprises (SOEs) such as Transnet, Telkom and Eskom, 'continue to be at the heart of the economy'. He argues that privatisation has not 'been pursued with any vigour'. Rumney suggests that it is only in the area of suburban property that there has been visible change, with the black middle class evacuating the townships for the formerly white suburbs.

Space does not permit a detailed summary of this important macro-analysis but it is worth noting Rumney's conclusion, particularly with regard to the foreign presence in the economy:

> The South African obsession with race has obscured the increasing foreign ownership of the economy and increasing concentration within sectors. For better or worse, our biggest firms have their headquarters overseas and foreigners own much bigger chunks than they used to. Foreign ownership of property in wine farms and beachfront homes in Cape Town has soared, though this pales into comparison with the substantial ownership foreigners have of the JSE Securities Exchange.

Little wonder then that the debate over the emotive issue of foreign ownership has surfaced recently.

In her article, Miriam Altman returns to the themes of employment and un-employment explored in the 2003 edition. In this 2004 volume, she addresses the issue of job-creating growth and whether South Africa is experiencing this phenomenon. She argues that unemployment and employment are not nec-essarily inversely related, and that the South African case illustrates that it is possible to experience both phenomena simultaneously. Their relationship depends on the rate of employment growth in relation to that of the labour force and the working-age population. In tracing the experience of employ-ment and unemployment in South Africa between 1996 and 2002, Altman argues that the rate of unemployment creation has been too slow in relation to the requirements of a sustainable growth path.

The other three articles in this section adopt a more microeconomic perspective and address issues central to the government's anti-poverty project – income disparities and the provision of services in the form of housing, water, electric-ity and sanitation.

Roger Southall identifies the goals of BEE as being an increase in black owner-ship, control and management of state, parastatal and private economic activity. This he sees as part of a broad state-driven interventionist strategy designed to overcome the dual nature of the South African political economy (rich white, poor black). He tracks how over time the state's pursuit of BEE has shifted from persuasion to assertion and regulation and, in the process, he examines the possibilities for the emergence of 'crony capitalism', in which the prime beneficiaries of BEE are ANC heavyweights and those connected to them. While Southall finds the case here as being still open and fluid, he concludes that there is a need to harden the 'present porous borders between state and black business' and to solidify the distinction between the practice of politics and economics.

Benjamin Roberts reviews the achievements and shortcomings of the government's poverty policies over the last decade and outlines possible trajectories for poverty alleviation in the next ten years. He shows that – despite irrefutable evidence of an improvement in the quality of life for some – high levels of poverty and inequality persist. To ameliorate this situation, Roberts argues for an improvement in what he calls the 'reach, reasoning and range of anti-poverty policies'. By reach, he means those groupings within the ranks of the disadvantaged not yet touched by the state's unfolding social net; his use of the term 'reasoning' involves a plea for a more accommodating attitude by government to criticism; while 'range' refers to a need for increased public participation in poverty 'policymaking'.

Finally, David Hemson and Kwame Owusu-Ampomah assess the status of the government's ambitious post-1994 service-delivery plans. While they concede that much that is positive has been achieved, overall they conclude that the delivery of basic services has been uneven and less dramatic than anticipated. They also express reservations about the adequacy and sustainability of some of the services provided. They attribute the slow pace of delivery to the inability of the poor to meet the costs of operating and maintaining the services provided or on offer, and this, of course, is linked in turn to issues of employment and income. In the final analysis, the authors argue, the backlog in service provision comes down to a question of sustainability. As they put it, 'the mediating factor between service delivery and poverty alleviation is employment which ... remains elusive to many South Africans.'

What these five chapters all point to is the political centrality of the assault on poverty in South Africa. This is a battle that has to be won and it is for this very reason that the editors in the overall introduction to this volume identified President Mbeki's second 'State of the Nation' speech, and the targets laid out therein, as of such significance to the future of South Africa and its democratic project.

14 An overview of the South African economy

Stephen Gelb

In its review of the decade since 1994, the government was unable to reach a clear conclusion about South Africa's economic growth record, arguing that, 'in comparison to strong growing economies, it is a mediocre performance, although it is steady but unspectacular compared with most developing economies' (PCAS 2003:35). The average rate of growth between 1994 and 2003 was in fact 2.77 per cent per annum, but since population growth averaged 2 per cent, the annual *per capita* increase was barely positive at 0.77 per cent per annum. This is indeed 'unspectacular', and with an unemployment rate in 2003 of 42.1 per cent (on the broad definition), a 'mediocre' rating is not unjustified.

This paper examines economic policy and performance primarily at the macroeconomic level, with some reference to sectoral and enterprise issues. But I start with some brief (given space limitations) comments on post-apartheid political economy which has framed economic policymaking.

The political economy of growth in post-apartheid South Africa

The most common explanation of economic policy choices over the past decade focuses on the inadequacies of the African National Congress (ANC) leadership: one or both of a lack of will, that is, the abandonment or 'sell-out' of liberation movement principles in favour of wealth and power accumulation for a few cronies; or a lack of skill, that is, the inability to use its political power to introduce progressive policies, against the wishes if necessary of reluctant democrats in the white and business communities (Bond 2000; Marais 1998; Terreblanche 2003). The result of either analysis is the same: political defeat for progressive forces signified by the dropping of the Reconstruction and Development Programme (RDP) and the adoption of the Growth, Employment and Redistribution (GEAR) strategy, and a commitment by government to pro-market policies. Focusing on 'agency' at the expense of 'structure', these arguments ignore the nature and distribution of economic and political power in South Africa at the point of transition, and the structural problems – crisis – which beset the economy for two decades prior to the transition. While it provided (black) interest groups with new political resources, shifting the terms of their engagement in the policy debate, the transition was not a *tabula rasa* in which any policy option could be chosen. Instead, political and economic imperatives ruled out some options and weighted choices towards others, in other words, these imperatives defined the parameters of the policy debate.

On the one hand, both economic and political imperatives pushed economic policy towards international openness. Profitability and productivity problems in the manufacturing sector were reflected in trade and balance of payments problems from the 1970s, which were heightened by international commodity price volatility and trade sanctions. Even worse, the financial 'sanctions' imposed in the mid-1980s meant that capital inflows were no longer available to finance current account deficits. Whatever the growth strategy during the 1990s, its sustainability would depend upon relaxing the external constraints, in other words, a significant increase in exports and capital inflows. Policy to raise exports needed to address production costs and international competitiveness, while increasing capital inflows depended on re-entry to international capital markets for South Africa. Thus there was also a political imperative for international openness in post-apartheid South Africa: the shift in the late 1980s by South African business to support negotiations was motivated by a desire to end sanctions, especially in finance, which depended on successful democratisation. With the ascendance of big business, which ironically had occurred in the context of economic decline and greater class differentiation, business' support was critical in reaching the point of transition. The form of the transition – negotiations rather than an overthrow of the apartheid state – reflected the prevailing balance of class power, and implied recognition of whites' inclusion in the social structure and their property rights. Thus business demands helped to frame the negotiation process, and a resumption of capital inflows was one of the top priorities.

On the other hand, there were social and political imperatives to reverse racial discrimination in the distribution of wealth, income and goods and services in both public and private sectors. The top priority in deracialising economic power was 'capital reform' (equivalent to land reform), or opening the owner-ship and management of private corporations and the direction of state insti-tutions and public corporations to the black middle classes, who were certain to be the most mobile distributionally in the transition, obtaining access to power, influence and remuneration. The negotiated nature of the transition meant that capital reform would necessarily be an incremental, market-focused process, engaging with current owners of capital. A second imperative was the reallocation of public expenditure on goods and services to reflect the racial composition of the population, to address social exclusion and poverty.

These imperatives underpinned what I have called an 'implicit bargain' or accommodation between white big business and the ANC, involving the ANC committing to macroeconomic stability and international openness, and business agreeing to participate in 'capital reform' to modify the racial structure of asset ownership, which would come to be called 'black economic empowerment' (BEE). The broad outlines of this accommodation emerged in 1990, and policy planning and implementation of trade and financial liberal-isation began well before the 1994 elections. By the end of 1994, inflation was down to single digits, fiscal deficit targeting had been explicitly adopted, Reserve Bank independence had been included in the interim Constitution, GATT commitments on trade liberalisation were formally agreed, legislation opening the banking system and the Johannesburg Stock Exchange (JSE) to international participation had been passed, and the plan for gradual relaxation of capital controls designed (Gelb 1999a; Gelb & Black 2004a).

Thus the debates which took place in the early 1990s about economic models for the 'new South Africa' – the basic needs model usually identified with the RDP, and the export-led manufacturing model usually identified with neo-liberalism – took place *within the framework* of this accommodation, and the RDP was itself formulated at the same time as policies for international open-ness. Though the policy specifics were of course influenced by the reigning international conventional wisdom on economic policy – in the early 1990s, obtaining private international capital required trade and capital account liberalisation and macroeconomic stability – the need for capital inflows and reform of ownership and control of capital arose from South Africa's eco-nomic and political realities. The basic needs approach could not satisfy the accommodation, not simply because it did not fit the current orthodoxy, but also because it did not credibly address the external constraint on growth sustainability – it focused on manufacturing for domestic consumer markets, and was at best ambiguous about short- to medium-term external constraints – while its approach to capital reform (far-reaching challenges to property rights, such as breaking up the major business conglomerates) could not win business consent (Gelb 1990).

On the other hand, the export-led model *formally* addressed the requirements, and its essential elements were implemented early on. The combination of macroeconomic stability and international openness, on one hand, with BEE, on the other, aimed to build mutual trust between 'old South African' business and new political stakeholders, creating an environment for generalised gains through rising fixed investment and sustainable growth, and reinforcing the alliance between them.

Macroeconomic policy post-apartheid

There were two flaws in the logic underlying the 'political economy of growth' defined during the transition. One was the absence of 'feedback' within the growth model from distribution (taking the form of BEE) to investment to support growth. The other was that the accommodation was implicit and informal, and its link with rising private fixed investment (and hence growth) unenforceable, since investment rests on decentralised corporate decisions rather than collective action by firms. Individual firms had to be persuaded of the new regime's commitment to the accommodation with business, leading to a risk of co-ordination failure as firms held back from investment in the face of uncertainty about the stability and predictability of policy and about other firms' strategies.

The new government inherited relative price stability but a difficult fiscal position. Following a fierce policy-induced recession between 1989 and 1993, inflation was down to single digits, after cycling around 15 per cent since 1973. But politically-related spending – higher public service salaries and massive pension payouts as the National Party (NP) prepared to exit government, vote-catching expenditure on social services for blacks, and rising police spending to maintain law and order – meant the fiscal deficit rose from 1.4 per cent of gross domestic product (GDP) in 1991, to 7.3 per cent in 1992 and 10.1 per cent in 1993, and government debt from 29 per cent of GDP in 1990–91 to 48 per cent in 1995–96 (see Figure 14.1 on p 373).

Table 14.1 *Government budget: size and distribution*

	1990/1	1995/6	1998/9	2001/2	2002/3	2003/4[a]	2004/5[b]	2005/6[c]	2006/7[c]
Growth, real non-interest expenditure (%)	n.a.	n.a.	-5.1	7.1	6.7	9.5	5.0	4.3	3.4
Percent of GDP									
Current non-interest expenditure	23.2*	23.6	22.5	22.2	22.9	24.9	25.0	25.1	24.6
Interest expenditure	4.3*	5.9	5.7	4.7	4.1	3.9	3.8	3.7	3.6
Capital expenditure	1.7*	1.6	0.8	1.1	1.2	1.3	1.3	1.4	1.3
Net government debt	29.0	48.0	47.6	42.1	36.3	36.8	38.0	38.8	39.0
Percentage share of budget									
Education	18	21	22	20	20	20	20	19	19
Health	9	10	11	11	11	11	11	11	11
Social security, welfare	6	10	12	12	14	15	16	16	17
Housing, other soc services	13	5	3	4	4	5	5	5	5
Social services (total)	46	46	48	48	49	50	51	51	52
Protection services	20	17	16	17	17	17	16	16	16
Economic services	14	11	9	11	12	13	13	13	13
Interest	12	19	20	17	15	13	13	13	13
Other	8	7	8	7	6	7	6	6	6
Total	100	100	100	100	100	100	100	100	100
Shares of total tax revenue									
Company income tax	21.5	13.9	16.4	23.6	26.1	25.6	n.a.	n.a.	n.a.
Personal income tax	33.6	40.2	42.1	35.8	33.4	32.4	n.a.	n.a.	n.a.
VAT	25.4	25.7	23.8	24.2	24.9	26.7	n.a.	n.a.	n.a.
Other	19.4	20.2	17.7	16.3	15.6	15.2	n.a.	n.a.	n.a.
Total	100.0	100.0	100.0	100.0	100.0	100.0	100.0	100.0	100.0

Source: Author's calculations from National Treasury (various years) *Budget review*
Notes: Fiscal years, ending March 31. a estimated. b budgeted. c projected. n.a. = not available. * 1991–92.

Given the ANC's historical orientation towards socialism, and its political base amongst the working classes and the poor, it sought to convince international and domestic investors of its commitment to openness and macroeconomic stability – 'build credibility' – by stressing continuity in macroeconomic policy, retaining both the contractionary stance and the Reserve Bank Governor (Stals) and Minister of Finance (Keys, who had introduced fiscal deficit targeting in 1993). Macroeconomic policy was effectively separated from the RDP, and ANC ministers publicly committed to fiscal stringency in 1994, stressing that expenditure reprioritisation would occur within lower public debt and fiscal deficit levels. This reflected the orthodox strategy of insulating fiscal decisions from popular political pressures. Similar considerations resulted in ANC leaders explicitly ignoring the Congress of South African Trade Unions (Cosatu) in 1996 when formulating the GEAR policy which reinforced the 'fiscal discipline' stance. The labour movement's exclusion from this, and subsequent macroeconomic policy processes, was perhaps successful with portfolio investors, but since labour remained an active constituent of the ruling alliance, the resulting political infighting within the alliance heightened uncertainty about the *long-term* stability and predictability of economic policy, producing the very opposite of the intended effect on fixed capital formation.

Secondly, as many other 'emerging markets' have found after embracing financial openness, efforts to build credibility by adopting and sticking to the 'right' policies – tight monetary and fiscal policies favoured by portfolio investors, restricting aggregate demand even when domestic cyclical conditions support a more relaxed approach – have not enabled South Africa to avoid the volatility and destabilisation associated with external capital flows. Macroeconomic conditions have been dominated by three foreign exchange crises involving a capital flow reversal and exchange-rate collapse, in 1996, 1998 and 2001. The inconsistent signals to producers provided by interest-rate and exchange-rate fluctuations have undermined any positive growth impact of successful stabilisation of the fiscal deficit and inflation rate.

Thus building credibility has been much slower than expected, particularly with investors in the real economy. Despite private profitability and productivity improving significantly, private investment – and therefore growth – have been sluggish. In the rest of this section, I look in more detail at fiscal policy, monetary policy and exchange-rate policy.

Fiscal policy: the success story

Fiscal policy must be regarded as one of the major successes in the post-apartheid era, in terms of meeting its own objectives. The National Treasury has completely reconstructed the budgetary and expenditure processes. Though this was partly imposed by new post-1994 sub-national provincial and local government structures, the Treasury has gone well beyond this aspect, introducing new systems of financial planning, expenditure management, reporting and accountability. Since 1997–98, budgeting has taken place within a medium-term expenditure framework (MTEF), a three-year rolling framework intended to provide greater certainty to line departments to plan and implement policy programmes, which are budgeted and evaluated on the basis of output-linked performance indicators rather than on inputs. For the Treasury it enables a combination of aggregate fiscal restraint with strategic reprioritisation for allocative efficiency. The MTEF is supported by the Public Finance Management Act (PFMA) passed in 1999, which imposes strong controls over financial management in all public sector institutions, with stiff penalties for transgressions. The PFMA requires departments to set measurable objectives for their spending, including details of outputs and service delivery indicators. The Treasury has imposed stringent discipline on provincial governments which have overspent budgets, though at the same time, many departmental budgets, at both national and provincial levels, have been underspent due to capacity constraints in the public sector.

Figure 14.1 *Fiscal balances as share of GDP, 1990–2003*

Percentage GDP

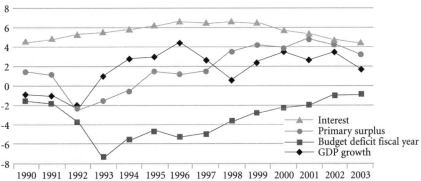

These reforms have contributed to the steady decline, since 1994, in the fiscal deficit, and since 1999 it has been kept below 3 per cent of GDP, as spelled out in GEAR (Figure 14.1). This was one of the only GEAR targets achieved, perhaps reflecting that a powerful ministry had direct control over the policy variable. Figure 14.1 also illustrates the inconsistent increase in the primary surplus (revenue less non-interest expenditure), which is one index of the fiscal policy stance *vis-à-vis* GDP growth; comparing their movements shows erratic shifts between pro- and anti-cyclical stances. In a context of sudden capital flow reversals and exchange-rate declines, fiscal policy cannot easily be used to stabilise activity levels in the real economy.

Government argues that since 2001, 'a more expansionary fiscal stance has been adopted' (National Treasury 2004:56), and real growth in non-interest expenditure grew 7.8 per cent per annum on average over the next three years, after real cuts of almost 2 per cent per annum the previous three years (Table 14.1). However, the primary surplus has actually declined since 2001, suggesting policy has remained contractionary, rather than becoming expansionary as advertised (Figure 14.1). For the 2004–5 fiscal year, with growth expected to dip below 2 per cent, a large real increase of 5 per cent in non-interest spending is budgeted, pushing the deficit above the threshold to 3.2 per cent (National Treasury 2004:67). Over the cycle as a whole though, the 3 per cent deficit target remains in place. Table 14.1 also shows that since 1999–2000, public debt levels have been substantially reduced from levels close to 50 per cent of GDP to below 40 per cent, where there need be little concern about sustainability.

Lowered debt levels have helped to bring down interest expenditure, though lowered nominal interest rates have been more significant here. Capital expenditure by government has been cut to make room within the budget for the increased share of social spending. Van der Berg (2001) shows that between 1993 and 1997, overall per capita social spending increased 23.8 per cent in real terms, with significant redistribution across income and racial categories: per capita spending on the lowest income quintile increased 28 per cent, and on the next two quintiles, 56 per cent and 31 per cent respectively. Allocations to social security and welfare increased dramatically, but at the expense of housing. In contrast, capital spending dropped to very low levels, and investment spending for the overall public sector fell below 5 per cent of GDP from 1992, compared with an average of 10 per cent during the 1980s (see Figure 14.7). It can be argued that the Treasury's successful institutional reforms have privileged the financial dimension of public expenditure over its substantive outcomes.

The substantial improvement in revenue collection has been essential in making fiscal policy successful in its own terms. The South African Revenue Service (SARS) was given organisational autonomy from the Treasury in 1997, and has since reorganised and modernised itself, resulting in increased efficiency in revenue collection, greater compliance by taxpayers and a significant widening of the tax base. Efficiency improvements are reflected in the smaller backlog of unassessed returns at the end of the tax-year: in March 1998, the backlog was 49 per cent of the 4.69 million returns, but in March 2003, it was only 5.4 per cent (SARS 1998, 2003). Compliance measures include risk-profiling of taxpayers, more extensive and integrated taxpayer auditing, improved enforcement and debt collection. The number of taxpayers in the tax base has been widened substantially: over the four years from 1998–99 to 2002–03, the number of individual and company income taxpayers each grew an average of around 12 per cent per annum. There may still be much room for further growth: in 1998, SARS estimated (probably conservatively) that the tax base in South Africa comprised 5.3 million individual taxpayers, 13 per cent of the population, but in 2003, only 3.9 million taxpayers filed returns.

Tax revenue declined as a share of GDP during the early 1990s, reaching a low of 22.6 per cent in 1995–96. It then increased and since 2001–2 has been maintained just below the GEAR-specified ceiling of 25 per cent (24.8 per cent in 2003–4). Government has had a formal commitment to promote growth and employment through private investment, and officials have often expressed the view that tax cuts on company profit (income) are the most effective mechanism to increase investment. Surprisingly then, the strong per-formance on the revenue side of the budget has been directed to tax cuts for the middle and formally-employed working classes, enabling these groups to increase their consumption spending, rather than to possible alternatives which might directly or indirectly – via provision of public goods and services, or increased private investment to create jobs – have benefited the informally employed and unemployed. According to the Treasury, R72.8 billion in tax relief has been given since 1994–95, of which R62.8 billion (86 per cent) has gone to individuals and only R6 billion to companies (National Treasury 2004:79). Table 14.1 shows that the relative contribution of company income tax first fell and then rose during the 1990s, while the share of personal income tax increased substantially to a peak of 42.6 per cent in 1999–2000, before falling as a result of tax relief. Over the six years to 2003–04, the income tax burden – the share of aggregate personal income paid in tax – fell from almost 15 per cent to below 12 per cent, while the value of total revenue collected in personal income tax paid fell by an average 0.9 per cent per annum in real terms, despite the growth in the tax base and improvement in tax collection efficiency. At the same time, revenue from company income tax grew by 12.3 per cent per annum in real terms.

Monetary and exchange rate policy: moving goalposts

Monetary and exchange-rate policy should be considered together with each other and with capital account liberalisation, because capital mobility places limits on monetary and exchange-rate policies. In general, macroeconomic policymakers in any economy would choose, if they could, to have an open capital market to enable access to external finance, a stable nominal exchange rate to underpin international trade, and the freedom to adjust interest rates via monetary policy to achieve domestic objectives such as output growth or price stability. The problem is that these three goals constitute a 'trilemma': achieving all three simultaneously is not possible, at least not in the medium to long term, and policy authorities must decide which two to prioritise and abandon the third (Obstfeld 1998).

Capital account liberalisation from March 1995 re-posed this choice, and subsequent monetary and exchange-rate policy can be divided into two phases. During the first phase, policymakers tried to pursue all three objectives, an inevitably unsustainable strategy, and by September 1998, the costs of trying to avoid the trilemma had become too high. In the second phase, from mid-1998, exchange-rate stability has been abandoned in favour of monetary policy autonomy in the form of inflation targeting.

From the early 1990s until 1999, the Reserve Bank set formal targets for money supply (M3) growth, though in practice monetary policy was 'eclectic' (its term) with the nominal exchange rate sometimes also implicitly targeted. High interest rates were used to lower inflation, together with a slowly depreciating nominal exchange rate to stabilise the real exchange rate for export competitiveness (Figures 14.2 and 14.4). Prior to the 1994 elections, South Africa's

Figure 14.2 *Exchange rate volatility, 1982–2003, percentage change in effective rates, quarterly*

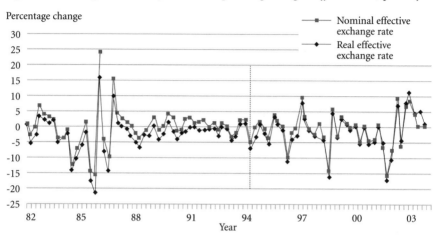

capital account had of course been closed. Exchange controls restricting capital outflows were in place on and off from 1961, and were re-imposed during the debt standstill in 1985, together with the dual exchange rate (commercial and financial rand rates), which discouraged disinvestment by foreigners. The removal of restrictions on South Africans' investing abroad was a major concern for domestic business as part of the re-entry to global financial markets. In his annual address in August 1994, the Reserve Bank Governor responded to the pressure for the early and total removal of controls by re-affirming the Bank's commitment to their removal, but in an orderly and gradual process of financial reintegration (Stals 1994).

But even with the capital account still closed, South Africa experienced massive capital inflows in the wake of the 1994 election, fulfilling the expectation that democratisation would relieve the growth constraint. Between July 1994 and June 1995, a *net* R18.6 billion flowed in to the economy, around 3.8 per cent of GDP, compared with the accumulated net outflow of R50 billion between 1985 and 1993 (Stals 1995). Given its size, the inflow was undoubtedly driven in part by supply factors, that is, pressure within the global financial markets for funds to find profitable outlets, especially within emerging markets in the wake of the Mexican crisis from late 1994. Notwithstanding the need for external capital to sustain long-term growth, the size, rapidity and composition of inflows (mainly into short-term assets) alarmed the Reserve

Bank: its efforts to lower inflation and enhance international competitiveness could be undone by excessive money supply growth and pressure for currency appreciation.

The Bank began to emphasise these *disadvantages* of capital inflows. But though it referred approvingly to controls on capital inflows adopted in other emerging markets, it opted instead for capital account liberalisation in March 1995, as a strategy to reduce the size of *net* short-term inflows, by offsetting large *gross* inflows with capital outflows. The dual exchange rate was unified to remove restrictions on non-residents' transactions, and a series of steps begun (and are still ongoing) towards the relaxation of restrictions on residents' foreign investment. For the Reserve Bank, the unified exchange rate carried the additional substantial advantage that capital inflows would now occur on the same basis as commercial transactions, adding to forex reserves and enabling the reduction of its 'forward book' and 'net open foreign currency position', which posed major risks to the policy authorities.[1] In the next 12 months, the net open foreign currency position (NOFP) was reduced by about two-thirds from US$25.8 billion to US$8.5 billion (Mboweni 2004).

The strategy was based on the assumption (hope?) of ongoing large capital inflows with a longer-term maturity profile, to avoid the dangers of net outflows. This was remarkably optimistic, more so in light of the Mexican peso crisis from December 1994, the first big emerging market financial crisis of the 1990s globalisation. Furthermore, although South Africa's liberalisation strategy has been praised for being gradual (IMF 1997),[2] the freeing of foreigners' transactions in a once-off 'big bang' led to a substantial increase in capital-flow volatility, underlined by three foreign exchange crises with a destabilising impact on real output growth. Figure 14.2 clearly shows wider fluctuations and increased volatility in quarterly changes in the nominal exchange rate after 1994, impacting directly on the real rate also. The three troughs reflect the forex crises: in 1996, triggered by domestic political uncertainty though government may have shared the then-consensus that the Rand was overvalued and been planning a devaluation; in 1998, in the wake of the Asian crisis; and in 2001, when the causes remain unclear despite the Myburgh inquiry.

Figure 14.3 shows quarterly levels of gross capital inflows, again suggesting instability after 1994, particularly of portfolio investment. The greater size of

Figure 14.3 *Capital inflows, quarterly 1990–2003*

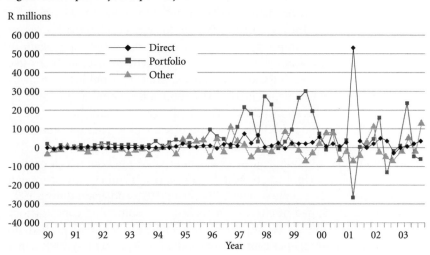

R millions

portfolio inflows compared with direct and 'other' investment (mainly bank loans) is related in part to the sequencing of liberalisation. Direct investment, the banking system and equity and bond markets were all opened at about the same time, in line with the prevailing international consensus, though also perhaps reflecting a lack of policy co-ordination in the transitional state. By the late 1990s, the international consensus had shifted to recommend first liberalising direct investment, the 'least footloose' flow, and the various financial markets much later (Eichengreen 2000). But relying on direct investment inflows would have meant much smaller inflows with limited impact on either the external constraint on growth or the South African Reserve Bank's forward book.

Notwithstanding capital account liberalisation in March 1995, the Reserve Bank continued to pursue its existing policy goals of cutting inflation, together with nominal exchange-rate stability (or, at most, slow depreciation) to maintain a competitive real exchange-rate. This implied a combination of high real interest rates and some 'sterilisation' of net capital inflows to limit money supply growth. In other words, the Bank attempted to pursue both monetary and exchange-rate targets, despite having shifted to an open capital account. Such evasion of the trilemma was possible while net capital inflows were sufficient to finance current account deficits and reduce the Bank's forward forex exposure, which was the case between March 1995 and January 1996, and again from September 1996 through April 1998. But the open capital market meant that net inflows could drop very abruptly, as in February 1996, and again in May 1998: expecting a Rand depreciation, foreign portfolio investors' herd-like behaviour – rushing to sell Rand-denominated assets to avoid losses in own-currency value – led to depreciation expectations becoming a self-fulfilling prophecy. On both occasions, the Reserve Bank tried to stem the outflow by absorbing exchange-rate risk from both importers and foreign investors, selling dollars into the market and increasing its NOFP (Stals 1996, 1998). In 1996, it sold about US$14 billion, and in 1998, about US$10 billion, which pushed the NOFP back up close to its March 1995 level. In other words, foreign exchange purchased to reduce the NOFP during 1995 and again during 1997 through April 1998, had in effect been wasted. In a somewhat contradictory move, given the support to importers, real interest rates were pushed up substantially – about 2.5 per cent in 1996 and a full 7 per cent in 1998 – in a vain effort to attract foreign portfolio flows back. In both crises, the rand eventually restabilised at levels about 20 per cent below the pre-crisis level, and net inflows rose again (Figure 14.4).

Figure 14.4 *Effective exchange rate indices, monthly 1990–2003, 1995=100*

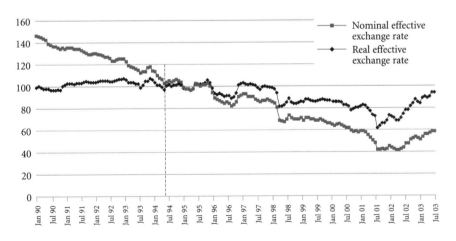

Late in the 1996 crisis, the GEAR policy statement was issued to restore (port-folio) investor credibility. The policy explicitly restated commitments to all three trilemma objectives: 'consistent monetary policy to prevent a resurgence of inflation ... [a nominal] exchange rate policy to keep the real effective rate stable at a competitive level ... [and] a further step in the gradual relaxation of exchange controls, that is, an open capital market' (Department of Finance 1996). After the 1998 crisis, in contrast, the costs of trying to maintain all three objectives and ignore the trilemma had become clear, and monetary and exchange-rate policy shifted to a new phase. Since capital account liberalisa-tion was not open for reconsideration, the choice was between targeting the nominal exchange rate and maintaining monetary autonomy. Given the already heavy investment in low inflation, and the perceived constraint of a large NOFP, it was no surprise that the authorities opted for the latter, abandoning efforts to target the nominal exchange rate by taking 'a decisive decision ... to reduce the NOFP to zero', and establishing an inflation-targeting regime, the 'best practice' monetary policy, according to the late-90s international consensus (Mboweni 2004).

Figure 14.5 *Interest rates and inflation, 1983–2003*

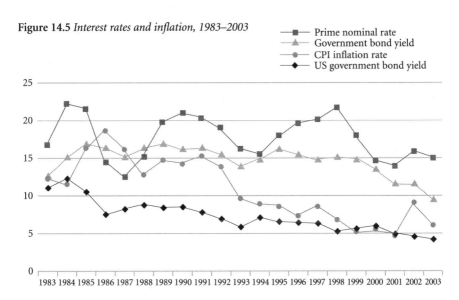

Inflation targeting was instituted in February 2000, with the target set by the Minister of Finance and the Reserve Bank, using interest-rate adjustments as the main policy instrument to meet it. The inflation targeting setup includes mechanisms for broader participation (a semi-annual Monetary Policy Forum) and monetary policy transparency (statements after each meeting of the Bank's Monetary Policy Committee). The initial target was to bring inflation (the CPIX rate, which excludes mortgage interest rates) within a range of 3–6 per cent by April 2002. Inflation inertia had been broken by the mid-1990s and the consumer price index (CPI) had dropped steadily from 10 per cent between 1993 and 2000, helped by tariff liberalisation and increased product market competition (Figure 14.5). But the Rand's nominal depreciation of 25 per cent in late 2001 pushed price increases above 10 per cent, especially for food, and the April 2002 inflation target was missed. Nominal interest rates had dropped from 1998 until 2000, before rising slightly during 2001. But the Reserve Bank pushed rates up steadily through most of 2002, to address the uptick in inflation from late 2001. The absence of inflationary expectations meant the increase was a temporary blip: by the second half of 2003, inflation was within the target band and interest rates were dropping.

Although the 2002 interest rate increase was the appropriate response within the inflation targeting regime, it was pro-cyclical rather than anti-cyclical, that is, monetary policy destabilised the real economy. The rate hike coincided with the start of the strong Rand appreciation, reinforcing the impact on output of the extreme exchange-rate volatility from the last quarter of 2001. This raises the issue of whether inflation targeting is too rigid a framework: while it allows for monetary policy autonomy, it focuses on a single objective, ignoring output, and the need, from time to time, for rapid reflation to counter a cyclical downturn. Figure 14.4 illustrates the fluctuations of the real trade-weighted exchange rate: a 25 per cent depreciation between August and December 2001 followed a depreciation of 25 per cent during the preceding three years, and was itself followed by a 45 per cent appreciation in the next 18 months until mid-2003. Over the three years since mid-2001, the Rand has been perhaps the most volatile currency in international markets.

According to the Finance Minister, 'government has chosen to follow a flexible exchange rate to act as a shock absorber against global developments. Exchange rate adjustments help cushion the economy from external trade and capital shocks and mitigate the impact of economic contraction, especially for the poor' (Manuel 2002). The problem is that any mitigating effect may be asymmetric – true for depreciations, but not appreciations – and also require that monetary policy act in concert. Further, the argument may hold only for adjustment from one 'long-run equilibrium' position to another, in which the direction of capital flows remain stable, allowing time for the offsetting effects of exchange-rate adjustment to work themselves through.

The situation since early 2001 does not appear to warrant the description of a 'shift between equilibria'. The international financial markets have experienced increased turbulence since the dotcom bubble burst in April 2001, and was followed by '9/11', rising commodity prices, the war in Iraq and the weakening of the US dollar. During this period, capital flow volatility has increased for South Africa, with five abrupt and large reversals from one quarter to the next in the subsequent two years: for example, an outflow of 0.4 per cent of GDP in Q1:2003 was followed in Q2 by an inflow of 2.4 per cent of GDP (SARB 2003).

Capital inflows since 1994, including foreign borrowing by government, have allowed the rebuilding of the economy's 'balance sheet': in February 2004, the NOFP was 'closed out' so that the Reserve Bank was no longer exposed to the risk of exchange-rate depreciation. The foreign exchange reserves were rebuilt by late 2002, with the help of capital inflows and foreign loans. This has certainly removed a 'structural' constraint from macroeconomic policy and has contributed to the further upgrading of South Africa's credit rating by international agencies. The stronger financial basis is also reflected in the dropping long-term bond yield and the narrowing of the differential between US and South African yields (Figure 14.5).

But the positive financial impact must be counterbalanced by the conclusion that macro policy has, intentionally or not, privileged financial concerns over problems in the real economy, and portfolio investment over fixed investment. Capital account openness has produced exchange-rate volatility, which worsened after the explicit float since 1998 but, throughout the decade, has meant inconsistent signals from the exchange rate to producers of tradables, increasing uncertainty and encouraging 'waiting' in production and investment decisions. At the same time, interest-rate policy has been concerned narrowly with lowering inflation, so that it is hard not to conclude that domestic price and fiscal stability have been achieved only at the expense of external instability, giving the lie to the repeated claims by the monetary and fiscal authorities that overall macroeconomic stability has been achieved, with the implication that microeconomic reforms should be the focus in future.

Macroeconomic performance post-apartheid

Growth

As already noted, GDP growth averaged only 1.7 per cent per annum between 1990 and 2002, and 2.77 per cent per annum between 1994 and 2003. Since the population growth rate has been 2 per cent per annum, per capita incomes have grown very slowly from 1994 at 0.77 per cent per annum. The growth rate has been very unstable but has never risen above 4.3 per cent per annum – the economy is apparently firmly trapped on a 'low growth' path (Figure 14.6). Fluctuations of GDP growth are tied to both changes in capital formation (fixed investment) and to the level of economic activity reflected in capacity utilisation.

Figure 14.6 *GDP growth, consumption growth and changes in capital formation, 1983–2003*

Percentage change year-on-year

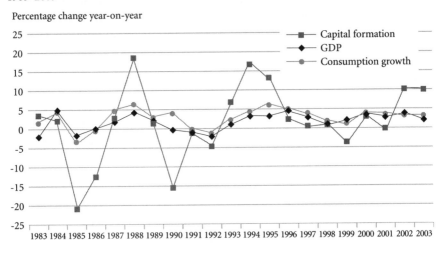

Investment

Figure 14.6 illustrates the volatility of fixed investment: the rapid growth in investment from 1993 is tied to the recovery of GDP growth, but with external volatility from 1996 through 2001, investment slowed down markedly. The strong rise of fixed investment from 2002 may be linked to currency appreciation reducing the cost of imported equipment.

In longer-run perspective, even though profitability and productivity in the private sector have improved significantly during the 1990s (Nattrass 2003), private investment has averaged only 12.1 per cent of GDP between 1994 and 2003, compared with more than 13 per cent in 1982 and 14 per cent in 1988 (after the foreign debt standstill), and 10.6 per cent average between 1990 and 1993, when the economy was in deep recession and the political situation in deep uncertainty (Figure 14.7). While the investment outcome may be in part due to sluggish aggregate demand as a result of contractionary fiscal policies, exchange-rate volatility and interest rate fluctuations, lack of (fixed) investor confidence has also been influenced by uncertainty regarding other factors of a longer-run nature. In the National Enterprise Survey of 1 400 firms carried out for the Office of the President in 1999–2000, firms identified a number of individual factors – labour regulations, the tax regime, crime and social policy, uncertainty over economic policy and infrastructure – as investment constraints. More systematic statistical analysis grouped these particular issues together as

Figure 14.7 *Investment as share of GDP, 1982–2003*

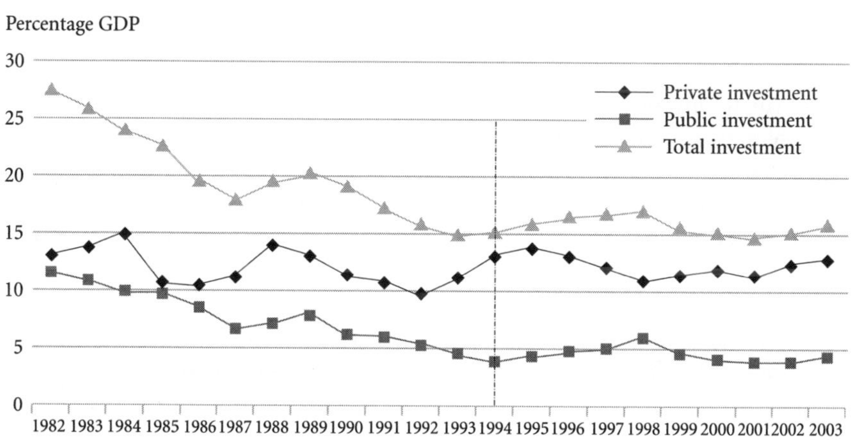

Percentage GDP

a *single* factor creating uncertainty amongst potential investors and holding back investment. This factor – the 'socio-political environment' – can be interpreted as a reflection of high inequality: potential long-term productive investors fear that if the political balance were to tilt towards the poor, and result in far-reaching policy shifts, or if property-related crime levels were to rise, the security of their claims to the returns from their investments could be undermined, so they hold back from making such long-term commitments (Gelb 1999a, 2001).

This problem in the broad investment environment has severely limited the success of various firm-level policy strategies to raise investment. One strategy has been to try to overcome 'co-ordination failure' amongst investors by communication and mobilisation for collective action. Investment accords or social contracts have been actively promoted and discussed and two national economic summits held, but these have not resulted in *binding* commitments on the 'social partners' (business and labour). Further efforts have focused on business organisation directly, supporting unification of peak associations across racial, linguistic, regional and sectoral lines, and establishing high-level Presidential working groups for domestic and foreign business. Targeted industrial policy interventions in the form of spatial development initiatives (SDIs) – corridors focusing government planning and financial resources – tried to address co-ordination failure through investor forums, extensive dialogue sessions between government and private investors, and as important, amongst the latter. The forums tried to build confidence and 'lock in' individual firms' investments by demonstrating the beneficial impact for markets, suppliers and low-cost infrastructure if all firms committed. Inevitably, these forums focused primarily on large firms.

Investment incentives have been a second strategy, but over and above the debate about the actual impact on firms' decisions, they have suffered from inconsistency of both instruments and targets. Several schemes have come and gone during the 1990s. In the early 1990s, incentives focused on natural resource-based materials exports, and the link between industrialisation and cheap energy – identifying large capital- and energy-intensive materials processing plants as 'anchor' projects. These '37E' incentives were scrapped in 1993, but the SDIs continue their commodity- and capital-intensive focus. A Tax Holiday Scheme was introduced via GEAR to provide incentives for employment creation and investment in specific regions, but withdrawn in

1999 due to low take-up rates. A general export incentive scheme was established in 1990 and halted in 1998, to be replaced by duty drawback programmes for exporters, but only in two sectors – autos and apparel.

Finally, foreign investment has been encouraged by liberalising the investment regime (including the removal of capital controls) and establishing investment promotion agencies to actively pursue potential investors. Domestic policymakers have focused too narrowly on the macroeconomic argument for foreign direct investment (FDI), as an apparently less volatile form of capital inflows to address a putative savings constraint on growth, ignoring possible dynamic efficiency impacts of foreign firms' presence (Department of Finance 1996). In light of this emphasis in policy reforms, new FDI since 1994 has disappointed, with gross inflows averaging $1.86 billion per annum between 1994 and 2002, while net inflows were 1.5 per cent of the developing country total (UNCTAD 2003). On a per capita basis, FDI inflow was about $41 per annum, close to developing countries' average, though South Africa's per capita income is about 2.5 times larger than the developing country average. South Africa differs from most middle-income countries in receiving far smaller direct investment than portfolio inflows: between 1995 and 2002, South Africa received 3.3 per cent of gross market-based capital flows to developing countries and 22 per cent of net portfolio equity flows (World Bank 2003). Firm-level survey evidence confirms this picture of small FDI inflows – the median capital stock in 2000 of foreign firms which had entered South Africa since 1990 was only US$2 million. (Gelb & Black 2004b)

As Figure 14.7 also shows, the 'slack' in investment demand has not been filled by the public sector. From 1994 to 1997, public investment rose in real terms by 9 per cent per annum, and from 3.7 per cent to 4.7 per cent of GDP. Although private investment and GDP growth were also slowing from 1998, the broad fiscal stance imposed a pro-cyclical approach to public investment, which also declined, notwithstanding a once-off telecommunications investment in 1998 as part of the sale of 30 per cent of Telkom to a US-Malaysian strategic partner. After the 2001 Budget signalled an intention to raise public investment, it grew by close to 10 per cent annually in the following two years, but remains well below its 1980s levels both in real terms and as a share of GDP. However, it is worth noting that since 1994, growth in investment in social infrastructure has been stronger than in economic infrastructure.

Savings

Turning to national savings, Figure 14.8 shows that South Africa's national savings have remained between 14.5 and 17 per cent of GDP since 1994, which is well below savings levels in the 1980s. Macroeconomically, if the domestic economy generates insufficient savings to finance investment, foreign savings equivalent to the current account deficit (or to net capital inflows less changes in foreign reserves) must make up the difference. But large current account deficits cannot be sustained for very long, unless capital inflows are large and stable, so investment is forced to rely mainly on domestic savings. The central question is whether savings represent a long-run constraint on investment and hence growth (as neo-classical economists argue), or whether a rise in investment would itself generate higher savings via its impact on income growth (as Keynesian theory suggests). South African policy since 1994 has been premised on the former view: a key justification for the tight fiscal stance from 1993 was to raise government savings, which had become negative during the early 1990s spending spree, but have been above 2.5 per cent since 1999. But it is hard to argue, more generally, that investment has been held back by lack of savings, since overall domestic savings have been enough to finance fixed capital formation[3] in all but two years. In addition, corporate

Figure 14.8 *National savings as share of GDP, 1982–2003*

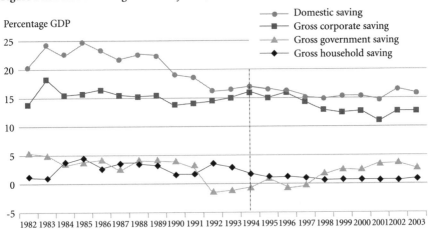

savings have been sufficient to finance corporate investment: the corporate sector (the major contributor to domestic savings) had a financial surplus – an excess of savings over investment within the sector – between 1994 and 2000, and near-balance (tiny surpluses or deficits) since 2001.

It does not automatically follow that an investment increase would be unconstrained by lack of savings, however, since the argument about the direction of causality between savings and investment assumes a stable propensity to save out of income. However, this coefficient may have dropped for both corporations and households over the past decade, so that income growth yields a smaller volume of savings than before. The corporate sector's savings has declined in real terms and as a share of GDP since 1996, notwithstanding a rise in net profit as a share of GDP from 24.7 per cent in the 1980s to 31.1 per cent since 1994. This suggests that firms have increased dividend payouts to equity-owning households relative to retained earnings to fund investment. At the same time, households have been increasing consumption rather than savings. Household savings were already very low in 1995, just above 1 per cent of GDP, and have fallen away further, hovering just above zero since 1999 compared with a 1980s average of 2.8 per cent of GDP. Consumption growth since 1994 has been 3.33 per cent per annum, faster than GDP growth of 2.77 per cent per annum, and much faster than growth of household disposable income per capita of only 0.83 per cent per annum (Figure 14.6). During the 1980s, dropping household savings were linked to rising debt levels, as households borrowed to maintain both consumption levels and contractual savings (insurance and pension funds). But the links between household wealth, debt and savings shifted after 1993, as household wealth rose as a result of lower inflation and rising asset values, especially for housing. At the same time, trade liberalisation encouraged higher consumption of imports. This led to a consumption spurt in the mid-1990s, and further declines in household savings. Consumption growth continued to be strong during the late 1990s, with the decline in interest rates from 1998, which meant household debt levels and debt-to-assets ratios dropped further (Prinsloo 2002).

The balance of payments

Since 1994, South Africa has returned to the 'normal' developing economy situation with a current account deficit and net capital inflows, after the debt standstill period between 1985 and 1993, when the current account was in surplus and foreign savings negative because of foreign debt repayment. Figure 14.9 shows that the current account deficit (the contribution of foreign savings to overall savings) has remained very small since 1994, never rising above 2 per cent of GDP. Since 1999, the current account has been more or less in balance. The chart supports the 'Keynesian' view that investment is constrained not by lack of savings, but by the other factors identified above. Had investment levels warranted it, a larger current account deficit would have been possible, in the sense that net capital inflows, though volatile, were sufficient to finance it. Instead, capital inflows in excess of the external deficit have been used to build foreign reserves, as Figure 14.9 illustrates. A small external deficit and rising reserves are desirable outcomes, of course, but there is a trade-off since reserves are unutilised resources from an investment and growth perspective.

Figure 14.10 shows the various components of the current account balance as shares of GDP. Both non-gold exports and imports have risen by around 50 per cent since 1993, though volume indices show that imports grew very rapidly until 1997 in the wake of trade liberalisation, but levelled off thereafter, as slow growth has limited imports of investment goods. Non-gold exports have

Figure 14.9 *Balance of payments, 1982–2003*

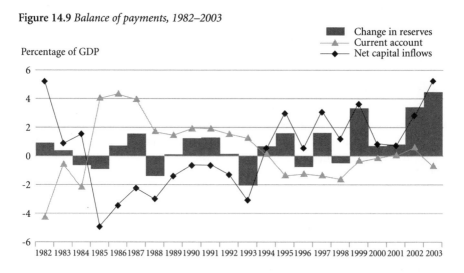

Figure 14.10 *Trade components as share of GDP,*
1982–2003

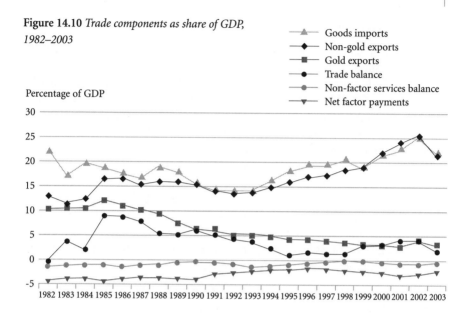

Percentage of GDP

risen more steadily, and the improvement in export performance – partly driven by currency depreciation – reflects a major post-1994 shift, particularly given the greater weight of manufacturing exports, rather than primary commodities. Gold exports have been in a long-term decline, and the gold production index dropped from 120.7 in 1986 to 86.6 in 1999 (IMF 2004). Taking account of a tiny, if consistent, non-factor services deficit, the trade balance (including goods and non-factor services) has been in surplus, averaging just over 1 per cent of GDP between 1995 and 1998, but then rising to 3 per cent since 1999. The difference between the trade surplus and the current account deficit is the factor services deficit, a persistent problem in the balance of payments for several decades. This rose from 1.9 per cent of GDP in 1995 to 2.6 per cent in 2000, driven by profit and dividend outflows, in part due to the relocation to the UK and US of the head offices of several major South African corporations. But as the figure illustrates, the factor services deficit after 1994 was below its 1980s levels, and indeed is 20 per cent lower in US dollar terms.

Sources of aggregate demand change

To summarise this discussion of macroeconomic outcomes, it may be helpful to examine changes in aggregate demand over the period since 1989, distinguishing between the private, public and foreign sectors as sources of demand. Following Taylor (1998), aggregate demand can be decomposed into components reflecting the 'stance' – expansionary versus contractionary – of each of the three sectors and the 'weight' of each sector in determining aggregate demand.[4] The stance reflects the direct impact on demand from the sector, taking account of both injections – private investment, public (current and capital) spending and exports for the three sectors respectively – *and* leakages to savings propensity, tax rate, and import propensity. The weight reflects the sector's importance relative to the other two in impacting on aggregate demand, measured by its share of total leakages. In essence, the stance reflects the net direct effect of the sector's injections and its leakages together, while the weight adjusts the stance to give the sector's overall impact on aggregate demand.

Table 14.2 presents the decomposition of aggregate demand for three sub-periods between 1989 and 2003. The stances are expressed as percentages of real output, so that stances above 100 per cent are expansionary, and those below 100 per cent contractionary. The weights are sector shares of total leakages and sum to 100. The sector components are the product of sector stance and weight,

Table 14.2 *Decomposition of aggregate demand, 1989–2003*

Average level	1989–1993	1994–1997	1998–2003
Private stance	75	106	132
Private weight	32	24	18
Private sector component	24	26	24
Public stance	103	92	76
Public weight	40	39	44
Public sector component	41	36	33
Foreign stance	126	106	114
Foreign weight	28	37	38
Foreign sector component	35	39	43
Change in output (% p.a.)	0.27	4.69	2.38

Source: Own calculations from SARB (2004)
Notes: Data is in constant 1995 prices. Stances are percentages of output; weights and components are percentage shares of overall leakages and output respectively.

showing the sector's contribution to overall demand, and also sum to 100 down the column. Annual average changes in real output (not GDP) are in the last row: between 1989 and 1993, annual output increased by 0.27 per cent annually on average, accelerating to 4.69 per cent between 1994 and 1997, but then slowing to 2.38 per cent per annum in the last six years of the period.

In the first sub-period, the foreign stance is expansionary as the debt standstill imposes an export surplus, but the stance is offset by the sector's low weight as imports were compressed. The increase in public spending during constitutional negotiations makes the sector's stance just expansionary, while dropping private savings and imports through the 1980s mean that taxes (the public sector's weight) are the largest proportion of leakages, though they average only 19 per cent of real output. With monetary policy aimed at demand compression, the private sector's stance is contractionary and in fact becomes more so through the sub-period: both private investment and savings fell in real terms, the former's faster fall reducing the stance, while the latter's fall reduces the sector's weight and moderates the demand impact of the falling stance. During this period, the public sector is the most important of the three sectors in contributing to demand.

During the second sub-period, there are substantial shifts in the sectoral sources of demand as sectors' stances and weights adjust to reflect the ending of external debt standstill and constitutional negotiations, and the start of external liberalisation and the democratic era. The private and public stances diverge during the sub-period – the private sector stance increases strongly and becomes expansionary, driven by further declines in private savings, which reinforce the injection from a strong investment upturn, while the public sector stance becomes contractionary, as fiscal discipline is adopted with no relief from lower taxes, so the weight remains basically constant, and the public sector component drops markedly. The drop in private savings lowers the private sector's weight significantly, and its share of overall leakages is taken up by the foreign sector, whose weight increases strongly as imports rise strongly due to trade liberalisation. Thus, even though the foreign stance is less expansionary than before (given the rise in imports), this sector becomes the main contributor to demand. There is no change in the private sector's overall impact.

By 1998, the adjustment of stances and weights across sectors was completed, so that a third sub-period to 2003 can be distinguished, characterised by less inter-sectoral variability in contributions to overall demand, though each sector's stance and weight fluctuate *over time* during this period of output volatility. The private sector stance is now very strongly expansionary, as savings continue to decline (private investment growth slows), but for the same reason there is a significant drop in its weight, so the sector's overall contribution to demand in fact drops slightly. The public sector's weight rises significantly because of the increase in tax revenues due to improved collection efficiency (see above). Continued tight fiscal expenditure re-inforces the contractionary effects of higher tax leakages, so the sector's stance is much lower than before, with the net overall contribution to demand somewhat smaller. In the foreign sector, strong exports and a slower rise in imports (see above) mean the stance is more expansionary, while the weight increases slightly. The foreign sector's contribution to demand is by far the largest of the three sectors, as in the second sub-period, but the rise in the foreign sector stance is not enough to maintain the same rate of output growth as in the previous sub-period.

This discussion shows that the apparent shift in sector components from the public to the foreign sector has in fact been mediated by the private sector: the two sub-periods had investment and export growth respectively, but what is common across the full period is the significant drop in private savings, linked to consumption-led growth which has sucked in imports. This points to the limits of consumption-led growth. As the earlier discussion of savings suggests, there has been a downward shift in the savings propensity of both corporations and households, which is linked in turn to changes in import and tax propensities, rather than simply a temporary adjustment in the wake of economic opening, since the savings, tax and import coefficients at the end of the first sub-period after 1994 were maintained into the post-1998 period rather than re-adjusting back to earlier levels. This implies that private savings may not respond strongly to rising income even if invest-ment were to increase, which would mean reliance on foreign savings and possibly 'stop-go' cycles. Raising investment is of course a separate problem, and the decomposition exercise shows that investment stayed flat during the second sub-period even though export demand increased, suggesting that there are also limits to export-led growth, and reinforcing the earlier argu-ment that expanding demand components may not be sufficient to bring about sustained growth.

Sectors

Space constraints allow only a very brief look at the changing sectoral composition of output and of trade which were significant between 1990 and 2003, as shown in Tables 14.3 and 14.4, and which have exacerbated the impact of low growth on employment levels and skills composition in the labour market. The shares in output of both mining and manufacturing declined, as did 'other industry' (construction and utilities), while services increased, with transport and communications and financial services growing particularly strongly. Within manufacturing, there were also composition shifts. Labour-intensive sectors (food and beverages, textiles and clothing and footwear) grew slowly, at around 0.2 per cent per annum, and declined from 23 per cent of manufacturing value-added (MVA) in 1990 to 20 per cent in 2000. At the same time, basic metals, wood products and chemicals were the fastest-growing sectors, basic metals and wood growing by more than 4 per cent per annum and increasing their shares of MVA, basic metals by over three percentage points to 16 per cent, and wood by half a percentage point to 3.9 per cent of the total (Kaplan 2003).

The shift to more capital-intensive sectors was linked in part to international trade. The share of exports from capital-intensive sectors rose from 56.1 per cent in 1993 to 60.8 per cent in 1997, while import penetration in labour-

Table 14.3 *Sectoral output shares, 1995 prices*

| | Share of gross value added, percentage | | | Growth rate, |
	1990	1994	2003	1990–2003
Agriculture	5.0	5.0	4.0	0.3
Mining	7.3	7.4	5.5	-0.2
Manufacturing	22.0	20.5	19.8	1.2
Other Industry	6.9	6.7	6.7	1.7
Transport & Communication	7.9	8.3	12.2	5.5
Financial services	15.6	16.3	19.6	3.8
Govt. & community services	16.0	16.5	13.7	1.0
Trade & other Services	19.4	19.3	19.3	1.7
Total	100.0	100.0	100.0	2.0

Source: SARB (2004)

Table 14.4 *Percentage shares of merchandise exports, by sector*

	1990	1995	2000	2002
Agriculture	4.5	4.9	4.1	5.5
Minerals	61.3	50.7	45.6	36.1
Food, beverages	3.0	3.1	4.0	4.3
Textiles and clothing	3.1	3.1	2.7	3.1
Basic processed goods	21.9	28.1	27.4	29.7
Machinery and equipment	5.9	8.5	14.7	19.3
Other manufactured goods	0.1	1.6	1.5	2.0
Total	100.0	100.0	100.0	100.0

Source: TIPS (2003)

intensive sectors rose from 55.5 per cent to 67.5 per cent in the same period, squeezing domestic production and employment (Edwards 1999).

Table 14.4 shows the change in the sectoral composition of merchandise exports between 1990 and 2002, in particular the significant shift from minerals to basic processed goods and to machinery and equipment. This reflects, in large measure, the growth of domestic beneficiation of natural resources to allow the export of materials rather than raw ores and resources. Basic processed goods include chemicals and plastics, wood products and basic metals. Machinery and equipment shows the biggest increase in export share. This category includes vehicle components, exports of which have grown rapidly since the mid-1990s in the context of the Motor Industry Development Plan. The overwhelming bulk of component exports have been catalytic converters and leather car seats, constituting 48 per cent (1994: 9.4 per cent) and 13 per cent respectively of motor exports in 2001. Both the converters (ceramic moulds imported until 2000 and platinum-coated in South Africa) and the seats are beneficiated natural resources rather than assembled products. Since 1999, the South African auto industry has also rapidly increased its exports of assembled vehicles, these rising from 25 900 in that year to over 100 000 by 2001 (Black 2002). But critics of the programme argue that the sector has seen a limited rise in productivity growth and international competitiveness, with the export success due to the Motor Industry Development Plan subsidy, the cost of which is ultimately borne by South African consumers (Kaplan 2003).

Conclusion

The shifts in output and export composition reflect the export-led growth model toward which, it was suggested above, South Africa was pushed by powerful political and economic imperatives in the course of the transition to democracy. Ten years on, the model has been implemented and the flaws in its logic are apparent, both the lack of a link from distribution (in the form of BEE) to growth (which has not been discussed here), and the difficulties of ensuring an increase of investment, which have been examined in detail.

Improving the growth performance will require an increase in *both* invest-ment and savings, which are independent processes, though both involve the lengthening of economic agents' decision-making time horizons. Short time horizons have been, in part, the consequence of the transition itself, bringing into power a new government in a new regime, with an associated rise in uncertainty for both firms and households. As time has passed without fun-damental change in the government's broad policy stance, and in particular its commitment to the accommodation with business, some of this uncertainty may begin to recede. Notwithstanding the difficulties and controversies associated with the BEE process, the progressive 'blackening' of business will have contributed to big business' growing belief in government's policy credentials, while the long-term confidence expressed by foreign organisa-tions – for example, in FIFA's selection of its World Cup 2010 venue – will help significantly to lengthen horizons of domestic actors.

Even if this assessment is correct, however, two difficulties remain. The first is that another aspect of uncertainty arises from external volatility, which, I argued above, has not been addressed by monetary and exchange-rate policy. Indeed, the authorities have adopted the view that it is simply 'a fact of life' beyond their control, which, translated, means that neither closing the capital account nor attempting to fix the exchange rate were even on the policy menu. In late 2003 and early 2004, vocal opposition to high interest rates and Rand strength elicited very little reaction, notwithstanding that within the lobby for policy change to support real economic growth were once-powerful gold mining and manufacturing interests. Interest rates have subsequently declined, but a more enduring solution to the problem is required. This leaves government, on the one hand, desperately looking for more FDI inflows so as to reduce external volatility, and on the other, seeking a solution to capital flow volatility at the level of the international financial system. Neither route is very promising in the short to medium term.

Finally, the second problem is that of domestic savings, and to resolve this, short household time horizons need to be lengthened so that consumption will be cut, not just by the rich but also by the poor. The recent emphasis on addressing poverty and inequality is very welcome in this respect, particularly if it involves adjustments to the fiscal stance on the revenue side, as well as the expenditure side, though again, it will be some time before savings behaviour begins to show a difference.

Notes

1   These were contingent liabilities on its balance sheet, reflecting the 'insurance' against Rand depreciation which the Bank provided to South African public and private sector organisations after 1985 to encourage them to make full use of the few channels of international credit still open to South Africans, such as trade credit, so as to maximise foreign funds inflows. If the exchange rate depreciated, the Bank would compensate the borrower for the additional debt service burden, but the cost would ultimately be transferred to the fiscus, and thus the taxpaying public.

2   Gradualism now being part of the orthodoxy, though it was not at the time.

3   But not capital formation in total, which includes changes in inventories.

4   The decomposition updates Gelb (1999b). Davies and van Seventer (2003) also use this methodology, but reach different results.

References

Black A (2002) The export 'success' of the Motor Industry Development Programme and the implications for trade and industrial policy. Paper presented at TIPS Annual Forum 9–11 September, Johannesburg.

Bond P (2000) *Elite transition*. London: Pluto Press.

Davies R & van Seventer D (2003) A gap and macro decomposition analysis for SA. Paper presented at TIPS Annual Forum.

Department of Finance (South Africa) (1996) *Growth Employment and Redistribution: A macroeconomic strategy*. Pretoria: Department of Finance.

Edwards L (1999) Trade liberalisation, structural change and occupational employment in South Africa. Paper presented at TIPS Annual Forum 20–22 September, Johannesburg.

Eichengreen B (2000) Taming capital flows, *World Development* 28:1105–1116.

Gelb S (1990) Democratising economic growth: Crisis and alternative growth models, *Transformation* 12:25–41.

Gelb S (1999a) Sustaining the nation: Economic growth, people and the environment. In G Maharaj (ed.) *Between unity and diversity: South Africa & the national question.* Cape Town: David Philip.

Gelb S (1999b) South Africa: Macroeconomic overview. Paper presented at Conference on Globalisation and Social Policy, New School for Social Research.

Gelb S (2001) Socio-political risk, confidence and firm investment in South Africa. Paper presented at Conference on New Industrial Realities and Firm Behaviour in Africa, Oxford.

Gelb S & Black A (2004a) South African case studies. In S Estrin & K Meyer (eds.) *Investment strategies in emerging markets.* Cheltenham, UK: Edward Elgar.

Gelb S & Black A (2004b) Globalisation in a middle-income economy: FDI, production & the labour market in South Africa. In W Milberg (ed.) *Labor and the globalization of production.* London: Macmillan.

IMF (International Monetary Fund) (1997) *South Africa: Selected issues.* Staff Country Report 97/82.

IMF (2004) *International financial statistics.* Available at <http://www.imf.org>. Accessed on 20.3.04.

Kaplan D (2003) Manufacturing performance and policy in South Africa – A review. Paper presented at TIPS Annual Forum.

Manuel T (2002) Closing remarks to the Commission of Inquiry into the Rapid Depreciation of the Exchange Rate of the Rand, 24.05.02. Available at National Treasury <http://www.finance.gov.za>.

Marais H (1998) *South Africa: The limits to change.* London: Zed.

Mboweni T (2004) Announcement regarding the Foreign Forward Exchange Book. South African Reserve Bank. Media release 1.03.04. Available at <http://www.reservebank.co.za>.

National Treasury (South Africa) (2004) *Budget review.* Pretoria: National Treasury.

Nattrass N (2003) The state of the economy: A crisis of employment. In J Daniel, A Habib & R Southall (eds.) *The State of the Nation: South Africa, 2003–2004.* Cape Town: HSRC Press.

Obstfeld M (1998) The global capital market: Benefactor or menace? *Journal of Economic Perspectives* 12:9–30.

Prinsloo JW (2002) *Household debt, wealth and saving,* South African Reserve Bank Quarterly Bulletin No. 226.

PCAS (Presidency Policy Co-ordination and Advisory Services, South Africa) (2003) *Towards a ten year review synthesis report on implementation of government programmes: Discussion document.* Pretoria: Government Communication and Information Systems.

SARB (South African Reserve Bank) (2003) *Quarterly economic review,* Quarterly Bulletin No. 229.

SARB (2004) *Online statistical and economic time series.* Available at <http://www.reservebank.co.za>.

SARS (South African Revenue Service) (1998) *Annual report.*

SARS (2003) *Annual report.*

Stals C (1994) Governor's address at the ordinary general meeting of shareholders, SARB.

Stals C (1995) Governor's address at the ordinary general meeting of shareholders, SARB.

Stals C (1996) Governor's address at the ordinary general meeting of shareholders, SARB.

Stals C (1998) Governor's address at the ordinary general meeting of shareholders, SARB.

Taylor L (1998) *Revised methodology for country studies.* New York: New School for Social Research.

Terreblanche S (2003) *A history of inequality in South Africa, 1652–2002.* Pietermaritzburg: University of Natal Press

TIPS (Trade & Industry Policy Strategies) (2003) *South Africa HS export value database.* Available at <http:// www.tips.org.za >.

UNCTAD (United Nations Conference on Trade & Development) (2003) *World Investment Report.* Geneva: UNCTAD.

Van der Berg S (2001) Trends in racial fiscal incidence in South Africa, *South African Journal of Economics* 69:243–268.

World Bank (2003) *Global development finance 2003: Striving for stability in development finance.* Washington DC: World Bank.

15 Who owns South Africa: an analysis of state and private ownership patterns

Reg Rumney

> When the whites came we had the land and they had the Bible.
> They asked us to close our eyes and pray. When we opened them
> again, we had the Bible and they had the land.
> *Xhosa proverb*

Introduction

Discussion of ownership, particularly of land, stirs up all sorts of emotions in South Africa: above all, memories of great wrongs wrought, resentment at theft on a grand scale, and insult on a pettier but no less wounding level. Twisted into a sense of identity and politics, these emotions are probably not unique. The violence of dispossession ripples from history into the present in many lands, Ireland and Israel being just two that flicker on television screens into our daily awareness.

Both arthritic tyrants and unsullied revolutionaries can deftly tap the force of that emotion for political skullduggery. State-sponsored and clumsily inept farm invasions across the border in Zimbabwe certainly underline the phenomenon, and have, in recent years, conjured up the magic somehow forgotten by its arch-proponent, the Pan Africanist Congress (PAC), of the call of the land.

Ten years ago 'ownership' in South Africa called to mind something different. Yes, informal settlements unsettled the descendants of the settlers, and the PAC's rhetoric about *Boers* caused concern in farm communities, but the big question was how the African National Congress (ANC) would approach the 'commanding heights' of an economy owned by whites, and controlled by conglomerates and state-owned entities or parastatals.

The issue of who owns whom had, since the late 1980s, underlined the growing control of companies on the Johannesburg Stock Exchange (JSE, later renamed the JSE Securities Exchange), as disinvestment threw prized companies into its lap and the laps of other conglomerates with their roots in mining. At one stage, the average white South African could barely escape consuming products associated with the Anglo American Corporation, from fruit juice and cereal at breakfast, through the Ford or Mazda car he or she drove to work, to the glass of wine with supper.

Why control rather than ownership? Control of companies has always been as important, if not more important, than ownership. Witness the late Harry Oppenheimer's ability to direct the fortunes of the Anglo American monolith – and benefit from those fortunes – while owning legendarily only 8 per cent of the shares.

Ten years ago, Anglo, a still dominant conglomerate, controlled 43 per cent of the JSE's market capitalisation (the worth of all the shares). The top five groups – Anglo American, Afrikaans firm, Rembrandt, and life assurers, Sanlam, Old Mutual and Liberty Life – controlled 84 per cent of the JSE (McGregor 2004).

In 1994, the ANC government inherited a country whose commanding heights were controlled by a few big companies, no matter what the nominal ownership. Where the private sector did not dominate, parastatals of one sort or another did. For instance, the South African Broadcasting Corporation owned all the really freely viewable TV stations and all radio stations, with one or two exceptions which had slipped in under the cover of the homeland system, such as Radio 702. Eskom and Telkom had legal monopolies, and Transnet ran all the rail and owned the dominant national airline.

Moreover, and more to the point, the ANC found itself at the helm of a country famous for inequality and little else beside, to paraphrase poet Roy Campbell. The apartheid state was, after all, well designed to keep economic and political power in the grasp of whites, no matter what hole it had blown in the hull of the ship of state.

Building on colonial exploitation and exclusion, the systemised oppression and expropriation of property under apartheid left a racially skewed economy in South Africa, if not unparalleled then certainly among the most unequal in the world. South Africa shares with Brazil, among other things, a sense of rhythm, great natural beauty and enormous income inequality.

The income inequality present at the dawn of democracy grimly persists. It may have improved slightly from the apartheid years, but not dramatically so. South Africa's Gini coefficient, the main measure of inequality of income, stands around 0.6, where 1 would be complete inequality and zero complete equality. Moreover, the divide has grown within racial groups, as a small group of black people has become exceedingly rich.

Traditionally, though, the real measure of wealth has been property in one form or another, from cattle or precious metals and gems, through tracts of land, and ownership of shares in companies. By that measure too, the country was somewhat unsurprisingly, a playing field tilted 45 degrees in favour of whites, so much so that no one had ever really made much of an attempt to measure this form of inequality.

President Thabo Mbeki's largely uncontroversial and backward-looking 'State of the Nation' address in 2004 focused on his government's self-imposed approach to combating inherited imbalances, that of delivery of basic needs to the masses of poor, such as housing, water, sanitation, electricity and tele-communications. He spent almost no time on the bolder and more difficult part of government's drive to put right inherited imbalances, black economic empowerment (BEE). Land reform, for restitution of property expropriated under apartheid, redistribution and land tenure, an essential component of empowerment, was not mentioned at all.

How black economic empowerment was born

The very question of who owns South Africa leads to another: who should own the economy?

The Freedom Charter, the poetically phrased ANC policy document which inspired generations of ANC cadres, frames the response in terms which could be associated with British socialism of that era:

> The national wealth of our country, the heritage of South
> Africans, shall be restored to the people; the mineral wealth
> beneath the soil, the banks and monopoly industry shall be
> transferred to the ownership of the people as a whole; all other
> industry and trade shall be controlled to assist the wellbeing
> of the people; all people shall have equal rights to trade where

they choose, to manufacture and to enter all trades, crafts and professions.[1]

In government, the ANC has abjured nationalisation of the banking industry, though 'the mineral wealth beneath the soil', has, along with water, indeed been nationalised. The Minerals Act that accomplished this is linked to another national intervention to redress imbalances, BEE – BEE and nationalisation have more than a coincidental link.

Nationalisation, for redistribution or for state control, still lurks in the shadows as an unarticulated and unfashionable rejoinder to growing liberal economic policies that emphasise private ownership of property. Indeed, African countries, such as Mozambique, reversed previous socialist policy to the extent of privatising state assets. But there is reluctance to ditch national ownership of land immediately. This is ostensibly because of the politically unpalatable consequences of large parts of very cheap real estate ending up in foreign hands, once more an emotive issue. Zimbabwe has, in a sense, skipped the phase of nationalising land before redistributing it.

Aside from mineral rights and water, the South African government has shown no great taste for nationalisation. But that does not mean enthusiasm for letting go of the reins of state-owned enterprises (SOEs) that, in pure economic terms, contribute little to the economy, but are nonetheless at the heart of the economy.

SOEs have been both a major resource for the government as well as powerful symbols of nationhood. A lot is now expected of SOEs. They have come under pressure from all angles – on the one hand, to supply basic services and implement government strategies such as the New Partnership for Africa's Development (Nepad), the grand plan for Africa's economic leap into the twenty-first century, and on the other, through privatisation, to broaden ownership and enhance economic efficiency.

As Centre for Policy Studies analyst Steven Friedman has noted, the ANC in government's embrace of privatisation, even in a cautious manner, came with an explicit understanding that BEE would fill the gap left by the party's abandonment of nationalisation as an option for creating greater equality.

One of the first real BEE companies – in the sense that the emphasis was on the conscious creation of black owners of shares as well as a black-managed company – was the privatisation of the state's sorghum or traditional beer interests in 1990, in National Sorghum Breweries (NSB). It was also the first – though not the last BEE company created by privatisation – to come a cropper.

BEE appears as a concept in 1994, in the Reconstruction and Development Programme (RDP). Around the same time, the ANC started to accept privatisation as one option for SOEs, as part of a general acceptance that, at the end of the twentieth century, aspects of a free market economy were unavoidable at best, and might even open new avenues for racial equality. Afrikaner capital, in the form of the visionary Marinus Daling, had by 1993 already started the process of trying to get black capitalists to mimic the growth of Afrikaner capital, through the sale of 10 per cent of Metropolitan Life to a consortium led by Dr Nthato Motlana, to plant the seed of what would become New Africa Investments Ltd.

Importantly, BEE presented another inspired trade-off by Anglo American Corporation and the other conglomerates. Support for BEE can be seen as a way of buying political credibility to make, for instance, government look more kindly on allowing Anglo American Corporation to move its head office to London. It could also be seen as a move to help create a black 'buffer' middle class to protect the interests of the capitalists.

State ownership of South Africa

Free market fundamentalist and founder of the Free Market Foundation, Leon Louw (1996) argued, 'Regrettably, the ruling African National Congress has failed to use several tools at its disposal to effect a massive, virtually cost-free and instant black empowerment. It can redistribute to blacks some of the vast amounts of land now under state ownership.'

The state's ownership of the economy starts, but by no means ends, with land. The state owns around 20 per cent of South Africa's land, excluding land owned by parastatals and 'tribal' land. Including the tribal, 'coloured' rural trust land and *Ingonyama* trust land, the percentage rises to around 25 per cent, though 4 per cent of this 25 per cent is marked for land reform.

However, the state does own – for example, through parastatal land ownership – even more than this. As Spoornet real estate arm Intersite has shown, excess state and parastatal land can be put to good use. However, state land cannot answer whatever demand there is for land.

Firstly, demand would be for land suitable for farming, or for residential accommodation. By no means all the available state land can be suitable for the intended purposes, since under 13 per cent of South African land is arable. The former residents of the Lohatla army training ground are claiming back their land under the government's policy of restitution. The South African army has a point in arguing that residents should tread lightly – figuratively and literally – in claiming land rife with unexploded munitions. Moreover, demand for land for housing is predominantly in or near urban areas, close to work opportunities, not necessarily in the homeland available.

Secondly, some state land ownership is legitimate. US federal and state owner-ship of land exceeds South Africa's, at around 40 per cent.

Privatisation problems and prospects

Since Louw's suggestion, privatisation of land is barely mentioned, though in a real sense, giving people tenure of the land on which they live and should have title, is privatisation of a far-reaching sort. Most of the debate, for or against, has focused on privatisation of the SOEs themselves.

According to the BusinessMap Foundation, SOEs (wholly owned or partially privatised) in South Africa have around R312 billion in assets.

The state and public corporations together still have 44 per cent of the coun-try's fixed capital stock. While the state's share of the economy has shrunk significantly since 1988, the public corporation share of fixed capital stock has grown.

Three SOEs have been, and continue to be, at the heart of the economy, despite either being partly privatised or due for part-privatisation: the trans-port and energy utilities are state-owned, and the state has a sizeable chunk of the former state fixed-line monopoly, Telkom.

For a group ranging from neo-liberals to libertarians, privatisation of state assets for redistribution to create more equal ownership in South Africa is an obvious solution. However, unlike in Eastern Europe or other former socialist states, the state in South Africa was never so extensive as to be able to give all citizens anything but a small piece of the action. The private sector is where the real wealth is, as is attested most sharply by the regular defection of public servants to the private sector. Ditching the prestigious title of director general for plain board director is an enriching experience, it would seem, judging by the roll-call of those who have done so; to name but a few, pioneers Khetso Gordhan and Mac Maharaj from the Transport Department, and former Communications Director General Andile Ngcaba.

It is clear, sometimes dramatically so, that privatisation can dramatically exacerbate inequality. The new class of oligarchs in the former Soviet Union is the most searing example, and a warning to South Africa. Socialism in the old days at least offered the prospect of equality of poverty.

Privatisation has not, despite its critics, really been pursued with any vigour in South Africa, so there is not much chance of that happening here. But how has privatisation contributed to redistribution of assets for BEE so far?

The answer is that the only major, high-profile privatisation to date has not led to new black ownership of assets, or even much wider ownership of assets. Smaller privatisations have achieved more in themselves, but alone will not do much for BEE.

The 'retail offering' of shares in Telkom to the public was accompanied by the so-called Khulisa scheme. The Khulisa scheme was designed specifically to put shares in the hands of new black owners. It resulted in less than 1 per cent of Telkom's shareholding being black.

The total retail offering, Khulisa and non-Khulisa, comprises around 2 per cent of Telkom's total number of issued shares – most of Telkom remains in state or corporate hands. As an exercise in empowerment of the broader populace, the Iscor privatisation of the 1980s did a better job, even though it was confined to the white population.

On top of this, the other Telkom gesture at empowerment – the 3 per cent of shares held by small empowerment consortium Ucingo, set aside from the initial privatisation – vanished after the listing. The Ucingo stake reverted to financiers because of Ucingo's inability to finance the shares, in a manner uncomfortably common for the first wave of empowerment deals, built as they were on the assumption of a surging share price. The net result is that Telkom has no significant block of empowerment shareholding. To date, nothing has come of the plan to reserve 5 per cent of Telkom shares for transfer to the National Empowerment Fund for financing of BEE.

Opportunities for using privatisation for BEE to broaden ownership of the economy appear limited, to say the least. Simply put, privatisation is on the back burner, though there is no actual policy change. Most tellingly, government betrays a new hesitance about privatising its core assets, making a fuss of dividends received from Eskom, for instance, rather than privatisation proceeds.[2]

Liberalisation, or restructuring in the sense of reshaping the economy to be more competitive, also seems to have stalled in 2003. True, the listing and further sale of Telkom shares went ahead in calendar 2003, but the state is still heavily involved in telecommunications through the Eskom and Transnet shares of the proposed competition for Telkom, the second national operator. Through its continued holding in Telkom, the state is involved in cellular telephony through Vodacom, 50 per cent owned by Telkom.

Privatisation of Eskom electricity generation itself is understandably being handled gingerly, though the first small steps have been taken to introduce competition in electricity generation through the privatisation of, for example, the former Kelvin Power Station outside Johannesburg. But Eskom Enterprises, Eskom's private sector arm, continues to be state-owned. State information technology (IT) firm Arivia.kom, which competes with other IT firms in the private sector, has not even been mentioned as a candidate for privatisation.

After ten years, the state has loosened its grip slightly on central areas of the economy but it has by no means let go.

This might not be important, but for the peculiar fondness South Africa – birthplace of one of the longest-lasting global cartels, De Beers – has for monopolies and market dominance. Robin McGregor has inherited from his crusading father, Who Owns Whom founder Robin McGregor, the task of monitoring monopolistic tendencies. In the 2004 edition of *Who owns whom*, he notes that the market control by the top five companies, referred to earlier, has dropped from around 83 per cent ten years ago to 44 per cent today. The big conglomerates have unbundled, simplifying their structures and letting companies loose to be bought by others or survive on their own.

Yet McGregor (2004:67) remarks that, 'concentration of control in sectors of the South African economy is still unacceptably high'. 'In 1977', he writes, 'the

Mouton Commission found that in 37 sectors, three or fewer producers shared more than 75% of the sector's market.' Disturbingly, McGregor notes that a recent study by Who Owns Whom finds the degree of sectoral concentration has increased. 'It is now hard to find sectors where there are not three or fewer dominant players.' In this situation, Rand strength is important to allow imported competition, since limited local competition gives local producers far too much leeway.

The nub of private ownership

In 1994, visitors to South Africa could be shown the stark reality behind the statistics of inequality simply by driving from Sandton to nearby Alexandria township. It is not that simple now. True, Alexandria is still there, and informal settlements still jostle the formal housing in what remains a ghetto. Residential property ownership is still highly stratified in South Africa, ranging from informal ownership of congested shack settlements through modest suburbs of single-story houses to faux-Tuscan mansions in gated golf estates where property prices run into the millions.

The focus since 1994 has not been on ownership so much as housing, with the President able to boast of substantial improvements. A decade ago, 'Estimates of the housing backlog ranged from 1.4 million to 3 million units and people living in shacks were between 5 million to 7.7 million.' By February 2004, 'About 1.9 million housing subsidies have been provided and 1.6 million houses built for the poor of our country'.[3] Whatever targets the ANC may have had, building almost two million houses for the poor is no mean feat.

Even the boom in informal settlements means that black people living there have a form of wealth, since they probably have some form of tradeable value.

Apartheid laws mostly cramped black economic activity in the homeland areas, and black ownership of property in most of South Africa was prohibited for decades. This, combined with persistent poverty, should mean that whites own most of the housing in traditional residential areas. In 1994 it was expected that a rapid influx of black buyers would boost housing prices massively. The house price boom did not come. Instead, a housing market recession plunged prices to levels so low it was joked that either South Africa had the cheapest houses in the world, or the most expensive cars. What happened to the expected flow of black buyers from the townships?

Racial ownership patterns did change after 1994. Even before 1990, some areas had rapidly become mixed or changed their racial nature entirely, becoming *de facto* black suburbs with a sprinkling of white people. But the creation of an African middle class able to afford to leave the townships did not happen overnight. Even the wealthier Indian communities needed some time to say goodbye to the apartheid-designated areas such as Lenasia and poorer, 'mixed' suburbs such as Mayfair, which were a transition from Lenasia, before helping to boost house prices in formerly genteel middle-class white areas like Greenside to unheard-of levels.

The influx of the new black middle class, including Africans, has happened, though the evidence is largely anecdotal – except for the surge in house prices. According to ResearchWorldwide.com, South African house prices rose by 22.7 per cent year-on-year, the highest among the countries monitored, including star performers like Australia and the UK. ResearchWorldwide.com puts this down to, 'Low interest rates, the emergence of a rapidly growing black middle class and the longest period of uninterrupted economic growth in half a century.'[4]

There is no obvious way of quantifying the exact value of this new black ownership of residential property, since property records do not require racial classification. At the other end of the scale, there is little information available now on the value of the low-cost housing programme that the President boasted created many new homeowners in the first decade of freedom. And the value of housing in the 'mixed' or newly black suburbs decreased sharply, as a result of a banking reluctance to lend in what were perceived as risky suburbs, together with problems of non-payment by new tenants.

What statistical surveys do show is that African ownership of residential property is not insubstantial. Around half of South African households own a housing asset; 63 per cent of those households are urban, and 67 per cent are black. Half of these households have a mean household income of R2 300, and so fall into the category of low income.

Ownership for poorer people has not translated easily into a stepping-stone into the middle class. As Ros Gordon and Matthew Nel of Shisaka Development

Management Services noted in BusinessMap's review of empowerment (Reddy et al. 2003b), low-income households cannot use their housing units to raise capital.

Real estate with capital-raising value exists in the residential suburbs, and with pressure being put on banks not to red-line newly black suburbs, owners may not be trapped with the 'dead capital' Peruvian economist Hernando de Soto (2000) reckons is the drag on the urban poor converting their property into working capital.

Gordon and Nel argue that home ownership among the poor represents an opportunity for them to improve their financial circumstances, but a secondary market for low-income housing has not materialised, and lenders see low-income areas as high risk. They conclude that while government has done a wonderful job of delivering housing, 'it is now necessary to turn the attention to making such housing a recognizable and economically useful asset for its owners. Only then will housing begin to contribute properly towards alleviating poverty in SA' (Reddy et al. 2003b:37).

The burning issue that isn't such a burning issue

Land dispossession lies at the heart of the country's history, and its heritage of inequity may well curse the land well into the future. Though focusing on the land alone now will not necessarily put matters right, land reform is acknowledged as a necessity, even by staunch proponents of property rights like Leon Louw. Property rights and land reform are seen as complementary. Land reform has three important parts: land restitution of land taken away under apartheid; land redistribution to create more equal ownership of land; and land tenure reform to give people ownership of land they live on under tribal systems.

When the ANC came to power ten years ago, South Africa had one of the most skewed patterns of land distribution in the world, with some 87 per cent of land owned by a minority of the five million whites and only 13 per cent of it owned by blacks.

As former Surplus People's Project head Stephen Hulbert (2002) has pointed out, black people not only held *less* land, the land they did hold was generally of inferior productive quality. More than 12 million black people inhabited only 17 million hectares of land: less than 60 000 almost exclusively white-owned farms occupied 86 million hectares, including most of the limited high-potential arable land.

To make matters worse, around 15 per cent, or about 2.6 million hectares of the 17 million hectares held by blacks, was potentially arable. Most was classified as being of low to medium potential. By contrast, white-owned farms included over six times that amount, or some 16 million hectares of potentially arable land, of which nearly two-thirds was of medium to high potential (Hulbert 2002).

Yet land reform, in the sense of redistribution, has been low on the agenda, and what has been undertaken since 1994 has been concentrated in the area of land restitution.

In February 2004, the *Financial Mail* could say that the Department of Land Affairs has to date settled around 43 000 or more than half the claims lodged with government before a cut-off date for applications in 1998, at a cost of R1.9 billion. In the process, around 477 000ha has been given back to victims of apartheid's forced removals (*Financial Mail* 20.02.04).

In 2000, the *Financial Mail* noted, government undertook to make good on the RDP promise of redistributing a third of South Africa's 85 million hectares of agricultural land within 15 years. Compared to this, the million or so hectares of land demanded for restitution will be a drop in the ocean.

That ownership of agricultural land does not play a bigger role in South African politics may be due to the relatively high urbanisation of the country, and to the decline of the political party whose rallying cry was traditionally the return of the land to the pre-colonial inhabitants – along with the slogan 'One settler one bullet'. That the ANC in government has been able to put a number of other spending items higher up the priority list – including arms – is testimony to the lack of influence of the PAC. Also, the ANC has been pragmatic in recognising the economic importance of agriculture, as did the Zimbabwean government for many years until the fruit of economic mismanagement led the Zimbabwe African National Union-Patriotic Front President to use populist measures to shore up his support.

Another reason for government not rushing into land redistribution is that it has been persuaded of the economic importance of farming. Primary agriculture, according to a Department of Agriculture Strategic Plan produced in 2001, contributes 4.5 per cent of South Africa's gross domestic product, while the larger agro-food complex accounts for another 9 per cent. The 50 000 mostly, but not exclusively, white, large, commercial farming operations exported about R16 billion worth of products, or nearly 10 per cent of South Africa's total exports.

Undoubtedly, this thinking has contributed to what could be construed as 'excruciatingly slow' delivery on land reform. But some of the slow pace could be explained by low level of resources, reinforced by the inability to spend the money.

Some may have been due to the Department of Land Affairs (DLA) shifting its focus from trying simply to hand over land to black communities without ensuring the necessary 'aftercare' to ensure their success. The present Minister of Land Affairs prefers to concentrate on creating a class of black commercial farmers, a way of thinking more in line with developments in BEE.

Whatever the case, land reform has been given new impetus by the chaos next door surrounding 'fast-tracked land reform', the Zimbabwean government's euphemism for illegal land expropriation later given force by law. The spectre of land invasions effectively ending certainty on property rights has hung over South Africa ever since President Robert Mugabe gave the nod to illegal occupations by 'war veterans' of farmland in neighbouring Zimbabwe.

And because of the violent Zimbabwe farm occupations and what they represent, at least for white South Africans and the West, the Bredell land invasions in Kempton Park in July 2001 started to bring land issues back into the headlines in the South African and foreign media. The South African government was quick to point out that the invasions, apparently sponsored by the PAC, were driven by the need for accommodation, not by land hunger. But this misses the point somewhat.

As University of the Witwatersrand political studies professor Tom Lodge (2003:7) pointed out in October last year, 'Arguably with two-thirds of the population living in towns and with a relatively efficient agricultural system, the minor significance assigned to land reform may seem justified.' He quite rightly goes on to point out the political dangers of ignoring land, 'If we want a democracy in ten years' time we need to spend more, much more, on land reform directed at poor people now. Otherwise, in the year before the ANC's fifth-term election, state-sponsored illegal land seizures will make perfectly good sense to government leaders whose first priority, as with politicians anywhere, is retaining office.'

Growing discontent about the speed of land redistribution, if not land restitution, led to the ascendancy of the Landless People's Movement (LPM) as the main voice, according to HSRC senior research specialist Michael Aliber, writing in BusinessMap's annual review, 'for black people wanting to see a completely different version of land reform', one not only speeded up, but concentrating on the poor rather than the 'well-resourced and capable local elites', as the DLA's land redistribution for agricultural development does, in Aliber's view (Reddy et al. 2003b:38–39).

Whether the land redistribution for agricultural development approach, which is essentially BEE, is the correct approach, needs further examination.

Finance Minister Trevor Manuel's latest Budget seemed to acknowledge that government is listening, at least with half an ear, upping the amount devoted to land reform by R700 million. Money devoted to land reform and restitution rises over the three-year budgeting process, even after the 2005 deadline for settling all restitution claims. Moreover, the government has amended legislation to give itself even more power to expropriate, bypassing the 'willing seller, willing buyer' route that has, it is argued, in some cases delayed and made more expensive the land redistribution process.

Clearly land redistribution will increase in importance, though there are doubts whether political pressures have retarded land tenure reform, alluded to by Leon Louw (1996) in calling for increased emphasis on private ownership of land: 'The Mandela administration also could call for the summary conversion of all forms of apartheid title into full ownership.'

Black economic empowerment: to BEE or not to BEE?

Lodge has contrasted the importance of land reform with that of BEE as it is more generally understood:

> Generally the very visible inequities in land ownership are politically dangerous, more so, probably, than the racial inequalities in

share ownership on the stock exchange, the current focus of government empowerment policies. Poor people's resentment of white wealth is much more likely to be triggered into violent retribution by a racial land monopoly than the less visually obvious racial configurations of company ownership. (2003:7)

Racial ownership of the JSE Securities Exchange is a proxy for ownership of the economy in general, especially in the absence of other indicators. A glance at the glossy pictures of the boards of most companies on the JSE will show mostly middle-aged – and mostly male – white faces. The new black multi-millionaires are very much visible, clutching cellphones to do deals while driving a range of luxury cars, or paying high prices for cigars and liquor at ultra-modern venues glittering with glass and blonde wood paneling in Rosebank's Hyatt hotel or Melrose Arch.

So what is the racial ownership of the JSE? Do the new black millionaires and billionaires – the Tokyo Sexwales, Patrice Motsepes and Mzi Khumalos – signal a seismic shift in ownership, the new black face of capitalism in South Africa? Not quite.

BusinessMap Foundation research estimated that, at the end of September 2002, 12 per cent to 15 per cent of the value of shares listed on the JSE Securities Exchange was held, directly and indirectly by black people (Reddy et al. 2003a).

This far from reflects demographics, with the white population only representing around 10 per cent of the population. But it may be misleading, because that 15 per cent is a percentage of the entire ownership of the JSE's share capital.

Foreigners hold a large proportion of the shares on the JSE. According to the study, foreign ownership of the JSE stood at 32 per cent at the end of 2002. Since foreign investors cannot be expected to bear the burden of a policy designed to correct historical imbalances they had no role in creating, this leaves 68 per cent for BEE. Direct foreign investment is long term by nature and can, in many cases, help South African firms tap into foreign networks for exports, as well as access new skills and technology. No one disputes that it should be encouraged. Yet a policy that amounts to ownership 'indigenisation' – such as the 25 per cent sale of mostly foreign-owned oil companies by the Liquid Fuels Charter – automatically does just that.

Some of the unintended consequences can be laid at the door of the nature of BEE. It was not a carefully prepared policy. BEE has evolved from a voluntary and ad hoc initiative by the private sector in the years before and after 1994, to a programme driven by the state's buying and licensing power and more clearly guided by state policy. Much of the focus in the early years of BEE was on 'direct empowerment stakes'.

However, in most of the developed world, ownership of shares directly by individuals, firms, or consortia is small compared to investment through institutions such as life assurance companies. BusinessMap has tracked direct investment since 1996, specifically the listed black-controlled companies' share of JSE's market capitalisation. This has hovered around 3 to 4 per cent in recent years.

Institutional investors own 35 per cent of the JSE, and the Government Pension Fund owns at least 10 per cent. Unsurprisingly, this is where most black ownership is concentrated, rather than in direct shareholding, specifically that of ordinary black people.

Lodge is incorrect in thinking that BEE concerns only equity transfers in listed companies (though this will continue to be an important part of BEE). Government's Broad-Based Black Empowerment Act, and its attending broad-based BEE strategy, aims to de-emphasise equity transfers and dramatically increase the racial transformation of business by buttressing other legislation aimed at affirmative action ('employment equity' in South Africa), skills training, and procurement of goods and services from black people.

It is true that in the popular imagination BEE is still associated with the high-profile deals involving listed companies of the mid-90s. The 'art of the deal', to use the title of American wheeler-dealer Donald Trump's book, was highly prized. These deals often fell apart because of faulty financial engineering assembled to transfer equity from those who had money to those who did not. Some deals put together recently to satisfy government demands for transformation in industries such as mining – that have been subjected to 'charters' where companies have agreed to targets on equity transfer over a certain time – bear features suspiciously similar to past deal structures, and sometimes with new structures whose sustainability is open to question.

Nonetheless, the equity deals that have passed and those still to pass cannot be dismissed out of hand as not contributing to transformation. Those deals contribute to a process where ordinary black people own, as white people do, a stake in the economy through retirement funds, endowments, unit trusts and – it is to be hoped now that government is introducing legislation to make such schemes more tax-friendly – employee share-ownership schemes.

It is true that overall measures of black equity as a proxy for transformation are better than the direct measures that have possibly misled commentators in the past – the 3 or 4 per cent of the JSE now held by black individuals, black companies or the 'broad-based' consortia that at times evaporate, leaving the shares in the hands of black individuals.

As direct black ownership increases, this will help the process of entrenching employment equity and black skills development. This, in turn, will mean indirect ownership will increase, as more of those newly employed black people take out pension policies and invest their earnings in insurance and life assurance policies.

Along with other interventions to bring more black people into the mainstream of the economy through spreading ownership, by creating a real property market for the newly housed, and by land reform to create new viable black-owned farms, BEE holds out the hope of normalisation of the economy if it is pursued carefully. But while BEE will naturally seduce the newly empowered with the charms of fly-fishing and single malt whiskies, it cannot stop there.

It is disappointing that the idea of employee share-ownership schemes and other broader incentives to give ordinary people a stake in the economy float to the top of public debate occasionally, are mentioned in official documents, and then disappear again from consciousness. True, the first two schemes to try to broaden black ownership – Johnnic's Ikageng scheme and M-Net's Phuthuma scheme – were badly timed, but the concept was correct. In Eastern Europe, schemes to give workers and the public shares in newly privatised companies were notorious for their failure, as the new shareholders sold on their shares immediately. But in South Africa, the Khulisa scheme, as we have seen, did not even attempt much in the way of broad-based ownership.

Conclusion

Ownership is a broad and complex topic, and one chapter is not enough to even begin to find hard solutions. But we can get an overview of the road travelled and the road ahead.

Ten years after the first democratic elections, ownership patterns have changed, dramatically in some areas and little in others. And in some areas it is hard to judge how far we have come because the measurement is recent. How much of the JSE was owned indirectly by black people in 1994, for instance? A lack of measurement also underlines some deeper political issues. One is gender. Though government has gone out of its way to ensure gender representation at the highest levels – in Cabinet, for example – and the paras-tatals have a good record of promoting women, this has not leaked into the private sector, where women chief executive officers are notable by their absence. And in BEE, complaints about the first draft of the Broad-Based BEE Bill led to the specific inclusion of black women as candidates for empower-ment. White women, however, are now explicitly excluded in terms of the provisions of the Broad-Based BEE Act.

This points to a problem for the grand project that is BEE. Why the continual emphasis on direct equity, on black groupings and already empowered indi-viduals, despite government's scorecard approach that demands a range of changes along with equity? Could this be because of pressure from vested interests, the black middle class whom the President's brother, Moeletsi Mbeki, believes need no empowering, but who are being aided and abetted in enrichment by BEE?

With government's broad-based BEE strategy finally having officially defined BEE, it may be thought that the intellectual contest over the content of this aspect of 'transformation' is finally over. Government has had to sail between the Scylla and Charibdis of too broad or too narrow a definition, neither of which would be much used. It defines BEE as: 'an integrated and coherent socio-economic process that directly contributes to the economic transfor-mation of South Africa and brings about significant increases in the numbers of black people that manage, own and control the country's economy, as well as significant decreases in income inequalities' (DTI 2003).

It seems to me urgent that BEE be rethought, not in relation to transformation in the broad sense, but in relation to ownership patterns. I believe land reform, land tenure, creating a market for RDP houses and boosting the market for township housing, are all as much a part of BEE as changing ownership of Anglo American Corporation, and likely to be more successful in enlarging the middle class in South Africa. The government strategy document acknowledges this, but even its scorecard approach has not managed to deflect the political pressure for direct equity to be transferred, mainly to a relatively small number of black people who have the drive, knowledge or political connections. The question is: will this achieve even the wealth owned by white South Africans, never mind the economic growth necessary for re-distribution of wealth through spending on social services and the like?

The wealth of most white South Africans does not lie in having shares in specific companies on the JSE. Successive cycles of boom and bust tend to dissuade most people from putting hard-earned savings in stocks. They own houses, or are in the process of paying bonds on houses. What money white South Africans have put away is usually in the form of contractual savings, amounts taken from bank accounts through debit order or by their employers to be funnelled into life assurers to invest on their behalf.

Beyond the scope of this paper is the other thing that white South Africans own – though not to the extent that Europeans or Americans do – skills, and disparities are still racially based. The South African Institute of Race Relations (SAIRR 2002) has noted that nearly 15 per cent of working-age whites hold a higher degree, whereas only 1.5 per cent of Africans have such a qualification, though SAIRR notes that the divide will narrow as African enrolment now exceeds that of whites at both universities and technikons. That educational edge will have to be used by whites to stay within the middle class. Anecdotally, the thought is that the shutting off of easy options for employment is causing young white males either to emigrate or to become entrepreneurs. There is some evidence that entrepreneurship has surged among whites, coloureds and especially Indians. What this attests to is the importance of not neglecting education as a tool for equality as well as for economic growth, as the export thrust of the economy demands skilled workers.

Related to that is the precious new jewel that is intellectual property. President Robert Mugabe has attempted to return many of his countrymen to a hard life of subsistence agriculture through parcelling out farms confiscated haphazardly and illegally, under the guise of finally putting right an old wrong. Many, mainly black people, both in Zimbabwe and, significantly, in South Africa, refuse to acknowledge the moral and financial damage done – and the not coincidental human rights abuses that accompanied this last gamble – and the economic mismanagement that preceded the desperate move.

Mugabe, with a world view formed by the last part of the nineteenth century, never mind the twenty-first, had not grasped or did not care that in the modern world of cash economies and information zipping around the world in seconds, a piece of land is not the prize it used to be.

Microsoft founder Bill Gates has become one of the wealthiest men in the world through ownership, initially, of little more than closely guarded computer software code. Ownership of intellectual property, and the ability to use modern technology to advantage, is a source of wealth often neglected in discussions on ownership, mired in past visions of Satanic mills or vast estates from which to seek rents. In that sense, only recently has there been some glimmer of the importance attached to open-source software, the bane of Bill Gates' corporation because of the threat it contains to intellectual property in the world of computerisation. Ironically, now backing that movement is 'Afronaut' Mark Shuttleworth, who became a billionaire by selling software developed in South Africa to US-based Verisign some years ago.

The final point for changing ownership patterns is the South African obsession with race, which has obscured the increasing foreign ownership of the economy and increasing concentration of ownership within sectors. For better or worse, our biggest firms have their headquarters overseas and foreigners own much more than they used to. Foreign ownership of property in wine farms – even President Bongo bought one – and beachfront homes in Cape Town has soared, though this pales in comparison with the substantial ownership foreigners have of the JSE Securities Exchange. And while opening up the economy has brought imported competition, which in times of Rand strength helps combat inflation, it has also implied that local industries have become more concentrated to fight off foreign competition. This may be temporary, and was unavoidable, but it does point to a need to throw a lot of political weight behind our newly reformed competition authorities to offset the unintended consequences of what seemed like a good idea at the time.

Notes

1   The Freedom Charter was adopted by the Congress of the People in June 1955 at Kliptown. Available at <http://www.anc.org.za/ancdocs/history/charter.html>.

2   Presentation of Eskom's annual financial statement, speech by shareholder representative of Eskom Holdings Limited, Mr Jeff Radebe, 10.03.03. Available at <http://www.dpe.gov.za>.

3   Quoted in the *Address of the President Of South Africa, Thabo Mbeki, to the First Joint Sitting of The Third Democratic Parliament,* Cape Town, 21.05.04. Available at <http://www.gov.za>.

4   According to 'Worldwide house price indices', compiled by ResearchWorldwide.com.

References

Adam H, van Zyl Slabbert F & Moodley K (1997) *Comrades in business – post-liberation politics in South Africa.* Cape Town: Tafelberg.

Cargill J et al. (2000) *Empowerment 2000: New directions.* Johannesburg: The BusinessMap Foundation.

Cargill J et al. (2001) *Empowerment 2001: Better outcomes.* Johannesburg: The BusinessMap Foundation.

de Soto H (2000) *The mystery of capital: Why capitalism triumphs in the West and fails everywhere else.* New York: Basic Books.

DLA (Department of Land Affairs, South Africa) (2001) *Strategic plan for South African agriculture.* Pretoria: DLA.

DTI (Department of Trade and Industry, South Africa) (2003) *South Africa's economic transformation: A strategy for broad-based black economic empowerment.* Pretoria: DTI.

Hitzeroth L & Reddy C (2003) *Black ownership structure of the JSE.* Study commissioned by Anglogold. Johannesburg: The BusinessMap Foundation.

Hulbert S (2002) Zimbabwe-style land grabs – could they happen here? Unpublished paper.

Innes D (1981) *Anglo American and the rise of modern South Africa.* Johannesburg: Ravan.

Landman JP (co-ordinator) assisted by H Bhorat, S van der Berg & C van Aardt (2003) *Breaking the grip of poverty and inequality in South Africa 2004–2014. Current trends, issues and future policy options.* Available at <http://www.sarpn.org.za/documents/d0000649/P661-Povertyreport3b.pdf>.

Lodge T (2003) Land reform, *Arena Magazine* 10:6–7.

Louw L (1996) Property rights and democracy, *Economic Reform Today No. 1.* Available at <http:www.cipe.org/publications/fs/ert/e19/louw.htm>. Accessed 18.08.04.

McGregor R (2004) *McGregor's Who owns whom in South Africa 2004.* Johannesburg: Who Owns Whom.

Riley T (1993) *South Africa: Characteristics of and constraints facing black business in South Africa – survey results.* World Bank Discussion Paper No 5. Washington: World Bank Group.

Reddy C et al. (2003a) *Phase 1: Black ownership structure of the JSE.* Study sponsored by Anglogold, The BusinessMap Foundation, April 2003.

Reddy C et al. (2003b) *Empowerment 2003: State and market initiatives gain momentum.* Johannesburg: The BusinessMap Foundation.

Rumney R et al. (2002a) *Empowerment 2002: The state steps in.* Johannesburg: The BusinessMap Foundation.

Rumney R et al. (2002b) *Restructuring 2002: A sense of movement.* Johannesburg: The BusinessMap Foundation.

SAIRR (South African Institute of Race Relations) (2002) *Fast Facts* No. 11.

Stats SA (Statistics South Africa) (2002) *Report on the survey of large and small scale agriculture.* Pretoria: Stats SA.

16 The state of employment

Miriam Altman

Introduction

What is job-creating growth? At what point can we say that we have jobless or job-creating growth? If 200 000 jobs are created in a year, is that job-creating growth? What about 50 jobs? Or 50 000 jobs? The idea of job-creating growth does not necessarily relate to positive job growth, but rather to the sustainability of that growth in relation to its role in generating employment. Most economies require that some minimum proportion of the population work to support output, taxation, household livelihoods and income distribution – and to support the rest of the population that are not working, especially children and the elderly.

Relatively low levels of economic participation may be possible in economies with strong fiscal systems and a sufficient tax base, assuming there are generous income transfers through the state, and assuming that this is seen as desirable. Countries that do not have this access to earnings must depend on high levels of economic participation to guarantee minimum livelihoods.

Low levels of economic participation, and the resulting social dislocation, are not generally sustainable in the long run. In countries with similar per capita income levels, about 50–68 per cent of the working age population participates in the labour force, with unemployment ideally not rising above about 10–15 per cent (see UN 2004 and Table 16.1).

Let's look at what job-creating growth means.

If there is positive job creation, does this indicate that there is 'job-creating growth'? *Jobless growth generally indicates that the gross domestic product (GDP) is growing, while employment is stagnant or falling.* But job-creating

Table 16.1 *Unemployment rates by region and gender, 2003 (percentages)*

	Total	Female	Male
World	6.3	6.5	6.2
Industrialised economies	6.8	7.0	6.7
Transition economies	9.4	9.3	9.5
East Asia	3.1	2.6	3.6
South East Asia	7.1	7.8	6.5
South Asia	4.8	6.1	4.2
Latin America & Caribbean	9.0	11.2	7.6
Middle East & North Africa	11.9	16.2	10.4
Sub-Saharan Africa	10.8	9.5	11.8

Source: Extracted from ILO 2004: Table 2
Note: Different aggregation techniques and methodologies may lead to differences
in aggregate figures. These should be seen as indicative only.

growth is not merely a situation where employment is rising. To identify job-creating growth, we need to define what stagnant employment growth means.

Positive job creation would mean something very different for a small economy like Mauritius, with a labour force of less than 1 million – than it does in a larger economy, such as Mexico or Brazil, with a labour force of about 70 million and 121 million people respectively. Creating an extra million jobs over ten years could create a labour shortage in Mauritius, and would hardly be noticed in Mexico or Brazil.

The rate and scale of employment creation needs to be measured in relation to the size and average growth of the labour force. If these are not growing in line, then unemployment will rise. So, employment may be rising, but by such a small amount relative to the labour force that it might still be thought of as stagnant.

Any economy undergoing change, and especially a developing one, will experience major shifts between sectors – often a painful uneven process. South Africa is going through a process of structural change and development, which is an inherently uncertain time. This means that some sectors will lose jobs, and hopefully others will gain. Net employment losses or gains must be understood in this context.

This paper contributes to debates on jobless growth – insofar as it seeks some indicators that might be tracked to determine whether SA is on a sustainable growth path – here defined as a path where there is a sufficient rate of employment growth at any rate of economic growth.

Job-creating or jobless growth?

Some indicators of a sustainable (job-creating) growth path are identified as:
- GDP growth, with stable rates of unemployment (at acceptable rates), or else falling unemployment – remembering that it is possible to have rising employment and unemployment if the labour force is growing faster than can be accommodated by the economy.
- Employment expansion sufficient to sufficiently absorb new labour market entrants (and possibly some unemployed).
- GDP growth, with concomitant increases in employment.

Unemployment and growth

Unemployment is the first indicator of the sustainability of a growth path. We know that unemployment by any measure in SA is very high. Is there any indication that it might be slowing or reversing?

Table 16.2 presents the growth in unemployment over the period 1994–2002. Year-on-year changes in unemployment are not always reliable, but the overall trend is one of growing unemployment – increasing by about 1 to 2 per cent per annum. Figure 16.1 compares GDP and unemployment. We can see that unemployment has been rising despite economic growth.[1]

Table 16.2 *Unemployment trends (percentages)*

	1994	1995	1996	1997	1998	1999	2000	2001	2002
Strict definition	20.0	16.9	19.3	21.0	25.2	23.3	25.8	29.5	30.5
Broad definition	28.6	26.5	34.9	38.9	37.5	36.2	35.9	41.5	41.8

Source: Calculated from electronic data made available by Stats SA, OHS 1994–99; Sept LFS 2000–01

Figure 16.1 *GDP and unemployment*

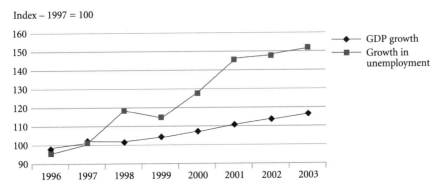

Index – 1997 = 100

Source: Calculated from electronic data made available by SARB and Stats SA, OHS 1996–99; Sept LFS 2000–02

Figure 16.2 shows how unemployment has been rising for all race groups, but markedly less for whites than for others. As is well known, unemployment hits the African labour force harder than other race groups – rising to 36.8 per cent by 2002. However, the rates of unemployment for coloureds and Indians have also risen quite substantially – to more than 20 per cent by 2002.

Figure 16.2 *Unemployment by race*

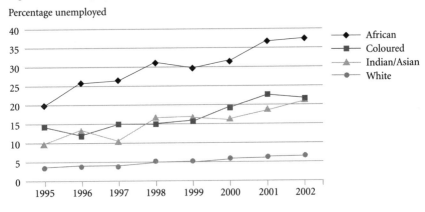

Percentage unemployed

Source: Calculated from electronic data made available by Stats SA, OHS 1995–99; Sept LFS 2000–02
Note: this figure uses the strict definition of unemployment

One-third to half of the 'strictly-defined' unemployed had been out of work for more than three years. Although some argue that many of these people may well be working in small piece jobs or in the formal sector, the Labour Force Survey (LFS) covered any and all economic activity, including unpaid labour, so should capture this possibility. Figure 16.3 shows that a greater proportion of the labour force is looking for work.[2] This is surprising in the context of structural unemployment, and may mean that people are more hopeful, or alternatively more desperate, as the picture is still quite bleak. Figure 16.4 may partly explain why a growing proportion of people are looking – the majority of the unemployed are young and recent entrants to the labour market. Figure 16.4 presents unemployment by age, comparing 1995 and 2002. While approximately 75 per cent of the unemployed were less than 35 years old in both years, the sheer growth in numbers shows the burden that the jobs queue imposes on young entrants.

Rapid labour force growth between 1997 and 2000 is one contributor to unemployment – with a growing gap between labour force entry and the ability of the economy to create jobs. Figure 16.5 compares total job creation to labour force growth between 1996 and 2000 – and shows how the labour force growth outstripped employment expansion.

However, labour force entry does not help to explain growing unemployment after 2000, since the labour force participation rate (LFPR) stabilised, as seen

Figure 16.3 *Comparing strict and broad unemployment*

Unemployed (thousands)

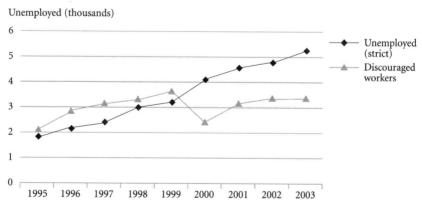

Source: Calculated from electronic data made available by Stats SA, OHS 1995–99; Sept LFS 2000–02

in Figure 16.5. The growing gap between the number of entrants to the labour market and available jobs appears to rely on an understanding of weak employment expansion. This will be discussed in the following section.[3]

Figure 16.4 *Number of unemployed by age*

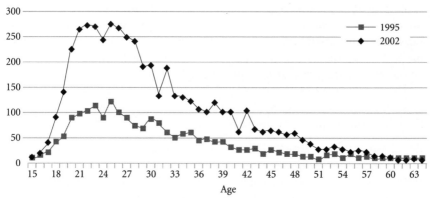

Source: Calculated from electronic data made available by Stats SA, OHS 1995; Sept LFS 2002
Note: This figure uses the strict definition of labour force and unemployed

Figure 16.5 *Employment and labour force*

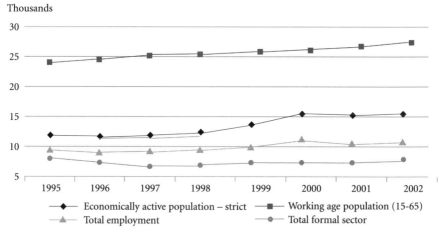

Source: Calculated from electronic data made available by Stats SA, OHS 1995; Sept LFS 2000–02
Note: This figure uses the strict definition of labour force

It is difficult to know the extent to which the rising labour force growth rate over the 1990s was real, as opposed to a result of changes in measurement. The way questions were posed shifted, where the surveys delved deeper into economic activity – it is possible that many people, such as housewives or subsistence farmers, viewed themselves as not economically active at one point, but with more probing, were later categorised as unemployed or employed (see Altman & Woolard 2004). An alternative way of tracking unemployment would therefore be useful – one that does not rely on labour force participation as a mediating factor.

Figure 16.6 shows the proportion of the working age population (15–64) that is *not working*.[4] We see a different trend to that seen in Figure 16.2 – for most race groups, the proportion in the working age population that was not working did fluctuate, but was essentially stable. This is particularly surprising for Africans. More than the unemployment figure, the relation to the working age population gives a sense of the extent to which the employed support the rest of the population. A second measure shows the ratio of the population that is not working to those that are working. This measure of dependency falls from 3.5 in 1996 to 3.4 in 2002. This means there were 3.4 people to every one working person in the population in 2002.[5]

In summary, despite a positive GDP growth rate between 1996 and 2002, the unemployment rate continues to grow by about 1–2 per cent per annum. By this

Figure 16.6 *'Not working', as a percentage of working age population, by race*

Percentage of working age population that is not working

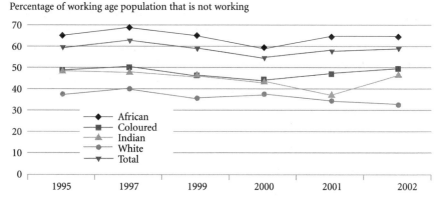

Source: Calculated from electronic data made available by Stats SA, OHS 1995–99; Sept LFS 2000–02

measure, we find that we do not have a sustainable employment growth path. However, the unemployment rate partly increased as a result of a rapid expansion in labour force participation in the 1990s. As we are not sure whether or not this is a real or measured phenomenon, we looked at the ratio of the economically active population that were not working to those that were working. This measure ignores whether a person is (or believes they are) participating in the labour force – so that it eliminates the possible measurement problem. Here we find a surprising result – that the percentage of non-working people relative to working people has been quite stable. This means that the dependency of non-working people on working people is about the same in 2002 as it was in 1996. This is a positive result. However, it does not mean that the growth path is sustainable from an employment perspective, as will be shown in the following section, where we find that the employment-generating capacity of the economy is simply too small in relation to the size of the labour force.

Employment and growth

We have already seen that unemployment rates are continuing to rise, by about 1–2 per cent a year, reaching about 30.5 per cent by September 2002. There is some evidence to show that unemployment growth may be slowing, but it is still to early to say whether the trend is actually reversing.

An analysis of employment trends will give us a sense of whether we might expect to turn the corner any time soon. There is considerable confusion in the understanding of employment trends, owing to variations accross different data sets.

Figure 16.7 offers a direct comparison of GDP and formal private non-agricultural employment. This is a useful representation as it eliminates confusion and cyclical variations arising from agriculture and the informal sector. Two sources of employment data are shown. The most frequently used representation of GDP employment involves the use of data from the Survey of Earnings and Employment (SEE). This representation – showing GDP rising and employment falling since 1995 – is a chart often cited from the South African Reserve Bank (SARB) publications. It depicts a fairly dire picture of a dramatically widening gap between employment and GDP since 1994.

Then compare the employment figures as extracted from the October Household Survey (OHS) and the September LFS, also in Figure 16.7. This shows important increases in formal private non-agricultural employment since 1998, seeming to grow at a similar rate as GDP. Over this period, the OHS and LFS offer better employment estimates than the SEE due to the latter's exclusion of many parts of services industries – the main source of employment growth in the 1990s. Indeed, the leap in the SEE figures in 2002 is really a discontinuity, when the statistical agency updated its business register, upon which its survey is based.

Figure 16.7 *GDP and employment growth – comparing formal non-agricultural private sector employment in the LFS and SEE*

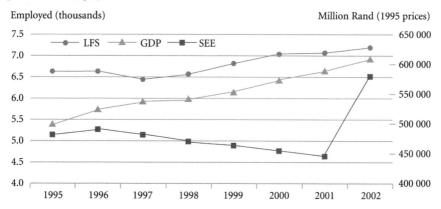

Source: Calculated from electronic data made available by Stats SA, OHS 1995–99; Sept LFS 2000–02; SEE 1995–2002

Figure 16.8 presents total employment, with a breakdown by private, public and non-formal employment. This latter category includes domestic workers and the informal sector.[6] Subsistence agriculture is reported separately. The value of disaggregating trends becomes clear. On face value, the totals would make us believe that total employment fell after 2000 – a very desperate finding. Yet, the reader will see that this apparent trend is led by non-formal employment. While the picture is still not a happy one – stagnant total employment between 2000 and 2003 – we at least find that there has not been job loss overall. Identifying underlying trends then bears fruit – here we find that formal private sector employment has been growing slowly, but relatively consistently, since 1997 – a very important indicator of health and sustainability.

Figure 16.8 *Employment in formal and non-formal sectors*

Number of employed (thousands)

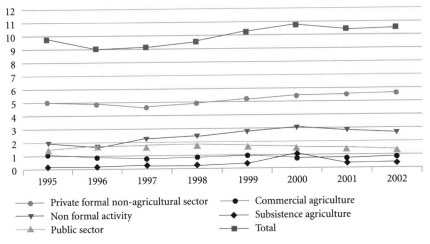

Source: Calculated from electronic data made available by Stats SA, OHS 1995–99; Sept LFS 2000–03
Note: These figures are adjusted as explained in Altman & Woolard 2004

Figure 16.9 and Figure 16.10 show how employment has varied by sector.[7] Figure 16.9 presents the change in formal employment in the private non-agricultural sector, commercial agriculture and the public sector. While public sector employment has dampened growth, the changes are over-shadowed by the private sector. In the formal economy, it is clear that the private non-agricultural sector has been the main source of employment growth – although it is far from spectacular. Table 16.3 shows that the labour force grows by about 500 000 to 600 000 each year, as compared to an average 115 000 jobs created annually between 1995 and 2002. Over this period, the formal and informal sectors contributed about equally to job creation, albeit in different periods. The informal sector appears to have been an important job creator between 1996 and 1999. The private sector took over as the main employment creator from 1997. The formal private sector was the more important contributor to employment, generating about 1.1 million jobs after 1997. The majority of new formal jobs were created (in order of importance) in finance, insurance and information

Figure 16.9 *Change in formal employment*

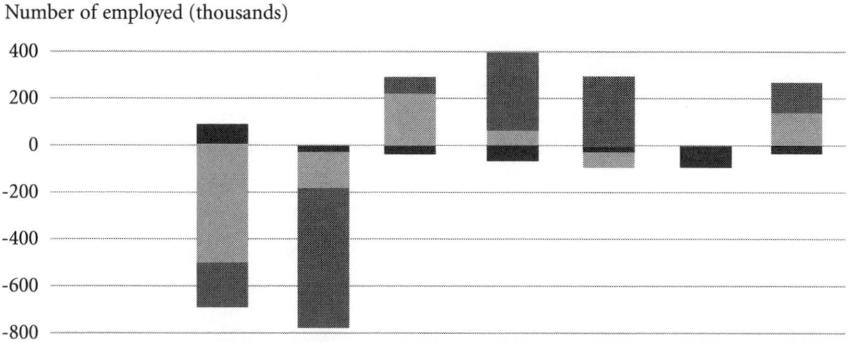

Number of employed (thousands)

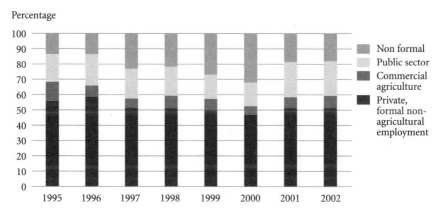

	1996	1997	1998	1999	2000	2001	2002
Private sector	-206 000	-595 000	89 000	320 000	299 000	-15 000	145 000
Commercial agriculture	-489 467	-171 950	218 258	72 765	-85 882	1 358	136 981
Public sector	86 000	-16 000	-23 000	-63 000	-7 000	-69 000	-36 000

Source: Calculated from electronic data made available by Stats SA, OHS 1995–99; Sept LFS 2000–02

Figure 16.10 *Distribution of employment, broad sectors*

Percentage

Source: Calculated from electronic data made available by Stats SA, OHS 1995–99; Sept LFS 2000–02

technology-related industries, retail and wholesale manufacturing, and community and social services.

Surprisingly, the demand for lower- and middle-skilled workers had grown more rapidly than for other groups between 1997 and 2002. This represents a reversal of trends found in the early 1990s, when many low- and mid-skill jobs were lost in mining, agriculture and, to a lesser extent, in some manufacturing industries.

Table 16.3 *Summary of net employment creation (thousands)*

Jobs created	Between 1995–2002		Between 1997–2002		Between 1995–1999		Between 1999–2002	
	Total	per annum	Total	per annum	Total	per annum	Total	per annum
Formal sector	173	25	1 084	217	-285	-71	458	153
Non-formal sector	1 109	158	717	143	1 038	260	71	24
Non-formal, excluding subsistence agriculture	648	93	416	83	760	190	-112	-37
Total	1 282	183	1 801	360	753	188	529	176
Total (excl. subs agric)	821	117	1 500	300	475	119	346	115
Labour force growth	4 295	614	4 253	851	2 143	536	2 152	538

Source: Calculated from electronic data made available by Stats SA, OHS 1996–99; Sept LFS 2000–02

This is hardly enough to maintain the unemployment rate at its current rate, and certainly will not reduce it. It is worth reiterating that this is not merely a problem of rapid labour force entry. The rate of labour force entry has not grown since 2000. This is a problem of the underlying ability of the economy to absorb labour. While it does not represent a 'jobs blood bath', it does give us a sense of being in an environment that, given the status quo, does not yet offer a sustainable growth employment path.

The private sector will be a good marker of the underlying capability of the economy to create jobs. Commercial agriculture is unlikely to make a large sustained contribution to job growth, as it will more likely offer cyclical upturns and downturns.[8] Government has had an active strategy to cut back personnel – this may also turn around in subsequent years, but without a substantial shift in policy it is unlikely to create many more jobs.

The main sources of employment growth will be the private non-agricultural sector – as the driver – and the informal sector. A sustainable growth employment path arises where the private sector and informal sectors grow hand-in-hand. If the informal sector grows faster than the formal sector, there may be an indication of displacement, representing a vicious circle, with falling incomes. If the formal sector and informal sector are growing, it may indicate a virtuous circle, where rising incomes from the formal sector result in expanded expenditure on goods and services provided by the informal sector.

Figure 16.10 shows the distribution of employment across these sectors. Here we see that the non-formal sector, comprised of domestic workers, the informal sector and subsistence farmers, account for a rising proportion of employment. The implications of this are discussed below. Counter to the prevailing view about a skills-intensive economy, Figure 16.11 shows that the proportion of low and high skill workers in the formal sector has hardly changed since the mid-1990s.

Figure 16.11 *Formal employment by skill level*

Number of employed

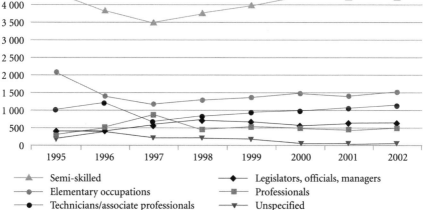

Source: Calculated from electronic data made available by Stats SA, OHS 1995–99; Sept LFS 2000–02

STATE OF THE NATION 2004–2005

The character of employment and underemployment

Productive and unproductive labour

Why does it matter if the informal sector grows faster than the formal sector? Don't they both create jobs? We have an intuitive sense that people should work, but could we live with high rates of unemployment – through a reliance on social transfers? Some economies do accept this notion. However, the South African government has adopted a distributional target which aims to halve unemployment by 2014 – this would mean that public policy supports the aim of having about 15 per cent unemployment, and 85 per cent employed. Does it matter how the 85 per cent are employed?

Figure 16.12 represents the balance between the formal sector, non-formal sector and strictly unemployed between 1995 and 2002. The formal sector can broadly be defined to offer 'productive employment', the non-formal sector to be 'low productivity employment' and those that are unemployed are 'unproductive labour'. Here we see that the formal sector accounted for 72 per cent of employment in 1995, as compared to 51 per cent in 2002. Unemployment rose from 16 to 31 per cent of the labour force over the same period. So, about 18 per cent of the labour force worked in the non-formal sector in 2002, as compared to 12 per cent in 1995.

These comparisons show us that a shrinking proportion of the labour force fully participates in the economy, contributes to the tax base, supports their households, and are involved in a positive context often associated with the social aspects of work. This point does not only refer to the unemployed. A large portion of those working in the non-formal sector have lower earnings than their counterparts in the formal sector.

The quality of work

What is happening to the quality of work in the formal sector? We offer some indications below. Figure 16.13 offers data on average hourly earnings in the formal sector by broad skill level. These figures are deflated to 2000 prices. We find that most groups experienced very little change in real earnings between 1995 and 2002. There are some exceptions – in particular female managers became better paid over this period.[9] From an employment promotion perspective, Figure 16.13 shows that rising low- and medium-skill wages are not

Figure 16.12 *Proportion of labour force, productive and unproductive*

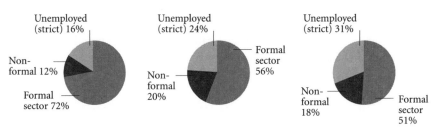

Source: Calculated from electronic data made available by Stats SA, OHS 1994–99; Sept LFS 2000–02
Note: Formal sector includes domestic workers; unemployed by strict definition.

causing a disincentive – as they are either stagnant or falling over the period. However, in a context where a declining proportion of the labour force has formal jobs, the lack of real wage growth, or even its slight decline, may represent a welfare loss to poor households.

Figure 16.13 *Wage trends by skill level in the formal sector, 2000 prices*

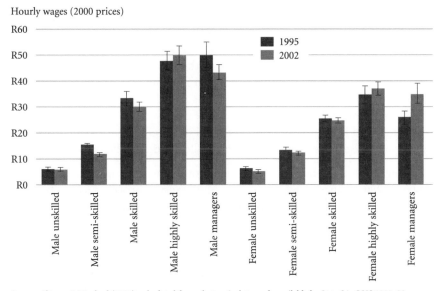

Source: Altman & Woolard (2004), calculated from electronic data made available by Stats SA, OHS 1995–99; Sept LFS 2000–02
Note: The thin lines at the tops of each bar represent confidence levels

Women are finally starting to earn more. Table 16.4 presents women's earnings as a percentage of their male counterparts in the formal sector. Working women have gained considerably over the 1990s. Semi-skilled female workers appear to be earning more than their male counterparts – possibly reflecting on the growing demand for women in services sectors. And yet, in most areas of work, women still earn less than their male counterparts.

Table 16.4 *Female earnings as a percentage of male earnings, formal sector 2002*

Unskilled	87.0
Semi-skilled	106.4
Skilled	82.8
Highly skilled	73.8
Managers	80.3

Source: Calculated from electronic data made available by Stats SA Sept LFS 2002
Note: Calculated as mean hourly earnings

Figure 16.14 and Figure 16.15 offer representations of formal sector work conditions – essentially giving a sense of the strength of contracts and the extent to which workers are covered by private benefits. We look at measures related to contracts, but also review other questions with the possibility that some workers are not sure whether or not certain provisions cover them. The figures are presented by skill category, as the lower skill workers are, on the one hand the most vulnerable, and on the other, are the main point of concern when the problem of regulation is raised. We show information for unskilled, semi-skilled and skilled. The coverage by contracts and pensions for managers and highly skilled workers are similar to those for skilled workers. So, a comparison between skilled, semi-skilled and unskilled is offered.

Although this is a short period of time over which to measure change, it appears that an increasing proportion of workers are covered by contracts at work – with 58 per cent of workers having written contracts in 1999 as compared to 70 per cent in 2002. The growth was particularly marked for the lower skill categories. This change directly coincides with amendments to the Basic Conditions of Employment Act in 1998, that required employers to have witten contracts with employees.[10] However, looking at pension plan coverage offers a different picture. Comparing Figure 16.14 and Figure 16.15 we see that the expansion in contracts for unskilled and semi-skilled workers does not necessarily translate into benefits – possibly indicating that while more workers have contracts (or are aware that they have contracts), they are not necessarily of a very binding or long-term nature. The number of workers covered by private pension plans – a benefit they may be more aware of – hardly changed from its coverage of between 55 to 60 per cent of the formal

Figure 16.14 *Formal sector workers with written contract, by skill category*

Percentage of formally employed in each skill category

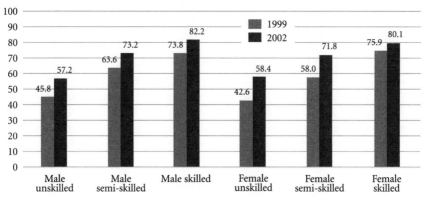

Source: Calculated from electronic data made available by Stats SA, OHS 1999; Sept LFS 2000–02

Figure 16.15 *Formal sector workers with pension plan, by skill category*

Percentage of formally employed in each skill category

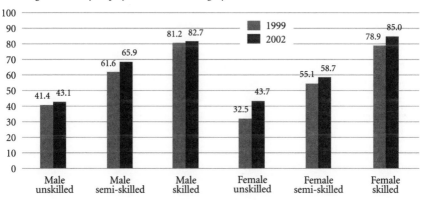

Source: Calculated from electronic data made available by Stats SA, OHS 1999; Sept LFS 2000–02

workforce, over the period from 1999 to 2002. Since half of the labour force works in the formal sector, this means that about 32 per cent of the labour force have written contracts, and about 29 per cent have private pension plans.

The different quality of work in the formal and informal sectors is made evident in Table 16.5, which compares formal and informal earnings in urban and rural areas. The variations by race are also quite substantial.

Informal sector workers earn between one-fifth and almost half of what their counterparts earn in the formal sector. Mean monthly incomes in 2002 are presented in Table 16.5, while Figure 16.16 compares earnings in the formal and informal sectors by level of educational attainment.

Mean formal wages for African workers ranged from about R500 to R3 000 per month or between R6 000 and R36 000 per annum. It is estimated that more than 4 million formal sector workers earn less than R23 000 per year. As many households depend on only one wage earner, the sector worked makes a very large difference to poverty levels. Relative wages for African workers in the informal economy, domestic work and agriculture have dropped considerably over a short period of time.

Table 16.5 *Mean monthly incomes*

	2002 Rand		1999 As % of formal urban African male earnings		2002 As % of formal urban African male earnings	
	Men	Women	Men	Women	Men	Women
White workers			%	%	%	%
Formal (urban)	9 328	6 150	341	217	318	210
African workers						
Formal (urban)	2 931	3 092	100	94	100	105
Informal (urban)	1 055	655	46	38	36	22
Informal (non-urban)	723	436	32	24	25	15
Domestic (urban)	524	544	41	24	18	19
Domestic (non-urban)	410	399	16	18	14	14
Agricultural (formal)	698	497	46	27	24	17
Agricultural (informal)	480	424	18	14	16	14

Source: Altman & Woolard (forthcoming), calculated from electronic data made available by Stats SA, Sept LFS 2002

Figure 16.16 shows us relative earnings in the formal and informal sectors for those with the same educational attainment. We see that formal sector workers generally earn more than informal ones. The gap becomes more pronounced, the more education a person has. So we see that the greater the proportion of people in the informal sector, the less relative wage income earned, and the less that households and the economy benefits from education.

Figure 16.16 *Earnings in the formal and informal sector, by level of education, 2002*

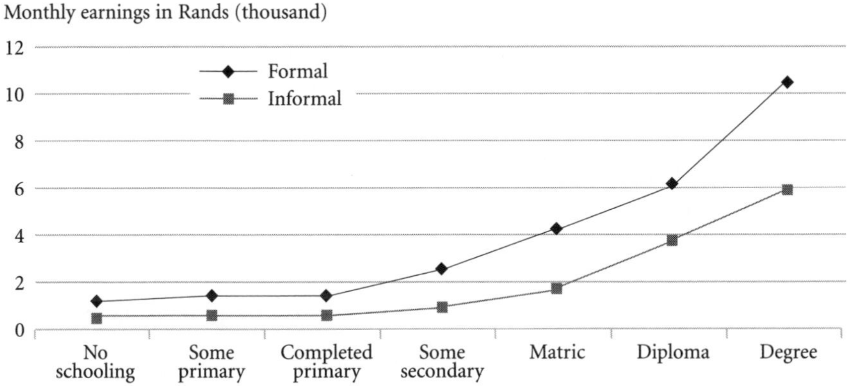

Monthly earnings in Rands (thousand)

Source: calculated from electronic data made available by Stats SA, Sept LFS 2002

Explaining slow employment growth

It is generally positive that some indications of employment growth are emerging after dramatic declines in the early 1990s. But, there is still not enough evidence to warrant celebration. The growth is not that rapid, is only found in some quarters, and does not seem to translate into positive overall employment growth. In particular, while formal non-agricultural private sector employment has been growing, total employment has been relatively stagnant since 2000.

To what extent is slow employment growth caused by labour market phenomena, as opposed to other factors contributing to weak demand of SA goods and services more generally?

Formal employment growth in a small economy like South Africa's will rely substantially on export growth. The domestic market will always be a constraint on growth – SA had already reached a barrier in import substitution by the late 1970s. SA has experienced quite substantial growth in its exports, but without concomitant improvements in employment absorption. Why not?

Insofar as employment is constrained by inequality, government may play a role in stimulating demand for basic wage goods and services, such as food and social welfare services. This is an important area, where government can promote expansion of non-traded goods and services. Government policy over the 1990s has focused on improving efficiencies in the civil service, and this has resulted in job loss. While there may be some job growth in the public sector in future, it appears that policy will emphasise indirect employment.

In instances where there is a positive link, informal sector employment growth will indirectly depend on the expansion of formal sector wage earners – who in turn buy goods and services and reinvest in family micro businesses. Yet formal sector employment has been stagnant overall since 2000.

What explains slow job creation in the formal private sector?

Rising unemployment in the context of positive employment creation is sometimes attributed to a dramatically expanded labour force – that is, where labour force participation rates are growing fast. There is evidence to show that this was partly the case in SA in the 1990s, but certainly not so since 2000. It is possible that the expansion in the labour force in the latter part of the 1990s was partly related to counting, as the survey questions became more probing. Even so, the labour force participation rate of 59 per cent now falls within an international norm and the rate of participation has not increased since 2000. This means that the rate of job creation is simply not enough in the context of the scale of the SA labour force.

A second labour market question relates to rising wages and regulations and possible disincentives to employ. While the proportion of workers in the formal sector covered by contracts has grown, the proportion covered by pensions has not. This might indicate that either workers previously were not aware that they had contracts, or that they are not very tight or permanent.

Coverage is primarily found in formal unionised environments, but this relates to about 30 per cent of those employed (Stats SA LFS Sept 2002). The majority of union members are found in mining, public service and a small number of manufacturing subsectors, as seen in Table 16.6. It is worth noting that employment in these sectors has grown, albeit slowly. Otherwise, coverage by contracts and benefits is very limited in non-unionised formal sector environments, and barely found at all in the informal sector (Watkinson & Horton 2001). There is no clear overarching connection between rates of unionisation and employment creation. Therefore, debates about labour regulation would benefit from a focus on specific manifestations in specific sectors – and a move away from broad statements about the entire economy.

Wage growth, whether in a unionised or non-unionised context, can also act as a disincentive to employ. The central issues relate to the relative price of labour versus capital, the availability of new technologies or processes (that allow for labour replacement) and the extent to which wages and productivity grow together. We do not have room to discuss the full spectrum of issues, and so

Table 16.6 *Unionisation*

Main industry	Total no. in workforce ('000s)	Total no. in workforce unionised ('000s)	Percentage of workforce unionised
Agriculture, hunting, forestry and fishing	884	60	6.8
Mining and quarrying	494	378	76.5
Manufacturing	1 425	481	33.8
Electricity, gas and water supply	80	42	52.5
Construction	410	53	12.9
Wholesale and retail trade	1 281	246	19.2
Transport, storage and communication	462	154	33.3
Financial intermediation, insurance, real estate & business services	884	198	22.4
Community, social and personal services	1 888	1 114	59.0
Private households with employed persons	1 040	12	1.2
Total	**8 899**	**2 750**	**30.9**

Source: Calculated from electronic data made available by Stats SA, Sept LFS 2002
Note: Table excludes employers, self-employed and those working without pay

focus only on the productivity-wage relationship. Figure 16.13 showed that average real wages for low, semi-skilled and skilled workers in the formal economy did not grow between 1995 to 2002. But, competitiveness does not rely simply on input costs, but also on productivity which influences the final cost of goods and services. Countries with low input costs may still be expensive if their productivity is poor – similarly, high cost economies are sometimes more competitive where productivity is high. Table 16.7 compares productivity and wage growth over the period from 1971–2002.[11] Here we see that productivity has outstripped wage growth in every period. Notably, the changes were very small in the 1970s and 1980s, and productivity growth is only really seen from the 1990s. This may mean that productivity improvements have been an important contributor to job loss, as suggested by Edwards (2000). It may also indicate growing competitiveness in the SA economy. It certainly does not point to a problem of wage growth exceeding productivity.

Table 16.7 *Average year-on-year growth rates of productivity and real wages*

Variable	1971–1979	1980–1989	1990–2002
Productivity	0.30%	0.22%	3.38%
Real Wages	-0.40%	0.26%	2.04%

Source: Wakeford (2003), calculated from SARB Quarterly Bulletin, June 2003

A third labour market problem relates to skills availability. The concern stretches back into primary and secondary education, especially in relation to maths and science education. Then there is concern about whether tertiary education institutions are delivering sufficient numbers of the quality required. The particular constraint refers to the availability of black commerce and science graduates. While there is considerable emphasis on the number of graduates, Altman (2004a) argues that the number of black enrolments and graduates in commerce and science and engineering has grown tremendously over the past period of years. However, the majority of African graduates attend historically disadvantaged universities, technikons and distance education institutions. These are not the institutions favoured by employers, so the racial bias in opportunity is further entrenched. The limited interaction between firms and a wider set of education institutions is an important contributor to the mismatch of curricula. Poor secondary education preparation and very limited access to finance and information also means that black students attend education institutions that diminish their labour market prospects. Whether graduating from advantaged or disadvantaged institutions, we find that black graduates fare more poorly than their white counterparts – we believe this is partly caused by weak networks, poor search skills, insufficient information about labour market opportunities, but also the recruitment behaviour of companies themselves (Moleke 2004).

Employment and exports

Exports have grown in the 1990s, so why haven't they led to job growth? Considerable blame for the lack of growth in labour-intensive exports is placed on the functioning of the labour market, and more specifically, real wages growth and inflexibility. Some of these arguments were addressed in the previous section.

There is already substantial evidence to show that sectors having expanded exports have tended to a greater capital intensity, partly due to a shift to more capital-using sectors, but mostly because of technological change (Edwards 2000). This has resulted in some scepticism that employment will be expanded on the back of trade. However, in the long run, this really is South Africa's main opportunity for formal sector employment due to the small size of its domestic market. Understanding why export growth has leaned to capital intensity, and why expansion has been less than spectacular, is therefore essential.

We will not penetrate deeply into this question here, except to point to two important questions. As with most economies, trade will depend considerably on intra-regional market growth. South Africa has benefited considerably from improvements in its trade relations with Africa. Indeed, Africa has been the main source of market growth for South African value-added exports over the 1990s. How fast will these markets grow in future? The initial boom rose from a very small base of activity. The benefits from trade in Africa still accrue to resource-based and construction firms and, more recently, forays into telecommunications. These are generally small and poor consumer and producer markets. Moreover, it is generally hard to do international business in Africa – also potentially slowing trade growth.

A second concern relates to the slow growth in the trade of services. Services are a fast growing area of international trade, accounting for about 25 per cent of global trade. Approximately one-quarter of foreign direct investment to developing countries is directed to services. Moreover, services tend to be more labour intensive than manufacturing, so more jobs will be created per Rand invested. Although there has been some growth in trade in SA services, generally less than 4 per cent of services output is exported – this means that services industries are largely constrained to the size of the domestic market.

Government's direct role in promoting employment

Government plays a number of roles in generating employment. A large portion of these roles is quite indirect – where it lays the foundation for industrial growth. Here we want to focus on the more direct role in creating employment. In this first instance, it is an employer itself, through the civil service. In South Africa, the civil service is not as large an employer as one finds in many other developing countries. In 2002, approximately 1.556 million people worked for government, (including all levels of government and the parastatals). This accounts for about 19 per cent of formal employment and 14.9 per cent of total employment. While new workers have been absorbed into public service over the 1990s, the restructuring and streamlining programme has resulted in a net loss of about 214 000 public sector jobs between 1997 and 2002. Government's stated policy is to keep a tight civil service – so there may be some expansion in future, but it is unlikely to be very substantial.

Government can also play an influential indirect role through procurement of goods and services. Special public works programmes are the most well-known instrument and most popularly referred to. However, the position of these special programmes must be contextualised within the important role that government spending plays within the construction industry generally. For example, there is considerable emphasis on government's poverty relief programmes. In 2001–02, R1.35 million was spent on these programmes. Compare this to the R52 billion allocated to public sector capital expenditure in the same year (Altman & Mayer 2003).

Infrastructure expenditure is dominated by the public sector, approximately equally divided between that by public enterprises and government directly. The construction industry experienced a secular decline between the 1980s and 1990s, substantially caused by falling expenditure by government and public corporations. It is estimated that formal construction employment fell from about 450 000 to 200 000 between 1981 and 2001. The informal sector has grown to about 35 to 50 per cent of construction employment (Teljeur & Stern 2002). There is a view that the contraction in government spending on infrastructure was a consequence of an oversupply of infrastructure during the 1970s. However, evidence of infrastructure backlogs suggests that the replacement of infrastructure is now necessary (Merrifield 2002).

In fact, government has committed itself to a massive expansion in its capital budget, from about R58 billion in 2002–03 to R74 billion in 2003–04. Approximately R28 billion more will be spent in real terms over the three-year period between 2003–04 and 2005–06, than was spent between 2000–01 and 2002–03 – this is an increase of 30 per cent (see Altman & Mayer 2003). A large portion of this increase will be allocated to civil construction, which is typically capital intensive. So it is anticipated that this spending, in combination with the Department of Public Work's programme to intensify labour use in infrastructure projects, should together have an important impact on employment. There are two key challenges faced by government in maximising the impact of its infrastructure spending on employment. The first relates to its ability to spend its budget. For example, a survey by Eskom of local government found that in 2001, only 71.5 per cent of local government's capital budgets was actually spent (Altman & Mayer 2004). A second challenge relates to how widely the labour-intensive methods programme is promoted.[12]

Increasingly, attention is being devoted to the role of social services in government's programme to meet basic needs and generate employment, as evidenced by its inclusion in the Growth and Development Summit's agreements (Altman & Mayer 2003). Dramatic social and economic dislocation, weak community care for children, the aged, the disabled and HIV/AIDS sufferers, and a dearth of basic services in waste collection, education, health and welfare, amongst others, characterise the South African situation. It is therefore easy to justify the expansion of community goods and services. The expanded provision of community services provides long-term jobs and also contributes to human capital development and social cohesion. Given that women workers are disproportionately represented in the social services sector, creating new social service jobs, as well as improving the quality and security of existing jobs, also has important implications for women's empowerment and gender equity.

A large portion of government spending, especially that through provinces, is already allocated to social expenditure. The gap identified relates to the para-professional class of workers who can provide better community access to public services. Examples include early child development and education, home care, after-school care, care for disabled, care for aged, or mental health care. The Department of Education's Early Child Development programme (or its reception year programme) is the most developed and has a budget allocated to it of about R500 million in 2003–04. On the other hand, the HIV/AIDS home-care programme is extremely small – with only R66 million allocated to the Department of Social Development for community-based care in 2003–04 (Altman & Mayer 2003). The growing attention devoted to these areas in 2004 will hopefully lead to important expansions from 2005.

The key issue confronting government is how to utilise increased expenditure on social services to enhance the delivery of basic needs and create employment. Challenges in this regard include enhancing government's capacity to effectively design and implement specific programmes, and developing a pool of suitably skilled and accredited suppliers of these services. There is substantial complexity in taking these programmes to scale, partly because they are often provided in a combination of home-based, community-based, residential and institutional modes of delivery and a wide range of actors – government, non-governmental organisations, faith-based and private institutions – provide these services. While they often don't require a high qualification level, quality assurance is critically important as these are sensitive services with substantial potential consequences for the health and welfare of clients.

Informal sector

The South African informal sector is quite small by international standards, accounting for about a quarter of total employment. There is evidence to show that it grew substantially over the 1990s. There is contention over the actual extent of its expansion, but a conservative estimate might be about 612 000 jobs created between 1997 and 2002. This is not surprising, with improved population mobility and relaxed controls over trading. Unfortunately, it did not grow between 2000 and 2002. It is very difficult to anticipate whether its growth will revive or not. Critically, we have little understanding in relation to whether it is mainly entrepreneurial activity that arises as the economy grows, or alternatively survivalist activity that takes place when formal jobs are lost. The entrepreneurial form may still be marginal, but grows in conjunction with the formal sector, resulting in a virtuous dynamic circle, while the survivalist activity may grow in inverse proportion to the formal sector, leading to a vicious static circle.

Conclusions

The South African economy generated at least 115 000 jobs annually between 1996 and 2002. This contrasts sharply with the view of jobless growth, or even severe job losses. Does this mean South Africa is now experiencing job-creating growth? Is it sustainable growth? This can be answered, first by looking at the scale of job creation relative to the labour force, and by assessing the quality of these jobs and their contribution to household livelihoods.

The pace of labour force growth offers the most important and stark contrast. The economy is only absorbing 20 to 30 per cent of the 500 000 to 600 000 people added to the labour force each year. This explains why the unemployment rate rises each year. This in itself indicates that South Africa is not yet on a sustainable employment growth path.

Are the underlying trends starting to point to greater labour absorption? The information about jobs growth is very uneven and confusing. Much depends on measurements used and periods chosen. If taken between 1995 and 1999, about 426 000 net new jobs were created. But if measured between 1996 and 1999, we find that 1.151 million net new jobs were created! Either way, the story is one of some jobs growth over the second half of the 1990s. This is positive news. Unfortunately, the total number of employed was relatively stagnant between 1999 and 2002. This negative picture can be tempered by the knowledge that private non-agricultural sector employment has been growing since 1997 – this sector is the best measured, and certainly the most important marker of economic sustainability.

Government's stated objective is to reduce unemployment to 15 per cent by 2014 – this might be used as a benchmark of satisfactory redistributive norm. If the labour force grows at 2.2 per cent per annum, then approximately 420 000 net new jobs would need to be created each year.[13] The South African

economy is running well short of this target. We therefore find unemployment rates rising by 1–2 per cent every year. Even amongst the employed, a
diminishing proportion work in the formal sector where relative earnings are
higher. This has serious implications for household welfare, since wage
income is the single most important contributor to shifting families out of
poverty. So, even where positive employment creation is found, it is not yet
possible to say that South Africa is on a sustainable employment growth path.

The possible contributors to rising unemployment and slow employment
creation were reviewed. From the labour market perspective, it is often argued
that rising wages of low-skill workers and labour market regulation create disincentives to employ. The evidence points to stagnant growth in unskilled and
semi-skilled real wages. While a rising proportion of formal sector workers
have contracts, this is not reflected in other benefits such as private pension
coverage. This may indicate that workers are either becoming more aware of
the fact that they have contracts, or that they have relatively loose contracts.
Only a few sectors are highly unionised. Debate about wages and labour market regulation would benefit from increasing focus on specific subsectors, and
a move from generalised statements.

Surprisingly, this paper showed that a large portion of new employment since
1997 was accounted for by low- and semi-skilled workers. This may indicate
that the discouragements to hiring low-skill workers is less than previously
thought, or it may also indirectly reflect unmet demand for higher-skill labour.

Employment arises from the demand for goods and services – while there is
much emphasis on labour market contributors to unemployment, it is clear
that demand is growing too slowly. Government has been one contributor
to job loss, both directly by cutting the civil service, and indirectly, through
cutbacks in expenditure. It is expected that government will expand its
budget dramatically for infrastructure and social services from 2003–04.
Manufactured and agricultural exports have grown quite rapidly, but the
expected increase in employment has not happened. More importantly, South
Africa has not kept up with the rapid growth in global services exports – a
more likely avenue for job creation. The informal sector has not grown since
2000 – which is very difficult to understand.

The overall picture is still uncertain. The 'jobs bloodbath' is long over, and there
are certainly some positive underlying trends in the private sector particularly.

However, a sustainable employment growth path is still elusive. Bolder policy will be required to improve the workings of labour markets, and also to fast-track private and public sector-linked employment promotion.

Notes

1   While it appears that unemployment growth may be slowing since 2000, the trend may be misleading. The HSRC is currently involved in a process to review the data on employment, unemployment and labour force participation to identify trends underlying these figures. At the outset, it is important to note that a new survey was introduced in 2000, so the figures reported from 1995–99 (sourced from Stats SA's OHS Surveys), and 2000–02 (sourced from Stats SA's September LFS) are not directly comparable. We have not made use of the 2003 LFS as they have been re-weighted in light of the 2001 census. New weights for 2000– 02 had not yet been made available by the time this article was written. The March and Sept 2003 LFS data will not be directly comparable to the 2000–02 figures until this re-weighting is done.

2   The strict definition of unemployment refers to those that want to work and are actively searching. The broad definition of unemployment also includes those that want to work, but are not searching.

3   See how the labour force varies with employment? We believe that some variation in employment and the labour force may arise from changes in the way surveys were conducted. In particular, the questions about economic activity deepened considerably over time, assisting those who were unsure of their answer – better capturing those who are involved in relatively marginal activities and work done in-kind. We are still not sure to what extent these trends are related to the different character of Stats SA's OHS (1995–99) and LFS (2000–02) surveys.

4   Normally, one measures the percentage of the working age population that is working. This may give us a better sense of economic participation. Note that the calculation of 'not working' includes those categorised in 'subsistence agriculture'.

5   See Altman 2004a for further discussion.

6   The 'informal sector' is a self-definition where respondents say their activity lies in the informal rather than formal sector. It includes all such activity, except domestic work and subsistence agriculture.

7   The employment figures in 1995 and 1996 for agriculture and community, social and personal services may not be accurate, and the trend presented here requires some investigation. Also note that the category 'unspecified' varies considerably

between 1995 and 1997, and we are not sure how workers falling here would have been correctly allocated across the sectors.

8   Of course, the expansion of high-value agriculture – for example, in cut flowers or mariculture – may be able to generate output and employment that is less linked to commodity prices and so forth.

9   It should be noted that the category of manager is very imprecise and does not necessarily denote high-skill personnel – only 35 per cent of managers have a tertiary qualification.

10   More specifically, in November 1998, the Basic Conditions of Employment Act was amended to require an employer to give an employee who was in employment the written particulars of employment required by Section 29, to be enforced within six months of the date on which the Act came into effect. This was promulgated in terms of the Basic Conditions of Employment Act, No. 75 of 1997, under Government Notice No. R1438 of 1998 in Government Gazette No. 19453 of 13.11.98.

11   Employment and productivity figures over the past ten years suffer from the exclusion of many services sectors. The Reserve Bank data used by Wakeford relied on the SEE, which excluded parts of trade and construction, and particularly the financial sector which was severely underestimated until the third quarter of 2003. It is unclear to what extent the overall productivity figures would be influenced by their inclusion, as neither Stats SA nor the Reserve Bank have attempted to re-weight previous years.

12   As regards the objective of *drawing significant numbers of the unemployed into productive work*, the government's Expanded Public Works Programme target of one million job opportunities over the five-year period from 2004–05 to 2007–08 would account for about 7 to 9 per cent of the net new jobs required to enable the reaching of an interim target unemployment rate of about 23 per cent (from the strict definition) or 32 per cent (by the broad definition), assuming a labour force growth rate of about 2 per cent (this is the interim target of halving unemployment by 2014). Note that this contribution refers only to *additional* opportunities created. The contribution would be less than the million jobs if existing programmes are simply grouped under the Expanded Public Works Programme.

13   While previous projections put labour force growth as falling to below 1 per cent due to AIDS, the 2001 census showed that population and labour force growth has not varied as expected and labour force growth continues to grow in the 2 per cent range. As government rolls out its anti-retrovirals there is more expectation that labour force growth may not diminish as previously expected.

References

Altman M (2001a) Employment promotion in a minerals economy, *Journal of International Development* 13:1–19.

Altman M (2002a) Employment policy in a 'minerals economy'. In E Carlson & W Mitchell (eds.) *The urgency of full employment*. Sydney: CAER-UNSW Press.

Altman M (2002b) Progress in addressing employment and unemployment. Paper prepared for the Policy Co-ordination and Advisory Services, Office of the Presidency, as part of a ten-year policy review and strategic planning. Pretoria.

Altman M (2004a) Employment and growth – a sustainable employment path? Forthcoming working paper. HSRC.

Altman M (2004b) Meeting equity targets – are there enough graduates? Forthcoming working paper. HSRC.

Altman M & Mayer M (2003) Sector strategies for employment creation: Construction, social services and food. Paper presented to the Trade Industry Policy Strategies (TIPS) and Development Policy Research Unit (DPRU) Forum on 'The challenge of growth and poverty: The South African economy since democracy, Johannesburg, 8–10.09.03.

Altman M & Mayer M (2004) Basic needs and employment. Forthcoming working paper. HSRC.

Altman M & Woolard I (2004) Employment and unemployment in SA, 1995–2002. Forthcoming working paper, HSRC.

Bell T & Cattaneo N (1997) *Foreign trade and employment in South African manufacturing industry*. Occasional Report No. 4, Employment and Training Department, International Labor Organization (ILO), Geneva.

Bhorat H & Hodge J (1999) Decomposing shifts in labour demand in South Africa, *South African Journal of Economics* 67:348–380.

Black A & Kahn B (1998) Growing without gold? South Africa's non-traditional exports since 1980. Mimeo, Department of Economics, University of Cape Town.

Edwards L (2000) Globalisation and the skill bias of occupational employment in SA, *South African Journal of Economics* 69:40–71.

Edwards L & Golub S (2002) *South Africa's international cost competitiveness and productivity: A sectoral analysis*. Report prepared for the South African National Treasury under a USAID/Nathan Associates SEGA Project.

Fallon P & Pereira de Silva L (1994) *South Africa: Economic performance and policies*. World Bank Discussion Paper, No. 7, Southern Africa Department, World Bank.

Fallon P & Lucas R (1998) *South African labor markets: Adjustments and inequalities.* Discussion Paper 12. Washington. World Bank Southern Africa Department.

Fedderke JW, Henderson S & Kayemba J (1999) *Changing factor market conditions in South Africa: The capital market – a sectoral description of the period 1970–1997.* Report prepared for the TIPS, European Regional Science Association Paper No. 5, University of the Witwatersrand.

Galbraith JK, Conceição P & Ferreira P (2000) Inequality and unemployment in Europe: The American cure, *New Left Review* 237:28–51.

ILO (International Labor Organization) (2004) *Global labor trends.* Geneva: ILO.

Lewis J (2001) *Policies to promote growth and employment in South Africa.* Informal Discussion Papers on Aspects of the Economy of South Africa, No. 16, World Bank.

Merrifield A (2002) The investment in construction goods and services – Final report. Unpublished paper, University of Wolverhampton.

Meth C (2001) Unemployment in South Africa – what the latest figures tell us. Unpublished paper, University of Natal.

Moleke P (2004) The employment experiences of graduates. Forthcoming working paper, HSRC.

National Treasury (South Africa) (2001) *Budget review.* Pretoria: National Treasury.

SARB (South African Reserve Bank) (2003) *Annual economic report.*

Stats SA (Statistics South Africa) (various) *Labour force surveys* (LFS). Pretoria: Stats SA.

Stats SA (various) *October household surveys* (OHS). Pretoria: Stats SA.

Stats SA (various) *Survey of Employment and Earnings* (SEE). Pretoria: Stats SA.

Teljeur E & Stern M (2002) *Understanding the South African construction services industry.* TIPS Annual Forum Paper. Available at http://www.tips.org.za/research/papers/showpaper.asp.

UN (2004) *Indicators on income and economic activity.* Available at http://unstats.un.org/unsd/demographic/social/inc-eco.htm.

Wakeford J (2003) The productivity-wage relationship in South Africa: An empirical investigation, *Development Southern Africa* 21:109–132.

Watkinson E & Horton C (2001) *Characteristics of the South African labour force.* Naledi working paper, Johannesburg.

17 Black empowerment and corporate capital

Roger Southall

In late 2003, President Thabo Mbeki lashed out at Sasol Chief Executive Pieter Cox for citing black economic empowerment (BEE) as a risk factor in a document that the company had to compile in terms of New York Stock Exchange (NYSE) regulations. Sasol, he raged, was guilty of 'bigotry' and had 'an outdated mindset' (*Business Day* 8.12.03). His argument was subsequently developed by Essop Pahad, Minister in the Presidency, who posed the question:

> whether BEE can remotely be listed as a risk factor. When one considers the enormous advantages of BEE – with another SA company currently running a commercial celebrating the fact that BEE can increase its client base by 5 million people – it defies logic, surely, that a company can trumpet it to the world as a risk factor. BEE should be viewed as the engine of our economic future and the factor that, more than any other, will link our two, disparate economies. (*Financial Mail* 12.12.03)

Presidential insiders indicated that the complaints about Sasol reflected the fact that big business had been slow to buy into transformation. However, it was the follow-up explanation of Pieter Cox which was more demonstrative of the dilemma that faces South African industry:

> We believe empowerment is a risk. But we also know that it is a bigger risk if we don't do empowerment. (*Financial Mail* 12.12.03)

Whatever the rights or wrongs of Sasol's record, Cox manifestly highlighted the fact that large corporations in South Africa, domestically owned and multinational, are having to meet the enormous challenges posed by a highly competitive, globalised environment at the same time as they seek to cope with the economic disadvantage of blacks which is the legacy of apartheid.

This paper is an attempt to provide one assessment of their progress as well as an analysis of the risks of BEE as they are perceived by large corporations.

Defining black economic empowerment

In common parlance, BEE has come to mean the empowerment of blacks within the private sector of the economy. In short, to what extent is black ownership of the formal economy increasing? And to what extent are blacks upwardly mobile within South African corporate capitalism? However, whilst this focus upon the private sector is understandable in so far as it trains gunsights upon the principal structures which generate wealth, it clearly misses the target if the overall advance of blacks within the political economy is to be understood. To this end, it is helpful to argue some very basic points.

The first point is that whilst, conventionally, there are 'minimalist' and 'maximalist' approaches to defining BEE, neither is adequate. The former concentrates upon the promotion of black business and black businessmen within the private sector. It is probably the definition of BEE which is most widely (albeit implicitly) adopted, and the one which tends to feature most in journalistic commentary. It is also the one which, because it commonly highlights limits to the advances made by blacks within the corporates, leads easily to the widespread accusations that BEE has favoured only a small elite of blacks, who by one means or other have accumulated considerable wealth and private sector power. Yet the problems with this narrow definition of BEE are manifest, for black economic activity so obviously entails much more than direct involvement in formal, private business. The economy is made up of both the public and private sectors. Consequently, any meaningful measurement of BEE must attempt to assess black advance across both.

Given these drawbacks of the minimalist approach, it has become fashionable to pursue a maximalist definition of BEE which emphasises the 'comprehensive restructuring of institutions and society ... rather than the replacement of white individuals' and which aims at the 'simultaneous empowerment of ... black people as a collective and the individual as an entity' (Edigheji 1999). However, although superficially attractive, this more inclusive approach risks the danger of BEE being defined in such enormously sweeping terms that virtually any black economic activity can be included in it, including for instance, an increase in the number and availability of menial jobs. Black empowerment suddenly runs the risk of including any extension of 'black helotry', which is clearly absurd!

Consequently, a more precise definition of BEE, which will be used here, centres around a sociological perspective, which focuses upon *the increase of black ownership, control and management of state, parastatal and private economic activity in the formal sector.* This is wide enough to be adequately inclusive, yet is parsimonious to the extent that it excludes the bulk of employed wage labour from the definition, except to the extent that shop-floor supervisors and foremen can be considered as junior management, even whilst raising operational problems to the extent that ownership, control and management functions are often merged within small businesses. Meanwhile, it excludes the informal sector, not because the latter is insignificant (indeed its overall contribution to black economic survival may well be growing), but rather because it is the resort of those who have been pushed out of the formal sector (through loss of jobs, retrenchments and so on) or who are too poor or disadvantaged to enter it. More particularly, however, this definition has the marked advantage of shifting the focus to the 'power' element in the term empowerment, whilst diverting the focus of the term away from the rather woolly implication of psychological and/or economic 'upliftment' of blacks which tends to predominate at the moment.

Although easily stated, this definition of BEE outlines a formidable agenda: indeed, it leads towards an examination of the distribution of power throughout the South African political economy as a whole. However, the much more limited intent of the present chapter is only to trace the progress of black advance within the corporate sector, and to ask how the latter is responding.

Towards an assertive state: black empowerment after 1994

South Africa is a post-colonial, semi-industrialised economy, which has been famously characterised by President Thabo Mbeki as divided into two nations, one white and wealthy, one black and poor. In essence, the settlement in 1994 transferred political power to the black majority, whilst leaving the economy dominated by the white minority. The government's strategy of BEE has been designed to overcome these divides through a series of state interventions intended to promote black ownership and management of the economy, most notably of public enterprise and of the private corporate sector.

These interventions have moved from being largely *persuasive* to becoming more *assertive and regulatory* (Southall 2004). In broad summary, this relatively measured transformation reflects a variety of factors discussed below.

The negotiated nature of the 1994 settlement

The principal emphasis of the Mandela government (1994–99) was upon national reconciliation, the promotion of domestic peace, and the extension of assurances to international and domestic capital that newly democratic South Africa was a safe place in which to invest. On the one hand, this required efforts to secure the support for the new order of the white minority, notably through recognition of property rights and such devices as 'sunset clauses', which guaranteed high levels of protection to whites in state employment. On the other, it entailed the adoption of economic strategies which eschewed nationalisation and socialisation in favour of those which viewed foreign and domestic private investment as the principal generators of economic growth. Conventionally, this is presented as lying behind the shift away from the Reconstruction and Development Programme (RDP), which envisaged a strong but slim state correcting market failures to cope with poverty and effect social redistribution, towards the Growth, Employment and Distribution (GEAR) strategy, which, from around 1996, adopted neo-liberal prescriptions which placed emphasis upon an investor-friendly macro-environment through strict fiscal discipline, deregulation of industry, privatisation and the opening up of what had been a relatively closed economy to world competition (see for example, Bond 2000).

The associated ideological re-orientation of the ANC

Historically, the African National Congress (ANC) had envisaged the liberation of South Africa as entailing the capture of the commanding heights of the economy and the nationalisation of at least some of the principal means of production. This was most famously expressed by the Freedom Charter, which was adopted in 1955. The national democratic revolution (NDR) which would ensue, as envisaged not just by (elements of) the ANC but its allies in the South African Communist Party (SACP), would provide, *inter alia*, for the necessary expansion of an African middle class, (which had been stunted by apartheid), as well as the development of a progressive, black, capital-owning bourgeoisie. Together, these shifts in production relations would provide the basis for a transformation of capitalist relations of production in favour of the working class and its allies, and open the eventual way to socialism.

Such thinking was to be greatly strengthened by the support given to the liberation struggle by the Soviet Union and other self-proclaimed socialist states. However, with the changed balance of global forces brought about by the implosion of state socialism in the Soviet Union and Eastern Europe, and the need for the ANC-in-government to adapt to the post-1990 neo-liberal environment internationally, the interpretation of the NDR has been shifted in a much more conservative direction. Hence, instead of tilting the economy towards socialism, the NDR is now seen as: (i) legitimating the 'historic role' of the party in leading South Africa; (ii) validating the need for an interventionist state within the context of a mixed economy; (iii) encouraging the existence, expansion, wealth and function of a black bourgeoisie; (iv) endorsing the need for close co-operation with capitalists of the old order some (at least) of whose 'objective' interests (for instance, in political stability) coincide with those of the liberation movement; and (v) quietly emphasising the role in 'transformation' of party elements which control the state, alongside the 'patriotic' bourgeoisie, at the expense of the working class and its allies (Southall 2004).

The stunted nature of black capitalism

Segregation and apartheid deliberately inhibited the development of black capitalism. Whilst this did not fully prevent the development of an Indian merchant class in Natal, it had crippling effects on African capitalism more specifically. In the late nineteenth and early twentieth centuries, the competitive threat of African agricultural competition was broken by the appropriation by whites of the vast majority of land; and subsequently, significant capital accumulation by blacks was denied by a maze of restrictive legislation, as well as by a lack of education and skills training alongside job reservation and access to loans. To be sure, under the policy of 'separate development' promoted by the National Party (NP) after 1948, African petty capitalism was to be encouraged in the various ethnic homelands through assistance proffered to aspirant African businessmen by development corporations and competitive restrictions placed on white economic activity within the homelands; and after the Soweto uprising, the government was to cautiously enact a series of measures to promote African business as part of its strategy to develop an urban black middle class as a buffer between white minority capital and the black masses. Yet this serves only to confirm that, whilst African capitalism had an ambiguous relationship with the apartheid state, it was simultaneously deeply politically entangled in the latter's strategies for securing white domination. Overall, therefore, for all that Indian capital enjoyed something of a more favourable development trajectory, it remains the case that black capitalism was severely under-developed and ill-equipped to develop independently after the end of apartheid.

The monopolised structure of the South African economy

The commanding heights of the South African economy have long been dominated by just a handful of companies. By the early 1980s, eight private conglomerates could be identified as 'the controlling forces within South African capitalism, together with state corporations and a small number of foreign multinationals' (Davies 1988:175). Subsequently, a series of major takeovers and other developments was to further a centralisation of the economic power in the hands of domestic conglomerates, a process which was further accelerated by withdrawals by foreign multinationals from direct investments during the terminal crisis of apartheid. To put this another way: whereas in 1981 the top eight corporations in South Africa controlled 61.66 per cent of the total assets of non-state corporations, by 1985 the top six controlled 71.26 per cent (Davies 1988:177). What this records is not only the expanding asset base of the domestic conglomerates, but the shift in the relative weight of local and foreign capital in favour of the former.

Despite the fact that democratic South Africa has been able to shed the burden of sanctions against apartheid, and has presented itself as a now stable and friendly site for foreign investment, the trend towards the concentration and centralisation of capital has not been significantly disturbed, even though the shape and composition of the leading conglomerates has changed through 'unbundling'. Meanwhile, given the decision of the exchange control authorities that the global expansion of South African corporates would hold significant benefits for the economy as a whole, five major corporations (Billiton, South African Breweries, Anglo American, Old Mutual and Dimension Data) have moved their primary listings from the Johannesburg Stock Exchange (JSE) to the London Stock Exchange since 1997. Whilst this was actually accompanied by an increase in their market capitalisation in South Africa (from R1.129 billion in 1997 to R1.771 billion in 2001) (Walters & Prinsloo 2002:63), this nonetheless rendered their domestic assets as now wholly or partly-owned subsidiaries of foreign companies, increasing the country's liabilities to foreign shareholders commensurately (Walters & Prinsloo 2002). In short, there has been a shift back in the relative weight of foreign ownership in the South African corporate sector, even though the firms which have shifted their base overseas retain a heavy South African imprint (*Financial Mail* 28.11.03).

The high level of concentration and centralisation of South African capital has posed enormous problems for BEE. There have been major obstacles to black empowerment, including the desperate lack of blacks who have acquired the necessary training and skills to assume middle- and high-level management positions in business, especially given the particular counter-attractions offered by state employment during the early years of the democratic transition. Meanwhile, the most formidable barrier to a significant increase of black ownership within the corporate sector has been blacks' lack of capital. As I have argued elsewhere, black businessmen are often, in effect, *capitalists without capital,* who need either to be given or lent capital at highly advantageous rates if they are to emerge as property-owning industrialists. Not surprisingly, therefore, the standard indicators which have been put forward to measure the progress of BEE ownership have recorded minimal impact upon the overall structure of South African capitalism. Hence whilst some reports suggested that black business had captured 10 per cent of the shares on the JSE between 1994 and 1997, this was recorded as having fallen to between 1 and 4 per cent by early 2002, according to the source (and the precise nature of what was being measured) (see Southall 2004 for a review). From this point of view, whilst there were most certainly some spectacular examples of individual success and enrichment amongst black businessmen, the number of such achievers was extremely few.

Given that in advanced industrial capitalism major shareholdings in leading companies tend to be held by institutional rather than individual investors, and given the vast amount of wealth required to make any significant penetration of the JSE, it is in retrospect far from surprising that the impact of any initial black assault upon the South African corporate structure should have been so limited. Indeed, there could scarcely have been any other outcome.

This serves to stress that the route to increasing black ownership, control and management of the economy lies, inevitably, through the *deployment of state power*. This has already been significantly realised through the appointment, by the government, of blacks to senior management positions within the parastatals.

Black control over the parastatal sector

According to the Ministry of Public Service and Administration, there are at present some 336 public entities employing about 250 000 people outside the public service (*Business Day* 12.02.04). After 1948, an expansion of the public sector was undertaken to increase Afrikaner control over the economy. Between 1946 and 1973, the share of state corporations in gross fixed investment in the South African economy rose from 6.2 to 11.5 per cent, with Afrikaner businessmen being appointed to key positions on state economic boards, and to senior management positions in state industries and key public corporations, such as South African Railways and Harbours (SAR&H), Eskom, Iscor and Sasol. 'After a decade of NP rule, just as in the public service, the middle and upper echelons of the wide network of parastatal organizations were virtually monopolized by Afrikaners' (O'Meara 1996:79).

The ANC's commitment to GEAR included a determination to restructure state assets in order to optimise investment resources and address service deficiencies and backlogs by an expansionary infrastructure programme. This was to entail both a streamlining of public enterprises, and where appropriate, a strategy of privatisation. Within this context, the ANC was also committed to utilising the public sector as an instrument of black empowerment, just as its predecessor NP government had turned to the parastatals to promote Afrikaner empowerment during the 1950s and 1960s. Hence it is that affirmative action (now referred to as 'employment equity') strategies have been used aggressively since 1994, with middle management and leading positions in parastatals increasingly awarded to blacks.

Extensive research needs to be done upon this aspect of state transformation in contemporary South Africa. However, cursory examination indicates that the major parastatals are now all significantly subject to black control. Thus today, six out of nine directors of the Industrial Development Corporation (IDC) (development finance), 12 of 23 directors of Denel (defence industry),

11 out of 15 directors of Eskom Holdings and 9 out of 12 directors of Eskom Enterprises (electricity) are black. Similarly, 13 out of 17 directors of Transnet and seven chief executives of its nine operational divisions are black, as are seven out of 11 directors of Telkom. Six out of nine South African Airways – another public enterprise – directors are also black, three of them having major connections with other public companies.[1] Interestingly, many such board numbers also have positions on the boards of private companies, indicating considerable cross linkages between the parastatals and a variety of private firms, many of them with extensive black interests. Altogether, the top 15 state owned enterprises (SOEs) deployed assets of R291 billion in 2003, and hence exert considerable weight throughout the economy (*Financial Mail* 6.02.04), a factor which needs to be factored in to any calculation of the effect and extent of BEE.

Against this, the government's efforts to use privatisation to boost BEE have had limited impact, notably because of a lack of qualified equity partners and available capital to would-be black buyers. The BusinessMap Foundation, an organisation which tracks BEE, opined in late 2003 that, 'Where BEE is concerned, actual privatization has delivered little when compared to the potential to use SOEs for black advancement in management and in procurement.' Indeed, the very first privatisation under the ANC, that of Sun Air, ended in the company's liquidation, whilst the biggest attempted privatisation to date, Telkom, which was listed on the JSE in 2002, 'has no significant block of empowerment shareholding' (*Business Day* & *Sowetan* 6.02.04).

Not surprisingly, given the limited gains for BEE through privatisation, state strategy has more recently begun to place more emphasis upon the state taking a prominent role in directly generating economic growth. Importantly, much of this effort is directing state contracts towards companies which are black owned or partially owned. Hence the Department of Trade and Industry (DTI) has recently reported that it has increased its procurement to BEE companies from 15 to 30 per cent over two years (2001–03), whilst Public Enterprises Minister Jeff Radebe has similarly reported that Eskom increased its BEE procurement from 1.8 per cent in 1996 to 21 per cent in 2002, this representing some R5.4 billion worth of business being placed in the hands of black business over the space of a few years. Transnet's contribution to BEE is likewise reported to have increased to 54 per cent, this representing a total spending of R4 billion (presumably over the same period) (*Sowetan* 13.02.04).

If this level of state spending is directed to BEE companies consistently over the next few years, it will clearly go some considerable way to compensating for the present lack of capital available to blacks. Overall, it is expressive of a much more assertive state strategy which has been adopted since the year 2000, not least because of deliberate promptings by a lobby which has been arguing that, given the limited black advance within the private sector since 1994, the government should adopt a far more active role in promoting BEE.

The Black Economic Empowerment Commission

The ANC's post-transition embrace of black capitalism was particularly associated with two more or less concurrent developments. The first was the shift from the RDP to GEAR. The second was when a number of leading former political activists, most notably former ANC Secretary-General Cyril Ramaphosa (who at this time joined New African Investments Limited), chose to move from politics into business (Macozoma 2003). Taken together with growing impatience at the slow rate of black entry into the corporate sector, these changing currents prompted the appointment in 1997 of the Black Economic Empowerment Commission (BEEC), chaired by Ramaphosa, to promote a new vision for BEE. Operating under the aegis of the Black Business Council, an umbrella body of 11 black business organisations, this was to recommend the adoption of a wide-ranging, state-driven programme to outline guidelines, regulations and obligations for the private, public and civil society sectors regarding BEE over a period of ten years.

Noting that neither state nor private sector efforts to achieve a meaningful transfer of economic resources into black hands had hitherto been successful, and that racial barriers continued to distort the efficient functioning of the market, the BEEC report – which was presented to President Mbeki in April 2001 – recommended concerted activity by the state to provide a more enabling environment for black empowerment. This, it was argued, should include the forging of an *Investment for Growth Accord* to earmark assets from business, labour and government for investment in projects which would enhance black economic participation; a *Black Economic Empowerment Act* to establish indicators and targets against which the public and private sectors could measure their attainment of BEE; a *National Procurement Agency* to revamp the national tendering and licensing system to ensure the centrality of empowerment in allocation of government contracts; a *National Empowerment Funding Agency* to improve and co-ordinate government efforts to assist black entrepreneurs; and an *Empowerment Framework for Public Sector Restructuring* to facilitate transfer of 30 per cent of state assets to black companies within ten years. Together with other suggestions, these proposals constituted a major bid to shift government towards concerted intervention within the economy in favour of BEE (BEEC 2001; Southall 2004).

The reaction of the government, which was caught between its increasing desire to promote BEE and its fears about scaring off domestic and foreign investment, was initially cautious. However, given growing political pressures from within its own political constituency, and increasing realisation of the limited advances that had hitherto been made by blacks regarding ownership and control of the economy, it moved surely but steadily towards the adoption of the BEEC's interventionist philosophy. Hence it was that, at the ANC's 51st National Conference in December 2002, President Mbeki committed the government to drawing up a 'Transformation charter' which would set BEE benchmarks, timeframes and procedures and eliminate uncertainly amongst investors (Southall 2004).

This was soon to have dramatic consequences in the form of the drafting of empowerment charters by significant sectors of private industry.

Empowerment charters: pre-emption or partnership?

Black advance within the corporate sector may have been slow, yet this did not mean that corporate capital in South Africa was standing aside from meeting the challenges posed by BEE. For a start, the major conglomerates, whether domestic or foreign, were acutely aware that their operations were taking place within a context of *political* economy. They might, ideologically, preach the need for the state to minimise regulation of the market. However, they were acutely aware, not just of the precedent of Afrikaner economic empowerment (of which some of them were a product), but of the way in which the corporate structure of South Africa had been affected by the imposition of sanctions in the 1980s. They were therefore acutely aware of the need to adjust to the new style, rules, impositions and demands of democratic politics, and most notably those of the ANC, which were to take centre stage after 1994.

As Said and Simmons point out, the relationship between multinational corporations and nation states is almost infinitely adaptable, and formed 'out of
a relative advantage-disadvantage calculus which will vary with every specific
situation' (1975:17). This would seem to apply no less to the large-scale
domestically oriented conglomerates in South Africa. Hence it was that
throughout the 1990s, the established corporate sector began to feel its way
towards insinuating itself with the new powers-that-be through such devices
as loans to, and joint ventures with, BEE companies, as well as scrambling to
compete for the dismally small pool of qualified black managers. Nonetheless,
not least because of the volatile global market conditions of the late 1990s
(which saw the crash of many early BEE companies), the overall impact upon
the structure of the capital market in South Africa was extremely limited:
BusinessMap argues that by 2002 little more than 2 per cent of equity of firms
listed on the JSE was in black hands, whilst fully 98 per cent of executive directors of such companies were white (*City Press* 11.0503).

Made increasingly aware of the mounting pressures to adapt politically by the
flurry of expensive, champagne-laden BEE conferences where established
business executives hobnobbed with the aspirant black elite, key corporate
players responded with an array of industrial sector empowerment charters.
Taking their lead from the sort of ideas that were to emanate from the report
of the BEEC and from later government action to prescribe BEE targets, the
charters were in essence a device to *pre-empt* what was considered to be potentially damaging government intervention by lining up with government and
black business interests as *partners.*

The first industrial sector off the block, in early 2002 – the liquid fuels sector
– would require of its signatory companies that 25 per cent of its equity would
be in black hands by 2010 (*Sunday Times* 14.12.03). However, the charter
movement really came to the fore with a major controversy precipitated by the
leak of a mining charter which was to be put to the industry by government.
This proposed that all mining operations would have to be 51 per cent owned
by blacks within ten years, whilst to secure a new mining licence a company
would have to have an empowerment partner with at least 30 per cent stake in
existing operations. Given that this was linked to a Mineral and Resources
Development Bill, whose basic intent was to vest sovereignty over South
Africa's natural resources in the hands of the state (which the mining companies decried as an attempted erosion of property rights), there was a massive

negative response on the stock market, and share prices in South African mining companies immediately slumped. Intense negotiations between the mining houses and government – which were spurred by calls by the Congress of South African Trade Unions (Cosatu) for state involvement in the industry and *worker* empowerment – followed, resulting in the emergence of a considerably milder charter in which it was agreed that all mines should be 15 per cent black-owned in five years and 26 per cent in ten years, with the industry agreeing to raise R100 billion to fund the transfer. In addition, it was agreed that companies should aspire to achieving a target of 40 per cent of blacks in management within five years, although flexibility was promised in the form of adoption of a scorecard approach to such goals as ownership, employment equity, improved community and rural development, worker housing and living conditions, procurement and beneficiation and so on, which, within limits, would be able to be offset against each other (Southall 2004).

The leak of the proposed mining charter and the resultant wiping of R11 billion off the share prices of mining companies over the next six months, had been salutary to both the government and industry. For its part, the Presidency had responded by approaching the mining houses to consider what business could do to ensure that such a situation was not repeated and to undertake transformation in a rational and orderly matter.

A particular initiative was taken by magnate Nicky Oppenheimer, Chairman of De Beers (the diamond giant), who, with his son (also a director in the company), approached the London-based Bain & Company consultancy to consider how the government's initiatives aimed at accelerating BEE could be used to strengthen, not weaken, investor confidence. The outcome, the Brenthurst Initiative (with a foreword by President Mbeki), was unwrapped with fanfare before prominent decision-makers and 'opinion-makers' at the Oppenheimer's family home in August 2003. Placing the need for growth at the centre of debate on the need for the narrowing of racial inequality, the plan highlighted uncertainty about BEE and lack of partnership between government and industry as the major causes of lack of investor confidence. It therefore proposed a three-pronged strategy which revolved around the idea of transformation scorecards (that is, giving weightings to black equity ownership, management representivity, employment profiles and so on); the creation of corporate tax incentives linked to transformation performance; and a plan to close the black empowerment funding gap (including introduction of tax-effective employee share options, mandated levels of savings and increased pension fund investments). These ideas, claimed the Oppenheimers, were designed to overcome short-term thinking, and stimulate debate about how South Africa could beat daunting odds (*Business Day* 6.8.03).

The response to the Brenthurst Initiative was mixed. Broadly speaking, big business (both black and white) loved it, whilst the union movement and radical critics loathed it. On the one hand, business lauded the Oppenheimer family ('When it comes to business dynasties none looms larger in South Africa') for coming up with proposals that dovetailed with the government's own plans and promised a 'second Codesa' (*Financial Mail* 8.08.03). On the other, Cosatu and the SACP slammed the Oppenheimers, who were linked to companies that had de-listed offshore, as unpatriotic and as attempting to get black workers to pay for the creation of a class of black capitalists (*Business Day* 7.08.03; *Mail & Guardian* 8–14.08.03).

Running for cover amidst the flak, the government politely backed off, explaining that tax incentives would adversely affect tax revenues, which would have to be collected elsewhere. Nonetheless, it was looking at reducing tax *disincentives* to BEE, and it might make an appropriate adjustment in the next Budget (*Financial Mail* 21.11.03). When the Budget came, business commentators were eventually disappointed in Finance Minister Trevor Manuel's lack of attention to a tax regime, which, they argued, penalised empowerment transactions above 25 per cent of a company's shares. Nonetheless, the introduction of tax relief on employment share schemes, which was expected to encourage BEE, suggested that the Oppenheimers' views on manipulating tax structures to boost employment resonated with the government more than it was openly prepared to admit, and suggested the possibility of future benefits to come (*Business Day* 19.02.04; *Financial Mail* 20.02.04).

In the meantime, the charter movement had taken root. Following on from the brouhaha around the mining industry, the financial sector had sought to pre-empt direct state intervention by drawing up its own charter, a draft of which it presented to DTI in July 2003. Like the mining charter, this adopted the scorecard approach to empowerment with regard to categories such as access to financial services, empowerment in management and procurement, employment equity and so on. Hard negotiations with government followed, notably over DTI's recommended target of 25 per cent black equity ownership within ten years, with the industry blanching at the vast amounts of finance this would entail. Subsequently, when the charter was finalised, a target of 25 per cent black ownership by 2010 was revealed, which was both higher and sooner than commentators had expected. Yet this was not so fierce as it immediately appeared. Only 10 per cent of equity (estimated as costing R20 billion over seven years) needed to be owned *directly* by blacks by 2010, the additional 15 per cent (which could be owned directly or *indirectly* by blacks, for instance through membership of pension funds) was optional. Meanwhile, foreign institutions, which had baulked at selling up to 25 per cent of their shares to black investors and had claimed that they were constrained by head office policies, were exempted from selling part of their South African businesses to blacks if they had a global policy in place precluding them from doing so. However, in return for this concession, they were to be expected to direct proportionately higher amounts of loan capital towards the financing of empowerment deals.

Otherwise, there was an additional list of targets to be attained: there was to be 33 per cent black representation at board level; 25 per cent at executive level; 20–25 per cent at senior level; 30 per cent at middle level; and 40–50 per cent at junior level; 50 per cent of procurement expenditure was to be directed to black companies by 2008 and 70 per cent by 2014; empowerment financing, which could amount to over R75 billion, was to be heavily (66 per cent) directed towards low-income housing, transformational infrastructure and small and medium businesses, whilst massive efforts were to extend financial services to the huge numbers of poorer people who are presently beyond their reach. Finally, 0.5 per cent per annum of after-tax operating profits was to be directed towards black groups as social responsibility expenditure (*Sunday Independent* & *Sunday Times* 19.10.03). Black business, in the person of Tendai Musikavanhu, Chief Executive Officer (CEO) of Umbono Fund Managers, waxed lyrical: the charter was a chance 'to set the seal on the South African miracle' (*Business Day* 24.10.03).

Other industries followed where the fuel, mining and finance sectors had already led. The private medical schemes, scrambling to boost their empowerment credentials ahead of a government plan to introduce a single, mandatory scheme for its employees, took an early lead with moves to create a charter (*Business Day* 19.05.03). Mutual suspicion between hospital groups, medical scheme administrators, professional bodies and pharmaceutical companies hindered progress, but key players were pushing for progress in order to forestall government intervention (*Business Day* 25.02.04). The maritime industry formally adopted a charter in September 2003, announcing this as a step on the road to a single charter for the entire transport sector (*Business Day* 23.09.03). The commercial property sector announced plans for a charter in early 2004, commentary noting that without it, 'the industry would be unlikely to be able to benefit from lucrative state development projects' (*Business Day* 27.01.04). Agricultural, wine and construction industry charters were likewise planned for early agreement (*Business Day* 23.01.04, 19.02.04), although concerted resistance by Dell, IBM, Hewlett-Packard, Microsoft and Oracle to transfer of equity slowed progress towards a charter in the information and communications technology (ICT) industry. These major global players were arguing, in contrast, that empowerment objectives could be equally well met by other methods such as assisting black entrepreneurs, reinvesting profits in South Africa, forming consortia with black partners and achieving black management targets (*Business Day* 17.09.03, 23.01.04). The prospect of government intervention was cited as likely to prompt arrival at an industry-wide consensus, yet the ICT experience – alongside that of the financial sector – indicates that the securing of multinational corporations' agreement to equity ownership targets remains highly problematic, and conceivably a bar to the investment-friendly environment in South Africa that the government proclaims it is attempting to create.

Empowerment charters are now the chosen vehicle whereby different industries can attest their commitment to BEE and keep in the government's good books. Rather more to the point, they are forcing the pace of change, and rapidly opening new vistas to South Africa's black business. Yet this in turn is posing a new set of urgent questions about the *nature* of this change, and the overall impact upon the performance of the South African economy.

In particular, is the *politically-induced* nature of BEE likely to produce a parasitic or a productive black bourgeoisie?

Politics and economics: is South Africa moving towards 'crony capitalism'?

It is precisely the centrality of the state to the current promotion of BEE and a black bourgeoisie that with fair regularity leads to the charge that South Africa is in danger of moving towards 'crony capitalism'. This highly charged term is borrowed primarily from critiques of Southeast Asian developments, and centres around notions that emergent business elites operate within a context in which:

- those who wield state power and authority are pivotal in the development process (notably via their ability to allocate resources);
- business relations between private and state capitalism closely interlock, resting upon personal and political connections which blur the lines between legal and illegal methods;
- business is carried out by informal groupings of capitalists, often joined by family or 'crony' linkages which are often regional and international; and
- finally, there is a further implication that such an elite is unlikely to shed their primary reliance upon those who wield political power in favour of basing their expansion as a group upon a normal basis of capital accumulation.

In short, 'crony capitalists' do not have it in them to become a Weberian-style, productive bourgeoisie (Clad 1991; Jones 1997; Robison & Goodman 1996). Meanwhile, the suggestion that BEE is pointing towards crony capitalism is closely related to wider critiques that emergent capitalist classes elsewhere in Africa are likewise state-dependent and kleptocratic, and are more extractive and exchange-oriented in their activities than productive and developmentally-oriented (see for example, Himbara 1994). Finally, there are suggestions that the artificially forced pace of BEE distorts the market, creating a culture of dependency and entitlement among black business, and hence inhibits and distorts rather than promoting growth and development (*Business Day* 24.02.04).

These are fundamental and serious charges, to which no easy or short answers can be given at the present time. However, there are two preliminary points which can usefully be made.

First, it needs to be recognised that participation in the market in South Africa has, for well over a century, been politically and racially structured. BEE therefore evinces strong elements of continuity with, as well as disjuncture from, the past. Differing perspectives on BEE and its outcomes are therefore a reflection of divergent approaches to desirable relationships between market and state, between social interventionists and economic liberals. At the heart of this aspect of the debate is the issue of how the legacy of racial inequality can be overcome without simultaneously inhibiting economic growth.

Second, it also needs to be appreciated that whereas there is an assumption in the critique of crony capitalism that 'normal capitalism' operates upon a basis of rational and legal Weberian-style behaviour by business elites, advanced industrial capitalism – as illustrated by massive business scandals (Enron and so on), often illustrative of intimate connections between corporations and governments – also systematically throws up instances of shady dealings that defy and tax norms of sound corporate governance. Critiques of the current restructuring of the South African capital market therefore need to be historically and sociologically aware, concerned with a search for an appropriate combination of legitimacy (racial redress) and efficacy (does it inhibit or promote economic growth?).

Against this background, the argument here is that the black capitalist class being promoted by BEE is highly dependent upon state policies, protection and preferences, and operates extensively through political networks associated with the ANC. Indeed, it is upon these grounds that it is being systematically courted by, and forging interrelations with, established ('white') corporations, both domestic and multinational. This does *not* mean that all black capitalists and corporate managers are paid up members of a political elite, for as Randall (1996) has indicated, there are significant streams which have emerged from other routes, be it through a professional and educational route to expertise, or through direct recruitment and training by established corporations. What is argued, rather, is that the black capitalist class operates within a sphere of capital accumulation which is fostered and nurtured by close connections with the state.

Broadly speaking, there are two main ways of arguing this case. First by looking at the direct political involvements of senior members of the ANC in business. Second, by examining the political and/or state background of senior members of the emergent black business elite. At this stage, findings can only be suggestive.

ANC crony capitalism?

The *Mail & Guardian* has recently decried what it considers to be the alarming degree to which 'crony capitalism and influence peddling is reaching high into the African National Congress' (6–12.02.04). It highlighted, in particular:

- The role of Minister of Public Enterprises Jeff Radebe in pushing a privatisation tender towards Skotaville Publishing, an empowerment company which was favoured after agreeing to sell an ANC Trust 20 per cent of its share capital at a heavily discounted price (*Mail & Guardian* 14–20.02.03).

- Allegations that the ANC, senior party figures and their relatives benefited from a deal in which a company, the South African Oil Company, which was registered in the Cayman Islands, secured a favourable oil deal from the Nigerian authorities, after personal recommendation by President Thabo Mbeki, which brought no benefit to South Africa.

- Revelations concerning 'empowerment businessman' Sandi Majali, who, in 2000, secured favourable oil allocations from President Saddam Hussein at a time when the Iraqi leader was offering Iraqi crude oil in exchange for diplomatic support to subvert UN sanctions against his country. Majali's activities were apparently sponsored by ANC Secretary General Kgalema Motlanthe and Treasurer Mendi Msimang. Meanwhile, not only does Majali's company, Imvume, support a fundraising trust for the trust (whose trustees are Motlanthe, Msimang and Radebe), but Majali is also known to have benefited from two massive state oil tenders, one issued by the Strategic Fuel Fund (valued at R1 billion), the other by Petro SA. Suspicions remain about the probity of the tender process entailed in the allocation of at least the former contract.

Other dubious deals include:

- Serious unanswered questions about the notorious arms deal. These revolve around allegations that Deputy President Jacob Zuma attempted to secure a bribe of R500 000 from the French defence company, Thomson-CSF (now named Thales), through the offices of Schabir Shaik, in return for his protection of the company's interests. Shaik, a former head of ANC intelligence, is a partner of Thales in the latter's local subsidiary, African Defence Systems (Crawford-Browne 2004).

- Conflict of interest issues surrounding the Minister of Defence, Mosiuoa Lekota, who failed to declare to Parliament, as required, his interests in fuel and wine businesses that had either done business with the government or had attempted to secure state or parastatal contracts. Lekota later apologised and resigned from the board of the fuel company, BZL, in which he had been given shares, free of charge, by the Managing Director 'as a friend'(*Mail & Guardian* 23–29.05.03).

- Involvement of the former Minister of Defence, the late Joe Modise, in a deal, driven by former South African Defence Force Major-General Ian Deetlefs, who in 1997 recommended to his co-directors of JSE-listed Log-Tek Holdings that they purchase Anglo-American's Conlog, which was available for a favourable price. Deetleefs then negotiated to buy Conlog's *business* rather than the actual company itself for R34 million, with money borrowed from a Malaysian bank. However, he did this on behalf of Charleston Marketing, which he then proceeded to rename Conlog (Pty) Ltd. He then returned to Log Tek, and recommended the purchase of Conlog (Pty) Ltd, which it subsequently bought for R124 million! The fortunate shareholders gaining this R90 million profit were a number of trusts, of which the trustees and ultimate beneficiaries included not only Modise and Deetlefs, but former Armscor boss Ron Haywood (*Noseweek* December 2003/January 2004).

- Ownership by Smuts Ngonyama, ANC spokesman in the President's office, of a stake in a consortium, Genesis Telecom, bidding to buy between 15 and 20 per cent of a R1 billion joint venture formed by Econet Wireless and IT giant Altech. Ngonyama is linked to Genesis through a company called Crestwave, of which he is a director together with three other individuals. These latter are all business partners of Charles Ngqula, CEO of the state finance company, IDC, from which Genesis is attempting to borrow money to purchase the shares (*Mail & Guardian* 20–26.02.04).

- The direct or indirect involvement of the ANC Youth League in a series of business ventures which appear designed to take advantage of special access to government. The principle vehicle, the South African Youth Development Trust, stands at the centre of a web of some 12 subsidiaries which have interests in many sectors of the economy, including mining, finance and property (*Mail & Guardian* 5–11.03.04).

Connections of the black business elite

Just as marked a feature of contemporary South African politics is the manner in which powerful individuals amongst the black elite are moving from politics and government to the private sector, where the increasing imperative to attain healthy BEE credentials is opening up impressive avenues for personal advance.

Undoubtedly the most prominent amongst those who have forsaken politics is Cyril Ramaphosa, who left his position as Secretary General of the ANC in 1996, and now serves as Chairperson of the major media and entertainment group, Johnnic Holdings, the cellphone company MTN, the Molope Group and Millenium Consolidated Investments, as well as serving as CEO of Millenium Resources and a director of other companies, including investment company Alexander Forbes. Following closely behind him in the public eye is Tokyo Sexwale, a former Robben Island prisoner who resigned as Premier of Gauteng in 1997, and is now Chairperson of the black mining group, Mvelaphanda Holdings and three other companies, whilst also being, *inter alia*, a director of Absa Bank and Gold Fields of South Africa. Meanwhile, a fellow luminary and former ANC Member of Parliament, Saki Macozoma, who was controversially appointed a member of the party's National Executive Committee in 1997 when he was still serving as Managing Director of Transnet, is now CEO of media giant New Africa Investments Ltd and Deputy Chair of the Standard Bank.

Whilst there are various other companies like Dyambu, New Line Investments, Ituseng Mining and Ikamva which are also led by former ANC activists (Southall 2004), it is also the case that, after having gained experience and contacts through public service, leading civil servants and parastatal managers are exiting the state for private business. Prominent amongst these are former Transnet CEO Mafika Mkhwanazi, who recently became non-executive Chair of Western Areas gold mining (whose CEO, Brett Kebble, is an associate of Schabir Shaik and recently made a major donation to the ANC's 2004 election fund) (*Business Day* 4.09.03). Also on the move was Andile Ngcaba, Director General (DG) of the Department of Communications, who left the civil service, probably to join the IT sector. Previously, the DG of Public Enterprise, Sivi Gounden, had left the civil service to become CEO of engineering company Bateman; Tami Soukou, DG of Public Works, had left for the African Bank; Sipho Pityana, DG of Foreign Affairs, had left for banking group Nedcor; and Roger Jardine, DG of Science and Technology, had quit for Kagiso Media (*Sowetan* 3.12.03). In addition, Jakes Gerwel, formerly DG in the President's office under Mr Mandela, has recently become Chair of the private health care company Afrox (*Business Day* 18.11.03). Meanwhile, numerous other black businesspeople similarly have close connections to the political elite, these including, of course, mining magnate Patrice Motsepe, Chairperson of ARMGold, who is brother-in-law to both Public Enterprise's Minister Jeff Radebe and Cyril Ramaphosa.

The point about these connections is not, it must be stressed, that they indicate corruption. However, what they do suggest is the fluidity, overlapping and intimacy of South Africa's new black elite, which is still relatively small, amongst whom personal and political linkages across political, state and business boundaries provide for a constant flow of exchanges and illuminate a sense of community.

Parasitic or productive capitalism?

It is evident from the above that aspects of BEE, as encouraged by government strategies, and as most particularly instanced by official or unofficial ANC involvements in business, verge dangerously near to the description of crony capitalism provided above. However, against this, as argued previously (Southall 2004), the sheer number and the magnitude of the empowerment deals being enacted suggests that Randall (1996) may be correct in arguing that, unlike in the rest of Africa, the complexity and size of the economy foreshadows non-state opportunities, which will make for the development of a relatively independent black capitalist class in South Africa. Even so, the political context in which South African business is presently located clearly poses sharp dilemmas for the established corporates, which not surprisingly, view BEE as an inevitable risk.

Conclusion: the necessary risk of black empowerment

It was recently reported that South Africa has slipped from 19th to 22nd out of 37 countries ranked by the Global Entrepreneurship Monitor 2003, indicating that 'the country has failed to create a competitive climate in which emerging businesses can grow and thrive' (*Business Day* 24.02.04). Meanwhile, results of a survey by Standard Corporate & Merchant Bank of 800 leaders from the corporate and public sectors indicated that 60 per cent of respondents believed that living standards would remain the same or decline if

President Mbeki retained his office for the next five years (*Business Day* 24.02.04). And although it was Sasol which drew President Mbeki's ire for labeling BEE a risk, parastatal Telkom was also revealed as having declared empowerment, alongside unemployment, poverty and crime, as a potential investment hazard to the New York Stock Exchange (*Business Day* 9.12.03).

The counter-argument, of course, is that whilst 'BEE cannot be realized without costs to white capital … it is a cost that is necessary investment in growth and stability', and one which will 'yield opportunities for capital across the racial spectrum' (editorial, *Sowetan* 6.11.03).

Present indications, as illustrated by the empowerment charter movement and by increasing mutual interaction and investment connections between black ventures and established firms, suggest that large-scale corporate capital is adapting to BEE as both an economic and political imperative. After all, the corporations, foreign and domestic, have massive investments in South Africa from which they seek to profit, and which the spectre of Zimbabwe suggests to them will be endangered unless they accommodate to the demands of a government which is largely regarded in investment circles as moderate and sensible, and under whose aegis, a remarkable expansion of South African capital into Africa is being facilitated. The danger remains, however, that the massive opening up of easy opportunities for advance to blacks which is being engineered by BEE will place a scramble for personal enrichment ahead of a drive for entrepreneurship and productive investment, and that black capitalism will veer down the barren path of crony capitalism, encouraged by the more unscrupulous elements of established business.

Whether that route can be avoided will depend much upon whether the present *porous* borders between state and black business under the ANC can be *hardened*, and more rigorous distinctions between politics and economics *solidified*.

Notes

1   See 2003 annual reports of IDC, Denel, Eskom, Transnet and Telkom. See also <http//business.iafrica.com/news/49835.htm>.

References

BEEC (Black Economic Empowerment Commission) (2001). *Executive summary report of the BEEC 2001*. Available at <http://www.bmfonline.co.za/bee_rep.htm>.

Bond P (2000) *Elite transition: From apartheid to neoliberalism in South Africa*. London: Pluto.

Clad J (1991) *Behind the myth: Business, money and power in Southeast Asia*. London: Grafton.

Crawford-Browne T (2004) The arms deal scandal, *Review of African Political Economy*, 31:313–328.

Davies R (1988) Nationalisation, socialisation and the Freedom Charter. In J Suckling & L White (eds.) *After apartheid: Renewal of the South African economy*. London: James Currey.

Edigheji OM (1999) Rethinking black economic empowerment in the post-apartheid South Africa. Trade Industry Policy Strategies (TIPS) Annual Forum, Muldersdrift, 19–22.09.99.

Himbara D (1994) *Kenyan capitalists, the state and development*. Nairobi: East African Educational Publishers.

Jones D (1997) *Political development in Pacific Asia*. Cambridge: Polity.

Macozoma S (2003) From a theory of revolution to the management of a fragile state. In D Everatt & V Maphai (eds.) The real state of the nation: South Africa after 1990. *Development Update* 4:11–30.

O'Meara D (1996) *Forty lost years: The apartheid state and the politics of the National Party, 1948–1994*. Johannesburg: Ravan.

Randall DJ (1996) Prospects for the development of a black business class in South Africa, *The Journal of Modern African Studies* 34:661–86.

Robison R & Goodman D (eds.) (1996). *The new rich in Asia: Mobile phones, McDonalds and middle class revolution*. New York: Routledge.

Said A & Simmons L (1975) *The new sovereigns: Multinational corporations as world powers*. Englewood Cliffs, New Jersey: Prentice Hall.

Southall R (2004) The ANC and black capitalism in South Africa, *Review of African Political Economy*, forthcoming.

Walters SS & Prinsloo JW (2002) The impact of offshore listings on the South African economy, *South African Reserve Bank Quarterly Bulletin*, September: 60–71.

18 'Empty stomachs, empty pockets': poverty and inequality in post-apartheid South Africa

Benjamin Roberts

> For the black, and especially African majority, suddenly a new
> dawn broke. After these masses had cast their votes, they still
> had nothing in their stomachs and their pockets … [b]ut yet
> they had a spring in their step because they knew that a new
> dawn had proclaimed the coming of a bright day.
> *President Thabo Mbeki, 'State of the Nation' address, February 2004*

For South Africa, 2004 represents a salient benchmark in poverty discourse for a number of reasons. Most importantly, the celebration of the country's first decade of democracy signifies an opportune moment to reflect upon the progress that has been made in redressing the pervasive and multifaceted poverty and inequality affecting the majority of the population. Similarly, it allows for a critical discussion on the adequacy of the suite of policy measures and interventions that have been introduced as part of the government's strategy to reduce poverty. This year also marks the 20th anniversary of the conference of the Second Carnegie Inquiry into Poverty and Development. This event mobilised those critically engaged in the poverty challenge and focused not only on documenting the extent, nature and dimensions of poverty amongst the African population, but also on the development of strategies for action against poverty. Being an election year, the politics of poverty reduction have again come to the fore. The African National Congress's (ANC's) election manifesto proposes a series of ambitious socio-economic objectives and targets for the next decade of democracy: of particular note is the intent to halve both poverty and unemployment through economic development; comprehensive social security; land reform; and improved household and community assets. With an overwhelming electoral victory, the ANC has rapidly begun to concentrate on its responsibility to deliver on electoral promises. Therefore, in addition to looking backwards at the achievements and shortcomings of post-apartheid poverty policy and praxis, there is the opportunity to begin to look prospectively at possible trajectories for the next decade.

This chapter begins by briefly outlining the state-driven policy initiatives introduced to redress the multidimensional and deeply rooted inequalities that proliferated under colonial, segregationist and apartheid dispensations. This is followed by an examination of poverty trends and the emerging disagreements among those concerned with poverty reduction. A review of evidence on the evolving nature of inequality is then presented, focusing especially on the gradual shift in the relative importance of racial and employment and earnings-based determinants. The chapter concludes by assessing whether the vision for the second decade of liberation will serve to reduce South Africa's pervasive impoverishment, confront the burgeoning class divide within race groups, and provide relief to persistently marginalised groupings in society.

Anti-poverty policy in post-apartheid South Africa

With the election of the democratic government, there emerged a strong and committed policy concern with poverty. The reduction of mass impoverishment and social inequality was *explicitly* incorporated into the 1994 Reconstruction and Development Programme (RDP). The strategy to address the legacy of poverty and inequality rested upon the RDP's four pillars, namely building the economy, meeting basic needs, developing human resources and democratising the state. Government departments were subsequently expected to fulfil the poverty reduction mandate articulated within these policy frameworks, most especially by directly targeting the poor through service delivery.

Public spending on the poor over the decade has assumed two predominant forms, namely mainstream social expenditures and separate, specialised poverty relief funds. Most of the financing for poverty reduction in South Africa is designed to occur through the regular budget of the various government departments. These mainstream interventions can be disaggregated into three basic forms of social development programmes (Pieterse & van Donk

2002). Firstly, there are infrastructure programmes directed at the provision of basic household and individual needs, incorporating local public goods and services such as water, sanitation, energy, housing, health and education. Secondly, there is the well-developed social security system, which extends safety nets to certain cohorts. These include the three dominant types of non-contributory and means-tested social assistance grants provided by the state to vulnerable groups that are unable to fulfil their basic needs, namely child grants,[1] the old age pension and the disability grant, along with other measures such as school feeding programmes. The third type of social expenditure focuses on job-creation measures and entails skills training, the promotion of small, medium and micro enterprises, job summit programmes and land redistribution. In addition, it has involved the pursuance of measures designed to maintain macroeconomic stability, such as fiscal prudence, debt reduction and managed trade liberalisation. A range of social and human rights have also been secured through an internationally lauded Constitution, offering legal protection to the poor, vulnerable and marginalised.

Despite the state-driven programme of development directed at alleviating the legacy of poverty and inequality, the ANC government formulated a fairly orthodox neo-liberal macroeconomic policy package. The adoption of the Growth, Employment and Redistribution strategy (GEAR) in 1996 – which differed substantively from the original developmental ethos of the RDP – entailed stringent measures to maintain fiscal discipline as a means to deficit reduction and stimulating economic growth. While the rationale for this policy shift continues to be vigorously debated, the emphasis on economic growth laying the basis for the reduction of unemployment and a more equitable distribution of income and wealth came to be increasingly challenged. By 1997 it was becoming apparent that departments had not been sufficiently able to reprioritise their budgets to overcome the developmental challenge. Moreover, there was an increasing realisation that market liberalisation was likely to have a disproportionate impact on the poorest, and that GEAR was severely limiting any enhancement in existing redistributive programmes. In response to this mounting social deficit, the Poverty Alleviation Fund[2] was introduced during the 1997–98 financial year by the National Treasury as a *short-term* intervention directed at fulfilling two fundamental objectives. It aimed firstly to address poverty directly by providing funding for departments to perform functions they would not conventionally have undertaken or budgeted for, and secondly to assist departments in fast-tracking the re-orientation of their services to the poor (Aliber 2003; de Bruyn 2001). The special allocation thus emerged as a measure for temporary employment creation and poverty alleviation until GEAR produced sufficient growth to enable the market itself to create jobs.[3]

The ANC's 50th national conference acknowledged that poverty represents the 'single greatest burden' confronting South Africa's population and that 'attacking poverty and deprivation is the first priority of the democratic government' (ANC 1997). It further reaffirmed the importance of the relationship between economic growth and human development, and prioritised the identification and removal of inefficiencies in markets, institutions, spatial structure and delivery mechanisms that operate against the poor in order to create a macroeconomic climate conducive to sustainable growth. Other resolutions included commitments to enhancing the delivery of physical and social infrastructure to the poor, and improving the collection of social, economic and demographic data to monitor changes in poverty.

In 1995, Cabinet agreed that a comprehensive poverty assessment be undertaken, after which the then Deputy President, Thabo Mbeki, convened an inter-ministerial committee to oversee the study. Finally, a consortium of South African researchers was commissioned in 1997 to produce the Poverty and Inequality Report (PIR). The purpose of the study was to redress the dearth of information on South Africa's poor by developing a comprehensive profile of poverty and inequality, in addition to analysing the coherence and effectiveness of the post-apartheid state's policy response to these challenges (May 1998). The report noted that low investment, low employment and low growth have resulted in progress that has not lived up to the expectations of the poor or the policymakers, but did laud the tremendous range of government programmes, pilot projects and grants relevant to the reduction of poverty and inequality being implemented. Nonetheless, a lingering concern was the fact that the policies were not integrated into a coherent poverty reduction framework, according to which priorities and sequencing are mapped out.

The Minister of Welfare and Population Development articulated the government's response to the PIR in 1998, which described the state's policy approach to poverty and inequality as consisting of five components, namely macroeconomic stability (as enshrined in GEAR), meeting basic needs (basic education and health, water and sanitation, housing and basic services for municipalities), providing social safety nets (comprehensive social security as a safety net), human resource development and job creation (Fraser-Moleketi in Meth 2003). This policy trajectory was further consolidated at the ANC's 51st national conference. Facing mounting criticism, it reaffirmed that 'the central challenge remains the eradication of poverty and inequality through economic growth and development, job creation and social equity' (ANC 2003). Despite openly acknowledging low economic growth, mass poverty and rising unemployment, it was concluded that the 'right policies', including the GEAR framework, are in place.[4] Consistent with this belief, the recommended approach for social transformation is a scaling up of the roll-out of comprehensive social security, free basic services, an expanded public works programme and an integrated food security programme, combined with improvements in financial resources and government capacity.

Impoverished numbers and contested realities: the extent and nature of poverty

How has poverty changed in the post-transition period and what are the drivers underlying these dynamics? As the first decade of democracy drew to a conclusion and empirical evidence on well-being in South Africa proliferated, the extent to which government action has served to address the key challenges of poverty and inequality received increasing attention in public policy discourse. Despite advances in poverty measurement and the emergence of a voluminous literature on the subject, the patterns and dynamics of poverty and inequality have become the subject of much debate. The key issue of contention relates to whether poverty has increased or decreased over the period. This situation has developed partly due to insufficient recognition of the fact that different measurement techniques yield divergent estimates of poverty and inequality. This is compounded by the absence of an official national poverty line, resulting in poverty estimates that fluctuate within quite a broad range, even when referring to a single dataset.[5] A lack of conceptual and definitional specificity in relation to poverty in South Africa, particularly the apparent lack of consensus on the meaning and measurement of poverty among senior level government officials, further complicates the picture (Everatt 2003). Even more important is the quality of the data that has been collected over the decade. Problems of data comparability, reliability and credibility have become an increasing barrier to meaningful inter-temporal analysis. As the 1990s progressed, household surveys were modified with the aim of achieving improvements in both clarity and the consistency of reporting, but these amendments to the survey design make the measurement of social phenomena, such as food insecurity or unemployment, increasingly difficult. The implication is that observed changes may end up being technique driven or determined by data anomalies, rather than reflective of actual societal dynamics.

The debate on progress in poverty reduction has also been influenced by the availability of regular, nationally representative survey data on income and expenditure patterns. Despite commendable strides, such surveys still occur intermittently and there are significant time lags in the release of data, which has constrained the ability to conduct poverty and inequality analysis in the 2000–2004 period. As such, much of the existing documentation on money-metric measures of poverty in the country rely on statistics that either predate the 1994 democratic elections or only enable us to comment on the first couple of years of democracy. For example, the government poverty estimates in *Measuring poverty in South Africa* (Stats SA 2000) utilised 1995 data, while the most recently published estimates provided in *Earning and spending in South Africa* (Stats SA 2002) relate to 2000, though the quality and reliability of these data have been widely contested. While not a representative sample, the KwaZulu-Natal Income Dynamics Survey, a panel study of approximately 1 200 African households over 1993–98, represents one of the better indications of post-apartheid poverty trends. Using expenditure-based measures, the poverty rate for the cohort rose from 27 per cent to 43 per cent, whereas the distribution of wealth became less equal (Carter & May 2001). Nonetheless, assessing the impact of policy change remains circumscribed by the reality that observable impacts are only likely to manifest a relatively long period after the changes, as well as the poor availability of timely credible data.

The official release of the results of the 2000 Income and Expenditure Survey (IES) in November 2002 provoked strident debate about the nature of the gains to the poorest of the first ten years of freedom. It concluded that, 'South Africans, on average, became poorer between 1995 and 2000. Increases in social spending have not as yet translated into higher average incomes and expenditures' (Stats SA 2002:32). This finding contrasts with national accounts and demographic statistics, and was disputed by the Office of the President in favour of the more sanguine results of the All-Media Products Survey (AMPS).[6] The latter revealed that, between 1994 and 2001, the population share falling in the lowest category of the living standard measure (LSM) had decreased from 20 to 5 per cent (Schlemmer 2002).[7] Since government has persistently acknowledged that the fight against poverty is one of the most important tasks confronting it, it could be argued that the sensitivity displayed by government and party spokespersons in response to suggestions that poverty is worsening is rather unsurprising (Meth & Dias 2003). This led to pronouncements such as the following by Joel Netshitenzhe, Chief Executive Officer of the Government Communication and Information System (GCIS), who expressed the intention to 'correct mistaken views that the poor were worse off than they were during apartheid years'.[8] Similarly, a media briefing following the 2003 Cabinet *Lekgotla* boldly stated that 'massive progress had been made … in attacking the poverty and neglect that characterised social relations under apartheid' (GCIS 2003). The situation was further complicated by the discovery of flaws with the 2000 IES data, which lent credence to the government's claims of statistical measurement error.[9]

Another government response to the claims of mounting impoverishment has been to underscore the importance of factoring in the contributory role of the 'social wage' to poverty reduction. The social wage is essentially 'a measure of how much better off individuals are with the provision of publicly funded welfare services than they would be without these "in kind" benefits' (Sefton 2002:1). A sizeable share of government's spending is devoted to social grants, such as the child support grant, in addition to improved public services for all, including healthcare, education, electricity, water, sanitation and housing. The value of such services can be conceived as an income in kind, or a social wage, representing a substantial supplement to the cash income of individuals or households, most especially for those towards the lower end of the income distribution. Although most conventional measures of poverty and inequality ignore the value of benefits in kind, their inclusion is potentially very significant in monitoring the impact of government policies on the poorest households. The social wage is therefore of great policy relevance given government's concern with inequality and a more specific commitment to reducing poverty.

The emphasis of the government has progressively shifted away from income poverty towards the successes achieved in relation to the social wage. For instance, during the 2003 'State of the Nation' address, President Mbeki (2003) stated that 'the "social wage"... has improved with each passing year'. The massive research endeavour commissioned by the Office of the President in 2003 to document progress over the decade, *Towards a ten year review*, focused quite explicitly on the various components of the social wage. This focus was carried over into the 2004 'State of the Nation' address, where improvements in access to housing, electricity, clean water, adequate sanitation and education were the only social statistics cited by President Mbeki.

While it is evident that substantial progress has been made in the provision of social services over the last decade, a salient question remains to be addressed, namely: to what extent the social wage has translated into reductions in the incidence of poverty in the country? The IES 2000 report states that, 'there are indeed benefits being accrued from the social wage. But these are not yet impacting on monetary poverty' (Stats SA 2003:26). Yet given the statistical anomalies with this dataset, the reliability of this conclusion needs to be questioned. In one of the rare studies that have probed this matter in any depth, Meth and Dias (2003) examine poverty trends and the role that the social wage plays in these estimates. Their analysis suggests that while the social wage has undeniably played a salient contribution to the well-being of South Africans over the last decade, an estimated 4 million people have become poor between 1999 and 2002, even if generous assumptions are made in the valuation of the social wage. More specifically, the study indicates that the social wage has a limited impact on the spending power of the poor, as rapidly increasing numbers needing assistance are negating accomplishments in social provision.

Exploring the multiple dimensions of poverty

While the debate about aggregate poverty trends rages on, there is nonetheless more agreement as to the factors associated with being poor in South Africa. Living standards have been shown to be closely associated with race, with poor Africans accounting for the overwhelming majority of the poor. There is also a distinctive spatial dimension to poverty in the country, with the incidence of poverty in rural localities significantly higher than for residents of secondary cities and the metropoles. Substantial provincial disparities also exist, with those containing former homelands bearing a disproportionately larger share of the poverty burden as shown in Figure 18.1 (see Gelb 2004).

Given apartheid spatial engineering, the racial character of poverty relates closely to the spatial dimension of poverty in the country.

Figure 18.1 *Incidence of poverty by province (percentage of households)*

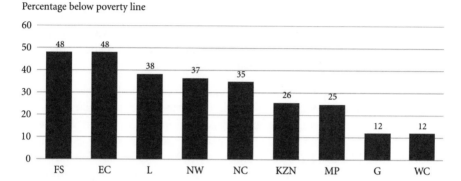

Percentage below poverty line

Source: Stats SA 2000
Note: Household poverty line based on monthly consumption expenditure of R800 or less in 1996 prices.
Eastern Cape (EC), Free State (FS), Gauteng (G), KwaZulu-Natal (KZN), Limpopo (L), Mpumalanga (M), Northern Cape (NC), North West (NW), Northern Province (NP), Western Cape (WC)

There is a strong relationship between employment and poverty and inequality. The unemployment rate for individuals from poor households is higher than the national average, while the labour force participation for the poor is demonstrably lower for poor relative to non-poor households (Woolard & Leibbrandt 2001). In 1995, more than half of the economically active in poor households were outside the labour market, which is supported by evidence that poverty deters job-search activities in South Africa (Kingdon & Knight 2004). This signifies that poor households are not only likely to have a greater number of unemployed adults relative to richer households, but also more adults who are unavailable for work. Access to wage income is also an important correlate of poverty, with poor households generally characterised by a lack of earnings, some due to unemployment among potential breadwinners and others due to the poorly-paid nature of work secured, especially in the domestic and agricultural sectors (Bhorat, Leibbrandt, Maziya, van der Berg & Woolard 2001; Seekings 2003). One estimate has reported the proportion of South African households in the bottom quintile of the income distribution without any members in employment as being as high as 83 per cent (DoSD

2002). The incidence of such workerless households seems to be rising, as suggested by the increase of workerless African households from 32 per cent to above 38 per cent between 1995 and 1999.[10] This corresponds to a shift from 1.9 to 3.1 million African households (DoSD 2002). In consequence, and as a risk-aversion strategy, the sources of income on which the poor depend tend to be more varied than the non-poor, with remittances and state transfers accounting for a sizeable share – 45 per cent in 1995 (Woolard 2002). However, it is important also to consider that approximately 60 per cent of the poor receive no social security transfers (DoSD 2002).

This situation may have worsened over the decade, particularly since the South African economy has been unable to create jobs at a sufficiently rapid rate to absorb the growing economically active population. According to official sources, the number of employed people rose from 9.6 to 11.2 million between 1995 and 2002, representing an increase of 1.6 million jobs, whereas the number of unemployed grew by 2.3 million due to the large number of labour market entrants (PCAS 2003).[11] This shortfall has translated into low labour absorption rates and rising unemployment, with a startling 72 per cent of the unemployed under the age of 35 years in 2002 (Altman 2003). The disjuncture between increases in employment and the economically active population is especially pronounced for Africans as well as for women (see Figure 18.2). Further demonstrating the close correlation between poverty and the labour market, the KwaZulu Income Dynamics Survey survey revealed that a household member losing a job or receiving reduced labour earnings was the principal determinant for 51 per cent of the households that became poor between 1993 and 1998. Conversely, 56 per cent of households escaping poverty did so primarily because a household member gained employment or experienced an increase in earnings (Budlender 2003:173).

The performance of government programmes aimed at addressing capability and asset poverty, especially those pertaining to health, education, housing, land, basic services and access to credit, are considered 'well conceived and potentially well targeted' (DoSD 2002:299), but constrained by various challenges to their efficacy. Educational attainment is an important determinant of employment status and, by extension, impoverishment. In 1995, individuals with no education or less than a primary school education were more prone to poverty, with the incidence of poverty dropping as educational attainment increases (Woolard & Leibbrandt 2001). As for health, in spite of

Figure 18.2 *Change in employment and economically active population by race and gender, 1995–99 (percentage)*

Percentage

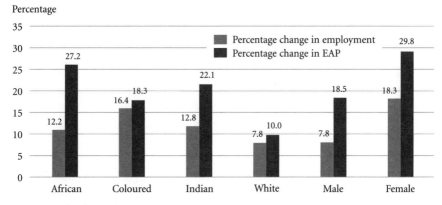

Source: McCord & Bhorat 2003

the government's bold moves to tackle the inequities inherited from the apartheid era by restructuring the public health system and promoting equity, household data indicate the continuing influence of barriers to access on healthcare demand. These include distance to the nearest healthcare facility and cost of care, medication and transportation, especially given that many lack a basic income to cover food and other essential non-food spending requirements. Lower socio-economic groups seek care less frequently than other groups, despite their generally worse health status, even through primary healthcare is free. There is a growing burden of chronic illness, including HIV/AIDS, and injuries, even whilst poverty-related illness persists. As a consequence, poor African households in particular have had to cope with the triple burdens of health system restructuring, increased levels of chronic illness and broader economic shocks over the last decade. The impact of HIV/AIDS is likely to exacerbate the burden over the next decade. The percentage of adult deaths that could be attributed to AIDS-related diseases has increased from about 9 per cent in 1995–96 to about 40 per cent by 2000–01, and is expected to rise steadily and peak around 2010 (van Aardt in Woolard 2002).[12]

Despite a considerable improvement in the expansion of physical infrastructure, access to basic services tends to be negatively associated with poverty in the country, with poorer households having slightly lower levels of safe drinking water and significantly lower access to adequate sanitation than the non-poor. Household access to electricity has increased from 32 to around 70 per cent by 2001. Nonetheless, the backlog in urban areas stands at an estimated 34 per cent, possibly driven by the growth of informal settlements, whereas 51 per cent of rural areas remain unconnected. Public service provision has tended to be target-driven rather than outcomes-driven, resulting in an emphasis on quantity over quality of the service rendered. As such, water interruptions and the maintenance of other existing infrastructure is becoming an increasing concern. As Hemson and Owusu-Ampomah assert in this volume, the matter of the sustainability of service delivery to the poor remains largely unresolved, especially the ability of the poor to pay for services beyond a basic minimum level and the provision of publicly provided services that are affordable to the poor. The policy of fiscal prudence adopted under GEAR has meant cutbacks for local government, which in turn has resulted in escalating costs of services in urban and rural areas due to stringent cost-recovery policies. Faced with this mounting cost burden, service disconnections and evictions due to non-payment have become commonplace, especially among the poor, with often severe ramifications on quality of life (Kotzé 2003).

In South Africa poverty is correlated with certain vulnerable groupings. Female-headed households are over-represented among the poor, with substantially higher poverty rates among *de jure* and *de facto* female-headed households than for households with a resident male head.[13] Some of the factors underpinning these gendered differentials include the greater probability that female-headed households are rural based, where poverty is concentrated, with fewer adults of working age in female-headed households, higher female unemployment rates, and the persisting wage gap between male and female earnings (Woolard 2002). Children are also disproportionately represented among the poor, with more than 40 per cent of those aged 14 or younger falling below the international poverty line of $1 per day in 1995 (Dieden & Gustafsson 2003). As with the poor population in general, the poverty incidence among this cohort has strong racial and spatial dimensions, is shaped by the educational level of the household head and the household's access to regular wage income, and is associated with household structure. Labour market trends and the growing prevalence of orphanhood attributable to the HIV/AIDS pandemic suggest that child poverty is unlikely to have diminished substantially over the decade or to diminish in the near future (Dieden & Gustafsson 2003).

Malnutrition has been worsening, with the prevalence of underweight children increasing from 9.3 per cent to 10.3 per cent during the late 1990s (Stats SA & UNDP 2003). Stunting also rose, from 22.9 per cent of children aged 1–6 in 1994, to 23.3 per cent in 1999 (Bradshaw, Masiteng & Nannan 2000). This inability of many South Africans, especially children, to secure their recommended dietary requirements is further corroborated by available data pertaining to *subjective* measures of food insecurity.[14] Despite inconsistent phrasing hampering comparability over time, certain patterns can be discerned. Between one-quarter and one-third of households are unable to purchase food to meet the dietary requirements of children at any given time. This phenomenon is more acutely felt amongst rural households and in poorer provinces, most especially the Eastern Cape and Mpumalanga (see Table 18.1).

Table 18.1 *Subjective assessment of food insecurity in South African households by province and area of residence, 1995–2002 (percentage)*

Province	Did not have enough money to feed children in household	Could not afford to feed children in the household			Children aged <7 went hungry because there was not enough money to buy food	Children aged <=17 went hungry because there was not enough food
	1995	1996	1997	1998	1999	2002
WC	23.1	22.9	20.6	25.7	18.0	17.2
EC	42.8	39.2	31.8	47.0	31.2	49.7
NC	27.3	25.6	22.8	26.9	13.8	29.2
FS	32.4	17.5	31.2	28.7	26.5	35.5
KZN	35.2	25.4	27.2	32.2	26.9	29.8
NW	25.3	20.2	27.6	26.6	25.1	37.7
G	22.0	27.7	18.7	22.0	14.6	18.8
M	39.5	24.5	29.0	33.7	32.0	36.6
L	43.7	28.2	24.0	30.2	16.1	31.8
Urban	–	25.5	22.3	26.4	19.1	23.4
Rural	–	29.1	29.9	37.2	27.6	40.3
National	31.7	27.0	25.5	31.1	23.4	30.8

Source: Calculations from electionic data made avilable by Stats SA, OHS 1994–99 and General Household Survey 2002

Social assistance has an important role to play in alleviating child poverty. However, while the number of beneficiaries of the child support grant has risen dramatically over the decade, relative to the estimated number of children entitled to grants the uptake remains rather low. Woolard (2003) indicates that the number of recipients increased from 321 906 to 2.1 million between 1999–2000 and October 2003, though approximately 4 to 5 million children under seven are eligible. Recent analysis using 2002 data from a demographic surveillance site in a remote rural district of Kwa-Zulu Natal revealed that a third of age-eligible children were receiving the grant, that most of these beneficiaries had parents that are less educated and less likely to be employed, and reside in households with few assets (Case, Hosegood & Lund 2003). This suggests that while the uptake could be improved, the child support grant has over five years managed to achieve notable success in reaching the rural poor. However, improved understanding of who qualifies for benefits is required over forthcoming years (Case et al. 2003).

The 1990s saw the rapid expansion to, and equalisation of, the state old age pension across race groups. Nonetheless, despite being considered generous by international standards, the real value of the grant has steadily begun to decline, partly due to the fiscal limitations imposed by the introduction and scaling up of the child support grant in 1998 (Woolard 2003). The old age pension is an effective tool for redistribution and for reaching predominantly poor households (Case & Deaton 1998). Moreover, it is often the sole source of income for rural African households. A study of the Eastern and Western Cape shows that the majority of African pensioners pool their pension together with other household income to meet the survival needs of the family (Møller & Ferreira 2003).

Divide or conquer: patterns of inequality

That South Africa has high levels of income inequality – amongst the highest in the world – is generally well known. This is unsurprising given that discriminatory practices during the apartheid era served to engender a racial divide in wage earnings. Depending on their racial classification, individuals would be paid different wages for the same job, irrespective of qualification. Differences in access to and quality of education, location and economic sector have also influenced this racial wage gap (Nattrass & Seekings 2001). In addition to the range of redistributive measures introduced by the democratic government to raise incomes and improve human capital and asset accumulation among the previously disadvantaged, further efforts have been exerted to overcome this legacy of inequality by means of affirmative action policies directed at correcting labour market imbalances, and black economic empowerment policies to encourage asset transfer. Recently, there has been much speculation about whether inequality has been worsening and increasing reference to a '50 per cent solution' (Morris 1993). The argument here is that the historical racial divide is being supplanted by a class divide, since democratisation and the subsequent neo-liberal embrace has effectively only deracialised the apex of the class structure (Habib, Daniel & Southall 2003).

While substantial uncertainty exists regarding recent poverty trends in South Africa, there appears to be more consensus about the dynamics of inequality over the past ten years, at least when disaggregated by race. Whereas the Gini coefficient[15] for the country has been shown to have remained at a consistently high level between 1975 and 1991, this aggregate trend obscured the reality that the richer became wealthier whereas the poor became more deprived, as well as a widening gulf within race groups. Since the 1970s, the wages of African workers began to rise, a phenomenon that has been ascribed to the confluence of a number of factors. These include the rise of trade unionism and the associated increase in bargaining power, declining wage discrimination and the resulting gains in occupational mobility, and rising education and training (Leibbrandt, Woolard & Bhorat 2001). However, parallel to these encouraging developments, there was a sizeable rise in unemployment as a result of poor economic growth and the growing cost of labour relative to capital. These factors have served to produce a segmented labour market, with a yawning gap between those with access to formal employment and those in the informal sector, engaging in subsistence farming or unemployed. Therefore, the divide between poor and rich Africans and between poor and rich whites is increasing (Bhorat et al. 2001; Whiteford & McGrath 1994).

A number of estimates produced for the period following the democratic transition show that there has been a consistent upward trend in real per capita incomes for all population groups (see Figure 18.3). It is evident that there has been a small and gradual narrowing of the gap in African incomes relative to white incomes over the period (See Table 18.2). Nonetheless, despite this observed decline in inter-racial inequality, it must be noted that

Figure 18.3 *Real annual per capita income by race group, 1970–2000 (constant 2000 Rands)*

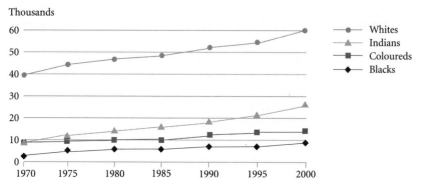

Sources: van der Berg & Louw 2003:11; *Business Report* 25.02.04

Table 18.2 *Annual per capita income by race group (percentage of white level)*

	1970	1975	1980	1985	1990	1995	2000
African	8.0	10.1	10.9	11.2	11.6	12.5	12.9
Coloured	20.9	19.5	18.9	20.4	22.0	23.6	22.3
Indians	24.5	25.4	28.5	31.2	33.9	38.2	41.4
White	100.0	100.0	100.0	100.0	100.0	100.0	100.0

Sources: van der Berg & Louw 2003:11; *Business Report* 25.02.04

African per capita income is still approximately 7.7 times lower than white annual per capita income.

Whiteford and van Seventer (2000) found that between 1991 and 1996, the incomes of the poorest 40 per cent of African households dropped by over 20 per cent. In contrast, the richest 10 per cent of African households experienced an equivalent increase over the period. They also reveal that a remarkable two-thirds of overall inequality in South Africa is due to skewed distribution of income *within* population groups (intra-racial inequality), with the remaining third attributable to the skewed distribution of resources *between* the population groups (inter-racial inequality). Leibbrandt et al. (2001) further observed that both intra- and inter-racial components are important contributors to overall inequality, with intra-racial inequality accounting for more that 60 per cent of overall inequality. The largest within-race contributor to inequality is among African households. Table 18.3 provides estimated Gini coefficients for each separate race group between 1970 and 2000.

Table 18.3 *Gini coefficients by population group using per capita income*

Year	1970	1975	1993	1995	1996	2000
African	–	0.49	0.56	0.57	0.68	0.59
White	0.43	–	0.47	0.47	0.52	0.49
Indian	0.42	–	0.50	0.49	0.53	0.51
Coloured	0.53	–	0.47	0.52	0.57	0.55

Source: van der Berg & Louw 2003:15, based on estimates from various surveys and censuses

Therefore, race-based components of income inequality in South Africa between 1994 and 2000 are characterised by two divergent trends. Inequality between race groups has been slowly declining, but this has been effectively offset by increasing inequality within groups, notably for the African population. But what does this imply for overall inequality in the country over the interval? Again, as with the poverty trends, there are a number of different contrasting and competing interpretations. While estimates such as those previously outlined point towards a more static trend in inequality since 1994, there are also certain actors using Gini coefficients derived from disputed Statistics South Africa (Stats SA) data to substantiate their claim that overall inequality has widened over the period (Bhorat 2003; Friedman 2004; Gelb 2004; van der Berg & Louw 2003). Nonetheless, irrespective of which estimates are cited, with a Gini coefficient ranging between 0.58 and 0.68, South Africa remains one of the world's most inequitable societies.

As with poverty, wage income remains one of the key determinants of inequality in the country (see Table 18.4). An individual's location in the distribution of income is influenced by access to employment, or the type of employment he or she is able to get. For those below the poverty line, where many households are workerless, it is access to income that is likely to be the key driver of inequality, compared with those above the poverty line where the issue is likely to be more about the highly skewed character of earnings. Aside from wage income, the other dominant driver of inequality is access to state transfers for the poor and self-employment for the non-poor.

Table 18.4 *Decomposition of national income by income source and poverty status (percentage share in overall Gini)*

Income source	Proportion of household receiving source		Proportional share in total income		Percentage share in overall Gini	
	Below PL	Above PL	Below PL	Above PL	Below PL	Above PL
Remittances	0.23	0.09	0.12	0.02	5.64	-0.27
Wage income	0.50	0.79	0.49	0.68	63.00	63.30
Capital income	0.09	0.21	0.04	0.10	5.51	9.90
State transfers	0.49	0.26	0.33	0.04	22.03	-0.91
Self-employment	0.04	0.11	0.03	0.18	3.86	27.98
Total	1.00	1.00	1.00	1.90	100.00	100.00

Source: Bhorat et al. 2001:33, using 1995 IES data
Note: PL refers to poverty line, which was defined as income per adult equivalent

Pushing back the frontiers of poverty: towards Vision 2014

During the 1990s, poverty reduction efforts in sub-Saharan Africa have been hampered by poor economic growth, political instability, livelihoods failure, and persistently high levels of income inequality (UNDP & Unicef 2002). The reality is that for many countries in the region, the prospect of halving poverty over the next decade is likely to remain an elusive aspiration. This has prompted the call for countries to 'endogenise' the Millennium Development Goals (MDGs)[16] in order to reflect what can feasibly be attained. As a signatory of the 2000 Millennium Declaration, South Africa has in effect committed itself to achieving the MDGs and the associated set of targets by 2015. Foremost amongst these is the challenge of eradicating extreme poverty and hunger.

As part of its 2004 electoral manifesto, the ANC articulated its vision for the second decade of democracy, entitled Vision 2014. Supposedly guided by the developmental ethos enshrined in the RDP, the vision focuses on the creation of a truly united, non-racial, non-sexist and democratic society. Vision 2014 also comprises a set of objectives and targets, the most important being halving unemployment, halving poverty, providing skills, protecting constitutional rights, massively reducing cases of tuberculosis, diabetes, malnutrition and maternal deaths, turning the tide against HIV/AIDS, striving to eliminate malaria and significantly reducing crimes (ANC 2004).

Unlike other states in the region, many of which have begun to set more modest poverty reduction targets for the next decade, the South African government has thus effectively recommitted itself to the MDG poverty reduction target. Moreover, it has gone a step further and linked this to a similar aspiration of halving unemployment. The obvious question that this raises is: given the mixed evidence of poverty reduction efforts during the last decade, by what means does the government intend to bring about these impressive gains? At the 2002 ANC policy conference, it was concluded that the policies needed to overcome the country's colonial and apartheid legacy were largely in place. Based upon an arguably sanguine reading of empirical evidence emerging from the comprehensive *Ten year review*, the 2004 'State of the Nation' address reaffirmed this view, by stipulating:

> unequivocally that the policies we required to translate what President Mandela said in May 1994 are firmly in place. Accordingly, *we do not foresee that there will be any need for new and major policy initiatives.* The task we will all face during the decade ahead will be to ensure vigorous implementation of these policies. (Mbeki 2004, emphasis added)

This emphasis on scaling up existing policy and programmatic interventions signifies that the primary mechanisms through which the government aims to fulfil the 2014 poverty reduction objective include 'economic development, comprehensive social security, land reform and improved household and community assets' (ANC 2004). On this basis, the remainder of this section will reflect critically upon the extent to which the policy prescriptions underpinning Vision 2014 are likely to significantly push back the frontiers of poverty and inequality, or alternatively, whether they ultimately represent a famished road to prosperity.

The stipulation that the policies needed to realise Vision 2014 are cast in stone raises a number of concerns. Firstly, there is mounting evidence to suggest that poverty is not a static or homogenous phenomenon. Despite the existence of a group of persistently or structurally poor individuals and households, there is a substantial amount of dynamism and churning, with people moving into and out of poverty over time (Roberts 2001). Consequently, the policy mix required to effectively address the diverse needs of these groupings of chronic and transitory poor is going to have to be equally diverse and adaptive to changing needs and a range of 'poverties', especially as the socio-economic impact of HIV/AIDS escalates. Recognising this, to prescriptively assert that more of the same is necessary is somewhat short-sighted and demonstrates a tenuous grasp of the nature of poverty in South Africa.

A second, and fundamentally interrelated, consideration is that there has been a lack of public discussion and consultation on the appropriate policies required to make Vision 2014 a reality. Other African countries that have recently developed similar national visions have premised their policy formulation on widespread consultations (see Roberts 2003). Some commentators have observed that in South Africa there is an apparent mismatch between anti-poverty policy and programmes on the one hand, and the circumstances and the needs of the poor on the other, a phenomenon that is determined at least in part by the lack of voice and limited active participation of the poor. Therefore, in order to improve the efficacy of social spending in meeting the needs of the poorest, a co-ordinated national dialogue is perhaps warranted to openly debate South Africa's current policy trajectory and examine whether the range of policies being pursued are sufficient to substantively address the obdurately high levels of poverty and unemployment (*Business Day* 5.04.04; Friedman 2004).

In April 2004 on a current affairs programme, *Asikhulume/Let's talk*, Deputy President Jacob Zuma indicated that the government would welcome such debate, provided that it is coupled with suggestions about 'sensible' policy or programmatic alternatives. Though open to interpretation, this statement could arguably be seen as reflective of government's tendency to prevent those it perceives as being too hostile to state policy from having a voice. Recent examples include the state's denial of the Anti-Privatisation Forum's right to protest, and the Treatment Action Campaign's (TAC's) tireless, though until recently ignored, lobbying for the roll-out of anti-retroviral drugs.[17] An important challenge over forthcoming years is whether participatory democracy can be made to work, especially in relation to the selection of the suite of poverty reduction measures to be introduced. This will require that the voices of the Basic Income Grant Coalition, TAC and other poor groups and representatives be heard.

In terms of the dominant policy measures to reach the Vision 2014 goals, the Growth and Development Summit (2003) emphasised that the main route to reducing poverty and unemployment was by means of an Expanded Public Works Programme. Yet, how realistic is it to assume that a scaled-up version of the public works programme that was initially introduced in 1994 will make considerable inroads into the challenges of unemployment and poverty? Evaluations conducted during the mid- to late-1990s characterised the Community-Based Public Works Programme as having a generally inequitable geographic spread of projects, an imbalance in project type, lacking a monitoring and evaluation system, inadequate administrative co-ordination between ministries with jurisdiction over public works, and insufficient capacity for implementation (DoSD 2002). While the Department of Public Works has since made commendable strides in attempting to address these deficiencies, the type of employment offered by the public works programme is temporary in nature rather than offering sustainable livelihoods.[18] This poor track record in the creation of sustainable employment poses real questions in relation to the objective of halving unemployment in a decade.

The Expanded Public Works Programme, with its additional financial allocations and an increased emphasis on skills training, will probably produce a greater number of workdays and employment opportunities relative to the existing programme. Nonetheless, it is misleading to assume that it will necessarily be able to meet the various socio-economic objectives enshrined in Vision 2014. The experience over the last decade has shown that while a public works programme is an undoubtedly noteworthy component of social security provision for the poorer echelons of society, it is unlikely to significantly address poverty and unemployment, unless the share of social spending allocated to the programme substantially increases and associated institutional constraints in both the public and private sectors are addressed (McCord 2003a). Other arguments against such a programme as the principal means of poverty and unemployment reduction note the fact that the poorest households often have limited labour resources, and question the extent to which the poorest are represented amongst the participants in the programme, and hence its adequacy as a social safety net (McCord 2003a).

Since access to wage income is shown to be a critical component of poverty and inequality reduction, the anticipated rise in morbidity amongst the economically active over the next decade is of grave concern. Over the next decade, the cumulative impact of HIV/AIDS is also likely to bear negatively on the public works programme. As economically active household members are affected by illness and death, both directly and indirectly, their capacity to participate in physically demanding activities is going to diminish. This effect is going to be especially acute for poor households where access to healthcare, a nutritionally balanced diet and essential medication, is often limited. Morbidity and mortality may also serve to produce diminishing returns to the skills-training component of the programme. Furthermore, poorest households, especially female or child-headed households, may not have an adult who is able to work, particularly given the incidence of HIV/AIDS. These households are thereby excluded from the benefits of participation in public works programmes.

A number of aggregate social trends have served to complicate the processes of service delivery over the last decade. With a growth rate of approximately 2 per cent per annum between 1996 and 2002, the population has increased from 40.4 million to 44.8 million, and the number of households has trebled. Therefore, while government has been rolling out the delivery of basic public services, a parallel development has been an exponentially growing demand for these services that is attributable to the pace of population growth. Similarly, the country's economically active population grew by a dramatic 4 per cent between 1996 and 2002, the consequence being that the net number of new jobs created in recent years has failed to keep apace of the number of new labour market entrants. Unemployment has thus been showing a marked upward trend. This increasing demand for state-provided services and employment is further compounded by the intensified migration over the period from rural localities to urban centres. The important lesson for the next decade, especially in relation to meeting the ambitious social targets that the government has set itself, is that unless the pace of service delivery and job creation exceeds the rate of natural population growth, then we are going to be confronted with a situation of mounting pressure on existing services and a qualitative decline in a host of social indicators, especially those pertaining to poverty, inequality and unemployment – a reality that policymakers are growing ever cognisant of. As the *Ten year review* document eloquently expresses, if the current trajectory is maintained 'we could soon reach a point where the negatives start to overwhelm the positives' (PCAS 2003:102).

Conclusion

At a recent international development forum, Nobel laureate Amartya Sen articulated that the three factors that would most concern him if tasked with initiating and implementing a major reform would be reach, range and reason (Sen 2004). This represents a useful and simple heuristic lens through which we can view the important reforms of the first decade of freedom in South Africa.

With regard to the *reach* of poverty reduction policies, there are three domains upon which we can focus, namely the economic, social and political. The economic reach of any reform is concerned with the poverty-reducing character of economic growth, the basic issue being what growth does for the poor rather than about attaining a higher rate of economic growth. In South Africa, the GEAR strategy has been successful in securing macroeconomic stability, but it has failed to address the poor long-term growth and employment performance of the economy. As a result of this situation of 'stabilisation without growth', unemployment and poverty remain resolutely high, and economic inequality has begun to intensify (Lewis 2001; McCord 2003b). Therefore, the economic reach of reforms in South Africa appears to have slackened over the decade. As for the social reach, the political change of 1994 ushered in improvements in social spending. Social assistance has been equalised and extended, basic social services have been extended, especially in relation to education, public health-care, clean water and electricity, while housing and land reform programmes have attempted to address the lack of capital assets among the poor. While (some of) the poor have undoubtedly benefited from these interventions, the reality is that a significant gap remains between the poor and the non-poor in relation to access to basic public goods and services. The increase in the incidence of evictions and water and electricity disconnections also threatens to reverse the gains already made. As such, despite a strong social commitment and the attendant financial commitment to a suite of poverty reduction reforms, the social reach may not have been as even-handed as it could have been, in the sense that a sizeable share of the disadvantaged has yet to benefit from such reforms. Moreover, unless care is taken, the improvements in the social reach of public action to address poverty and inequality may begin to erode.

The political reach of reform relates to the informational and incentive roles of democracy on public policy, operating primarily through open public discussion.[19] South Africa has a rather mixed experience with regard to open public debate as the government has tended to treat groups that publicly scrutinise its social failures with a certain amount of hostility. A more constructive approach would be to view this criticism as a healthy part of the democratic process and as an opportunity to improve service delivery in forthcoming years.

Unlike reach, which focuses on the ends or outcomes of policy change and reform, the *range* of reform relates to the ways and means to pursue those ends. It is widely accepted that there is a need for an adequately broad range of reforms in order to accommodate the diverse and interrelated nature of social changes. Rather than advocating a few 'magic bullets', an incontrovertibly wide range of policy and programmatic interventions have been introduced in South Africa with the aim of producing a more equitable distribution of income and wealth in the country. The government has employed a range of instruments covering social security, education, healthcare, infrastructure and housing provision, and land reforms, while simultaneously attempting to make intelligent use of domestic and global markets. In spite of this, the fit between anti-poverty programmes and policies and the circumstances, needs and different categories of the poor is an area where improvement is required. Similarly, there is also a need for differentiated policy responses to address labour market failure among the different categories of the unemployed, especially since the characteristics of, and obstacles confronting, the inexperienced unemployed youth, for instance, are substantively different to those of the poorly educated rural unemployed (McCord & Bhorat 2003).

It should be recognised that range does not refer exclusively to a broad range of policies or instruments, but also to the involvement of a variety of institutions. In spite of efforts in recent years to improve policy co-ordination between the different spheres of government, progress in increasing broader participation of the poor has been less than impressive. According to Friedman (2004), a lack of bargaining power and the means of organisation among the poor have inhibited political participation. In turn, the lack of voice of the poor in South Africa has adversely affected the implementation of anti-poverty policy (as discussed above). Despite the emergence of new social movements in response to the perceived hostility of government policy and practices towards the poor (Desai 2002), and the success some of these have enjoyed in shaping policymaking, the absence of a strong, organised support base of many of these movements effectively curtails their ability to speak for the majority of the poor. The pressure for effective implementation could thus be seen as being driven by organised sections of society, whose policy concerns and priorities may not necessarily address the diverse array of needs of the poor. During the next decade, an important challenge will thus be for government, civil society organisations, donor agencies and other influential lobbies to recognise that poverty reduction is not merely a bureaucratic or technical exercise, but is inherently about politics (Booth & Lucas 2001) and, as such, help create a conducive environment where the voices of the poor can be expressed and heard.

The last factor of concern is that of *reason*, which pertains to asking the critical question of *why* a particular reform is being undertaken or chosen. With the build-up to the 2004 general election, the South African public was assailed with multiple manifestos, slogans and promises for reform, many of which directly or indirectly related to reducing poverty.[20] However, an adequately conceived programme of reforms to address poverty requires the development of detailed, empirically informed and well-reasoned policy packages, and cannot rest on a disparate set of such epigrams and axiomatic musings. The outcomes of government interventions on the poor is effectively determined by a reasoned assessment of the nature of economy, society and indeed poverty. In South Africa, policy formulation has yet to be firmly based on such a nuanced understanding of social dynamics. Government departments have experimented with, and continue to initiate, monitoring systems that provide information on the impact of policies and programmes.[21] Nonetheless, there is not yet a deeply-rooted culture of evidence-based policy-making whereby decisions about policy and programmatic reforms are based on empirical evidence of the outcomes on the intended beneficiaries. This is particularly true of poverty monitoring at the aggregate level. The Poverty and Inequality Report (1997) lamented the absence of an effective form of monitoring and evaluating delivery programmes in the country and recommended that 'a system and procedures for monitoring the impact of government policy on poverty and inequality be established as a matter of priority' (May 1998:277). It is disheartening that, more than half a decade later, a co-ordinated poverty monitoring system has not been effectively instituted, though discussions have occurred on the possibility of establishing a poverty monitoring unit in the National Treasury. Unless this situation is addressed, the ability for policy to remain adaptive to the needs of the poor, and make a sustained impact on poverty, will continue to remain elusive objectives.

In summing up, there exists incontrovertible evidence of improvements in the quality of life of many South Africans over the last decade, and a resolute commitment to meeting the poverty and inequality challenges inherited from decades of segregation and apartheid. Yet despite these gains, high levels of poverty and inequality appear to have persisted. Consequently, over the next decade, serious effort needs to be exerted by government and other development partners in order to improve the reasoning, range, and ultimately, the reach of anti-poverty policy. A failure to do so will result in a proliferation of empty pockets, empty stomachs and the gradual eclipse of the jubilant spirit that accompanied the dawn of the 'bright day'.

Notes

1   These include child support grants, foster care grants and care dependency grants.

2   The full title of the fund was the Special Allocation for Poverty Relief, Infrastructure Investment and Job Summit Projects.

3   Apart from the Poverty Alleviation Fund, a number of other special funds have emerged that are of relevance to the discussion of poverty relief efforts in South Africa, including the National Development Agency, Umsobomvu Trust, the National Lottery and National Skills Fund.

4   Ironically, this adherence to the GEAR framework continued despite the reality that the statistics suggested at the conference in order to benchmark progress in economic policies, including economic growth rate, reduced unemployment, increased real gross domestic product per capita, the human development index and the poverty gap index, mostly showed reversals during the 1990s.

5   For instance, Woolard and Leibbrandt (2001) use 1993 data from the South African Labour Development Research Unit (Saldru) and different definitions of poverty to provide six estimates of the country's poverty incidence, which vary between 26 and 57 per cent.

6   The AMPS is produced by the South African Advertising Research Foundation.

7   The living standard measure is a composite index consisting of assets and socio-economic characteristics.

8   *Business Day* 26.03.03.

9   The problems identified with the IES 2000 include: (a) credibility, with nominal decreases in both income and expenditure since 1995; (b) aggregation error; and (c) an apparent problem with the sample weights. According to van der Berg and Louw (2003:2), the 2000 IES is considered a poor dataset principally due to evidence of sloppy work in the collection and management of data, with an estimated 25 per cent of records useless for analytical purposes. Even Stats SA has since admitted that it does not consider the survey as being comparable with the IES 1995.

10 Only a minority of these African workerless households are pensioner households.

11 In the 1995 to 1999 period alone, 3.1 million South Africans entered the job market (McCord & Bhorat 2003).

12 HIV/AIDS is also impacting negatively on human capital realisation, skills availability and skills shortages in South Africa. It is expected to have dire consequences for household income and expenditure patterns, particularly as the productivity levels of ill wage earners or care givers diminishes, and as the costs of medication, care and funerals rises.

13 *De jure* means that the head is officially female, which includes situations where the head is unmarried, a widow, a divorcee or separated from her husband. In contrast, *de facto* means that the household is in practice female, since the official male head is absent for most of the year. Based on the 1993 Saldru survey, a resident male-headed household had a 28 per cent probability of being poor, whereas a *de jure* female-headed household had a 48 per cent chance of being poor and a *de facto* female-headed household had a 53 per cent chance of being poor (Woolard 2002).

14 The October Household Surveys (1995–99) and the General Household Survey (2002) each contained a question on the ability of households to feed children as an indicator of food insecurity.

15 The Gini coefficient is the most widely-used measure of income inequality that ranges from 0 (perfect equality, where everyone has the same income) to 1 (where one person has all the inequality).

16 The MDGs are a set of eight inter-connected and mutually-reinforcing targets adopted by 191 countries at the 2000 Millennium Declaration. Building on various world summits and global conferences during the 1990s, these goals focus on eradicating poverty and hunger, achieving universal primary education, promoting gender equality and empowering women, reducing child mortality, improving maternal health, combating HIV/AIDS, malaria and other diseases, ensuring environmental, sustainability and lastly, developing a global partnership for development.

17   The Anti-Privatisation Forum is an organisation that has resisted evictions and electricity and water disconnections.

18   The *Ten year review* documents that, while expenditure on the public works programme increased ten-fold between 1998 and 2002 and an estimated 125 000 people received jobs, the majority of this employment was temporary in nature (PCAS 2003).

19   By way of example, Sen (2004) discusses how intense criticism of health services in India represents a social opportunity to make amends and is ultimately a source of the country's strength, in contrast with the lack of open public discussion in China, which played an important contributory factor in the spread of the SARS epidemic in 2003.

20   Examples include the following: A better life for all, Create work, Fight poverty (ANC), More jobs and less crime, 1 million *real* jobs and Free AIDS drugs (Democratic Alliance).

21   For example, in the late 1990s, the Monitoring and Evaluation division of the Department of Land Affairs initiated what it termed the 'Quality of life' surveys. The results from these surveys indicated that while the land reform programme fell short of the quantitative goals set, it was targeted to the poor and has created a significant number of projects that generate sustainable revenues (Deininger & May 2000). Unfortunately, the surveys were discontinued following a policy shift early in the new millennium. Similar exercises include the monitoring and evaluation of government's social security programme by the Monitoring, Evaluation and Audit Directorate in the Department of Social Development and the establishment of a Food Insecurity and Vulnerability Information and Mapping System under the umbrella of the National Department of Agriculture.

References

Aliber M (2003) Chronic poverty in South Africa: Incidence, causes and policies, *World Development* 31:473–490.

Altman M (2003) The state of employment and unemployment in South Africa. In J Daniel, A Habib & R Southall (eds.) *State of the Nation: South Africa 2003–2004*. Cape Town: HSRC Press.

ANC (African National Congress) (1997) *Report of the 50th National Conference*. Johannesburg: ANC.

ANC (2003) *Briefing notes on the ANC 51st National Conference, December 2002.* Johannesburg: ANC.

ANC (2004) *Manifesto 2004: A people's contract to create work and fight poverty.* Johannesburg: ANC.

Bhorat H (2003) *Labour market challenges in post-apartheid South Africa.* Cape Town: Development Policy Research Unit (DPRU).

Bhorat H, Leibbrandt M, Maziya M, van der Berg S & Woolard I (2001) *Fighting poverty: Labour markets and inequality in South Africa.* Cape Town: UCT Press.

Booth D & Lucas H (2001) *Desk study of good practice in the development of PRSP indicators and monitoring systems: Initial review of PRSP documentation.* Report for the Strategic Partnership with Africa. London: Overseas Development Institute.

Bradshaw D, Masiteng K & Nannan N (2000) Health status and determinants. In *South African Health Review 2000.* Durban: The Press Gang.

Budlender D (2003) The social and human development context. In Human Sciences Research Council (HSRC) *Human resource development review 2003: Education, employment and skills in South Africa.* Cape Town: HSRC Press.

Carter M & May J (2001) One kind of freedom: Poverty dynamics in post-apartheid South Africa, *World Development* 29:1987–2006.

Case A & Deaton A (1998) Large cash transfers to the elderly in South Africa, *The Economic Journal* 108:1330–1361.

Case A, Hosegood V & Lund F (2003) *The reach of the South African child support grant: Evidence from KwaZulu-Natal.* Research Program in Development Studies Working Paper No. 223, Princeton University.

de Bruyn J (2001) Special allocation for poverty relief infrastructure investment and job summit projects: An overview. Paper presented at the International Conference on the Role of Adult Education in Sustainable Development, 27–29 November 2001.

Deininger KW & May J (2000) Can there be growth with equity? An initial assessment of land reform in South Africa. *World Bank Policy Research Working Paper* No. 2451.

Desai A (2002) *We are the poors: Community struggles in post-apartheid South Africa.* New York: Monthly Review Press.

Dieden S & Gustaffson B (2003) Child poverty in South Africa: An assessment based on microdata for 1995, *International Journal of Social Welfare* 12:326–338.

DoSD (Department of Social Development, South Africa) (2002) *Transforming the present: Protecting the future. Report of the Committee of Inquiry into a Comprehensive System of Social Security for South Africa* (Taylor Committee Report). Pretoria: DoSD.

Evaratt D (2003) The politics of poverty. In D Evaratt & V Maphai (eds.) The real state of the nation: South Africa after 1990, *Development Update Special Edition* 4:75–100.

Friedman S (2004) The silent citizen: Poverty, participation and the health of our democracy. Presentation for Foundation of Human Rights Conference 'In Pursuit of Justice: Celebrating a Decade of Democracy', Durban, 25.01.04.

GCIS (Government Communication and Information System, South Africa) (2003) Notes on Cabinet *Lekgotla*, 23–29 July.

Gelb S (2004) *Inequality in South Africa: Nature, causes and responses*. Johannesburg: The EDGE Institute.

Habib A, Daniel J & Southall R (2003) Introduction. In J Daniel, A Habib & R Southall (eds.) *State of the Nation: South Africa 2003–2004*. Cape Town: HSRC Press.

Kingdon G & Knight J (2004) Unemployment in South Africa: The nature of the beast, *World Development* 32:391–408.

Kotzé H (2003) Responding to the growing socio-economic crisis? A review of civil society in South Africa, *Development Update* 4:1–32.

Leibbrandt M, Woolard I & Bhorat H (2001) Understanding contemporary household inequality in South Africa. In H Bhorat et al. (eds.) *Fighting poverty: Labour markets and inequality in South Africa*. Cape Town: UCT Press.

Lewis J (2001) *Policies to promote growth and employment in South Africa*. Discussion paper No. 16, Southern Africa Department, World Bank.

May J (ed.) (1998) *Poverty and inequality in South Africa. Report prepared for the Office of the Executive Deputy President and the Inter-Ministerial Committee of Poverty and Inequality*. Durban: Praxis Publishing.

Mbeki T (2003) State of the Nation Address of the President of South Africa at the opening of Parliament, Cape Town, 14.02.03.

Mbeki T (2004) State of the Nation Address of the President of South Africa at the opening of Parliament, Cape Town, 6.02.04.

McCord A (2003a) An overview of the performance and potential of public works programmes in South Africa. Paper presented at the Trade Industry Policy Strategies (TPIS) and Development Policy Research Unit (DPRU) Forum, Johannesburg, 8–10.09.03.

McCord A (2003b) Overview of the South African economy. In HSRC *Human resource development review 2003: Education, employment and skills in South Africa.* Cape Town: HSRC Press.

McCord A & Bhorat H (2003) Employment and labour market trends. In HSRC *Human resource development review 2003: Education, employment and skills in South Africa.* HSRC Press.

Meth C (2003) What to do until the doctor comes: Relief for the unemployed and for poorly paid-workers. University of KwaZulu-Natal, draft manuscript, available at <http://www.nu.ac.za/csds>.

Meth C & Dias R (2003) Increases in poverty in South Africa, 1999–2002. Paper presented at the DPRU/TIPS Forum, Johannesburg, 8–10.09.03.

Møller V & Ferreira M (2003) *Getting by ... Benefits of non-contributory pension income for older South African households.* Cape Town: University of Cape Town, Institute of Aging in Africa.

Morris M (1993) Who's out? Trying to side-step a 50% solution, *Work in Progress* 87:6–9.

Nattrass J & Seekings J (2001) 'Two nations'? Race and economic inequality in South Africa today, *Daedalus* 130: 45–70.

PCAS (Presidency Policy Co-ordination and Advisory Services) (2003) *Towards a ten year review synthesis report on implementation of government programmes: Discussion document.* Pretoria: GCIS.

Pieterse E & van Donk M (2002) *Capacity building for poverty reduction.* Dark Roast Occasional Paper No. 8, Cape Town: Isandla Institute.

Roberts B (2001) Chronic and transitory poverty in South Africa: Evidence from KwaZulu-Natal, *Journal of Poverty* 5:1–27.

Roberts B (2003) Exploring the PRSP process in Lesotho: Reflections on process, content, public finance, donor support and capacity need. Paper prepared for the Third Meeting of the African Learning Group on the Poverty Reduction Strategy Papers, Addis Ababa, 3–5 December 2003.

Schlemmer L (2002) A better life for all? Poverty trends in South Africa, *Focus* 26:20–23.

Seekings J (2003) The reproduction of disadvantage and inequality in post-apartheid South Africa. Paper presented at the North Eastern Workshop on Southern Africa, University of Vermont, Burlington, 6.09.03.

Sefton T (2002) *Recent changes in the distribution of the social wage.* Centre for Analysis of Social Exclusion (CASE) Discussion Paper No. 62, London School of Economics.

Sen AK (2004) Remarks at the Inaugural Meeting of the GDN Conference on Understanding Reform, New Delhi, 27.01.04.

Stats SA (Statistics South Africa) (2000) *Measuring poverty in South Africa.* Pretoria: Stats SA.

Stats SA (2002) *Earning and spending in South Africa: Selected findings and comparisons from the income and expenditure surveys of October 1995 and October 2000.* Pretoria: Stats SA.

Stats SA (2003) *General Household Survey July 2002.* Pretoria: Stats SA.

Stats SA & UNDP (United Nations Development Programme) (2003) *Social development indicators for the government of South Africa's 10-year review: Millennium Development Goals.* Pretoria: Stats SA/UNDP.

UNDP & Unicef (United Nations Children's Fund) (2002) *The Millennium Development Goals in Africa: Promises and progress.* New York: UNDP/Unicef.

Van der Berg S & Louw M (2003) Changing patterns of South African income distribution: Towards time series estimates of distribution and poverty. Economic Society of South Africa Conference paper, Stellenbosch, 17–19.09.03.

Whiteford A & McGrath MD (1994) *The distribution of income in South Africa.* Pretoria: HSRC.

Whiteford A & van Seventer DE (2000) South Africa's changing income distribution in the 1990s, *Studies in Economics and Econometrics* 24:7–30.

Woolard I (2002) *An overview of poverty and inequality in South Africa.* Pretoria: DFID South Africa.

Woolard I (2003) Social assistance grants, poverty and economic growth in South Africa. Paper presented at DPRU/TIPS Forum, Johannesburg, 8–10.09.03.

Woolard I & Leibbrandt M (2001) Measuring poverty in South Africa. In H Bhorat et al. (eds.) *Fighting poverty: Labour markets and inequality in South Africa.* Cape Town: UCT Press.

19 A better life for all? Service delivery and poverty alleviation

David Hemson and Kwame Owusu-Ampomah

[Our country] was a place in which squalor, the stench of poverty, the open sewers, the decaying rot, the milling crowds of wretchedness, the unending images of a landscape strewn with carelessly abandoned refuse, assumed an aspect that seemed necessary to enhance the beauty of another world of tidy streets, and wooded lanes, and flowers' blossoms offsetting the green and singing grass, and birds and houses fit for kings and queens, and lyrical music, and love.
Thabo Mbeki, Presidential Inauguration Address, 27.04.04

I'm glad that I have a house even if it's too small.
A middle-aged woman chatting with President Thabo Mbeki

Service delivery in South Africa looms large in political discussion and evaluation of government's achievements. In the President's speeches it has become the critical focus of human development and a measure of effective government. To both opposition and the ruling party itself, it is the key indication of whether the country is moving ahead and the prospect of a better future will be realised. The arguments about delivery in parliamentary debates run to exchanges over broken pipes and failed systems, but there is also the wider, and certainly more heated, debate between social movements in the poorest urban centres over water cut-offs, levels of service and privatisation. Service delivery, in short, brings together administrative, political and social issues in a combustible combination.

In many ways the political element is to the fore. Black South Africans have been denied their birthright – starting with secure residence, decent houses, water, electricity and other services, during apartheid – and the expectation is that all this should change. A fast turnaround was not only expected, but also demanded, particularly by the urban constituencies. The African National Congress (ANC) government was elected in the first elections on a manifesto of social demands captured in the Reconstruction and Development Programme (RDP) in land restitution, houses, health facilities, water and sanitation. These were cast within the short and medium term; there was a sense of impatience to overcome the apartheid legacy and to move on to the plane of social advancement. At the time few thought of the longer term; in ten years time it was thought all would have been achieved.

In the past ten years, much has been achieved. In many rural communities piped water is available for the first time, in urban areas the landscape is one of huge stretches of RDP municipal housing. The social spending in the Budget on health, education, welfare, housing and other social services now accounts for 58.3 per cent of non-interest expenditure, up from 52.9 per cent a decade ago and close to 60 per cent, a proportion which the Minister of Finance, Trevor Manuel, states cannot be increased any further.[1]

These achievements have been enumerated in the *Ten year review* by government and the details of achievement in each sector have been chronicled. Compared to the record of the apartheid government, these are achievements indeed, but how do they measure against the expectations of the people, the promise of the RDP, and the actual requirements of a modern social democratic state? In heated debates on delivery, what objective measures can there be of improving the lives of ordinary people? Apart from quantifying the roll-out in specific sectors and measuring achievements against promises, in what way can government's performance be gauged? Where practice has fallen short of promise, can the explanation of government be an excuse or a reasonable answer to the accusations of shortcomings?

In South Africa, and most developing countries, service delivery has a wider definition and greater urgency than in developed countries where it is often associated with 'those activities associated with the direct provision of a service which meets the needs of an individual older person and/or caregiver'.[2] In South Africa the definition certainly is more encompassing and includes not only the ability to provide users with services needed or demanded, but also a sense of redress; that the services should raise the standard of living of the majority and confirm their citizenship in the new South Africa.[3] In a society of growing inequality and uneven advances in education and training, service delivery is seen, at times, as an instrument for leaping over the contradictions and ensuring a 'social contract' with the people.

The sense of social inclusion arising from a combination of welfare, higher levels of social spending and a pro-poor stance, characteristic of social democratic countries, is to be found in South Africa, which, almost alone on the African continent, provides broad social welfare to the population. The Bill of Rights in the Constitution spells out a range of entitlements in terms of access to housing, water, work, freedom of movement, for workers to strike, and so on. These rights have, in turn, been strengthened by crucial Constitutional Court rulings such as the Grootboom decision, which has been 'the first building block in creating a jurisprudence of socio-economic rights.'[4] Although these entitlements have to be fought to be realised by individuals, landless people and civic groups, they do exist. In appeals to court they are being reinforced through legal action even if the state itself often tries at times to avoid its liabilities. A culture is being created of socio-economic rights and a Constitutional Court judge can complain that aggrieved people in terms of these established rights are making insufficient use of the Constitutional Courts.[5] The course of justice is long and tedious, and the judgements at times imprecise (allowing various spheres of government, at times, endless opportunities for delay), but there is a culture of human rights and entitlements which is an important advance socially, and a check on government.

In this chapter, the data on delivery will be explored against the varying criteria of human need and official commitments. The questions will be placed within the wider setting of South African society, the question of social environment and institutional capacity, and the articulation of basic needs through civil society.

Some important controversies and contradictions are at debate and will be explored. These include the problem of declining or stagnant incomes among the poorest in society, which has raised the profile of communities experiencing cut-offs as individuals or groups, and put immense pressure on the delivery agents to ensure free services. As a basic level of free services has been introduced, there have also been assertions made about the proportion of people's incomes now coming from the state in terms of a social wage, as welfare issues have become more prominent. This matter cannot be comprehensively explored here, but has to be kept in mind.

Poverty alleviation: floods, leaks or trickles?

There are, and have been, three critical constraints to delivery: the resources committed in the fiscus; economic policy; and the instrument of delivery, the civil service and municipalities. South Africa has been variously appraised as the first possible developed country in Africa, a country rich in resources, and simultaneously, as a developing country that has to beware of the effects of globalisation. The various mental pictures of the economy and country tend to be related to the possibilities for redistribution and, in turn, the availability of public funds to be allocated to delivery. Economic growth and fiscal policy are the first two constraints.

The agency of delivery, the civil service, has, at times, been criticised by government itself in the commitment to change by individual members or in terms of bureaucratic inertia. This is a new criticism, as previously the arrows of anger had been aimed at white civil servants who were not seen to be committed to transformation. The current criticism follows evidence of considerable under-spending on housing and other services, either through a lack of commitment, bureaucratic delays in allocating funds, or incapacity mixed with indifference in the bureaucracy. Of this the President demonstrates his concern unequivocally, saying:

> We must be impatient with those in the public service who see
> themselves as pen-pushers and guardians of rubber stamps,
> thieves intent on self-enrichment, bureaucrats who think they
> have a right to ignore the vision of Batho Pele, who come to work
> as late as possible, work as little as possible and knock off as early
> as possible. (Mbeki 2004b:18)

This critical outlook in relation to the civil service is informed, to an increasing extent, by the World Bank's approaches to, and calculations of 'value for money' in relation to the provision of social services; where budgets are being cut through the preoccupation with the budget deficit, the best value possible should be squeezed from the proportion which remains. It is from this perspective that an emphasis on eliminating corruption and countering mismanagement has come.

The general point which is being made through the various methodologies to calculate the 'trickle down' phenomenon is to ensure that what funds are available are received by those who are targeted. In the ascription of 'pro-poor policy', which is widely applied to much of social policy, there is the expectation that state expenditure should be reaching the very poor. In fact the large proportion of expenditure in any line department goes firstly to cover the costs of bureaucracy, buildings, travel, computers and other overheads, before actual expenditure on the poor takes place. Schemes and plans are made for all forms of alternative payment systems to ensure that the idea of social welfare translates into a proportional individual or household benefit.

In addition to this problem of resources, there are also two other important considerations in relation to service delivery and state expenditure. Firstly, to ensure that the poor are able to participate by gaining some level of employment through capital expenditure on schools, dams, roads and water works, there should be a strong labour-intensive element in public expenditure. There is the celebrated case of Working for Water, which employs thousands of poor people to eliminate invasive species in rural areas. Unfortunately, not all capital projects are well monitored to provide maximum employment and, in addition, there are frequent complaints of councillors putting their friends, supporters and relatives in the front ranks of job applicants (Hemson 2002).

The second point is that the poor are often the last people to take up the opportunities available to them. This is a very evident anomaly in virtually all pro-poor initiatives. At one level this is a problem of access to new services through social disorganisation, abject status of the poor and scepticism often expressed of projects intended for the benefit of all. The phenomenon has been exhaustively examined and proven in a study of the access by the poor to health services in Brazil, which found that new public health interventions and programmes reach the better-off first, and only later the poor. It found inequity ratios for coverage, morbidity and mortality indicators, and that inequalities only improved when the rich had achieved the new minimum achievable levels for morbidity and mortality and the poor start to gain greater access to the interventions (Victora, Vaughan, Barros, Silva & Tomasi 2000). This is a peculiarly bleak view of the process of service delivery in health and invites comparison between the South African experience and other developing countries.

In South Africa, many poor households are unable to have access to service facilities such as clinics and hospitals as a result of distance from such facilities. It is estimated that people in the poorest quintile must travel almost two hours on average to obtain medical attention, compared to an average of 34 minutes for the richest quintile. Time spent away from economic activity represents much greater private opportunity costs for the poor, who, unlike their salaried counterparts, have to forgo income in order to obtain medical care. These costs can dominate the decision to seek care (Castro-Neal, Dayton, Demery & Mehra 1999).

Services may also fail the poor as a result of their inability to pay for the cost of medical care due to low-income levels or no income arising from unemployment. In South Africa, the high rate of unemployment, estimated at over 30 per cent, is a significant factor that explains why the poor may not access public services. In some cases poor quality of service has been mentioned, though this is less likely in the case of the poor than it is in the case of rich households.

Important services do not always reach the poor. In a recent study of an informal settlement, it was found that there was no school immediately available to the resident children, that they were unsure whether they were entitled to make use of the neighbouring schools, and that there were frequent absences from school due to illness and lack of parental support. Most daunting was the fact that the children felt that if they had not paid the school fees they could and should not attend school. In sum, the poorest of the poor had very poor access to education, to levering themselves out of the settlement and having sufficient education to get anything more than a 'piece' job (*ThisDay* 23.03.04). The funds aimed at relieving their poverty through education were mostly passing them by.

A similar phenomenon may be found with the anti-retroviral roll-out, with those better-off and more educated more likely to attend clinics and hospitals and ask for this treatment before the poor feel they are entitled to the same treatment.

Despite a considerable increase in social spending, all these factors tend to limit the effect of improved service delivery when inequality or income inequality is increasing. This, in turn, can have a marked effect on the results of service delivery; improved housing, water supply and sanitation should have a decisive effect.

One final perversity in service delivery is around the following awkward principle: to those who have shall be given. For complex social reasons, those who have higher levels of income are able to access services earlier and at a higher quality. Those with higher incomes are, for example, almost all to be found with the highest levels of service in piped water, and the poorest with the lowest levels. To some extent this can be explained by the places where people live, and more generally by the ability of people to pay the costs of connection and to meet their monthly bills.

The focus of the chapter will be on water and sanitation as a prime example of the advances and contradictions in policy, implementation and operation.

Ten years of delivery: water and sanitation

The scale of water and sanitation provision has been hailed as a great achievement of the ANC-led government. Water is a vital resource for life and, in principle, it is agreed that it has to be accessible to all. The question is: at what level, at what consumption and at what cost? Water and sanitation received a high priority in the RDP, both for reasons of lessening the drudgery of rural women and for health reasons. Both water and sanitation have an acute effect on child mortality rates and adults' as well. On the one hand, for those households which do not have piped water the child mortality rate is found to be twice as high. On the other hand, for those households which do not have flush sanitation the child mortality rate is four times as high. These are critical facts, which drive public concern with delivery in water and sanitation (Hemson 2003). Although water delivery is universally given priority, sanitation is even more closely related to the survival of children, but this is not reflected in budgets.

Within the past ten years, official records indicate that 9 million additional people have gained access to safe drinking water – about 3.7 million additional households between 1995 and 2003. The proportion of people who have access to clean water has risen from 60 per cent in 1996 to 85 per cent in 2001. The number of households that have access to sanitation has also risen from 49 per cent in 1994 to 63 per cent in 2003.

The figures of levels of access reproduced in Figure 19.1 below, show that access to clean water has improved since the ANC government has come to power, including for those regarded as 'ultra-poor', although progress is highly uneven. In the preliminary studies as background documents for the RDP, it was reported that 58.9 per cent of the national population had piped water connection to yard or house in 1993; this had risen to 63.7 per cent by 2004. Progress is indicated, but it is not stunning.

The statistics on sanitation show certain changes year to year, which are probably a reflection of problems of measurement. At times a sudden upsurge or decline in delivery is evident; highly unlikely in such relatively stable issues as access to services. The statistics presented below, for the sake of economy, draw on the statistics presented in Statistics South Africa's (Stats SA's) *South Africa in transition: Selected findings from October household survey of 1999 and changes that have occurred between 1995 and 1999* (2001b), which presents a number of tables summing up developments over the period 1995 to 1999. These are added to by the South African Labour Development Research Unit (Saldru) survey of 1993, and subsequent national surveys in the period since 1999. The trend lines are important to give some idea of the general direction of delivery as there are variations from survey to survey which do not necessarily indicate actual change, but rather statistical variations.

Taken as a whole, there has been progress in the provision of water services, a slightly inclining trend line from the closing year of the apartheid era to the present in relation to access to clean water (defined here as access to piped water). This incline has largely come from a shift from households accessing borehole/rain water rather than those who have no access to water at all; there is a steady decline in this category, while the proportion of households drawing water from streams, dams, wells and springs has remained more or less constant.

Although the trends are in the right direction, taken all in all there has not been a dramatic change in the situation of delivery; the liberation period opened with some 78 per cent of the population having access to piped water and closed the first decade with about 10 per cent increase in that figure. Most of the increase has, however, come from those accessing an 'improved' water source; evidently most moved from a 'safe' source to a more convenient source, rather than from potentially unsafe supplies to piped supplies. The proportion of the population drawing water from these potentially unsafe sources has remained remarkably constant over the whole period, fluctuating between 9–13 per cent.

From a broad perspective, progress is evident, but the vast inequality in consumption between those with the greatest need (the poorest and largest

Figure 19.1 *Progress over the period, water delivery, 1993–2003*

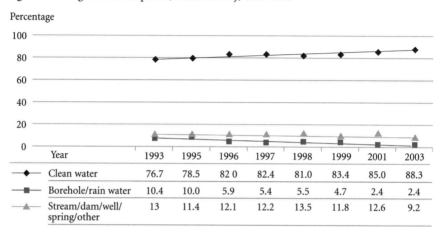

Year	1993	1995	1996	1997	1998	1999	2001	2003
Clean water	76.7	78.5	82 0	82.4	81.0	83.4	85.0	88.3
Borehole/rain water	10.4	10.0	5.9	5.4	5.5	4.7	2.4	2.4
Stream/dam/well/ spring/other	13	11.4	12.1	12.2	13.5	11.8	12.6	9.2

Source: Stats SA 2001b; Saldru 1993

families) and the wealthiest is equally clear. These differences are highly visible within a few kilometres in the ostentatious consumption of water in the suburbs in large swimming pools, water features and sprinklers, compared to women carrying water in buckets in the informal settlements. The vast differences in the scale of consumption of water is also marked in general health, domestic cleanliness and a relief of women from the drudgery of carrying water and having to take clothes and blankets to rivers and springs to do the washing. Some improvements have been made, others not.

In the very neglected sector of sanitation, improvement has been very modest indeed. Unlike the case of water delivery where the statistics are more or less consistent year on year, there are many variations in the short term and much greater reliance has to be placed on the trend lines to give a clearer idea of changes over time.

The increase in the proportion of households having access to flush toilets and chemical toilets has increased over time, but at a lower incline. Again the categories have been taken from Stats SA (2001b) and, unfortunately, contain some ambiguities. Chemical toilets, for instance, are not necessarily 'improved' as they are often the lowest level of service available to the people

Figure 19.2 *Progress over the period, sanitation, 1993–2003*

Percentage

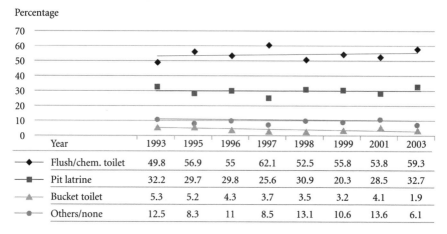

Year	1993	1995	1996	1997	1998	1999	2001	2003
◆ Flush/chem. toilet	49.8	56.9	55	62.1	52.5	55.8	53.8	59.3
■ Pit latrine	32.2	29.7	29.8	25.6	30.9	20.3	28.5	32.7
▲ Bucket toilet	5.3	5.2	4.3	3.7	3.5	3.2	4.1	1.9
● Others/none	12.5	8.3	11	8.5	13.1	10.6	13.6	6.1

Source: Stats SA 2001b; Saldru 1993

of informal settlements, and the category 'pit latrine' collapses ventilated improved privies (VIPs) and self-built long drops, which often are the source of fly infestation. The definition of categories of improved sanitation is critically important to understanding whether real change is being made.

Although there is visible progress in the delivery of clean water, there have been very evident lags, particularly in sanitation. The cholera epidemic, which exploded and then raged through KwaZulu-Natal in late 2000 through 2001, marked the fact that delivery had been dragging. The epidemic definitely brought sanitation to the fore and there has been a rush of 'cholera' projects, often introduced in communities which had suffered death or severe illness during the epidemic. Nothing fixes the mind better than an emergency. The question has been whether the emergency initiatives of the time are being translated into successful longer-term municipal services.

In Figures 19.1 and 19.2 above it is clear that improvement has been very uneven, and that, at times, there have been setbacks. The proportion of the population without any sanitation has remained remarkably constant. In line with policy, however, there has been a general reduction in bucket toilets, which has historically been favoured in small towns and settlements, from

5.2 per cent to 1.9 per cent over the whole period. The highest level of service, and the one expressly desired by most black people – that of flush toilets – has also not risen steadily over the past period; in the time of the ANC government coming to power there were about 57 per cent of the population with these toilets. This proportion has risen to a peak of 62.1 per cent in 1997, and fallen subsequently to a figure of 59.3 per cent in 2003. The pit latrines, a category that includes both 'unimproved' (unventilated and often structurally hazardous) and VIPs (ventilated and better constructed), has increased slightly over the whole period; not a general indication of improvement.

Unfortunately in Figure 19.2 there is not a distinction made between improved and unimproved pit latrines; the former (known as VIPs) are the approved level of sanitation in rural areas and often, informal settlements. Table 19.1 below, which presents more of these qualitative indicators, shows that there has not really been progress in the provision of flush toilets, or even in the improved pit latrines, and that there has been a tendency even for the number of households without any form of sanitation to rise.

Progress in sanitation has, to date, been almost imperceptible as the relatively slow delivery coupled with rapid population growth have kept the proportions of reasonable service unchanged, and inferior forms of sanitation such as chemical toilets persist.

The South African Social Attitude Survey (SASAS) on which the data in this chapter is based shows that 89.5 per cent of the respondents have access to piped tap water; and only 10.5 per cent do not have access to piped tap water. For the latter group of respondents, the most often-used sources of water include borehole, rainwater, river/stream, dam/pool, stagnant pond, well and

Table 19.1 *Forms of household sanitation 1995 and 2001 (percentage)*

Type of toilet	1995 (%)	2001 (%)
Flush toilet	58.6	51.9
VIP	7.8	5.7
Pit latrine	25.8	28.9
None	7.7	13.6
Total	100.0	100.0

Source: Stats SA 1995, 2001a

spring. Unfortunately, however, the category 'piped water' includes many varied levels of service, some with little health impact, and raises issues of continued drudgery for rural women.

Similarly SASAS's data on sanitation show that 63.6 per cent of the households in the survey had access to improved toilet facilities, defined to include flush toilet on-site, flush toilet off-site, chemical toilet and pit latrine with ventilation pipe (VIP). The proportion of households in the survey that has unimproved toilet facilities, that is pit latrine without ventilation pipe and bucket toilet, was 34.5 per cent, while 1.9 per cent had no form of toilet facility at all. This shows delivery has taken place, but generally at lower levels of access.

Free basic water service

Following the cholera epidemic, in October 2002 the government announced the free basic water service, in which households would receive supplies of up to 6kl of water per month. Although targeted on the poor, generally all households were included and increased consumption above 6kl charged for. By 2002, 57 per cent of the population in 214 out of 309 municipalities reporting were benefiting from the free basic water service. The South African Human Rights Commission (2003) hailed this as an improved level of delivery in a short time period, although recognising that the major obstacle for the poor was the lack of access to piped water at all. The free water debate highlights the policy problem between spending on free services or capital expenditure on extending services.

The free basic water service has not principally targeted rural households, which invariably need basic services most desperately, but are least capable of paying for them. As a rule rather than an exception, revenue received from beneficiaries has generally not been adequate for essential maintenence of water facilities in rural communities. Problems of sustainability continue in the management of projects on a stand-alone basis as revenue has generally been inadequate for maintenance and there are shorter or longer breakdowns in service in many projects (Hemson 2003). Most rural communities still do not benefit from free basic water, although it is here that the need is greatest.

The provision of free basic water is beginning to change the nature of sustainability of rural programmes (Hemson 2003). There is a decisive shift of responsibility for service provision from 'stand-alone' schemes with local communities providing labour and project management, to municipalities, which are also beginning to include 'stand-alone' schemes. The process is very uneven and incomplete.

The provision of free basic water in rural communities has led to consumption rising to levels equal to, and/or above, the RDP first-phase standard of 25l per person per day. The 2003 SASAS data provide a partial confirmation of this trend.[6]

If increasingly poor people are accessing free water, what effect is there on consumption? Figure 19.3 shows that from a preliminary calculation of the SASAS data, 63.3 per cent of adults consume 25 litres of water per person per day (lppd) or more, while 36.7 per cent of adults surveyed consume less than 25 lppd – that is, less than a bucket. This result is computed by regarding consumption in each household at the upper reach of each category (for example 100 litres in the category 25–100 litres) and thus exaggerates the calculated consumption per individual. Improved consumption of clean water has an effect on the health of poor communities, particularly the child mortality rate.

The limiting factor, however, remains poverty, as confirmed in Figure 19.4. The graph shows that of households whose income is between R0-R500 per month, 81 per cent have access to piped water whereas all households in the income range R5 000+ (and above) have access to piped water. Although there is a high proportion of poor people with piped tap water, it is clear from the graph that household access to piped water improves as income rises. Improvement in wage income is therefore positively linked to improved consumption of clean water and good health.

Similar conclusions can be drawn between income and access to sanitation. Figure 19.5 shows that amongst the group R0–500 household income, 12 per cent have no sanitation or access to a toilet, while few of the households earning R1 501 or more is without a toilet. The graph shows that the richer the household, the greater the access to improved sanitation: the proportion rises from 46.1 per cent among the lowest-income category to 94.4 per cent among the highest. Conversely, access to unimproved toilet facilities declines as household income rises.

Figure 19.3 *Consumption of drinking water*

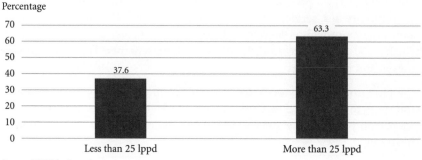

Source: HSRC forthcoming

Figure 19.4 *Access to piped water by household income*

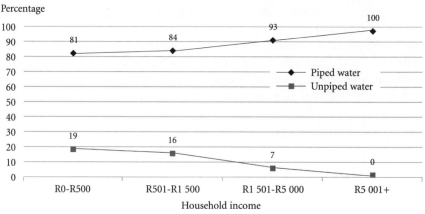

Source: HSRC forthcoming

Cost recovery and sustainability

The introduction of free basic water marks a shift from the cost-recovery policy introduced in 1994 as an incentive for better demand management and sustainability of services and infrastructure. This policy, and the increased emphasis on sanitation, has undoubtedly resulted from the cholera epidemic which undermined confidence that poor people had ready access to clean water.

Prior to this there was a deep tension between the imperative of providing basic services and the poverty of the people, shown most graphically with the

Figure 19.5 *Access to sanitation and household income*

Percentage

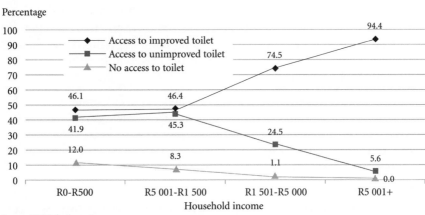

Source: HSRC forthcoming

seemingly very high level of disconnections. McDonald (2002:170), for example, in a scaled-up calculation, estimated that the number of people affected by water cut-offs was just fewer than 10 million, with the same number being affected by electricity cut-offs (and about 7.5 million people having experienced both). Using the same calculations, he also estimated that approximately 2 million people had been evicted from their homes for failure to pay their water and/or electricity bills, and a further 1.5 million people had had property seized.

The figure has been widely used, but has been hotly contested by Department of Water Affairs and Forestry (DWAF) officials, who argue that the question as directly posed to respondents invites an affirmative response. The respondents could really be indicating that they had experienced interruptions for other reasons, which they may be indicating as linked to payment only in a loose sense. The accuracy of McDonald's calculations, particularly on the water cut-offs, is the subject of an ongoing debate, which underscores the uncertainty over the number of people who have experienced cut-offs in the last ten years. Where there has been a prior question asking respondents whether they had experienced interruptions, followed by one asking for reasons with a range of possible responses, there are considerably fewer positive responses indicating cut-offs. On this basis, the number of cut-offs for non-payment of water services could be in the neighbourhood of 4–5 million in the last ten years, and a little over 1 million in 2002, and discussions are taking place over the appropriate questions and methodology in scaling-up from percentages. However, one thing is certain: there are frequent reports of incidents of cut-offs of individuals and communities, and this comes through the voices of ordinary people on radio at the pre-election *imbizos* called by President Thabo Mbeki.

Another point of certainty regarding water services is the relationship between wealth and cut-off for non-payment of water services. Table 19.2 shows that the proportion of adults reporting the main reason for interruptions as being cut-offs for non-payment is highest (10 per cent) amongst the poorest and lowest (3.6 per cent) amongst the wealthiest.

The conventional response to the financial sustainability of projects is to stress cost recovery for services provided. There is evidence, however, that cost recovery alone does not answer the questions of sustainability in rural areas – there is a clash between the poverty of the people and the meeting of costs, which requires widening the boundaries of responsibility. Very importantly, sustainability then becomes the responsibility of local municipalities which can access funding from the free basic services account provided in the Budget.

The recovery of costs in itself implies costs; a number of studies have shown how its technology and associated personnel can cost more than the revenue received.[7] Such contradictions highlight the problem of rural services; in many cases there is relatively low consumption of water or use of electricity, which in turn, means there are higher costs and less revenue. Free basic water has expanded consumption in rural projects by an order of two to three times. In the long run, programmes cannot be sustainable on the basis of cost recovery, without a

Table 19.2 *Main reason for interruption of water service for more than one day by monthly household income*

	R0–500	R501–1 500	R1 501–5 000	R5 001+	Total
Just stopped	35.2	37.3	36.9	26.6	37.2
Cut-off for non-payment	10.0	8.5	4.1	3.6	7.0
Interrupted for repairs	35.8	42.4	51.6	54.3	42.5
Other	19.1	11.7	7.4	15.6	13.2
					99.9

Source: HSRC forthcoming

considerable and consistent increase in rural incomes. Free services involve a loss in revenue, but they also reduce some costs; where electronic standpipes have been converted to provide free water, vandalism has declined and the costs of maintenance of these metered standpipes was reduced. These considerations have been some of the most powerful arguments for free services.

With the inauguration of free basic water in the rural areas, the stand-alone model is falling away, as water tariffs are no longer met and many standpipes are being changed to provide free water. There is growing pressure on municipalities both to provide free basic services and to clear the backlog in basic services (Hemson 2003).

Is delivery bold enough to make a difference?

For the hundreds of thousands of families who have houses for the first time, access to water and sanitation and a clinic nearby, there is no doubt that life has improved. But the question is whether the fundamental inequities of South Africa built over the past centuries have been reversed by these interventions.

How can long-term social progress be measured? Against the advances in services there is a corresponding decline in the labour market; although government states some 1 million jobs have been created over the past ten years, unquestionably most of these have been either in downgraded work as casual labour or in the informal sector. Wages for these workers are pitiably low. Of the 2.3 million people employed in the informal sector, for instance, 72 per cent were earning below R1 000 a month, 14 per cent earned nothing and should have been classified as unemployed, and 37 per cent earned less than R500 (Stats SA 2001a:27). As one commentator has stated about earlier figures: 'At worst the informal sector is near slavery or disguised unemployment. At best it's underemployment.'[8]

These statistics point to the continuation of appallingly low incomes among the African majority. Low incomes mean that improved rural services are difficult to establish and maintain, and that informal settlements are often the only alternative for casual workers or the unemployed.

At the core of the extensive debates on the government's performance to date is the claim that increased social spending over the past decade has improved the effective income or quality of life of the poor in South Africa by over 40 per cent. In other words, since 1994 South African society has become more egalitarian through redistribution in the form of increased social grants, public works and access to infrastructural services such as housing, electricity, education, health, water and sanitation. This implies a substantial reduction in South Africa's Gini coefficient, a measure of income inequality in society, from 0.68 in 1997 to 0.59 in 2000, in contrast to Stats SA's figures showing a worsening Gini from 0.56 in 1995 to 0.57 in 2000.[9] Taking taxes, transfers and other social spending into account, the Gini further reduces to 0.44, implying that the social wage is a critical determinant of the Gini coefficient and quality of life in South Africa, in contrast with wage income.

Much of the literature on inequality and poverty in South Africa (for example Leibrandt, Woolard & Bhorat [2001]) shows that the Gini coefficient in South Africa has for a long time been the highest recorded in the world, alongside Brazil's. South Africa's Gini coefficient has also always served as the starkest indicator of the country's highly skewed distribution of income. However, even when the Gini remained static, as it did between 1975 and 1991, it could mask the fact that the rich got richer while the poor got poorer. Looking at income inequalities within races, Whiteford and MacGrath (1998, cited in Leibrandt et al. 2001:23) found a widening gap between the richest Africans and the poorest Africans, the richest whites and the poorest whites. The income share accruing in the same period to the poorest 40 per cent of Africans fell by a disquieting 48 per cent, while the share accruing to the richest 10 per cent rose by 43 per cent (see also Gelb 2003:8).

Recent studies reinforce this observation, confirming that inequality generally and income inequality are increasing, despite considerable increase in social spending in the past decade. Reserve Bank statistics show that the share of labour income has declined from above 57 per cent in 1990 to below 52 per cent in 2002. According to Stats SA, the share of total income of the poorest 60 per cent of households also declined from 17 per cent in 1995 to 15 per cent in 2002, while the average income of an African household fell by 19 per cent. On the other hand, the average white household's income rose by 16 per cent (*Sunday Times* 29.02.04). Consequently, in keeping with Whiteford and McGrath's observation noted earlier, the rich have become richer while the poor have become poorer. The only difference is that there are now more rich black people, which hides the class aspect of Mbeki's reference to the existence of two nations in South Africa, the one predominantly white and developed, and the other predominantly black and underdeveloped (*Sunday Times* 29.02.04).

The uncertainties surrounding the Gini coefficient have influenced responses that shift emphasis to the overall argument about sustainable, equitable development strategy in debates over the *Ten year review* data. In this light, President Thabo Mbeki's faith in his government's existing policies is now being turned to emphasise stepping up service delivery. However, observers now regard it as imperative to take account of the cumulative effect of various development investments and social processes that accompany it, rather than taking the development challenge as merely a question of delivery (Isandla Development Communique 2004).

On the one hand, considerable fiscal and financial resources have been invested in human development, but the results have often been disappointing. For instance, education outcomes have generally been extremely poor in the past decade, often far behind some African countries, like Zimbabwe, despite increased access to classroom facilities, a decline of the learner-facility ratio from 43:1 in 1996 to 38:1 in 2002, and equalisation of education spending. In the Western Cape, for example, van der Berg and Burger (2002, cited in Gelb 2003:56) argue that in spite of an increase in overall spending in education – making it possible for education spending per pupil to be equalised across races, and the narrowing of pupil-teacher ratio since 1994 – the proportion of students passing the school-leaving matric examination is down from 35 to 30 per cent. The quality of service delivery in many sectors is generally poor, and in education part of the problem is that current spending on education and pupil-teacher ratios does not determine input quality: nationally, 40 per cent of schools are inadequately supplied with classrooms, and the same proportion have inadequate electricity, while 49 per cent are without textbooks (SAHRC 2003:33).

On the other hand, there is considerable under-spending on services, either as a result of lack of commitment, red tape in the process of fund allocation, or incapacity mixed with indifference in the bureaucracy. In 2003, for example, provincial housing departments failed to spend over R1 billion. The attitude to work of public servants, in many instances, mirrored that of the old regime. President Thabo Mbeki is reported to have slammed 'cruel and irresponsible' officials who had kept pensioners waiting for up to two years to be registered for grants and warned public servants to do their work or quit (*AEGiS-AFP* 14.02.02). 'Those who do not want to serve the people should leave the public service', he is reported to have said bluntly, apparently disgusted at the poor attitude to work of public servants. But disgust in itself may not work for the poor; policies that deliver, including those that produce committed, loyal and efficient public servants who make policies work, are what they need.

Human development index and life expectancy at birth

If delivery itself is not always certain to make a difference to the income and wealth divide, can it not make enough difference to extend life and health? The debate about life chances and expectancy, wealth and political responsibility is raging in the field of policies relating to HIV/AIDS, the economy and budgets, and in labour markets. Will accelerated service delivery eventually be reflected in greater well-being and longer life expectancy?

Social movements, some statutory bodies, opposing political parties and academics, point to the decline of South Africa's Human Development Index (HDI), a measure of progress towards a better life and health, as an indication of deteriorating conditions of life. Indeed, as shown in Table 19.3, the HDI for South Africa has been declining in the past ten years from a high of 0.741 in 1995 to 0.684 in 2001. This contrasts markedly with the upward movement of the measure from 1975 until 1995.

The downward movement of the country's HDI from 1995 to 2001 parallels the trend of the statistics for life expectancy at birth for the same period. From a high of 64.1 years in 1995, life expectancy has been declining steadily to a low of 50.9 years in 2001, except for a marginal rise in 1999.

By its very nature the HDI can be criticised for reductionism (Owusu-Ampomah 2004), conceptual weakness and empirical difficulties, involving serious problems of non-comparability over time and space, measurement errors and biases (Srinivasan 1994). Its central trend in South Africa, the decline in life expectancy and the health of the nation, is, however, beyond doubt. Estimates show that the probability at birth of a South African not surviving to the age of 40 (as a percentage of the cohort) has increased from 24.4 per cent between 1995 and 2000 to 44.9 per cent for the period 2000 to 2005 (UNDP 2003). Negative trends are also visible in the rates of underweight

Table 19.3 *Human Development Index and life expectancy trends*

Year	HDI	Life expectancy
1975	0.660	n.a.
1980	0.676	n.a.
1985	0.702	n.a.
1990	0.734	n.a.
1995	0.741	64.1
1997	n.a.	54.7
1998	n.a.	53.2
1999	0.702	53.9
2000	0.695	52.1
2001	0.684	50.9

Sources: UNDP 1999, 2000, 2001, 2002, 2003

Note: The World Health Organization's estimate of life expectancy for 1999 is 48 years
Dorrington et al. 2001)

children, stunted growth in children aged 6–7 months and wasting. The rate of underweight children has increased, though slightly, by 2.07 per cent, stunt by 0.9 per cent and wasting by 1 per cent between 1994 and 1999.

Health is a major preoccupation of the poor. Noticeable advances have been made in the not-so-distant and recent pasts, including free medical care for women and children aged under six, increase in the rate of immunisation and the number of targeted learners in the Integrated Nutrition Programme, which has reached 4.58 million children.

These advances have, however, been literally wiped out by HIV/AIDS. The prevalence of HIV/AIDS has increased from 0.7 per cent in 1990 to 26.5 per cent of the population in 2002, although by 2001 it appeared to be stabilising, with an overall prevalence rate of 24.8 per cent (RSA 2003). Projections suggest that between 4 and 7 million South Africans will die of AIDS between 2000 and 2010. Adult mortality has increased steadily in the 1990s, but the mortality of young adult women has increased rapidly in the last few years, with mortality rate in the 25–29 year age range in 1999–2000 being some 3.5 times higher than in 1985. Life expectancy is declining, particularly for African people, and most acutely for young African women (Dorrington, Bourne, Bradshaw, Laubscher & Timæus 2001).

Public perceptions: how is government performing?

A snapshot of statistics on public perception of the government's perform-ance reflects mixed reactions regarding delivery across the spectrum of sectors (HSRC forthcoming). A measure of public perception of the government's handling of service delivery, on a ten-point level of satisfaction scale ranging from 10 for complete satisfaction to 0 for complete dissatisfaction, yields an index of 5, indicating a general sense of satisfaction among the public.

Although the general level of satisfaction is not high, the government's performance, sector-by-sector, is best in electricity, water and sanitation, and refuse-removal sectors. The level of satisfaction index for each of these sectors is 6. In contrast to the general high level of approval of electricity services, water and sanitation and refuse removal, there are substantial levels of dissatisfaction with government performance in health, housing, crime and land reform. The satisfaction indices of these sectors are 4 for each of health and housing, and 3 each for crime and land reform. These figures relate fairly closely to the views generally expressed among black people about their living conditions, particularly those living in the urban informal and rural areas.

A better life for all?

There are concerted efforts to improve the quality of lives of all living in South Africa. These efforts have yielded modest gains in terms of access to services such as housing, water and sanitation, education, electricity and health. However, several questions remain unresolved, most of which revolve around the sustainability and adequacy of service delivery to the poor, particularly with the provision of free basic services. The question of sustainability is significantly economic, and at least two conditions need to be satisfied: the ability of the consumer to pay for services that maximise well-being, that is, beyond the point of free basic service delivery; and that of service providers to reduce the costs of service provision to make them affordable to the poor.

Managers of services have to undertake a balancing act in which falls, or breakdowns, are entirely possible. The dilemma between better services and sustainability can only be resolved if people have regular jobs and incomes above subsistence levels. Service delivery, as has been discussed above, is a function of poverty alleviation, but to what extent has it contributed, beyond social inclusion and ending the deprivation of life sustaining services, to the final incomes of the people? The mediating factor between service delivery and poverty alleviation, then, is employment, which, as observed in this chapter, remains elusive to many South Africans.

The political attitude of many towards government efforts has generally been one of recorded satisfaction, but there are two important reservations in the minds of the poor. Firstly, there is growing concern about the quality of delivery, as illustrated in the example of the woman quoted earlier, who was pleased to have a house, but was unhappy about its size. In the rush to get things moving there have been serious faults both in the size and sustainability of houses, which, among other failings, are often not built to receive the warmth of the sun during winter.

Secondly, there is a warning to government contained in the high levels of dissatisfaction on all fronts expressed by those living in the informal settlements. Caught on the urban periphery, this sizeable grouping lives in deep poverty without secure education for children, and with insecure access to health and the illusive promise of housing.

The entire rationale of service delivery is to improve the lives of the existing generation and life-chances of the rising generation of South Africa. Although HIV/AIDS appears as a separate health and treatment issue, its resolution also depends on better levels of access to social welfare, housing, water services, and ultimately, health facilities. The spread of the epidemic is unquestionably linked to deprivation and poor social conditions, and determined social reforms and an ending of poverty are the key to its solution.

Delivery in life-sustaining services has been a feature of the post-apartheid government, but its progress has been uneven and less dramatic than anticipated. The difficulties are very evident; the pace of delivery is undoubtedly hindered by the incapacity of the majority to meet the costs of operating and maintaining services. There would have been much greater advance if there were a steady improvement in employment, earnings and incomes generally; in the absence of such progress, service delivery is retarded by anxieties about, and real difficulties in, ensuring the continuation of services over time. Issues relating to sustainability and meeting costs are an increasing preoccupation as municipalities take over and extend essential services to the poor.

Notes

1 SAFM, post-budget interview, 2004.

2 See <http://www.aoa.gov/napis/definspr.html>.

3 Other formal definitions include the following: The ability to convey useful labor that does not result in a tangible product. See <http://www.nbrii.com/Create_/Questions/Definitions/definitions.html>. Service delivery means supplying users with services needed or demanded. This can be done by government institutions and organisations, parastatal organisations, private companies, non-profit organisations or individual service providers. See <http://www.gtz.de/agriservice/definitions/definitions.html>.

4 Judge Goldstone, quoted by Bonny Schoonakker, *Sunday Times* 21.03.04.

5 Judge Dennis Davis, Constitutional Court judge, SAFM interview, 2.02.04.

6 SASAS data (HSRC forthcoming) measured consumption of drinking water, although it has been regarded as a measure of general household consumption. Although it did not expressly measure use for other purposes, for example, washing clothes, bathing, cooking, gardening, and so on, it can, with these reservations, be used as a measure of household consumption and the derived individual consumption.

7 Presentation by Joe Ferreira at Masibambane Meeting, Assegay Hotel, 13.02.03.

8 Duma Gqubule quoted by Ashwin Desai. 'Mbeki lashes doomsayers.' Available at <http://www.nu.ac.za/ccs/default.asp?> 2, 40, 5, 367.

9 The Gini coefficient has a value between zero and one. The bigger the number, the greater the extent of inequality in society.

References

Atkinson D, Abrahams D, Buso N, Goldman I, Makgoba S, Meyer M, Mokgoro J, Olivier J, Pienaar D, Reitzes MN, Roefs MMI & Wiechers M (2003) *Review of schedules 4 & 5 of the Constitution, 29 March 2003*. Report to the Department of Provincial and Local Government.

Castro-Neal F (1996) *The impact of public health spending on poverty and inequality in South Africa*. Privatization Support Project Discussion Paper Series No. 101. World Bank, Poverty and Social Policy Department, Washington DC.

Castro-Neal F, Dayton J, Demery L & Mehra K (1999) Public social spending in Africa: Do the poor benefit? *The World Bank Research Observer* 14:49–72.

Dehn J, Reinikka R & Svesson J (2002) *Survey tools for assessing service delivery.* Washington DC: World Bank Research Group.

Department of Provincial and Local Government, South Africa (1998) *The White Paper on local government.* Pretoria: Department of Provincial and Local Government.

Department of Public Services and Administration, South Africa (1997) *'Batho Phele – people first' White Paper on transforming public service delivery.* Pretoria: Government Printers.

Dorrington R, Bourne D, Bradshaw D, Laubscher R & Timæus IM (2001) *The impact of HIV/AIDS on adult mortality in South Africa.* Pretoria: Medical Research Council.

Furtado X (2001) *Decentralization and capacity building: Understanding the links and implications for programming.* Occasional Paper No. 4, Canadian International Development Association, Policy Branch.

Gelb S (2003) *Inequality in South Africa: Nature, causes and responses.* Johannesburg: The EDGE Institute.

Hemson D (2003) Beating the backlog: Meeting targets and providing free basic water. Position paper for the National Treasury, Durban: Human Sciences Research Council (HSRC).

Hemson D (2002) Breaking the impasse, beginning the change: Labour market, unions and social initiative in Durban. In V Padayachee & B Freund (eds.) *(D)urban vortex: South African city in transition.* Pietermaritzburg: University of Natal Press.

HSRC (forthcoming) *South African Social Attitudes Survey.* Cape Town: HSRC Press.

Isandla Development Communique 1(1), March 2004.

Leibrandt M, Woolard I & Bhorat H (2001) Understanding contemporary household inequality in South Africa. In H Bhorat, M Leibrandt, M Maziya, S van der Berg & I Woolard (eds.) *Fighting poverty: Labour market and inequality in South Africa.* Cape Town: UCT Press.

Mbeki T (2004a) Address by the President of South Africa, Thabo Mbeki, on the occasion of his Inauguration and the 10th Anniversary of Freedom, 27.04.04, Pretoria.

Mbeki T (2004b) State of the Nation Address of the President of South Africa at the opening of Parliament, Cape Town, 21.05.04.

Mcdonald DA (2002) The bell tolls for thee: Cost recovery, cutoffs, and the affordability of municipal services in South Africa. In DA McDonald & J Pape (eds.) *Cost recovery and the crisis of service delivery in South Africa*. London: Zed.

Owusu-Ampomah K (2004) Human development paradigm and agenda: A wild goose chase. In S Adjibolosoo (ed.) *International development agenda and activities: What are we doing wrong?* Bloomington: 1st Books.

PCAS (Presidency Policy Co-ordination and Advisory Services) (2003) *Towards a ten year review synthesis report on implementation of government programmes: Discussion document*. Pretoria: Government Communications and Information Systems.

PRC (Presidential Review Commission) (1998) *Developing a culture of good governance: Report of the Presidential Review Commission on the reform and transformation of the public service in South Africa*. Pretoria: Government of South Africa.

SAHRC (South African Human Rights Commission) (2003) *4th Annual Economic and Social Rights Report: 2000–2002*. Johannesburg: SAHRC.

Saldru (Southern African Labour and Development Research Unit) (1993) *South African living standards survey*. Available at <http://www.worldbank.org/html/prdph/lsms/country/za94/za94home.html>.

Srinivasan TN (1994) Human development: A new paradigm or reinvention of the wheel? *American Economic Review* 84:238–249.

Stats SA (Statistics South Africa) (1995) *October Households Survey*. Available at <http:/www.sscnet.ucla.edu/issr/da/index/techinfo/M8771.htm>.

Stats SA (2001a) *Census 2001: Census in brief*. Available at <http:www.statsa.gov.za>.

Stats SA (2001b) *South Africa in transition: Selected findings from October household survey of 1999 and changes that have occurred between 1995 and 1999*. Pretoria: Stats SA.

Steinich M (2000) *Monitoring and evaluating support to decentralisation: Challenges and dilemmas*. ECDPM-GTZ Discussion Paper No. 19. Maastricht: European Centre for Development Policy Management.

UNDP (United Nations Development Programme) (1999) *Human development report* (HDR). Available at <http://hdr.undp.org/reports/global/1999/en>.

UNDP (2000) *Human development report* (HDR). Available at <http://hdr.undp.org/reports/global/2000/en>.

UNDP (2001) *Human development report* (HDR). Available at <http://hdr.undp.org/reports/global/2001/en>.

UNDP (2002) *Human development report* (HDR). Available at <http://hdr.undp.org/reports/global/2002/en>.

UNDP (2003) *Human development report* (HDR). Available at <http://hdr.undp.org/reports/global/2003>.

Victora CG, Vaughan JP, Barros FC, Silva AC & Tomasi E (2000). Explaining trends in inequities: Evidence from Brazilian child health studies, *Lancet* 356:1093–98.

Wallis M (2003) Promoting accountability. Paper presented to the colloquium on improving the health of school age children in an era of HIV/AIDS: Linking policies, programmes & strategies for the 21st century. Inkosi Albert Luthuli Hospital, Durban 16–19.03.03: HSRC.

Wesgro (2002) *Wesgro background report on the clothing industry in the Western Cape province of South Africa.* Available at <http://www.wesgro.org.za/uploads/BRboatbuildingApril2001.doc>.

Part IV: South Africa in Africa

South Africa in Africa: introduction

John Daniel, Roger Southall and Jessica Lutchman

Our review of South Africa's relations with the rest of Africa focuses on two particularly important issues. The first is upon the developing economic relationship between South Africa and Nigeria, two of Africa's economic giants. The second is upon South Africa's 'quiet diplomacy' with regard to Zimbabwe. Together they raise important issues about whether South Africa can be regarded as an emergent African 'hegemon'.

Daniel, Lutchman and Naidu follow up the study that was presented in last year's *State of the Nation,* which provided an overview of 'Post-apartheid corporate expansion into Africa'. Drawing upon a database belonging to the Human Sciences Research Council (HSRC), that chapter provoked a lot of interest. This year's more specialised chapter will similarly occasion attention. The three authors outline the major aspects of South Africa's corporate African thrust. They deal successively with Africa's growing status as an export destination for South Africa's products, noting how this has not yet been matched by a significant growth in imports from the continent, save with regard to oil imports from Nigeria and Gabon, and the remarkable extent to which Africa, notably those countries which belong to the Southern African Development Community (SADC), is becoming a site for South African investment. Much of this, they note, centres around investment in mining, yet banking and financial ventures are growing apace, whilst telecommunications, aviation and retail interests are also of considerable significance.

It is against this background that the authors focus upon the South Africa-Nigerian nexus, which they regard as of particular importance because Nigeria is South Africa's only major non-SADC trading partner, as well as because both countries are dominant within their respective sub-regions, and because a dynamic South Africa has much to contribute to a struggling Nigerian economy.

Overall, the authors demonstrate not only how trade between Nigeria and South Africa has expanded so significantly since 1992, but how a South

African trade surplus has been transformed into a deficit. However, whereas South Africa's exports to Nigeria are promoted by some 55 firms, and are highly varied (involving private and public enterprises, and ranging through involvements in telecommunications, electricity provision, natural gas extraction, retail and engineering and so forth), Nigeria's exports to South Africa are comprised almost exclusively of oil.

Daniel, Lutchman and Naidu use their discussion of the South African-Nigerian economic relationship to challenge those who have argued that the two powers are hegemonic in their regions. Nigeria, they conclude, has been too predatory and chaotic a state to establish domination over other states within its regional backyard. Meanwhile, although South Africa's Africa policy has been far more holistic and systematic under Mbeki than under Mandela, its growing economic influence has not been matched by a political agenda with an aggressive expansionary intent. Nor indeed, according to Le Roux and Boshoff, does it have the military capacity at the present time to assume the status of a hegemon.

If South Africa were a regional hegemon, then it would surely have had more success in dealing with the extended crisis in Zimbabwe than it has done. Nor perhaps would its diplomacy have been 'quiet'. However, as Lloyd Sachikonye notes, South Africa could not afford to stand aloof as Zimbabwe slid into a crisis of repression and economic meltdown from 2000 onwards. South Africa, under Mbeki, was aspiring to continental leadership through its promotion of the African Union (AU) and the New Partnership for Africa's Development (Nepad). Thus it could not afford to isolate itself from other SADC and African states, which were reluctant to condemn the country's controversial land reform, by loudly admonishing Mugabe and hence appearing to align with western imperialism. It therefore opted to pursue a low-key policy of promoting dialogue between the Mugabe regime, and its opponents, as represented by the opposition Movement for Democratic Change (MDC).

Sachikonye proceeds to identify successive phases in South Africa's policy on Zimbabwe. He notes how the relationship between the two countries when Mandela was President was marked by a simmering rivalry over regional leadership, and how during the period 2000 to 2002 – when the situation in Zimbabwe began to deteriorate swiftly following the land occupations, the 2000 election and the Zimbabwe African Union-Patriotic Front's defeat in the constitutional referendum – Mbeki sought to draw in third parties (notably President Obasanjo of Nigeria) to resolve the crisis, only to have Mugabe – in essence – twist his South African counterpart around his little finger. Thereafter, from 2002 until the present, South Africa's attempt to promote dialogue between the regime and its opponents has been highly compromised by South Africa's apparent endorsement of the legitimacy of the highly controversial 2002 presidential election, and its shift to a position whereby it seems to have been more strongly defending Mugabe than propelling him into meaningful negotiations with the MDC.

Sachikonye reinforces the perception that South Africa's quiet diplomacy has been ineffective and ambivalent and has fought shy of using the country's economic muscle to underpin its initiatives. He not only confirms the view of Daniel, Lutchman and Naidu that South Africa is reluctant to become a regional hegemon, but more alarmingly, that whilst South Africa's policy is rhetorically versed in terms of good governance and Nepad, its application in the peculiarly important case of Zimbabwe is a conspicuous failure.

20 South Africa and Nigeria: two unequal centres in a periphery

John Daniel, Jessica Lutchman and Sanusha Naidu

Like wildfire tearing through dry forest, South Africa is rapidly entrenching itself in every facet of the Nigerian economy: from construction, energy, aviation, entertainment to revenue collection, South African companies loom large and are still growing.
Aminu Mohammed, Weekly Trust 13.09.03

We have every reason to be upbeat as we meet with members of the Nigeria-South Africa Chamber of Commerce, given the remarkable increase in bilateral trade between our two countries. We have noted that the value of the bilateral trade has continued its sharp upward curve … I am also pleased at the growing presence of South African companies and parastatals in Nigeria … the presence of these companies in Nigeria has had a substantial impact on the sharp rise in the value of South African exports to this country.
Deputy President Jacob Zuma, Lagos, 11.12.03

Africa still doesn't have telephones and we are going to target this market.
Alan Knott-Craig, CEO of Vodacom, Business Day 08.06.04

Introduction

In the first *State of the Nation* volume (2003), Daniel, Naidoo and Naidu examined the growing post-apartheid importance of Africa as an export and investment destination for South African capital. They noted that:

* Africa's share of South Africa's global export trade had risen from 4 per cent in 1991 to 12 per cent in 2001, making it the country's fourth largest export market.

- South Africa had become a major source of new direct investment in Africa through a range of mergers, acquisitions, joint ventures and new 'greenfield' investments. In the countries making up the Southern African Development Conference (SADC), South Africa was the largest foreign direct investor, the volume of its foreign direct investment (FDI) exceeding that of the United States and United Kingdom combined. Views differed as to whether South Africa was also the largest source of FDI into the African continent as a whole, but if not, it was certainly the second largest.
- There was an across-the-board involvement of every sector (private and parastatal) of the South African economy in the African market.
- There was a considerable imbalance in the South African-African trade relationship ranging, in 2001, from 9:1 in South Africa's favour in regard to the SADC bloc, to 5:1 overall for Africa.
- Mozambique represented the fastest-growing area of South African economic involvement on the continent and seemed poised to eclipse Zimbabwe as South Africa's largest African trading partner.
- The above notwithstanding, Africa remained in many respects a difficult economic environment for outside traders and investors and some South African ventures on the continent had either collapsed or were failing to attain anticipated targets. Zimbabwe was noted as especially difficult economic terrain.
- There was little evidence that the South African government was utilising its growing economic muscle in the African marketplace to pursue a narrow and self-serving hegemonic political agenda. Instead, the most consistent feature of the Mbeki regime's foreign-policy agenda in Africa was the eschewing of the unilateralism of the apartheid past in favour of bi- and multi-lateral co-operation.

In the year since that chapter was drafted, little fundamental has changed in regard to the above. What there has been is continuity to the trends outlined above. The result has been a deepening of South Africa's corporate and parastatal involvement in the continent, albeit not uniformly across all sectors of the economy. The one exception has been construction where there has been a pulling back.[1]

Africa as an export destination

In regard to exports, the most significant development in 2002 – and confirmed in 2003 – was that Africa overtook the Americas (North, Central and South) in terms of trade volumes by continent or region, moving into third place overall in the export market stakes. This was achieved through a 28.2 per cent increase in exports to Africa, in contrast to a 15 per cent growth in exports into the Americas. What makes this development more remarkable is that this leap-frogging of the Americas occurred in the context of the enhanced opportunities to export into the United States through the African Growth and Opportunity Acts (Agoa 1 and 2) passed by the US Congress in 2000 and 2002 respectively. South Africa has taken good advantage of the Agoa provisions, earning, for example, an additional US$88 million in the export of textiles and apparels in 2002. Other industries to have benefited from Agoa are the automobile (sales of motor cars to the US are classified statistically as 'transportation equipment'), agriculture, minerals and metals such as ferromanganese, exports of which amounted to US$44 million in 2002.

Africa's share of South Africa's global export trade in 2002 was 16.74 per cent (compared to 16.1 per cent for the Americas), while as Table 20.1 and Figure 20.1 show, the percentages for 2003 were 16.48 per cent for Africa and 14.43 per cent for the Americas. The gap between the two is therefore widening slightly. Overall, it should be noted, the gross value of South Africa's exports to all continents except the Pacific dropped in 2003, due probably to deterio-rating global conditions (the war in Iraq), combined with the appreciation of the Rand against all major currencies. The overall percentages remained essentially unchanged.

While South Africa's export trade with Africa has flourished since the ending of apartheid, the same cannot be said of its African import trade. As Figure 20.2 indicates, this remains miniscule, with the percentages between the years 2000 and 2003 being 2.25, 2.62, 3.62 and 3.20 respectively. Given its remote-ness from South Africa, the fact that most of its members are tiny island economies like Fiji, and that both the New Zealand and Australian economies are structurally not unlike that of South Africa's, it is not surprising that the Pacific group's share of South Africa's import trade should be tiny. What is extraordinary, however, is that it was only in 2002 that the total value of South Africa's imports from Africa exceeded that of the Pacific group.

Table 20.1 *Rand value of South African exports by continent/region, 2000–03*

Region	Exports (R millions)					Rank	Proportion
	2000	2001	2002	2003	2003	Percentage total 2003	Percentage total 2002
Total Europe	70 786	85 592	105 699	92 019	1	38.88	39.68
Total Asia	45 885	53 268	67 412	65 176	2	27.54	25.31
Total Africa	28 109	34 709	44 580	39 000	3	16.48	16.73
Total Americas	31 122	37 331	42 936	34 161	4	14.43	16.12
Total Pacific	3 838	4 363	5 767	6 331	5	2.67	2.16
Total continents	179 742	215 264	266 396	236 688		100	100

Source: DTI economic data base, http://www.dti:gov.sa/econdb/

Figure 20.1 *Market share of South Africa's export trade by continent/region, 2003*

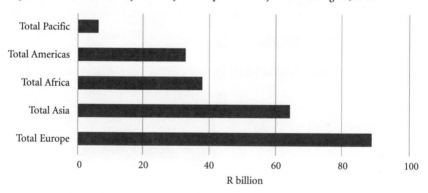

Source: DTI economic data base, http://www.dti:gov.sa/econdb/

It follows from the above that the trade balance in South Africa's favour is substantial. Earlier it was indicated that in 2001 that figure was in the region of 5:1 in favour of South Africa; in 2002 it dropped slightly to 4.5:1; and in 2003 it dipped to 4:1. What this reflects is first, the impact of the depreciation of the Rand, and second, the increase in South Africa's oil imports from Nigeria and Gabon. Figure 20.3 provides fuller details, and reveals that it is only with the African continent that South Africa enjoys a trade surplus.

Figure 20.2 *Market share of South Africa's import trade by continent/region, 2003*

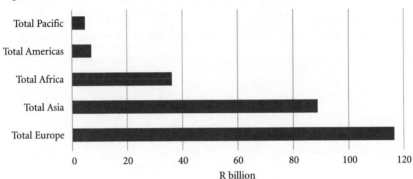

Source: DTI economic data base, http://www.dti:gov.sa/econdb/

Figure 20.3 *South Africa's trade balances by continent/region, 2003*

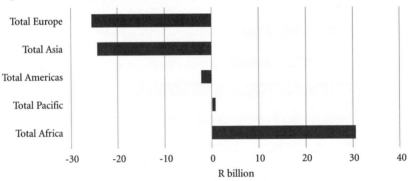

Source: DTI economic data base, http://www.dti:gov.sa/econdb/

In terms of overall trading partners (value of exports and imports combined), South Africa's top five African partners in 2002 and 2003 were Zimbabwe, Mozambique, Nigeria, Zambia and Angola. Table 20.2 presents a breakdown of the trade between South Africa and these five continents.

What is interesting about these figures is that, despite the acute and prolonged nature of the economic crisis in Zimbabwe, it retains its top ranking as South

Table 20.2 *South Africa's top five African trading partners (R billions)*

Country	2002 Exports from SA	2002 Imports into SA	2002 Totals	2003 Exports from SA	2003 Imports into SA	2003 Totals
Zimbabwe	7.30	2.16	9.46	6.55	2.65	9.20
Mozambique	6.42	0.40	6.82	5.67	0.28	5.95
Nigeria	2.73	3.62	6.35	2.54	2.76	5.30
Zambia	5.54	0.78	6.32	4.04	0.57	4.61
Angola	3.43	0.13	3.56	3.39	0.08	3.41

Source: Constructed from figures supplied by DTI economic data base, http://www.dti:gov.sa/econdb/

Africa's most important African trading partner. Perhaps even more interesting is the fact that, in 2003, the value of goods sold by Zimbabwe into the South African market exceeded that for 2002. It is also worth noting how skewed, in all but one case, the trade balance favours South Africa. Only one of the top five, Nigeria, has a favourable balance of trade with South Africa. This derives wholly from the fact that Nigeria sells huge amounts of oil, and very little of anything else, to South Africa. Nonetheless, this does give Nigeria a significance to its trading relationship with South Africa, which no other African country has.

Africa as an investment destination

According to figures supplied by the South African Reserve Bank, total South African foreign investment in Africa in 2001 amounted to R26.8 billion, an increase of approximately R2.7 billion over 2000, and a 300 per cent increase over five years. Just over half of this took the form of direct investment in new or ongoing operations, while less than 5 per cent was invested in Africa's stock markets. By contrast, 42 per cent of all African investment in South Africa is on the Johannesburg Stock Exchange (JSE) and only 10 per cent in the form of FDI.

Perhaps the most significant fact relating to the South African-African and African-South African investment pattern, however, is the fact that the bulk of it is invested within the SADC community. In our chapter in the first *State of the Nation* volume, the impression may have been given of a large-scale or even rampant investment pattern on the part of South African capital throughout most of the continent, and particularly beyond the SADC rim. If so, that was incorrect. In fact, the figures for 2001 reveal a drop in total South African investment into non-SADC Africa over the previous year (from R3 959 billion and 16.37 per cent of the total to R2 652 billion and 9.9 per cent of the total), while that into the SADC grew by R4 billion or 25 per cent to total R24.1 billion.

A number of other factors regarding South Africa's investment pattern merit comment. The first is that when outward and inward flows are combined, South Africa's largest African investment partner in 2002 was Mozambique (accounting for 48.4 per cent of South Africa's corporate investment in all of Africa). Mozambique was discussed as a special case in our previous *State of the Nation* chapter (2003) where it was noted that:

- South Africa had become the largest single investor in Mozambique in 2001, eclipsing the former metropole, Portugal; and
- in the period 1997–2001 over 250 South African companies had opened operations in Mozambique.

These South African companies have made important investments in the mining, aluminium, coal and telecommunications sectors. The biggest to date has been the Industrial Development Corporation's 25 per cent stake in the establishment of the Mozal I and II Aluminium Smelter. In the telecommunications sector, Vodacom has purchased a licence to operate in Mozambique and plans to pump US$200 million into the country over the next ten years. Sasol has also invested R10 million in the Pande and Temane gas-field project and is currently distributing gas from these fields to Secunda in South Africa.

Second to Mozambique, Mauritius has emerged as an important investment partner. Why this should be so is not clear but one explanation may lie in the fact that Mauritius is the site of an offshore banking operation, with South Africa's Standard Bank being one of the only two permitted offshore operatives. The other is the German Deutsche Bank. So it is possible that a good proportion of the outward flow of South African investment to Mauritius is ultimately destined for another, and possibly non-African, destination. Likewise, the inflow from Mauritius may well originate from beyond Africa or may be African monies using the Mauritian facility as a conduit and cover. Interesting too, is the fact that while the bulk of African investment in South

Africa comes in the form of portfolio capital, very little of the Mauritian inflow heads for the stock market (4.5 per cent in 2000, 7.1 per cent in 2001 and 2.4 per cent in 2002), while that which emanates from Africa's biggest single investor in South Africa – Namibia – does. In 2000, portfolio investment formed 79.6 per cent of Namibia's capital inflow into South Africa, rising to 82.9 per cent in 2001 and 90.8 per cent in 2002.

By contrast with its 'star-rating' as an investor, Mauritius ranks lower in the pecking order as an export-import trading partner. In 2002, it was South Africa's sixth largest importer of South African goods (worth R2.7 billion) and 13th as an African exporter into the South African market (worth R119.6 million). The balance in favour of South Africa was in the region of 22:1.

Finally, the steady decline of Zimbabwe as an investment partner should be noted. In 1997, Zimbabwe was South Africa's second largest investment destination in Africa, topped only by Namibia. Five years later in 2002, it had slipped to third place.

Table 20.3 *South African investments in Africa by region and investment type, value in R millions and by market share, 1997–2001*

Region	Direct[a]	Portfolio[b]	Other[c]	Totals	Percentage
SADC	37 458	4 028	35 538	77 024	80.1
	(48.6%)	(5.2%)	(46.2%)		
Other Africa	14 072	171	4 832	19 075	19.9
	(73.7%)	(0.9%)	(26.4%)		
Overall	51 530	4 199	40 370	96 099	100.0
	(53.6%)	(4.4%)	(42.0%)		

Source: Constructed from figures supplied by the South African Reserve Bank's *Quarterly Bulletins 1997–2003*
Notes:

a Investments by South African residents with undertakings abroad in which they individually, or collectively in the case of affiliated organisations or persons, have at least 10 per cent of voting rights (long-term investments)

b Investment that covers all outright securities transactions between residents and non-residents (for example, purchases of new issues, trading and redemptions)

c Investments that are mostly long-term and short-term deposits and loans not recorded under financial account items

Table 20.4 *African investments by region in South Africa, value in R millions and by market share, 1997–2001*

Region	Direct	Portfolio	Other	Totals	Percentage
SADC	9 280 (10.0%)	43 636 (46.8%)	40 132 (45.2%)	93 048	89.9
Other Africa	1 519 (14.4%)	324 (3.0%)	8 703 (82.6%)	10 506	10.1
Overall	10 799 (10.4%)	43 960 (42.4%)	48 835 (41.2%)	103 554	100.0

Source: Constructed from figures supplied by the South African Reserve Bank's *Quarterly Bulletins 1996–2003*

Figure 20.4 *South Africa's investment partners in Africa, 2002*

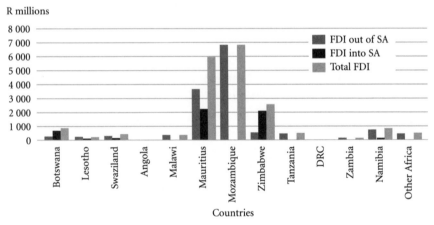

Source: SARB 2003

Africa as an overall market for South African capital

In our earlier *State of the Nation* chapter (2003), we attempted to portray the range and extent of South African corporate involvement in the African market by developing a table, which reflected the operations by sector of the larger players. This table has been updated in this volume as Table 20.5. Contrasting the two tables highlights a number of issues.

The first is the deepening of the mining sector's African operations, with the most dramatic development in 2003 being the announcement of AngloGold's merger through a 50 per cent shareholding acquisition with Ghana's largest and oldest mining company, Ashanti Goldfields. The new company will become the world's biggest gold producer with a presence in eight African countries. In the bidding war to acquire the shareholding in Ashanti Gold-fields, AngloGold was pitted against another South African mining giant, Randgold Resources. Randgold, however, had its successes when it was granted a licence to invest US$80 million in a second gold mining venture in Mali. Randgold also has mining operations in Tanzania and Senegal, while its pre-feasibility drilling programme in Cote d'Ivoire had to be suspended in late 2002 due to the conflict in that country. A *force majeure* declaration was made by the company and accepted by the government. Another South African mining company that experienced difficulties with an African operation was Anglovaal Mining (Avmin), which in 2003 sold off its Chambishi copper and cobalt operation in Zambia after incurring losses in excess of R2 billion.

A new and potentially major South African mining player entered the African mining scene in January 2004 when Mvelaphanda Holdings signed two agreements to enable it, in partnership with two at-the-time unnamed South African consortiums, to:
- explore, develop and exploit gold assets in the Ituri province of the eastern Democratic Republic of Congo (DRC); and
- acquire 100 per cent of the assets of the Ruashi copper and cobalt project.

Another sector to deepen its involvement in Africa was that of banking and financial services, with Investec and Metropolitan Life increasing their continental profiles, as did the state-owned Industrial Development Corporation (IDC). The latter continued its involvement in 20 African countries other than South Africa, but in 2003 increased its number of operations and levels of investment in five of them, namely, Namibia, Nigeria, Mozambique, Swaziland and Ghana.

An interesting feature of the increased role of South African banks in the African market is their growing involvement in the oil industry. Currently they are financing oil ventures in the DRC, Gabon, Nigeria and Angola. In the latter case, all the oil deals have been with Sonangol, the state-owned oil company, and have involved the IDC, Rand Merchant and Standard Banks, and Investec. Other significant developments involved:

- The telecommunications sector, with both MTN and Vodacom seeking to expand into new markets in Kenya and Nigeria respectively. In both these cases, MTN and Vodacom are rivals in an increasingly frenetic competition to dominate the African market. Vodacom's attempts to break into the Nigerian market to compete directly with MTN in an arena where previously it had feared to tread are discussed in more detail in the next section of the paper.
- The aviation market where South African Airways (SAA) was said, in 2003, to have acquired a 30 per cent share in Nigeria's bankrupt national carrier, thereby acquiring a west African hub to complement its eastern base in Tanzania. Recent reports, however, indicate that this is not yet a done deal and that the Nigerian government is reconsidering the deal after the South African government rejected a reciprocal agreement to allow Nigerians to buy 10 per cent equity in SAA. It was suggested that the Nigerian government might throw open the bid to other airlines (*ThisDay* 28.05.04).
- The continuing expansion of Shoprite Checkers. Excluding South Africa, Shoprite has opened branches in 15 countries in Africa and is planning a move into the Nigerian market sometime in 2004. With the recent announcement of its intention also to enter the Indian market, Shoprite can claim to be South Africa's only true multinational retail outfit.

Table 20.5 *Major South African companies in other African countries by sector (selected companies)*

Sector	Companies	Located
Aviation & airport services	Airports Company of South Africa (ACSA)	Management contracts in 9 countries
Airlines	South African Airways (SAA)	SAA has a 49% stake in Air Tanzania and is negotiating a 30% stake in Nigeria's national carrier, Eagle Airline. In all, SAA flies to 20 African destinations
	Nationwide Airlines	Contracts to provide aircraft for five national airlines (Tanzania, Malawi, Namibia, Zimbabwe and Mozambique)

Banking & financial services	Private enterprises	Stanbic	In 18 African countries
		Absa	In 5 countries
		Stanlib (joint venture between Standard Bank and Liberty Life)	In 9 countries
		First Rand (FNB) and its subsidiary Rand Merchant Bank	Retail operations in 4 countries; corporate operations in 25 countries and project financing in 12 countries
		Nedbank	In 7 countries
		Investec Ltd	In 4 countries
		Metropolitan Life	In 5 countries
	State-owned enterprises	DBSA	Funding ventures in 7 countries
		IDC	Funding ventures in 20 countries
Construction		Murray and Roberts	Permanent offices in 3 countries and 13 country contracts
		Group 5	13 country contracts
		Grinaker LTA	9 country contracts
		Concor	9 country contracts
Energy		Sasol	4 country contracts. Planned merger of its liquid fuels sector with Malaysia's Petronas marketing and distribution businesses means it will have operations in 14 sub-Saharan African countries
Manufacturing		Nampak	In 10 countries
		SAB Miller	18 beer breweries in 14 countries, 35 sorghum breweries in 5 countries
		Illovo Sugar	In 5 countries
		Barloworld	In 7 southern African countries
		AECI (subsidiaries African Explosives Ltd [AEL] & Dulux)	AEL companies in 7 countries Manufacturing Dulux products in 5 countries
Media & broadcasting		Multichoice	TV and subscriber services in 21 countries
Mining		Anglogold	The merger with Ashanti Goldfields and Anglogold gives it a mining presence in 8 countries
		Randgold Resources	In 3 countries

Retail trade	Shoprite Holdings Ltd	162 outlets in 15 countries with planned expansion into Nigeria in 2004
	Massmart (Makro, Game, Dion, Cash & Carry et al.)	Over 300 outlets in SACU states
	Metcash	In 3 countries
	Wooltru/Woolworths	52 stores in 19 countries
	Truworths Limited	Stores in 13 countries
	Famous Brands (Steers, Debonairs, Fish Aways, Church's Chicken, Pouyoukas Foods)	Franchises in 22 countries
	St. Elmo's	Franchises in 7 countries
	Pepkor Holdings (Pep Stores and Ackermans)	Present in 6 countries
	Ellerine Holdings Ltd. (Ellerines, Town Talk Furnishers, Furn City, Rainbow Loans, CPI, Foreign, Wetherlys, Osiers, Roodefurn)	94 stores in 5 countries
	JD Group (Abra, Barnetts, BoConcept, Bradlows, Electric Express, Hi-Fi Corporation, Joshua Doore, Morkels, Price and Pride, Russells)	28 stores in 4 countries
Research & development	V&A Waterfront	Contracts in Mauritius, Gabon, Nigeria for the construction of waterfront complexes
	CSIR	Conducting research projects in 17 countries
Telecommunications	MTN/M-Cell (MTN posted net profits of R4.3bn from revenues of R23.9bn from all of its African operations in fiscal 2003–04. Up 23% on previous year)	Cellular-fixed line contracts in 5 countries (Uganda 50%, Rwanda 31%, Nigeria 94%, Cameroon 100%, Swaziland (a joint venture). Has 9.5 million African customers. Its non-SA operations contribute 64% of revenue compared to Vodacom's 6.4%

		Vodacom		11.2 million African customers and contracts in 5 countries but only functional in 4: Lesotho, DRC (51%), Tanzania (65%) and Mozambique; its Zambian licence has been non-operational for two years. In 2003–04 it posted a profit of R3bn from Africa-wide revenue of R23.5bn. Attempts to move into Nigeria collapsed in May 2004	
		Transtel (a division of Transnet)		Runs a telecommunications network in 19 countries with South African multinationals including banks, railways, retailers, local telecoms, and civil and security networks	
Transport		Transnet: 9 divisions (African involvement is through divisions such as Spoornet International Joint Ventures and subsidiaries, Comazar, Transwerk and Transtel)		20 country contracts	
		Unitrans		7 country contracts	
Tourism & leisure services		Protea Hotels		Resorts in 10 countries	Collectively these
		Southern Sun		Resorts in 6 countries	hotels operate in
		Sun International		Resorts in 4 countries	14 countries
		Imperial Car Rental		110 outlets in 8 Southern African countries	
Utilities	Power	Eskom Enterprises		A presence in 33 African countries (via utility management contracts in Malawi, Mali, Uganda and Nigeria, joint venture companies in Morocco, Mozambique, Libya and Zambia and contracts in 25 other countries) means that Eskom is Africa's largest power utility. Its biggest initiative is the 'Grand Inga' project where, together with the national utilities of Angola, Botswana, the DRC and Namibia, Eskom has formed a joint venture company known as Westcor. The project aims to generate enough energy to light up Africa and create excess to export to Europe	
	Water	Umgeni Water		3 country contracts	
Information technology		Arivia.kom (state-owned)		3 offices in Nigeria, Ghana and Botswana, 1 joint venture with Seven Seas Technologies in Kenya Contracts in Namibia, Malawi, Zambia and Uganda	
		Mustek		Authorised dealerships in 8 countries	

Source: HSRC Corporate Mapping Database

The South Africa-Nigeria nexus

There are several good reasons for a focus on Nigeria. First, the fact that Nigeria is South Africa's only major non-SADC trading partner, as well as one of only a handful of African states whose trading balance with South Africa is positive. Then there are the more substantial facts that both countries are the dominant and potentially hegemonic states within their respective sub-regions, with both currently led by heads of states with extra-national ambitions. They both, moreover, have a history of co-operation and involvement in a range of continental and other (like the Commonwealth) projects, which makes their mutual commitment to the New Partnership for Africa's Development (Nepad) and the African Union (AU) ventures significant. The question arises as to whether this reflects a desire on their parts for regional and or larger hegemony. Is there an Ajuba-Pretoria axis emerging in at least sub-Saharan African politics?

Finally, there is the 'economic chemistry' between South Africa and Nigeria born of the fact that South Africa is Africa's strongest and most versatile political economy while Nigeria, with a population of 132.8 million, is Africa's largest consumer market. However, it is also Africa's most spectacular economic underperformer (Adebajo & Landsberg 2003). Potentially wealthy, four decades of maladministration and larceny on a grand scale has turned Nigeria into what is probably the world's 'richest' poor country. The consequence is that it is today an economy 'for the taking', and now that MTN has shown that money can be made in Nigeria, corporate South Africa is gearing into action. It is moving not quite like the wildfire described in the quote at the head of the paper, but the growth in South Africa's economic stake in Nigeria has been substantial in the past five years. The patient is not well, and South African capital appears to be the entity most willing and capable of breathing new life into the enfeebled body of the Nigerian economy. It expects, however, to extract a sizeable return in the process.

There is one other important factor for this focus on Nigeria and that is our view that in the decade or so ahead, South African investment in Africa will become more concentrated and centralised and that a 'big four' will emerge in the form of Nigeria, Mozambique, Angola and the Democratic Republic of the Congo (DRC). All four have in the past decades or more been ravaged by warfare or serious internal conflict as well as by corruption, but each has also, in the past decade, undergone a transition to peace or democracy (or both). They are now beginning to reap a peace dividend in the form of new investment mainly, as well as some trade. With the exception of Nigeria, South Africa played a role, sometimes the major role, in brokering the transitions and is likewise beginning to reap the bulk of the fruits of that peace. Of the projected big four, only the DRC stands outside of the top five in the league table of South Africa's African trade and investment traders. It is in tenth place, but very much on the outside looking in. We anticipate that if the peace holds, the DRC will move rapidly up the table as the series of trade and investment agreements signed in Kinshasa in early 2004 kick in and begin to bear fruit.

In future editions of the *State of the Nation* we will focus on the DRC and Angola. For now we think it is timely to look closely at the Nigerian case for the reasons we have outlined above.

South Africa in Nigeria

South Africa's accession to democracy coincided with the last years of military rule in Nigeria. Economic links in that period were minimal, while political relations hit rock-bottom after the execution of Ken Saro Wiwa in November 1995 and President Mandela's outspoken criticism of that action at a Commonwealth Summit in New Zealand. Trade and political relations changed and blossomed with the elections in the first half of 1999 of Presidents Obasanjo and Mbeki. Figure 20.5 illustrates the extent of the growth in trade post-1999.

As indicated earlier, MTN has been the trail-blazer in terms of large-scale South African operations in Nigeria. Its entrance into the Nigerian market came by way of the first telecommunications auctions process in Africa when, in January 2001, it was awarded one of Nigeria's Global Systems Mobile or GSM licences, for a fee of US$285 million. At the time, MTN's entrance into the Nigerian market was the company's single biggest investment outside of South Africa and by the end of 2003, it had spent more than US$1 billion in infrastructural and other start-up costs in Nigeria. By then, its subscriber numbers had topped the one million mark, with its customers spread across some 40 cities, more than 100 smaller towns and villages and more than 700 communities. As of June of 2004, its subscriber base had grown to

Figure 20.5 *South Africa's trade relations with Nigeria, 1992–2003*

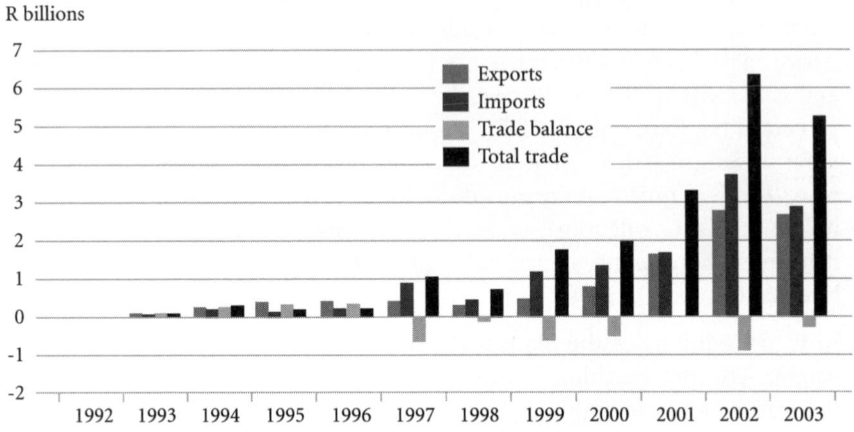

R billions

Source: Constructed from information contained in the DTI economic data base, http://www.dti:gov.sa/econdb/

1.65 million. Even so, its geographic coverage of the country was estimated at only 14 per cent and estimated population coverage of 38 per cent. It had, however, attained premier cellphone status with brand recognition of 95 per cent. Even more significantly, in 2003–04, MTN recorded an after-tax profit (PAT) from its Nigerian operation of R2.4 billion, representing just over 55.8 per cent of its total operating profit of R4.3 billion, and an 80 per cent improvement in its Nigerian PAT from 2002.

The activities of MTN notwithstanding, the real engine of South African-Nigerian trade has been the South Africa-Nigeria Bi-National Commission (BNC), signed into being in October 1999, and the Nigeria-South Africa Chamber of Commerce, which was launched in 2001. Set up as vehicles to promote and strengthen co-operation in such areas as defence and security, science, technology and infrastructure including communications tech-nologies, education, sports and culture, the Commission has met on five occasions and the Chamber three times. Together they have spawned some 20 agreements, the bulk of which have been ratified by the Parliaments of the two countries and are therefore operative. They cover each of the above areas, as well tax, investment promotion, immigration, extradition and other legal and criminal matters. In addition, there has in recent years been an exchange of industry visits to both countries, as well as an increased level of participation by the private sectors in South African and Nigerian trade fairs and exhibitions.

The net effect over the four years between 1999 and 2002 has been an approximately 540 per cent increase in South Africa's exports to Nigeria while South Africa's imports have grown by about 300 per cent. In 2002, discussions were initiated around the issue of a Nigeria-South Africa Free Trade Area, while at the December 2003 conference, a bi-national agreement was reached on the convening at the meeting in 2004 of a Business Investment Forum. Other significant agreements to emerge from the 2003 BNC involved closer co-operation between the customs authorities of the two countries, and between the respective Reserve Banks in regard to monetary managements, surveillance of financial institutions and external reserve management.

As of mid-April 2003, there were an estimated 55 South African companies doing business in Nigeria. Many of these are the major players whose activities in Africa are summarised in Table 20.5. One of these was Vodacom, which sought to go head-to-head with MTN in the Nigerian market by acquiring a 50 per cent stake in the Nigerian subsidiary of the South African-based Econet Wireless group. This was blocked by the parent company, to which the Nigerian subsidiary responded by awarding Vodacom a five-year management contract to run its local operations. This arrangement became operational in March 2004, but fell apart within weeks when corruption allegations against two senior Vodacom executives in Nigeria resulted in the company deciding to withdraw from the country altogether. MTN apart, the other major South African players in Nigeria are:

- Eskom Enterprises, which has taken a majority 51 per cent stake in the Nigerian state power authority, National Electric Power Authority (NEPA), and linked up with Shell in a contract to rehabilitate a cluster of power plants in the Rivers State. This contract is said to be worth US$540m.
- Sasol, which has invested US$1.2bn in a joint venture with Chevron Texaco to pursue commercial applications of Nigeria's reserves of natural gas.
- SAA, which has spent about US$460m to acquire a 30 per cent share in the new national carrier, Nigerian Eagle, which will replace the bankrupt Nigeria Airways. As indicated earlier in the paper, this deal may now be in jeopardy, although there has been no official statement on the part of the Nigerian government.

Other South African corporates with investments in Nigeria include Stanbic and Stanlib, Murray and Roberts, Umgeni Water, Mustek, Multichoice, Spoornet, Woolworths, Steers and Protea Hotels. An interesting newcomer to the African and Nigerian scene is the Victoria & Alfred Waterfront Group which, in a consortium with Entech, a Stellenbosch-based engineering consultancy, has won a US$1.08 billion tender for the re-development and rehabilitation of the Bar Beach area of Victoria Island off Lagos, as well as a tender to develop a Cape Town-style waterfront in Port Harcourt. Also included in the Victoria Island redevelopment is the construction of a retail centre in which Game and Shoprite will be the anchor tenants. This will represent the first entry of these two retailers into the Nigerian market. The South African property services company, JHI Real Estate, operating with a Nigerian architectural group, is developing this particular project. Once completed, they will also manage the complex, again in conjunction with a local Nigerian group.[2]

The setbacks involving Vodacom – and possibly SAA – notwithstanding, there is every indication that South African capital's engagement with the Nigerian economy is set to increase rapidly. Speaking in May 2004, the Nigerian Finance Minister announced that South African businesses would invest US$1 billion in Nigeria in the oil and gas, agro-industrial and services sectors in the nine-month period leading up to 2005 (*ThisDay* 25.05.04).

Nigeria in South Africa

By contrast with the South African presence in Nigeria, Nigerian business has a very modest profile in South Africa. Most publicly visible is the *ThisDay* newspaper, which, after a longer-than-anticipated gestation period, finally launched in October 2003. Moving into an over-traded market, the paper has been well received by the serious newspaper-reading public and it has breached the psychologically important 30 000-readership barrier far more quickly than had been expected. Its survival is not ensured, however, as it has not attracted the level or volume of advertising it had anticipated.

A second Nigerian newspaper operating in South Africa is the *FS African Standard,* which is geared to a readership comprised of an estimated 100 000 West Africans living in South Africa. Published monthly, the *Standard* is an offshoot of the Nigerian publishing company, Millenium Harvest Ltd which, *inter alia*, produces Nigeria's leading financial weekly, the *Financial Standard* (hence the FS in the South African paper's title).

The only other Nigerian companies of note operating in South Africa are two banks (Union Bank and First Bank) and Philips Consulting, which operates as an investment broker. However, according to African business consultant, Dianna Games, this paucity of companies only:

> masks the vibrant business relationship that Nigeria has with South Africa. For example, many Nigerian entrepreneurs have invested millions of Rands in South Africa and source products from the country. Training companies, particularly in the area of IT, get a lot of business from Nigerians and there are thousands of Nigerians working as professionals in a wide range of fields such as academia, human resources, property, accounting and the medical field. (*Business Day* 22.09.03:9)

And then, of course, there is the whole arena of organised and illicit crime in which it is widely conceded that significant numbers of other Nigerians are involved.

Conclusion: the issue of hegemony

Recently released statistics point to a continuing decline in Africa's role in the world economy. Its share of global trade has slipped to around 2 per cent (down by nearly 50 per cent over two decades) while the continent continues to attract less and less FDI. According to the World Trade Organization, Africa's share of global FDI in 2002 was only 1.7 per cent. It is little wonder that a recent World Economic Forum document described growth in Africa, or rather the lack thereof, as 'the economic tragedy of the twentieth century' (*Business Day* 03.05.04).

Thirty years ago, the dependency theorists conceptualised the global economy as being structurally divided into a centre (the First World) and a periphery (the Third World of Asia, Africa and Latin America). If it was accurate then, one would now have to describe Africa as the periphery of the periphery, given how far it has fallen behind both the Asian and most Latin American economies. Africa's economic statistics are sinking below the horizon and it is probably not unfair to suggest that, other than its oil sector, the African economy does not much matter globally.

What the dependency theorists also told us was that, within each sector, growth was unequal and that, within them, the centre-periphery pattern tended to reproduce itself. If one looks at the African political economy, this would seem to be the case, with South Africa and Nigeria standing out as dominant poles. This is particularly so in regard to their respective sub-regions.

But does this mean that the relationship of these two powers to their regions is hegemonic? Perhaps more pertinently, and particularly given that the South African economy is so much larger and more diversified than Nigeria's, does this mean that the South African-African relationship is a hegemonic one? The answer, in our view, is in both cases no. This is not a view shared by all South Africans, or South African-based analysts, but the weakness in their arguments is their failure to unpack the concept of hegemony. Being big and strong does not make an individual a bully, and neither does it, in the case of a country, make it a hegemon.

Hegemony means more than just being big. It refers, in conceptual terms, to a power relationship of domination and subordination between two or more parties; one which, if not intentionally crafted, is deliberately perpetuated. Intent, therefore, is the key aspect. Does the dominant power seek to exploit the fact of its bigness to its advantage and, if so, does it seek to protect and maintain that advantage?

Nigeria did not intentionally craft its domination of West Africa. It is not a product of the historical past or some form of colonial engineering. It is purely a fortuitous (or perhaps not if one looks at the sorry sight of Nigeria's modern political economy) product of the fact that it has oil resources, which came on tap soon after its independence in the 1960s. The prime state beneficiary of Nigeria's oil wealth has been its military (and a succession of corrupt military leaders) and there have been times in the last 30 years where it has employed its military strength, both to serve its interests and as a peace-keeping or stablilising force in the region.

But whether it has ever intended it or not, the post-independence Nigerian state has lacked the capacity to establish and maintain a power relationship of domination within its regional backyard. This is due to the predatory nature of the Nigerian state since the oil boom of the early 1970s. The vast fiscal resources generated by oil have been systematically looted by Nigeria's ruling elites, and never more so than during its periods of military rule.

Concurrently, other sectors of the economy, notably agriculture and infrastructure, have been neglected and allowed to decline, while any state-directed regulatory systems collapsed. The result is an enfeebled Nigerian state, today barely able to hold together a country riven by class, ethnic and religious tensions. Far from being a hegemon, Nigeria is a dysfunctional entity. This, in part, explains the success South African business is having in Nigeria. It produces commodities that work for a consumer market that wants them.

The South African situation is different in many respects from that of Nigeria. The democratic South African state inherited a hegemonic, imperialist-type relationship with the continent, and particularly with its southern African hinterland. Forged by colonial capital in the late nineteenth and early twentieth centuries, South Africa's domination of the region was aggressively defended in the 1970s and 1980s, as the apartheid state strove to contain the efforts of the South African liberation forces and their allies.

The question now, ten years on from liberation, is has the post-apartheid state changed the nature of its imperialist inheritance? We argued in our last *State of the Nation* article (2003) that it had. Some have disagreed, arguing that South Africa's hegemony has merely changed its form and that the post-apartheid state still uses its economic muscle to pursue 'South Africa-first' policies. They point to South Africa's reluctance to ease African access to the South African market through tariff concessions and the lifting or easing of trade barriers. They also frequently cite South Africa's military incursion into Lesotho as an exercise in hegemony.

Our response is that these critics fail to distinguish between the Mandela and Mbeki regimes and the key differences between them in regard to South African-African state relations. While the Mandela era was not hegemonic in intent, its foreign policy was ad hoc and sometimes contradictory. Some of the old apartheid habits continued, and it is correct to suggest that early trade negotiations with some of our regional partners were characterised by narrow self-interest. It is true too, that the Lesotho incursion was a rather crude show of force although, as we argued last year, it has had a positive political outcome for Lesotho.

The Mbeki era, we contend, is qualitatively different from that of its predecessor in that South Africa's Africa relations are now conducted within a coherent policy framework which specifically eschews hegemony and which places a premium on partnership and co-operation over narrow national advantage. This is in line with the principles which underlie the charter of the African Union and the Nepad framework. We contend that this is nowhere more evident than in the position adopted by South Africa in the recent re-negotiation of the Southern African Customs Union's (SACU) agreement.

This arrangement, originally negotiated in 1909, basically linked the economies of the former High Commission Territories of Bechaunaland (Botswana), Basutoland (Lesotho) and Swaziland to South Africa, in an economic union that was unequally skewed to South Africa's economic benefit. Namibia joined SACU after its independence in 1990. Symbolic of South Africa's domination of the Union was that it was located within the DTI in Pretoria where, effectively, all decisions were made, including the size of the amounts allocated annually to the partners from the common customs revenue pool.

In terms of the renegotiated arrangement, which took effect in April 2004, SACU's headquarters are being relocated to Namibia. All decision-making within the Union has been democratised and will now require consensus on the part of a Council of Ministers that will replace Pretoria as the Union's ultimate authority. The new agreement also provides for a new revenue-sharing formula to replace one that was perceived by the non-South African partners as unfair. It will result in their receiving a greater share of the pool, which in 2003, collected R22.7 billion in tariff revenue. According to the head of the DTI's SACU desk, the new agreement also makes provision 'for the development of common policies and strategies regarding industrial development, co-operation on agricultural policies and competition policy' (*Business Day* 06.04.04).

So the challenge to those who argue that the Mbeki government is pursuing a hegemonic agenda is to produce the evidence. Last year we argued that the 'leopard' of South Africa's aggressive interventionist foreign policy of the late apartheid era had changed its spots. Nothing has transpired in the last year to change our view. Indeed, this SACU renegotiation further confirms our view. That is not to dispute that there are not dangers in South Africa's increasing economic strength in Africa. Clearly there is a potential for hegemony, but at present we contend the intent is not there.

Finally, what of the Nigerian-South African relationship? Will it prevail and what form will it take? While Nigeria currently enjoys a positive trade balance with South Africa, the relationship in our view is unequal and actually favours South Africa. Nigeria's trade link with South Africa is monocultural – being based almost entirely on oil (98.3 per cent of Nigeria's exports to South Africa in 2003 was comprised of oil) – while South Africa's is diverse and includes a range of products that Nigeria's massive consumer market clearly wants. It is our view that, provided the Nigerian state holds firm and does not fragment in the face of sectarian violence, South Africa's trade into the Nigerian market can only grow. The opposite does not apply because, oil apart, Nigeria has little or nothing to offer to the South African consumer.

The inequality in the relationship will therefore grow and ultimately the trade balance will turn in South Africa's favour. As the CEO of Vodacom noted in June 2004, 'Nigeria is very important. It's the second-most important economy in Africa and it's very difficult not to be in Nigeria' (*Business Day* 08.06.04). An increasing number of South African businesses are recognising that fact and, as they enter that market, the gap between Africa's largest and second-largest economies will widen.

Notes

1   In January 2004, the construction group, Aveng, issued a profit warning and announced that it was withdrawing from all its African construction contracts. Aveng's roads and earthworks division forms part of Grinaker-LTA, South Africa's largest construction company. Aveng took this action after substantial losses on three of its African roads contracts. A spokesperson for Aveng was quoted in *Business Day* (3.02.04) as stating: 'In South Africa it is difficult enough managing a road project; in Africa it is impossible.' The same report quoted other roads contractors in Africa, Murray and Roberts and Group Five, as agreeing with this view, with the Murray and Roberts spokesperson stating that road contracts in Africa had become 'just too risky'. Group Five announced that it had restructured in order to downscale its activities in Africa.

2   JHI is also currently involved in three large construction projects in Ghana. Two are in Accra and involve the building of an office complex, hotel and retail centre, while in Kumasi, the company is developing a shopping mall.

References

Adebajo A & Landsberg C (2003): South Africa and Nigeria as regional hegemons. In M Baregu & C Landsberg (eds.) *From Cape to Congo: Southern Africa's evolving security challenges*. Boulder, Colorado: Lynn Reiner.

Daniel J, Naidoo V & Naidu S (2003): The South Africans have arrived: Post-apartheid corporate expansion into Africa. In J Daniel, A Habib & R Southall (eds.) *The State of the Nation 2003–2004*. Cape Town: HSRC Press.

SARB (South African Reserve Bank) (1996) *Quarterly Bulletin*, December, No. 202. Pretoria: SARB.

SARB (1997) *Quarterly Bulletin*, December, No. 206. Pretoria: SARB.

SARB (1998) *Quarterly Bulletin*, December, No. 210. Pretoria: SARB.

SARB (1999) *Quarterly Bulletin*, December, No. 214. Pretoria: SARB.

SARB (2000) *Quarterly Bulletin*, December, No. 218. Pretoria: SARB.

SARB (2001) *Quarterly Bulletin*, December, No. 222. Pretoria: SARB.

SARB (2002) *Quarterly Bulletin*, December, No. 226. Pretoria: SARB.

SARB (2003) *Quarterly Bulletin*, December, No. 230. Pretoria: SARB.

SARB (2004) *Quarterly Bulletin*, June, No. 232. Pretoria: SARB.

21 South Africa's quiet diplomacy: the case of Zimbabwe

Lloyd M Sachikonye

Introduction

In his 2004 'State of the Nation' address, President Mbeki did not even mention one of his major foreign policy challenges, Zimbabwe. However, it is common knowledge that political and economic conditions in Zimbabwe have deteriorated sharply since 2000. The term 'crisis' is often employed to describe the profound and complex set of developments that underlie this deterioration. From being one of the more industrialised economies in Africa and an agricultural breadbasket, Zimbabwe has experienced an economic contraction of more than 30 per cent since 2000, and a massive food deficit since 2002. Its political system has been characterised by state repression, election manipulation, draconian controls over the media, and human rights abuses, including the use of violence, torture and rape against opponents of the ruling party.

The international community, and especially the countries in the southern Africa region, could not afford to ignore the unravelling of the situation in Zimbabwe. The Zimbabwe crisis adversely affected economic and trade flows, investment and tourism in the region, as well as burdening neighbouring economies through significant flows of Zimbabwean migrants, legal and clandestine, of up to two million (about 16 per cent of the population). Organisations such as the Southern African Development Community (SADC) and the Commonwealth, amongst others, were naturally concerned about the crisis in Zimbabwe and its possible spill-over effects. By virtue (or accident!) of geography and history, perhaps no country was more exposed to, and therefore more concerned about, the unfolding situation in Zimbabwe than South Africa.

This chapter attempts to evaluate South Africa's policy towards Zimbabwe during the period between 2000 and early 2004. The policy itself – also termed 'quiet diplomacy' to distinguish it from what has sometimes been termed 'megaphone diplomacy' – has generated heated controversy both within and outside South Africa. There are not many instances in which one country's diplomatic efforts to facilitate a resolution of a spiralling internal crisis in another has evoked such an intense debate. The chapter begins by spelling out the principal elements of South African foreign policy towards Africa, and then briefly assesses the regional context and dynamics which have shaped its Zimbabwe policy. This entails a consideration of how the SADC countries have approached the Zimbabwe crisis and interacted with the government in that country during the period from 2000 to the present.

While the chapter does not ignore the importance of the first phase of the Zimbabwe policy under the Mandela government between 1994 and 1999, it is during the period 2000 to the present that quiet diplomacy became South Africa's principal response to the crisis. In particular, the quiet diplomacy approach came under critical scrutiny following the controversial 2002 presidential election in Zimbabwe. The chapter seeks to explore several inter-related issues. What have been the motivations and considerations behind this form of diplomacy? What are its strengths and weaknesses? How has this brand of diplomacy been assessed by the international community and within Zimbabwe?

South Africa's foreign policy towards Africa

The idea of an African Renaissance – and the vision outlined in the founding document of the New Partnership for Africa's Development (Nepad) – has been the defining concept of Mbeki's government. Because regional stability and integration are an important component of this concept and policy, Southern Africa and the African continent as a whole are identified as its major foreign policy focus (van Wyk 2002). The key goals of the policy are:

* The promotion of peace and security (entailing the strengthening of conflict prevention and resolution capabilities of the region and rendering assistance in monitoring and addressing issues that affect regional stability).

- The promotion of democratisation and human rights (including the monitoring of elections in the region and rendering assistance in this regard upon request).
- The pursuit of sustainable development and alleviation of poverty. (DFA 2001)

Foreign Minister, Dr Dlamini-Zuma, outlined the values underlying that policy as democracy, good governance, people-centred development, peace, stability and security, promotion of co-operation and partnerships, as well as good neighbourliness (Dlamini-Zuma 2001).

Why is the African Renaissance idea so central to South Africa's policy towards the continent and region? It has to do with Thabo Mbeki's vision of the potential future of the continent, and South Africa's role in shaping that future. The first interpretation of the African Renaissance idea links:

> South Africa's economic interests to Africa through the analytical register offered by meta-theory devised by globalisation with its seemingly endless vistas, shrinking horizons, and economistic logic ... The second interpretation involves using the African Renaissance to unlock a series of complex social constructions that are more immediate, and turn on issues of identity. (Vale & Maseko 2002:26)

The first interpretation has been termed 'globalist', while the second has been called 'Africanist'. In the globalist perspective, Africa is posited as a potentially expanding and prosperous market, alongside Asia, Europe and North America, and one in which South African capital is destined to play a special role via trade, strategic partnerships and the like. By virtue of its size, wealth and regional status, South Africa is endowed with resources to play a major leadership role on the continent:

> In hierarchical understandings of politics, it appears natural ... that South Africa should provide such leadership. Because of this, South African commentators have been odious in their belief that their country and their experience of political transformation and managing market economics in particular has everything to teach Africa and by implication, that Africa has nothing to teach South Africa ... These impulses have certainly fed wider international

understandings that South Africa is the only country that can offer leadership south of the Sahara – a point, incidentally, enthusiastically embraced by the United States as it seeks to implement a version of the theory of pivotal states as a central plank of its post-cold war foreign policy. (Vale & Maseko 2002:131–32)

Although this leadership role is not made explicit in policy statements and in pronouncements of its leaders, it is a role that South Africa would like to play. However, how to play such a role without arousing the hostility and non-co-operation of other countries with a similar ambition is a question that exercises the minds of the leadership in South Africa. It is also an issue that animates the debate on whether South Africa should or can play the role of a 'hegemonic power' or that of a 'pivotal state' (Daniel, Naidoo & Naidu 2003; Habib 2003; Landsberg 2003; Vale 2003). These considerations pertaining to its regional and hegemonic ambitions have a bearing on how South Africa approaches its relations with such groupings as SADC, the African Union (AU), the Commonwealth, and its neighbours such as Zimbabwe. Let us, however, begin by assessing how it has handled the issue of Zimbabwe in the councils of SADC.

Regional context of policy towards Zimbabwe

As we have already observed above, SADC countries could not afford to be aloof to Zimbabwe's slide into a crisis of repression and economic meltdown from 2000 onwards. The slide was epitomised by a land reform programme that was implemented in an environment of violence, lawlessness and chaos; and by the ruling Zimbabwe African National Union-Patriotic Front's (Zanu-PF) exploitation of political capital out of the programme in the 2000 and 2002 parliamentary and presidential elections respectively. As stated earlier, some of the immediate effects of the Zimbabwe meltdown were a decline in the volume of trade with neighbouring countries, increased flows of Zimbabwean migrants and decreased flows of investment and tourists. One estimate was that by 2001, the economies of SADC may have lost over US$36 billion in potential investment as a result of the situation in Zimbabwe (see *The Observer* 30.09.01).

Although SADC has no institutional mechanisms for intervening in the domestic affairs of a member state, the deteriorating situation in Zimbabwe warranted special attention – hence the series of SADC summit meetings held on the situation in 2001 and 2002. The SADC heads of state took positions on the land reform issue, and later on human rights, electoral and political issues. The wider international context in which they took these positions was one in which western governments, especially Britain, were very critical of the Mugabe government's handling of the land and human rights issues.

The dilemma of SADC states, including South Africa, was how to admonish the Mugabe government on these issues without appearing to side with the West against it. This partly explained the muted nature of their criticism of the government, and partly the divisions between them over a collective approach on Zimbabwe. Some countries, such as Namibia, Angola and the Democratic Republic of the Congo (DRC), were in support of the Zimbabwe government on most issues, apart from being allies in the Congo war. Following the controversial 2002 election result, the heads of state of Namibia, Zambia, Mozambique, Malawi and Tanzania lent legitimacy to it by attending Mugabe's inauguration.

It is against this background that we can examine South Africa's own cautious, and sometimes contradictory, approach to the issue. First, it had to contend with the issue of regional solidarity vis-à-vis the wider international community; second, with the need to ensure that the political and economic situation did not become more unstable within Zimbabwe; and third, that it could still play a catalytic leadership role despite the divisions within SADC. The issue of state-based regional solidarity was articulated in these terms:

> SADC would not go along with evil machinations of some
> Western powers using the neo-colonialist press locally and inter-
> nationally. SADC would remain on Zimbabwe's side because
> blood is thicker than water. (Lilian Patel, Malawi's Foreign
> Minister, quoted in *The Herald* 12.12.01)

The land issue formed a convenient cause around which to rally in the name of historical redress and justice for Zimbabwean people, and on which to criticise the seemingly dismissive approach that the Blair government had taken on the issue of 'historic responsibility' and compensation for white farmers. True, as the land reform programme degenerated into violence and elite 'land-grabbing', some SADC heads deplored the manner of implementation of land reform. This did not, however, disguise the bottom line that the grouping

backed the land reform programme. The Mugabe government itself was skil-
ful in ensuring that regional solidarity would provide cover for its repression
of the opposition under the guise of implementing land reform.

The rural areas, including commercial farms, were sealed off from the opposition parties, while the ruling party's war veterans, youth and militia
mobilised the population for the 2000 and 2002 elections by coercion and
intimidation. Mugabe himself warned other SADC leaders about what their
fate could be:

> There is a Western, and especially Anglo-American, plot to destroy
> Zanu-PF and evict it from power because it was a liberation
> movement. If this plot succeeded in Zimbabwe, it would then be
> applied successfully against all other ruling liberation movements
> in Southern Africa. (Quoted in Johnson 2002:8)

It is not unlikely that such a conspiracy theory might have found resonance
amongst some SADC heads of state.

It can be argued that faced with such currents of opinion on regional solidarity,
it would be difficult for South Africa to take a more forthright position on
Zimbabwe, if it had wanted to do so. South Africa would have risked isolation in
SADC, and perhaps further afield in the AU – such tags as 'regional big brother'
or 'superpower' would then have been derisively applied to it. The dilemma for
the Mbeki government then, as now, was how to juggle between sensitivities in
SADC and the AU, and the need to apply pressure on the Harare government. It
was not beyond Mugabe to play the different currents against each other:

> There is a view that Mugabe was prepared to isolate South Africa
> within SADC if it became too critical, thereby gaining leverage
> within the region. South Africa had already experienced the
> onslaught of propaganda levied against it when it spoke against
> Zimbabwe. (Field 2003:360)

The wish not to be outflanked by Mugabe on the regional and continental
platform would have entered the calculations of the South African leadership,
hence the toning down of its rhetoric. Much more was at stake in its role in
the AU and Nepad, and this could not be overshadowed by Zimbabwe.

Thus there was an aspect of a 'lowest common denominator' approach by
SADC, including South Africa, to the Zimbabwe crisis. However, this did not

prevent several initiatives aimed at healing the situation between 2000 and 2002. There were several meetings by SADC foreign ministers devoted to the Zimbabwe question. In addition, there was a task team, comprising Botswana, Mozambique and South Africa, appointed by SADC in 2001, to work with Zimbabwe. Although this team was constrained to a certain extent by the position of other SADC members, its brief was to move the Mugabe government to a more constructive programme of action (Field 2002). The team met with Zimbabwe government authorities, representatives of the opposition Movement for Democratic Change (MDC) and civil society; and it set a deadline for the restoration of the rule of law and resolution of the land crisis. The idea took hold that dialogue between the major political players, Zanu-PF and MDC, was imperative in resolving the crisis but it was not until after the 2002 presidential election that the dialogue was initiated. As we will see below, South Africa, initially together with Nigeria, and later largely on its own, would play a central role in encouraging what was termed 'inter-party dialogue'.

In sum, the baggage that South Africa brought to the Zimbabwe issue was not light. Rather than risk isolation and division, it needed to work alongside the other SADC countries in a slow and muddled process. It seemed to have learnt something from its unilateral approach to the Nigerian crisis, when it pursued a tough position on the Abacha dictatorship in the mid-1990s under Mandela. South Africa had assumed that there would be regional support for its position and that the West would impose sanctions on oil imports from Nigeria. When this failed, South Africa was left looking exposed and ineffective (Field 2003). As an ANC international relations expert put it:

> There is no way in which South Africa can stand alone and outrightly condemn (Zimbabwe), knowing that their condemnation will not have an impact but will actually worsen the situation. We did that with Nigeria when Madiba took a position without consulting the Commonwealth, without consulting SADC, and without consulting the OAU; and what happened? Everybody stood aside and we were isolated because it was a terrible mistake we made ... We acted as this bully, and people resent being bullied. (Myokayaka-Manzini, quoted in *Mail & Guardian* 2.03.01)

While Zimbabwe is not Nigeria, South Africa appears to have learnt its lesson too well on the side of caution, perhaps excessive caution, in the second time round! Clearly, an informed analysis of South Africa's policy towards Zimbabwe should take into account the kind of baggage it was carrying.

Phases in South Africa's policy on Zimbabwe

Relations under the Mandela presidency

During the Mandela presidency, relations between South Africa and Zimbabwe were reasonably good, though not warm. The transition to a democratic, post-apartheid government in 1994 marked not only a new phase in South Africa and the region, but the completion of the decolonisation process on the continent. However, there were undercurrents of rivalry between the two leading figures in the region, Nelson Mandela and Robert Mugabe. It is reported to have been famously stated by Mandela that 'Mugabe's problem is that he was the star – and then the sun came up' (Sparks 2003:269). The latter aspired to continue to play a central leadership role in the region, and he was reluctant to give up his chairmanship of the SADC Organ for Politics, Defence and Security. In 1998, Zimbabwe spearheaded a coalition of allies (together with Angola and Namibia) to send military inter-vention forces to prop up the Laurent Kabila regime in the DRC.

It has been observed that the chemistry between Mandela and Mugabe did not contribute to a warm relationship between the two leading countries in the region:

> Formalized relations between the region's sovereign states – for all their commonalities – were not, nor ever had been, close and intimate. Rather, their relations were always impersonal, always contractual, notwithstanding the ritual tributes paid to solidarity and struggle. One relationship – that between Mandela and Mugabe – exemplified the tension. Always terribly formal, the personal and professional intimacies necessary to draw the region's strongest two poles were simply absent. (Vale 2003:7)

The absence of a warm bond between them may have also affected certain aspects of the bilateral relationship – for instance, negotiations on the renewal of a trade agreement that had expired in 1992 took a long time to conclude.

This was a symptom of a certain inertia, combined with pressure of certain interest groups (such as textile manufacturers) on the South African government. The irony is that the two previous white governments hammered out out a trade agreement more quickly than two successor black governments. In sum, the first phase of the bilateral relationship of the two independent states was marked by a simmering rivalry over regional leadership, and this spilled over into trade and economic issues.

Relations under Mbeki: 2000 to 2002

No sooner had Thabo Mbeki assumed the mantle of leadership than the situation in Zimbabwe began to deteriorate rapidly, particularly from 2000 onwards. As we have already observed in passing, the land occupations and the 2000 election campaign following the referendum defeat of the Zanu-PF government were characterised by widespread violence and lawlessness. The Zimbabwe situation posed a difficult challenge to the Mbeki presidency – as it did to SADC. The series of initiatives that South Africa took in pursuit of its quiet diplomacy may be subdivided between those undertaken between 2000 and March 2002, and those since. Throughout 2000 there was some hope that the land question could be somehow resolved once the parliamentary elections were out of the way. The position of South Africa appeared to be that Zimbabwe had a genuine grievance in the land issue, and that the British government and white farmers should play facilitative roles in the resolution of the issue. At the same time, Mbeki called for an end to the violence in the land reform programme and in the 2000 election campaign.

There was a series of four visits to Harare by President Mbeki, and another to Bulawayo, to open Zimbabwe's International Trade Fair. Bilateral meetings after the 2000 election included the participation of senior South African ministers with their Zimbabwean counterparts on post-election plans for economic recovery, and a possible South African contribution to such a programme, with a particular focus on trade and finance issues (van Wyk 2002). More such ministerial meetings followed in 2001. South Africa also played a role in persuading the United Nations to despatch an envoy to Harare to discuss possible assistance for the land reform programme. The envoy, Mark Malloch Brown, visited Harare in December 2000 for high-level talks relating to the land issue.

At the same time, however, the Mbeki government sought to draw upon a third party from outside the region to weigh in on its diplomatic overtures. It was President Obasanjo who accompanied Thabo Mbeki to Harare to discuss both the land question and breakdown of the rule of law. This was the first of such visits by Mbeki-Obasanjo during 2001, 2002 and 2003. There is a sense in which the drawing of Obasanjo into the discussions with Harare was either an admission by Mbeki that he did not have the clout to convince Mugabe to change course, or an astute move to cover himself in case there was some negative fall-out from the discussions (particularly criticism of the 'big-brother syndrome') – there was a not unreasonable assumption that Mugabe would take seriously the overtures of the two largest powers on the continent. A great deal was at stake: the credibility of Nepad would partly depend on whether Mugabe would be nudged towards an abandonment of repression and lawlessness. In 2001 and 2002, both Mbeki and Obasanjo – through the Commonwealth – would pursue the same goal, but, with difficulty, trying to restrain the Commonwealth Heads of Government Meeting's then chairperson, John Howard, who pushed for tougher measures against the Mugabe government. It fell to the two African leaders to restrain the Commonwealth from taking a more hard-line position, such as the expulsion of Zimbabwe from that organisation.

Meanwhile, there was little to show for these diplomatic initiatives by the Mbeki government, and those in conjunction with the Obasanjo government. It appeared that it was not Mugabe's intention to reciprocate these overtures; he was bent on procrastinating on the issues of ending political violence and implementing land reform in an orderly and transparent manner. Sparks has observed that:

> Mugabe felt that he could twist Mbeki around his little finger. He seemed to enjoy publicly humiliating him. He did so right after the Victoria Falls summit of 2000. At that meeting, Mbeki thought he had negotiated a deal in which Mugabe agreed to withdraw the war veterans from the farms they had started invading and occupying, in return for South Africa interceding with Britain to reinstate a 1998 donors' agreement to provide money to compensate those whose land was to be expropriated. But a few days later, Mugabe reneged on the deal by publicly encouraging the war veterans to continue occupying white farms. (2003:268)

This must have been quite frustrating for Mbeki. In 2001, there appeared to be a shift in the focus of the quiet diplomacy approach. The new focus was on a possible post-Mugabe situation. Having identified Mugabe's leadership of Zanu-PF and his unreliability as a negotiating partner as problems, the shift was to identify moderate and pragmatic elements in Zanu-PF that could be prepared to work out a deal with the MDC. This shift would form the basis of the concept of inter-party dialogue that could lead to a government of national unity, or at least a transitional administration that could restore normalcy and prepare for legitimate elections.

From 2002 to the present

However, several developments beginning in March 2002 would put South Africa's mediating approach to severe test. The first related to its government's assessment of the 2002 presidential election, and the second, its response to the position taken by the Commonwealth on Zimbabwe – suspension in 2002 and extension of suspension in 2003. Both the assessment and response by South Africa were widely perceived as tacit siding with the Mugabe government. Hence the beginning of sustained criticism of the quiet diplomacy, both within South Africa and Zimbabwe.

Prior to the 2002 election, South Africa's approach to the Zimbabwe question had still appeared even-handed, befitting its potential role of mediator between Zanu-PF and the MDC. However, a puzzling development was the endorsement of the conduct and outcome of the election by a government-sponsored South African observer mission, headed by Sam Motsuenyane. The verdict that the result was 'legitimate' was made fairly quickly after the publication of the election outcome. This was contradicted by the assessments of the SADC Parliamentary Forum, the Commonwealth Observer Group and the Zimbabwe Election Support Network, which concluded that the election conduct and outcome were deeply flawed. Significantly, an examination of SADC's norms and standards for elections indicated that 11 of the most significant standards were flouted in the 2002 election. These included standards relating to voter registration, voter education, election monitoring, conduct of the election process itself in the cities of Harare and Chitungwiza and access to the public media.

The readiness of the South Africans to whitewash the election conduct and outcome was quickly followed by the undertaking (together with Nigeria) of a rapid initiative to persuade Zanu-PF and MDC to enter negotiations for a government of national unity. The Mbeki government received a great deal of flak for its somewhat enthusiastic endorsement of the controversial 2002 election.

A similarly puzzling position that South Africa took on the Zimbabwe question was during the Commonwealth summit in Abuja in December 2003. It would appear that the Mbeki government was deeply uncomfortable with having Zimbabwe raised as a major issue of debate at both the 2002 Brisbane and 2003 Abuja summits. As a matter of principle, it was against the suspension of Zimbabwe from the Commonwealth at both summits. The Mbeki government in fact pushed for the lifting of the suspension on Zimbabwe, despite the fact that the latter had ignored the corrective measures on governance and electoral reform recommended by the Commonwealth. The persistence of repression – with the enactment of more sweeping legislation such as the Public Order Security Act and the Access to Information Protection of Privacy Act – underscored Zimbabwe's arrogance towards the calls for reform from the Commonwealth and other international organisations. Nevertheless, it still came as a surprise that Zimbabwe's major defender at the Abuja summit was Thabo Mbeki.

The South African leader would have preferred a quiet diplomacy approach to ensure that Zimbabwe remained within the Commonwealth, instead of the extension of the suspension. However, the length to which South Africa went to oppose the line orchestrated by most Commonwealth states stirred surprise in many quarters – it not only backed a Sri Lankan candidate (unsuccessfully) against the incumbent Secretary General, Don McKinnock, but it (together with several SADC states) denounced the Commonwealth decision to extend Zimbabwe's suspension, to the chagrin of Obasanjo. This was a puzzling development, which Mbeki quickly followed with a visit to Harare in December 2003. While it may be explained as Mbeki's attempt to maintain the political bridge to Harare, it raised questions of judgment about the resolve of the Commonwealth and the arrogance, if not siege mentality, of the Mugabe government. It was scarcely suprising that there was considerable criticism of the tactics of the Mbeki government within South Africa, Zimbabwe and the international community.

By the end of 2003, there was not much to show for quiet diplomacy. The political and economic crisis showed no signs of abating. There were still no formal talks underway between the ruling Zanu-PF and the opposition MDC. The succession issue in Zanu-PF had been neutralised at its December 2003 conference, and repression continued. How then have the South African and Zimbabwean public and the international community assessed the quiet diplomacy approach to the Zimbabwe question? This is the focus of the next section.

Perspectives on quiet diplomacy

Perspectives on South Africa's quiet diplomacy range from the sceptical to the critical, to those that are supportive and passionately defensive about this approach – very few hold a neutral position on the issue. Those who hold sceptical and critical views point to the fact that there has not been a change in the political and economic situation in Zimbabwe since the inauguration of quiet diplomacy. In some instances, the situation has actually worsened. In South Africa, this position has been articulated by a section of the press, opposition parties and civil society. One example of a forthright critique of the policy was an editorial in the *Mail & Guardian* (23.02.01) that argued that:

> as the battle lines have been drawn one of the more puzzling reali-
> sations for democrats across the Southern Africa region has been
> that [Mugabe] does not fear the group of people with the power
> to bring him to his knees more quickly and peacefully than any-
> one else. This group is the South African government. Why? ...
> Is our own government frozen by fear on the cusp of a difficult
> decision? Does Mugabe know that the ANC is so wedded to
> the notion that former liberation movements alone constitute
> legitimate governments in post-struggle states that it will not do
> anything it believes might endanger Zanu-PF's hegemony in
> Zimbabwe? Or does our government have a cunning plan which,
> even as we ask these questions, is being quietly and secretly rolled
> out to bring the country to stability in the near future?

These sentiments appeared to have been shared in much of the mainstream press, and they were fuelled by the less than transparent communication of the government's policy on Zimbabwe. Some individual ANC leaders also expressed their exasperation with the policy, including figures such as Reserve Bank Governor, Tito Mboweni, and Minister of Defence, Mosioua Lekota. In

August 2001, Mboweni remarked that lawlessness and a collapsing economy in Zimbabwe were contributing to the depreciation of the South African Rand.

The opposition Democratic Alliance (DA) of Tony Leon was much more critical and called for concrete action. Charging that Mugabe was a serious threat to the African Renaissance and Nepad, the DP recommended that South Africa should reconsider its electricity supplies to Zimbabwe (provided at 25 per cent discount), and that the ANC Youth League should boycott a regional conference to be hosted by Zanu-PF's youth wing at Victoria Falls in 2001. There were similar calls from other quarters for South Africa to use its economic muscle to back up its quiet diplomacy. Civil society groups, such as the Congress of South African Trade Unions (Cosatu), called for tougher measures against Harare to demonstrate displeasure with the continued repression.

The independent Zimbabwean press, like that in South Africa, was also critical of the quiet diplomacy policy. An editor of the largest independent newspaper, the *Daily News*, which the government forced into closure for several months from September 2003 (and again in February 2004), observed that:

> Mbeki has virtually endorsed the two elections others have condemned as grievously flawed ... He has also pleaded for a chance to apply his quiet diplomacy, which many Zimbabweans believe to be responsible for Mugabe's mounting arrogance ... If the actions taken against (the *Daily News* and the *Daily News on Sunday*) result in their demise, it will be on Mbeki's head. Quiet diplomacy will have helped a ruling party to have staged one of the biggest frauds in history to silence its fiercest domestic critic. It may leave most Zimbabweans with little option but to wage their own struggle against quiet diplomacy. (*Mail & Guardian* 26.09.03)

True, quiet diplomacy began to be associated with developments for which it was not directly responsible, such as persistent repression that the Mbeki government itself condemned. Nevertheless, the view spread in Zimbabwe that the policy was an alibi, if not an excuse, for inaction. For its part, the MDC was generally sceptical towards quiet diplomacy; despite the fact that they were consulted by the Mbeki government, they showed little trust in the process. Its position, rightly or wrongly, was that the ANC government leaned towards the Zanu-PF government, and that recognition and consultation by the former were grudgingly extended to it late in the day. Like the DA, the MDC urged South Africa to employ its economic muscle, including sanctions, to force a change in policies by the Mugabe government.

On the whole, however, the critics of quiet diplomacy did not recommend an alternative credible approach to the policy, except that of coercive sanctions. This was often highlighted by those who defended the approach. The defence of quiet diplomacy has been led by the Foreign Ministers, Dr Dlamini-Zuma, and Aziz Pahad. As Dlamini-Zuma (2001) argued: 'Our goal in foreign affairs is good neighbourliness, we build bridges across countries. Don't advocate war with Zimbabwe, we won't do it.' This was echoed in Pahad's comments on the pressure from western countries for South Africa to take a stronger line against the Mugabe government: 'We don't believe that their megaphone diplomacy and screaming from the rooftops has helped ... If it is not diplomacy we pursue in Zimbabwe, then it is war. We will not go to war with Zimbabwe' (*Sunday Times* 29.09.02).

The Finance Minister, Trevor Manuel, was also credited with voicing similar sentiments. To be sure, none of the critics of the quiet diplomacy approach advocated military intervention. The colourful rhetoric about 'not going to war' must have been a device to pre-empt the basic criticism that the approach was not bearing fruit. In sum, the advocates of quiet diplomacy often appear to over-react to criticism. Some commentators have described this defensive reaction as a red herring: 'Contrary to what Mbeki says, we are not called upon to invade Zimbabwe ... but we are called upon to speak for the values upon which our democracy is built' (Kane-Berman, in *Business Day* 30.10.02).

For its part, the wider international community has not taken a single position on quiet diplomacy. There has been muted or little criticism of quiet diplomacy in much of Africa. Neither SADC nor the AU have made grand statements for or against the policy. Countries such as Britain and the United States, and organisations like the European Union (EU) and the Commonwealth have been more forthright in demonstrating their opposition to the Mugabe government, and targeted sanctions have been directed at the Zimbabwean political leadership and its business supporters. These western countries and organisations have increasingly become impatient with quiet diplomacy.

Finally, the Mugabe government itself has been ambivalent towards the policy. While the policy has allowed the Mugabe government to buy time during the past four years, it does not appear to fully trust the role of the Mbeki government. Whenever the latter has criticised Zimbabwe's policies or actions, there have been sharp comments from Harare. For instance, the state-owned newspaper, the *Herald*, remarked that the criticism:

> neatly dovetails into Britain's grand plan for a global coalition towards Zimbabwe ... A clear pattern is emerging of a build-up against Zimbabwe and South Africa's complicity in a plot to overthrow Zanu-PF ... a betrayal difficult to stomach. (3.12.01)

Some of the more acerbic comments on the South African government and press have emanated from Zimbabwe's Minister of Information and Publicity, Jonathan Moyo. His colourful rhetoric matches that of South African ministers when they talk of 'not going to war with Zimbabwe'. But the rhetoric from Zimbabwe does not disguise the fact that the government would be concerned if South Africa employed its economic muscle against it.

References

Biel R (2003) Imperialism and international governance: The case of US policy towards Africa, *Review of African Political Economy* 30:77–88.

Chothia F & Jacobs S (2002) Remaking the Presidency: The tension between co-ordination and centralization. In S Jacobs & R Calland (eds.) *Thabo Mbeki's world.* Pietermaritzburg: University of Natal Press.

Daniel J, Naidoo V & Naidu S (2003) South African expansion into Africa: Can the leopard change its spots? *South African Labour Bulletin* 27:14–16.

DFA (Department of Foreign Affairs, South Africa) (2001) *Southern Africa.* Pretoria: DFA.

Dlamini-Zuma N (2001) Minister of Foreign Affairs briefing, Cape Town, 16.02.01.

Field S (2003) When neighbours stray: Political implications for the SADC region of the situation in Zimbabwe. In K Colvard & M Lee (eds.) *Unfinished business: The land crisis in Southern Africa.* Johannesburg: African Century Publications.

Habib A (2003) South Africa: Hegemon or pivotal state? Paper presented at a debate organised by the Centre for Policy Studies and the Open Society Foundation for South Africa, Johannesburg, August 2003.

Johnson RW (2002) The final struggle is to stay in power, *Focus*, 1st quarter, 2002.

International Crisis Group (2002) Zimbabwe: The politics of national liberation and international division, *Africa Report* No. 52.

Landsberg C (2003) South Africa: The pivotal state. Paper presented at a debate organised by The Centre for Policy Studies and the Open Society Foundation of South Africa, August 2003.

Mbeki T (2003) State of the Nation Address of the President of South Africa at the opening of Parliament, Cape Town.

Mbeki T (2004) State of the Nation Address of the President of South Africa at the opening of Parliament, Cape Town, 21.05.04.

Pillay D (2003) Zimbabwe: Silence of the left, *South African Labour Bulletin* 27:61–62.

Raftopoulos B (2003) The political challenges in Zimbabwe. Mimeo.

Southall R (2003) Democracy in Southern Africa: Moving beyond a difficult legacy, *Review of African Political Economy* 96:255–272.

Sparks A (2003) *Beyond the miracle*. Johannesburg: Jonathan Ball.

Vale P (2003) Ending walls: Southern Africa in the new millennium. Paper presented at a Symposium organised by the CIIR, SACBC, ICS and NAJ, Windhoek, September 2003.

Vale P & Maseko S (2002) Thabo Mbeki, South Africa and the idea of an African Renaissance. In S Jacobs & R Calland (eds.) *Thabo Mbeki's world*. Pietermaritzburg: University of Natal Press.

Van de Walle N (2001) *African economies and the politics of permanent crisis 1979–99*. Cambridge: CUP.

van Wyk J (2002) The saga continues: The Zimbabwe issue in South Africa's foreign policy, *Alternatives* 1:176–230.

Contributors

Miriam Altman
Executive Director,
Employment and Economic Policy
Research Programme, HSRC

Henri Boshoff
Researcher,
Defence Sector Programme, Insitute
for Security Studies (ISS)

Linda Chisholm
Research Director,
Child, Youth and Family Development
Research Programme, HSRC

John Daniel
Research Director,
Democracy and Governance Research
Programme, HSRC
Chair of the Editorial Board
HSRC Press

Zimitri Erasmus
Senior Lecturer,
Sociology Department,
University of Cape Town

Stephen Gelb
Executive Director,
The EDGE Institute
Visiting Professor,
Development Studies Department,
University of Witwatersrand

Shireen Hassim
Senior Lecturer,
Political Studies Department,
University of Witwatersrand

David Hemson
Research Director,
Integrated Regional and Rural
Development Research
Programme, HSRC

Shamil Jeppie
Senior Lecturer,
History Department,
University of Cape Town

Ted Leggett
Senior Researcher,
Crime and Justice Programme, ISS

Len le Roux
Researcher,
Defence Sector Programme, ISS

Jessica Lutchman
Researcher,
Democracy and Governance
Research Programme, HSRC

Lynn Maree
Independent Consultant In Arts
and Education

Seán Morrow
Chief Research Specialist,
Democracy and Governance Research
Programme, HSRC

Sanusha Naidu
Chief Research Specialist,
Integrated Regional and Rural
Development Research Programme,
HSRC

Lungisile Ntsebeza
Associate Professor,
Sociology Department,
University of Cape Town

Kwame Owusu-Ampomah
Research Specialist,
Integrated Regional and Rural
Development Research Programme,
HSRC

Tim Quinlan
Research Director,
Health Economics and HIV/AIDS
Research Division,
University of KwaZulu-Natal
(Position funded by the Policy Project,
USAID)

Benjamin Roberts
Chief Researcher,
Integrated Regional and Rural
Development Research Programme,
HSRC

Reg Rumney
Director,
BusinessMap Foundation

Sam Sole
Senior Reporter,
Mail & Guardian

Roger Southall
Distinguished Research Fellow,
Democracy and Governance
Research Programme, HSRC

Lloyd Sachikonye
Senior Researcher,
Agrarian and Labour Studies,
Institute of Labour Studies,
University of Zimbabwe

Goolam Vahed
Associate Professor,
History Department,
University of KwaZulu-Natal

Sarah Willan
Project Director,
Health Economics and HIV/AIDS
Research Division,
University of KwaZulu-Natal

Luvuyo Wotshela
Lecturer,
History Department,
University of Fort Hare

Index